OHIO

MATTHEW CARACCIOLO

Contents

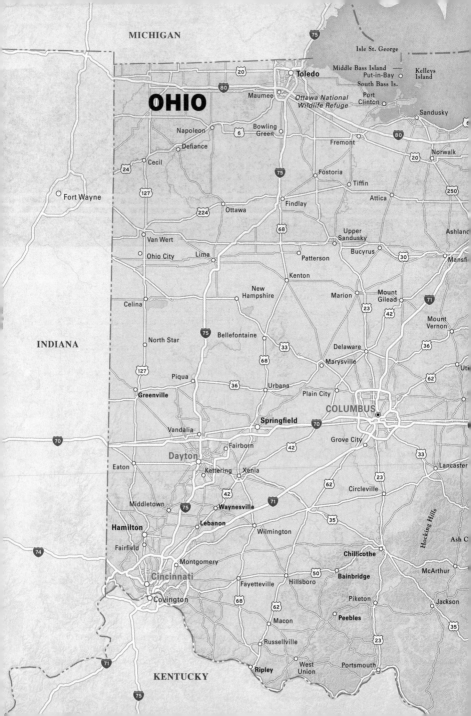

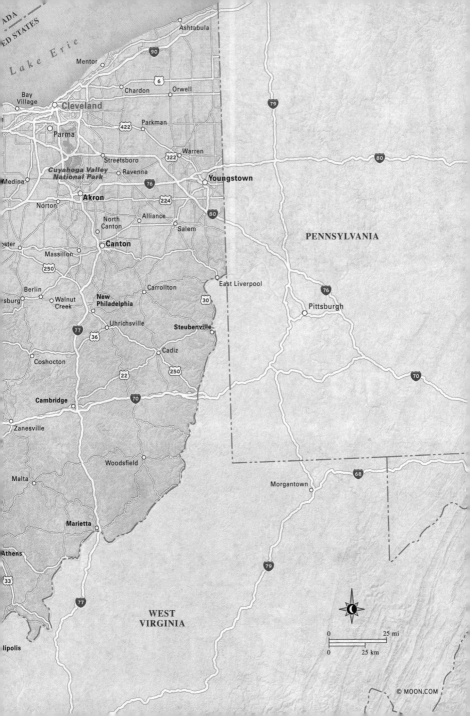

Ohio

There's no one way to define Ohio. Technically part of the Midwest, the Buckeye State's northeastern environs echo the industrial centers of New England, Cincinnati is just a river away from the South, and much of the state's rugged southeast is the entryway into Appalachia. From the 1980s to the 2000s, Ohio's official tourism slogan was "The Heart of It All," which told motorists where they'd arrived: the state where the country's cultures meet and mingle.

This mosaic of American temperament has produced some of the country's greatest figures. Eight presidents of the United States hail from Ohio. The first American to orbit the Earth and the first man to walk on the moon are from Ohio. Countless athletes, film stars, inventors, and business tycoons got their start here. "If I were giving a young man advice as to how he might succeed in life," said aviator Wilbur Wright, "I would say to him, pick out a good father and mother, and begin life in Ohio." This success, much of it made elsewhere, has perhaps fueled the misconception that Ohio is a great place to be *from* but not a great place to *be*. The truth is Ohioans have been building a terrific place to *be* for 15,000 years.

Clockwise from top left: Ash Cave in Hocking Hills State Park; Clifton Mill near Yellow Springs; Ohio wine country; Cleveland Museum of Art; Kings Island amusement park; downtown Cleveland.

For families, there's a lot of fun to be had for a fraction of the cost of many "premier" destinations. In one small state, you can find two top-shelf amusement parks (Cedar Point and Kings Island), excellent zoos, and innovative hands-on museums.

Then you have the cosmopolitan offerings of the Three C's: Cleveland, the Gilded Age cultural powerhouse; Columbus, the polished, fashionable capital; and Cincinnati, the old-world river town. Together they boast monumental museums and architecture, legacies of the industrial age. They tantalize with exciting food, brought here by those who have just arrived and those who have been here for generations. And there's plenty of beer to wash it all down, with over 300 craft breweries in the state. Another just opened while you were reading this paragraph.

But what of the countryside? Holmes County is the center of the second-largest Amish settlement in the world, a pastoral symphony of farmland, rolling hills, and touristed villages. The dense Appalachian foothills to the southeast conceal a world of cliffs, rock formations, and adventure sports. Lake Erie's shoreline and islands attract birders and those looking for a quiet retreat . . . or a party, depending on the island. And dotted across this land are remnants of mysterious mound-building civilizations long, long vanished.

So define Ohio however you like. Make it your own. In the United States, you'll be hard-pressed to find such a variety of things to do in a comparable amount of space.

Clockwise from top left: Ledges loop trail in Cuyahoga Valley National Park; National Veterans Memorial and Museum in Columbus; covered bridge in Ashtabula County; Amish Country.

10 TOP EXPERIENCES

1 Enjoy camping, boating, and summer fun at the **Lake Erie islands and shores** (page 212).

^
^
^

2 Walk Ohio's **unique neighborhoods:** Columbus's cozy **German Village** (page 49), Cleveland's artsy **Ohio City** (page 127), or Cincinnati's Victorian **Over-the-Rhine** (pictured, page 255).

3 Pay tribute to the classics at the **Rock & Roll Hall of Fame** in Cleveland (page 124).

4 Hike in **Cuyahoga Valley National Park,** a collage of woods, cliffs, and cultural heritage (page 170).

5 Escape to **Amish Country,** attracting visitors looking for antiques, cheese, and some peace and quiet (page 88).

>>>

6 Explore the history of flight at the **Dayton Aviation Heritage National Historical Park** and the **National Museum of the United States Air Force** (page 300).

>>>

7 See rare animals and learn about conservation at one of Ohio's **zoos,** regarded as some of the finest in the country, especially those in **Columbus** (pictured, page 79) and **Cincinnati** (page 260).

8 Scream on a roller coaster at **Cedar Point** (pictured, page 222) or **Kings Island** (page 289).

<<<

9 Sample more than 50 breweries in **Cincinnati's craft beer scene** (page 277).

>>>

10 Experience Ohio's take on Appalachia with rugged cliffs, hiking, and camping in the **Hocking Hills region** (page 352).

<<<

Planning Your Trip

Where to Go

Columbus and Vicinity

Ohio's **progressive capital** embraces art, technology, and a nationally recognized food and drink scene. Family attractions **COSI (Center of Science and Industry)** and the **Columbus Zoo and Aquarium** are top of the pack in their fields. **Walkable neighborhoods** surrounding downtown such as adorable **German Village** and the artsy, LGBTQ-friendly **Short North** inspire visitors to discover ample public art, coffee shops, and galleries.

Amish Country and Central Ohio

People come to **Amish Country** to browse the region's **bakeries, cheesemakers, craft stores,** and **restaurants,** as well as to learn about another way of life—**Holmes County** is the center of the second-largest Amish settlement in the world and is one of the only counties in the United States where nearly half the population speaks German at home. Beyond, this pleasant world of rolling hills and farmland offers **historic towns,** attractive **state parks,** and the shooting location for an iconic film, ***The Shawshank Redemption.***

Cleveland and Vicinity

Once one of the largest cities in the United States, Cleveland boasts the kind of cultural amenities typically seen in much larger cities. World-class **museums,** stunning **architecture,** and a strong **performing arts** scene draw people to a city evolving from its industrial past. The strongest **ethnic enclaves** in Ohio persist in

downtown Columbus

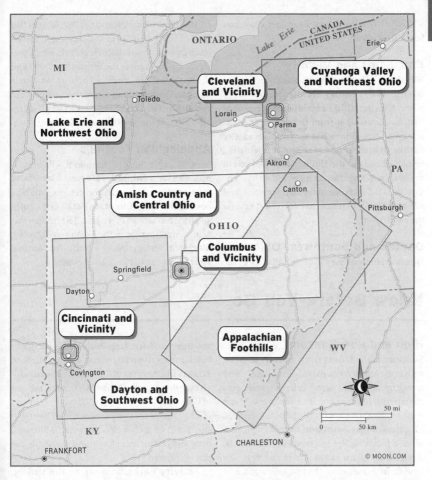

Cleveland, and with them their **cuisines** and **festivals.** If you want big-city trappings without being trapped in a big city, Cleveland is your place.

Cuyahoga Valley and Northeast Ohio

The area surrounding Cleveland is dotted with small to midsize industrial cities, each offering their own redemption story. **Ohio's only national park**—Cuyahoga Valley—cuts between Cleveland and **Akron** and protects cultural heritage as well as wildlife and natural features.

Ashtabula County is renowned as Ohio **wine country** and home to 19 **covered bridges,** and small maritime communities feature **beaches** and local history museums.

Lake Erie and Northwest Ohio

Surprising historical and cultural gems are dotted across this vast swath of farmland including **presidential sites** and **Neil Armstrong**'s hometown. **Toledo** punches above its weight with a surprising zoo and art museum. The real **vacation destination,** though, is the **Lake Erie** coast. **Cedar Point** beckons roller coaster lovers while **Put-in-Bay** draws a summer crowd on South Bass Island.

Cincinnati and Vicinity

Whether it's the abundant **German heritage,** colorful **19th-century architecture,** or **beer** scene, Cincinnati has an old-world demeanor that distinguishes it from the state's other cities. **Over-the-Rhine** has survived decades of decline to become one of the most fascinating neighborhoods in the United States and one of the country's largest intact historic districts. The **Cincinnati Zoo** is one of the country's best, and **Kings Island**'s 14 roller coasters lie just beyond the city's outerbelt.

Dayton and Southwest Ohio

Ohio's aviation history is on full display in the Dayton area with the **National Museum of the United States Air Force** and **Dayton Aviation Heritage National Historical Park,** which preserves sites relevant to the **Wright brothers** and the birth of flight. **Yellow Springs** is a hippie mountain town without a mountain, found amid cornfields. The area's state parks and preserves offer some of the best **hiking** in the state.

Appalachian Foothills

Visitors expecting flat farmland will be surprised to see a **rugged, forested hinterland** away from major population centers. Millions flock to **Hocking Hills State Park**'s caves, cliffs, and rock formations every year. The first permanent U.S. settlement in the Northwest Territory, **Marietta,** attracts history buffs. **Adventure sports** and **cabins** abound elsewhere.

Know Before You Go

High and Low Seasons

Summer is the **truest high season** in Ohio, with open amusement parks and beaches, busy campgrounds, a full events calendar, and parks operating at full capacity. It's also the easiest and most sensible time to visit the Lake Erie islands. This time of year is **hot and humid,** with **rain** often a factor in the July and August swelter, though late August can see some nice days. Try to **visit in June** before the real heat arrives, or **after mid-August** after schools reopen.

Though things tend to wind down in November, **fall** is a **secondary high season** of sorts: football is in full swing, peak fall foliage is mid-to-late October, and amusement parks stay open until Halloween, albeit with reduced or weekend-only hours. **September and October** are among the most beautiful times to visit Ohio, with **comfortable temperatures** and **drier conditions** to accompany the pretty leaves.

Things quiet down considerably for **winter,** by far Ohio's **lowest season.** Most outdoor attractions close or reduce their offerings for the season, and there are fewer large-scale events outside of holiday festivals and light displays in December. Winters in Ohio are **cold**—occasionally frigid—and varying degrees of **snowy.** The snow belt east of Cleveland sees upward of 100 inches (254 cm) of lake-effect snow every season, while Cincinnati sees about 22 inches (56 cm) a year. Museums, bars, and restaurants plow ahead as they do the rest of the year.

Activity perks back up in the **spring,** though outside isolated events such as St. Patrick's Day in Cleveland and Columbus's early-March Arnold Sports Festival, things stay relatively **quiet through March and April.** The weather can stubbornly oscillate between winter's last throes and warm fronts as soon as late February, though it's generally **wet** either way. Hikers are rewarded with wildflowers, though the leaves don't fully return until May. The summer season officially starts with the Memorial Day weekend.

All in all, the **best times** to visit Ohio are in the in-between months of **May-June** and **September-October.**

hiking in the woods at the Cleveland Metroparks

the Scotts Miracle-Gro Foundation Children's Garden at the Franklin Park Conservatory in Columbus

Advance Reservations

As far as attractions go, you can show up to nearly anything in Ohio without a prior reservation unless it's a special event or visiting exhibit you're after. **Accommodations,** especially on weekends from May through October, do book up or see drastically higher prices. To avoid frustration (especially for campgrounds, B&Bs, and other rural or small-town accommodations), book at least three months in advance. Weekday availability is typically easier to find.

Transportation

With ample highways and relatively few public transportation options, a **car** is the best way to see Ohio. All of Ohio's major airports feature car rental kiosks. In the major cities, it is possible to travel via intercity buses, though depending on the number of daily trips this may not be ideal.

What to Take

Ohio's **summer** is meant for the outdoors. Bring sunscreen, bug spray, a swimsuit, a good pair of walking shoes, plus your favorite camping gear if you plan to go camping. Come prepared for Ohio's **winter** with heavy winter coats, layers of clothing to wear underneath, hats, gloves, and the means to potentially dig your car out of snow or ice (an ice scraper and perhaps a shovel). Keep a sharp eye on the forecast in **spring or fall**—you could be in for just about anything! In general, a jacket or hoodie is good enough for the day, and an umbrella or rain jacket would be useful if long walks or hikes are in the plans. Though most occasions call for only **casual attire,** pack a **business casual outfit** for a nice dinner or cultural performance.

Ohio Getaways

Two Days in Cleveland

Cleveland offers the best of Ohio's urban sophistication. It also makes a great base for exploring both town and country. Choose the getaway that works best for you . . . or combine three getaways into a one-week itinerary (see sidebar on page 23) that balances rural charm with the best legacies of industry: mansions, art museums, and stunning architecture.

Day 1

Check into your hotel either in University Circle or downtown. Head to University Circle's green Wade Oval, a strollable park surrounded by top-notch cultural institutions, including the **Cleveland Museum of Natural History,** home to Balto, the famed dogsled husky. Eat lunch in **Little Italy** before returning to Wade Oval for the **Cleveland Museum of Art,** where you'll have the afternoon to explore one of the country's great art museums.

Once you've hit your threshold, take a stroll in leafy, Victorian **Lake View Cemetery** before dining in nearby **Cleveland Heights.** For some nightlife, head downtown to The Flats or Warehouse district for a drink or musical performance.

Day 2

Eat breakfast in trendy **Tremont.** Explore downtown Cleveland's **Gilded Age architecture** on foot: the **Arcade,** the former **Cleveland Trust Company** building (now a Heinen's grocery), and **Public Square,** for starters. Eat lunch in one of **Ohio City**'s brewpubs, **Great Lakes Brewing Company** or **Market Garden Brewery** in particular. Or put together a lunch at **West Side Market** and grab a drink after. In the afternoon, visit the **Rock & Roll Hall of Fame.** Grab dinner in **Lakewood** and head back to Ohio City for a cocktail and live music at speakeasy **Velvet Tango Room.**

Cleveland Museum of Art

Town and Country Road Trip

You can plan a weeklong road trip starting in Cleveland by combining three getaways. From bucolic Amish Country to the fascinating history of Ohio's industrial northeast, it's possible to see two very different sides of the state in just a few days. Here's a point-to-point itinerary:

CLEVELAND

Days 1-2

- Spend two days enjoying the city's many highlights.

WINE COUNTRY

Day 3

- From Cleveland, head northeast on I-90 to **wine country** and **Ashtabula County** (about 1 hour).

AKRON AND CUYAHOGA VALLEY

Day 4

- From Ashtabula County, head south on SR 11 to **Youngstown** (75 minutes).
- Head west on I-80 and I-76 to **Akron** (50 minutes).

Day 5

- From Akron, head north to **Cuyahoga Valley National Park** (20 minutes), and then back to Akron.

AMISH COUNTRY

Day 6

- From Akron, head south on I-77 to **New Philadelphia** (50 minutes).
- Head west on SR 39 to **Amish Country** (15 minutes).

Day 7

- From Amish Country, head north via I-71 or I-77 back to **Cleveland** (about 1.5 hours).

With more time...

- **Wine country** and **Ashtabula County** are about 1 hour northeast of Cleveland via I-90 (page 198).
- **Akron** is 50 minutes south of Cleveland via I-77 (page 175).
- **Cuyahoga Valley National Park** is about 30 minutes south of Cleveland via I-77 (page 170).
- **Amish Country** is about 1.5 hours south of Cleveland via I-71 or I-77 (page 88).
- **Cedar Point** and **Sandusky** are just over an hour west of Cleveland via SR 2 (page 220), with the **Lake Erie islands** just a short ferry ride away (page 212).

Wine Country

Head northeast on I-90 to Ohio's **wine country** (1 hour from Cleveland) and spend a leisurely day driving from winery to winery. Take in the view at **South River Vineyard** or get lunch or dinner at **Ferrante Winery and Ristorante.** Explore **Ashtabula County's covered bridges** in between, and stay the night in one of the area's bed-and-breakfasts, if you're so inclined. Walk the beach at **Geneva State Park** or find some cheap eats in summer resort town **Geneva-on-the-Lake** if you want to add to the day.

Akron and Cuyahoga Valley
Day 1

Head to **Youngstown** (1.25 hours from Cleveland), taking I-77 south to I-480 south to the I-80 turnpike east, and see works from Winslow Homer, John Singer Sargent, and other illustrious names at the impressive **Butler Institute of American Art.** Pick an Italian restaurant for lunch, perhaps the nearby **Cassese's MVR,** or eat at the café at **Fellows Riverside Gardens,** where you'll take an hour-long stroll, give or take. Hop on I-80 west to I-76 west to **Akron** (50 minutes from Youngstown), where you'll check into your hotel and find dinner and live music in downtown's **Akron Historic Arts District.**

Autumn is an excellent time to visit Ohio, especially during **mid-late October** when the colors are at their peak. Consider any of these locations for optimum fall foliage:

- **Mohican State Park,** with its covered bridge and Gorge Overlook, looks good in autumn yellows and oranges, as do the pastoral hills of nearby **Malabar Farm State Park** from the Mount Jeez Overlook.

- East of Cleveland, **Holden Arboretum'**s Murch Canopy Walk and Emergent Tower put you in and above the trees for an immersive autumn view.

- Youngstown's **Lanterman's Mill** is a popular photo destination during peak autumn colors.

- Waterfalls and foliage combine for splendid views at **Cuyahoga Valley National Park.**

- Sun shining through the autumn trees outside **Hocking Hills State Park'**s Ash Cave makes for a magical setting.

- The Buzzardroost Rock Trail in **Edge of Appalachia Nature Preserve** is one of the most commanding views in the state for fall colors.

historic Lanterman's Mill surrounded by colorful foliage

Day 2

Spend the morning exploring **Cuyahoga Valley National Park** (20 minutes from Akron) in whichever way strikes your fancy: a hike on the **Ledges loop trail** or to **Brandywine Falls,** a themed ride on the **Cuyahoga Valley Scenic Railroad,** or a bike ride on the **Ohio & Erie Canal Towpath Trail.** Just save enough energy for a walking tour back in Akron at the Tudor Revival **Stan Hywet Hall and Gardens,** one of the largest houses in America and the former home of F. A. Seiberling, co-founder of Goodyear Tire and Rubber Company. Find lunch in Akron's **Highland Square** neighborhood or at the estate's visitors center before you embark on the tour, which depending on your interest may take the rest of the day. Check the calendar for special events or evening concerts. Head back to Cleveland (50 minutes from Akron).

Amish Country
Day 1

Head south on I-77 to **New Philadelphia** (80 minutes from Cleveland) and admire the hand-carved steam engines at the **Ernest Warther Museum and Gardens,** or pick up some quality cutlery at the workshop as a souvenir. Then head west on SR 39 to **Amish Country** (15 minutes from New Philadelphia), eating a hearty lunch at **Dutch Valley's** restaurant and taking a look at the **World's Largest Cuckoo Clock** in Sugarcreek before doing some shopping in **Berlin,** where you'll also stay the night.

Day 2

Grab breakfast at popular **Boyd and Wurthmann** in Berlin or at a bakery of your choice before doing whatever shopping you didn't do yesterday: cheese, quilts, baked goods, antiques. **Hershberger's Farm and Bakery** has a little bit of it all, plus a petting zoo. If you're done shopping, head down SR 643 (winding, scenic, and the most direct way) to **Coshocton** for a look at the **Roscoe Village** restored canal town, with a ride on the canal aboard the *Monticello III.* Learn something about Amish culture at **Yoder's Amish Home** or the **Amish and Mennonite Heritage Center** before heading back to Cleveland (1.75 hours from Amish Country).

Two Days in Columbus

It's all about family time in Columbus during the day and exploring the city's eclectic neighborhoods and food scene by night.

Day 1

Eat a big, inexpensive breakfast in The Ohio State University district and get to the world-class **Columbus Zoo and Aquarium** first thing in the morning, while the animals are most active. If you brought your swimsuits, mosey over to the adjacent **Zoombezi Bay** water park for a late-afternoon splash. Or, do a little hiking at **Highbanks Metro Park** instead, searching for ancient mounds and eagle nests. You've earned a treat being outside all day; get a nice dinner and walk the suspended pedestrian bridge in nearby **Dublin**'s **Bridge Park** center, where you'll also find several family-friendly watering holes for a drink or dessert.

Day 2

Pick up some pastries or a big egg sandwich at **Fox in the Snow** before heading to the mind-bending museum **Otherworld.** Everyone can find what they want for lunch at **North Market** downtown before spending the rest of the afternoon in **COSI (Center of Science and Industry).** Make the short trek to **Franklinton**'s

Otherworld in Columbus

Fiona the Hippo at the Cincinnati Zoo

Family Fun

With best-in-class amusement parks and zoos alongside interactive museums and limitless outdoor recreation, Ohio is attractive as an affordable and accessible family vacation destination. Mix and match these top attractions for the ultimate family vacation.

- While most of Ohio's zoos are top-tier institutions, the world-famous **Columbus Zoo and Aquarium** and its **Zoombezi Bay** waterpark counterpart are quite the one-two punch. Two days are ideal to catch the more than 600 species of animals and 17 water rides.

- **COSI (Center of Science and Industry)** in Columbus is one of the largest and most respected science museums in the country, with a dinosaur hall, planetarium, and over 300 interactive exhibits.

- There are over 30 roller coasters between giant seasonal amusement parks **Cedar Point** and **Kings Island,** many of them among the longest, tallest, or fastest of their kind. The edge for best kids' area goes to Kings Island for its Planet Snoopy region (Cedar Point has one as well, but it's not as extensive). The roller coaster edge goes to Cedar Point. Both sport adjacent waterparks.

- For time in the great outdoors, rent a cabin (or a room in a castle) in the **Hocking Hills region,** with hiking, zip-lining, canoeing, and ropes courses within easy distance. You can do much of the same in the smaller **Mohican State Park** area.

- The **Cincinnati Museum Center at Union Terminal** is three museums in one, with just enough history and science to get your

Cedar Point roller coaster

feet wet before moving on to the Duke Energy Children's Museum and its climbable, touchable, throwable exhibits.

- In the Appalachian foothills, hop in a safari-style truck at **The Wilds** conservation center and travel through open grasslands in search of some of the rarest animals in the world.

- Stay the night in **indoor waterparks** in Sandusky and Mason, or at one of the **state park lodges** for beaches, swimming pools, and sports.

brewpubs **BrewDog** or **Land-Grant Brewing Company** for dinner, or head to historic **German Village** for a quieter dinner and an evening stroll along brick roads. Be sure to stop inside **The Book Loft** to get lost in a maze of literature. For some nightlife, head up to the **Short North** neighborhood for a drink or to glance inside some art galleries if they have extended hours (check the calendar for Gallery Hop!).

With more time...

- Browse the shops and markets in **Amish Country,** 1.75 hours east of Columbus via US-62 (page 88).

- Ride the roller coasters at **Kings Island,** 80 minutes southwest of Columbus via I-70 (page 289), or **Cedar Point,** 2.5 hours north of Columbus via US-23 and SR 4 (page 222).

- Go for a hike in the gorges and forests of the **Hocking Hills** region, just over an hour southeast of Columbus via US-33 (page 352).

Two Days in Cincinnati

Take advantage of the city's compactness with walking tours that highlight the best of Cincinnati's unique architecture, history, and cuisine.

Day 1

Start your day with a hearty breakfast at **Taste of Belgium**, then cross the street to the **National Underground Railroad Freedom Center** for a dose of local and national history. Take a leisurely walk through **Smale Riverfront Park** and cross the Ohio River to **Newport, Kentucky**, on the Purple People Bridge, which will take you straight to **Hofbräuhaus** for lunch, beer, and a long sit. Spend the rest of your afternoon inside the **Newport Aquarium,** then hop on a rideshare or a taxi back to Ohio and the **Carew Tower,** where you'll find your way to the observation deck for an evening view

of the city. Dinner is downtown at any of the swanky establishments near the intersection of 6th and Walnut Streets. You'll stick around here for drinks, or check the city's events calendar for shows at the **Aronoff Center for the Arts, Contemporary Arts Center,** or **21c Museum Hotel Cincinnati.**

Day 2

You'll spend more time in the car today. Grab an early breakfast at **Eckerlin's Meats** (try a goetta sandwich for a local specialty) or one of the other breakfast spots surrounding **Findlay Market,** which will open by the time you're finished with your coffee. Drive over to the art deco **Cincinnati Museum Center at Union Terminal** to spend the rest of the morning steeped in science, history, and creative playgrounds. Head north for lunch at **Camp Washington Chili** to try Cincinnati-style chili or west to the Price Hill neighborhood for a view of the city at **Incline Public House.** Get back to the **Over-the-Rhine** neighborhood in time for a Queen City Underground Tour at **American**

Smale Riverfront Park and the Roebling Suspension Bridge in Cincinnati

Cedar Point amusement park

Legacy Tours to hear about the history of the neighborhood and to tour rediscovered brewery tunnels. Or, if that's not your speed, check out the Cincinnati Zoo and Botanical Garden or the free Cincinnati Art Museum for a few hours. Either way, be back in Over-the-Rhine in time for dinner, where you'll have your pick from fashionable places to eat. Enjoy walking past the neighborhood's Italianate storefronts, houses, and the imposing Cincinnati Music Hall. Pick a craft brewery or two to settle for the evening, including Rhinegeist.

With more time...

- Explore the region's extensive aviation history in Dayton, one hour north of Cincinnati via I-75 (page 298).
- Ride the world's longest wooden roller coaster at Kings Island, 30 minutes northeast of Cincinnati via I-71 (page 289).
- Shop for antiques in Waynesville, 45 minutes northeast of Cincinnati via I-71 (page 321).

Lake Erie Road Trip

Sometimes even Ohioans forget that the state has a Great Lakes shore, yet Lake Erie boasts a maritime culture just like the rest of them. This itinerary takes travelers through the coast's top attractions, highlighting the beaches, history, and recreation that Lake Erie waters have invited over the centuries. Five days should be enough to explore resort islands, amusement parks, and metropolitan cities with a little time for leisure.

Day 1: Ashtabula County and Headlands Beach

Going east to west, start your trip by exploring Ashtabula County's covered bridges and tranquil wineries, picking one for lunch. Spend your afternoon on the beach at Headlands Beach State Park (40 minutes west of Ashtabula County's Geneva-on-the-Lake) and amble along the shore to the adjacent Headlands Dunes State Nature Preserve toward the lighthouse. When you've had your fill of sun, pick up SR 2 west to Cleveland (35 minutes from Headlands Beach) and check into your downtown hotel.

Splurge for dinner in **downtown** before sitting down for a drink at a **craft brewery** in The Flats district or in the **Ohio City** neighborhood.

Day 2: Cleveland

Today is about saturating yourself in culture in **University Circle.** Soak in as much as you can at the **Cleveland Museum of Art** in the morning before finding lunch in **Little Italy.** Pick a sight or two that suits your fancy in the afternoon, perhaps the **Cleveland Museum of Natural History, Cleveland Botanical Garden,** or **Lake View Cemetery.** Alternatively, head back downtown for the **Rock & Roll Hall of Fame.** Find dinner in the trendy **Tremont** or **Ohio City** neighborhoods. See what's on the calendar for the evening's entertainment: a **Cleveland Orchestra** concert or a performance at **Playhouse Square.**

Day 3: Cedar Point and Sandusky

Check out of your hotel and eat a hearty breakfast before heading west on SR 2 to **Sandusky** (just over an hour from Cleveland) for **Cedar Point,** where you'll be spending most of the day riding roller coasters. Eat snacks in the park to tide yourself until dinner in downtown Sandusky, then head to your hotel. If it's the off-season, trade in Cedar Point for **Kalahari Resorts Sandusky** and its massive indoor waterpark. If amusement parks and waterparks aren't your thing, explore downtown Sandusky on foot and get some lunch, and then continue on to **Marblehead** (25 minutes from Sandusky) for a look at the **Marblehead Lighthouse** and a stay at the **Red Fern Inn at Rocky Point Winery.** Dinner is at **Marblehead Galley** next door, or drive 20 minutes west to **Port Clinton** for more options.

Day 4: Put-in-Bay (South Bass Island)

Take SR 2 west again to **Port Clinton** (25 minutes from Sandusky or 20 minutes from Marblehead) and catch the Jet Express ferry to **Put-in-Bay** (30-minute ferry ride), where you can't miss **Perry's Victory and International Peace Memorial.** Rent a golf cart to look around and

Marblehead Lighthouse

Buckeyes in the Skies

With Orville and Wilbur Wright, John Glenn, and Neil Armstrong all hailing from Ohio, sites belonging to and inspired by these **pioneers of flight** and **space exploration** are sprinkled across the Buckeye State, ranging from humble homes to parks and museums.

CINCINNATI

Long before flight was possible, Ohioans observed the stars through the 19th-century **Cincinnati Observatory,** home to one of the world's oldest working telescopes. Learn about the historic Apollo 11 moon landing at the **Cincinnati Museum Center at Union Terminal** and its Neil Armstrong Space Exploration Gallery.

DAYTON AND SOUTHWEST OHIO

An hour north of Cincinnati, Dayton is the epicenter of Ohio's aviation history, preserving sites relevant to Orville and Wilbur Wright and the birth of flight within the **Dayton Aviation Heritage National Historical Park.** Within these locations, you'll find one of the original bicycle shops where the brothers tinkered with their designs, the original 1905 Wright Flyer III airplane, and the field in which the brothers conducted many of their tests. The massive **National Museum of the United States Air Force** chronicles the history of flight through the lens of armed conflict and science, featuring hundreds of fighter jets, space capsules, and presidential airplanes.

LAKE ERIE AND NORTHWEST OHIO

In the town of Wapakoneta, about an hour north of Dayton, is the **Armstrong Air and Space Museum,** devoted to Apollo 11 astronaut and native son Neil Armstrong. Many of his personal belongings, as well as the original Gemini VIII spacecraft, sit in this small museum. While not open to the public, **Neil Armstrong's boyhood home** evokes the humble beginnings of a monumental figure.

APPALACHIAN FOOTHILLS

On the eastern side of the state, the **John and Annie Glenn Museum** celebrates the achievements of John Glenn—the first U.S. astronaut to orbit the Earth—within the walls of his boyhood home in New Concord, outside Cambridge. About an hour south, in the Hocking Hills region, is the **John Glenn Astronomy Park,** a designated dark-sky park named in his honor with regular programming and a small observatory.

CLEVELAND

John Glenn's legacy continues at NASA's Glenn Research Center, which houses its official visitors center in Cleveland's **Great Lakes Science Center** with displays on the International Space Station, an original Apollo capsule, and a few of Glenn's personal effects.

---

relax in any of the island's bars or restaurants, or rent a Jet Ski or kayak to get on the water before heading back to Port Clinton on the mainland. Hop back on SR 2 again and head west to Curtice Road, which will take you to lakeside **Maumee Bay Lodge and Conference Center** (40 minutes from Port Clinton), where you'll check in and enjoy a late afternoon/evening stroll along the beach or on the boardwalks through the coastal marsh. Or, if you'd rather party, stay the night on the island.

Day 5: Toledo

Enjoy a leisurely morning at the lodge or at your island accommodation before heading west to **Toledo** (20 minutes from Maumee Bay Lodge via Cedar Point Rd., or 50 minutes from Port Clinton via SR 2) to grab an early lunch at **Tony Packo's.** After lunch, check out the nearby **National Museum of the Great Lakes** to board a freighter and put some of the sights you've seen into a larger perspective. If time allows, check out the expansive **Toledo Zoo and Aquarium** or the **Toledo Museum of Art.**

Craft Beer Scene

Ohio's three C's are Cincinnati, Columbus, and Cleveland, but you could easily add a fourth C: Craft beer. These three great beer cities have everything you need for an exciting and educational exploration of craft beer—breweries, walking tours, and even the world's first crowdfunded craft beer hotel. Cincinnati's Rhinegeist, Columbus's BrewDog, and Cleveland's Great Lakes Brewing Company are the state's flagship breweries, with brews found in grocery stores and bars throughout Ohio. In addition to the locations listed below, each of the Three C's is home to a **Hofbräuhaus** beer garden affiliated with the Bavarian original in Munich—but only Cincinnati's location is by a riverfront.

Cincinnati

Descend into a world of debauchery and brewing with **American Legacy Tours** and its Queen City Underground walking tour, which takes visitors to rediscovered 19th-century brewing tunnels while exploring neighborhood Over-the-Rhine's colorful history. Take your pick from Cincinnati's over 50 breweries, including **Rhinegeist**'s industrial digs and rooftop patio looking at the city, **Taft's Ale House**'s restored church building, and **MadTree Brewing**'s enormous heated patio and pizza. There are dozens to choose from in this authentic beer town steeped in German heritage.

In transit between Cincinnati and Columbus, **Dayton** is worth a stop. Taste beer history at **Carillon Brewing Company,** which brews using 19th-century recipes and techniques for unusual results (for modern taste buds, anyway). Then head to the Oregon District, a hipster haven where **Warped Wing Brewing Company** is leading the charge of a handful of quality breweries.

Columbus

Scottish company **BrewDog** chose the Columbus area as headquarters for its operations on this side of the pond. Its main production facility, southeast of the city in suburb Canal Winchester, sports a pub, a craft beer museum, and the 32-room **DogHouse Hotel,** the world's first crowdfunded craft beer hotel with taps in every guest room. Head into town for the city's burgeoning, respected beer scene: **Land-Grant Brewing Company** and **Seventh Son Brewing Company** top most lists. Or, head farther southeast toward Lancaster for sipping beers at **Rockmill Brewery,** housed in a former horse barn.

Cleveland

The big name in Cleveland is **Great Lakes Brewing Company,** which offers tours of the brewing facility along with a popular brewpub. Respected neighbor **Market Garden Brewery** also offers brewery tours and a gift shop. Both are located in the Ohio City neighborhood, the epicenter of brewing in Cleveland and home to half a dozen breweries. Downtown, look for friendly **Masthead Brewing Company** in a former auto showroom.

Carillon Brewing Company

Ohio and the Underground Railroad

During the early and mid-19th century, enslaved people in the southern United States utilized the Underground Railroad to escape to the relative safety of the North. "Conductors," such as Harriet Tubman, guided groups of freedom seekers along the route, stopping to eat and hide at safe houses run by "station masters," who were often free Black people, abolitionists, or clergy. By 1850, it's estimated that as many as 100,000 enslaved people utilized this network of safe houses and clandestine routes, which was neither underground nor a railroad.

Ohio played a pivotal role in the Underground Railroad network, with slave state Kentucky just on the other side of the Ohio River. Multiple routes crossed the state on the way to Canada, where freedom seekers would be safer after the passing of the Fugitive Slave Act in 1850. Today, you can learn more about this pivotal piece of U.S. history in Ohio's museums and former stations. In some cases, you can even stay the night. Cincinnati and southern Ohio in particular hold a number of relevant sites.

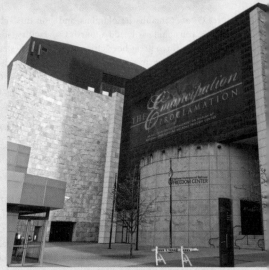

National Underground Railroad Freedom Center

SIGHTS

- **National Underground Railroad Freedom Center** (Cincinnati): Start at this contemporary museum for exhibits, videos, and artifacts depicting slavery in the United States and the operation of the Underground Railroad.

- **Harriet Beecher Stowe House** (Cincinnati): Famed author Stowe gathered much of her research for the controversial antislavery novel *Uncle Tom's Cabin* while living in this house.

- **John Rankin House** and **John Parker House** (Ripley, Southwest Ohio): Visit two former stations on the Underground Railroad, one the home of a Presbyterian minister and the other a free Black entrepreneur who had formerly been enslaved.

- **Hubbard House Underground Railroad Museum** (Ashtabula, Northeast Ohio): The only Underground Railroad terminus in Ohio open to the public, this house by the shores of Lake Erie was the final stop before a more secure life in Canada.

LODGINGS

- **Six Acres B&B** (Cincinnati): This Black-owned bed-and-breakfast repurposes the home of Quaker and station master Zebulon Strong. The innkeepers are very knowledgeable about the history of the house, and guests stay in rooms separate from where freedom seekers hid out of respect.

- **Safe House Bed and Breakfast** (Mansfield, Central Ohio): This sandstone house built in 1837 was the home of abolitionist Samuel Lewis, who used an underground tunnel to the stone house across the street to secretly move freedom seekers in and out. Today, this remains a peaceful place to rest.

Get Outside

Each of Ohio's regions offer their own inspiration to enjoy the outdoors, with plentiful opportunities for hiking, biking, paddling, and more.

Columbus and Vicinity

- Spend a lazy afternoon soaking up the sun and **swimming** at **Alum Creek State Park,** home to Ohio's largest inland **beach.**
- **Kayak** your way through the city on the **Scioto and Olentangy Rivers** with **Olentangy Paddle.**
- Go **rock climbing** at **Scioto Audubon Metro Park,** where you'll find the largest free outdoor climbing wall in the United States.

Amish Country and Central Ohio

- **Mohican State Park** is the center of the "Camp and Canoe Capital of Ohio," with thousands of **campsites** and several **canoe** liveries in the region, plus miles of **hiking** around the Mohican River gorge and a 25-mile (40-km) **mountain bike** trail.
- **Hikers** can explore canal ruins and disused railroad tunnels at **Blackhand Gorge State Nature Preserve.**
- Amish Country's rails-to-trails **Holmes County Trail** connects Amish communities through rolling farmland and is utilized by **hikers, bikers,** and buggies alike.

Cleveland and Vicinity

- Spend a day on the **beach** at **Headlands Beach State Park,** one of the state's most popular **swimming** destinations, and the adjacent **Headlands Dunes State Nature Preserve,** with trails meandering through beach grass. On the opposite side of the Grand River is the family-friendly beach at **Fairport Harbor Lakefront Park.**

camping in Mohican State Park

the shore of Lake Erie in Geneva State Park

- Cleveland's Metroparks offer dozens of miles of **hiking** through woods and cliffs, best of all at **Rocky River Reservation.**

Cuyahoga Valley and Northeast Ohio

- Over 100 miles (161 km) of **hiking** trails wind past cliffs, waterfalls, and dense forest in Ohio's only national park, **Cuyahoga Valley National Park.** The park's lovely 60-foot (18.3-m) **Brandywine Falls** is the tallest in Ohio.

- **Hike** or **bike** the multiuse **Ohio & Erie Canal Towpath Trail,** which runs 87 miles (140 km) from Cleveland, through the national park, south through Akron, and on to Tuscarawas County.

- Hit the slopes at **Boston Mills and Brandywine ski resorts,** sister resorts within the national park.

- Relax on the **beach,** go **zip-lining,** rent kayaks and paddleboards, or hire a **fishing** charter at **Geneva State Park,** on the shore of Lake Erie.

Lake Erie and Northwest Ohio

- **Boating** abounds along the **Lake Erie shoreline,** with marinas dotting the coast.

- **Camp** at **East Harbor State Park** and enjoy the sandy **swimming beach.**

- On **Put-in-Bay,** rent **kayaks** or **Jet Skis** and explore the small bluffs around the island, or hire a **fishing** charter to find some perch or walleye.

- Book a stay at the **lodge** or the **campgrounds** at **Maumee Bay State Park,** which also features **swimming beaches** as well as **hiking.** The park is a good **birding** spot, especially in the spring, as are the coastal marshes of nearby **Ottawa National Wildlife Refuge** and its surrounding nature preserves.

- **Kayak** the **Maumee River Water Trail,**

Brandywine Falls in Cuyahoga Valley National Park

zip-lining at Geneva State Park

a collection of over 30 access points for over 100 miles (161 km) of accessible waterways.

- **Hike** at Toledo's giant **Oak Openings Preserve Metropark,** which offers over 50 miles (81 km) of trails through the unusual oak savanna ecosystem.

Cincinnati and Vicinity

- Explore the wooded ravines racing down to the Ohio River in the large parks outside the city center. Go **hiking, mountain biking,** or **horseback riding** at **Mt. Airy Forest,** or visit its handicapped-accessible **tree house.** Look for 450-million-year-old trilobite **fossils** in the 100-foot (30-m) gorge within **Sharon Woods.**

- Take up a **paddle** at **Fifty West Canoe & Kayak** and head out on the Little Miami River.

Dayton and Southwest Ohio

- One of Ohio's best day-trip options, Yellow Springs features excellent **hiking** at **John Bryan State Park** and two adjacent preserves (**Clifton Gorge State Nature Preserve** and **Glen Helen Nature Preserve**) with gorges and waterfalls. John Bryan State Park also offers **mountain bike** trails and opportunities for **rock climbing.**

- The paved, multiuse **Little Miami Scenic Trail** makes for good **biking** in and between Cincinnati and Dayton.

- **Caesar Creek State Park**'s Caesar Creek Lake is one of Ohio's best **boating** spots, with five boat ramps and a marina.

- **Hike** to one of Ohio's best overlooks in **Edge of Appalachia Nature Preserve,** through old-growth forest in **Highlands Nature Sanctuary,** or among ancient Hopewell mounds at **Fort Hill Earthworks and Nature Preserve.**

Appalachian Foothills

- **Hike** past recess caves, waterfalls, and cliffs at **Hocking Hills State Park,** with **Ash Cave** the biggest highlight. **Camp** within the park or any of the region's nearby campgrounds.

Ash Cave in Hocking Hills State Park

canoeing down the Hocking River

- Go **backpacking** in **Wayne National Forest** or **Zaleski State Forest.**

- Add some **adventure sports** to the hiking: Go **zip-lining** at **Hocking Hills Canopy Tours.** Try **off-road driving** with **NevilleBillie Adventure Park**'s ATVs, or take on its massive **ropes course. Climb** up a cliff at **High Rock Adventures.**

- **Paddle** or **float** down the **Hocking River** with either of Logan's two liveries.

- Head to **Marietta** for the city's **mountain biking** trails or to **paddle** along the **Muskingum or Ohio Rivers.**

- Do a little bit of everything while staying at the lodge at **Salt Fork State Park,** with **boating,** a **beach, hiking,** and **golf.**

Columbus and Vicinity

Chances are you've thought very little about

Columbus. But now is a good time to start: All told, Columbus could be the best family destination in Ohio, with ample attractions, ease of getting around, and a central location that makes nearly the entire state possible as a day trip.

Columbus was long the buttoned-up government center of Ohio, with a state university football program whose reputation was larger than the city itself. Though old enough by Ohio standards—founded in 1812, it's only 24 years younger than Cincinnati—Columbus didn't grow as rapidly or develop the intense industry of its peers. Indeed, it wasn't even the first state capital. Its location on a perch of untamed wilderness referred to by locals as "wolf's ridge" was determined

Highlights

Look for ★ to find recommended sights, activities, dining, and lodging.

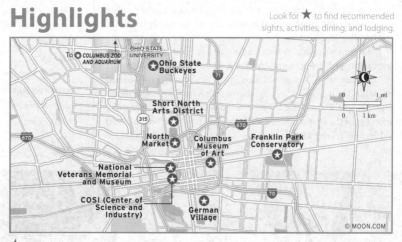

★ Engage your imagination at the **Columbus Museum of Art,** with a strong early modern art collection and a unique gallery known as the Wonder Room (page 43).

★ Stop and smell the flowers at the historic **Franklin Park Conservatory,** which boasts an expansive children's garden (page 45).

★ Explore hands-on exhibits about everything from outer space to the ocean at **COSI (Center of Science and Industry)** (page 46).

★ Honor the stories and sacrifices of service members at the thought-provoking **National Veterans Memorial and Museum** (page 46).

★ Stroll around **German Village,** a large district of 19th-century homes and brick roads

that offers some of the area's best dining (page 49).

★ Browse art galleries and boutiques and hit the rollicking nightlife scene in the dynamic **Short North Arts District** (page 52).

★ Cheer on the Scarlet and Gray at an **Ohio State Buckeyes football game** and enjoy some of the proudest traditions in the college football world (page 58).

★ Grab a bite at **North Market,** where over 30 vendors of specialty groceries and international cuisine represent what's newest and best to eat in town (page 62).

★ Witness cheetah run demonstrations and giraffe feeding time at the innovative **Columbus Zoo and Aquarium** (page 79).

Columbus

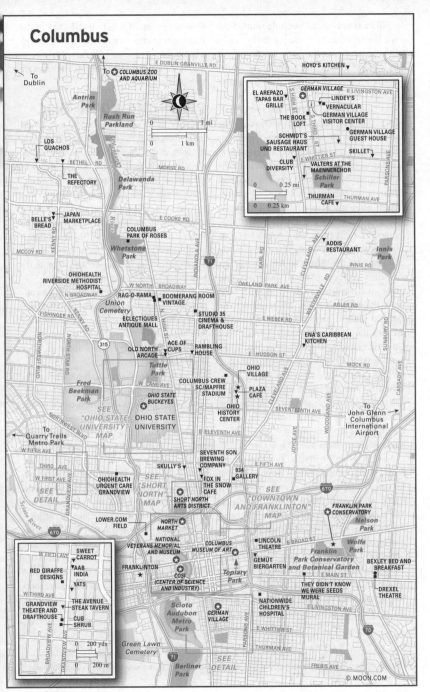

To Dublin

To ● COLUMBUS ZOO AND AQUARIUM

E DUBLIN GRANVILLE RD

HOYO'S KITCHEN ▼

Antrim Park

Rush Run Parkland

LOS GUACHOS ▼

BETHEL RD

MORSE RD

THE REFECTORY

Delawanda Park

0   1 mi
0   1 km

German Village inset:

EL AREPAZO TAPAS BAR GRILLE

GERMAN VILLAGE   E LIVINGSTON AVE

LINDEY'S ▼
VERNACULAR

THE BOOK LOFT

GERMAN VILLAGE VISITOR CENTER

E HIGH ST   E THIRD ST

SCHMIDT'S SAUSAGE HAUS UND RESTAURANT

● GERMAN VILLAGE GUEST HOUSE

SKILLET ▼

CLUB DIVERSITY ▼

E WHITTIER ST

VALTERS AT THE MAENNERCHOR ▼

Schiller Park

PARSONS AVE

0   0.25 mi
0   0.25 km

THURMAN CAFE ▼   THURMAN AVE

BELLE'S BREAD ▼
JAPAN MARKETPLACE

KENNY RD
MCCOY RD

E COOKE RD

COLUMBUS PARK OF ROSES ●

Whetstone Park

INDIANOLA AVE

KARL RD

ADDIS RESTAURANT ●

CLEVELAND AVE

Innis Park

INNIS RD

OHIOHEALTH RIVERSIDE METHODIST HOSPITAL ■

N BROADWAY   W NORTH   BROADWAY

OAKLAND PARK AVE

WESTERVILLE RD

AGLER RD

SUNBURY RD

FISHINGER RD

RAG-O-RAMA ▼   BOOMERANG ROOM VINTAGE

Union Cemetery

N HIGH ST

ECLECTIQUES ANTIQUE MALL ■

■ STUDIO 35 CINEMA & DRAFTHOUSE

E WEBER RD

ENA'S CARIBBEAN KITCHEN ■

315

OLD NORTH ARCADE ▼

ACE OF CUPS ▼

RAMBLING HOUSE ▼

E HUDSON ST

Tuttle Park

NORTHWEST BLVD
NORTH STAR RD

Fred Beekman Park

W LANE AVE

COLUMBUS CREW SC/MAPFRE STADIUM ■

OHIO VILLAGE

CLEVELAND AVE

MOCK RD

CASSADY AVE

SEE "OHIO STATE UNIVERSITY" MAP

NORTHWEST BLVD

OHIO STATE BUCKEYES ●

OHIO STATE UNIVERSITY

★ PLAZA CAFE

OHIO HISTORY CENTER ★

SEVENTEENTH AVE

WOODLAND AVE

To John Glenn Columbus International Airport

To Quarry Trails Metro Park

W FIFTH AVE

E ELEVENTH AVE

THIRD AVE

W FIRST AVE

SEE DETAIL

GRANDVIEW AVE

SEVENTH SON BREWING COMPANY ▼

E FIFTH AVE

934 GALLERY ■

JOYCE AVE

670

FRANKLIN PARK CONSERVATORY ●

OHIOHEALTH URGENT CARE GRANDVIEW ■

SKULLY'S ▼

SEE "SHORT NORTH" MAP

FOX IN THE SNOW CAFE ▼

SEE "DOWNTOWN AND FRANKLINTON" MAP

Nelson Park

SHORT NORTH ARTS DISTRICT ●

Scioto River

670

LOWER.COM FIELD ■

NORTH MARKET ●

NATIONAL VETERANS MEMORIAL AND MUSEUM ■

COLUMBUS MUSEUM OF ART ●

■ LINCOLN THEATRE   E BROAD ST

Wolfe Park

FRANKLIN PARK CONSERVATORY

BEXLEY BED AND BREAKFAST ■

Franklin Park Conservatory and Botanical Garden

Grandview inset:

W FIFTH AVE

SWEET CARROT ▼

RED GIRAFFE DESIGNS

▼ AAB INDIA

YATS ▼

W THIRD AVE

GRANDVIEW THEATER AND DRAFTHOUSE ■

THE AVENUE STEAK TAVERN ▼

CUB ▼
SHRUB ▼

BROADVIEW AVE
GRANDVIEW AVE

0   200 yds
0   200 m

FRANKLINTON ★

COSI (CENTER OF SCIENCE AND INDUSTRY) ●

GEMÜT BIERGARTEN ■

E MAIN ST

THEY DIDN'T KNOW WE WERE SEEDS MURAL ●

DREXEL THEATRE ■

Topiary Park

Scioto Audubon Metro Park

GERMAN VILLAGE ●

PARSONS AVE

NATIONWIDE CHILDREN'S HOSPITAL ■

E LIVINGSTON AVE

E WHITTIER ST

Green Lawn Cemetery

SEE DETAIL

71

Berliner Park

THURMAN AVE

FREBIS AVE

70

© MOON.COM

by political necessity. Everyone wanted the capital near them, so it was put in the center of the state. Columbus grew as Ohio grew, but it didn't develop the name brand or the population that Cincinnati and Cleveland initially did.

As Cincinnati and Cleveland lost prominence, industry, and population through the second half of the 20th century, Columbus gained all three. Buoyed by an aggressive land annexation policy that prevented the city from becoming landlocked by suburbs, Columbus preserved its tax base and diversified its economy with significant insurance, finance, and fashion industries. It quietly became the largest city in Ohio by the late 20th century and is now one of the fastest-growing cities in the United States, with a thriving tech and start-up scene. Artists, designers, and other creatives find ample opportunities to make their marks in a city unencumbered by the past. Indeed, in the United States, there are only more fashion designers in New York City and Los Angeles. The city feels polished in a way that Cincinnati and Cleveland do not, with less of the lived-in grit of those places. Overall, Columbus very much feels like a place looking toward the future instead of the past. Perhaps that's why Ernest Cline picked Columbus as the tech capital of the world in his dystopian novel *Ready Player One*.

So what is there to find in Columbus today? A surprising lineup of distinct neighborhoods, for one, led in stature by charming German Village and the chic Short North Arts District. You'll find the top-rated Columbus Zoo and Aquarium as well as COSI (Center of Science and Industry), one of the nation's top science museums. The Franklin Park Conservatory and Columbus Museum of Art have uniquely angled their exhibits toward children. And throughout the city, you'll find a burgeoning arts and culture scene, craft breweries, and a

diverse restaurant selection reflective of the increasingly international flavor of the city's population.

Oh yeah, and those Ohio State Buckeyes are no slouches either.

PLANNING YOUR TIME

Because of its central location, you could make Columbus the base for your entire trip to Ohio, depending on your interests. As for the city itself, four or five days is plenty of time to see the highlights and explore a couple neighborhoods, though at a faster pace you can hit up nearly all the highlights on a long weekend. Some opt to make the zoo and the water park a two-day affair (the duo offers a combo ticket to facilitate such plans). This is a car-centric city in a car-centric state, so it's best to have one to maximize your time.

Day-trip possibilities abound. Add a couple days to pick an excursion or two that suits your fancy. Cedar Point is only a little over two hours away. Kings Island is even closer. The Hocking Hills region is about an hour from downtown Columbus.

The calendar of events and activities picks up in May and lasts through October. May-June and September-October provide a combination of marquee events and pleasant weather. Summers can get toasty and humid, not to mention rainy, and winters are cold. Snow can be a problem, but it's not to the level of the snowbelt northeast of Cleveland. Nevertheless, winter is certainly the slowest part of the year and you may not get the full experience of the area's outdoor attractions. Throughout the year, you may find that some venues are closed either Sunday or Monday. Beware of the Arnold Sports Festival (a weekend-long bodybuilding and fitness event) in early March and marquee Ohio State football games during the fall—hotels can book up quickly.

Previous: *Short North Gothic* mural by Steve Galgas and Mike Altman; rotunda entrance to Ohio Stadium; Columbus Commons.

ORIENTATION

Columbus is a straightforward city to navigate, with much of the city more or less following a grid and with easy access to major highways. I-70 crosses town east to west while I-71 cuts through northeast to southwest. The outerbelt I-270 circles the city and connects suburbs. An inner ring of unique neighborhoods—Short North to the north, German Village to the south, and Franklinton to the west—circles downtown, connected by High Street running north to south and Broad Street running east to west. The spine of the city, High Street is especially useful, continuing on to The Ohio State University campus, Old North Columbus, and Clintonville as you head north. Divided highway SR 315 runs parallel to High Street for a quicker drive between downtown and I-270.

Sights

DOWNTOWN

There have always been attractions in downtown Columbus, but not always a lot to keep you there. The 21st century brought a whirlwind of development to this formerly nine-to-five part of town. The Arena District, which began construction simultaneously with Nationwide Arena, ushered in a new wave of residential units. The Columbus Commons park brought some much-needed green space. The Scioto Mile brought even more. Further development followed, along with more bars, restaurants, and nightlife that attract people to the area during evenings and on weekends. Though there are still plenty of under-utilized parking lots, downtown Columbus boasts happening pockets along 4th Street, Gay Street, and the area surrounding Nationwide Arena and the Greater Columbus Convention Center.

Ohio Statehouse

The center of gravity in downtown Columbus is the formidable **Ohio Statehouse** (1 Capitol Square, 614/752-9777, ohiostatehouse.org, 8am-5pm Mon.-Fri., 11am-4pm Sat.-Sun., free). This Greek Revival building, completed in 1861, is one of the oldest working statehouses in the United States and is unusual for its lack of a dome. Visitors enter through the 3rd Street entrance, where they check in with security and head to the ground floor for the Ohio Statehouse Museum, a small but interesting display about state government and Ohio history. The real highlight is the hour-long **free guided tour** of the statehouse itself, which leaves every hour on the hour from the Map Room 10am-3pm Monday-Friday and noon-3pm Saturday-Sunday. The tour covers the impressive architecture, decisions that went into the building's design, and notable history—including visits from Abraham Lincoln. The Museum Shop is an excellent place to buy souvenirs, with locally sourced gifts and books about Ohio or political themes.

Scioto Mile

Technically a collection of small, contiguous parks, the **Scioto Mile** (233 S. Civic Center Dr., 614/645-3300, sciotomile.com, 7am-11pm daily, free) is Columbus's front stoop. Over 140 acres of parkland and paved pathways surround the Scioto River as it curves past downtown, providing a central location for outdoor play and some of the best views of the city. Walk past kids enjoying Bicentennial Park's large interactive splash fountain (complete with stainless steel halo towers and light and fog effects) or couples relaxing in swinging chairs along the promenade between Rich and Broad Streets on the east side of the river. Keep an eye out for three bronze statues of bipedal deer enjoying the scenery—one on the Rich Street bridge and two between COSI and the river. During the summer, this riverfront

Downtown and Franklinton

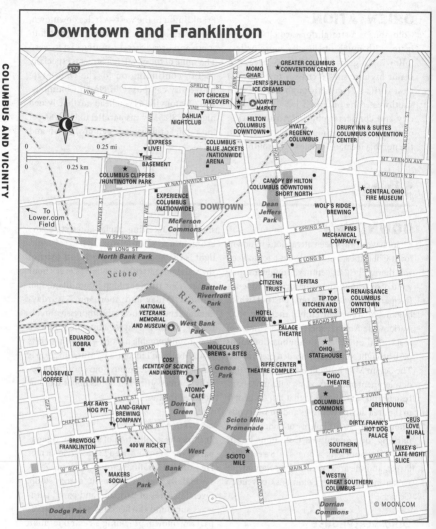

green space hosts large events such as the Columbus Arts Festival and Jazz and Rib Fest. Aside from such events, finding metered parking on the street is a breeze within a block or two of the river.

A good starting point for the Scioto Mile is **Milestone 229** (233 S. Civic Center Dr., 614/427-0276, milestone229.com, 11am-9pm Mon.-Thurs., 11am-10pm Fri.-Sat., 10am-3pm and 4pm-9pm Sun., $14-25), a restaurant in Bicentennial Park that serves up modern American cuisine and patio views of the river and splash fountain.

Columbus Commons

The land that is now the **Columbus Commons** (160 S. High St., 614/545-4701, columbuscommons.org, 7am-11pm daily, free) used to be the enclosed City Center Mall, which enjoyed all of a decade of area retail dominance before flashier malls arrived in the suburbs. Opened in 2011, this

6-acre lawn a block away from the statehouse hosts over 200 free events a year (mostly occurring May-Sept.) including live symphony concerts, fitness classes, and food truck food courts. The technology-driven NEOS playground promotes aerobic exercise with 10 programmed games. **Jeni's Splendid Ice Creams** (11am-4pm Mon.-Wed., 11am-6pm Thurs.-Sat.) and **Taquero Mad Street Food** (11am-8pm Mon.-Sat.) have set up permanent, though seasonal, locations on the south end of the park, next to the carousel ($1 per ride). A 4,500-space underground parking garage resides underneath the park, offering centrally located and inexpensive parking convenient to the park, Ohio Theatre, statehouse, and riverfront. Special events increase the rates.

★ Columbus Museum of Art

Though not as big as its peers in Cincinnati, Cleveland, and even Toledo, the **Columbus Museum of Art** (480 E. Broad St., 614/221-6801, columbusmuseum.org, 10am-5pm Tues.-Wed., 10am-9pm Thurs., 10am-5pm Fri.-Sun., $18 adults, $9 seniors, students, and ages 4-17, free for children 3 and under) sports a fine collection and a focus on engagement and visitor participation, making this a more intimate fine arts experience and one of the more interesting art museums in Ohio for children. The building is comprised of two distinct sections: the long-standing building constructed in 1931 and the striking, rectangular Margaret M. Walter Wing completed in 2015, which houses the museum's contemporary art collection and special exhibitions. The collection's strength resides in American and European art of the late 19th and early 20th centuries by artists such as Monet, Picasso, Miró, and Rockwell. The world's largest collections of works by Columbus artists George Bellows, Aminah Brenda Lynn Robinson, and Elijah Pierce figure prominently as well. Though most of the galleries encourage engagement, with open-ended questions and hands-on activities, kids will especially enjoy the Wonder Room, a unique gallery combining textiles with tactile art stations where they can, for example, design their own bug or engage in a Mad Max-inspired fashion activity.

The sleek **Museum Store** entices visitors with a curated assortment of locally and globally crafted gifts and jewelry. Equally fashionable is the contemporary **Schokko Café** with a short menu of elevated soups, sandwiches, and salads as well as a wine list. The museum is open into the evening on Thursdays, with $5 admission 5pm-9pm. Additionally, the museum is free on Sundays. Parking is $5 in the museum lot.

Topiary Park

Georges Seurat's famous painting *A Sunday Afternoon on the Island of La Grande Jatte* resides in the Art Institute of Chicago, but the three-dimensional version is in Columbus. Over 60 topiaries of people, animals, and boats recreate the scene at **Topiary Park** (480 E. Town St., 614/645-3300, columbus.gov/recreationandparks, 7am-11pm daily, free). An informational sign designates the best spot to take it all in, though you're welcome of course to stand among the carefully pruned bushes and take your place inside the "painting." This small park is framed by the main branch of the Columbus Metropolitan Library and the impressive Cristo Rey High School, housed in the former Ohio School for the Deaf, built in 1899. A small gatehouse (11am-3pm Tues., Thurs., and Sat., noon-4pm Sun. May-Nov.) houses a gift shop and information desk.

Central Ohio Fire Museum

The **Central Ohio Fire Museum** (260 N. 4th St., 614/464-4099, centralohiofiremuseum.wordpress.com, 10am-4pm Tues.-Sat., $8 adults, $7 seniors, $6 children) is housed in the former Engine House No. 16. The 1908 building displays antique fire engines, hoses, and other equipment to interpret yesteryear's firefighting. The museum is also a safety education center, with re-created displays of fire-burned bedrooms, kitchen fire demonstrations, and exhibits of household items that have experienced a fire. More on the fun side,

Flex and Pose with Public Art

The deconstructivist **Greater Columbus Convention Center** (400 N. High St.), designed by Peter Eisenman, is worth a gander in its own right, but there are two noteworthy pieces of public art in and near the center to keep on your radar if walking in the area.

In 1970, bodybuilder **Arnold Schwarzenegger** won the Mr. World competition at Columbus's Franklin County Veterans Memorial Auditorium, defeating three-time champion Sergio Oliva. It was an important early victory for Schwarzenegger, who would later begin a friendship with event organizer Jim Lorimer. Together, they established the Arnold Sports Festival in 1989, an international bodybuilding competition in Columbus that has expanded to include other elements of fitness, bikini, and strongman competitions. It's considered the second most prestigious bodybuilding event in the world, after Mr. Olympia, and draws 200,000 people over one weekend every March. To commemorate the city's long friendship with Schwarzenegger and its importance in the world of bodybuilding, a statue of young Schwarzenegger flexing his bulging arms was dedicated outside the auditorium in 2012. It was relocated outside the convention center, where the festival takes place, in 2014, when the auditorium was slated for demolition to make way for the new National Veterans Memorial and Museum. Today, you can find the statue at the front entrance to the convention center at the intersection of High Street and Spruce Street, perhaps with a line of people ready to flex their arms with the bodybuilder.

Have you ever wanted your face on a statue? *As We Are* is an interactive sculpture of a human head retrofitted with 3,000 LED light panels. Step inside the head, where a photo booth captures the image of your face, and wait for your face to appear on the sculpture minutes later. When the photo booth isn't in use, the sculpture circulates through thousands of pre-captured faces, showcasing a diverse lineup of faces from all colors, creeds, and nationalities. The sculpture resides inside the atrium of the convention center's northwest entrance, facing toward the atrium during the day and the streetscape at night.

kids can don firefighting costumes and climb into a modern fire engine.

★ Franklin Park Conservatory

Regarded as one of the finest botanical gardens in the United States by Thrillist and Travel Channel, the **Franklin Park Conservatory and Botanical Gardens** (1777 E. Broad St., 614/715-8000, fpconservatory.org, 10am-5pm daily, $19 adults, $16 seniors, $12 children 3-12) combines flora, art, and play to promote horticulture and a respect for nature. Over 400 species of plant are on display between the indoor greenhouses and the outdoor gardens. The greenhouses are divided into biomes, each a lush display of color and life. The Victorian-style Palm House is the oldest segment of the conservatory, constructed in 1895 and reminiscent of the World's Columbian Exposition architecture in Chicago. On permanent display throughout the conservatory are 19 pieces of Dale Chihuly's glass sculptures, the largest such permanent collection in a botanical garden. Outside, kids will get the most enjoyment out of the Scotts Miracle-Gro Foundation Children's Garden, a 2-acre natural playground with rock outcroppings, waterfalls, and interactive plant life displays. The *NavStar* sculpture, evoking a ship's sails, dominates the open Grand Mallway.

The **Garden Café** (11am-3pm daily) offers grab-and-go sandwiches, salads, and a small selection of soups and hot sandwiches to enjoy in the main atrium. **Botanica Gift Shop** sells houseplants, home decor, garden supplies, and other related items. Check the events calendar on the website for seasonal events and activities including butterfly releases and holiday displays. Parking at the conservatory is free.

1: downtown Columbus 2: the Scioto Mile Fountain

FRANKLINTON

You wouldn't know by looking at it, but Franklinton is the oldest part of Columbus. Settled in 1797, the neighborhood across the Scioto River from downtown, in fact, predates the city itself. The area has long been known derisively as "The Bottoms" both for its low-lying geography and its working-class roots. A flood plain, the area was hit hard by the Great Flood of 1913 and investors avoided the area for decades, wary of the potential for another disaster. The city completed a new flood wall in 2004 and development has once again returned to this prime location, filling in the blanks of neglect but ushering in gentrification to a low-income area. You'll see a mixture of shiny new buildings and old industrial buildings and houses, as development continues.

Franklinton's riverfront is home to some of the premier cultural institutions of the city. Craft breweries, coffee shops, and creative art spaces have moved in. Franklinton Fridays—the second Friday of each month—showcases the neighborhood's galleries and art studios with events and extended hours at art-minded places like The Vanderelli Room and 400 West Rich. More details can be found at franklintonartsdistrict.com.

★ COSI (Center of Science and Industry)

Rated the #1 science museum in 2008 by *Parent Magazine,* the Center of Science and Industry, or **COSI** (333 W. Broad St., 614/228-2674, cosi.org, 10am-5pm Wed.-Sun., $25 adults, $20 children 2-12), stands opposite downtown across the Scioto River. This massive science museum invites visitors to explore themed hands-on exhibits focusing on, among other things, outer space, energy usage, and the ocean. The Ocean section will certainly be memorable for children, featuring an enormous statue of Poseidon surrounded by an interactive water play area. Access to the **Planetarium** and the **National Geographic Giant Screen Theater** is an additional $5 each, but there are free demonstrations throughout the day; rat basketball is an ongoing favorite. In 2017, the museum began a partnership with New York's American Museum of Natural History, which established a permanent dinosaur gallery and attracts exciting traveling exhibits spanning scientific, historical, and cultural themes.

Though the museum caters to the entire family, a monthly evening event called **COSI After Dark** is a 21-and-over series that allows adults to explore the museum's offerings with drinks in hand and kids at home.

The **Atomic Café** offers sandwiches and grill options, and **Molecules Brews + Bites** outside of the Giant Screen serves up locally roasted Stauf's coffee for your mid-afternoon caffeine boost. A large gift shop in the central atrium features science experiments, books, and trinkets that speak to the geek in us all.

★ National Veterans Memorial and Museum

The round, futuristic building across the street from COSI is the moving **National Veterans Memorial and Museum** (300 W. Broad St., 614/362-2800, nationalvmm.org, 10am-5pm Wed.-Sun., $17 adults, $14 seniors, $10 ages 5-17, free for veterans of all nations). Light on artifacts and heavy on stories, the museum focuses on the people in the armed services and their contributions to the United States. The project was one of the last that astronaut and senator John Glenn had a hand in before his passing, and was recognized by *Architectural Digest* as one of 2018's most anticipated buildings. In the main gallery, a lengthy timeline to the left maintains a high-level rundown of the conflicts Americans have fought in, from the Revolutionary War onward. To the right is a series of human stories on joining the armed forces, life in the service, and the evolution of the military to include minorities and women. Thoughtful exhibits allow visitors to read letters to home,

---

1: Columbus Museum of Art **2:** COSI (Center of Science and Industry) **3:** Ohio Statehouse **4:** the Scotts Miracle-Gro Foundation Children's Garden at the Franklin Park Conservatory

The War Between Ohio and Michigan

Ohio and its neighbor up north, Michigan, have never seen eye to eye. In modern times, this feud has played out on the gridiron between the two winningest college football programs in the United States: the Ohio State Buckeyes and Michigan Wolverines, or as Buckeyes refer to them, "that team up north." The two play each other as the final game of the regular season every year, and it's been a back-and-forth affair over the years (though Ohio State has dominated in the 21st century). During the "Ten Year War" between 1969 and 1978, coaching juggernauts Woody Hayes (OSU) and Bo Schembechler (Michigan) led their respective teams through some of their most successful seasons. A Big Ten Championship, a trip to the Rose Bowl, and even a National Championship was often at stake when they met. The results were split, with four going Ohio State's way, five going Michigan's, and one tie.

It was neither Woody nor Bo that started the fight, though. A dispute over land nearly came to blows in 1835's Toledo War, when conflicting interpretations of Ohio's northern boundary led Michigan—then a territory—and Ohio to send militia to claim the city of Toledo. President Andrew Jackson signed a bill that granted Michigan statehood and the Upper Peninsula as part of the state in exchange for their claim to the "Toledo Strip." At the time, the Upper Peninsula was viewed as a worthless wilderness, so this was not seen as a fair exchange, but Michiganders nevertheless agreed. Michigan became the 26th state, and Ohio kept Toledo.

watch video interviews, leave questions or answers about military service, and honor the veterans in their own lives by inserting a name to temporarily display on a star. On the upper floor, an infinity mirror with a flag flown at Arlington National Cemetery's Tomb of the Unknown Soldier presents a haunting visual of the number of Americans who made the ultimate sacrifice. Outside in the memorial grove, shady elm trees and a long, limestone water feature create a peaceful spot to reflect on the museum's message of service. The memorial grove itself is free, as is walking along the ramp to the top of the building for a wonderful view of downtown Columbus. The walk from the parking lot up the ramp to the main entrance can be daunting for the elderly. Look for the much closer group entrance and buzz in at the post to be let in.

★ GERMAN VILLAGE

The largest privately funded historic district in the United States, 233-acre German Village is the city's preeminent historic neighborhood and the home of many of its favorite culinary destinations. A quieter, more residential counterpart to Cincinnati's massive Over-the-Rhine neighborhood, this district is marked by its cozy, red-brick houses and charming brick streets peppered with neighborhood taverns, cafés, and shops. The neighborhood was settled in the mid-to-late 19th century by the burgeoning German immigrant population, which by 1865 comprised one third of the entire population of Columbus. The village grew so rapidly, and without proper zoning regulations, that a real commercial zone never materialized. Pockets of retail and restaurants popped up on a corner here and there, much like it remains today, contributing to the residential nature. Large breweries set up shop in the adjacent Brewery District.

Xenophobia toward Germans, the onset of Prohibition, new zoning laws, and the demolition of the northern third of the neighborhood for the construction of I-70 ushered in an era

1: a 19th-century house in German Village
2: The Ohio State University 3: National Veterans Memorial and Museum

of decline for the area, which was largely blighted by the 1950s. Columbus residents fought to protect the historic structures that remained and, by 1974, the neighborhood was placed on the National Register of Historic Places. By the 1980s, restoration was nearly complete. Today, German Village is the most strollable neighborhood in Columbus and its Italianate houses are some of the most sought-after real estate in the city. To get your bearings before wandering, check out the **Visitors Center** (588 3rd St., 614/221-8888, germanvillage.com, 9am-4pm Mon.-Fri., 10am-2pm Sat., noon-3pm Sun. Apr.-Nov.).

Schiller Park

Schiller Park (1069 Jaeger St., 614/645-3156, columbus.gov/recreationandparks, 7am-11pm daily, free), opened in 1857, is the second-oldest park in Columbus after Goodale Park (established in 1851). Lawns, stately trees, landscaped gardens, and ponds provide a natural oasis within the urban grid of the neighborhood, all anchored by a statue of German poet Friedrich Von Schiller (1759-1805) in the center and a floral promenade brandishing his quotes. A smaller statue on the northwest corner of the park, *The Umbrella Girl*, is a recreation of a mysteriously lost statue of a girl caught in a perpetual rain shower.

THE OHIO STATE UNIVERSITY

One of the largest college campuses in the United States, The Ohio State University often draws admiration or ire, depending on what stance you take on college football. As a major research institution, though, the university is so much more than its football team. Founded in 1870 as a land-grant university, the school has evolved into a flagship institution for the state.

Countless politicians, prominent scientists, CEOs, entertainers, and athletes have attended Ohio State. Notable Buckeye alumni include 19th U.S. President Rutherford B. Hayes, track-and-field athlete Jesse Owens, golfer Jack Nicklaus, actress Patricia Heaton,

artist Roy Lichtenstein, musician Dwight Yoakam, and author R. L. Stine.

The leafy campus north of downtown includes historic buildings, museums, and the impressive Thompson Library, with its sleek lobby and stately Grand Reading Room. The eastern edge of campus along High Street buzzes with coffee shops and restaurants catering to the student population, live music, and art museums. Start at the central Oval and let your feet wander. (The closest public-parking option to the Oval is the Ohio Union North Garage at 1780 College Rd. S.)

Ohio Stadium

Affectionately known as The Horseshoe, or simply "The Shoe," **Ohio Stadium** (411 Woody Hayes Dr., 614/292-6330, ohiostatebuckeyes.com) is a temple to college football. Opened in 1922, the stadium is on the National Register of Historic Places and has maintained many of its original flourishes despite having undergone several expansions to increase the seat total to its current 102,000. The north-entrance rotunda is the most attractive, with Buckeye-themed stained-glass windows standing guard over the entry gates. A buckeye tree is planted to honor every OSU All-American football player in the Buckeye Grove on the southwest corner of the stadium.

Tours of the stadium are organized by **Ohio State Stadium Tours** (ohiostadiumtours.com). Visit the press box, roam the sidelines, and peek into other unique spots unavailable to ticketholders. Tours are by appointment only and require a minimum two-week notice. It costs $200 for 10 people or fewer, plus $20 for each additional adult.

Wexner Center for the Arts

The postmodern **Wexner Center for the Arts** (1871 N. High St., 614/292-3535, wexarts.org, 11am-6pm Tues.-Wed., 11am-8pm Thurs.-Sat., noon-5pm Sun., $9 adults, $7 seniors, free for college students and children) is a multidisciplinary gallery promoting contemporary art in various mediums. This bold,

The Ohio State University

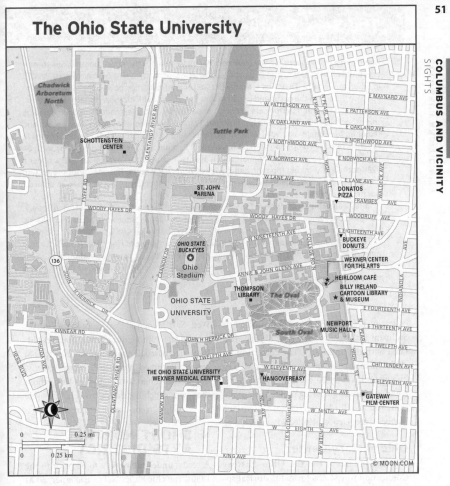

deconstructivist building (designed by Peter Eisenman, who also designed the convention center) houses flexible exhibition spaces, bringing in visiting artists, traveling programs, and temporary exhibits spanning art, film, theater, and music.

Within the center is **The Heirloom Café** (theheirloomcafe.com, 8am-4pm Mon.-Fri., $6-11) which offers healthy breakfasts, sandwiches, and salads as well as café beverages. There's a focus on locally sourced ingredients, including some produce grown on campus.

Admission to the center is free on Thursdays after 4pm and on the first Sunday of every month. Tickets for special events include admission to the gallery.

Billy Ireland Cartoon Library and Museum

Named after a beloved early-20th-century cartoonist for *The Columbus Dispatch,* the **Billy Ireland Cartoon Library and Museum** (1813 N. High St., 614/292-0538, cartoons. osu.edu, 1pm-5pm Tues.-Sun., free) houses the largest collection of comic and cartoon art in the world, including comic strips, original art, political cartoons, comic books, and more. Only a small percentage of the enormous

The Sells Brothers Big Show of the World

Impressed by other circuses and convinced that they could pull their own together, Sells brothers Ephraim, Allen, Lewis, and Peter started the Sells Brothers Big Show of the World in Columbus in 1872. Their first season went well enough that they pooled their life savings to increase the size of the circus and began to tour the country with increasingly large numbers of animals and stunning performers. Among the performers for an extended engagement were sharpshooter Annie Oakley and her husband, Frank Butler, who were noticed by a scout and recruited for Buffalo Bill's Wild West Show. At its height, the circus was the second largest in America, directly competing with names like P. T. Barnum and the Ringling Brothers, with 64 performers, 50 cages of wild animals, 13 elephants, 7 camels, and over 300 workers under a 328-foot-tall (100-m) big top tent, along with six other large tents. This enormous production wintered in Columbus near the Olentangy River and King Avenue in what was then an unincorporated area known as Sellsville.

In 1895, Peter built a mansion at 755 Dennison Avenue at the northwest corner of Goodale Park. Designed by prominent Ohio architect Frank Packard, the Romanesque-style house immediately stands out for its pointed roof reminiscent of a circus tent. The "circus house," as locals often call it, spent time as a Fraternal Order of Police lodge, the House of Hope for Alcoholics, and a nursery before returning to life as a private residence. In 2010, in commemoration of the Sells brothers and their circus, the City of Columbus installed a new fountain in Goodale Park featuring two elephants spraying water below.

collection is viewable by the public in historic Sullivant Hall; this is a research library affiliated with the university. The collection includes historic cartoons from Winsor McCay, known for his early-20th-century *Little Nemo* comic strip and pioneering projects in animation, and the Bill Watterson (of *Calvin and Hobbes* fame) Deposit Collection.

Ohio History Center

The headquarters for the Ohio History Connection (the state's formal historical society), the Ohio History Center (800 E. 17th Ave., 614/297-2300, ohiohistory.org, 10am-5pm Wed.-Sun., $13 adults, $11 seniors, $7 children) is the foremost museum of Ohio history, with dedicated exhibits covering Ohio's ancient cultures, nature, and political and cultural progress. Highlights within the stately, brutalist structure are a full mastodon skeleton, Hopewell culture effigy pipes, and a 1950s-era all-steel Lustron house.

The Plaza Café (11am-2pm daily) serves Mexican favorites, sandwiches, and build-your-own bowls.

Outdoors is Ohio Village (10am-5pm

Wed.-Sun. Memorial Day-Labor Day). This re-created late-19th-century village features old-fashioned baseball games and holiday special events. Costumed interpreters engage with visitors through hands-on activities throughout the town, which includes a town hall, bicycle shop, village green, chapel, and more.

★ SHORT NORTH ARTS DISTRICT

A seedy, undesirable place to be prior to the 1980s, the chic Short North has emerged as one of Ohio's most unique urban districts and as the neighborhood that put Columbus on the map of arts and fashion destinations. A dense assortment of art galleries, bohemian shops, fashion boutiques, coffee houses, bars, nightclubs, and upscale restaurants lines High Street, bridging downtown with The Ohio State University campus. Stretching over High Street are 17 steel, LED-lit arches, paying homage to the old wooden, gaslit arches built in 1888 when Columbus was known as "The Arch City." Victorian Village and Italian Village complement the busy street on either side with late-19th-century and

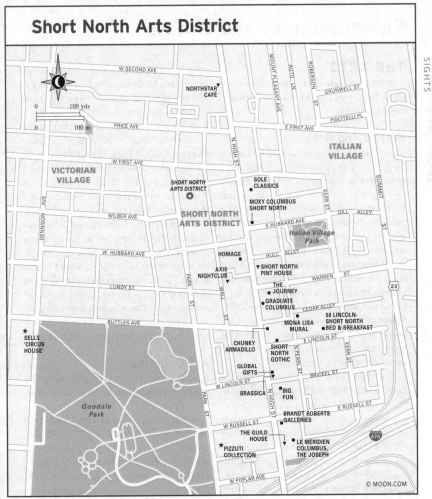

Short North Arts District

early-20th-century housing and a sprinkling of additional retail. This area is the most LGBTQ-friendly area of the city, with many businesses affirming or catering to the local population.

Pizzuti Collection

An extension of the Columbus Museum of Art, the **Pizzuti Collection** (632 N. Park St., 614/221-6801, columbusmuseum.org/pizzuti-collection, 10am-5pm Thurs. and Sun., 10am-8pm Fri.-Sat., $8 adults, seniors, and children over 4) houses the private art collection of developers Ron and Ann Pizzuti. The small, three-story building was constructed in the 1920s. Its spartan galleries display only a small percentage of the over 2,000-piece collection of bold, contemporary art, along with rotating exhibitions from national and international artists. There's a strong emphasis on sculpture, as evidenced by the small sculpture garden in the front of the building. More of the collection is housed in the nearby Le Meridien Columbus, The Joseph hotel a block away.

Entertainment and Events

THE ARTS

Columbus maintains a vibrant, busy arts scene that has only grown since the arrival of the 21st century.

Performing Arts

The opulent 1928 movie palace **Ohio Theatre** (39 E. State St., 614/469-0939, capa.com) is a restoration success story. Saved from demolition in 1969, this nearly 2,800-seat Spanish Baroque-style theater was built by prolific movie palace-architect Thomas W. Lamb and, upon its restoration, converted for performing arts operations. Today, the theater is home to the **Columbus Symphony Orchestra** (columbussymphony.org) and **BalletMet** (balletmet.org). Don't have the stomach or budget for the fine arts? The theater hosts the **CAPA Summer Movie Series** (capa.com), an opportunity to watch a classic blockbuster as the masses used to, complete with cartoons and a live organ performance.

The Ohio Theatre isn't the only game in town. Nearby **Palace Theatre** (34 W. Broad St., 614/469-9850, capa.com) is another of Lamb's movie palace turned performing arts centers. Less ornate and slightly smaller than the Ohio, the Palace maintains a busy schedule of traveling live performances, including Broadway shows. Older than both is the **Southern Theatre** (21 E. Main St., 614/469-1045, capa.com), dating back to 1896 as part of the "Great Southern Fireproof Hotel and Opera House." This two-balcony 933-seater, restored and reopened in 1998, is home to **Opera Columbus** (operacolumbus.org), **Columbus Jazz Orchestra** (jazzartsgroup.org) and **ProMusica Chamber Orchestra** (promusicacolumbus.org). The Egyptian-revival **Lincoln Theatre** (capa.com), opened in 1928, boasts a history as a major jazz center, having hosted performances by Duke Ellington, Miles Davis, and Etta James, to name a few. It received a major restoration in

2009 and is once again a prominent fixture in the city's African American community as well as a busy multipurpose performance and education center.

Aside from music, a few notable acting troupes keep things lively. Professional theater company **CATCO** (catco.org) performs at the modern **Riffe Center Theatre Complex** (77 S. High St., 614/460-7214, capa.com), which boasts the 903-seat Davidson Theatre and three studio-style theaters. During the summer months, **Actors' Theatre of Columbus** (theactorstheatre.org) performs primarily Shakespearean plays on Schiller Park's open-air stage. Bring lawn chairs! **Short North Stage** (shortnorthstage.org) breathes life into the former Garden Theatre, a small movie palace that suffered decades as a dingy burlesque. Today, the theater seats 138 for an eclectic variety of comedies, musicals, and cabarets.

Art Galleries

Most of Columbus's best art galleries are located either in the Short North or Franklinton.

In Franklinton, AJ Vanderelli curates shows by local artists at **The Vanderelli Room** (218 McDowell St., 614/403-4689, thevanderelliroom.com), the gallery she founded, as well as at **400 West Rich** (400 W. Rich St., 614/454-1287, 400westrich.com), an early-20th-century warehouse turned creative arts space with over 100 tenant artists.

In the Short North, **Brandt-Roberts Galleries** (642 N. High St., 614/223-1655, brandtrobertsgalleries.com) is one of the Columbus area's premier contemporary galleries for regional and national artists. **934 Gallery** (934 Cleveland Ave., 934gallery.org) hosts quirky contemporary shows from around the world and wins points for its colorful outdoor murals.

1: Ohio Stadium at The Ohio State University
2: Ohio Theatre

Murals

Dozens of Instagrammable murals color the streetscape with fanciful depictions of familiar paintings, quirky characters, and representations of the city's cultures. Many are centered around the Short North, with an increasing number in downtown and Franklinton. All reflect the city's growing reputation as an art and design destination. Below are some of the highlights.

- The *CBus Love Mural* (257 S. Young St.), designed by Alex Haldi and produced by NKDSGN, boldly spells out COLUMBUS in black and white, but by night is lit up to reveal the word "love" within the lettering.

- *Short North Gothic* (8 E. Lincoln St.) by Steve Galgas and Mike Altman puts a fun twist on the classic *American Gothic* painting.

- Likewise, the *Mona Lisa Mural* (28 Bollinger Pl.) by Brian Clemons presents the famous painting from a different perspective.

- A rallying cry for the oppressed, *They Didn't Know We Were Seeds* (1340 E. Main St.) by Patrick Torres and Julie combines a popular quote in bold letters with a growing garden.

- There is tons of street art around and on the ultra-modern Gravity building (500 W. Broad St.), most notably the enormous **self-portrait** of Brazilian street artist **Eduardo Kobra.**

- Just as impressive is *The Journey* (750 N. High St.) on the side of the Graduate Columbus hotel. Designed by Ryan "Yanoe" Sarfati and Eric "Zoueh" Skotnes, the mural celebrates the large Somali population in the Columbus area. Download the app The Journey AR Mural for an augmented reality experience with the artwork.

Cinema

Columbus features several quality independent movie theaters. The largest is the modern **Gateway Film Center** (1550 N. High St., 614/247-4433, gatewayfilmcenter.org), located next to the Ohio State campus and named one of the 20 best North American arthouses by Sundance. The varied theater sizes show anything from the latest blockbuster to the smallest art house flick. Keep an eye on the event calendar for movie marathons and other intriguing programming. Clintonville's **Studio 35 Cinema and Drafthouse** (3055 Indianola Ave., 614/262-7505, studio35.com) is a more intimate neighborhood theater, serving pizza and over 40 beers on tap representing a wild mix of local and national craft breweries. There are two screens—a 195-seater and a 28-seater—allowing the cinema to host a mix of blockbusters, independent flicks, and late-night programming.

FESTIVALS AND EVENTS

The Columbus calendar is bursting with events year-round, though Memorial Day through October is particularly busy. One longstanding date, **Gallery Hop** (shortnorth.org), is the first Saturday of every month. High Street in the Short North bursts with street performers and visitors as art galleries, bars, and restaurants stay open late, though the official Gallery Hop hours are 4pm-9pm.

Late June's progressive, volunteer-run **ComFest** (comfest.com) takes over the Short North's Goodale Park with music, art, food, and a come-as-you-are attitude for a weekend. The **Ohio State Fair** (ohiostatefair.com), which runs for 12 days in late July and early August, is one of the largest state fairs in the country and includes an extensive concert lineup, a large number of rides, and a renowned butter calf.

Many of the city's biggest events take place along the riverfront. The prestigious **Columbus Arts Festival** (columbusartsfestival.org) pulls in hundreds of local, national, and international artists and craftworkers for a weekend in mid-June. Grab a spot early for **Red, White, and Boom!** (redwhiteandboom.com), the largest Independence Day fireworks display in the Midwest. The fireworks are released from behind COSI. Late July's **Jazz and Rib Fest** (hotribscooljazz.org) combines award-winning barbecue joints and live musical performances over a weekend along the Scioto River.

A significant outlier on the schedule, Arnold Schwarzenegger's **Arnold Sports Festival** (arnoldsportsfestival.com) is a major international bodybuilding and fitness expo that pulls in over 20,000 athletes and hundreds of thousands of visitors to the Greater Columbus Convention Center area over one weekend in early March.

Recreation

PARKS

Columbus boasts over 20 metro parks, mainly outside I-270, that feature thousands of acres of woods, prairies, and wetlands, with opportunities for hiking and other recreational activities.

One of the most popular hiking spots is **Highbanks Metro Park** (9466 Columbus Pike, 614/906-3149, metroparks.net), 16 miles (26 km) north of downtown and named after the 100-foot (30-m) bluffs off of the Olentangy River. Hiking trails pass through deep ravines, past ancient earthworks, and through prairies. A bald eagle nest is distantly visible at the end of the moderate **Overlook Trail** (2.3 mi/3.7 km round-trip). Larger still is **Battelle Darby Creek Metro Park** (1775 Darby Creek Dr., 614/370-6254, metroparks.net), 18 miles (29 km) southwest of downtown, preserving a stretch of Big Darby Creek, a National Scenic River. Trails hug the creek or wander into the park's woods and prairies. The modern nature center features live animals, engaging displays on creek life, and an overlook over the resident bison herd, reintroduced into the park in expansive enclosures.

Currently under development is **Quarry Trails Metro Park** (metroparks.net), which will reclaim a former quarry 8 miles (12.9 km) west of downtown, at the corner of Trabue and Dublin Roads, and provide some of the most unique rock climbing, mountain biking, kayaking, and hiking opportunities in the city.

For more of an urban oasis, check out Clintonville's **Columbus Park of Roses** (3901 N. High St., 614/645-3391, parkofroses.org), 7 miles (11.3 km) north of downtown. One of the largest public rose gardens in the United States, the 13-acre garden incorporates five different themes, including the Formal Rose Garden and Perennial Garden, and over 12,000 rose bushes. The colorful, curated garden is a popular wedding venue for locals.

Alum Creek State Park (3365 S. Old State Rd., Lewis Center, 740/548-4039, ohiodnr.gov), 19 miles (31 km) north of town, has hiking trails, campgrounds, a large reservoir for boating and fishing, and most popularly a 3,000-foot (914-m) swimming beach.

CYCLING

The combined **Olentangy** and **Scioto Trails** are over 24 continuous miles (39 km) along woodsy riverside and connect Worthington (north of the city), the Ohio State campus, downtown, and German Village. Many of the city's attractions are a short distance from the trail. There are many trailheads, but some helpful ones with parking are at Antrim Park (5800 Olentangy River Rd.), Park of Roses (3901 N. High St.), and Scioto Audubon Metro Park (400 W. Whittier St.). Additionally, the

31-mile (50-km) **Alum Creek Trail** offers a scenic ride through neighborhoods, woodlands, and wetlands, with helpful trailheads at Three Creeks Park (3860 Bixby Rd., Groveport) and Wolfe Park (105 Park Dr.). For more information on the area's bicycle trails, visit centralohiogreenways.com. For bike rentals, you'll find plenty of **COGO** (cogobikeshare.com) stations near the trails. A single 30-minute ride is $2; a day pass costs $8.

KAYAKING, CANOEING, AND PADDLEBOARDING

Olentangy Paddle (855/643-8611, olentangypaddle.com) offers four kayaking itineraries on the Scioto and Olentangy Rivers, including one downtown that leaves from the boat ramp in Scioto Audubon Metro Park (400 W. Whittier St.). Tours are guided, run about 2.5 hours, and cost $40 for adults and $20 for kids. The outfitter also provides bike rentals.

Southwest of the city in a rural corner of Franklin County is **Trapper John's Canoe Livery** (7141 London Groveport Rd., Grove City, 614/877-4321, trapperjohnscanoeing. com). Situated on the scenic Big Darby Creek, the livery offers self-guided kayak and canoe trips of varying length, from 1-2 hours to 5-6 hours, as well as shuttle pick up.

ROCK CLIMBING

Scioto Audubon Metro Park (400 W. Whittier St., 614/202-5197, metroparks.net) is an industrial brownfield turned urban playground and popular haunt for birding enthusiasts. The highlight is the largest free outdoor climbing wall in the United States. Climbers must bring their own equipment. Smaller boulders that don't require equipment are available for young ones.

SPECTATOR SPORTS
★ Ohio State Buckeyes

The **Ohio State Buckeyes** (ohiostatebuckeyes.com) **football** program is one of the most successful in the country, made even more legendary by the massive **Ohio Stadium** (411 Woody Hayes Dr.,

614/292-6330) on the banks of the Olentangy River. Columbus lacks a National Football League team, though you would hardly notice; the city treats its Buckeyes, for better or worse, like its home team. The Buckeyes serve as a rallying point for the entire state, though. In some ways, the campus is the beating heart of Ohio.

Attending a game at Ohio Stadium is a bucket list item for many football fans, Buckeye or not. If you manage to grab tickets to a game, make sure to arrive early enough to watch the beloved **Ohio State University Marching Band,** known as "The Best Damn Band in the Land" (or TBDBITL) in their traditional pregame performances. Doors at **St. John Arena** (410 Woody Hayes Dr.) open four hours prior to kickoff for the "Skull Session," a final rehearsal/pep rally, with the band starting two hours and 20 minutes before the game. Seating is first-come, first-served and attendance is free. If you're not that committed, be in your seat in the stadium at least 20 minutes before game time to watch the band march into the stadium for their pregame show, including the "Script Ohio" tradition in which the band gradually spells "Ohio" in cursive lettering. The band is also known for its half-time shows complete with outlandish formations and pop culture references.

The university sponsors a large number of men's and women's teams. Second in popularity to the football program is the **men's basketball team** (ohiostatebuckeyes.com), which has enjoyed its own share of success and plays in the massive **Schottenstein Center** (555 Borror Dr., schottensteincenter.com). More successful is the **women's basketball team**, which also plays in the arena.

Soccer

Columbus is an important American soccer city as a frequent host site for the U.S. National Team and as home of the **Columbus Crew**

1: an Ohio State Buckeyes football game 2: Nationwide Arena, home of the Columbus Blue Jackets 3: Columbus Park of Roses 4: Scioto Audubon Metro Park

SC (columbuscrewsc.com), one of the original Major League Soccer teams. The team plays in **Lower.com Field** (96 Columbus Crew Way, lowerfieldcbus.com) in the Arena District.

Hockey

The NHL's **Columbus Blue Jackets** (nhl.com/bluejackets) maintain a devoted following, playing games in the Arena District's **Nationwide Arena** (200 W. Nationwide Blvd., 614/246-2000, nationwidearena.com). Games are lively, with a replica cannon—referencing the team's Civil War theme (Blue Jackets is a reference to Union soldiers)—that fires every time the home team scores.

Baseball

As far as minor league baseball goes, it's hard to beat the **Columbus Clippers** (milb.com/columbus). The Triple-A affiliate of the Cleveland Indians is one of the most valuable minor league teams in the country and plays at handsome **Huntington Park** (330 Huntington Park Ln., 614/462-5250) in the Arena District.

Shopping

GERMAN VILLAGE

Booklovers may spend hours perusing **The Book Loft** (631 S. 3rd St., 614/464-1774, 10am-11pm daily), a conglomeration of pre-Civil War buildings and a local favorite. Hallways, nooks, and crannies in this labyrinthine 32-room bookstore are filled to the brim with every genre imaginable. Those who are claustrophobic may want to enjoy the outdoor courtyard and its small book selection instead. Check the website for coupons and special seasonal deals.

Women's apparel boutique **Vernacular** (177 E. Beck St., 614/228-2316, 11am-7pm Mon.-Sat., 11am-5pm Sun.) mixes modern, approachable apparel with accessories and fragrances, as well as home decor and kitchen accessories. Another location is in Grandview Heights.

SHORT NORTH ARTS DISTRICT

Many of Columbus's best **boutiques** operate one, if not their only, location in the Short North. You'll find dozens of apparel, gift, vintage, and bookshops along High Street, marching in a line from I-670 almost all the way north to the Ohio State campus.

If you spend any amount of time walking in the city, you're bound to see locals sporting shirts from **Homage** (783 N. High St., 614/706-4254, 10am-8pm Mon.-Sat., noon-6pm Sun.). Specializing in Ohio-themed and vintage pop culture apparel, Homage puts a uniquely Buckeye spin on designer tops and accessories. Prices are a little steep, but the quality is also quite high. There are six locations throughout the state, including one in Easton Town Center.

Sole Classics (846 N. High St., 614/299-2290, 11am-8pm Mon.-Sat., noon-6pm Sun.) is a full-service sneaker boutique that sells fresh streetwear, including apparel. The store's vibe—and its wares—is contemporary and retro, with funky alien characters adorning the walls. The store sells original, local designs and a curated selection of brands.

"Everything a modern, wild-hearted gypsy diva needs" is how **Chunky Armadillo** (726 N. High St., 614/826-0041, chunkyarmadillo. com, 1pm-7pm Tues., noon-7pm Wed.-Sat., 1pm-5pm Sun.) brands itself. Part country charm, part celebration of bohemia, this expressive boutique carries clothing, locally made gifts, and rustic, repurposed decor that, all together, shapes a vibe that is unique to the Short North.

Non-profit **Global Gifts** (682 N. High St., 614/621-1744, 10:30am-6pm Mon.-Sat.) promotes fair-trade and sustainable economic opportunities, with artisans and farmers from over 40 countries. Products include an eclectic arrangement of home goods, toys, jewelry, coffees and teas, and other gifts from around the world.

Toy lovers young and old will not want to miss out on **Big Fun** (672 N. High St., 614/228-8697, 11am-7pm Tues.-Sun.). This vintage toy shop is jam-packed with action figures, collector items, and novelty gifts in a spunky celebration of geek culture.

CLINTONVILLE

High Street continues north past the Ohio State campus and the Old North Columbus district to this well-to-do neighborhood of early- to mid-20th-century homes. Many of the city's best **secondhand and vintage shops** reside here, as do locations of many of the city's popular restaurants (Hot Chicken Takeover and Northstar Café, for example).

Eclectiques Antique Mall (3265 N. High St., 614/447-2242, eclectiquesantique-mall.com, 11am-6pm daily) occupies two large floors and covers all the essentials of antiquing: long-gone kitchen accessories, vintage decor, and wacky odds and ends. Additionally, you'll find secondhand clothing and a solid collection of mid-century modern

furniture. Across the street from Eclectiques Antique Mall is the equally browse-worthy **Boomerang Room Vintage** (3274 N. High St., 614/262-9661, boomerangroom.com, noon-5pm Sun.-Fri., 11am-6pm Sat.), also with a good selection of artwork, decor, and furniture fitting the mid-century modern aesthetic.

Hip **Rag-O-Rama** (3301 N. High St., 614/261-7202, ragorama.com, 11am-8pm Mon.-Sat., noon-7pm Sun.) curates an eclectic assortment of recycled men's and women's clothing, accessories, handbags, and jewelry. It may look like a thrift store, but don't expect similar prices; these are gently used designer brands.

Trendy boutique **Tigertree** (3284 N. High St., 614/299-2660, 10am-5pm Tues.-Sat., 11am-4:30pm Sun.) is one of the city's favorite gift shops, with playful accessories, games and puzzles, stationery, and decor for the youthful spirit in us all.

MALLS
Easton Town Center

You have **Easton Town Center** (160 Easton Town Center St., 614/337-2200, easton.com) to thank, or blame, for the profusion of outdoor malls that have largely replaced enclosed malls

The Book Loft

in the 21st century. Opened in 1999, Easton was an early adopter of the concept, combining traditional mall retail with upscale dining, entertainment options, and a re-creation of a mid-20th-century town square. The mall boasts more than 240 retail shops, which include a good mix of typical mall stalwarts, upscale shops with little or no other presence in Ohio, and satellite locations of local favorites such as Homage and Hot Chicken Takeover. Designed to resemble a railroad terminal, the central building is dominated by a massive AMC Theater, along with a **Legoland Discovery Center** (614/407-7721, columbus.legolanddiscoverycenter.com).

Polaris Fashion Place

The largest enclosed mall in the area is **Polaris Fashion Place** (1500 Polaris Pkwy., 614/846-1500, polarisfashionplace.com), which includes a mix of local, regional, and national retailers—some unique to Columbus or Ohio, such as Where I'm From, which sells locally inspired attire.

Food

Columbus's food scene reflects the state's rich agricultural heritage; recent immigration waves from Latin America, Asia, and Africa; and The Ohio State University's consistent draw of international students. The big name in town is Cameron Mitchell, whose restaurant empire includes 20 upscale concepts throughout the metropolitan area.

DOWNTOWN

Downtown Columbus has a nice mix of inexpensive quick bites and upscale, destination-dining options, though you'll notice some choices disappear after lunchtime. You'll find most of the places you want in a few livelier corridors, namely Gay Street between High Street and 3rd Street, near the intersection of 4th Street and Main Street, and the area in front of the convention center.

★ North Market

If you grab a bite in one place in Columbus, make it **North Market** (59 Spruce St., 614/463-9664, northmarket.com, 9am-7pm Tues.-Sat., 10am-5pm Sun.-Mon.). Dating back to 1876, North Market is the last surviving public market in Columbus. It has bounced between locations over the years but has been situated on Spruce Street in an old thresher warehouse since 1995. As both an incubator for small businesses and an attractive satellite location for local favorites, the market presents Columbus at its most up-to-date; more than 30 vendors reflect long-standing institutions and the latest concepts. More a food hall than Ohio's other public markets, it offers your traditional butchers, bakers, and cheesemongers interspersed with Vietnamese, Italian, Thai, and other culinary options.

North Market is the birthplace of what is arguably Columbus's most famous culinary export: **Jeni's Splendid Ice Creams** (jenis.com). Jeni Britton Bauer opened her artisan ice cream stand in the market in 2002, serving unique flavors of ice cream such as Brown Butter Almond Brittle and Wildberry Lavender using Ohio's agricultural pedigree to her advantage. Today there are over 40 Jeni's scoop shops across the country, including 10 in Columbus. Another concept made popular in the market, **Hot Chicken Takeover** (hotchickentakeover. com), is as much a social enterprise as it is a Nashville-style hot chicken concept, giving folks with barriers to employment a shot at a new start. There are two additional locations in Clintonville and Easton and another in Cleveland. Two examples of restaurants that started elsewhere in the city and then came to the market are Nepalese **Momo Ghar** (facebook.com/momogharohio), which has received national attention for

Somali Food in Columbus

There are an estimated 38,000 Somali immigrants and refugees residing in the city, a population second only to the Minneapolis-St. Paul metropolitan area. Somalis began arriving in the city in the mid-1990s as a result of the horrific civil war devastating their home country. Their numbers have since swelled, with significant communities in several corners of the city, most prominently the northeast part of town. It was roundabouts here that fast-casual **Hoyo's Kitchen** (5788 Columbus Sq., 614/899-8800, hoyoskitchen.com, 11am-9pm Mon.-Tues. and Thurs.-Sat., 11am-8pm Sun., $10-13), now also a popular stand at North Market, found its start and still operates its original location. Opened in 2014, family-owned Hoyo's Kitchen is the most visible Somali restaurant in Columbus, serving up build-your-own bowls with beef, chicken, and goat as well as samosa-like *sambusas*. There are other restaurants serving Somali food as well, most of them in the northeast quadrant of the city. The cuisine is a vibrant mix of East African, Arabian, Indian, and Italian influences. In total, there are over 600 Somali-owned businesses throughout Columbus as the population integrates itself into the city, and the city embraces their contributions.

its dumplings, and **Hoyo's Kitchen** (hoyoskitchen.com), a popular fast-casual Somali food stand.

There is plenty of seating on the market's 2nd floor—accessible by elevator—as well as outdoor seating on either side of the building. The market's parking lot is off Vine Street and offers cheap parking with a validated ticket. (The lot may not be long for this world as there are plans in development to build a high-rise.) Additional street parking is best found on Park Street or down farther south on Goodale Street.

Contemporary

One of the most exceptional fine dining choices in Columbus is **Veritas** (11 W. Gay St., 614/745-3864, veritasrestaurant.com, 5pm-10pm Tues.-Sat., $18-30), housed in a former bank building. The experimental kitchen constantly churns out audacious tasting menus (around $55-95 pp depending on the menu) as well as a rotating menu of smaller plates, and the restaurant is known for exemplary wine pairings. If you can't stay for dinner, at least grab a drink at **The Citizens Trust** (thecitizenstrust.com, 4pm-11pm Wed.-Thurs., 4pm-midnight Fri.-Sat.), Veritas's sister cocktail bar in the former bank's luxurious, high-ceilinged lobby.

Gastropub

★ **Wolf's Ridge Brewing** (215 N. 4th St., 614/429-3936, wolfsridgebrewing.com, 11am-9pm Tues.-Fri., 10am-9pm Sat.-Sun., $10-27) has carved a name for itself as one of the city's most well-regarded drinking and dining establishments, combining popular craft brews that you'll find in area bars and groceries with elevated American cuisine. There are actually two dining experiences to choose from in this industrial-chic space. The Tap Room is the more accessible, with meaty sandwiches and burgers dominating the menu. For a more sophisticated experience, the Dining Room offers tasting menus alongside such sumptuous offerings as quail and braised lamb shank pie.

Hot Dogs

An alternative to downtown's fancy eats is the delightfully tacky **Dirty Frank's Hot Dog Palace** (248 S. 4th St., 614/824-4673, dirtyfranks.com, 11am-2am daily, $7-10), an inexpensive choice for daytime meals and late-night noshes. Choose from one of the over 30 specialty dogs and customize with any number of toppings (or have your dog wrapped in bacon), available for a small extra charge. Beer and liquor are on hand as well. Wiener Wednesdays feature a $5 wiener-and-fries deal.

Pizza

Have a hankering for pizza at midnight? Near Dirty Frank's Hot Dog Palace is one of four **Mikey's Late Night Slice** (268 S. 4th St., 614/737-3801, latenightslice.com, 11am-3am Sun.-Thurs., 11am-4am Fri.-Sat., $4-6 per slice) locations. Order by the slice—one or two will do you just fine—or by the whole pie. A dozen craft beers are on tap to add to your night in this irreverent Columbus staple.

German

Just across I-71 from downtown is unique brewpub **Gemüt Biergarten** (734 Oak St., 614/725-1725, gemutbiergarten.com, 4pm-10pm Mon.-Thurs., 4pm-midnight Fri., 11am-midnight Sat., 11am-10pm Sun., $9-18). The family-friendly brewery's beers are inspired by Norse mythology characters, the likenesses of whom are reflected in stunning stained-glass windows behind the bar. A large biergarten outside features a gazebo, kids' area, and plenty of shade. The menu is smaller than at other German restaurants in town but covers the basics and is the most flexible with those coveted German side dishes.

FRANKLINTON

Franklinton does not yet have the density of retail and restaurants that serves places like the Short North. A number of developments are in various stages of construction or proposal which will add significantly to the number of offerings.

Barbecue

The best barbecue in town is at food truck **Ray Ray's Hog Pit** (424 W. Town St., 614/404-9742, rayrayshogpit.com, 11:30am-8pm Thurs. and Sun., 11:30am-10pm Fri.-Sat., $9-16). Featured on the Food Network, Ray Ray's maintains a relationship with **Land-Grant Brewing Company,** serving as the brewery's official food provider. Stand in line next to the smoker and take your St. Louis-style ribs or sandwich inside the brewery for a seat. There are three other permanent food truck locations, each with a side dish particular to that location. Prices and portions are reasonable.

Coffee

The mission of **Roosevelt Coffee** (462 W. Broad St., 614/892-9633, roosevelcoffee.org, 7am-5pm Mon.-Fri., 8am-5pm Sat.-Sun.) mixes java with justice. Profits from the fresh, sustainably sourced coffee, roasted down the street, support initiatives fighting hunger, unclean water, and human trafficking. The walls in this location, inside the ultra-modern Gravity building, feature Instagram-worthy murals (and the building's exterior features murals as well).

GERMAN VILLAGE

Nearly all of German Village's dining options are held in high regard, so you should have no trouble finding something tasty.

Surf and Turf

Fine-dining establishment ★ **Lindey's** (169 E. Beck St., 614/228-4343, lindeys.com, 11am-10pm Sun.-Thurs., 11am-11pm Fri.-Sat., $15-47) beckons with what is arguably Columbus's best patio experience, with trickling fountains, romantic lighting, shady trees, and lush greenery promoting an intimate, secret garden vibe. Inside is no less exquisite, with chandeliers and wood decor. The classy surf-and-turf menu covers expected territory, all done up with creative flourishes. And, of course, there's a long wine list to pair with your delicacies. Save room for Lindey's Post Mortem, a chocolate brownie topped with coffee ice cream and Kahlua hot fudge. Lindey's has been a favorite special occasion destination for four decades; reservations are recommended.

Burgers

Featured on *Man v. Food*, divey **Thurman Café** (183 Thurman Ave., 614/443-1570, thethurmancafe.com, 11am-1am daily, bar open

1: cream puff at Schmidt's Sausage Haus und Restaurant 2: stained-glass window in the Gemüt Biergarten 3: North Market 4: Roosevelt Coffee

to 2:30am daily, $8-20) is well known as a favorite destination of bodybuilders during the Arnold Fitness Classic held in the city every March. The massive three-quarter-pound hamburgers aren't for the faint of heart, and neither is the Thurmanator challenge. It's worth upgrading the kettle chips you get with your burger to fries. You should also count on a wait during peak times.

German

Dating back to 1886, **Schmidt's Restaurant und Sausage Haus** (240 E. Kossuth St., 614/444-6808, schmidthaus.com, 11am-9pm daily, $10-23) is a Columbus institution. You'll find Schmidt's food trucks present at festivals and sporting events year-round, but the real deal is in an old livery stable in German Village. There's oompah music, brick and wood decor, and plenty of families and large parties contributing to the busy, jovial atmosphere. The restaurant is particularly famous for its Bahama Mama sausages and gigantic cream puffs. Though the menu covers an extensive list of German favorites, many opt for the Autobahn buffet, which features a highlight reel of the menu.

For a more intimate neighborhood experience, check out **Valter's at the Maennerchor** (976 S. High St., 614/444-3531, valtersatthemaennerchor.com, 11am-10pm Mon.-Thurs., 11am-11pm Fri., 9am-11pm Sat., 9am-11pm Sun., $10-33). Set up in a 1907 brick house, Valter's serves authentic German food and beer in a couple of cozy rooms adorned with vintage memorabilia like old-world coats of arms. The menu includes nicely portioned plates and an affordable sandwich menu with brats, fried bologna, and schnitzel. The restaurant is the home venue of the **Columbus Maennerchor** (maennerchor.com), the nation's largest and longest continually active German singing club. Check the club's website for a performance schedule.

Latin American

El Arepazo Latin Grill (515 S. High St., 614/471-7296, elarepazolatingrill.com,

11am-2pm and 5pm-9pm Mon.-Thurs., 11am-2pm and 5pm-9:30pm Fri., 1pm-8:30pm Sat., $9-18) specializes in Venezuelan and Colombian cuisine, particularly arepa pocket sandwiches. Creative cocktails and sangria are the highlights of the bar offerings. The decor is chic without being pretentious, making for an approachable choice for a date night. Grab a bottle of the cilantro sauce to go.

Breakfast

Neither simple nor complicated, hole-in-the-wall **Skillet** (410 E. Whittier St., 614/443-2266, skilletruf.net, 8am-2pm Wed.-Sun., $9-14) bills itself as "rustic urban food" and offers one of the city's most sought-after brunch menus. Side dishes such as cheese grits and Cincinnati-style *goetta* (meat-and-grain sausage), as well as trendy breakfast beverages, allow visitors to customize their meals more than at most places, though prices can add up quickly. The restaurant's decor matches the theme of its food, with exposed brick walls and simple wooden tables.

SHORT NORTH ARTS DISTRICT
Contemporary

Cameron Mitchell's **The Guild House** (624 N. High St., 614/280-9780, theguildhouse-columbus.com, 6:30am-10pm Mon.-Thurs., 6:30am-11pm Fri.-Sat., 6:30am-9pm Sun., $20-40) is an urban rustic counterpart to the chic **Le Meridien Columbus, The Joseph** hotel in which it resides. Locally sourced but globally inspired, the menu of this high-end dining establishment covers pasta, elegantly prepared meat entrées, and a lengthy list of sumptuous starters and appetizers. Sides are purchased separate from entrées. Cocktails and an extensive wine list are available to pair with your meal, all of which you'll enjoy in a modern, yet comfortable dining room.

Northstar Café (951 N. High St., 614/298-9999, thenorthstarcafe.com, 9am-9pm daily, $10-18) is known for its elevated diner food, cocktail and local craft beer selection, and brunch menu. Vegans will be happy to find several options to choose from. There are five locations in all, each with a slightly different menu, so choose wisely! The Short North's location is a good spot for people-watching, with a bright and airy dining room and large windows facing High Street.

Gastropub

The **Short North Pint House** (780 N. High St., 614/429-3986, shortnorthpinthouse. com, 3pm-2am Mon.-Thurs., 11am-2am Fri.-Sun., $10-14) has a biergarten conviviality, a sports-bar-worthy number of TVs, and above-average pub food. The menu covers pizza, burgers, sandwiches, and an interesting variety of shareables, including short rib nachos and Reuben quesadillas. The weekend brunch menu adds even more options. Beer lovers will find more than 75 options to choose from between drafts, bottles, and cans.

Mediterranean

From the folks at Northstar Café, **Brassica** (680 N. High St., 614/867-5885, brassicas. com, 11am-10pm daily, $8-14) combines a fast-casual, build-your-own pita sandwich or bowl concept with bold Mediterranean flavors and trendy decor. Minty pink lemonade and a small selection of local craft beer rounds out an interesting drink selection. This place gets busy during the rush—you may find the locations in the suburbs Bexley and Upper Arlington have more seating available.

Breakfast

There are three locations of local roaster ★ **Fox in the Snow** (1031 N. 4th St., 614/372-5677, foxinthesnow.com, 7am-5pm Mon.-Fri., 8am-5pm Sat.-Sun.), but this Italian Village location is the first. Named one of the best coffee shops in America by *Food & Wine Magazine,* this welcoming café is as known for its exquisite baked goods and egg sandwich as it is for its coffee. The atmosphere is jovial, with both large and small tables in the naturally lit space to accommodate groups of all sizes. Note: there is no wi-fi, an intentional

decision to encourage conversation and time away from the screen.

LINDEN

Those with palates for African cuisine ought to take a side trip to the predominately African American neighborhood of Linden and the area near Morse Road, which is one of the most multicultural parts of the city, with newly arrived refugees, immigrants, and long-established families all co-mingling on the east side of town and benefiting from an eclectic variety of restaurants.

Ethiopian

Though the place itself is rather modest, **Addis Restaurant** (3750 Cleveland Ave., 614/269-8680, addis-restaurant.com, noon-9pm Sun.-Thurs., noon-10pm Fri.-Sat., $10-15) is one of the most popular Ethiopian restaurants in town, with reasonable portions and a seasoned hand in the kitchen. Feel free to request a less-spicy version of what's on offer.

Jamaican

Ena's Caribbean Kitchen (2444 Cleveland Ave., 614/262-0988, enascaribbeankitchen. com, noon-7pm daily, $10-14) has been a Linden stalwart since 1999, owned and operated by Jamaica native Ms. Ena, who immigrated to Columbus in the 1980s. The counter-service restaurant has limited seating inside and also does a Sunday brunch.

THE OHIO STATE UNIVERSITY

High Street near the university features some of the city's favorite cheap eats. Though some feel downright collegiate, others are only in the area to benefit from the constant influx of young, hungry bellies.

Pizza

The city lays claim to "Columbus-style pizza": edge-to-edge toppings on a thin-crust pie cut into squares. Though this style of pizza can be found in much of the Midwest, Columbus arguably features a fair number of pizzerias offering the style. The most popular and ubiquitous is local chain **Donatos Pizza** (2084 N. High St., 614/294-5371, donatos.com, 11am-midnight Sun.-Thurs., 11am-1am Fri.-Sat., $7-13), which was founded in 1963 and has locations across the city and beyond. The pizzeria is especially known for its substantial pepperoni coverage. Eat in the clean but unremarkable dining area or take your pizza to the Oval and people-watch.

Breakfast
Like its name implies, **HangOverEasy** (1646 Neil Ave., 614/586-0070, hangovereasy.com, 8am-3pm daily, $7-12) is a "breakfast cures all" type of place, as the wall reminds groggy students and locals looking for a bite with friends. Pull up a stool at the bar or sit at one of the tables (they're easy to move around to accommodate groups of all sizes). Eggs feature heavily on the breakfast menu, and the lunch menu has typical diner sandwich options. There are three other locations: near downtown, in Athens, and in Cincinnati.

The 24-hour donut shop **Buckeye Donuts** (1998 N. High St., 614/291-3923, buckeyedonuts.net., 24 hours daily, $6-9) was opened in 1969 by Greek immigrants and has been a staple of campus culture ever since. The snug dining room doesn't seat many, but students depend on this diner for cheap Greek eats, all-day breakfast, and, of course, a wide variety of donuts.

NORTHWEST COLUMBUS
There's not a lot to see in northwest Columbus; this suburban extension of the city is full of condo developments and strip malls. A more discerning eye, though, will notice the Asian groceries, halal markets, and mom-and-pop restaurants filling the neighborhood's commercial spaces. This is one of the most diverse corners of the city, and the eats reflect the population. If you're passing between the zoo and the inner city, you'll find some of the city's best ethnic food here.

Japanese
You'd likely pass the Kenny Centre strip mall if you weren't looking for the ★ **Japan Marketplace** (1169 Old Henderson Rd., japanmarketplace.com). Four restaurants for all budget levels, the largest Japanese market in Ohio, and a quirky gift store compose this window into East Asia, all owned by the same family corporation. **Tensuke Express** (614/451-4010, tensukeexpress.com, 11am-2:30pm and 4pm-8:30pm Mon.-Fri., 11am-8:30pm Sat.-Sun., $8-11) is the most affordable lunch option, offering ramen, udon, and other simple dishes fast-casual style. **Belle's Bread** (614/451-7110, bellesbread. com, 10am-7pm Mon.-Sat., 11am-6pm Sun.) is a French-inspired Japanese bakery, with made-from-scratch pastries—both sweet and savory—ready for you to put on your tray. The front counter will further entice you with cakes, cookies, and a full café drink menu of coffee, smoothies, and floats. There's also **Sushi Ten** (614/451-9100, sushiten.us, 3pm-7pm Mon.-Thurs., 11am-7pm Fri.-Sun., $4-11 per roll) and casual sit-down restaurant **Akai Hana** (614/451-5411, akaihanaohio.com, 11:30am-2:30pm Mon.-Sat., 5pm-9pm Mon.-Thurs., 5pm-9:30pm Fri.-Sat., 4:30pm-9pm Sun., $12-20), which has party boats of sushi as well as some Korean menu options.

Mexican
Popular counter service joint **Los Guachos** (5221 Godown Rd., 614/538-0211, losguachostaqueria.com, 11am-midnight Sun.-Thurs., 11am-1am Fri.-Sat., $2-10) serves up authentic *al pastor* (marinated pork) street tacos and a host of cheesy, meaty authentic Mexican eats in a cozy dining room. There are two other locations, including one nearer the zoo, but this is the original. Lines can get long on Mondays, when the restaurant offers buy-one-get-one-free *al pastor* tacos.

French
★ **The Refectory** (1092 Bethel Rd., 614/451-9774, refectory.com, 4:30pm-9pm

Mon.-Thurs., 4pm-9:30pm Fri.-Sat., $28-50) is a AAA Four-Diamond restaurant and has been a mainstay of the Columbus fine-dining scene since 1981. Housed in a historic 19th-century church building and featuring a kitchen run by Richard Blondin, who hails from Lyon, France, this white-tablecloth establishment offers wine tastings, a music series, and other events to connect with its exquisite French cuisine and over 700 wines in its cellar. Stained glass windows illuminate a warm, rustic wood and brick interior.

Bars and Nightlife

There's no shortage of things to do at night in the Columbus area, including over 50 craft breweries and an LGBTQ-friendly club and bar scene, especially in the Short North and German Village. Downtown activity is mainly focused near the Arena District, Gay Street, and the intersection of 4th and Main Streets.

CRAFT BREWERIES

Consistently ranked by locals as one of the best breweries in Columbus, the Short North's **Seventh Son Brewing Company** (1101 N. 4th St., 614/421-2337, seventhsonbrewing.com, 4pm-10pm Mon.-Wed., 4pm-midnight Thurs., noon-midnight Fri.-Sat., noon-10pm Sun.) specializes in ales and IPAs and has plenty of seating between a large patio, taproom, and enclosable rooftop patio. A different food truck supplies the food every day of the week.

In 2017, ambitious Scottish brewing company BrewDog built its American headquarters in the suburb of Canal Winchester and has since sprinkled its influence throughout the Columbus area. **BrewDog Franklinton** (463 W. Town St., 614/908-3077, brewdog.com, 11am-10pm Sun.-Thurs., 11am-midnight Fri.-Sat.) is in a former Franklinton car mechanic shop, with a contemporary taproom and rooftop patio with downtown in plain view. There are 48 drafts to choose from, including notable IPAs Elvis Juice and Punk, and a menu of burgers and pizza to go with your choice.

Across the street from BrewDog Franklinton is **Land-Grant Brewing Company** (424 W. Town St., 614/427-3946, landgrantbrewing.com, 3pm-10pm Tues.-Wed., 11am-10pm Thurs., 11am-midnight Fri.-Sat., 11am-8pm Sun.), one of the more prolific microbreweries in Columbus; you'll find its beer—a nice variety of brews—in area groceries and at professional sporting events. Keep an eye out for the Bread Crumbs dark stout, a hearty drink for Ohio winters. Long wooden tables fill the polished taproom, and there's a large outdoor biergarten with **Ray Ray's Hog Pit** (11:30am-8pm Thurs. and Sun., 11:30am-10pm Fri.-Sat.) serving up the best barbecue in the city from its food truck.

BARS

This ain't your dad's bowling alley. Downtown's hip **Pins Mechanical Company** (141 N. 4th St., 614/464-2255, pinsbar.com, 4pm-11pm Wed.-Thurs., 4pm-midnight Fri., 2pm-midnight Sat., 2pm-11pm Sun.) is part bar, part duckpin bowling destination. If bowling's not your thing, there's foosball, an arcade, and other activities to keep you entertained as you savor over 30 draft beers. There's also the world's largest ping-pong paddle to gawk at. A rotating lineup of food trucks keeps chow options open. The brand has begun to expand to other cities, including nearby Dublin.

Tip Top Kitchen and Cocktails (73 E. Gay St., 614/221-8300, tiptopcolumbus.com, 11am-2am daily) in downtown has a little bit of everything: 22 beers on tap, locally themed cocktails, and affordable comfort food, all in a warm, historic wood and brick tavern.

DIY projects plus alcohol? Enter Franklinton's **Makers Social** (461 W. Rich

St., 614/309-1663, makerscolumbus.com, 5pm-11pm Tues.-Fri., 11am-11pm Sat., 11am-5pm Sun.), an unusual mash-up of bar and craft workshop. Choose from over 30 projects spanning leather, textiles, jewelry, and basic home decor. Grab a specialty cocktail or local craft brew while you're at it. Projects run $35-45 and reservations are recommended, though not required.

German Village's LGBTQ-inclusive **Club Diversity** (863 S. High St., 614/224-4050, clubdiversity.com, 4pm-midnight Mon.-Thurs., 4pm-2:30am Fri.-Sun.) sits in an 1880s house and prides itself on its welcoming vibe, martinis, and event calendar, which includes a standing Thursday night piano performance and movie nights in the gazebo on Tuesdays.

Old North Arcade (2591 N. High St., no phone, oldnortharcade.com, 4pm-2:30am Mon.-Fri., noon-2:30am Sat.-Sun.) is a cavernous space stuffed with 60 nostalgic first-person shooter, pinball, and other classic arcade games, free to play with the purchase of a drink. You'll also find consoles, air hockey tables, and Skee-Ball to choose from between your game-themed cocktails and craft beer. North of campus in the Old North Columbus neighborhood, the barcade is family-friendly

every day until 8pm, after which guests must be 21 and over.

CLUBS

Dahlia Nightclub (147 Vine St., 614/224-3002, dahliacolumbus.com), around the corner from Nationwide Arena, pulls in big name DJs and has an intimate party vibe.

Axis Nightclub (775 N. High St., 614/421-2233, axisonhigh.com) is the largest LGBTQ dance club in Columbus, with stiff drinks, loud music, and a busy event calendar that includes drag shows and cabarets. Two levels of viewing space pack in the crowds at this popular Short North venue.

Skully's (1151 N. High St., 614/291-8856, skullys.org) and its Ladies '80s throwback Saturdays has been voted Columbus's best ladies night by Columbus Alive for over a decade. Sitting in the Short North, this lively dance club hosts regular themed nights and attracts shows that range from hip-hop to rock, pop, and beyond. A full menu keeps people fed in between dancing.

LIVE MUSIC

Express Live! (405 Neil Ave., 614/461-5483, promowestlive.com) in downtown's Arena District is a combined indoor venue (2,200

a concert at Express Live!

guests) and outdoor venue (5,200 guests) that hosts national and international acts. Concertgoers at the outdoor stage are treated to great views of downtown. Next door is sister operation **The Basement** (391 Neil Ave., 614/461-5483, promowestlive.com), which hosts up-and-coming national acts in a more unvarnished and intimate setting. Artists such as Chance the Rapper, The National, and the Local Natives played early gigs here.

Closer to the Ohio State campus is **Newport Music Hall** (1722 N. High St., 614/461-5483, promowestlive.com), the longest continually operating rock club in the United States. This 1,700-capacity former movie house has seen the likes of REO Speedwagon, Green Day, Foo Fighters, and Red Hot Chili Peppers grace the stage.

Cozy **Rambling House** (310 E. Hudson St., 614/468-3415, ramblinghousemusic.com) in Old North Columbus hosts live Americana music five nights a week. The venue is also a small-batch soda shop, providing an interesting alternative to beer (though there's that too).

Ace of Cups (2619 N. High St., 614/262-6001, aceofcupsbar.com), also in Old North Columbus, sports an eclectic lineup of live local and national bands. This edgy bar features 16 craft brews, a patio, and a permanent location for **Ray Ray's Hog Pit** (11:30am-8pm Thurs.-Sat.).

Accommodations

Most of Columbus's most interesting places to stay the night are located in the downtown and Short North neighborhoods. Cheaper chain hotels can be found on almost any exit around I-270. Better yet is a handy few north of downtown along SR 315 between Grandview Heights and Riverside Methodist Hospital, offering a good combination of location, pricing, and free parking.

DOWNTOWN
$150-200
The **Westin Great Southern Columbus** (310 S. High St., 614/228-3800, marriott.com, $166-288) began life in 1897 as the Great Southern Fireproof Hotel and Opera House (the opera house portion is now the connected Southern Theatre). Today, this restored redbrick building maintains the elegance of a late-19th-century luxury hotel, with an airy lobby, grand ballroom, and three restaurants. Unlike the historic central spaces, the 188 guest rooms are contemporary.

The large **Hyatt Regency Columbus** (350 N. High St., 614/463-1234, hyatt.com, $139-164) is connected to the convention center and offers city views from its modern, spacious guest rooms. An enormous ballroom and ample business meeting space make this a popular extension of the convention center.

One of the more affordable convention center and downtown options is the **Drury Inn and Suites Columbus Convention Center** (88 E. Nationwide Blvd., 614/221-7008, druryhotels.com, $140-180), offering clean, comfortable guest suites and easy access to Nationwide Arena. An indoor and outdoor pool is on the premises, and rates include a free hot breakfast. On-site covered parking is $15 per night, which is easily half the cost of larger hotels nearby.

Over $200
It's hard to beat the location of ★ **Hotel LeVeque** (50 W. Broad St., 614/224-9500, marriott.com, $176-222), a block away from the Scioto River and inside Columbus's most distinctive skyscraper, the Art Deco LeVeque Tower. This 150-room boutique hotel, a member of Marriott's Autograph Collection line, deftly combines historic aesthetics with contemporary conveniences. Within the hotel is **The Keep** (614/745-0322, thekeepcolumbus.com), a French brasserie (7am-2pm and

5pm-10pm Sun.-Thurs., 7am-2pm and 5pm-11pm Fri.-Sat., $19-54) and liquor bar (11am-11pm Sun.-Thurs., 11am-midnight Fri.-Sat.) designed to evoke the Roaring '20s.

The swanky ★ **Hilton Columbus Downtown** (401 N. High St., 614/384-8600, hilton.com, $198-236) sits in the middle of a lot of action; the convention center, North Market, Short North, and Nationwide Arena are all only steps away. Inside this modern hotel you'll find a large fitness room, indoor pool, and stylish bistro and bar. A 28-story addition is slated for completion in 2022, which will bring the total number of rooms to 1,000.

Opened in 2019, the **Canopy by Hilton Columbus Downtown Short North** (77 E. Nationwide Blvd., 614/223-1400, hilton.com, $189-241) is a short walk from the convention center and arena. The sleek guest rooms in this mid-rise hotel include window-side chaise lounges and walk-in showers. The rooftop features a fitness room and a cocktail bar and restaurant with excellent views of the city.

The **Renaissance Columbus Downtown Hotel** (50 N. 3rd St., 614/228-5050, marriott.com, $204-252) is at the edge of a small but lively section of Gay Street, with local restaurants and bars, and is convenient to some of the nightlife on 4th Street. This modern, upscale hotel comes complete with a restaurant, a bar, and an outdoor rooftop pool. Rooms are contemporary, practical, and clean.

SHORT NORTH
$100-150

Tailored for the 20-something crowd is the **Moxy Columbus Short North** (808 N. High St., 614/412-7664, marriott.com, $121-169), a playful, contemporary hotel designed for mixing and mingling. Check in at the bar and pick up your free drink token. Join a game of over-sized Jenga in the lobby. Head to the game room for billiards. Bedrooms feature walk-in showers and big-screen TVs, though storage space is limited. Those looking for a traditional hotel experience may not appreciate the hotel's let-loose vibe.

An alternative to the hustle and bustle of High Street can be found at **50 Lincoln Short North Bed & Breakfast** (50 E. Lincoln St., 614/299-5050, columbus-bed-breakfast.com, $144). Seven guest rooms—each with a private bath and comfortable bed—are tucked into a large 1917 Italianate house a block and a half away from the hubbub. Guests can enjoy their breakfast in the dining room or screened-in porch, and the off-street parking is free.

Hotel LeVeque

$150-200

More Scarlet and Gray than sophisticated, the **Graduate Columbus** (750 N. High St., 614/484-1900, graduatehotels.com, $153-224) puts a classy spin on Ohio and Ohio State Buckeyes-related decor. One of the more unique hotel offerings in town, Graduate Columbus is located in the thick of the Short North and features a coffee shop with breakfast pizzas, 24/7 fitness center, and Shake Shack. Check out the north side of the building to see *The Journey,* an enormous mural celebrating the city's Somali refugee population. Guest rooms are on the small side, though none lack for curated charm.

Over $200

Postmodern and chic, ★ **Le Meridien Columbus, The Joseph** (620 N. High St., 614/227-0100, marriott.com, $230-467) is strategically located between the Greater Columbus Convention Center and the Short North Arts District. The boutique hotel's 500-plus pieces of contemporary art throughout the bar and reception areas are an extension of the Pizzuti Collection located a block away. Additional pieces from 15 contemporary artists adorn the guest rooms. (Want the art? Pull out your checkbook.) Floor-to-ceiling windows in all of the rooms offer unobstructed views of downtown Columbus and High Street. There is a spa on-site and on the ground floor is **The Guild House** (614/280-9780, theguildhousecolumbus.com, 6:30am-10pm Mon.-Thurs., 6:30am-11pm Fri.-Sat., 6:30am-9pm Sun., $20-40), one of restaurateur Cameron Mitchell's more luxurious offerings, featuring creative American cuisine for breakfast, lunch, and dinner in a rustic, urban dining room.

GERMAN VILLAGE
$150-200

There aren't many accommodations in German Village outside of Airbnb, but the **German Village Guest House** (748 Jaeger St., 614/437-9712, gvguesthouse.com, $194-244) is a convenient and intimate alternative to the large downtown hotels. Three contemporary guest rooms, each with an en-suite bathroom, are located inside a historic brick house. Outside, visitors have a garden, courtyard, and outdoor fireplace at their disposal. In another brick house a few blocks south on Whittier Street, the guest house operates two private suites that come with full kitchens.

Information and Services

TOURIST INFORMATION

Experience Columbus (614/221-6623, experiencecolumbus.com) operates two visitor centers: in the Arena District (277 W. Nationwide Blvd., 8am-5pm Mon.-Fri., 10am-4pm Sat., noon-5pm Sun.) and in the lower level of Easton Town Center's Station building (188 Easton Town Center, 10am-9pm Mon.-Sat., noon-6pm Sun.).

HEALTH AND EMERGENCY SERVICES

Columbus is home to a number of fine hospitals. The sprawling **Ohio State University Wexner Medical Center** (410 W. 10th St., 614/293-8000, wexnermedical.osu.edu) is centrally located and offers a comprehensive level of services. Large but less daunting is **OhioHealth Riverside Methodist Hospital** (3535 Olentangy River Rd., 614/566-5000, ohiohealth.com). **Nationwide Children's Hospital** (700 Children's Dr., 614/722-2000, nationwidechildrens.org) is one of the top 10 children's hospitals in the country.

If you're just looking for an urgent care clinic, there are plenty around. A centrally located one is **OhioHealth Urgent Care Grandview** (895 W. 3rd Ave., 614/437-0278, ohiohealth.com).

Transportation

Like the rest of Ohio, Columbus is less than a day's drive from half of the population in the United States. Additionally, as the most centralized large city in the state, Columbus is an easy drive from most of Ohio; nearly any Ohioan can get here in 2.5 hours or less. The city is connected by air to most major hubs.

GETTING THERE
Air

Growing **John Glenn Columbus International Airport** (CMH, 4600 International Gateway, 614/239-4000, flycolumbus.com) is located only 6 miles (9.7 km) northeast of downtown. Eight airlines including Southwest, Delta, and American connect the city to most hubs and coastal vacation destinations down south, though daily service to Toronto and seasonal service to Cancun keeps the "international" in the name relevant.

Allegiant Airlines flies out of **Rickenbacker International Airport** (LCK, 2295 John Circle Dr., 614/491-1401, flycolumbus.com), a primarily cargo airport 15 miles (24 km) south of downtown.

Train
Columbus is the largest city in the United States without passenger rail of any kind. The city is a leading contender to receive the first Hyperloop sometime in the not-too-distant future.

Long-Distance Bus
Greyhound (greyhound.com) is the most comprehensive bus option, with an easily accessible downtown station (111 E. Town St.). Also setting up shop at the Greyhound station are **Flixbus** (flixbus.com), which operates a route between Columbus and New York City; **Barons Bus** (baronsbus.com), which also has a stop at the Ohio State campus; and **GoBus** (ridegobus.com), connecting Ohio's Three C's with smaller rural cities.

Car
I-70 runs east-west and connects Columbus with much of the nation, most immediately to Dayton (72 mi/116 km) to the west. Busy **I-71** connects Columbus to Cleveland, just over two hours (143 mi/230 km) to the northeast, and Cincinnati, 1.5 hours (107 mi/172 km) to the southwest. **US-33** is helpful to reach the southeast part of the state, including the Hocking Hills region about an hour (60 mi/96 km) away. **US-23** runs straight through Columbus from the north, becoming High Street through the city and returning to divided highway to the south. This road will be most useful getting to Toledo, about 2.25 hours (142 mi/229 km) to the northwest, and Cedar Point, about 2.25 hours (123 mi/198 km) to the north.

GETTING AROUND
To and from the Airport
John Glenn Columbus International Airport is only 6 miles (9.7 km) from downtown Columbus via I-670, a roughly 10-minute drive. COTA's Air Connect bus route (6am-9pm daily, $2.75) leaves every 30 minutes and connects downtown's High Street with the airport. A full list of charters and shuttle services is available at flycolumbus.com. Taxis and rideshares are available 24/7. A ride to downtown will run you about $25.

Getting to and from Rickenbacker International Airport is a little trickier. Enterprise's southeast Columbus office (614/836-2500) is nearby. Call to arrange transportation to its office for a rental car. Otherwise, taxis and rideshares are your best option.

Car

Compared to other cities its size, Columbus is a relative breeze to drive in, with flat topography, wide streets, and clear signage throughout most of the city. Downtown has plentiful and cheap parking; only valet parking at the city's most upscale hotels could be considered anything close to pricey. It's easy to find rental cars from Hertz, Enterprise, and any other major car rental company either at the airport or within the city.

Bicycle

Bikeshare company **COGO** (cogobikeshare.com) offers over 600 bikes between more than 80 stations throughout inner Columbus as well as Easton. A single 30-minute ride is $2, or you can purchase a day pass for $8.

Local Bus

The Central Ohio Transit Authority, or **COTA** (cota.com), runs Standard (15-30 minutes apart), Frequent (every 15 minutes or better), and Rush Hour routes. Fares are $2 (except Rush Hour, which is $2.75) and can be purchased on the bus or the COTA Connector app. Day passes are $4.50 and can be purchased at the airport, the COTA North Terminal (33 W. Spring St.), and a long list of locations throughout the city available on the website. Transfers are free for up to two hours.

In general, the bus can be an infuriating way to traverse the city if you're going beyond downtown and the inner circle of neighborhoods. The best COTA route is the **free CBUS circulator** (7am-10pm Mon.-Thurs., 7am-midnight Fri., 9am-midnight Sat., 10:30am-6pm Sun., free), which connects the Short North, downtown, and northernmost edge of German Village. It arrives every 10-15 minutes daily. No need for a ticket—just hop on!

Taxi

Taxis are around but are not ubiquitous in Columbus like they are in larger, denser cities, so it's best to call one if you need one. **Express Cab of Columbus** (614/822-8666) and **Columbus Taxi Service** (614/262-4444) have some of the best reviews. You should have no problem taking one from John Glenn Columbus International Airport without calling.

COGO bike rental station

Vicinity of Columbus

Columbus city limits look rather like a hand with fingers reaching out to annexable land and suburbs fitting in between. The farther you get from the inner city, the more difficult it is to determine if you are in a suburb or a "suburban" part of Columbus. Nevertheless, there are a number of top destinations away from the city center including arguably the most popular: the Columbus Zoo and Aquarium in Powell. Otherwise, several suburbs have historic, interesting downtowns in their own right, with terrific restaurants, bars, and shops as an alternative to downtown Columbus.

GRANDVIEW HEIGHTS

Surrounded on all sides by Columbus city limits, suburb Grandview Heights looks and feels like an affluent city neighborhood rather than a separate municipal entity. Less than 4 miles (6.4 km) from downtown Columbus, Grandview (most people drop the "Heights") features Grandview Avenue, a dense main street of boutiques, cafes, and restaurants, presenting an inviting, walkable option for an evening on the town. The strip is anchored by the **Bank Block Shopping Center,** one of the country's first shopping centers, built in 1927. Parking is behind the building, making for a better window-shopping experience than your average suburban strip mall.

Entertainment and Events
GRANDVIEW THEATER AND DRAFTHOUSE

Single-screen **Grandview Theater and Drafthouse** (1247 Grandview Ave., 614/670-4102, grandviewtheater.com) is run by the same folks at Studio 35 Cinema and Drafthouse, which is in Columbus's Clintonville neighborhood. Typically playing blockbusters (or Blue Jackets playoff games), the theater features 40 beers on tap, a small arcade, and a menu that includes pizza, subs, and inexpensive concessions.

Shopping

Adorable **Cub Shrub** (1257 Grandview Ave., 614/725-1900, 11am-6pm Mon.-Sat., noon-6pm Sun.) is brought to you by the California-transplant duo behind Clintonville's popular boutique, Tigertree. The pair brings the same buoyant vibe to clothes, toys, books, and accessories all catering to children up to age 6.

Red Giraffe Designs (1419 Grandview Ave., 614/705-5749, noon-6pm Tues.-Thurs. and Sun., 11am-7pm Fri.-Sat.) specializes in handmade, customizable jewelry for the Etsy crowd. It's easy on the wallet, and there are three other locations throughout the city.

Food

For the fast and inexpensive option, **Yats** (1386 Grandview Ave., 614/486-9287, yatscajuncreole.com, noon-8pm daily, $8-11) serves up heaps of spicy Cajun and Creole favorites, though a rotating menu keeps things interesting. The Drunken Chicken is the most popular menu item. A small selection of craft beer is available to pair with your meal.

At about the same price point is **Sweet Carrot** (1417 W. 5th Ave., 614/488-7151, sweetcarrot.com, noon-7pm Thurs.-Fri., 9am-7pm Sat., 9am-2pm Sun., $8-12), though portion sizes are smaller. This counter-service comfort food joint serves up delicious build-your-own plates of barbecue, meatballs, and salads. Corn cakes are a popular choice as a base for your protein. A handful of cookies and alcohol options add to the comfort level.

Aab India (1470 Grandview Ave., 614/486-2800, aabindiarestaurants.com, 11:30am-2:30pm and 5pm-10pm Mon.-Wed., 11:30am-2:30pm and 5pm-10:30pm Thurs.-Fri., noon-3pm and 5pm-10:30pm Sat., noon-9:30pm Sun., $13-20) serves award-winning northern Indian cuisine including tandoori dishes, curries, and plenty of vegetarian options in a classy dining room. The restaurant features decent happy hour deals Monday-Thursday and a lunch buffet daily. A second location is in Bexley.

The Avenue Steak Tavern (1307 Grandview Ave., 614/485-9447, theavenuesteaktavern.com, 4pm-9pm Sun.-Thurs., 4pm-10pm Fri.-Sat., $15-48) beckons with a classic demeanor and a shaded patio. The elegant wood accents and dimly lit chandeliers match the sophisticated surf-and-turf menu, which also has a few affordable sandwich options. A second location sits in Old Dublin near the river.

Transportation

COTA's frequent Route 5 traverses 5th Avenue, which skirts along the northern edge of Grandview. Less frequent is the 31 bus, which rolls straight up Grandview Avenue. Parking can get a little obnoxious during popular dinner times. Make sure to read signs along residential streets carefully if you're unable to find a spot in a parking lot; the police are known to enforce parking.

DUBLIN

For a glance at how the other half lives, head to Dublin. Avid golf fans will know of Dublin via the prestigious **PGA Tour Memorial Tournament,** held every year in conjunction with Memorial Day weekend at the private, Jack Nicklaus-designed Muirfield Village Golf Club. This sprawling, upper-class suburb—the second largest city in Franklin County after Columbus—has dedicated considerable resources to redefining its downtown core, and the result is a walkable neighborhood of upper-crust restaurants, riverfront parks, and specialty boutiques. On the west side of the Scioto River is **Old Dublin,** a mishmash of 200-year-old storefronts, stone houses, and tasteful new developments. On the east side is the surprisingly dense **Bridge Park,** a 21st-century mixed-use district featuring pricey condos, upscale dining, and a sleek hotel. Connecting the two is the stunning **Dublin Link Bridge,** a suspended pedestrian bridge that curves high above the water. If for whatever reason a night in downtown Columbus isn't in the cards, central Dublin offers some of the same experiences with the added benefit of free parking. Indeed, it seems almost designed that way as businesses such as Pins Mechanical Company and North Market operate satellite locations here away from their original downtown locations.

Recreation
INDIAN RUN FALLS

If you're already in Dublin or need a quick, easy hike, **Indian Run Falls** (700 Shawan Falls Dr., 614/410-4700, dublinohiousa.gov/parks-open-space), a series of smallish cascades, burbles quietly behind the hubbub of Old Dublin and busy Bridge Street. The address given is for the dedicated parking lot, which is located directly next to the falls. However, you can park near the library and walk along the gorge first for a longer, more dramatic reveal—it's an easy hike, about 0.5 mile (0.8 km) one-way.

Food

Cap City Fine Diner (6644 Riverside Dr., 614/889-7865, capcityfinediner.com, 11:30am-9pm Mon.-Thurs., 11:30am-10pm Fri., 11am-10pm Sat., 11am-9pm Sun., $13-25) is one of restaurateur Cameron Mitchell's more accessible dining options, with an elevated diner menu catering to the meat-and-potatoes crowd with finer tastes. A patio—heated during the winter months—overlooks busy Riverside Drive and the park and pedestrian bridge beyond. Reservations are a good idea. Other locations are in Grandview and northeastern suburb Gahanna.

Fukuryu Ramen (4540 Bridge Park Dr., 614/553-7392, fukuryuramen.com, 11am-2:30pm and 5pm-8pm daily, $10-13) serves up piping hot bowls of authentic ramen and rice bowls in its modern, somewhat industrial dining space. A small outdoor patio curves around the storefront. An additional location is in Upper Arlington, closer in to the city.

Across the river in the Old Dublin portion of town is **Harvest Pizzeria** (45 N. High St., 614/726-9919, harvestpizzeria.com, 11am-10pm Mon.-Thurs., 11am-11pm Fri.-Sat., noon-9pm Sun., $14-20). Either build your own pizza or choose from any of the high-end concepts on the menu, which also includes salads and burgers. The lunch special is significantly cheaper than dinner prices.

High-end **Tucci's** (35 N. High St., 614/792-3466, tuccisdublin.com, 3pm-10pm Mon.-Thurs., 10am-11pm Fri.-Sat., 10am-9pm Sun., $17-45) serves elegantly prepared pasta, steak, and seafood dishes in an intimate but comfortable dining room. Additionally, a shaded brick patio fronts the restaurant, which is known for its expansive wine selection and nightly live music. Tucci's also offers brunch on weekends.

Accommodations

The **AC Hotel by Marriott Columbus Dublin** (6540 Riverside Dr., 614/798-8652, marriott.com, $180-259) is a contemporary mid-rise hotel with views of the Scioto River, Bridge Park, and the pedestrian bridge. This stylish hotel offers spacious guest rooms and the rooftop tapas bar **Vaso** (614/698-2525, vasodublin.com, 4pm-10pm Mon.-Thurs., 4pm-midnight Fri.-Sat., $7-18), with an outdoor patio overlooking all of central Dublin. The bar busts out special igloos for patrons who still wish to enjoy the patio during winter's chill.

Transportation

Dublin is located 13 miles (20.9 km) northwest of downtown Columbus and is crisscrossed by I-270 and US-33/SR 161. Driving is by far the best option, and there is plenty of free, covered parking on either side of the river (though more on the Bridge Park side). Though infrequent, COTA's 33 line runs through the center of Dublin.

1: Dublin Link Bridge 2: Indian Run Falls
3: Otherworld

POWELL

An affluent bedroom community northwest of Columbus, Powell is home to the famous Columbus Zoo and Aquarium and its affiliated water park and golf course. The small downtown area surrounding the cross-section of Powell Road and Liberty Street offers local restaurants and boutique shops for those not interested in amusement park concessions or the abundant fast-food options off of Sawmill Road.

Sights

TOP EXPERIENCE

★ COLUMBUS ZOO AND AQUARIUM

When Jack Hanna flew into Columbus in 1978 to interview for the new director position at the Columbus Zoo, the cab driver who picked him up said, "We don't have a zoo." Such was the esteem of the park. These days, the **Columbus Zoo and Aquarium** (4850 Powell Rd., 614/645-3400, columbuszoo.org, 10am-4pm daily Jan.-Feb., 10am-5pm daily Mar. and Oct.-Dec., 9am-5pm daily Apr.-May and Sept., 9am-7pm daily Memorial Day-Labor Day, $21.99 adults, $16.99 seniors and children 3-9, free for children under 3) is truly a world-class zoo, named the best in the country by USA Travel Guide in 2009 and again in 2012 by Besties Readers' Choice. Over 2.3 million people visit the zoo annually. Jack Hanna's reputation grew alongside the zoo as a frequent guest on late-night shows and the host of television series including *Jack Hanna's Into the Wild* and *Jack Hanna's Wild Countdown*. Today, the zoo's staff stars in National Geographic's *Secrets of the Zoo*. Though Hanna retired in 2020, he is credited for leading the transformation of the zoo into the top-notch institution it has become.

The zoo is home to nearly 10,000 animals representing over 600 species spread across eight zoo regions. **Polar Frontier** is home to some fertile polar bears that frequently birth adorable offspring. An underwater viewing platform allows for some pretty unique vantage points. The next-door neighbors, the grizzly bears, also enjoy a refreshing pond, and visitors enjoy the opportunity to stand inches from their wrestling matches. **Heart of Africa** is perhaps the most unique exhibit, a sweeping expanse home to lions, ostriches, zebras, and various bird and antelope species living in a simulated shared savanna. Giraffe feeding times are posted every day, as are the cheetah run demonstrations. Opened in 2020, **Adventure Cove** features a 360-degree viewing tunnel for sea lions and harbor seals. Other highlights include the gorillas, manatees, and the Australian section, which features species such as koalas, Tasmanian devils, and kiwis found in few American zoos.

A collection of typical amusement park dry rides once known as Jungle Jack's Landing is now **Rides at Adventure Cove.** Tickets can be purchased individually for the rides ($1-2 each), or you can purchase a Zoo More wristband ($14.99) that covers all the rides in addition to other attractions throughout the zoo, including a 4D theater, camel rides, and a train ride.

Be prepared to walk. Some of the regions are quite large and the only shuttle service is a short-cut ride from the front of the park to the far east side of the zoo. Food service is located intermittently throughout the park, with the Congo River Market serving the widest selection. The food is neither cheap nor especially pricey. There is a picnic shelter available in front of the main gate to drop off your coolers while you enjoy the zoo. Parking is $10.

Recreation
ZOOMBEZI BAY
Connected to the zoo is its water park, **Zoombezi Bay** (4850 Powell Rd., 614/724-3600, zoombezibay.columbuszoo.org, 10:30am-7pm daily late May-mid-Aug. 10:30am-7pm Sat.-Sun. mid-Aug.-Labor Day, $34.99 adults, $26.99 seniors and children 3-9, free for children under 3). Water attractions—all 17 are roughly zoo-themed—occupy over 22 acres, accessible via the zoo's main gate. Jam to some tunes while splashing down the Soundsurfer water slide. Get dropped into a funnel on Cyclone. Ride Python Plunge, an unusual uphill water coaster. Other highlights include a wave pool (look for a movie night schedule on the website), an adults-only lazy river, and Baboon Lagoon, an interactive kids' play area with nine slides, heated pools, and a 1,000-gallon bucket that tips onto excited children.

The entrance to the zoo and water park is the same, so head to what appears to be the front gate of the zoo to purchase your ticket and enter the water park. Regular admission to the water park includes admission to the zoo the same day the ticket is valid. Discounted tickets are available on the website. A two-day ticket option includes admission to the zoo and water park on both days at a heavy discount. Parking is $10.

SAFARI GOLF CLUB
As if a zoo and a water park weren't enough, the Columbus Zoo also operates **Safari Golf Club** (4850 Powell Rd., 614/645-3444, safarigolf.columbuszoo.org, 7am-dusk Mon.-Fri. and 6:30am-dusk Sat.-Sun. Apr.-Sept., call for hours Oct.-Mar., $35 for 18 holes, $25 for 9 holes), an 18-hole public course across the street from the zoo's parking lot. The 72-par facility includes a shop, clubhouse, practice green, driving range, and the Safari Grille, which offers inexpensive burgers, sandwiches, and wraps for lunch and dinner.

Food
Sawmill Road snakes from I-270 to Powell Road, passing every conceivable retail establishment on its way (sometimes twice). Taking a right on Powell Road instead of a left toward the zoo will put you in Powell's "downtown," such as it is, with more local options.

Family-friendly **Nocterra Brewing Company** (41 Depot St., 614/896-8000,

---

1: Columbus Zoo and Aquarium 2: Baboon Lagoon at Zoombezi Bay

nocterrabrewing.com, 2pm-10pm Mon.-Wed., 11:30am-10pm Thurs.-Sat., 11:30am-8pm Sun.) feels very Midwestern, with its farmhouse-like taproom and quarter-acre beer garden. Adults can choose from 15 beers on tap, and hand-crafted sodas are available for the kiddos. Rotating food trucks offer bites to go with your beer, including the local barbecue favorite **Ray Ray's Hog Pit** (rayrayshogpit.com) from Thursday to Sunday.

Patriotically themed **Liberty Tavern** (50 S. Liberty St., 614/825-0500, libertytavernpowell.com, 11am-9pm Sun.-Thurs., 11am-10pm Fri.-Sat., $10-21) boasts a thoroughly American menu of burgers, salads, and sandwiches. Inside you'll find a typical bar and grill atmosphere, albeit with a small Liberty Bell replica. Those looking for a drink will find a solid beer list as well as cocktails, wines, and whiskeys.

Transportation

Powell is 17 miles (27 km) northwest of downtown Columbus. COTA runs a **Zoo Bus** (cota.com/zoobus) May-September that connects downtown Columbus and the zoo with a handful of stops in between. Otherwise, you need a car for this suburb.

SOUTHEAST SUBURBS

From old-money suburb **Bexley** to bedroom communities **Canal Winchester** and **Pickerington,** the Southeast suburbs offer a sprinkling of interesting sites, though not necessarily a dense corridor that you'd want to spend the majority of your day around. Amid the sprawl you'll find two truly original attractions: the mysterious museum Otherworld and the world's first craft beer hotel.

Sights
OTHERWORLD
Go further and further down the rabbit hole in, without a doubt, the oddest attraction in Columbus. The artists and visionaries behind **Otherworld** (5819 Chantry Rd., 614/868-3631, otherworldohio.com, 11am-8pm Mon.,

11am-10pm Thurs.-Fri., 10am-10pm Sat. 10am-8pm Sun. Memorial Day-Labor Day, 10am-8pm Sun.-Mon. and Wed., 10am-10pm Thurs.-Sat. off-season, $22 adults, $20 seniors, $18 children 3-12) reclaimed part of an abandoned strip mall and filled it with Jim Henson-esque dreamscapes, infinity mirrors, and interactive technology. The thinnest of plots places visitors as beta-testers for Otherworld Industries and its "alternate realm tourism." What this amounts to is exploring nearly 50 rooms of weirdness at your own pace. There are secret passageways, Burning Man-type sculptures, and atmospheric music throughout. It's mostly kid-friendly, though some rooms may be unsettling for younger kids. A small café at the entrance serves coffee and snacks. Parking is free (it's a strip mall, after all).

MOTORCYCLE HALL OF FAME MUSEUM
Run by the American Motorcyclist Association, the snug **Motorcycle Hall of Fame Museum** (13515 Yarmouth Dr., Pickerington, 614/856-2222, americanmotorcyclist.com/hall-of-fame, 9am-5pm daily, $10 adults, $8 seniors, $3 students, free for children 11 and under) is located right off I-70 and honors individuals who have promoted the design and racing of motorcycles in the United States. You'll find uniforms, historic motorcycles, and memorabilia from hall of famers such as Evel Knievel within this two-floor museum. Admission for AMA members is free.

Entertainment and Events
DREXEL THEATRE
Since 1937, the Art Deco **Drexel Theatre** (2254 E. Main St., Bexley, 614/231-1050, drexel.net) has served the Bexley community. Today, you'll find primarily independent, foreign, and classic films on the theater's three screens. The building went through an extensive renovation in 2016 to restore some of the original features and increase amenities and comfort for 21st-century moviegoers.

Food

Popular sports bar **Shade on the Canal** (19 S. High St., Canal Winchester, 614/837-9873, shaderestaurants.com, 11am-10pm Mon.-Thurs., 11am-11pm Fri.-Sat., 11am-9pm Sun., $9-15) is a good alternative to the chain restaurants nearer the highway. The menu includes a lengthy shareables list and just about any food you'd want out of a sports bar (wings, pizzas, burgers, subs). The casual joint's long bar and many TVs ensure you're never too far from whatever action you're trying to watch.

For "Columbus-style" pizza outside of the Donatos chain, try old-school **Rubino's Pizza** (2643 E. Main St., Bexley, 614/235-0712, 11am-10:30pm Tues.-Thurs., 11am-11:30pm Fri., 4pm-11:30pm Sat., 4pm-10:30pm Sun., $6-13). You can't miss the giant neon sign on the far east end of Bexley's attractive Main Street corridor pointing the way to the diminutive joint, which has been slinging pies since 1954. The dining room is no-frills, and the menu is one page long. A handful of inexpensive pasta, sub, and salad options are available, but pizza is the main star here.

Accommodations

The main attraction pulling outsiders to Canal Winchester is ★ **The Doghouse Hotel and Brewery** (100 Gender Rd., Canal Winchester, 614/908-3054, brewdog.com, $172-304). The world's first crowdfunded craft beer hotel, this 32-room curiosity features in-room taps, beer-stocked fridges, a craft beer museum, and, of course, a brewery. As for the more typical hotel niceties, the establishment has a gym, continental breakfast featuring local Stauf's coffee, and a lobby bar.

With its stately houses, classy Main Street, and proximity to downtown, Bexley is a fabulous place to base yourself for a Columbus trip, so it's curious there aren't many accommodations available. Enter **Bexley Bed and Breakfast** (519 S. Drexel Ave., Bexley, 614/203-7558, bexleybedandbreakfast.com, $179) with modern, minimalist rooms, ensuite bathrooms with walk-in showers, and a continental breakfast. The Drexel Theatre and Main Street are two short blocks away.

Transportation

Bexley is the closest of the Southeast suburbs to downtown—just 3 miles (4.8 km) east down Broad Street or I-70. Being an inner ring suburb, Bexley is well-integrated into the existing public transportation options. COTA's Line 2 travels up Bexley's Main Street, and COGO has three Bexley bikeshare stations.

Beyond Bexley, a car is the best bet as there are no bus stops near Otherworld or the area's other attractions. Head east on I-70 from downtown to find Otherworld off the Brice Road exit (12 mi/19.3 km from downtown) and the Motorcycle Hall of Fame Museum off the SR 256 exit (14 mi/22.5 km from downtown). For Canal Winchester, take I-70 to US-33 south toward Lancaster (16 mi/26 km from downtown).

Amish Country and Central Ohio

Forming a donut around the Columbus metro area, Central Ohio encompasses the transition between the Midwest corn belt to the west and the first inclinations of Appalachia to the east, where farms spill into the forested foothills. The result is a pastoral, Shire-like region. John Chapman, better known as Johnny Appleseed, spent much of his time wandering these parts during Ohio's early pioneer days. Though much of the region is tied to Columbus as a statistical area, the stark contrast between the city's sensibilities and the quaint life of small-town Ohio cannot be discounted: Central Ohio holds more than just the capital city.

Small cities like Mansfield, Newark, and Lancaster have separated themselves in character, with rich histories in industry,

Highlights

Look for ★ to find recommended sights, activities, dining, and lodging.

★ Browse an endless supply of shops and markets in **Amish Country**—and be sure not to miss the region's cheesemakers (page 92).

★ Tour the **Ohio State Reformatory,** the Victorian prison that was the primary filming location for *The Shawshank Redemption* (page 97).

★ Hike, canoe, and camp in and around the scenic river gorge at **Mohican State Park** (page 101).

★ See interesting combinations of stalactites, stalagmites, and rock formations at the colorful **Ohio Caverns** (page 105).

★ Wander the 2,000-year-old **Newark Earthworks,** the remains of the world's largest complex of geometric mounds (page 107).

★ Explore canal and railroad ruins in the remote **Blackhand Gorge State Nature Preserve** (page 110).

Amish Country and Central Ohio

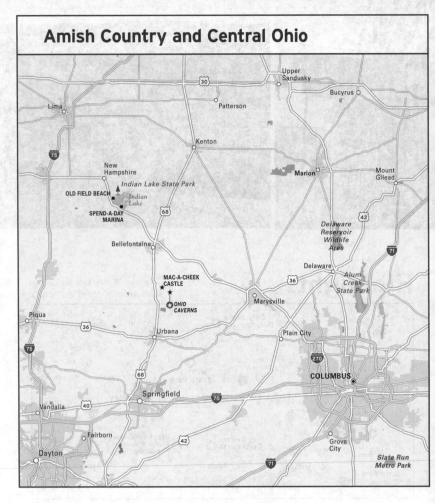

transportation, and, in Newark's case, ancient mounds that were built by the Hopewell culture. Heading farther east, passing the ruined locks of the former Ohio & Erie Canal, you can find this history still living at Coshocton's Roscoe Village, a revitalized canal town. Blackhand Gorge State Nature Preserve safeguards more heritage, and Mohican State Park maintains miles of trails through the region's deepest woods.

Carving out a home for themselves in Ohio's heartland is the Amish community. Lancaster, Pennsylvania, may be more well known as an Amish tourist destination, but Ohio has roughly the same number of Amish people, and much of that population is congregated around Holmes County. Folks in search of a peaceful respite will find a smorgasbord of hearty food, country shopping, and all the cheese you could want.

Previous: World's Largest Cuckoo Clock in Sugarcreek; the Historic Carrousel District in Mansfield; fall in Central Ohio.

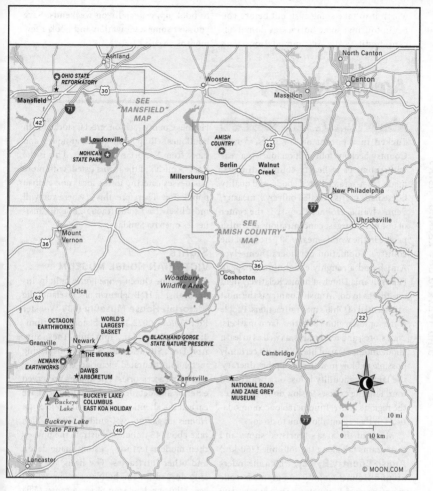

© MOON.COM

If you came to Ohio expecting endless farms and a rural lifestyle, you've found the part of the state where this is the most true. What you may not have expected is how downright agreeable it all is.

PLANNING YOUR TIME

With few marquee attractions or large cities, this is the easiest part of Ohio in which to slow it down. You can pick a base such as Newark or Mansfield and make excursions into Amish Country, or base yourself in Amish Country and take your time exploring. Alternatively,

practically anywhere in this region is an easy day trip from Columbus, though Amish Country's distance from major highways does make the drive a bit onerous. In general, 2-3 days is plenty of time to experience some Amish culture and take in a few sights.

As most of this region's delights center around outdoor activities, you'll get the most out of your experience May-October. It also bears mentioning that in Amish Country virtually everything is closed on Sundays. As a result, Saturdays attract big, sometimes maddening crowds of day-trippers. It's also worth it to take some cash out before you begin touring; some businesses do not accept credit cards. Accommodations tend to book up, especially on weekends. Save yourself some aggravation and book a few months ahead.

Amish Country

Tucked in a pocket of low hills, Amish Country beckons four million tourists a year with promises of hearty country dinners, made-from-scratch baked goods, and quality homemade crafts. Rivaled only by Lancaster, Pennsylvania, Holmes County is the center of one of the largest concentrations of Amish people in the world—nearly 50 percent of the county's population considers themselves Amish and a roughly equal number speak Pennsylvania Dutch at home. Relatively light on "things to do," Amish Country is the most experiential of Ohio's main attractions. People come for the region's bakeries, farm markets, craft stores, and restaurants, as well as to learn about another way of life. While it's certainly possible to blow in with a shopping itinerary, the land's tranquility is lost on a whirlwind tour. Finding excuses to slow down enhances the region's allure. Innumerable accommodations in the region allow you to do so.

Much of the area's touristed shops and restaurants fall along the 160-mile (260-km) **Amish Country Byway,** which meanders around Holmes County and grants bucolic country views. Best not to be in a hurry—you never know if a horse-and-buggy is trotting around the corner.

There is no public transportation to Amish Country (with the exception of Sugarcreek) or around the region, so a car is your best bet.

Note that some addresses in this area list one town (such as Millersburg) though physically they are nearer—or even within—another (such as Berlin).

MILLERSBURG

With 3,000 people, Millersburg is the largest town in Amish Country and the county seat of Holmes County. Jackson Street is stocked with boutiques selling home goods, antiques, and more from Victorian storefronts. This is the least "Amish" of the towns listed, with more businesses catering to the local non-Amish population. Therefore, this is where you will most likely find some (though not all) businesses open on Sundays.

Sights

VICTORIAN HOUSE MUSEUM

A handsome Queen Anne house built by industrialist L. H. Brightman of Cleveland, the **Victorian House Museum** (484 Wooster Rd., 330/674-0022, holmeshistory.com, 1pm-4pm Sat.-Sun. Mar., 1pm-4pm Tues.-Sun. Apr.-Dec., $10) features 28 rooms displaying meticulously curated Victorian-era furniture and home accessories. The house's preserved exterior and detailed finishing touches have earned the attention of HGTV and *Victorian Homes* magazine. Self-guided tours, which take about 45 minutes, illustrate the house's then-modern features, custom-made decor, and other intricacies. The halls are suitably decked for the holiday season, which sees a busy calendar of festive events. (The house closes for two weeks in early October for decorating.) Adjacent to the house is the **Millersburg Glass Museum** ($5, or $13 for both museums), a small display of locally made glasswork. Ticketing is within the Victorian House.

HOLMES COUNTY OPEN AIR ART MUSEUM

Set upon the woodsy grounds of The Inn at Honey Run, the **Holmes County Open Air Museum** (6920 County Rd. 203, 330/674-0011, innathoneyrun.com, 24 hours daily,

Amish Country

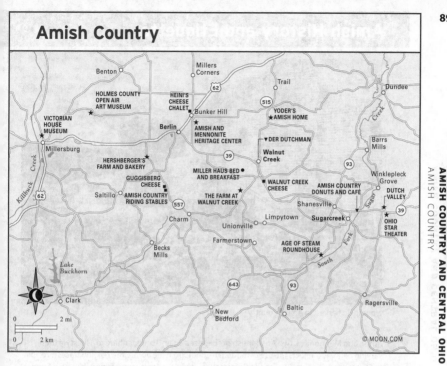

free) is more like a hike with art. A trail weaves 1.5 miles (2.4 km) through the woods to eight intermittent sculptures by local and regional artists. The sculptures range in style and material, with a good deal of natural themes integrated. There is some uphill climbing involved (those rolling hills and all). The park is open to inn guests and non-guests alike.

Recreation

Perhaps the best way to appreciate this region's slow pace is to walk it. Stretching 22 miles (35 km) from Killbuck to Fredericksburg, with Millersburg in the center, the paved **Holmes County Trail** (holmestrail.com) is a rails-to-trails multiuse path utilized by hikers, bikers, and buggies alike. There are several access points, including Millersburg's **Hipp Station** (62 N. Grant St.).

Shopping

Homestead meets shabby chic at **Farmhouse Frocks** (45 W. Jackson St., 330/231-8475, farmhousefrocks.com, 10am-5pm Mon.-Sat.), a woman's clothing boutique that mixes urban sensibilities with country comfort.

Starlight Antiques and Gifts (66 W. Jackson St., 330/674-5111, starlightantiques. com, 10am-5pm Mon.-Sat., 10am-4pm Sun.) mixes secondhand furniture, collectibles, and other antique accessories with a gift shop and canvases by local artist Billy Jacobs.

Food

Millersburg Brewing Company (60 E. Jackson St., 330/674-4728, millersburgbrewing.com, 11:30am-9pm Tues.-Thurs., 11:30am-11pm Fri.-Sat., noon-7:30pm Sun., $9-14) offers half-pound burgers, sandwiches, and flatbreads as well as over 20 draft beers representing a nice variety of styles. Nachos are an interesting side option.

Tarragon at The Inn at Honey Run (6920 County Rd. 203, 330/674-0011, innathoneyrun.com, 8am-2pm and 5pm-9pm daily, $17-37) is a white-tablecloth alternative

Amish History and Etiquette

a pumpkin harvest in Amish Country

Amish and Mennonites, two Anabaptist (or "baptized again") sects, adhere to a lifestyle that—by varying degrees—rejects the use of modern technology in the home. The religion traces its origin to Switzerland concurrent with the Reformation, when Anabaptists were persecuted in Europe by both Protestants and Catholics for following the practice of adult baptism, also known as believer's baptism, rather than the traditional practice of baptizing infants. They immigrated to the New World, Pennsylvania in particular, to practice their faith in a place with more religious freedom. Today, there are approximately 350,000 Amish in the world, with the vast majority living in the United States. Though different subgroups have differing opinions on theology and restrictions, in general Amish and Mennonites speak the Pennsylvania Dutch language, worship in the home, adhere to pacifism, and wear plain clothes.

If traveling to Amish Country, please be mindful that you're treading on their home territory and that the Amish are not costumed interpreters. Here are some simple etiquette rules:

- Do not take pictures or videos of Amish people. If you would like a picture of their buggy or their farm, ask for permission. Your consideration is greatly appreciated.

- Respect the privacy of Amish people you encounter. Nobody appreciates being stared or pointed at; imagine someone stopping you in the middle of running errands to ask you to represent your entire culture. If you'd like to ask an Amish person about their culture, your best bet is a shopkeeper or tour guide.

- Assume that you shouldn't trespass on private property, even if a No Trespassing sign is missing—but if there's a sign advertising goods, then by all means stop by! Some Amish homes sell homemade crafts, baked goods, and other items for travelers.

- Keep an eye out for bicyclists and horse-drawn buggies. Give them plenty of room as you pass, keep your lights on low at night, and don't honk! You'll spook the horses.

to Amish Country's predominately meat-and-potatoes choices. The New American menu covers upscale versions of breakfast and lunch staples, with the dinner menu divided into three courses and dessert. The Juniper Lounge features luxurious small plates such as duck taquitos and baked brie.

Accommodations

In the thick of Millersburg's main strip is **Hotel Millersburg** (35 W. Jackson St., 330/674-1457, hotelmillersburg.com, $109-159). Built in 1847, this historic hotel maintains its Victorian-era charm. The guest rooms, all laid out differently, are set up to accommodate different group sizes. Hallways have antique furniture and 19th-century photographs and calendars. A tavern is on-site.

Had Frank Lloyd Wright designed J. R. R. Tolkien's Hobbiton, it likely would've resembled the adults-only **Inn at Honey Run** (6920 County Rd. 203, 330/674-0011, innathoney-run.com, $199-289), with its 12 modern Honeycomb suites built into the earth. There are also 25 inn guestrooms and two cottages set amid 56 acres of woodlands, with walking trails, a fine-dining restaurant, and cozy shared spaces.

Transportation

Millersburg is an hour and forty minutes (84 mi/135 km) east of Columbus via SR 161 east and US-62 north. It's about a 50-minute drive (36 mi/58 km) west of Canton, the nearest major city to Amish Country. From Canton take US-62 west to US-30 west past Massillon to SR 241/Millersburg Road SW, which will take you directly to Millersburg, though keep an eye out for turns to stay on SR 241 when you cut through small towns.

There is no public transportation to or within Millersburg.

BERLIN

Tiny Berlin is a touristy, centrally located focal point for Amish Country visitors, with shopping, restaurants, and hotels within walking distance. Fans of the country aesthetic will find plenty to buy here: farmhouse decor, handmade quilts, quality crafts.

Sights
AMISH AND MENNONITE HERITAGE CENTER

It's worth remembering that though tourists mainly come to these parts to shop and eat, there is a real culture with a deep-rooted faith in Holmes County. The **Amish and Mennonite Heritage Center** (5798 County Rd. 77, 330/893-3192, behalt.com, 9am-5pm Mon.-Sat. Apr.-Nov., 9:30am-4:30pm Mon.-Sat. Dec.-Mar., free) is a good place to learn about the history of the Amish and Mennonite faiths and to ask your questions. There is a bookstore and small museum with old Anabaptist hymnals and contextual information about Amish culture, but the highlight is the 265-foot (81-m) cyclorama painting *Behalt,* meaning "to keep," with 1,200 characters depicting the Christian faith and the journey of the Amish community. The 30-minute *Behalt* presentation ($7) is a crash course on the history of Christianity and Anabaptists, but the information will help guide your experience in Amish Country. Presentations are every hour on the hour, while a separate historic school and barn tour (free) begins at the bottom of every hour.

HERSHBERGER'S FARM AND BAKERY

Hershberger's Farm and Bakery (5452 SR 557, 330/674-6096, hershbergersfarmand-bakery.com, bakery and farm store 8am-5pm Mon.-Sat., petting area 10am-5pm Mon.-Sat.) pulls in quite a crowd. Part bakery, part food trough, part antique store, part farm, there's something to enjoy (or eat) for everyone here. The retail portion features fresh produce along with shelves of preserves and homemade baked goods. Purchase an entire pie off the shelf or from the freezer to bake later. The farm features horse-and-buggy rides ($5) as well as a zany petting zoo ($3) including every conceivable farm animal, some of which are free to leave their pens.

☆ Cheese in Amish Country

Heini's Cheese Chalet

One of the most popular items to shop for in Ohio's Amish Country is cheese. There are a few quality cheesemakers that craft dozens of varieties and offer free tours and samples—you can't really go wrong.

- **Heini's Cheese Chalet** (6005 County Hwy. 77, northeast of Berlin, 330/893-2131, heinis. com, 9am-6pm Mon.-Sat.) looks straight out of the Swiss Alps from the outside. The store has been making and selling more than 30 types of cheese under its Bunker Hill Cheese brand since 1935, offering visitors free samples, tours, and windows into the cheesemaking floor. The store sells other locally made goods to pair with your cheese selection as well.

- **Guggisberg Cheese** (5060 SR 557, south of Berlin, 330/893-2500, babyswiss.com, 9am-5pm Mon.-Sat.) holds the distinction of having invented baby swiss cheese in the 1960s. The factory churns out award-winning cheeses, with over 60 varieties for sale and available for sampling.

- **Walnut Creek Cheese** (2641 SR 39, Walnut Creek, 330/852-2888, walnutcreekcheese.com, 8am-7pm Mon., 8am-6pm Tues.-Fri., 7:30am-6pm Sat.) is more of a grocery store than a cheese shop. While it sells plenty of its own cheese, the giant roadside market also sells local baked goods, meats, jams, and fresh produce, and hosts a restaurant.

Recreation

Amish Country Riding Stables (5025 SR 557, 330/893-3600, amishcountryriding-stables.com) brings visitors on 45-minute guided horseback rides through the scenic rolling hills of Amish Country. When not giving guests rides, the horses roam freely throughout the grounds. The stables are open April-October, depending on the weather.

Shopping

Helping Hands Quilt Shop (4818 W. Main St., 330/893-2233, helpinghandsquilts.com, 9am-5pm Mon.-Sat. summer, 10am-4pm Mon.-Sat. winter) sells beautiful locally made quilts and other embroideries. It's also a good resource if you want to take a stab at your own, with fabric, patterns, and tools.

Craft enthusiasts will want to check out the giant **Sol's in Berlin** (4914 W. Main St.,

330/893-3134, solsinberlin.com, 9am-5pm Mon.-Thurs., 9am-6pm Fri.-Sat.), brimming with country-styled textiles, decor, apparel, candles, and more.

Food

There's nearly always a line out the door at **Boyd and Wurthmann** (4819 E. Main St., 330/893-4000, boydandwurthmann.com, 5:30am-7:30pm Mon.-Sat., $5-13), but it manages a high turnover rate and the wait isn't as long as the line suggests. This wood-paneled, Mennonite-owned diner has served country breakfasts, lunches, and dinners since the 1940s. The eatery accepts cash or checks only.

The much larger **Berlin Farmstead** (4757 Township Rd. 336, 330/893-4600, dh-group.com, 11am-8pm Mon.-Wed., 7am-8pm Thurs.-Sat., $11-16) is part of the Dutchman Hospitality group of Amish-cooking restaurants, which offers big tables, larger portions, and a killer buffet of meat-and-potatoes comfort food.

Accommodations

The **Berlin Grande Hotel** (4787 Township Rd. 366, 330/403-3050, berlingrandehotel.com, $169-199) is steps away from Berlin's main retail strip and offers over 100 contemporary rooms and suites, an indoor saltwater pool, and a hot breakfast buffet.

An idyllic Amish Country view awaits from the front porch of the **Hillside Inn** (5676 Township Rd. 362, 330/893-1122, hillsideinn.com, $99-199) with six modern, comfortable bedrooms that can be reserved separately or together.

Transportation

Berlin is 11 minutes (7 mi/11.3 km) east of Millersburg via US-62. It's 45 minutes southwest (32 mi/52 km) from Canton, also via US-62. From Columbus, take US-62 northeast from SR 161 near New Albany, a drive of about an hour and 50 minutes (90 mi/145 km).

There is no public transportation to or within Berlin.

WALNUT CREEK

Like nearby Berlin, little Walnut Creek is on the touristy side, with large-scale markets and modern hotels catering to visitors. Centrally located as it is, though, it's not a bad base for a stint in Amish Country.

Sights

THE FARM AT WALNUT CREEK

With over 500 animals, **The Farm at Walnut Creek** (4147 County Rd. 114, 330/893-4200, thefarmatwalnutcreek.com, 8:30am-6pm Mon.-Sat. Apr.-Oct., $11.75 adults, $8.75 seniors and children) is the closest thing to a zoo in Amish Country. Feed free-roaming giraffes, zebras, camels, exotic deer, and more from a horse-drawn wagon (for an additional fee; reserve ahead for a large group) or the comfort of your own car along a 2.3-mile (3.7-km) route. A walk-through area features enclosures with smaller animals and a petting zoo. The business is also a working farm. There's no restaurant on the premises but there is a bakery. Credit cards are not accepted.

YODER'S AMISH HOME

A much more subdued experience than The Farm at Walnut Creek, **Yoder's Amish Home** (6050 SR 515, 330/893-2541, yoders-amishhome.com, 10am-5pm Thurs.-Sat., $13 adults, $9 children) allows visitors to tour a working Amish home and farm with a barn dating to 1885. The 1.5-hour tour answers questions about the Amish lifestyle and visitors have the opportunity to ride in horse-drawn buggies with Amish drivers open to sharing about their culture. A buggy ride-only option is also available ($4.75).

Shopping

Coblentz Chocolate Company (4917 SR 515, 330/893-2995, coblentzchocolates.com, 9am-6pm Mon.-Sat. July-Oct., 9am-5pm

94

Mon.-Sat. Nov.-June) is an old-fashioned chocolatier with rows of hand-dipped sweets and confectionaries. You can also take a peek at employees making the next batch.

Food

Another member of the Dutchman Hospitality group, ★ **Der Dutchman** (4967 Walnut St., 330/893-2981, dhgroup.com, 6am-8pm Mon.-Sat., $11-16) features generous meat-and-potatoes meals as well as a giant buffet. The atmosphere oozes country comfort, with big tables and an attached bakery. There are two other locations, one close to Mansfield and the other on the northwest side of Columbus in Plain City.

Rebecca's Bistro (4986 Walnut Rd. 330/893-2668, rebeccasbistro.com, 8am-3pm Mon.-Sat., $6-9) is a local breakfast and lunch spot with specialty café beverages, a Saturday morning breakfast casserole, sandwiches, and quiches served in a renovated 19th-century log cabin.

Accommodations

A quiet, scenic alternative to the modern hotels, **Miller Haus Bed and Breakfast** (3135 County Rd. 135, 330/893-3602, millerhaus. com, $129-169) beckons with a home-cooked country breakfast (and evening dessert) and nine rooms authentically appointed with Amish furniture. The 10.5-acre surrounding grounds are lovely.

The **Wallhouse Hotel** (2870 Cove Ln., 330/852-6105, wallhousehotels.com, $145-185) rejects the area's country aesthetic for a sleek, contemporary look. Every guest room and suite comes with a seating area and walk-in tiled shower, and some come with a private balcony.

Transportation

Walnut Creek is a 6-minute drive (4 mi/6.4 km) east of Berlin via SR 39. It's about a 45-minute drive (36 mi/58 km) from Canton via I-77 south and SR 39 west.

There is no public transportation to or within Walnut Creek.

SUGARCREEK

The "Little Switzerland of Ohio," Sugarcreek is on the eastern edge of Ohio's Amish Country, just barely tripping into neighboring Tuscarawas County. This town of 2,000 prides itself on its Swiss heritage, so much so that much of the small central district is fashioned to look like Swiss chalets. Aside from shopping, the main draw here is the world's largest cuckoo clock.

Sights
WORLD'S LARGEST CUCKOO CLOCK

Sitting on a tidy corner in the middle of town, the **World's Largest Cuckoo Clock** (100 N. Broadway St., 24 hours daily, free) was commissioned by a Swiss-themed restaurant in the 1970s but, when the restaurant folded in 2009, the clock was refurbished and relocated to the center of Sugarcreek. The 23-foot by 24-foot (7-m by 7.3-m) clock's two dancing figurines and oompah band come alive as the cuckoo sounds every 30 minutes (9am-9pm daily Apr.-Nov., weather permitting).

ALPINE HILLS MUSEUM

Also in central Sugarcreek, the small **Alpine Hills Museum** (106 W. Main St., 330/852-4113, alpinehillsmuseum.org, 10am-5pm Mon.-Sat. Apr.-Oct., 10am-5pm Thurs.-Sat. Nov., donation suggested) includes three floors of artifacts and audiovisual exhibits to explore at your own pace. The museum focuses on the town's Swiss and Amish heritage, with an Amish kitchen, antique fire equipment, and a re-creation of a cheese house circa 1890. The museum also functions as a visitors center, with up-to-date information on local events and attractions.

1: Alpine Hills Museum in Sugarcreek **2:** a line out the door at Boyd and Wurthmann in Berlin **3:** the *Behalt* cyclorama at the Amish and Mennonite Heritage Center

AGE OF STEAM ROUNDHOUSE

The **Age of Steam Roundhouse** (213 Smokey Lane Rd. SW, 330/852-4676, ageofsteamroundhouse.org, tour times and prices vary) houses the private steam engine collection of Jerry Jacobson, who constructed the 18-stall roundhouse and functioning turntable to preserve railroad heritage. Among the collection are locomotives, passenger cars, and freight equipment, all of which the staff dutifully continues to repair and restore. This is a working site, so you'll need to take a tour to experience it. A variety of options are available, including a basic roundhouse tour (10am, noon, and 2pm Thurs.-Sat. May-Oct., $20 adults, $17 seniors, $12 children) that lasts 1-1.5 hours. More in-depth, hands-on tours allow additional time for interested minds to learn about the mechanics of steam engine machinery. Check the website for details.

DUTCH VALLEY

If you're driving along I-77 and need a quick Amish Country fix, **Dutch Valley** is more or less a one-stop shop. This complex—a mere 10-minute drive west from I-77 via SR 39—features a large Amish restaurant, a high-ceilinged gift shop stuffed with farmhouse decor, and a market of local goods, all accessible from one parking lot. If you have a little more time on your hands, catch a show at the **Ohio Star Theater** (1387 Old SR 39, 855/344-7547, ohiostartheater.com), which programs a busy lineup of music, comedy shows, and traveling artists.

Shopping

The deeper you wander into **Secret Garden** (108 W. Main St., 330/852-0716, 10am-6pm Mon.-Sat.), the more eclectic the selection gets. Aside from quilts, you'll find free-spirited garden decor, ornaments, and fairy-related gifts.

Carlisle Fabric and Quilts (108 E. Main St., 330/852-2264, 8:30am-5pm Mon.-Fri., 8:30am-4pm Sat.) sells quilts, and the materials to make one, from its Swiss chalet storefront.

Food

The contemporary **Amish Country Donuts and Café** (522 Dover Rd. E., 330/852-5214, amishcountrydonuts.com, 7am-9pm Tues.-Thurs., 7am-5pm Fri.-Sat., $7-11) features large, wheel-like donuts, a breakfast menu, sandwiches, and salads.

Accommodations

Part of the Dutch Valley complex east of town, the **Carlisle Inn Sugarcreek** (1357 Old SR 39, 855/411-2275, dhgroup.com/inns, $139-224) has 69 comfortable, country-style guest rooms, each with a patio. Breakfast is included in the rate.

One of the more unique accommodations in Amish Country, the **Sugarcreek Village Inn** (206 Factory St. NE, 330/852-9900, sugarcreekvillageinn.com, $75-105) is located within town. The rooms are split between the inn and some refurbished train cars.

Transportation

Sugarcreek is a 9-minute drive (6 mi/9.7 km) east of Walnut Creek via SR 39. It's a 10-minute drive (8 mi/12.9 km) west of I-77 and the New Philadelphia area via SR 39. From Canton, take I-77 south to SR 39 west, a total of about 30 minutes (32 mi/52 km).

Greyhound (greyhound.com), **Barons Bus** (baronsbus.com), and **GoBus** (ridegobus.com) stop at the Eagle Truck Stop (217 County Hwy. 21, New Philadelphia) about 15 minutes (10 mi/16.1 km) east of Sugarcreek. **Performance Taxi** (330/204-7393) is a 24/7 taxi service located in New Philadelphia serving the greater area.

There is no public transportation in Sugarcreek.

Central Ohio

Forming a donut around the state capital Columbus, Central Ohio is dotted by small farm communities, historic county seats, and quaint college towns. The geography makes a distinct shift here: West of Columbus is largely flat and undistinctive, while east of Columbus the first bumps of the Appalachian plateau mix with farms and forests, making for pleasant scenery. Anything in this transitional section of Ohio makes for an easy day trip from Columbus.

MANSFIELD

A former manufacturing city, blue-collar Mansfield is the largest city and midpoint between Columbus and Cleveland on I-71, with a population hovering around 50,000. Mansfield's claim to fame is courtesy of Hollywood; nearly the entire movie *The Shawshank Redemption* was filmed in the city and its environs, in particular at the intimidating Ohio State Reformatory. Downtown features more filming locations in addition to the **Historic Carrousel District,** with family-friendly shops and restaurants both new and established surrounding the Richland Carrousel Park and its old-fashioned fun. There's plentiful free parking at the lot on 4th and Main Streets, right in the center of the historic district.

Sights
★ OHIO STATE REFORMATORY

A primary filming location for the film *The Shawshank Redemption,* the **Ohio State Reformatory** (100 Reformatory Rd., 419/522-2644, mrps.org, 11am-4pm daily Apr.-Dec., 11am-4pm Thurs.-Sun. Jan.-Mar., $25 adults, $23 seniors and children) was an operating prison up until its closure in 1990. Constructed between 1886 and 1910, the massive structure combines elements of Gothic, Romanesque, and Queen Anne architecture

and is open for both self-guided and guided tours as a museum. The interior has not been restored—folks expecting an intact Victorian prison will instead find a haunting, peeling maze of prison cells, offices, and shared spaces. Money generated from tours is going toward restoration of the building.

Audio wands ($5) provide information for self-guided tours, in addition to the occasional placards that mark scenes in the film. Expect to spend an hour wandering on your own, or perhaps longer if you're a big *Shawshank* fan or a dutiful listener to the audio wand.

Guided tours (price, duration, and frequency vary) highlight film scenes shot here, which extend beyond *Shawshank* to movies such as *Air Force One* and *Tango and Cash,* as well as the building's famed paranormal activity and life within the prison. For additional filming locations, the museum offers a 4.5-hour bus tour (8am and noon Sat.-Sun.) that travels throughout the area.

Ghost enthusiasts will want to check the calendar for the building's Halloween events.

BIBLEWALK

Ohio's only life-sized wax museum, **Biblewalk** (500 Tingley Ave., 419/524-0139, biblewalk.us, 10am-5pm Tues.-Sat. Apr.-Oct., reduced winter hours, tour prices vary) holds over 300 figures in 78 different scenes depicting stories from the Bible and moments of church history. There is also a small selection of historic bibles and art. Pick one of six themed itineraries, all taking 30-60 minutes each ($5.50-6.50), or see all of them ($33). There are two meal options available: the Dinner with Grace dinner theater and the Guess Who is Coming to Dinner? lunch, featuring a mystery guest from the Bible—advance reservations are recommended. The museum is largely volunteer-run and is frequented by church groups and bus tours.

Mansfield

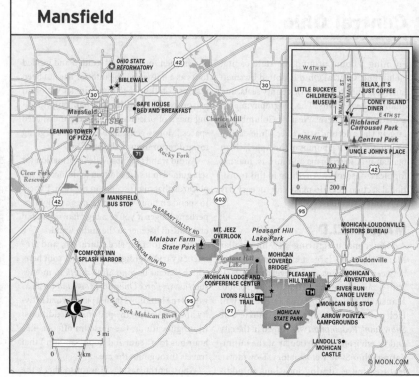

© MOON.COM

LITTLE BUCKEYE CHILDREN'S MUSEUM

The **Little Buckeye Children's Museum** (44 W. 4th St., 419/522-2332, littlebuckeye.org, 10am-4pm Mon.-Fri., 10am-5pm Sat., noon-5pm Sun. Memorial Day-Labor Day, 10am-4pm Wed.-Fri., 10am-5pm Sat., noon-5pm Sun. Labor Day-Memorial Day, $9 ages 2 and up) makes a nice pairing with the Richland Carrousel Park a block away. Catering to children ages 2-10, the small museum features over 40 interactive stations for children to play, climb, build, and explore. Many of the exhibits are modeled after places kids might visit with their parents, such as the grocery, bank, mechanic's shop, and even a McDonald's. There's also the Blue Room, where kids can build forts with giant soft blocks. Free parking is located at 4th and Main, only a block away from the museum.

RICHLAND CARROUSEL PARK

The centerpiece of downtown's Historic Carrousel District is the **Richland Carrousel Park** (75 N. Main St., 419/522-4223, richland-carrousel.com, 11am-5pm Tues.-Sun., $1 per ride, $5 for 6 rides). Opened in 1991 as the first new hand-carved merry-go-round in the United States since the 1930s, this family attraction lives in a handsome pavilion with plenty of rocking chairs from which to enjoy the old-fashioned fun. Purchase a ticket in the gift shop, which sells toys, Ohio-themed souvenirs, and other gifts. The carrousel's 52 horses, rabbits, ostriches, and other friendly creatures were all carved locally, and the 18 painted panels atop the ride depict local sites and history.

Food

A frequent recommendation by locals is **Uncle John's Place** (18 S. Main St.,

The Shawshank Trail

The former Ohio State Reformatory was a primary filming location for *The Shawshank Redemption.*

Hollywood took over Mansfield in the summer of 1993, when principal photography for *The Shawshank Redemption* took place throughout the region. The film follows banker Andy Dufresne (Tim Robbins), convicted of murdering his wife and sentenced to life in prison, and fellow inmate Ellis Boyd "Red" Redding (Morgan Freeman) while they serve time in a corrupt prison. Though not initially successful, the film built a cult following and, in 2015, the Library of Congress selected the film for preservation in the National Film Registry, an honor bestowed on movies it designates "culturally, historically, or aesthetically significant." Today, fans of the film can follow **The Shawshank Trail** (shawshanktrail.com), which identifies 16 filming locations with splashy signs. Most are found within Mansfield city limits as well as in nearby Malabar Farm State Park.

- The **Ohio State Reformatory** (100 Reformatory Rd.) is the most obvious location, serving as the film's penitentiary.

- **Downtown Mansfield** holds a handful of locations. Start at the bench in **Central Park** (29 Park Ave.), where former inmate Brooks fed the birds, and then head north on Main Street.

- **Malabar Farm State Park** (4050 Bromfield Rd., Lucas) and nearby roads were also used as filming locations, including the cabin in the opening scene. Sadly, the massive oak tree from a pivotal scene was struck by lightning and blown down in 2016.

419/526-9197, 11am-9pm Mon.-Sat., $8-20). This favorite is most known for its creative burgers but also offers a wide variety of sandwiches and meaty dinner platters. There's plenty of alcohol to choose from behind the bar to pair with your burger.

The smell of freshly baked homemade dough wafts in your face as you walk into **Leaning Tower of Pizza** (180 Lexington Ave., 419/525-3462, leaningtowerofpizzamo.

com, 11am-10pm Sun.-Thurs., 11am-11pm Fri.-Sat., $5-10). This long-standing pizza joint hasn't changed much over the years—the counter service-only room is plastered with vintage posters. The only seating is a handful of picnic tables outside.

Coney Island Diner (98 N. Main St., 419/526-2669, famousconeyisland.com, 6:30am-7pm Mon.-Fri., 6:30am-4pm Sat., $6-14), traces its roots back to 1919. On top of coney dogs, burgers, and all-day breakfast, this diner (with an authentic neon sign out front) does banana splits and sundaes.

Relax, It's Just Coffee (105 N. Main St., 419/522-1521, 7am-5pm Mon.-Fri., 9am-5pm Sat.-Sun.) resides in a distinctive balconied building in the Historic Carrousel District. It's a quintessential neighborhood coffeehouse, with friends chatting under a white tin ceiling. The delectable baked goods are provided by local Blackbird Bakery.

Accommodations

Most of Mansfield's accommodations are chain motels found off I-71 or US-30. One option that stands out, **Comfort Inn Splash Harbor** (855 Comfort Plaza Dr., Bellville, 419/719-6072, choicehotels.com, $112-151), is a little south of town off I-71 and features a small indoor waterpark suitable for young children, with a short slide and splash pad.

One independent choice, the **Safe House Bed and Breakfast** (291 Stewart Rd., 419/961-1098, safehousebandb.com, $105-135), is an 1837 sandstone house with two guest rooms (the owners live on-site as well). Once a stop on the underground railroad, the house sits on 10 acres of woods with a stream, pool, and hammock for guest use.

Transportation

Mansfield is just over an hour's drive north (67 mi/108 km) of Columbus on I-71 and about 1.25 hours (80 mi/129 km) south of Cleveland via the same road.

Greyhound (greyhound.com) and **Barons Bus** (baronsbus.com) stop off I-71 south of the city at the Marathon Gas Station at 2424 Possum Run Road. **GoBus** (ridegobus.com) takes you into town with a stop at the **Stanton Transit Station** (74 S. Diamond St.). Tickets are not sold in either location.

Richland County Transit (richlandcountytransit.com) connects Mansfield with the smaller communities that comprise its tiny metropolitan area. Fares are $2 and payable in exact change. Ask for a free transfer when paying your fare. Day passes are $5. Lyft operates in the city, as does **Ontario Cab Company** (567/560-5228).

MALABAR FARM STATE PARK

One of Ohio's more unusual state parks, **Malabar Farm State Park** (4050 Bromfield Rd., Lucas, 419/892-2784, malabarfarm.org, 8:30am-5pm daily, free) preserves the historic working farm of Pulitzer Prize-winning author Louis Bromfield. The writer, who was in all the big circles, entertained thousands of visitors a year on his farm and hosted Humphrey Bogart and Lauren Bacall's wedding in 1945. Next to the farm, which produces beef, pork, and maple syrup, is Bromfield's 32-room Western Reserve-style "Big House." Both are open for tours (house tour $6, farm wagon tour $4), though you can walk around the farm and view the animals at your leisure. The idyllic spot is surrounded by woods and hills—explorable by car, by horse, or on foot—and the grounds are home to a handful of filming locations for *The Shawshank Redemption*, in particular the Pugh Cabin.

Hiking

There are over 10 miles (16.1 km) of hiking trails, 7 miles (11.3 km) of which are shared with the **Pleasant Valley Bridle Trail,** circling the park and passing by open farmland, woods, rock formations, and a waterfall. The hike is moderately difficult and shared with visitors on horseback. Also moderate, the 0.8-mile (1.3-km) loop **Butternut Trail** wanders through a beech-maple forest and passes rock outcroppings.

Other Recreation

The **Mt. Jeez Overlook** hardly qualifies as a mountain, but provides an idyllic, open view of the farm and surrounding wooded hills. The entrance is to the east of the main park entrance on Pleasant Valley Road.

Food

The **Malabar Farm Restaurant** (3645 Pleasant Valley Rd., Lucas, 419/938-5205,

11am-8pm Tues.-Thurs., 11am-9pm Fri.-Sat., 11am-7pm Sun.), in a brick Federal-style stagecoach inn, offers seafood and steaks as well as homemade bread and desserts.

Information

Start your tour at the **Visitor Center** (8:30am-4:30pm daily) to grab tickets for tours, look at the small museum on Bromfield and the farm, and browse the gift shop (noon-4pm daily), which sells Bromfield's books, toys, and produce from the farm.

Transportation

Malabar Farm State Park is 8 miles (12.9 km) off I-71 from the SR 13 exit, about 20 minutes (11 mi/17.7 km) southeast from Mansfield, a little over an hour from Columbus via I-71 north (70 mi/113 km), and just under 1.5 hours (85 mi/137 km) from Cleveland via I-71 south and the SR 39/Lucas Road exit.

★ MOHICAN STATE PARK

The Mohican River cuts a 300-foot-deep (91-m) gorge (large by Ohio standards) through **Mohican State Park** (3116 SR 3, Loudonville, 419/994-5125, ohiodnr.gov, dawn-dusk daily, free), with 1,110 acres of hilly woods, rock formations, and waterfalls on either side of the river. The popularity of the park and nearby Malabar Farm State Park has spurred the development of canoe liveries, campgrounds, and bed-and-breakfasts that make this pocket of Ohio something of a major recreational area, and a more centralized one at that compared to the larger Hocking Hills region in southeast Ohio.

Sights and Hikes

Between the state park and the adjacent Mohican Memorial State Forest, there are 13 miles (20.9 km) of hiking trails. A popular trailhead is at the **Mohican Covered Bridge** parking lot, from which you can venture on an easy riverside amble on the 0.75-mile (1.2-km) one-way **Pleasant Hill Trail.** On the opposite side of the covered bridge is the trailhead for

the **Lyons Falls Trail,** which edges along the river before heading up the hill to rock formations and two small waterfalls; the moderate-to-difficult trail is 2 miles (3.2 km) each way. Johnny Appleseed once had his name and the date etched on the wall next to the falls, but the etchings have worn away over time. The **Gorge Overlook** off SR 97 provides the best view of the park's Clearfork Gorge.

Other Recreation

Mountain Bike Action Magazine named the 25-mile (40-km) **Mohican Mountain Bike Trail,** which makes a scenic loop around the gorge, the best in Ohio. The park also features bridle trails and snowmobile trails, though there are no rentals.

There are multiple liveries and kayak rental agencies in the area. **River Run Canoe Livery** (3069 SR 3, Loudonville, 419/994-5204, riverrunfamilycampground. com) is located near the state park entrance, as is **Mohican Adventures** (3045 SR 3, Loudonville, 419/994-4097, mohicanadventures.com), which—on top of unguided river trips via canoe, kayak, rafts, and tubes—offers miniature golf, an Aerial Adventures ropes course, and go-carts.

Pleasant Hill Lake Park (3431 SR 95, Perrysville, 419/938-7884, pleasanthillpark. mwcd.org), just northwest of Mohican State Park, features hiking trails and a marina with boat and kayak rentals.

Accommodations

Mohican Lodge and Conference Center (1098 Ashland County Rd., 419/938-5411, mohicanlodge.com, $170-260) sits within the state park and features heated indoor and outdoor pools, a paved bike trail, tennis courts, a restaurant, and a lounge. Rooms are fairly basic, though the public areas exude a warm, rustic allure.

The enchanting **Landoll's Mohican Castle** (561 Township Rd. 3352, Loudonville, 419/994-3427, landollsmohicancastle.com, $219-329) is nestled deep in the woods southeast of the state park. Spend the night like

royalty in any of the elegant suites with fireplaces, heated bathroom floors, and Jacuzzis. There are additional suites in the Stables and Highland Building, a luxurious restaurant on-site, and ghost tours on offer.

CAMPING

The Mohican region bills itself as the "Camp and Canoe Capital of Ohio," and with approximately 4,500 campsites and cabins in the area, it's hard to argue against that claim.

Just north of the SR 3 entrance to the park, **Mohican Adventures** (3045 SR 3, Loudonville, 419/994-4097, mohicanadventures.com) offers 40 acres of primitive campgrounds, RV hookups, and 45 cabins, in addition to river trips and other fun-filled activities, including a heated indoor pool. Rates start at $25 per night for two people.

East of the park, **Arrow Point Family Campground** (6270 Twp. Rd. 208/Wally Rd., Loudonville, 419/994-5374, arrowpoint-campgrounds.com, Apr.-Oct.) offers riverside sites for RVs. Rates start at $30 per night for two people.

Mohican State Park (3116 SR 3, Loudonville, 419/994-5125, ohiodnr.gov) has 51 full hookup sites, 35 electric sites, and 10 non-electric sites as well as heated and air-conditioned cabins. Rates start at $25. Just northwest of the state park, **Pleasant Hill Lake Park** (3431 SR 95, Perrysville, 419/938-7884, pleasanthillpark.mwcd.org) features 440 campsites and 10 log cabins. Rates start at $43 per site.

Information

The **Mohican-Loudonville Visitors Bureau** (544 North Union St., Loudonville, 419/994-2519, discovermohican.com) is a good resource on the attractions, accommodations, and dining in the Mohican region. It runs a visitors center (9am-6pm daily) northeast of the state park.

1: Malabar Farm State Park **2:** the Historic Carrousel District in downtown Mansfield **3:** Gorge Overlook at Mohican State Park **4:** Mohican Covered Bridge in Mohican State Park

Transportation

Mohican State Park is 1.25 hours (72 mi/116 km) north of Columbus via I-71 and SR 97. From Cleveland, it's a 1.5-hour drive (83 mi/134 km) south along I-71 to the US-250 exit for Ashland, from which you jump on US-42 south to SR 511 south to SR 39—a bit of a country drive, all told.

Though a car is by far the best method of transportation for the area, there is a **Greyhound** (greyhound.com), **Barons Bus** (baronsbus.com), and **GoBus** (ridegobus.com) stop at 3175 SR 3 in Loudonville, near the campground entrance to Mohican State Park.

MARION

Marion somehow achieves the contradiction of being in the middle of the state without being very near anything. An epicenter of popcorn production as early as World War II with companies Wyandot Snacks and ConAgra, the city of 36,000 maintains its legacy with the Wyandot Popcorn Museum and Marion Popcorn Festival in September. The city's other claim to fame is as the longtime base of President Warren G. Harding, whose home is still an attraction.

Sights

WARREN G. HARDING HOME AND MEMORIAL

Warren G. Harding largely conducted his presidential campaign from his front porch, with over 600,000 people traveling to Marion to hear him speak. Today, the **Warren G. Harding Home and Memorial** (380 Mt. Vernon Ave., 740/387-9630, www.hardinghome.org, 9am-5pm Wed.-Sat., noon-5pm Sun., $16 adults, $15 seniors, $8 students) preserves the 29th president's home (and porch). Inside the Queen Anne house, his personal effects are on display, with the rooms organized as Warren and wife Florence had them when they lived in the house from 1891 to 1921. The guided tours last approximately one hour.

Adjacent to the home is the **Warren G. Harding Presidential Library & Museum,** opened in 2021. It houses an exhibit gallery that tells the story of the president and first lady through artifacts, photos, and videos. Admission to the Harding Home includes access to the presidential library (library only $10 adults and seniors, $8 students).

The **Harding Memorial** (corner of Vernon Heights Blvd. and Delaware Ave., 24 hours daily, free), 1.5 miles (2.4 km) south, resembles a Greek temple, with marble Doric columns making a circle around the final resting place of both Warren and Florence Harding. Parking is available on both Vernon Heights Boulevard and Delaware Avenue.

WYANDOT POPCORN MUSEUM

One of the most specific museum collections in Ohio, the **Wyandot Popcorn Museum** (169 E. Church St., 740/387-4255, wyandotpopcornmus.com, 1pm-4pm Wed.-Sun. May-Oct., 1pm-4pm Sat.-Sun. Nov.-Dec. and Mar.-Apr., $6 adults, $5 seniors, $3 children) sits in Marion's old post office and displays antique popcorn wagons and peanut roasters under a colorful big top circus tent. Built and operated in the late 19th and early 20th centuries, the wagons recall years long gone. To end the time on a tasty note, each visitor receives a bag of freshly popped popcorn at the end of the tour. The Greek Revival building is also home to the **Marion County Historical Society** (740/387-4255, marionhistory.com), which is included with admission to the popcorn museum, operates during the same hours, and features local history exhibits.

Food

Sansotta's Fresh Italian (1292 Delaware Ave., 740/751-6596, sansottasitalian.com, 10:45am-8pm Mon.-Sat., 10:45am-5pm Sun., $7-12) is a local Italian American staple with inexpensive subs, salads, and pastas served out of an unassuming strip mall. You're free to build your own pasta or salad bowl if none of the menu items suit your taste.

Blink-and-you-miss-it **Carlyle's Restaurant** (1116 Mt. Vernon Ave., 740/386-6333, 11am-3pm Mon.-Fri., $5-12) does a typical diner menu and some steak entrées not far from US-23, once you've gotten past all the chain restaurants. The made-from-scratch pies are popular.

Accommodations

There are several chain motels off the Marion/Mt. Gilead Road exit off US-23.

Transportation

Marion is an hour's drive (50 mi/81 km) north of Columbus via US-23.

There is currently no bus service to Marion, and the city doesn't operate a fixed-route bus system. The **Marion Area Transit (MAT)** (740/382-9850, marionohio.us/transit) operates a demand response service for the city if needed, with fares starting at $1.25.

BELLEFONTAINE AND WEST LIBERTY

Bustling Logan County seat Bellefontaine (pronounced "Bell-fountain") is home to some surprising superlatives. At 1,550 feet (472 m) above sea level, Campbell Hill just east of town is the highest point in Ohio, though searchers looking for an actual hill to summit will be disappointed to find the marker and plaza hiding behind Ohio Hi-Point Career Center with nary a view. Bellefontaine also lays claim to the country's first concrete street, quite literally paving the way toward the modern roads that we enjoy today across the United States. Though the central business district is a good place to stroll, with boutiques and restaurants, the main attractions in the area lay outside the city near the tiny village of West Liberty, including Ohio's largest and most striking cave.

"America's Oldest Concrete Street"

You don't get much more roadside attraction than a literal road, but Bellefontaine is justifiably proud of the role it played in modernizing the nation's streets.

Like many of the country's rural streets in the late 19th century, Bellefontaine's were made of dirt. Concrete entrepreneur George Bartholomew convinced the Bellefontaine city council to try paving a small portion of road with concrete, at the time an unproven material for road construction. To combat the council's skepticism, Bartholomew donated the concrete and paid a $5,000 bond to ensure that the road would last at least five years. In 1891, the first 8-foot (2.4-m) patch went up, followed by the remainder of the roads surrounding the county courthouse. The roads turned out to be a success and concrete would eventually become popular as a road surface. Today, "America's Oldest Concrete Street" has, of course, been repaved over time, but a marker and arch at Court Avenue and Main Street designate the site's significance in improving the country's road system.

A bit more arbitrary is "America's Shortest Street," a 15-foot (4.6-m) plot of asphalt known as McKinley Street, cutting a corner between Garfield Avenue and Columbus Avenue just west of the central business district. A marker under the McKinley Street sign indicates the road's significance.

Sights

★ OHIO CAVERNS

Ohio Caverns (2210 SR 245 E., West Liberty, 937/465-4017, ohiocaverns.com, 9am-5pm daily May-Sept., 10am-4pm daily Oct.-Apr., tours $19 adults, $10 children) is the state's largest cave and one of the more colorful you're likely to find anywhere, with hues of red from iron oxide and bright white stalactites creating majestic designs. Discovered in 1897 by a farmhand, the cave's interesting—and in some cases very rare—combinations of stalactites, stalagmites, and rock formations were immediately utilized as a tourist attraction, though much of the cave wasn't excavated until decades later. The cave is a brisk 54°F (12°C) year-round and tours, whichever of the three you choose, run roughly an hour, with the Limestone tour suitable for those with limited mobility, including people using wheelchairs (reservations are required). The Natural Wonder tour takes visitors through about 1 mile (1.6 km) of caverns and past the Crystal King, the largest stalactite in Ohio. Other highlights include a reflective pool and the magical Palace of the Gods, where nearly every cave formation is represented in one dynamic room. Above ground is a gem mining station and a gift shop.

MAC-A-CHEEK CASTLE

The French Huguenot-descended Piatt family built two castle-inspired homes in the Bellefontaine region in the late 19th century, as curious then as they are now. While Mac-O-Chee was auctioned off in 2019, the family is using the funds from the auction to restore the **Mac-A-Cheek Castle** (10051 Twp. Rd. 47, West Liberty, 937/465-2821, piattcastle.org, 10am-5pm daily Memorial Day-Labor Day, 10am-4pm Sat.-Sun. mid-Apr.-Memorial Day and Labor Day-Oct., $13 adults, $11 seniors, $7 children), which is still open to the public. Self-guided tours of the gothic home take about 45-60 minutes and lead you through rooms appointed with Piatt family furnishings and art collections as well as exhibits and artifacts depicting local history.

Entertainment and Events

HOLLAND THEATRE

While in town, try to catch a show at the **Holland Theatre** (127 E. Columbus Ave., Bellefontaine, 937/592-9002, thehollandtheatre.org), perhaps the most unique performing arts space in Ohio. The interior of the 1931 movie palace was designed by Dutch immigrant Peter Hulsken to resemble a Flemish village square, with facades of storefronts and

Annual Events in Ohio's Heartland

Central Ohio's small towns host some of the state's most popular annual events and festivals. Though some towns aren't always destinations on their own, these festivities offer a perfect opportunity to venture into Ohio's rural farm communities for a glimpse of local culture and an excuse to escape the city.

- The Lancaster Festival (lancasterfestival.org) is a 10-day music and arts festival in late July with individually ticketed shows to local, regional, and national acts. While classical music forms the backbone of the festival, events branch into pop music, country, Broadway, and more.

- One of the newer additions to the long list of local festivals, the Coshocton Sunflower Festival (coshoctonsunflowerfestival.com) provides ample opportunities for Instagram-worthy shots. The festival runs for a weekend in mid-August, though look for sneak peek events during the weekends leading up to it.

- Held the weekend after Labor Day and drawing upward of 250,000 people, the Marion Popcorn Festival (popcornfestival.com) is the largest popcorn festival in the world and features rides, popcorn cooking contests, and a popcorn parade. There's an emphasis on attracting big musical acts for free entertainment, with performers such as Boyz II Men, Foreigner, and REO Speedwagon visiting in previous years.

- Butler's Prairie Peddler Festival (prairietown.com) assembles 200 artisans and food vendors in the tranquil hills near Mohican State Park. The event is held on two weekends in late September/early October.

- Delaware's Little Brown Jug (littlebrownjug.com) is a classic harness race that's been going strong since 1937 and is one of the most prized trophies for Standardbred horses. The race goes on during the Delaware County Fair in late September over the span of five days.

- The Circleville Pumpkin Show (pumpkinshow.com) draws 400,000 people over one weekend to see gigantic pumpkins, eat pumpkin-flavored foods (some unusual ones are sprinkled in the mix), and enjoy live music and a parade. This is one of Ohio's largest and oldest festivals, always running the third Wednesday of October through the following Saturday.

windmills constructed into the walls. The theater reopened in 2019 after decades of neglect and a local campaign to save the local landmark, which sees country, gospel, folk, and other acts come through.

Recreation
INDIAN LAKE
The small Indian Lake region, 11 miles (17.7 km) northwest of Bellefontaine, is an easy weekend getaway for Central Ohioans year-round, with campgrounds, marinas, and vacation homes surrounding a 5100-acre reservoir.

Indian Lake State Park (12774 SR 235, Lakeview, 937/843-2717, ohiodnr.gov, dawn-dusk daily, free) features a large campground with some lakeside sites, a boat ramp, and two swimming beaches. Old Field Beach (11252 SR 235, Lakeview) is the larger of the two and comes with a handful of picnic shelters and a disc golf course.

There are a few boat rental businesses ready to send you out into the water, including Spend-A-Day Marina (9481 SR 708, Russells Point, spendaday.com) with pontoons and watersports.

Food
★ Six Hundred Downtown (108 S. Main St., Bellefontaine, 937/599-6600, 600downtown.com, 11am-9pm Tues.-Thurs., 11am-10pm Fri.-Sat., noon-8pm Sun., $9-15) is easily the town's most famous restaurant, having been featured on Food Network's *Guy's*

Grocery Games. Housed in a historic building with the Logan County Courthouse in full view, the restaurant offers classic Detroit- and Sicilian-style pizzas, along with gluten-free and cauliflower options, and the beer list is on point with 11 taps of mostly local craft beer.

Not to be outdone in the beer department, **Brewfontaine** (211 S. Main St., Bellefontaine, 937/404-9128, brewfontaine. com, 11am-10pm Sun.-Thurs., 11am-midnight Fri.-Sat., $7-10) has 20 taps of craft beer, some local and some from afar, plus more in bottles and cans. Cocktails and sandwiches are also available at this congenial subway-tiled taproom.

Accommodations

There's not much in town but two chain motels, a **Super 8** (1117 N. Main St., Bellefontaine, 937/404-5820, wyndhamhotels.com, $80-95) and a **Comfort Inn** (260 Northview Dr., 937/595-0631, choicehotels. com, $79-90).

CAMPING

If you'd prefer to stay next to Indian Lake in a campground or cottage, **indianlake.com** includes a list of what's on offer.

Indian Lake State Park (12774 SR 235, Lakeview, 937/843-2717, ohiodnr.gov) features a large campground with 443 electric sites suitable for tents or RVs, including 20 lakeside boat camping spaces. Rates start at $29.

Transportation

Bellefontaine is nearly an hour northwest of Columbus via US-33 (58 mi/93 km) and just over an hour northeast of Dayton (56 mi/90 km) via I-70 east and US-68 north, which also goes directly through West Liberty. There is no public transportation to or within Bellefontaine and West Liberty.

NEWARK

The county seat of Licking County, Newark boasts a growing population of 50,000 and is the largest of the small satellite cities a short drive from Columbus. Well-connected in the 19th century by canal and railroad, Newark built successful industries in glass and still attracts big corporations with its proximity to Columbus and affordability. The Victorian town square is well-maintained, with restaurants, boutiques, and cultural amenities steps away from the central lawn—including the **Canal Market District** (canalmarketdistrict. org), a pavilion and green space built over the former Ohio Canal, and its summer farmers market on Tuesdays and Fridays.

The most impressive sight in Newark has nothing to do with canals or railroads. The Hopewell culture built an immense complex of geometric mounds 2,000 years ago throughout what is today Newark. Though much was destroyed, the remainder of the Newark Earthworks still astonish with their scale and ingenuity.

Sights
★ NEWARK EARTHWORKS

Part of a 4-square-mile (10.4-sq-km) complex that was once the world's largest set of geometric earthworks, the **Great Circle Earthworks** (455 Hebron Rd., Heath, 740/344-0498, ohiohistory.org, dawn-dusk daily, free) encompass 30 acres of tranquil lawn just south of Newark—large enough to hold the entire Great Pyramid of Giza. Making a perfect circle, the 14-foot-tall (4.3-m) mound and moat (now a ditch) has a diameter of 1,200 feet (366 m) and was used for ceremonial purposes by the Hopewell culture. Built over 2,000 years ago, the site was actually used as the county fairgrounds for some time in the 19th century, which ironically preserved it while much of the rest of the complex, also used for ceremonial purposes, was lost to development. The small **museum** (noon-4pm Wed.-Sun. Memorial Day-Oct., noon-4pm Fri.-Sun. Jan.-Memorial Day, free) provides context through photographs, maps, and a handful of artifacts that depict the complex's scale and usage. A paved path skirts the eastern side of the circle, though you are encouraged to wander the inner lawn (but not the mound itself) via the entrance near the museum to appreciate the scale of the earthen undertaking. An hour is plenty of time to wander the mounds and peek inside the museum. **Guided tours** (10am and 2pm Fri.-Sat. July-Oct.) meet in front of the museum.

Another remnant of the massive complex is 2 miles (3.2 km) northwest of the Great Circle Earthworks. The **Octagon Earthworks** (125 N. 33rd St., dawn-dusk daily, free) feature both an octagon and a circle designed to align with moon positions. There is a viewing platform where you can get a better look at the mounds, though only a part of the complex is open to the public daily. The mounds are on the grounds of the Moundbuilders Country Club, which closes on select days to allow people to freely wander them in their entirety; consult the employees at the Great Circle Earthworks for these dates. **Guided tours** (3:30pm Fri.-Sat. July-Oct.) are available.

Along with the state's other Hopewell culture sites, the Newark Earthworks are under consideration as a potential UNESCO World Heritage Site.

THE WORKS

One of Ohio's more comprehensive local museums, **The Works** (55 S. 1st St., 740/349-9277, attheworks.org, 9am-5pm Tues.-Sat., $12 adults, $10 seniors, $8 children) fills a former steam engine factory with exhibits on science, local industry and history, and art. Kids can build and race K'nex cars, take apart computer towers and other electronics in the Invent Lab, and experiment with magnets. The 2nd floor features local human and natural history finds; an exhibit on native daughter Jerrie Mock, the first woman to fly around the world; and more about Licking County's transportation and industrial heritage. There are daily shows in the museum's SciDome Planetarium, which are included in admission, as are the glassblowing demonstrations in the Glass Studio (register to make your own glass decoration as well). The gift shop is well-stocked with glass-blown art and other trinkets, and parking is free.

DAWES ARBORETUM

Dawes Arboretum (7770 Jacksontown Rd., 740/323-2355, dawesarb.org, 9am-7pm daily Mar.-Oct., 9am-5pm daily Nov.-Feb., $10 adults, $5 children) is unmissable from an airplane, with the words "Dawes Arboretum" spelled in giant hedge lettering (a 36-ft/11-m observation tower sits next to it for those who

the Great Circle Earthworks, part of the greater Newark Earthworks complex

Side Trip to Granville

restaurants and boutiques in charming Granville

There's no shortage of adorable college towns in Ohio, but for a touch of New England small-town charm head to little Granville, just 6 miles (9.7 km) west of Newark. Settled in 1805, this town of around 6,000 people is home to **Denison University,** which overlooks the town on a bluff and counts Steve Carell and Jennifer Garner among the alumni of its theater program. The town exudes a relaxed pace and feeling of seclusion. The storefronts on Broadway, the main thoroughfare, maintain the idyllic persona of centuries past. Homey gift shops **Green Velvet** (130 E. Broadway, 740/587-0515, 11am-5pm Mon.-Sat.) and **Kussmaul Gallery** (140 E. Broadway, 740/587-4640, kussmaulgallery.com, 10am-5:30pm Mon.-Sat., noon-4pm Sun.) are long-standing favorites to pick up local art and gifts. Now a multistate franchise, **Whit's Frozen Custard** (138 E. Broadway, 740/587-3620, whitscustard.com, seasonal hours) got its start in Granville and still operates a tiny shop in town, with umbrella-ed seating on the wide sidewalk.

There are multiple bed-and-breakfasts, and not one but two storied inns across the street from one another. In business since 1812, the **Buxton Inn** (313 E. Broadway, 740/587-0001, buxtoninn. com, $129-229) is one of Ohio's oldest and has seen the likes of Abraham Lincoln and Harriet Beecher Stowe stay the night, along with a high volume of reported specters; the 25-room inn is reputed to be one of the country's most haunted hotels. Non-guests are welcome to join for dinner in the four dining rooms. The **Granville Inn** (314 E. Broadway, 740/587-3333, granvilleinn. com, $92-188) likewise exudes historic charm and features a respected dining room. Opened in 1924, the Tudor-style inn feels downright modern compared to the stagecoach-inn feel of the Buxton, with 36 comfortable rooms and complimentary bathrobes to use during your stay.

didn't bring an airplane). At nearly 2,000 acres, this massive arboretum is suitable for both walking and driving tours. The park is especially known for its buckeye and maple trees, providing stunning colors during the fall. Visitors will also find native woodlands and wetlands, one of the northernmost bald cypress swamps in the country, and a Japanese garden.

Stop by the visitors center for the bonsai collection, bird-watching garden, and gift shop.

WORLD'S LARGEST BASKET
In the 1990s, the upscale wood baskets from The Longaberger Company were all the rage with consumers who subscribed to a country-chic aesthetic. Riding the wave of success, the

company built the **World's Largest Basket** (1550 E. Main St.) in 1997, a seven-story office building complete with 150-ton handles to resemble a Longaberger basket. Sadly, a downturn in the economy and shifting preferences in the 21st century have drastically reduced the company's footprint; Longaberger moved out of the building in 2016. As of this writing the basket is empty and for sale, but you're free to look at it from the parking lot.

Recreation
★ BLACKHAND GORGE STATE NATURE PRESERVE

We don't normally equate Ohio with archaeological ruins but, 8 miles (12.9 km) east of Newark, within **Blackhand Gorge State Nature Preserve** (2200 Gratiot Rd. SE, ohiodnr.gov, dawn-dusk daily, free), hikers can explore an old canal lock from the 1820s, a 700-foot-long (213-m) railroad "deep cut" through a sandstone cliff dating back to 1850, and a disused interurban tunnel from the early 20th century, all within manageable distance of one another. Named after a hand-shaped Native American petroglyph that was lost during the construction of the canal, the park features hiking trails as well as the 4-mile (6.4-km) one-way **Blackhand Trail,** an easy, paved multiuse trail (open to hikers, bikers, and strollers) that snakes along the Licking River, through the deep cut, and into a low gorge. To access the canal lock and interurban tunnel, look for the trailhead of the 0.5-mile (0.8-km) one-way **Canal Lock Trail** across the Licking River from the main parking lot. The trail is an unpaved but flat path through the woods, leading past the canal lock and, soon after, to the ominous entrance of the tunnel, dead-ending at the other side. There's also a small, somewhat hidden parking lot across the road from the trailhead. A (not especially clean) bathroom is located by the main parking lot at this off-the-beaten-path gem.

BUCKEYE LAKE

The Buckeye Lake region south of Newark once boasted an amusement park and dance hall, but today is mostly the destination of anglers and watersports-lovers. There are house and cottage rentals, campgrounds, and marinas along the 35-mile (56-km) shoreline. **Buckeye Lake State Park** (2905 Liebs Island Rd., Millersport, 740/467-3690, ohiodnr.gov, dawn-dusk daily, free) features a 4-mile (6.4-km) walking path along the lake, and two small swimming beaches: Fairfield Beach to the south and Crystal Beach to the north.

Food

Franks and Sammies (34 S. 3rd St., 740/915-1812, franksandsammies.com, 11am-9pm Tues.-Sat., $6-11) keeps the oldies rolling with records for sale and posters of old acts on the walls. The jumbo hot dogs—wrapped in grilled tortillas with whatever assortment of toppings you choose—are music-themed too. There are cans and bottles of craft beer available.

A trendy craft brewery by appearances, with hanging lightbulbs and exposed brick, **Market Street Soda Works** (14 E. Market St., 740/877-6417, marketstreetsodaworks.com, 3pm-8pm Tues. and Fri., noon-4pm Sat.) keeps four drafts of root beer and other soda—produced locally and by specialty soda makers—and 160 different bottled varieties for a build-your-own six-pack. A rotation of food trucks provides the chow.

North of town is the historic Ye Olde Mill, which since 1960 has been the home of **Velvet Ice Cream** (11324 Mt. Vernon Rd., Utica, 800/589-5000, velveticecream.com, seasonal hours, $8-10). On the 20-acre grounds of the mill there's an ice cream parlor, restaurant featuring sandwiches and salads, free factory tours, an ice cream museum, and walking

---

1: preserved canal-era buildings in historic Roscoe Village **2:** draft root beer at Market Street Soda Works in Newark **3:** canal ruins at Blackhand Gorge State Nature Preserve

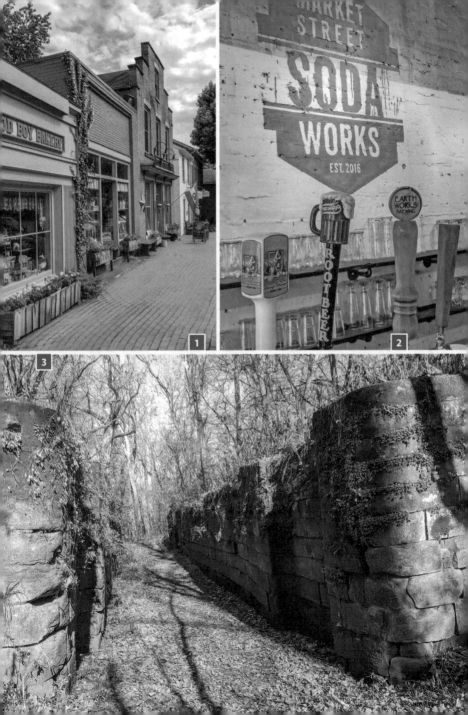

trails. Founded in 1914 by Lebanese immigrant Joseph Dager, Velvet ships its ice cream to hundreds of grocery stores.

Accommodations

Between Newark, Granville to the west, and Heath to the south, the area sports a fair number of chain hotels and motels. The **DoubleTree by Hilton Newark Ohio** (50 N. 2nd St., 740/322-6455, hilton.com, $104-127) is steps away from Newark's town square and Canal Market District and features an indoor swimming pool and free parking.

The area's most unique lodging choices are in nearby Granville, including the **Buxton Inn** (313 E. Broadway, Granville, 740/587-0001, buxtoninn.com, $129-229) and **Granville Inn** (314 E. Broadway, Granville, 740/587-3333, granvilleinn.com, $92-188).

CAMPING

The **Buckeye Lake/Columbus East KOA** (4460 Walnut Rd., 740/928-0706, koa.com/campgrounds/buckeye-lake) is within walking distance of the state park's lakeside trail and has 270 campsites, cabins, and an assortment of amenities such as a swimming pool and game room. Rates start at $28 for a nonelectric site.

Transportation

Newark is about a 40-minute drive (40 mi/64 km) east of Downtown Columbus and about 30 minutes from the northeast corner of I-270 along SR 161, which turns into SR 37 and then SR 16. Newark is 20 minutes north (10 mi/16.1 km) of I-70 via SR 13.

Greyhound (greyhound.com), **Barons Bus** (baronsbus.com), and **GoBus** (ridegobus.com) stop at 900 University Drive on the Ohio State University Newark and Central Ohio Technical College campus. There are no facilities or ticket sales on-site.

There's no fixed-route bus service in Newark. **Licking County Transit Services** (740/670-5185, lickingcounty.gov) provides demand-service public transportation. Call ahead to arrange a ride. **Safe Cab Co** (740/345-5436) operates in the area, though service can be spotty. Overall, it's best to drive yourself around town.

COSHOCTON

Originally a Lenape village, destroyed by American militia during the Revolutionary War, Coshocton attracted white settlers around the turn of the 19th century for its ideal position along the Tuscarawas and Muskingum Rivers. The Ohio & Erie Canal

the Buxton Inn in Granville, west of Newark

reached the area in 1830, in particular Roscoe Village just across the river. Roscoe Village thrived and waned with the canal system until it was devastated by the Great Flood of 1913. Restoration and preservation of the village began in the 1960s and has continued to the present day, with Roscoe Village now a regional tourist destination.

Though you'll find a handful of restaurants and shops near the city's courthouse, Roscoe Village is the primary reason to visit Coshocton.

Sights
ROSCOE VILLAGE

Restored **Roscoe Village** is one of Ohio's best-preserved canal towns, with shops, restaurants, living history exhibits, and a canal boat ride all within walking distance of one another and depicting life in a mid-19th-century transportation hub.

Start at the **Visitor Center** (600 N. Whitewoman St., 740/622-7644, roscoevillage.com, 10am-4pm daily) to purchase your Living History tickets ($11 adults, $10 seniors, $7 children), which grant you access to the village's restored museum buildings such as a schoolhouse, craftsman's house, and blacksmith shop, where interpreters (some costumed, some not) greet you and share information about their trade and the lives of residents past. The center also has informative dioramas, a video, and a gift shop. Visitors can wander the village on their own Memorial Day-Labor Day, and the rest of the year take a guided tour (10:30am and 1:30pm daily Labor Day-Memorial Day).

It's free to stroll Whitewoman Street and browse the retail shops and restaurants at your leisure. Within the restored buildings you'll find a general store, as well as antique, gift, and specialty shops.

At the far end of the village, the **Johnson-Humrickhouse Museum** (300 N. Whitewoman St., 740/622-8710, jhmuseum. org, noon-5pm daily Memorial Day-Labor Day, noon-4pm Tues.-Sun. Mar.-Memorial Day and Labor Day-Dec., noon-4pm Fri.-Sun.

Jan.-Feb., $5 adults, $4 children) displays the artifacts of well-traveled brothers David M. Johnson and John H. Johnson along with donated artifacts relevant to local history. The museum's holdings include Native American, European, and Asian art, weapons, and tools.

In the other direction, a long walk behind the visitor center, the **Monticello III** (23166 SR 83, 740/622-7528, 1pm, 2pm, and 3pm Tues.-Fri., 1pm, 2pm, 3pm, and 4pm Sat.-Sun. Memorial Day-Labor Day, $8 adults, $7 seniors, $6 students) takes guests on a lazy, horse-drawn canal boat ride down a resurrected portion of the canal while the captain regales riders with tales of the old canal life. The ride lasts about 45 minutes.

Food

Family-owned **McKenna's Market** (403 N. Whitewoman St., 740/291-8000, mckennasmarket.com, 10am-6pm daily, $6-10) has a little bit of everything—a deli counter, a grocery with Amish goods, and a freezer of local Velvet Ice Cream. There's a secluded patio behind the building with seating.

It's not all about Roscoe Village in Coshocton. **The Railroad Restaurant and Saloon** (509 Main St., 740/575-4151, railroadrestaurantandsaloon.com, 11am-10pm Tues.-Fri., 4pm-10pm Sat., $13-40) offers hefty surf-and-turf entrées in an old-timey saloon, with billiards free to play for guests. The lunch menu offers sandwiches and burgers for under $15.

Accommodations

Coshocton Village Inn and Suites (115 N. Water St., 740/622-9455, christopherhotels. com, $96-106) is just across the highway from Roscoe Village and features 64 basic but comfortable rooms, an indoor pool and hot tub, and a complimentary hot breakfast.

Transportation

Coshocton is about a 1.5-hour drive (76 mi/122 km) east of Columbus, taking SR 161/ SR 37/SR 16 all the way from I-270. Coshocton is an hour's drive (59 mi/95 km) southwest of Canton, taking I-77 south to US-36 west. There is no bus service to Coshocton.

ZANESVILLE

Ohio's second capital city (1810-1812), Zanesville once carved a niche for itself as a major pottery manufacturing center. This city of 25,000 sits on the cusp of Appalachia, with a compact downtown that includes several historic churches and an unusual Y-Bridge that carries traffic over the confluence of the Licking and Muskingum Rivers.

Sights

NATIONAL ROAD AND ZANE GREY MUSEUM

Honoring two staples of local Zanesville history in one museum, the **National Road and Zane Grey Museum** (8850 E. Pike, 740/826-3305, ohiohistory.org, 10am-5pm Wed.-Sat., 1pm-5pm Sun. May-Sept., $7 adults, $6 seniors, $3 children) is located just off I-70. Proposed by George Washington, the National Road (now US-40) was the first major road undertaken by the federal government and connects Cumberland, Maryland, with Vandalia, Illinois. The museum depicts the construction and evolution of the highway through a series of intricate dioramas, as well as displays a Conestoga wagon and other artifacts. It also commemorates Western author and Zanesville native Zane Grey (a descendant of the town's founder, Ebenezer Zane), whose books were wildly popular in the early 20th century and the basis for over 100 films. His books are for sale in the gift shop.

ALAN COTTRILL SCULPTURE STUDIO

Over 300 bronze sculptures live at the **Alan Cottrill Sculpture Studio** (110 S. 6th St., 740/453-9822, alancottrill.com, 9am-5pm Mon.-Sat., free), where Alan continues to sculpt commemorative statues, bells, and more from his studio. The former businessman left it all to become a sculptor, devoting significant time to the study of sculpture and anatomy to pursue a second career. Today,

Alan's commissions can be found across the country, including at The Ohio State University and the United States Military Academy. You may find Alan hard at work on his latest project during your visit.

Food

Tom's Ice Cream Bowl (532 McIntire Ave., 740/452-5267, tomsicecreambowl.com, 11am-10pm Sun.-Thurs., 11am-11pm Fri.-Sat., $7-12) has served Zanesville since 1948 and has only changed hands once—from the founder to his manager. Along with hefty scoops of over 25 varieties of ice cream, the menu includes sandwiches and burgers and is served in a classic mid-century modern dining room.

Old Market House Inn (424 Market St., 740/454-2555, adornettos.com, 4pm-9pm Tues.-Sat., $13-32) is located in a building from 1919, though the medieval English tavern-style dining room dates to the 1970s. There's something for everyone here: pub sandwiches, pizzas, steaks, seafood, and pastas.

Accommodations

There are several chain hotels and motels near downtown. Try the **Holiday Inn Express and Suites Zanesville North** (1101 Spring St., 740/297-4751, ihg.com, $106-123), which comes with an indoor pool, a hot tub, and a breakfast bar.

Transportation

Zanesville is about an hour's drive (56 mi/90 km) east from Columbus on I-70.

Greyhound (greyhound.com) and **Barons Bus** (baronsbus.com) stop at the **Zanesville Bus Station** (224 Main St.).

South East Area Transit (SEAT) (seatbus. org) operates a fixed-route bus system around the city. Regular fares are $1 and payable in exact change.

LANCASTER

Historic Lancaster boasts a Civil War-era downtown, elegant Italianate houses, and numerous small museums, one of which is the home of its most famous native son: controversial General William Tecumseh Sherman of the Union Army. The city of 40,000 sits in between Columbus, just 40 minutes north, and Hocking Hills, less than 30 minutes south.

Sights
SHERMAN HOUSE MUSEUM

The Shermans were quite an overachieving family, with William Tecumseh Sherman arising as one of the principal generals of the Union Army during the Civil War and his brother John serving as a U.S. senator. The general's most famous contributions—capturing Atlanta and pursuing a scorched-earth campaign to the Georgia coast known as "Sherman's March to the Sea"—made him a divisive figure. At any rate, the brothers' birthplace is now the **Sherman House Museum** (137 E. Main St., 740/687-5891, shermanhouse. org, tours at noon, 1pm, 2pm, and 3pm Tues.-Sun., $6 adults, $2 students), a modest 1811 frame house that's been added onto over the years. Exhibits feature Sherman's personal effects, furniture, and Civil War memorabilia. One bedroom re-creates Sherman's field tent, decorated with his belongings. Volunteers tend to the small era-appropriate gardens, which are free to the public.

MOUNT PLEASANT

Mount Pleasant is the main draw to **Rising Park** (1120 N. High St., 740/687-6651, fairfieldcountyparks.com, dawn-dusk daily). The 250-foot (76-m) sandstone bluff has an unimpeded view of the city, the flat farmlands to the west, and the hills of Appalachia to the south—a distinct shift marking the effect of glaciers past. Reach the peak via a short but bracing hiking path from the parking lot (0.7 mi/1.1 km one-way). The park also features a playground and fishing pond.

Food

Just west of town is the rustic ★ **Rockmill Brewery** (5705 Lithopolis Rd. NW, 740/215-5874, rockmillbrewery.com, 4pm-9pm Thurs., noon-9pm Fri.-Sat., noon-8pm Sun.). This family-owned, small-batch brewery is housed in a former horse barn, with inviting nooks and tables at which to sit and sip beers with a group of friends. The atmosphere is low-key and family-friendly. The grounds include an outdoor patio and pond on the edge of the woods, making for a tranquil scene, and rotating food trucks provide edible options. Down the road a few paces is the actual Rock Mill, dating to the early 19th century and set atop a small waterfall.

Back in the historic city center, gastropub **Ale House 1890** (149 W. Main St., 740/277-6053, alehouse1890.com, 4pm-11pm Mon.-Sat., $10-20) keeps it simple, with a menu focusing on salads, burgers, and steaks sold at market price with "made-from-scratch" recipes. Mostly local craft beer is on the 18 taps in this building that has been a Lancaster gathering space since (perhaps you've guessed) 1890.

Accommodations

A handful of chain hotels and motels are on the northwest side of Lancaster along the business route headed into town. The **Holiday Inn Express and Suites Lancaster** (1861 Riverway Dr., 740/654-4445, ihg.com, $110-160) garners the best reviews, with a free breakfast and an indoor pool.

Transportation

Lancaster is about a 40-minute drive (31 mi/50 km) southeast of Columbus via US-33.

Greyhound (greyhound.com), **Barons Bus** (baronsbus.com) and **GoBus** (ridegobus. com) stop at the **Dogwood Crossing Travel Center** (4400 Coonpath Rd. NW) northwest of town.

Cleveland and Vicinity

You want a city that feels "lived in"? Cleveland's done some living. Through prominence, struggle, and renewal, Cleveland has emerged as a cultural powerhouse that has reinvented itself while honoring its history.

While pioneers under the supervision of the Ohio Company of Associates swarmed the Ohio River valley, the Connecticut Land Company—led by Moses Cleaveland—surveyed the northeast quadrant of Ohio and quietly settled Cleveland in 1796. A small outpost until the completion of the Ohio & Erie Canal in 1832, Cleveland found its groove as a major transportation hub between the East Coast and the Midwest.

The city's population exploded in the latter half of the 19th century,

Highlights

Look for ★ to find recommended sights, activities, dining, and lodging.

★ Take in iconic views at **Public Square,** a central plaza adorned with monuments and water fountains, surrounded by impressive, historic buildings and the city's tallest skyscrapers (page 121).

★ Pay homage to the greatest musicians in rock and other genres at the one-of-a-kind **Rock & Roll Hall of Fame,** designed by I. M. Pei (page 124).

★ Wander around **Ohio City,** a resurgent neighborhood west of downtown with street art, galleries, trendy restaurants, and several breweries, led by Great Lakes Brewing Company (page 127).

★ Sample Eastern European cuisine and more at **West Side Market,** open since 1912 (page 128).

★ Appreciate fine arts, pieces of antiquity, and special exhibits at the **Cleveland Museum of Art,** one of the largest art museums in the United States (page 129).

★ Travel to distant biomes at the indoor/outdoor **Cleveland Botanical Garden,** with two giant greenhouses home to butterflies, reptiles, and birds (page 131).

★ Discover dinosaur fossils, learn about evolution, and view live animals native to Ohio at the **Cleveland Museum of Natural History** (page 133).

★ Go for a serene walk in leafy **Lake View Cemetery,** the final resting place of President James A. Garfield and oil baron John D. Rockefeller (page 134).

★ Spy orangutans, sloths, ocelots, and more at the **Cleveland Metroparks Zoo**—its giant RainForest building is one of the largest indoor zoo exhibits in the country (page 134).

★ Walk among the leaves at expansive **Holden Arboretum**'s Emergent Tower and Murch Canopy Walk (page 160).

Cleveland

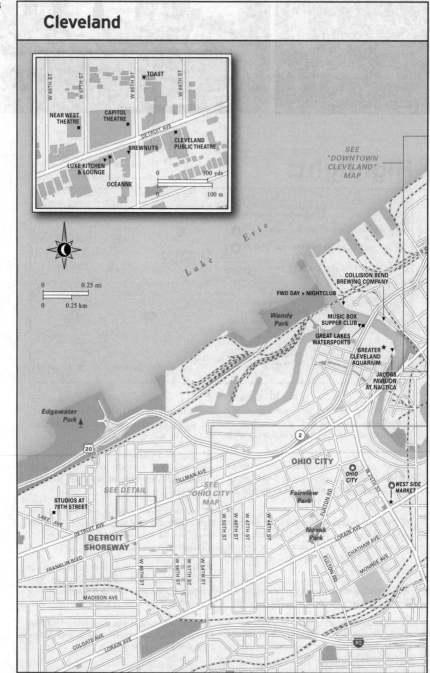

W 69TH ST
W 67TH ST
W 65TH ST
W 48TH ST

TOAST

NEAR WEST THEATRE

CAPITOL THEATRE

DETROIT AVE

CLEVELAND PUBLIC THEATRE

BREWNUTS

LUXE KITCHEN & LOUNGE

OCÉANNE

0   100 yds
0   100 m

SEE "DOWNTOWN CLEVELAND" MAP

Lake Erie

COLLISION BEND BREWING COMPANY

FWD DAY + NIGHTCLUB

Wendy Park

MUSIC BOX SUPPER CLUB

GREAT LAKES WATERSPORTS

GREATER CLEVELAND AQUARIUM

JACOBS PAVILION AT NAUTICA

0   0.25 mi
0   0.25 km

Edgewater Park

20

2

OHIO CITY

OHIO CITY

W 72ND ST

WEST SIDE MARKET

STUDIOS AT 78TH STREET

SEE DETAIL

SEE "OHIO CITY" MAP

Fairview Park

FULTON RD

LAKE AVE

DETROIT AVE

DETROIT SHOREWAY

W 50TH ST
W 48TH ST
W 47TH ST
W 44TH ST

Novak Park

LORAIN AVE

CHATHAM AVE

FRANKLIN BLVD

W 65TH ST
W 58TH ST
W 57TH ST
W 54TH ST

FULTON RD

MONROE AVE

MADISON AVE

COLGATE AVE

LORAIN AVE

90

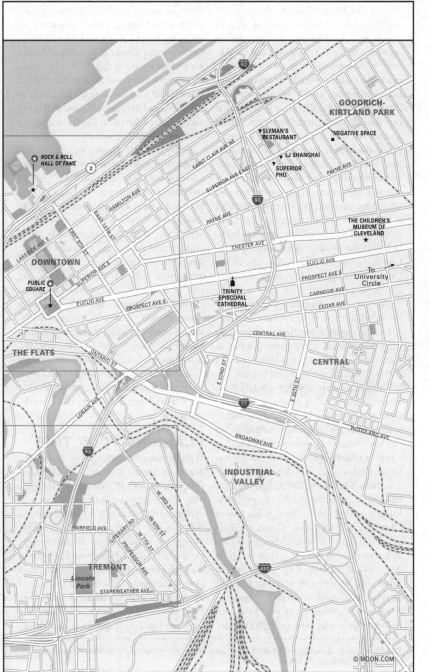

© MOON.COM

with waves of immigration from southern and eastern Europe as well as African Americans migrating from the South for job opportunities in the city's steel and iron industries, booming since the Civil War. Titans of industry such as John D. Rockefeller generated enormous wealth; his Standard Oil, which he founded in Cleveland in 1870, made him the richest man in the world. Rockefeller and his ilk built their homes on a stretch of Euclid Avenue known as Millionaires' Row, blowing past New York's 5th Avenue and comparing more favorably to Paris's Champs-Élysées in accumulated wealth and Gilded Age glamour. The street was heralded as "The Showcase of America" to European tourists, and the city for a moment was home to half of the world's millionaires. By 1920, Cleveland was the fifth-largest city in the United States and would remain in the top 10 into the 1970s.

You may know what happened next. It's the same story as in every Rust Belt city: Cleveland's population fled to suburbs or sunnier locales and its industries dried up or moved abroad. The city entered the 21st century with half the souls it had at its peak.

Those same souls have stewarded the city's assets to an astounding renaissance. Few cities have bones as good as Cleveland's. Rather than a punch line for deindustrialization, the city has become the poster child for adaptive reuse—a grocery or cocktail bar in a bank, a brewery in an auto dealership, a museum in a mansion, a hotel in a grandiose government building. Reinvestment in the city's core has led to a swell of construction in downtown, Ohio City, and University Circle, ushering population growth in neighborhoods that had seen nothing but decades of decrease. And, well, all that Gilded Age money bought something. Victorian shopping arcades and Beaux-Arts skyscrapers pepper a dynamic downtown. Cultural institutions built with philanthropic money in the early 20th century are at the top of their class: Playhouse Square is the second-largest performing arts center in the United States, and the Cleveland Orchestra and Cleveland Museum of Art are easily in the top five of their respective worlds. In 1995, the rebellious Rock & Roll Hall of Fame joined long-standing favorites such as the Cleveland Museum of Natural History and Cleveland Botanical Garden among the city's attractions.

Today, Cleveland boasts an array of cultural amenities unmatched in Ohio, a stylish dining scene, an "Emerald Necklace"—a constellation of attractive ravine-filled parks—and more than enough beer, led by the enterprising Great Lakes Brewing Company. With dense, walkable neighborhoods, intact ethnic enclaves, and the most comprehensive public transportation in Ohio, Cleveland looks, acts, and feels the most like a "big city" of the Three C's. The economy moves forward with an emphasis on the arts and a strong medical industry anchored by the famous Cleveland Clinic, consistently ranked one of the finest hospitals in the country. Being this much closer to the Northeast than Columbus or Cincinnati, people here have a whiff of Boston brashness—if only a whiff. If you'd lived as much as Clevelanders, maybe you would, too.

PLANNING YOUR TIME

With its many museums, parks, and neighborhoods, there's a bit more to Cleveland than Columbus and Cincinnati. It's also near a lot of highlights elsewhere in the state—all of Northeast Ohio as well as Cedar Point and the Lake Erie islands are doable day trips. Though a long weekend is sufficient to catch the best of the city, 4-5 days would be better to see all the highlights (you could burn 3 days around University Circle alone if you wanted to), catch a concert, and relax in a park or two. If you want to dive in deeper or add some day trips, you could easily spend a week up here.

Previous: Cleveland Museum of Art; the Soldiers' and Sailors' Monument at Public Square; Cleveland Script sign on North Coast Harbor.

ORIENTATION

Navigating Cleveland isn't quite as straight-forward as, say, Columbus, with the city split by the squiggly Cuyahoga River (though the presence of Lake Erie helps to designate north). Downtown is easy—it's set on a grid, with east-west throughfares Euclid Avenue (from the east) and Detroit Avenue (from the west) meeting at Public Square. Euclid Avenue is a direct route to University Circle on the city's east side, while Detroit Avenue runs to west-side neighborhoods Ohio City and Detroit-Shoreway and streetcar suburb Lakewood. Tremont lies directly south of downtown, with Old Brooklyn farther south.

Sights

DOWNTOWN

With resplendent architecture from the city's zenith combined with contemporary culture and cuisine, downtown Cleveland is a delight. Public spaces, distinct nightlife districts, and flashy sports complexes create a busy, walkable, metropolitan atmosphere. Over $7.5 billion in development has gone into downtown Cleveland since 2010, rescuing deserted gems and transforming them into posh hotels, residential spaces, and new retail, or else contributing to the development of flashy new additions such as the Hilton Cleveland Downtown. Adding to the energy are the number of people living downtown, who keep businesses afloat along with people coming in from the suburbs and out-of-town visitors. Connecting it all is Euclid Avenue, with Playhouse Square to the east, 4th Street's pedestrian zone in the middle, and Public Square to the west, from which nightlife districts The Flats and the Warehouse District are just a couple of blocks away. Like all great neighborhoods, downtown Cleveland demands to be explored by foot.

★ Public Square

Both a central gathering place and event venue, **Public Square** (50 Public Sq., 216/503-8103, clevelandpublicsquare.com, 24 hours daily, free) offers a quintessentially Cleveland view, with the three tallest skyscrapers looming over a plaza of fountains, monuments, and urban green space. The Beaux-Arts **Terminal Tower** is especially striking from this angle,

framing the square with imperial grandiosity. Public Square is not so much an attraction as an inevitability—with its central location and nearby parking, it's practically the front door of downtown Cleveland. It's difficult not to at least pass through, and you'd be doing yourself a disservice by not lingering for a moment or two.

In the east corner of the plaza is the **Soldiers' and Sailors' Monument**, constructed in 1894 and dedicated to those who fought in the Civil War. The 125-foot (38-m) column, with the personification of Liberty perched on top—sword and shield in hand—is hard to miss. Within the monument is a reverential space of bronze plates naming the Civil War veterans of Cuyahoga County, as well as reliefs depicting the war and the emancipation of enslaved people.

Public Square's green space hosts hundreds of events throughout the year, from yoga to major festivals. Check the event calendar on the website to see if anything's scheduled while you're in town.

Greater Cleveland Aquarium

The **Greater Cleveland Aquarium** (2000 Sycamore St., 216/862-8803, greaterclevelandaquarium.com, 10am-4pm daily, $19.95 adults, $13.95 children) has set up shop in the former FirstEnergy Powerhouse; the 1892 industrial building is an unusual yet educational counterpoint to the facility's environmental message. Eight themed galleries display aquatic life from Ohio and beyond,

Downtown Cleveland

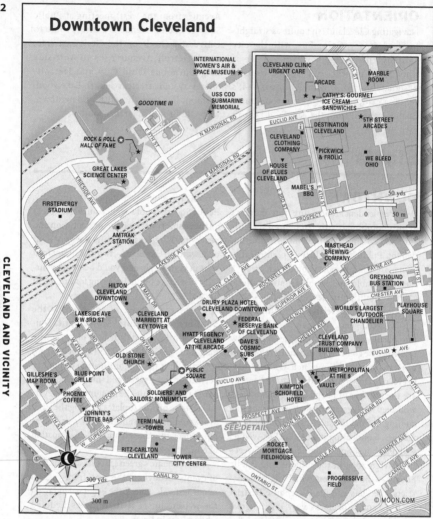

with the highlight being the Shark Gallery and SeaTube, a 175-foot-long (53-m) acrylic glass tunnel underneath a 230,000-gallon tank with sand tiger sharks, moray eels, and other creepy but magnificent fish. The Nautica Café offers personal pizzas, hot dogs, and sandwiches, and the Coral Cove gift shop sells souvenirs like stuffed animals, apparel, and more. This being a smaller aquarium, the focus is fish: visitors in search of charismatic mammals such as dolphins or sea lions may be underwhelmed.

North Coast Harbor

Cleveland's answer to Chicago's Museum Campus, similarly nestled between a Great Lake and skyscrapers, is the North Coast Harbor. Immediately north of downtown, it hosts a walkable collection of some of the city's marquee attractions—the Rock & Roll

Historic Architecture in Downtown Cleveland

The Arcade

With money to spend and people willing to spend it, Cleveland had no trouble erecting grand buildings in the late 19th and early 20th centuries, when the city was at its peak population and power. Much of that legacy is still around today, though not always used for its original purpose.

Any search for historic structures ought to start at Public Square (50 Public Sq.), a center of activity in downtown Cleveland with fountains, events, and the Soldiers' and Sailors' Monument (3 Public Sq.), which commemorates the Civil War with a 125-foot (38-m) column, sculptures, and a memorial inside. The oldest structure standing along the square is the Old Stone Church (91 Public Sq.); the current iteration dates back to 1884. The church is open for tours on weekdays 9am-4pm. Standing sentinel over all is the Beaux-Arts Terminal Tower (50 Public Sq.), completed in 1930 as the tallest building in the world outside of New York City at the time.

A few blocks east of Public Square on Euclid Avenue is The Arcade (401 Euclid Ave.), an opulent, high-ceilinged, Victorian shopping mall built in 1890 that today holds retail and a Hyatt hotel. The smaller 5th Street Arcades (530 Euclid Ave.) are just a short walk across the street and also date from the turn of the 20th century. Farther east on Euclid is the Cleveland Trust Company Building (900 Euclid Ave.), designed by New York Stock Exchange designer George Post and featuring a Tiffany dome and murals painted by Francis Davis Millet, who perished on the *Titanic*. The ground floor is now a Heinen's grocery, from which the impressive dome is visible. Away from Euclid Avenue, the marble Federal Reserve Bank of Cleveland (1455 E. 6th St.) features a chandeliered main lobby and the small Learning Center and Money Museum (clevelandfed.org, 9:30am-2:30pm Mon.-Thurs., free), which conveys the history of money through interactive exhibits and displays.

Not historic but worth noting is the world's largest outdoor chandelier hanging over the intersection of Euclid Avenue and 14th Street, installed in 2014 to beckon visitors to Playhouse Square.

Cleveland's oldest congregation worships at the Gothic Trinity Episcopal Cathedral (2230 Euclid Ave.), a few blocks east of Playhouse Square and completed in 1907.

Hall of Fame, Great Lakes Science Center, and FirstEnergy Stadium chief among them. One of the popular Cleveland Script signs, installed in 2016 by Destination Cleveland, sits in Voinovich Bicentennial Park and makes for a memorable picture, with the museums, stadium, and city skyline in the background.

TOP EXPERIENCE

★ ROCK & ROLL HALL OF FAME

Perhaps the most iconic building in Cleveland is I. M. Pei's postmodern, geometric **Rock & Roll Hall of Fame** (1100 E. 9th St., 216/781-7625, rockhall.com, 10am-5:30pm daily, check extended seasonal hours, $28 adults, $18 children). Opened in Cleveland in 1995 after a petition from Northeast Ohioans and a tasty financial package from the city, the museum is a more anarchic counterpart to Canton's reverent Pro Football Hall of Fame, an hour to the south. The museum is much larger than it looks, with a significant portion underground.

Start your tour by heading down the escalator to the permanent gallery, where a sensory feast awaits, with music, videos of live performances, costumes, memorabilia, and instruments from the biggest names in popular music—anything from Buddy Holly's acoustic guitar to Lady Gaga's outlandish outfits. The gallery tells the story of rock and roll's evolution, starting by recognizing early influencers in blues, gospel, country, and folk and moving through every decade to the present.

The actual Hall of Fame Gallery is on Level 3, with an exhibit on the year's inductees and the Power of Rock Experience, a 15-minute compilation of some of the induction ceremony's musical highlights through the years.

Elsewhere in the museum, try your hand at playing some classics (following video prompts) with real instruments in The Garage, design your own logo at the Brand Your Band kiosk, and shop for apparel and souvenirs in the massive gift shop.

The All Access Café, a bit on the expensive side, has snacks, pizza, coffee, and alcohol with nice views of the harbor and city from the airy atrium.

GREAT LAKES SCIENCE CENTER

The **Great Lakes Science Center** (601 Erieside Ave., 216/694-2000, greatscience.com, 10am-5pm Tues.-Sat., noon-5pm Sun., $16.95 adults, $13.95 children) is much smaller than Columbus's Center of Science and Industry but comes with two advantages: a more robust space exhibit and the **Cleveland Clinic DOME Theater** ($5), a six-story high OMNIMAX screen that folds over the auditorium.

The museum came by the space stuff via Cleveland's NASA Glenn Research Center. Along with a great deal of information about life on the International Space Station and the kind of research that goes on at Glenn, the exhibit features an Apollo command module, space suits, a moon rock, and some of astronaut John Glenn's personal effects.

Upstairs you'll find unique musical exhibits and opportunities to experiment with weather in the Science Phenomena and Polymer Funhouse areas. The Cleveland Creates Zone encourages kids of all ages to flex their STEM muscles with stations devoted to rocket building, light sculptures, and even duct tape hats. Downstairs, the Spark Kitchen offers a short menu of snacks, pizza, and sandwiches.

Not to be forgotten is the *William G. Mather* Steamship ($8.95 adults, $6.95 seniors, $5.95 children). Built in 1925, the 618-foot (188-m) freighter is docked just outside the museum and available for touring. You can buy tickets for the boat only or at a discount with admission to the museum. Either way, purchase tickets inside the museum.

The parking garage attached to the building will validate your ticket, reducing the fee to $8.

1: the Beaux Arts-style Terminal Tower looming over Public Square **2:** West Side Market **3:** Rock & Roll Hall of Fame

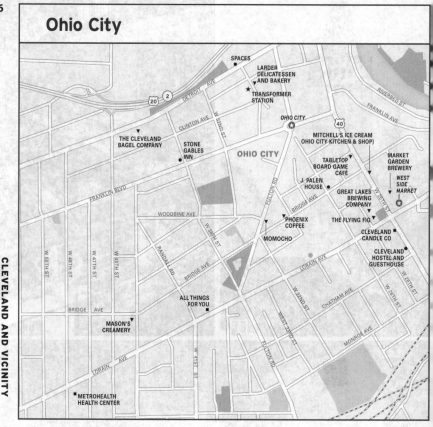

Ohio City

SPACES

LARDER DELICATESSEN AND BAKERY

★ TRANSFORMER STATION

DETROIT AVE

20 2

RIVERBED ST

FRANKLIN AVE

CLINTON AVE

W 32ND ST

OHIO CITY 40

MITCHELL'S ICE CREAM
OHIO CITY KITCHEN & SHOP

THE CLEVELAND BAGEL COMPANY

STONE GABLES INN

OHIO CITY

TABLETOP BOARD GAME CAFÉ

MARKET GARDEN BREWERY

WEST SIDE MARKET

J. PALEN HOUSE

GREAT LAKES BREWING COMPANY

FRANKLIN BLVD

FULTON RD

BRIDGE AVE

W 25TH ST

WOODBINE AVE

PHOENIX COFFEE

THE FLYING FIG

W 38TH ST

MOMOCHO

CLEVELAND CANDLE CO

W 50TH ST

W 48TH ST

W 47TH ST

W 45TH ST

RANDALL RD

BRIDGE AVE

LORAIN AVE

W 32ND ST

CHATHAM AVE

WEST 25TH ST

MONROE AVE

W 29TH ST

W 28TH ST

CLEVELAND HOSTEL AND GUESTHOUSE

ALL THINGS FOR YOU

BRIDGE AVE

MASON'S CREAMERY

LORAIN AVE

W 41ST ST

FULTON RD

METROHEALTH HEALTH CENTER

USS *COD* SUBMARINE MEMORIAL

A short walk from the Rock & Roll Hall of Fame, the **USS *Cod* Submarine Memorial** (1201 N. Marginal Rd., 216/566-8770, usscod. org, 10am-5pm daily May-Sept., $12 adults, $10 seniors and veterans, $7 children) allows visitors to enter a docked WWII submarine and view the vessel's torpedo rooms, control room, and other cramped confines. The 312-foot (95-m) ship saw action in several engagements in the Pacific theater of the war, including sinking a Japanese destroyer. The submarine served as a training vessel during the Cold War and was towed to Cleveland in 1959, where it sits today.

INTERNATIONAL WOMEN'S AIR AND SPACE MUSEUM

It feels very strange to just waltz into an airport terminal, but that's precisely what you do at the tiny Burke Airport to find the **International Women's Air and Space Museum** (1501 N. Marginal Rd., 216/623-1111, iwasm.org, 8am-8pm daily, free). This low-key display honors the female aviators, test pilots, NASA employees, and astronauts who smashed barriers for future generations of women to contribute to the fields of aviation and space research. Profiles on such figures as Katharine Wright (who worked with her aviation-pioneer brothers, Orville and Wilbur), aviator Amelia Earhart, astronaut Sally Ride, and NASA mathematician

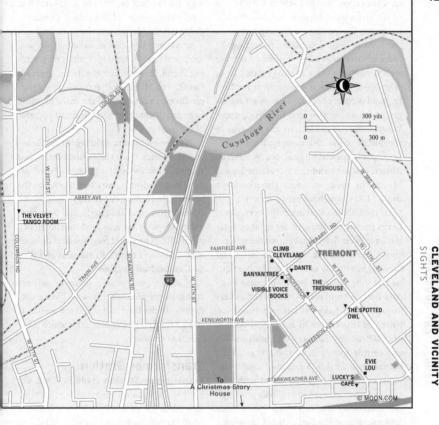

Katherine Johnson, along with some artifacts, help show an underrepresented side of aviation history. Walk through the main entrance of the terminal to start your tour.

GOODTIME III BOAT TOURS

Enjoy Cleveland from a waterborne perspective with the *Goodtime III* (825 E. 9th St. Pier, 216/242-4865, goodtimeiii.com, times and prices vary), the city's largest sightseeing ship. This quadruple-deck vessel takes passengers on tours up and down Lake Erie and the Cuyahoga River. Prices start at $25 per person, or you can spend more and get a lunch or dinner buffet with your journey. There are also entertainment cruises with live music and dancing.

TOP EXPERIENCE

★ OHIO CITY

You may spend your day in the museums, but the evening is for Ohio City. Arguably Cleveland's trendiest neighborhood and one of the most walkable and dynamic in the state, Ohio City shines as a model of Cleveland's resurgence, with a 21st-century building boom accommodating renewed interest in the area for its breweries, restaurants, and cultural amenities.

The 42-foot-tall (12.8-m) Guardians of Traffic, a pair of art deco figures carved into the pylons of Hope Memorial Bridge, welcome motorists coming from downtown to Ohio City. Its own municipality until its annexation in 1854, Ohio City is one of the city's most historic neighborhoods. Italianate, Queen Anne, contemporary—no one housing style dominates, reflecting the years of building and re-building on these streets opposite the Cuyahoga River from downtown. What was a settlement for New England pioneers became a haven for immigrants from Germany and Eastern Europe. When those groups left for the suburbs in the middle of the 20th century, the area became predominately populated by African Americans. Jobs and infrastructure lagged behind the needs of the neighborhood—a similar tale throughout urban America.

In 1988, Ohio's first microbrewery, Great Lakes Brewing Company, set up shop near stalwart West Side Market, sparking a revival that has reinvigorated 25th Street and the neighborhood as a whole. In particular, brewing seems to be the popular business here, with Market Garden and others joining Great Lakes as beer destinations. North of this center of activity, a stretch near Detroit Avenue named Hingetown has also seen redevelopment, with art galleries, breweries, and cafés. A neighborhood walking tour rewards inquisitive feet with murals and rebellious street art. Today, though gentrification remains a blessing and curse for its long-time residents, Ohio City is a socioeconomically and culturally diverse community, and perhaps the best spot to glimpse Cleveland—its past, present, and future—in one spot.

★ West Side Market

Great Lakes Brewing Company brought people to 25th Street in 1988, but **West Side Market** (1979 W. 25th St., 216/664-3387, westsidemarket.org, 8am-5pm Mon., Wed., and Fri., 7am-5pm Sat., 10am-4pm Sun., free) has been doing it since 1912 as the primary anchor for Ohio City. More an actual market than a food hall, unlike its peers in Columbus and Cincinnati, this Byzantine, Grand Central-like emporium is hard to miss with its 137-foot (42-m) clock tower. Over 100 vendors—some of them third- or fourth-generation independent businesses—sell meat and poultry, cheese, baked goods, seafood, and international specialties representing Polish, Russian, Slovene, Irish, German, Greek, and Middle Eastern cuisines. Fresh produce stands surround the main building in an arcade along the north and east portions of the market.

It's possible, and tantalizing, to cobble together a lunch from the various stalls, but seating is somewhat at a premium (read: almost non-existent). Grab a bench between the building and arcade, or better yet, look for the stairs up front and head to the 2nd floor for a view and spot to set your food (but not to sit). A handful of prepared food vendors do offer meals, notably **Frank's Bratwurst** and **Kim Se Cambodian Cuisine.**

Note that some vendors prefer or only accept cash, for which there is an ATM on-site. Parking in the large lot behind the market is free for the first 90 minutes, after which it becomes $1 an hour.

Transformer Station

Transformer Station (1460 W. 29th St., 216/938-5429, transformerstation.org, 11am-5pm Wed.-Sun., 11am-8pm Thurs., free) is a small space for contemporary artwork housed in a 1924 train substation. Shows change quarterly in the two spartan galleries and can vary from photography to mixed media to film. The Cleveland Museum of Art partners with the museum for some of the exhibitions.

TREMONT

Artsy Tremont has, like next-door neighborhood Ohio City just to the west, seen a renaissance in the 21st century, with a flurry of restaurants, boutiques, and galleries catering to a gentrifying population. One of the oldest neighborhoods in the city, Tremont boasts impressive churches built by waves of German and Slavic immigrants past, and a house most famous for its leg lamp in the window.

A Christmas Story House

Cleveland was a primary filming location for the classic 1983 film *A Christmas Story*. Indeed, the city seems to wear this badge with pride; drive around long enough and you'll begin to notice the famous leg lamp in window after window. **A Christmas Story House** (3159 W. 11th Ave., 216/298-4919, achristmasstoryhouse.com, 10am-5pm Thurs.-Mon., $15 adults, $13 seniors, $10 children) invites visitors to explore the house used for exterior and some interior shots of the Parkers' home. Inside you'll find the home suitably stuck in the 1940s and outside perpetually decorated for Christmas. Across the street, a museum houses props and costumes from the film as well as photographs taken during principal photography. Buy your own leg lamp at the gift shop, which is a must-stop for anyone in search of tacky Christmas decorations or gifts from *A Christmas Story* and other holiday classics. Parking is free in the lots adjacent to the house and the museum, as well as along the street, and you can actually stay the night in the house and the house next door, home of the hillbilly Bumpus family in the film. The museum extends its hours during the holiday season.

ASIATOWN

Though originally a Chinatown, this neighborhood east of downtown warranted a name change by 2006, after Korean, Vietnamese, and other Asian immigrants settled into the enclave. It's primarily experienced through its shops and eateries, with the Asia Plaza complex (Payne Ave. and E. 30th St.) catering to the local population.

The Children's Museum of Cleveland

An empty mansion turned civic asset, the **Children's Museum of Cleveland** (3813 Euclid Ave., 216/791-7114, cmcleveland.org, 9am-4pm Mon.-Wed. and Fri., 10am-5pm Sat., noon-5pm Sun., $12 adults and children) is an interactive, small child-oriented alternative to the museums of University Circle. Seven themed areas encourage little hands to play and little feet to explore. The Wonder Lab allows kids to experiment with water (an extra set of clothes might be useful) or send colorful scarves up vacuum chutes nearby. Additional play areas revolve around construction, art, music, and theater, and the Center Stage brings in professional troupes to perform age-appropriate music, theater, and dance. There are a couple of vending machines in the building, but guests are encouraged to pack a lunch or have one delivered. Parking is free in the museum lot.

UNIVERSITY CIRCLE

What most cities wouldn't give for a place like University Circle. A nearly unparalleled assortment of top-notch cultural institutions is clustered east of downtown around a strollable park, **Wade Oval**, with the Cleveland Museum of Art and Cleveland Orchestra (who play at Severance Hall) leading the charge. The neighborhood's cultural and economic energy is buoyed by the main campus of the prestigious Cleveland Clinic and the humming private research school Case Western Reserve University. Put together, University Circle is nearly a second downtown, a center of metropolitan creativity, learning, and commerce.

★ Cleveland Museum of Art

With over 130,000 square feet (12,077 sq m) of gallery space and over 60,000 pieces of art, the **Cleveland Museum of Art** (11150 East Blvd., 216/421-7350, clevelandart.org, 10am-5pm Tues.-Sun., free) is one of the largest and finest art museums in the United States. Financed by industrial philanthropists and founded in 1913 "for the benefit of all the people forever," the neoclassical building—which has a soaring glass atrium from a 21st-century expansion—invites visitors to enjoy works from all over the world. The collection is split between the museum's original 1913 building, West Wing and East Wing expansions,

Cleveland's Street Art Scene

Colorful street art abounds throughout Cleveland's neighborhoods, hearkening to both the ethnic history and contemporary spirit of the city.

Ohio City in particular boasts a density of murals by local and international artists and is worthy of a self-guided walking tour (plus there are breweries when you need a break). If the Cleveland Script signs are a little too touristy for your tastes, check out *Greetings from Cleveland* (2104 W. 25th St.) by Victor Ving, with icons of the city painted into the letters spelling "Cleveland." It's part of a series found in cities across the United States. A whimsical castle with the disclaimer "this is what it sounds like when I'm thinking" draws photographers to one of brewery **Market Garden's murals** (1849 W. 24th St.), on the side of its building. This one was put up by artist duo The Bubble Process. In the Hingetown side of Ohio City, there's the **Shoreway mural** (Washington Ave. between W. 25th St. and W. 28th St.) by Brazilian artist Ananda Nahu. The largest mural in Ohio, this striking piece stretches over 600 feet (183 m) and depicts children in a local arts program. Kick it with **Prince** (corner of W. 25th St. and Main Ave.) by artist Glen Infante, whose clients include LeBron James, Machine Gun Kelly, and Eminem.

In **Asiatown,** local artist Lauren Pearce explores themes of womanhood and race in her **wall of faces** (36th St. and Euclid Ave.). The **Graffiti HeArt building** (4829 Superior Ave.) is adorned with a color-wash spectrum of color by Kelly "RISK" Graval. Just a few doors down is *Guardian* (4823 Superior Ave.) by Beau Stanton, a surreal depiction of an angelic figure holding a flower.

Elsewhere in **East Cleveland, *Vote!*** (9107 St. Clair Ave.) by Gary Williams, Robin Robinson, and David Hayes empowers young people to vote. Thanks to artists mr.soul and his collaborators, **Maya Angelou** (11701 Buckeye Rd.) makes an appearance. A stuffy old bank building really "pops" with Camille Walala's **Pop Life building mural** (15619 Waterloo Rd.) on three walls, adding stark, colorful geometry to this design brand headquarters.

and contemporary North Building, with 16 themed areas displaying old masters such as Caravaggio, Botticelli, and Rubens as well as more modern favorites like Van Gogh, Monet, Renoir, Matisse, and Picasso. Ohio native George Bellows is featured, including one of his more famous works—the dramatic boxing ring of *Stag at Sharkey's.* You'll also find a strong collection of Asian ceramics and art, Mediterranean and Middle Eastern antiquities, Medieval iconography and armor, Central and South American artifacts, and African art spanning more than 300 pieces and a dozen tribes.

You'll need a sustenance break before you take it all in. Luckily, there's **Provenance Café** which, beyond the traditional light lunch options and coffee, offers pastas, pizzas, "melty" sandwiches, and international dishes to enjoy in the glass atrium. The classy **Provenance** fine-dining restaurant, adjacent to the café, presents a globally inspired menu

of entrées and a diverse drink menu. There's also the Museum Store, with depictions of art pieces from the collection in the form of posters and postcards. An hourly parking garage is attached to the museum.

Museum of Contemporary Art Cleveland

A geometric diamond of a building, **Museum of Contemporary Art Cleveland** (11400 Euclid Ave., 216/421-8671, mocacleveland. org, 11am-6pm Tues.-Wed. and Fri., 11am-9pm Thurs., 11am-5pm Sat.-Sun. free) is a non-collecting museum showcasing a rotation of exhibits from up-and-coming as well as established contemporary artists. Come to the small, four-story building for provocative displays and the latest in photography, mixed media, sculpture, painting, and film. There is no designated parking for the museum, but there is a visitor drop-off and nearby parking in the garage catty-corner to the museum on

University Circle

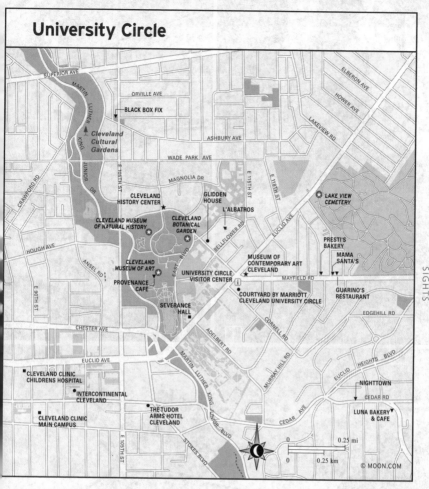

Ford Drive. You can also find two-hour metered spots along Ford and Euclid.

★ Cleveland Botanical Garden

Built atop the bones of the original Cleveland Zoo, the **Cleveland Botanical Garden** (11030 East Blvd., 216/721-1600, cbgarden.org, 10am-5pm Tues.-Sat., noon-5pm Sun., $15 adults, $10 children) transports visitors to the scrubby deserts of Madagascar and the lush rainforests of Costa Rica in its two futuristic conservatory greenhouses, with 50 species of butterflies, birds, and reptiles fluttering, flying, and crawling about, lending authenticity to these tropical realms. A highlight is the Madagascar greenhouse's giant baobabs, the legendary African trees that live for as many as 3,000 years.

There's as much to see outside as inside, with winding paths taking explorers through handsomely landscaped gardens of perennials, herbs, and exotic plants. Kids will enjoy the Hershey Children's Garden, where they can search for life in the pond, play in the sand, and complete a gnome scavenger hunt.

The Garden store stocks garden-themed apparel, kitchen utensils, and home decor as well as supplies for green thumbs to bring

home. An underground parking lot serves the garden, as well as nearby metered spots along Wade Oval Drive and East Boulevard. Note that the front entrance faces Wade Oval rather than the road.

★ Cleveland Museum of Natural History

Avoiding the staid atmosphere that can pervade natural history museums, the delightful **Cleveland Museum of Natural History** (1 Wade Oval Dr., 216/231-4600, cmnh.org, 10am-5pm daily, $17 adults, $14 seniors and children) offers a combination of playful displays and one-of-a-kind specimens. It's a good size, too—not so small that you wonder about getting your money's worth and not so large as to be overwhelming. The exhibits follow a loop, starting with the fossils and casts of dinosaurs and other prehistoric critters and moving on to exhibits on climate and geology.

Whereas some natural history museums separate their exhibits on cultural history and rows of stuffed animals, this museum groups them geographically in the Sears Hall of Human Ecology, a refreshing decision. A highlight in this gallery is the now-taxidermied canine Balto, the famous sled dog who led a dogsled team to Nome, Alaska, in 1925. Rescued from a sideshow to live out the remainder of his days at Cleveland's zoo, the famous canine now calls the museum home. In the Human Origins gallery, another famous resident is a skeletal cast of Lucy, the famous remains of an *Australopithecus afarensis* hominid that painted a clearer picture of man's evolution to bipedalism. Downstairs, the Smead Discovery Center features hands-on stations for little explorers. Outside, the Perkins Wildlife Center displays live native Ohio animals such as otters, coyotes, raptors, and raccoons in a network of natural enclosures.

1: Haserot Angel at Lake View Cemetery
2: Cleveland Museum of Art 3: Cleveland Botanical Garden

Planetarium shows are $6 for nonmembers. **Exploration Café** ($5-10) features an elevated grill menu as well as snacks. A parking garage is attached to the museum, though there are metered spots on Wade Oval Drive as well. The visitor engagement Current Science exhibit, a space for rotating exhibits on relevant and timely topics, opened in 2020. As of this writing, a campaign is underway to fund a bold vision of renovation to both the interior and exterior of the building. By the time renovations are complete, the museum's layout may differ entirely from its previous configuration.

Cleveland History Center

In a city of heavy-hitting museums, the local museum doesn't get as much attention. It's a shame, because the **Cleveland History Center** (10825 East Blvd., 216/721-5722, wrhs.org, 10am-5pm Tues.-Sun., $10 adults, $9 children, $6 children) is quite nice. "Cleveland Starts Here," as the museum likes to say, and visitors can get a sense of how the city came to be, how it grew into an industrial powerhouse, and how it had to reinvent itself afterward. Though there are fun artifacts such as LeBron James's championship sneakers and the working carousel from the old Euclid Beach Park, the highlight is the vintage cars and airplanes of the **Crawford Auto Aviation Museum.** With over 100 auto manufacturers in Northeast Ohio, Cleveland led the world in auto manufacturing—until Henry Ford's Model T and assembly line revolutionized the industry and spirited the capital of the automotive world to Detroit. The museum's large collection tells the story of the region's dominance of a nascent automotive industry, with rare specimens of early electric cars, vehicles from long-lost manufacturers, and more. You can even peek inside a gondola of a Goodyear blimp. Elsewhere, the museum incorporates two mansions into the floorplan, one utilized as additional exhibit space and one preserved as it was during the Gilded Age and accessible by guided and self-guided tours.

A café and gift shop are on hand toward the

front. There's a museum parking lot ($8 for two hours); if you're also visiting the natural history museum, you may just prefer to park in its garage, which is located across the street between both museums.

★ Lake View Cemetery

Leafy, historic **Lake View Cemetery** (12316 Euclid Ave., 216/421-2665, lakeviewcemetery. com, 7:30am-7:30pm daily Apr.-Oct., 7:30am-5:30pm daily Nov.-Mar., free) covers an expansive 280 acres and is a popular spot for a peaceful walk. Pull your car to the side of the meandering road and let your feet respectfully wander among the headstones, mausoleums, and funerary statues. (Despite the cemetery's name, views of the lake are limited.)

Of particular note is the **James A. Garfield Memorial,** dedicated in 1890. This 180-foot-tall (55-m) sandstone tower features 110 bas-relief figures depicting important moments of this then-popular president's life. The inside is equally marvelous, with gold mosaics, stained-glass windows, and a statue of the assassinated president. Another famous resident, oil baron **John D. Rockefeller,** rests underneath the watchful eye of a giant obelisk down the hill. The small, neo-classical **Wade Memorial Chapel** features an interior designed by Louis Comfort Tiffany, with *The Flight of Souls* stained-glass window and mosaics on the walls. The chapel was built in 1901 and dedicated to the memory of Jeptha Wade, a founding member of the Western Union Telegraph Company. People often search for the **Haserot Angel,** a life-size bronze statue over the burial ground of a local entrepreneur. Due to the corrosive effect of weather on bronze (akin to the Statue of Liberty's discoloration), the woman unsettlingly appears to weep black tears that pour down her neck. The grave is located in Section 9 on Lot 14.

OLD BROOKLYN

Drew Carey's old stomping grounds, Old Brooklyn is a primarily residential neighborhood with an increasingly diverse population. The draw to this somewhat far-flung neighborhood south of downtown is the very fine zoo operated by the Cleveland Metroparks system.

★ Cleveland Metroparks Zoo

The hilly **Cleveland Metroparks Zoo** (3900 Wildlife Way, 216/661-6500, clevelandmetroparks.com/zoo, 9:30am-4pm daily, $16.95 adults, $14.95 seniors, $12.95 children) does more than hold its own in a state with excellent zoos. More than 600 species are represented, and the zoo has one of the strongest collections of primates in the country.

The highlight, undoubtedly, is the RainForest building, with two acres of floor space filled with over 600 creatures from the world's tropical forests, including orangutans, capybaras, sloths, ocelots, and a number of monkey species. There's really not another exhibit on this scale anywhere in the state, not to mention most zoos anywhere, with lush foliage throughout and mood-setting mist in some spots.

Elsewhere, Australian Adventure features a giant walkabout with free-roaming kangaroos and wallabies. Wilderness Trek's focus on large, cold-weather mammals expanded with a beautiful snow leopard exhibit in 2018. Up the hill (take a free shuttle or walk up a series of ramps and steps), the Primate, Cats and Aquatics building rounds out the zoo's monkey and ape collection with gorillas, lemurs, and the creepy-looking, long-fingered aye-aye. Another unusual find is Madagascar's fossa, a cat-like carnivore. Freshwater and saltwater aquatic life such as piranhas and Australian lungfish are featured in 35 tanks.

At 185 acres, the zoo stretches its arms a bit: prepare for some walking, at times with not much to look at other than generally nice, woodsy scenery. There are concessions available in every region of the zoo, with the Welcome Plaza Food Court notably occupied by McDonald's, Pizza Hut, and Dave's Cosmic Subs. Parking is free.

Cleveland in the Marvel Cinematic Universe

Perhaps because Cleveland looks like a bigger city than its population would suggest, Hollywood occasionally uses it as a less-expensive stand-in for other metropolises. No one has done this more often than Marvel Studios. Many of the scenes shot here are fast-paced action sequences that make identifying a recognizable landmark tricky, but there are some notable exceptions. By far, *Captain America: Winter Soldier* (2014) utilized the city the most, with much of the street-level action and car chases occurring in and around downtown Cleveland.

Spider-Man 3 (2007)

- The Sandman whips Spider-Man around with his own web on **Euclid Avenue,** and the standoff ends in front of the **Cleveland Trust Company Building** (900 Euclid Ave.).

The Avengers (2012)

- Standing in for an opera house in Stuttgart, Germany, is the iconic **Terminal Tower** (50 Public Sq.), with the outdoor crowd scenes filmed just outside the entrance in **Public Square.**

- **E. 9th Street** doubles as New York City during the climactic battle.

Captain America: The Winter Soldier (2014)

- Just behind the Terminal Tower, Captain America and Black Widow kiss on an escalator and escape from Hydra agents in **Tower City Center** (230 W. Huron Rd.) shopping mall.

- The lobby for SHIELD's headquarters is the main atrium of the **Cleveland Museum of Art** (11150 East Blvd.).

- Captain America, Black Widow, and Falcon battle the Winter Soldier at the intersection of **Lakeside Avenue and W. 3rd Street.**

- Captain America regroups at a dam in **Lake View Cemetery** (12316 Euclid Ave.).

Entertainment and Events

THE ARTS

The city's cultural attractions and performing arts have played a large part in both stewarding Cleveland's identity through rough waters and catalyzing redevelopment. Between world-class institutions like the Cleveland Orchestra and cutting-edge galleries in artsy neighborhoods like Detroit-Shoreway, the city buzzes with creativity.

In the performing arts center world, only New York City's Lincoln Center is larger than the 1920s-built **Playhouse Square** (1501 Euclid Ave., 216/241-6000, playhousesquare. org), with seven resident companies including the **Cleveland Ballet** (clevelandballet.org), the classics-leaning **Great Lakes Theater** (greatlakestheater.org), and **Cleveland Play House** (clevelandplayhouse.com), founded in 1915 as America's first professional regional theater troupe. Playhouse Square has 10 performance venues in total, ranging from simple black-box spaces to the Italianate, 3,200-seat **KeyBank State Theatre** (1519 Euclid Ave.). On top of resident companies, Playhouse Square frequently hosts traveling Broadway shows. The 1501 Euclid Avenue address is the front of the primary building, holding most of the venues.

One of the elite "Big Five" orchestras in the United States and regarded as one of the

finest in the world, the **Cleveland Orchestra** (clevelandorchestra.com) plays the bulk of its concerts in **Severance Hall** (11001 Euclid Ave., 216/231-7300, clevelandorchestra.com), known for its art deco auditorium and neoclassical touches elsewhere.

Karamu House (2355 E. 89th St., 216/795-7070, karamuhouse.org) is the nation's oldest African American theater, operating since 1915. Meaning "a joyful gathering place" in Swahili, Karamu features high-quality performances and provides arts education to area children from its theater close to the University Circle area.

Detroit-Shoreway's **Gordon Square Arts District** (gordonsquare.org), centered at the intersection of Detroit Avenue and 65th Street, is a more contemporary alternative to Playhouse Square, hosting three cultural spaces interspersed with trendy dining and retail options. **Cleveland Public Theatre** (6415 Detroit Ave., 216/631-2727, cptonline.org) performs innovative, socially conscious shows highlighting local talent. **Near West Theatre** (6702 Detroit Ave., 216/961-9750, nearwesttheatre.org) emphasizes accessibility, inclusion, and affordability to provide a positive theater experience for the community, with popular musicals and diverse casts regularly appearing on stage. **Capitol Theatre** (1390 W. 65th St., 216/651-7295, clevelandcinemas.com) converted a 1921 single-screen theater into three digital auditoriums showing a mix of blockbusters and art films.

Near the Gordon Square Arts District are the **78th Street Studios** (1300 W. 78th St., 216/931-7931, 78thstreetstudios.com), a 170,000-square-foot (15,793-sq-m) arts incubator with cosmopolitan studios, performance spaces, and galleries. The facility coordinates an open house every Friday (11am-4pm) with several of the galleries open for walk-ins. The big to-do, though, is Third Fridays. From 5pm to 8pm on the third Friday of every month,

many of the studios open and are joined by pop-up vendors and food purveyors.

Numerous galleries operate throughout the city. **SPACES** (2900 Detroit Ave., 216/621-2314, spacescle.org) showcases provocative new works by international artists, both up-and-coming and established, in an industrial, minimalist space. The east side's **Negative Space** (3820 Superior Ave., 216/470-6092, negativespacecleveland.com) welcomes visitors to its inclusive open-mic nights and sketch nights as well as gallery space.

FESTIVALS AND EVENTS

Like Ohio's other large cities, Cleveland puts on a full summer of annual events and festivals, from bustling music festivals to ethnic celebrations. However, the city also embraces the drab winters with some of the state's best cold-weather festivals.

Brite Winter (britewinter.com) lightens up a Saturday in late February with rollicking live music, art installations, and fire.

A sort of Slovenian Mardi Gras, **Cleveland Kurentovanje** (clevelandkurentovanje.com) rejoices in the upcoming spring with Eastern European food, music, and cultural performances. Events occur during the week leading up to the festival's highlight, a parade held on the Saturday before Ash Wednesday, with folks dressed as the mythical Kurents—furry, horned creatures with bells on their waists that look like something out of Maurice Sendak's *Where the Wild Things Are*. The festival takes place in the St. Clair-Superior neighborhood on the east side.

To finish winter out with a bang, downtown Cleveland puts on one of the largest **St. Patrick's Day** parades in the country, with 10,000 participants and 500,000 spectators for the mid-March celebration.

In June, bring lawn chairs for eastern suburb Shaker Heights' **Larchmere Porchfest** (larchmereporchfest.org). This day-long, family-friendly music festival puts local and regional folk, Americana, funk, and hip-hop artists on residential front porches.

1: Cleveland Museum of Natural History **2:** the world-class Cleveland Orchestra performing at Severance Hall **3:** Rocky River Reservation **4:** Cleveland Metroparks Zoo

Suburb Avon, west of Cleveland, is home to ShurTech, which produces the famous Duck Tape brand of duct tape. Thus, the weekend-long **Duck Tape Festival** (duckbrand.com/duck-tape-festival) celebrates the utilitarian staple in mid-June with over-the-top sculptures and fashion using duct tape, duct tape crafts and contests, carnival rides, and a parade.

Sponsored by Great Lakes Brewing Company, music festival **Great Lakes Burning River Fest** (burningriverfest.org) sets up shop at the mouth of the Cuyahoga River and raises funds for clean-water initiatives. (Thanks to a legacy of unregulated pollution, the river famously caught fire in summer 1969, spurring recognition of the need for environmental protection.) Traditionally held on a mid-August weekend,

the festival features primarily local and regional acts spanning several genres of music including indie rock, hip-hop, and country.

For one weekend in mid-August, large crowds gather in Little Italy for Holy Rosary's **Feast of the Assumption Festival** (holy-rosary.org), or "The Feast," featuring Italian food and music. Carnival rides take over the church's parking lot. The festival culminates in a mass and procession through the neighborhood's narrow streets.

Lake Erie is the perfect setting for the **Cleveland National Air Show** (clevelandairshow.com), a Labor Day weekend tradition with parachuters, aerobatic jet maneuvers, and formations, including appearances by the U.S. Navy Blue Angels. Back on the ground, visitors can view airplanes, peek into cockpits, and more.

Recreation

PARKS

Not unlike traversing Washington D.C.'s Rock Creek Park, Martin Luther King Jr. Drive east of downtown winds in between neighborhoods and under historic bridges and continues as a verdant parkway past the **Cleveland Cultural Gardens** (10823 Magnolia Dr., 216/220-3075, culturalgardens.org, dawn-dusk daily, free), a collection of roughly 30 nationality-themed gardens, most with designers native to that country or of relevant heritage. You may park on the west side of Martin Luther King Jr. Drive, or you could park at the **Rockefeller Park and Greenhouse** (750 E. 88th St., 216/664-3103, rockefellerparkgreenhouse.org, 10am-4pm daily, free), a botanical garden and conservatory near the northern end of the cultural gardens, and walk from there.

Cleveland Metroparks oversees some fantastic green spaces and shoreline. The most popular is probably **Edgewater Park** (6500 Cleveland Memorial Shoreway, 216/954-3408, clevelandmetroparks.com, dawn-dusk daily,

free), with its sandy swimming beach on Lake Erie and its Cleveland Script sign in front of a scenic view of downtown. Note that to drive between the parking lots for the lower beach area and the upper area where the sign is, you must use the highway (though there are also sidewalks connecting the two).

CYCLING

Cleveland is a good biking city, with relatively flat terrain (the closer you stick to the lake) and a growing number of dedicated bike lanes. The **HOPR** (gohopr.com) bikeshare network is the best option for rentals.

The Cleveland Metroparks offer over 100 miles (161 km) of all-purpose paths and mountain biking trails between them, with some connectivity. **Rocky River Reservation** (Valley Pkwy., 440/734-6660, clevelandmetroparks.com) features a 13.6-mile (21.9-km) asphalt trail along Valley Parkway through woods, past cliffs, and over the Rocky River.

The northernmost trailhead for the **Ohio**

& Erie Canal Towpath Trail (ohioanderie-canalway.com) is at Harvard Avenue east of its intersection with Jennings Road. It's a bit of an industrial eyesore for a trailhead, but the 87-mile (140-km) trail runs through woods and continues south through Cuyahoga Valley National Park and then veers to downtown Akron and all the way to Stark County. Or head north on Jennings and pick the trail back up after Beltline Street to sneak through Tremont and reach the Scranton Flats.

For a unique indoor mountain biking experience, **Ray's Indoor Mountain Bike Park** (9801 Walford Ave., 216/631-7433, raysmtb. com) has 120,000 square feet (11,148 sq m) of warehouse space with mountain bike trails for all levels. Some parts resemble a skate park more than a mountain trail, while other features utilize more natural construction materials. You can rent a bike here or bring your own. Coinciding with the cold and wet Cleveland winters, this is a seasonal business operating October-April.

HIKING

It's a treat to drive along Valley Parkway west of downtown through the **Rocky River Reservation** (Valley Pkwy., 440/734-6660, clevelandmetroparks.com), marked by hills and ravines the farther you go from Lake Erie. Park at the nature center (24000 Valley Pkwy.) for a dramatic peek at the 100-foot-plus (30-m) shale cliffs along the Rocky River. You can ascend the stairs (a strenuous climb) of the 0.75-mile (1.2-km) **Fort Hill loop** for a closer look, though going around the loop the other way is a slightly more gradual climb up. Better yet, cross the Valley Parkway bridge and find an opening in the brush down to the river-bank for a more commanding look, though this is more easily done when the water level is low.

East of the city, the heavily forested **North Chagrin Reservation** (3037 Som Center Rd., Willoughby Hills, 440/473-3370, cleveland-metroparks.com) features **Squires Castle** (2844 River Rd.), a shell of an 1890s gate-house that's fun to treat as ruins of a more romantic era. The wide lawn in front of the castle is a popular picnic spot. The castle is a brief, easy walk from the Squires Castle Picnic Area parking lot.

It also bears mentioning that **Cuyahoga Valley National Park** is less than 30 minutes south from downtown Cleveland.

KAYAKING, CANOEING, AND PADDLEBOARDING

Take kayaks and pontoons out for an urban adventure at **Great Lakes Watersports** (1148 Main Ave., 216/644-0272, glwaters-ports.com), a first-come, first-served operation along the Cuyahoga River in The Flats district.

ROCK CLIMBING

Climb Cleveland (2190 Professor Ave., 216/906-4186, climb-cleveland.com) is a bouldering gym, with short climbing walls meant to extend endurance rather than scale serious height. Day passes are $14.

SPECTATOR SPORTS

Clevelanders stand by their storied sports teams, despite the championship drought that lasted from 1964 to 2016 when LeBron James and the **Cleveland Cavaliers** (nba.com/cav-aliers) won the 2016 NBA championship. The team plays basketball at **Rocket Mortgage FieldHouse** (1 Center Ct., 216/420-2000), an arena seating more than 19,000.

The National Football League's **Cleveland Browns** (clevelandbrowns.com) maintain a devoted following, though the team has struggled through much of the 21st century to maintain a winning culture. Originally founded in 1945, owner Art Modell infamously moved the Browns—a more competitive team at that point—to Baltimore in 1996. After an understandable uproar from the city, Modell agreed to leave the Browns' intellectual property for Cleveland to pick back up with an expansion team, and what were the Browns became the successful Baltimore Ravens, a situation that makes Clevelanders a bit grouchy toward their Maryland rival.

The Browns play at the lakeside **FirstEnergy Stadium** (100 Alfred Lerner Way, 440/891-5001, firstenergystadium.com).

The **Cleveland Guardians** (mlb.com), known for over 100 years as the Cleveland Indians, have a long history in Major League Baseball dating back to 1901 and have permeated popular culture numerous times, most notably in the film *Major League* and its sequels. They play at **Progressive Field** (2401 Ontario St., 216/420-4487), opened in 1994 as Jacobs Field.

The **Cleveland Monsters** (cleveland-monsters.com) play in the American Hockey League and are the top affiliate with the Columbus Blue Jackets. Like the Cavaliers, they play at Rocket Mortgage FieldHouse.

Unlike Columbus and Cincinnati, Cleveland does not have a strong college sports scene. The **Cleveland State Vikings** (csuvikings.com) primarily compete in the NCAA Division I Horizon League in 16 men's and women's sports.

Shopping

DOWNTOWN

The flagship location for **Cleveland Clothing Company** (342 Euclid Ave., 216/736-8879, cleclothingco.com, 11am-7pm Mon.-Thurs., 11am-8pm Fri.-Sat., noon-6pm Sun.) has an enviable spot on the high-traffic corner of Euclid Avenue and E. 4th Street. Both a local favorite and a good place for a Cleveland souvenir, the store carries its own brand of apparel and accessories with local pride slogans and logos. You'll also find similarly themed accessories, art, and souvenirs by local artists. Smaller outposts are at the Crocker Park mall and Van Aken District.

Smaller, family-owned **We Bleed Ohio** (530 Euclid Ave., 440/941-1178, webleedohio. com, 11am-6pm Mon.-Fri., 11am-4pm Sat.), inside the 5th Street Arcades, serves a similar purpose as Cleveland Clothing Company, with Cleveland- and Ohio-themed apparel, but at a slightly cheaper price point. For $35, you can also print your own shirt. Book your "printing party" ahead of time.

OHIO CITY

Explore the Scent Wall, with over 200 options, and craft your own candle at **Cleveland Candle Company** (2032 W. 25th St.,

216/471-8477, clecandleco.com, 11am-8pm Mon.-Fri., 10am-8pm Sat., 11am-6pm Sun.), or stick to the ones made by the professionals spanning food, floral, nature, and thematic aromas.

Vintage. Antique. Mid-century modern. It's all at **All Things For You** (3910 Lorain Ave., 216/273-7761, allthingsforu.com, noon-4pm Wed.-Fri., 10am-4pm Sat.-Sun.), one of Cleveland's largest vintage stores. Specializing in furniture, the owners love to talk shop about interior decoration. Pick their brains while you browse the unique decor and statement pieces from decades past.

DETROIT-SHOREWAY

What started as French designer Anne Harrill's side hustle making vintage-inspired jewelry has blossomed into **Oceanne** (6519 Detroit Ave., 216/862-7043, oceanne.net, 11am-5pm Thurs.-Sun.), a minimalist space of empowering jewelry and apparel. The shop also offers personalized items such as necklaces, cuffs, and bookmarks.

TREMONT

Visible Voice Books (2258 Professor Ave., 216/961-0084, visiblevoicebooks.com, noon-8pm Tues.-Wed., noon-10pm Fri., 11am-10pm Sat., 11am-5pm Sun.) takes its role as a community gathering space seriously, with a busy

1: FirstEnergy Stadium, home of the Cleveland Browns **2:** Presti's Bakery in Little Italy

slate of author events, panel discussions, and musical performances as well as a café stocked with local coffee and pastries. There's free parking in a lot behind the store.

Contemporary women's boutique **Evie Lou** (2509 Professor Ave., 216/696-6675, evielou.com, 11am-6pm Mon.-Wed., 11am-7pm Thurs.-Sat., noon-4pm Sun.) balances fashion and comfort with its curated collection of brands. Besides clothing, the store stocks shoes and accessories.

Fellow women's boutique **Banyan Tree** (2242 Professor Ave., 216/241-1209, shopbanyantree.com, 11am-7pm Mon.-Thurs., 11am-8pm Fri.-Sat., 11am-4pm Sun.) sits on the opposite end of the artsy Professor Avenue corridor. The store's chic collection stresses comfort and muted colors, perfect for gallery hopping or low-key evening events.

MALLS

There are quality malls in any direction you go away from the city center. Most notable is **Crocker Park** (177 Market St., Westlake, 440/835-9343, crockerpark.com),

an upscale, outdoor lifestyle center roughly 20 minutes west of downtown via I-90. It has outposts of some of Cleveland's favorite boutiques, including Cleveland Clothing Company and Banyan Tree, as well as dining options and a movie theater. On the east side of town, the **Van Aken District** (3401 Tuttle Rd., Shaker Heights, 216/491-8800, thevanakendistrict.com) straddles urban and suburban sensibilities and emphasizes local and regional brands (again with an outpost or two of Cleveland favorites such as Cleveland Clothing Company). It also features a 21,000-square-foot (1,951-sq-m) market hall among its several dining options. **Tower City Center** (230 W. Huron Rd., 216/623-4750, towercitycenter.com) sits within the historic confines of Tower City, just off Public Square in downtown Cleveland. It's seen better days and its stores are mostly modest national chains, but its food court is a cheap option in an expensive neighborhood, and there's a movie theater. Also, it features prominently in the film *Captain America: The Winter Soldier*.

Food

Hip, urbane, whatever you want to call it, Cleveland's culinary scene embraces innovation. Often found in rehabilitated old spaces—banks, houses, firehouses—Cleveland's restaurants reflect an "anything's possible" mentality, with New American cuisine leading the charge. Concurrently, you'll find long-standing ethnic spots, serving in particular Polish and other Eastern European cuisines. If you've ever wanted to try a pierogi, this is the place. A local specialty known as a Polish Boy—a French fry-, slaw-, and sauce-laden kielbasa on a bun—is typically found in no-frills neighborhood barbecue joints.

DOWNTOWN

Downtown is flush with ritzy fine-dining destinations, and so the price for a dinner

is much higher here than in other neighborhoods. Most downtown restaurants at a more affordable price point are chains.

Barbecue

When celebrity chef Michael Symon's flagship restaurant Lola became a COVID casualty, it was a great loss to the Cleveland dining scene. Luckily, his fellow concept ★ **Mabel's BBQ** (2050 E. 4th St., 216/417-8823, mabelsbbq.com, noon-9pm Tues.-Thurs., noon-10pm Fri.-Sat., $15-25) is still here to hold down the fort. Utilizing a particular mustard, Eastern European spices, and fruitwood for smoking, Symon has created a barbecue style unique to Cleveland. Order meat by the half pound and pick from 10 sides in this high-ceilinged, communal space. The lengthy alcohol list includes over 20 drafts of local and regional beer and quite the bourbon selection.

Surf and Turf

Put yourself in the middle of Gilded Age Cleveland's opulence in the ★ **Marble Room** (623 Euclid Ave., 216/523-7000, marbleroomcle.com, 4:30pm-11pm Tues.-Sat., 11pm-4pm Sun., $38-70), a raw bar and steakhouse located in a former bank building. With its lofty ceiling, Corinthian columns, and intricate molding, it's hard to imagine a more extravagant or awe-inspiring place to sit down for a steak dinner.

Seafood

Another downtown staple for fine dining, **Blue Point Grille** (700 W. St. Clair Ave., 216/875-7827, bluepointgrille.com, 3pm-9pm Mon.-Thurs., 3pm-10pm Fri., 4pm-10pm Sat., 4pm-9pm Sun., $29-59) boasts a white-tableclothed, chandeliered dining room with a business casual dress code, a view toward Public Square, and a reputation for fresh seafood.

Sandwiches

Don't let the stoic facade fool you; this location of **Dave's Cosmic Subs** (1918 E. 6th St., 216/861-4199, davescosmicsubs.com, 10:30am-3pm Mon.-Fri., $6-12) is no less groovy than the others, serving eccentric subs from a tiny, classic rock-themed dining room. Started in suburb Chagrin Falls, the franchise has grown to more than 20 locations, nearly all of them in Northeast Ohio. This particular spot is a cheap lunch alternative to the pervasive high-end options in this part of town.

Dessert

As if a peek inside the Victorian interior of The Arcade wasn't reason enough to visit, the landmark building is fronted by **Cathy's: Gourmet Ice Cream Sandwiches** (401 Euclid Ave., 216/452-7821, cathyscle.com, 2pm-9pm daily, $5-10). Build your own sandwich (choose your cookie and ice cream, and any extras you want sprinkled on top) or order a pint of cookie dough to go. The ice-cream sandwiches, though pricey, are quite large and a messy business to eat. There's little seating inside the small parlor.

OHIO CITY

Like downtown, Ohio City's offerings lean toward the pricey side. If you're not in the mood for the latest hipster haven, the neighborhood's brewpubs (see the *Bars and Nightlife* section) are more down-to-earth and offer pretty robust menus.

New American

The Flying Fig (2523 Market Ave., 216/241-4243, theflyingfig.com, 3pm-9pm Mon., 11am-10pm Wed.-Thurs., 11am-11pm Fri.-Sat., 11am-9pm Sun., $12-24) is a hip foodie destination, as recommended for its food as for its convivial atmosphere. The menu is split between small, shareable plates and individual large plates, with more affordable sandwich options on offer for weekday lunch. The front patio is a good people-watching spot, with Great Lakes Brewing Company and West Side Market steps away.

Eastern European

Established in 2018, **Larder Delicatessen and Bakery** (1455 W. 29th St., 216/912-8203, noon-6pm Tues.-Sat., $9-15) is housed in the old Ohio City Firehouse, dating back to 1854. The sandwich menu changes daily in tune with the seasons and the whims of the culinary team, but most always features pastrami. Baked goods and a small selection of locally purveyed meat, dairy, and produce round out a foodie paradise. There's indoor and outdoor seating to enjoy your picks.

Mexican

Momocho (1835 Fulton Rd., 216/694-2122, momocho.com, 4pm-8pm Tues., 4pm-10pm Wed.-Sat., $13-24) serves modern Mexican food in a dimly lit, wrestling-themed dining room. The drink menu is as long as the food menu, with Mexican beer, cocktails, and a lengthy list of tequila. Even if a pricey dinner isn't in the cards, it's worth going in for a drink or one of the specialty guacamoles.

Breakfast

Grab a fresh, hand-rolled bagel or twelve at **The Cleveland Bagel Company** (4201 Detroit Ave., 216/600-5652, clebagelco.com, 6:30am-1pm Tues.-Sun., $5-11). Buy them on their own, as sandwiches, or with schmears and lox. The small, unpretentious digs have limited seating, but the takeout line moves fast. A second location is near the Cleveland Clinic campus.

Coffee

Local coffee roaster **Phoenix Coffee** (3000 Bridge Ave., 216/400-7901, phoenixcoffee. com, 7am-4pm Mon.-Fri., 7:30am-4pm Sat., 8am-4pm Sun.) is an employee-owned co-op with six locations, each boasting freshly brewed, responsibly sourced coffee as well as a small selection of pastries and other goodies from local bakeries. This Ohio City outpost has a small, secluded patio.

Ice Cream

Ohio makes good ice cream, and Cleveland is no exception. Ohio City has two quality local parlors, the most noticeable being the flagship **Mitchell's Ice Cream** (1867 W. 25th St., 216/861-2799, mitchellshome-made.com, noon-10pm daily), in a recommissioned old movie theater that also serves as a sustainability-driven production space for its 10 shops; you can watch the staff at work through a window behind the counter. Mitchell's serves handmade ice cream made largely from Ohio ingredients.

Mason's Creamery (4401 Bridge St., 216/762-1095, masonscreamery.com, 2pm-10pm Tues.-Sun.) is a small-batch shop that cranks out unusual ice cream flavors like Ube, Popcorn, and Black Sesame (along with more typical flavors). You can also get your ice cream on an egg waffle. The parlor pivots to a ramen shop in the winter months called **Mason's Ramenry.** There are several picnic

tables next to the building, but indoor seating is limited.

TREMONT

Look for longstanding favorites as well as fashionable 21st-century concepts in Tremont, where young professionals and hipsters enjoy the low rents of this formerly downtrodden pocket of town.

New American

Michelin-starred Dante Boccuzzi has had a significant hand in reshaping Northeast Ohio's culinary scene. Tremont's **Dante** (2247 Professor Ave., 216/274-1200, danteboccuzzi. com/dante-tremont, 5pm-10pm Wed.-Thurs., 5pm-11pm Fri.-Sat., $16-36) serves luxurious takes on Italian, American, and seafood dishes from behind the Greek Revival facade of a former bank. Japanese restaurant **Ginko** and pizza/brunch spot **Dante Next Door,** two fellow concepts, reside next to his signature restaurant at the same address and come at a similar price point.

A bit more pared down is **Lucky's Café** (777 Starkweather Ave., 216/622-7773, luckyscafe.com, 9am-2pm daily, $12-15), a comfortable place for breakfast and lunch, with elevated dishes like gingerbread waffles and a top-notch macaroni and cheese. There's also a full café drink menu and a counter of pastries and desserts if you're in the mood for something sweet. Seating is both indoors and outdoors.

DETROIT-SHOREWAY

Detroit-Shoreway's offerings mainly fall near Gordon Square, with hip, artsy eateries to match the hip, artsy entertainment at the intersection's theaters.

Wine Bar

Warmly lit and cozy, **Toast** (1365 W. 65th St., 216/862-8674, toastcleveland.com, 4pm-10pm Mon. and Wed.-Sat., 11am-3pm and 4pm-10pm Sun., $13-23) is a romantic choice for a before-show meal or after-show drink. Primarily a wine bar, the restaurant also features a sizeable beer list, small plates, a brief list of high-end comfort food entrées, charcuterie boards, and Sunday brunch. Additional seating is outdoors behind the building and along the alley.

Mediterranean

The vogue **Luxe Kitchen and Lounge** (6605 Detroit Ave., 216/920-0600, luxecleveland.com, 5pm-10pm Mon.-Fri., 11am-2pm and 5pm-10pm Sat.-Sun., $12-22) throws together an accessible menu of elevated Italian and Mediterranean classics as well as a handful of beers on draft, handmade cocktails, and wine. It also serves brunch on weekends. There's a secluded back patio, and free parking at the neighboring Pioneer Savings Bank for customers.

Breakfast

Donuts infused with coffee or beer, you say? That's how they do it at **Brewnuts** (6501 Detroit Ave., 216/600-9579, brewnutscleveland.com, 6:30am-sold out Wed.-Fri., 8am-sold out Sat.-Sun.). At $3 each, the donuts are a bit more expensive than most, but they are also much bigger. Pair your donuts with a beverage either way—coffee or beer—in the bamboo-lined dining room. Donuts typically sell out by early afternoon.

UNIVERSITY CIRCLE/ LITTLE ITALY

Cleveland's Little Italy—a tight-knit community with a dense corridor of trattorias, bakeries, and old-world eateries—technically falls within the eastern half of the University Circle neighborhood. The western half of University Circle nearer the museums favors chains over local restaurants. The RTA Red Line separates the two halves.

Italian

There's no finer people-watching spot in Little Italy than the front patio of ★ **Presti's Bakery** (12101 Mayfield Rd., 216/421-3060, prestisbakery.com, 6am-7pm Mon., 6am-9pm Tues.-Thurs., 6am-10pm Fri.-Sat., 6am-4pm

Sun., $5-10), open since 1903. Eavesdrop on friendly conversations while enjoying pizza by the slice, pasta, sandwiches, or immaculate-looking pastries and cookies from the bakery. Additional seating is inside.

Casual, family-operated restaurant **Mama Santa's** (12301 Mayfield Rd., 216/231-9567, mamasantas.com, 11am-9pm Mon.-Sat., $9-18) hearkens to yesteryear with checkered tablecloths and inexpensive Italian American favorites, most notably pizza. Build your own or choose one of the specialties.

Since 1918, **Guarino's Restaurant** (12309 Mayfield Rd., 216/231-3100, guarinoscleveland.com, 11:30am-9pm Tues.-Thurs., 11:30am-10pm Fri.-Sat., 11:30am-7pm Sun., $10-19) has served the community with old-world recipes of Italian standards. The Victorian interior and garden patio often get as much attention as the food.

French

Within the Case Western Reserve University campus is **L'Albatros** (11401 Bellflower Rd., 216/791-7880, albatrosbrasserie.com, 4pm-9:30pm Tues.-Sat., 3pm-8pm Sun., $16-28), a brasserie that features a distinctly European menu of French, German, and Italian entrées to be enjoyed in either the classy dining room (formerly a carriage house) or on the sizeable patio. Wine and beer—a good mix of local craft beer and imports from Europe—are available.

Sandwiches

Located a couple blocks north of Wade Oval in Glenville, one of Cleveland's most prominent African American neighborhoods since the mid-20th century, is **Black Box Fix** (1400 E. 105th St., 216/282-1900, blackboxfix.com, noon-6pm Mon.-Fri., $12-20). This location, one of three, does what the others do: build mouth-watering sandwiches including the OMG Philly, with grilled chicken, jumbo shrimp, and spicy crab mayo on a hoagie. A wall in the indoor seating area pays homage to neighborhood greats such as comedian Steve Harvey and successful NFL athletes who attended football powerhouse Glenville High School.

ASIATOWN

Korean, Vietnamese, and a good variety of Chinese restaurants dominate Asiatown, most of them modest joints and refreshingly affordable compared to nearby downtown.

Vietnamese

Tucked in the back of a small building of Asian businesses is a hole-in-the-wall called **Superior Pho** (3030 Superior Ave., 216/781-7462, superiorpho.com, 10:30am-8pm Tues.-Sat., 10am-7pm Sun., $9-12), frequently listed as the best place in Cleveland for the Vietnamese soup. The banh mi sandwiches are also highly praised, with particularly crunchy bread. There's free parking in the lot behind the building off Danford Court.

Chinese

One block east of Superior Pho is **LJ Shanghai** (3142 Superior Ave., 216/400-6936, ljshanghaicle.com, 11:15am-8:30pm Tues.-Sun., $6-12), a Shanghainese eatery with a simple yet comfortable dining room. The soup noodles and dumplings are popular.

Deli

Corned beef fans ought to try **Slyman's Restaurant** (3106 St. Clair Ave., 216/621-3760, slymans.com, 6am-2pm Mon.-Fri., $10-20), a deli specializing in overstuffed corned beef sandwiches and Reubens. For breakfast, try the corned beef hash. The no-frills restaurant has quite a following, frequents "best sandwich in Cleveland" lists, and drums up decent lunch crowds.

OLD BROOKYLN

If you're hungry before or after a trip to the zoo, you'll find a handful of enticing food options nearby that reflect the neighborhood's diverse citizenry.

Jamaican

Near the entrance to the zoo, **Irie Jamaican Kitchen** (4162 Pearl Rd., 216/291-7488, iriejakitchen.com, 11am-8pm Tues.-Fri., noon-8pm Sat., $7-16) serves pleasing portions of authentic Jamaican cuisine in a blink-and-you'll-miss-it blue building. Plenty of side options allow you to venture into new territory without spending too much money. A second location is out in eastern suburb Euclid.

Guatemalan

A fast-food restaurant by outward appearance, friendly **El Rinconcito Chapin** (3330 Broadview Rd., 216/795-5776, elrinconcito-chapin.com, 11am-9pm Mon. and Wed.-Sat., 11am-6pm Sun., $8-15) is also close to the zoo and serves inexpensive Guatemalan sandwiches, seafood, and more, alongside some familiar Mexican favorites. Look for the *pupusas,* pancake-like corn tortillas stuffed with cheese and other good things.

Bars and Nightlife

Ample live music, a sturdy craft beer scene, friendly neighborhood watering holes: There's no shortage of nightlife in Cleveland. It's just a matter of where you want to spend the evening.

DOWNTOWN

From dives to posh cocktail bars to kinetic DJ parties to live music, there's a good variety of nightlife in downtown Cleveland.

Much of the livelier action takes place in The Flats area along the river and the Warehouse District just behind it, with its dance clubs and bars. E. 4th Street is another hot spot, with a pedestrian-only road connecting stylish bars and restaurants.

Bars and Breweries

In a former auto showroom, **Masthead**

Brewing Company (1261 Superior Ave., 216/206-6176, mastheadbrewingco.com, noon-9pm Tues.-Thurs., noon-10pm Fri.-Sat., noon-7pm Sun.) is well set up for big groups of friends with its lengthy biergarten tables and casual atmosphere. Over 20 drafts are on hand, along with pizzas, sandwiches, and shareables. An outdoor patio fronts the street as well.

Collision Bend Brewing Company (1250 Old River Rd., 216/273-7879, collisionbendbrewery.com, 11:30am-10pm Mon.-Thurs., 11:30am-midnight Fri.-Sat., 11:30am-8pm Sun.) in The Flats has a nice spot along the Cuyahoga River, with the Main Avenue Viaduct looming over the patio. The draft beer spans a nice variety, and the elevated menu offers a few options not always found in brewpubs, such as a poke bowl and some innovative burgers.

Part of the luxury hotel Metropolitan at the 9, **Vault** (2017 E. 9th St., 216/239-1200, metropolitancleveland.com, 4pm-10pm Wed.-Sat.), as its name suggests, inhabits an early-20th-century bank vault. This chic underground speakeasy serves over 30 handmade cocktails as well as beer and a long list of spirits.

In a neighborhood of high-concept eateries and pricey steakhouses, there's **Johnny's**

Little Bar (614 Frankfort Ave., 216/861-2166, 11:30am-2:30am Mon.-Sat., 4pm-9pm Sun.), sticking with the tried-and-true beer-and-burger combo and doing it swimmingly, from a brick-and-wood tavern in the Warehouse District. Over 40 beers are on tap.

The slender **Gillespie's Map Room** (1281 W. 9th St., 216/621-7747, maproomcleveland. com, 11am-2am daily), with its international flags and airplane hanging from the ceiling, exudes an explorer atmosphere, though in reality it's a low-key neighborhood watering hole and a good place to catch a game in the Warehouse District. Some 20 drafts cover local, regional, and national brews, and the menu is renowned for its pizza and Polish Boys.

Clubs

FWD Day + Nightclub (1176 Front Ave., 216/990-2300, fwdnightclub.com, 6pm-11pm Thurs., 9pm-2:30am Fri.-Sat., noon-7:30pm Sun.) in The Flats is open seasonally and hosts high-energy outdoor parties with DJs pumping music late into the night with the skyline as a backdrop. A pool adds to the fun. Dress to impress (check the website for the club's dress code).

Cleveland boasts a number of comedy clubs attracting touring stand-up comedians.

Downtown's pedestrian 4th Street is home to trendy bars and restaurants.

Pickwick and Frolic (2035 E. 4th St., 216/241-7425, pickwickandfrolic.com) is among the best, having hosted the likes of Dave Coulier, the Wayans Brothers, and Craig Robinson. Part restaurant, part comedy club, part cabaret, the complex also hosts other entertainment. Its Hilarities 4th Street Theatre accommodates 400 between the mezzanine and main floor, and Frolic Cabaret puts on murder mysteries and burlesque shows in a more intimate space.

Live Music

House of Blues Cleveland (308 Euclid Ave., 216/523-2583, houseofblues.com/cleveland) keeps a busy calendar of national and international rock and blues acts in a mid-sized but cozy performance space.

Jacobs Pavilion at Nautica (2014 Sycamore St., 216/622-6557, livenation.com) is a covered outdoor pavilion open early summer to early fall. Big-name rock, hip-hop, and pop acts perform with the Cuyahoga River and Cleveland skyline as a backdrop.

In The Flats, Music Box Supper Club (1148 Main Ave., 216/242-1250, musicboxcle.com) hosts up-and-coming national touring acts as well as local musicians spanning the rock, Americana, roots, blues, and jazz genres. The views from the windows cover the river and skyline.

OHIO CITY

Beer. That's what you're probably coming to Ohio City for, whether at one of the half-dozen craft breweries or a concept bar. Cleveland's reputation as a beer city is largely thanks to what people are up to in this neck of the woods.

Bars and Breweries

Cleveland's beer scene wouldn't look like it does today if it weren't for ★ Great Lakes Brewing Company (2516 Market Ave., 216/771-4404, greatlakesbrewing.com, noon-10pm Mon.-Sat., noon-6pm Sun.), which began operations in 1988 as Ohio's first microbrewery. Known for its Dortmunder Gold

Lager (and seasonal Christmas ale), the company operates a cozy brewpub across the street from West Side Market. Tours of the brewery ($6) run on Fridays and Saturdays and start at the Beer Symposium (1951 W. 26th St.) around the corner from the brewpub. The company is also known for its sustainability efforts, particularly in clean water.

Fellow staple Market Garden Brewery (1947 W. 25th St., 216/621-4000, marketgardenbrewery.com, 3pm-10pm Wed.-Thurs., 2pm-11pm Fri., 11am-11pm Sat., 11am-10pm Sun.) also runs a well-regarded brewpub and operates tours of its brewing facility located on the opposite side of the West Side Market parking lot, where there's also a gift shop.

Is it a bar? Is it a café? It's kind of neither. Tabletop Board Game Café (1810 W. 25th St., 216/512-3053, tabletopcleve.com, 4pm-9pm Wed.-Thurs., 11am-11pm Fri.-Sat., 11am-9pm Sun.) is Cleveland's first board game café, and a friendly place to play a favorite with friends or learn a new one from an employee (there are over 1,200 games in the library). A tempting menu of sandwiches, flatbread pizzas, snacks, café beverages, and local beers on tap keep you satiated during those long Risk campaigns.

The Velvet Tango Room (2095 Columbus Rd., 216/241-8869, velvettangoroom.com, 4:30pm-1am Mon.-Fri., 5pm-1am Sat.) shows up on most lists of top bars in Cleveland. The intimate cocktail bar features live jazz nightly care of its house band at 5:30pm and an additional act at 9pm. The hand-crafted cocktails are a bit steep at $18, though there's no cover charge.

TREMONT

Something of a counterpoint to the neighborhood's upmarket restaurants are its comparatively relaxed and homey bars, more pub than posh. Long-established neighborhood joints comingle with recently refurbished spaces.

Bars

The Treehouse (820 College Ave., 216/696-2505, treehousecleveland.com, 4pm-2:30am

Mon.-Thurs., 11am-2:30am Fri.-Sun.), has a rustic interior (which, appropriately, includes a tree behind the bar), shady patio, and vaguely Irish theme. Come for the 20 drafts, pub menu, and live folk music on Sunday evenings.

Conversation is as valued as the drinks at **The Spotted Owl** (710 Jefferson Ave., 216/795-5595, spottedowlbar.com, 5pm-2am daily), a rustic brick cocktail bar with stained-glass windows and a Cocktail Wheel for when you're not quite sure what you're feeling.

Across the street from A Christmas Story House is the no-nonsense **Rowley Inn** (1104 Rowley Ave., 216/795-5345, therowleyinn. com, 7am-10pm Mon.-Thurs., 7am-midnight Fri.-Sat., 7am-9pm Sun.). A neighborhood gathering spot since 1904, this dive proudly boasts a large drink menu and hearty food, covering breakfast, lunch, and dinner.

Accommodations

If you want to stay in Cleveland proper, downtown has by far the widest variety of options. University Circle has some upscale hotels and independent accommodations as an alternative base near many of the cultural institutions, and Ohio City has some small lodgings.

If you're looking for chain motels with free parking, the cluster that makes the most sense is just south of the intersection of I-77 and I-480 at the Rockside exit, about 9 miles (14.5 km) south of downtown and a 15- to 20-minute drive with no traffic. This location's also not a bad idea if you plan on spending some time at Cuyahoga Valley National Park; its northernmost corner touches Rockside near the hotels.

DOWNTOWN
$100-150

Perhaps the most historic accommodations in the city, the ★ **Hyatt Regency Cleveland at The Arcade** (420 Superior Ave., 216/575-1234, hyatt.com, $139-149) occupies the top three floors of the Victorian shopping center's atrium area as well as the towers on either side. The guest rooms are contemporary and face either the atrium or the city.

Taking over the former Board of Education building, which was built in 1931, the Beaux-Arts **Drury Plaza Hotel Cleveland Downtown** (1380 E. 6th St., 216/357-3100, druryhotels.com, $120-130) features an indoor pool, free wi-fi, and two restored Depression-era murals in the lobby.

$150-200

Across from the Drury is the **Cleveland Marriott Downtown at Key Center** (1360 W. Mall Dr., 216/696-9200, marriott.com, $159-169), with a sleek lobby, a bar and restaurant on the ground floor, a spa, a carry-out café, and modern rooms.

The posh **Hilton Cleveland Downtown** (100 Lakeside Ave. E., 216/413-5000, hilton. com, $151-183) is Cleveland's largest and tallest hotel, completed in 2016 in time for the Republican National Convention. Amenities include an indoor pool, a rooftop bar, and dining options.

Sitting in a bright red-brick building built in 1902, ★ **Kimpton Schofield Hotel** (2000 E. 9th St., 216/357-3250, theschofieldhotel. com, $138-208) has an interior that embraces a softer, more comfortable, but no less contemporary look than its peers. Some unusual amenities include a yoga mat in every guest room, complimentary guitar rental, and in-room spa services.

Over $200

Stylish and sexy, the **Metropolitan at the 9** (2017 E. 9th St., 216/239-1200, metropolitancleveland.com, $269-369) took an early-20th-century bank building and inserted bold design elements and luxurious nightlife.

Its 156 guest rooms and 65 suites come with walk-in showers (and some with soaking tubs). A rooftop bar and a cocktail bar within a bank vault are among the dining/drinking options.

The ultimate in sophistication, the **Ritz-Carlton Cleveland** (1515 W. 3rd St., 216/623-1300, ritzcarlton.com, $359-439) features expansive views of the city and lake, marble bathrooms, and guest rooms that set the standard for contemporary comfort. Stream what you'd like via your room's smart TV or step out of the hotel to the Tower City Center shopping mall in the building.

OHIO CITY
Under $100

Offering both shared and private guest rooms, the **Cleveland Hostel and Guesthouse** (2090 W. 25th St., 216/394-0616, theclevelandhostel.com, $67-78) is homey and comfortable. Shared rooms (4-8 beds, $26 pp) are convenient for groups. Off-street parking is free and the rooftop deck has stellar views of the city. Only some of the private rooms have their own bath.

$100-150

The low-key **Stone Gables Inn** (3806 Franklin Blvd., 216/961-4654, stonegablesinn.com, $139-159) sits in a painstakingly restored 1883 mansion several blocks away from the energy of 25th Street. The five quaint guest rooms all come with private baths.

Over $200

A five-minute walk from 25th Street and its breweries and shopping, the **J. Palen House** (2708 Bridge Ave., 216/664-0813, jpalenhouse.

com, $189-279) features nine guest rooms, suites, and lofts full of Victorian character, unique layouts, and modern comfort. The three-course breakfast included in the rate is served at 9am.

UNIVERSITY CIRCLE
Under $100

The **Tudor Arms Hotel Cleveland** (10660 Carnegie Ave., 216/455-1260, hilton.com, $83-95), part of the DoubleTree by Hilton brand, dates back to 1933. The rooms are spacious and modernized, though the bathrooms are on the tight side. A free shuttle does a loop around University Circle, putting you within steps of what you came to see.

$150-200

Enjoy a sumptuous breakfast buffet at the ★ **Glidden House** (1901 Ford Dr., 216/231-8900, gliddenhouse.com, $159-169), a turn-of-the-20th-century mansion turned boutique hotel within easy walking distance of Wade Oval's museums. Rooms are comfortable and come with free wi-fi and big-screen TVs.

The next closest hotel to the museums after the Glidden House is the **Courtyard by Marriott Cleveland University Circle** (2021 Cornell Rd., 216/791-5678, marriott.com, $149-169), which feels a bit more business-like. The modern hotel features a small indoor pool and an outdoor terrace.

The elegant **Intercontinental Cleveland** (9801 Carnegie Ave., 216/707-4100, intercontinentalcleveland.com, $185-193), not to be confused with the Intercontinental Suites located at 8800 Euclid Avenue, sits next to the Cleveland Clinic and features 294 bright, spacious guest rooms.

Information and Services

TOURIST INFORMATION

Destination Cleveland (334 Euclid Ave., 216/875-6680, thisiscleveland.com, 11am-7pm Thurs.-Sat., noon-6pm Sun.) operates a visitors center on the busy corner of Euclid Avenue and E. 4th Street and can provide tips, reservations, coupons, and itinerary assistance. Over in University Circle, the **Visitor & Circle Living Center** (11330 Euclid Ave., 216/707-4640, universitycircle.org, 10am-4pm Tues.-Wed., 10am-3pm Thurs.-Fri., 10am-2pm Sat. May-Oct., 10am-4pm Tues.-Wed., 10am-3pm Thurs.-Fri. Nov.-Apr.) can help you navigate the museums, restaurants, and transportation options of the east side.

HEALTH AND EMERGENCY SERVICES

The **Cleveland Clinic Main Campus** has an emergency room (9105 Cedar Ave., 216/445-4500, my.clevelandclinic.org) as well as a children's hospital (9500 Euclid Ave., 216/444-5437, my.clevelandclinic.org). The Cleveland Clinic also operates the **Lutheran Hospital** (1730 W. 25th St., 216/363-2128, my.clevelandclinic.org) in Ohio City, which has an emergency room. **Cleveland Clinic Urgent Care** can be found downtown (315 Euclid Ave., 216/442-6700, my.clevelandclinic. org, 8am-8pm Mon.-Fri., 8am-4pm Sat.-Sun.). Additionally, a **MetroHealth Health Center** (4757 Lorain Ave., 216/957-4848, metrohealth.org, noon-8pm Mon.-Fri.) operates in Ohio City.

Transportation

GETTING THERE

Air

Cleveland Hopkins International Airport (CLE, 5300 Riverside Dr., 216/265-6000, clevelandairport.com) is Ohio's largest and busiest airport. Located 15 minutes (12 mi/19.3 km) southwest of the city, the airport is served by United, Delta, American, Jet Blue, and several discount airlines and flies to most major cities in the United States and a handful of international routes to Canada and the Caribbean.

Train

The Amtrak *Capitol Limited* and *Lake Shore Limited* lines make a stop at the **Amtrak station** (200 Cleveland Memorial Shoreway, amtrak.com), which features ticket sales, a waiting room, and vending machines.

Long-Distance Bus

Greyhound (greyhound.com), **Barons Bus** (baronsbus.com), and **GoBus** (ridegobus. com) stop at the **Greyhound Bus Station** (1465 Chester Ave., 216/781-0520) near Playhouse Square.

Car

Cleveland is well-connected by highway to the rest of Ohio and cities in neighboring states.

From Columbus, take I-71 north until it spills into I-90 just south of downtown. All told, the journey is a little over two hours (143 mi/230 km). From Toledo, take either the I-80 toll road or SR 2 east for an approximately two-hour drive (115 mi/185 km). Either road bumps into I-90, which takes you into town, but SR 2 avoids the tolls. From Akron, take I-77 north for approximately 45 minutes (40 mi/64 km).

East of the city, I-90 follows the contour of Lake Erie past Erie, Pennsylvania, 1.5 hours away (100 mi/161 km), to Buffalo, New York, three hours away (189 mi/305 km). From Pittsburgh, take I-279 north to I-79 north, then hop on I-76 west to Akron, where you'll pick up I-77 north to Cleveland for a trip a little over two hours (146 mi/235 km). To shave a few minutes, you can hop on the I-80 west turnpike at Youngstown from I-76, which takes you to I-480 north/west to I-77 north. There are tolls this way, however.

GETTING AROUND
To and from the Airport
There are a few easy ways to get between Cleveland Hopkins International Airport and downtown. The **RTA Red Line** (riderta.com) light rail connects the airport's main terminal to Tower City with regular service, an approximately 30-minute ride. All the main car rental companies operate a kiosk at the airport's rental car facility. The airport website (clevelandairport.com) includes a lengthy list of limo and taxi services. You can also pick up an Uber or Lyft rideshare.

Car
Driving in Cleveland is relatively stress-free, with plentiful highways and well-marked, straight streets. Aside from perhaps Little Italy, parking is plentiful, though the garages in downtown and University Circle do add up. It could save you some money and a headache to come prepared with change—some meters only take coins. Otherwise, it's not difficult to find cheap or free street parking in most neighborhoods.

It's easy to grab a rental car at the airport, but you may find cheaper rates downtown, which has offices for **Budget** (1799 Superior Ave., 216/479-0125) and **Enterprise** (1802 Superior Ave., 216/348-0700).

Local Rail and Bus
The **Greater Cleveland Regional Transit Authority (RTA)** (riderta.com) moves people throughout Cleveland and surrounding communities via rail, bus, and trolley. Three **Rapid Transit light rail** lines connect downtown Cleveland with the rest of the city, the Red Line being especially useful for going to the airport, Ohio City, and University Circle. The light rail lines run daily from early morning to late night. Three **Bus Rapid Transit** lines, with dedicated bus lanes and fewer stops, also converge downtown. The HealthLine BRT going between downtown and University Circle along Euclid Avenue runs 24 hours daily, with peak hours seeing stops as often as every 10 minutes. The Cleveland State BRT heads west to Lakewood and the Crocker Park shopping mall. Downtown trolleys stop every 10 minutes 7am-7pm Monday-Friday, with the C line also running on weekends.

Fare is $2.50. Pay with exact change or with fare cards. Tickets are required on the Red Line and HealthLine BRT. Ticket vending machines are located at every stop on the Red Line and HealthLine BRT. If you plan on using public transportation often, purchase a daily pass ($5), two-day pass ($10), or four-day pass ($20) on the RTA website. Passes can also be purchased at any RTA vehicle farebox or ticket vending machine, or at area Giant Eagle, Dave's, and Marc's grocery stores.

Bicycle
HOPR (gohopr.com) operates bikeshare racks throughout Cleveland. Rides are $1 and an additional 15 cents per minute, or buy a day pass for $15.

Taxi
Several taxi companies operate throughout the Cleveland area, though they're not ubiquitous enough to easily hail from the street. **Ace Taxi** (216/361-4700) and **Cleveland Taxi Service** (216/856-0867) offer reliable transportation. **Uber** and **Lyft** also operate in the Cleveland area.

Vicinity of Cleveland

What are city limits to travelers but arbitrary, imaginary lines? Cleveland's urban mosaic seamlessly transitions to dense streetcar suburbs, some of them among the largest cities in Ohio. These communities are typically middle-class and diverse, with immigration stories that fit within the larger metropolitan area narrative. They also come with their own busy culinary and nightlife scenes, hiding some of the region's best dining and retail away from the biggest sights. Farther east, the suburbs become sparser and more affluent and the woods thicker and hillier, while the lakeshore regains a Great Lakes maritime atmosphere, with attendant beaches, industry, and port towns.

PARMA

The second-largest city in Cuyahoga County and the Cleveland metropolitan area, Parma is a dense inner-ring suburb and a coveted community in which to raise a family for its low crime rates and affordable housing. It continues to be shaped by strong ethnic communities, primarily Polish and Ukrainian. Visitors will most likely be drawn here by the restaurants serving these communities.

Sights
STEARNS HOMESTEAD

Trapped in a sea of development is the pastoral island that is the **Stearns Homestead** (6975 Ridge Rd., 440/845-9770, stearnshomestead.com, noon-4pm Sat.-Sun. May-Oct., free). The last working farm in Parma features a red Yankee-style barn and plenty of farm animals on its 48 acres. Two houses—the 1855 Stearns House and the 1940 Gibbs House—are museums filled with era-appropriate antiques. The old-fashioned Country Store sells antiques and "penny" candy and includes a farmers market stand. Not necessarily the largest or most exciting of Ohio's working farm attractions, its

free admission and plentiful animals may qualify as an alternative for young children if the Cleveland Zoo isn't an option or in the budget.

Food

As unpretentious as they come, one of the best places in the Cleveland area to try pierogis is Parma's **Little Polish Diner** (5772 Ridge Rd., 440/842-8212, 11am-7pm Tues.-Thurs., 11am-8pm Fri., 11am-6pm Sat., $7-11), whose name pretty much sums up the place. Pierogis, kielbasa, and stuffed cabbage dominate the menu in this straightforward, hole-in-the-wall joint.

Das Schnitzel Haus (5728 Pearl Rd., 440/886-5050, dshparma.com, 11am-9:30pm Mon.-Thurs., 11am-10:30pm Fri., noon-10:30pm Sat., noon-8pm Sun., $9-20) is known for having Cleveland's first covered biergarten (and it's heated, to boot). Wurst, schnitzel, and several kinds of spaetzle are highlights of the authentic menu, which also covers unfussy German beers and a handful of central European dishes (the owners are native to the former Yugoslavia).

Accommodations

A large bundle of chain hotels huddle along the Rockside Road exit off I-77 just east of Parma. Try the **Hyatt Place Cleveland/Independence** (6025 Jefferson Dr., Independence, 216/328-1060, hyatt.com, $109-129), with spacious guest rooms, an indoor pool, and a large breakfast spread included with the price. In general, this area is a good spot to base yourself if you are looking to save money and are thinking of splitting time between Cleveland and Cuyahoga Valley National Park.

Transportation

Parma is a roughly 15-minute drive (10 mi/16.1 km) south of downtown Cleveland via I-71 to SR 176 to I-480 west.

Vicinity of Cleveland

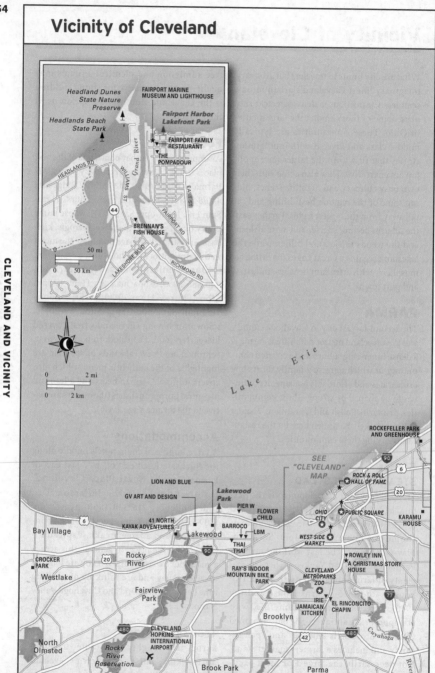

Headland Dunes State Nature Preserve

Headlands Beach State Park

HEADLANDS RD

WILLIAMS ST

Grand River

FAIRPORT MARINE MUSEUM AND LIGHTHOUSE

Fairport Harbor Lakefront Park

FAIRPORT FAMILY RESTAURANT

THE POMPADOUR

EAST ST

FAIRPORT RD

44

BRENNAN'S FISH HOUSE

LAKESHORE BLVD

RICHMOND RD

0   50 mi
0   50 km

Lake Erie

0   2 mi
0   2 km

ROCKEFELLER PARK AND GREENHOUSE

SEE "CLEVELAND" MAP

6

90

LION AND BLUE

GV ART AND DESIGN

Lakewood Park

PIER W

FLOWER CHILD

ROCK & ROLL HALL OF FAME

20

41 NORTH KAYAK ADVENTURES

BARROCO

OHIO CITY

PUBLIC SQUARE

KARAMU HOUSE

Bay Village

6

Lakewood

LBM

WEST SIDE MARKET

THAI THAI

CROCKER PARK

20

Rocky River

90

RAY'S INDOOR MOUNTAIN BIKE PARK

ROWLEY INN

A CHRISTMAS STORY HOUSE

Westlake

Fairview Park

CLEVELAND METROPARKS ZOO

77

IRIE JAMAICAN KITCHEN

EL RINCONCITO CHAPIN

77

North Olmsted

480

Rocky River Reservation

CLEVELAND HOPKINS INTERNATIONAL AIRPORT

Brooklyn

42

480

Cuyahoga River

Brook Park

Parma

SEE
DETAIL

To
Steele Mansion Inn
& Gathering Hub

Mentor

JAMES A. GARFIELD
NATIONAL HISTORIC SITE
LAWNFIELD

BEST WESTERN PLUS
LAWNFIELD INN & SUITES

Eastlake

MELT BAR
AND GRILLED

GREAT LAKES MALL

Mentor

HISTORIC KIRTLAND
VISITORS CENTER

Willowick

KIRTLAND
TEMPLE

BIGA
WOOD FIRED
PIZZERIA

Willoughby

Penitentiary Glen
Reservation

HOLDEN
ARBORETUM

THE
LOUIS PENFIELD
HOUSE

Waite
Hill

Wickliffe

Kirtland

Euclid

SQUIRE'S
CASTLE

CLEVELAND MUSEUM OF
NATURAL HISTORY

CLEVELAND MUSEUM OF ART

CLEVELAND BOTANICAL GARDEN

Wickliffe

North
Chagrin
Reservation

LAKE VIEW CEMETERY

Richmond
Heights

MAC'S BACKS BOOKS
ON COVENTRY

Mayfield

PACIFIC
EAST

Mayfield
Heights

East
Cleveland

Lyndhurst

Chesterland

BLANC
BOUTIQUE

Cleveland
Heights

BATTISTE
AND DUPREE

THE
GROG
SHOP

CEDAR LEE THEATRE

DOBAMA
THEATRE

Pepper
Pike

COVENTRY
VILLAGE
SHOPPING
DISTRICT

Shaker
Heights

Beachwood

Hunting Valley

VAN AKEN
DISTRICT

The West
Woods

SEE
"UNIVERSITY CIRCLE"
MAP

South Russell

Garfield
Heights

Moreland
Hills

Maple
Heights

Bedford
Heights

South Chagrin
Reservation

Bainbridge

Bedford

© MOON.COM

Chagrin River

Toni Morrison and Northeastern Ohio

The Cleveland metropolitan area stretches out past the streetcar suburbs and sprawl to satellite cities like Elyria and Lorain, themselves tied to the rise and fall of industry in much the same way Cleveland has been. One of these cities, Lorain, was where Ramah Willis and George Wofford moved from the Jim Crow South and gave birth to Pulitzer- and Nobel Prize-winning author Toni Morrison, arguably Ohio's most famous and prestigious voice in literature. Her works are renowned for their unflinching, often brutal, portrayals of African American life, and often take place in Ohio.

Born in 1931 as Chloe Anthony Wofford, Morrison grew up in Lorain in a neighborhood she labeled "neither plantation nor ghetto." She attended the integrated Lorain High School and went on to Howard University, where she graduated with a B.A. in English. She earned her M.A. from Cornell and taught English at the collegiate level. When she joined publisher Random House in 1967, she was the first African American woman to serve as editor in the company's history. Working in that role until 1983, she ushered African American voices into the world of mainstream literature.

She published her first novel, *The Bluest Eye*, in 1970. Set in Lorain, the story follows young Pecola Breedlove, who believes she's ugly and thinks she'd be prettier with blue eyes, like a Caucasian doll's. The book did not initially capture much attention but has since earned a spot in many classrooms as a catalyst for discussions about race. It has been banned from as many schools for its depiction of racism, rape, and incest. Her following novels, *Sula* (1973) and *Song of Solomon* (1978), drew more national attention.

Morrison's critical and commercial success exploded with her novel *Beloved* (1987), largely set in Cincinnati and inspired by the true story of Margaret Garner, who escaped enslavement. The novel earned enormous acclaim, including the Pulitzer Prize for Fiction in 1988, and was adapted into a 1988 film starring Oprah Winfrey. Throughout the remainder of the 20th and into the 21st century, Morrison continued to write and give voice to the marginalized. She passed away on August 6, 2019, due to complications with pneumonia.

Morrison's first job was at the **Lorain Public Library** (351 W. 6th St., 440/244-1192, 9am-8pm Mon.-Thurs., 10am-6pm Fri.-Sat.), where she ostensibly spent more time reading books than shelving them. When it was announced that Morrison had won the 1993 Nobel Prize in Literature, Lorain was anxious and uncertain as to how to honor her. Morrison contacted the library and said, "I want a reading room where people can sit and read and just think." **The Toni Morrison Reading Room** is precisely that, with comfortable chairs and a small collection of letters, notes, and newspaper clippings related to Morrison. You can also take a look at the modest gray house that was **Toni Morrison's birthplace** (2245 Elyria Ave.), though stay mindful that it's a private residence. It is, however, a reflective spot to consider little Pecola Breedlove's desire for blue eyes.

Greyhound (greyhound.com), **Barons Bus** (baronsbus.com) and **GoBus** (ridegobus.com) stop at a Shell Gas Station (13030 Brookpark Rd.) at the intersection of Brookpark and W. 130th Street, just south of I-480.

Parma is also accessible via the **Greater Cleveland Regional Transit Authority (RTA)** (riderta.com) public transportation system; the 51A Bus Rapid Transit line connects Parma with downtown Cleveland, terminating at the **Parma Transit Center** (8911 Day Dr.) along with the 45 and 79-79A bus routes.

LAKEWOOD

The densest city in Ohio, streetcar suburb Lakewood has a diverse and young population that energizes the west side of town with modish boutiques and a wide variety of restaurants that are often started by and cater to the collage of immigrants from Eastern Europe,

South Asia, and the Middle East. There are no real "sights" to this corner of the metro area other than popular parks, one-of-a-kind vintage shops and boutiques, and good food.

Shopping

The Cleveland and Ohio-themed apparel out of **GV Art and Design** (17128 Detroit Ave., 216/273-7188, gvartwork.com, 11am-6pm Mon.-Sat., 11am-3pm Sun.) has graced television screens on the chests of multiple professional athletes. The pop art-inspired designs speak to Clevelanders, sports enthusiasts, and streetwear fans alike. You'll also find artwork and impressive Etch A Sketch drawings in the bright, sports-themed store. Three other locations are spread across the region.

Located on the edge of the Lakewood/Cleveland border, quirky **Flower Child** (11508 Clifton Blvd., 216/939-9933, flowerchildvintage.com, noon-7pm Mon. and Wed.-Thurs., noon-8pm Fri.-Sat., noon-5pm Sun.) is an emporium of vintage clothing, accessories, furniture, and art. Almost museum-like in some of its displays, the store focuses on stuff from the 1930s to the 1980s.

Lion and Blue (15106 Detroit Ave., 216/529-2328, lionandblue.com, noon-6pm Mon.-Fri., 11am-6pm Sat.) stocks its shelves with unique fair-trade and hand-crafted gifts, decor, clothing, and other goods. Some are found globally, while others are solicited locally or even made in the store's workshop.

Recreation

Lakewood Park (14532 Lake Ave., 216/529-5697, onelakewood.com, 6am-11pm daily, free) is a terrific lakeside setting for a picnic or sunset, with views of distant downtown Cleveland from the promenade below, and the stone Solstice Steps curving along the shoreline and offering glimpses of the lake's bluffs. There's also a pool and a massive, state-of-the-art playground.

For scenic, guided tours of lakeside bluffs, rivers, and even the Lake Erie islands, look for **41 North Kayak Adventures** (1500 Scenic Park Dr., 866/529-2541, kayak41north.com). Or rent by the hour to explore the Rocky River (just west of Lakewood) or Lake Erie at your leisure.

Food

Perched precariously off a lake bluff, ★ **Pier W** (12700 Lake Ave., 216/228-2250, pierw.com, 11:30am-2:30pm and 5pm-10pm Mon.-Thurs., 11:30am-2:30pm and 5pm-11pm Fri., 5pm-11pm Sat., 9:30am-2:30pm and 5pm-9pm Sun., $21-40) is one of the region's premier romantic dinner spots, with fresh, responsibly sourced seafood, a lengthy wine list, and views of the water and downtown Cleveland from either the dining room or the deck.

Filled with bold wall art and murals, popular ★ **Barroco** (12906 Madison Ave., 216/221-8127, barrocoarepabar.com, 11am-9pm Sun.-Thurs., 11am-10pm Fri.-Sat., $10-22) serves an assortment of Latin American cuisine, including arepas, street tacos, and loaded plantains. Cocktails, live music, and a back patio keep things spirited.

Thai Thai (13415 Madison Ave., 216/226-4890, thaithailakewood.com, noon-9pm Mon. and Wed.-Thurs., noon-10pm Fri.-Sat., 4pm-9pm Sun., $9-13) serves up generous portions of authentic Bangkok street food from a small dining space, with the roasted duck noodle soup a particular highlight. Aside from noodles and curries, the restaurant also offers bubble tea.

In terms of nightlife, one of the area's most unusual haunts is **LBM** (12301 Madison Ave., 216/712-4692, lbmbar.com, 4pm-11pm Mon.-Sat., $10-16). Maybe the only Modern Viking-themed cocktail bar you'll ever come across, with Norse decor and loud music, the bar is a labor of love from food industry vets and sports a creative cocktail list, a small menu of elevated small and large plates, and an assortment of beer and mead.

Accommodations

There aren't really any recommendable accommodations in Lakewood. Your best bet is to grab an AirBnb or perhaps stay in one of Cleveland's Ohio City accommodations, which are about 15 minutes east.

Transportation

Lakewood is 15 minutes (6 mi/9.6 km) west of downtown Cleveland, continuing the city's grid along Lake Erie. Take either US-20/SR 2 west along the lake or hop on I-90 west to the 117th Street or Warren Road exits.

Lakewood is also connected to Cleveland's public transportation system, **RTA** (riderta. com), with the Cleveland State Bus Rapid Transit line and the 26 bus route in particular making stops in the suburb.

CLEVELAND HEIGHTS

Like Shaker Heights, its suburban neighbor to the south, streetcar suburb Cleveland Heights integrated better than most in the mid-20th century when communities began the tenuous journey of desegregation. Though not without tense moments, it managed to avoid the catastrophic racially motivated violence or emptying of neighborhoods that befell other communities, though the population continues to decrease, as it does for much of the region. Today, Cleveland Heights is a socio-economically and culturally diverse continuation of the urban grid, with early-20th-century main streets, tree-lined residential blocks, and a population that supports a healthy stock of local restaurants, nightlife, and shopping.

Entertainment and Events

The original home of the Cleveland International Film Festival, the historic **Cedar Lee Theatre** (2163 Lee Rd., 216/321-5411, clevelandcinemas.com) uses its six screens primarily for arthouse and foreign films, as well as specialty screenings and events. The seats are not the living-room recliners that you find at bigger cineplexes these days, but the prices are also cheaper. Beer, wine, and cocktails are available at concessions.

The small, professional **Dobama Theatre** (2340 Lee Rd., 216/932-3396, dobama.org) has

been producing meaningful, contemporary plays for over 60 years. Each season consists of six carefully selected plays that are performed in the 200-seat theater.

Shopping

Although you'll find interesting stores and boutiques throughout Cleveland Heights, the **Coventry Village Shopping District** (Coventry Rd. between Mayfield Rd. and Euclid Heights Blvd.) is a particularly walkable corridor of established bookstores, worldly gift shops, cafés, and vintage stores. Only 1 mile (1.6 km) east of Little Italy, the street is easily added to a University Circle itinerary.

Fostering an appreciation for literature and poetry since 1982, **Mac's Backs Books on Coventry** (1820 Coventry Rd., 216/321-2665, macsbacks.com, 10am-9pm Mon.-Thurs., 10am-10pm Fri.-Sat., 11am-8pm Sun.) features three cramped floors of new and used books. This friendly, neighborhood bookstore puts on author readings, twice monthly concerts, and other events from the loft space.

Fashion and function intersect at women's boutique **Blanc Boutique** (3104 Mayfield Rd., 216/321-1444, blancboutiquecle.com, noon-6pm Tues.-Fri., 11am-6pm Sat.). Two levels of apparel, jewelry, and gifts cater to a wide variety of sizes and lifestyles. The affordable prices match the laid-back nature of the merchandise.

Food

Put some New Orleans color into the drab Cleveland winter at **Battiste and Dupree** (1992 Warrensville Center Rd., 216/381-3341, battisteanddupreecajungrill.com, noon-9pm Tues.-Thurs., 2pm-10:30pm Fri.-Sat., $10-20), serving up seafood, po'boys, and the typical cast of Cajun favorites in a cozy dining room. This is also one of the best places to try a Polish Boy, a messy kielbasa with fries, slaw,

1: the Murch Canopy Walk at Holden Arboretum **2:** Headlands Dunes State Nature Preserve **3:** the Solstice Steps at Lakewood Park **4:** James A. Garfield National Historic Site

and sauce on a bun. Beer is on hand, as are cocktails in different sizes.

Pacific East (1763 Coventry Rd., 216/320-2302, pacificeastcoventry88.com, 11am-3pm and 5pm-10pm Mon.-Thurs., 11am-3pm and 5pm-11pm Fri., noon-3pm and 5pm-11pm Sat., 3pm-10pm Sun., $10-25) is frequently listed as the best place in Cleveland for sushi. The daunting menu at this Japanese/Malaysian restaurant also includes udon and other noodles, sashimi, and hot pot dishes. Wine, sake, and mostly Japanese beer fill the drink menu at this large but unpretentious gathering space.

With a sunny patio and health-conscious menu, **Luna Bakery and Café** (2482 Fairmount Blvd., 216/231-8585, lunabakery-cafe.com, 7am-4pm Mon.-Fri., 8am-4pm Sat.-Sun., $7-11) is one of the better breakfast and lunch options in town. Crepes—both savory and sweet—are the highlight of the menu, which also includes paninis, salads, and light breakfast choices.

Bars and Nightlife

The Grog Shop (2785 Euclid Heights Blvd., 216/321-5588, grogshop.gs) sits at the southern edge of the Coventry Village Shopping District and is one of the premier spots in the Cleveland area to catch touring alternative music acts. A full bar supports local craft breweries but also stocks name-brand stalwarts.

Open since 1965, **Nighttown** (12383 Cedar Rd., 216/795-0550, nighttowncleveland.com) is classy in an authentic, old-school club sort of way, with live jazz performances and clientele that includes musicians, C-level deal-makers, and doctors from nearby University Circle. A full-service restaurant and bar serving sandwiches, steak, and seafood, the establishment features a patio and late-night piano performances on Fridays and Saturdays.

Accommodations

There are no recommendable accommodations in Cleveland Heights. The best places to stay are in nearby University Circle in Cleveland.

Transportation

Cleveland Heights is easily accessible from adjacent Cleveland, connected by a 20-minute drive east down Euclid, Carnegie, or Chester Avenues (7 mi/11.3 km).

Cleveland Heights is also accessible via Cleveland's public transportation system, **RTA** (riderta.com), with the University Circle/Little Italy Red Line stop putting you within spitting distance (a brief Lyft or Uber from the station, perhaps) of the suburb. The 7, 9, and 32 bus routes cut through Cleveland Heights on their way to and from Cleveland.

KIRTLAND

Soon after Joseph Smith founded the Mormon church in 1830, he moved the church from upstate New York to little Kirtland, where congregations had already made substantial conversions. The Mormon church made its home here for much of the 1830s, its adherents building their first temple and adding to their numbers. However, when the economy went sour and local investors and even some church members grew disillusioned with Smith's prophetic capabilities, Smith left for his safety and, eventually, so did his followers. Today, the temple and other buildings from the Mormon settlement are open for tours in Historic Kirtland. Elsewhere, this well-to-do suburb is marked by quiet residential streets and thick pockets of woods, the largest preserved as Holden Arboretum.

Sights

★ HOLDEN ARBORETUM

An expansive mix of manicured gardens and natural woodlands, the 3,600-acre **Holden Arboretum** (9550 Sperry Rd., 440/946-4400, holdenarb.org, 9am-5pm Tues.-Sun., $15 adults, $10 children) encourages exploration and appreciation for plant life. Start your tour at the Corning Visitor Center, where you'll find information, restrooms, and the Treehouse gift shop. Behind, a patio overlooks the two small ponds of the lovely Holden Butterfly Garden. Walk farther afield for the Wildflower Garden, which re-creates environments found natively in Ohio.

Mesmerizing as the gardens are, the arboretum's highlights require a walk into the woods, where two opportunities exist for an elevated view of the forest. Get your heartbeat up climbing 202 steps to the top of the **Emergent Tower,** which provides an aerial view of the entire arboretum, the surrounding woods, and Lake Erie beyond. Nearby, the **Murch Canopy Walk,** opened in 2015, allows you to walk across a series of suspension bridges through the forest canopy, a colorful stroll during peak autumn foliage. Leaving these more developed parts, trails snake in every direction away from the center of action through the park's carefully managed woods.

There are no food options in the park, but there are a good number of picnic benches next to the parking lot. Come prepared for a lengthy walk, though most trails through the gardens are flat and easy, some even paved for wheelchair accessibility.

HISTORIC KIRTLAND

A small collection of historic buildings lives on as testament to Mormon settlers in Historic Kirtland. Start at the **Historic Kirtland Visitor Center** (7800 Kirtland Chardon Rd., 440/256-9805, history.churchofjesuschrist. org, 9am-8pm Mon.-Sat., 1pm-8pm Sun.) for interpretive exhibits on the Mormon settlement and a free tour of the surrounding buildings, including the N. K. Whitney house and store, where Joseph Smith lived for some time. The buildings have few educational placards, meaning a tour is most useful for context and history. Tours last 1.5-3 hours, though the missionaries can accommodate shorter tours if your time is limited.

Down the street from the Historic Kirtland Visitor Center, you can also visit the unadorned, very white **Kirtland Temple** (7809 Joseph Rd., 440/256-1830, kirtlandtemple.

org, 9am-5pm Mon.-Sat., 1pm-5pm Sun. May-Oct., seasonal hours vary Nov.-Apr., $10). Tours start from the temple's visitors center and last one hour.

Recreation

Several metro parks in these parts take advantage of the hilly woods. **Penitentiary Glen Reservation** (8668 Kirtland Chardon Rd., 440/256-1404, lakemetroparks.com) preserves the forests on either side of Penitentiary Gorge, so named for its steep 100-foot (30-m) walls that are difficult to climb out of. The easy, 1-mile (1.6-km) **Gorge Rim loop trail** gently descends to then follows the edge of a gorge; optionally, if you're game for a little sweat, take 141 steps down some stairs for a look at little, rippling Stoney Brook Falls. Near the parking lot is an informative visitors center, a wildlife center that takes in injured backyard critters, and a nature play area for little kiddos, with ponds for stomping, gardens for digging, and sand for building. (An extra set of clothes is probably wise.)

Food

Biga Wood Fired Pizza (9145 Chillicothe Rd., 440/379-7503, bigawoodfiredpizza, 3pm-9pm Wed.-Sat., $10-15) bakes its thick-doughed 10- to 12-inch pizzas—large enough to share between two, perhaps with a side—in five minutes. Ingredients are sourced locally. Seating is somewhat limited, though there is a small patio outside this converted house.

Kirtland has a quiet restaurant scene. You'll find a lot more options in nearby Mentor or Willoughby, both north of Kirtland on the opposite side of I-90.

Accommodations

Stay the night in a Frank Lloyd Wright home at the **Louis Penfield House** (2203 River Rd. #9685, 440/867-6667, penfieldhouse.com, $300-350). A unique commission for Wright, the house was designed with Penfield's height (6 ft 8 in/203 cm) in mind. The mid-century modern home comfortably accommodates five guests and is surrounded by woods. Guests have the entire house to themselves!

Transportation

Kirtland is about a 25-minute drive (22 mi/35 km) from downtown Cleveland without traffic. Take I-90 east to the Kirtland Road exit.

Kirtland is marginally connected to nearby lakeside communities via **Laketran** (laketran.com), a public bus system serving Cleveland's far east suburbs in Lake County. Many of the system's routes stop at Lakeland Community College, located off the Kirtland Road exit from I-90. From there, you will need to grab a taxi or rideshare to any of the listed destinations. Laketran connects to Cleveland's public transportation system, **RTA** (riderta.com), through park-and-ride routes and at Shoregate Town Center (29700 Lakeshore Blvd., Willowick) west of Kirtland.

MENTOR

The largest city in suburban Lake County, Mentor has a population of 47,000 people who enjoy easy access to Cleveland's amenities and jobs via I-90 and SR 2 as well as the Lake Erie shoreline for recreation. Headlands Beach State Park, located at the northern fringe of town, is one of the most popular natural beaches in Ohio, the longest in the state at 1 mile (1.6 km) long. The city is also the home of the James A. Garfield National Historic Site, a handsome stop on a presidential road trip through Ohio. Named one of the best places to live in 2010 by CNNMoney.com, Mentor nevertheless smacks of suburban sameness: a tangle of cul-de-sacs cut in half by SR 2 and further slashed by commercial corridors and endless retail.

Sights

JAMES A. GARFIELD
NATIONAL HISTORIC SITE

James A. Garfield conducted much of his campaigning for the 1880 presidential election from the front porch of his Lawnfield estate, which is preserved as the **James A. Garfield National Historic Site** (8095 Mentor Ave., 440/255-8722, nps.gov/jaga, 8am-4:30pm daily, free). Thousands traveled to Mentor to hear the talented orator expound upon old-fashioned virtues and the American Dream. If you need to bone up on your Garfield (and don't we all), start at the Visitor Center (10am-4pm Tues.-Sun.), housed in the estate's old carriage house, for exhibits on the man's military and political career, as well as his brief presidency before his assassination in 1881. It becomes clear that this man was, at the time, much more popular than his legacy suggests, which makes some sense of his grandiose resting place in Cleveland's Lake View Cemetery. Tours of the gingerbread house-like Lawnfield mansion begin in the Visitor Center, last approximately 45 minutes, and cost $10, though it costs nothing to visit the Visitor Center and roam the grounds. The tour is worth it for those with Victorian sensibilities: 10 wallpapers were painstakingly reproduced using old photographs and over 80 percent of the house's antique furniture belonged to the Garfield family during the 1880s.

Shopping

Not a minute's drive from the historic site is the **Great Lakes Mall** (7850 Mentor Ave., 440/255-8932, shopgreatlakesmall.com, 11am-7pm Mon.-Sat., 11am-6pm Sun.), a fairly standard enclosed mall albeit with a Round 1 Entertainment Center (round1usa.com) and a 16-screen cinema sharing a parking lot. A local store of note, **Hometown Clothing Co.** (440/567-3757, hometownclothingcompany.com) is located in the mall and a useful stop for Cleveland-themed apparel and accessories.

Recreation

The longest natural beach in Ohio makes **Headlands Beach State Park** (9601 Headlands Rd., 440/466-8400, parks.ohiodnr.gov) one of the most popular swimming destinations in the state. The beach is more pebbly than sandy, but that doesn't detract from the view of the lake. There are several bathrooms available and concessions closer to the west side of the beach. Attached to the eastern hip of the beach is **Headlands Dunes State Nature Preserve** (614/265-6561, naturepreserves.ohiodnr.gov). Here the beach narrows to a driftwood-strewn corridor, with the Fairport Harbor West Breakwater lighthouse plainly in view before you. Trails meander through the beach grass and other marshy plant species more typically found on the Atlantic coast. You would be forgiven for momentarily forgetting which state you were in.

Food

Spunky Cleveland-area favorite **Melt Bar and Grilled** (7289 Mentor Ave., 440/530-3770, meltbarandgrilled.com, 4pm-10pm Mon.-Thurs., 11am-10pm Fri.-Sat., 11am-9pm Sun., $7-15) has been featured on Food Network multiple times, with its outlandish grilled cheese concoctions (you can also create your own). Mentor's location is one of 10 spread across the state. Win a free T-shirt and more by completing the Melt Challenge (5 pounds of food) in one sitting.

It's easy to forget while lost in suburbia that you're near some legitimate maritime communities. **Brennan's Fish House** (102 River St., 440/354-9785, brennansfishhouse.com, 11am-8pm Mon.-Thurs., 11am-9pm Fri.-Sat., 1pm-8pm Sun., $12-25) puts you back in that mindset with nautically themed decor and fresh seafood caught from the lake and beyond. Open since 1973, the restaurant is located near the industrial mouth of the Grand River, a fitting scene for a low-key seafood joint.

Accommodations

There are a handful of chain motels in Mentor, mostly off SR 2. One outlier, both in location and appearance, is the **Best Western Plus Lawnfield Inn & Suites** (8434 Mentor Ave., 440/205-7378, bestwestern.com, $99-169), which has outfitted an 1880s home down the road from James A. Garfield's Lawnfield estate with a large extension and established a more boutique feel than the average Best Western. The guest rooms are well-appointed, and the Presidential and Bridal suites include jetted tubs. A heated outdoor pool and full breakfast are included in the rate.

Transportation

Mentor is well-connected to Cleveland, a nearly identical half hour drive (27 mi/43 km) east via I-90, or I-90 to SR 2.

Laketran (laketran.com) serves Mentor and connects the city to nearby towns with fixed-route buses as well as Cleveland through park-and-ride routes. Service is infrequent, arriving every hour or longer. Fares are $1.75 and can be paid using the EZfare app or exact change.

FAIRPORT HARBOR

It's easy to forget within Northeast Ohio's urban labyrinth the utility, wonder, and dangers of the ocean-like Lake Erie. Port town Fairport Harbor puts the lake back into perspective with its industry, lighthouses, beach, and fishing pier in sight of a U.S. Coast Guard station. The small town's pleasant but sleepy main street holds a handful of appetizing restaurants and curious shops to pair with a trip to the beach or lighthouse museum. Unlike practically anywhere else in Ohio, Fairport Harbor has a strong Finnish presence, as well as Hungarian and German.

Sights
FAIRPORT MARINE MUSEUM AND LIGHTHOUSE

The **Fairport Marine Museum and Lighthouse** (129 2nd St., 440/354-4825, fairportharborlighthouse.org, 1pm-4pm Wed. and Sat.-Sun. Memorial Day-Sept., $5 adults, $4 seniors, $3 children) was established in 1945, the first such lighthouse museum in the United States. It preserves the 1871 sandstone lighthouse and keeper's dwelling and has displays on Fairport Harbor's history as a port town, shipping on the Great Lakes, and shipwrecks. Highlights include the lighthouse's original lens; the pilot house of the carrier *Frontenac,* attached to the keeper's house; and a spiral staircase that takes you to the top of the 60-foot (18.3-m) lighthouse for a view of the town and lake. A strangely diverting feature on the website is a map that keeps tabs on ships currently sailing on Lake Erie.

Recreation

Fairport Harbor Lakefront Park (301 Huntington Beach Dr., 440/639-9972, dawn-dusk daily) is a smaller, tidier, and sandier beach than Headlands Beach State Park, on the opposite side of the Grand River. Restrooms, concessions, and a playground make this an easy family outing. Parking in the lot is $3.

Food

The easygoing **Fairport Family Restaurant** (212 High St., 440/354-7474, 7am-8pm Mon.-Sat., 7am-3pm Sun., $6-10) serves a simple menu of breakfast plates, seafood, and sandwiches at its homey dining room and patio on the town's main street, just steps away from the lighthouse and beach. The portions, price, and good-naturedness of the setting and employees make this a comfortable dining choice.

More contemporary is **The Pompadour** (320 High St., 440/639-0263, thepompadourbar.com, 5pm-9pm Tues.-Thurs., 5pm-10pm Fri.-Sat., $5-14), a tapas bar seemingly more at home in Cleveland's Ohio City neighborhood than a quiet port town, though the

easy-as-could-be parking and somewhat cheaper prices play to your advantage. This old dive bar turned restaurant serves elevated small plates and cocktails, and regularly sees large crowds; it's a good idea to make a reservation.

Accommodations

There are no accommodations in Fairport Harbor. A 10-minute drive south of town is the city of Painesville, which has the 1867 French Empire-style **Steele Mansion Inn and Gathering Hub** (348 Mentor Ave., 440/639-7948, steelemansion.com, $159-319), a 16-room boutique hotel with spacious, historic guest rooms and suites. Free wi-fi and a breakfast buffet are included in the rate.

Transportation

Fairport Harbor is 35 minutes east (30 mi/48 km) of downtown Cleveland. Take I-90 east to SR 2 and get off the Richmond Street exit to head north to town.

The village is served by Lake County's **Laketran** (laketran.com) public transportation system, with the Fairport Harbor Circulator making a loop down High Street past the beach and south to Painesville, where you can transfer to a different bus route. Service is hourly, so you're best served by driving to Fairport Harbor yourself.

Cuyahoga Valley and Northeast Ohio

Northeast Ohio offers what is arguably the

state's most diverse lineup of experiences. There's Ohio's only national park, for starters, with dozens of miles of hilly hiking, the state's tallest waterfall, and the ruins of the Ohio & Erie Canal. There are the fringes of the Cleveland metropolitan area and a trio of Rust Belt cities—Akron, Canton, and Youngstown—reinventing themselves in the 21st century with art, microbreweries, and innovative start-ups. Then there's Ashtabula County, one of the most unique regions in Ohio, home to summer resort Geneva-on-the-Lake, port city Ashtabula, wine country, and covered bridges.

The legacies left by the people in this region continue to shape the United States. "The Rubber Capital of the World" by 1920, Akron was

Highlights

Look for ★ to find recommended sights, activities, dining, and lodging.

★ Explore **Cuyahoga Valley National Park,** which delights with waterfalls, rock formations, and canal history (page 170).

★ Tour **Stan Hywet Hall and Gardens,** the exquisite Tudor-style estate and gardens that belonged to Goodyear co-founder F. A. Seiberling (page 175).

★ Pay tribute to the National Football League's best players at the extravagant **Pro Football Hall of Fame,** which also highlights the league's history and development (page 183).

★ Visit the **McKinley National Memorial,** the stately mausoleum for President William McKinley, which impresses from its lofty perch next to his **presidential library and museum** (page 183).

★ Find the work of practically any U.S. artist of note, from Thomas Cole to Andy Warhol, at Youngstown's **Butler Institute of American Art** (page 190).

★ Wander the down-to-earth strip at Ohio's first summer resort, **Geneva-on-the-Lake,** on the shores of Lake Erie (page 198).

★ Taste the fruit of local vineyards in Ohio's picturesque **wine country,** where most of the wineries are concentrated around the Grand River (page 202).

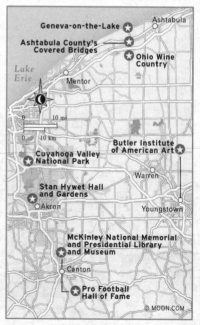

★ See **Ashtabula County's covered bridges**—the county has more than anywhere in the state, among them both the longest and shortest in the United States (page 204).

Cuyahoga Valley and Northeast Ohio

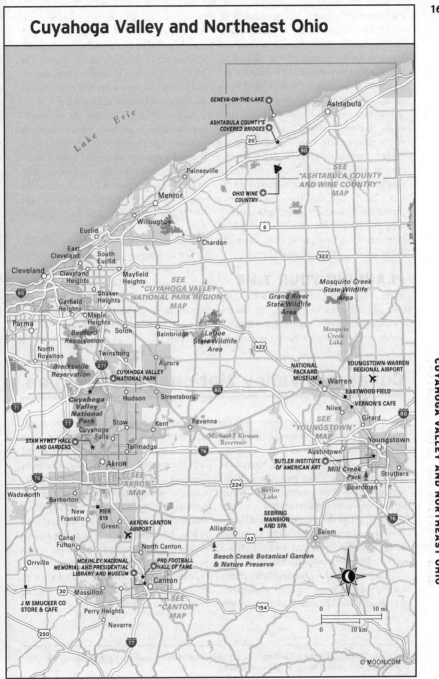

Lake Erie

GENEVA-ON-THE-LAKE

Ashtabula

ASHTABULA COUNTY'S COVERED BRIDGES

20

90

Painesville

SEE "ASHTABULA COUNTY AND WINE COUNTRY" MAP

Mentor

OHIO WINE COUNTRY

Willoughby

6

Euclid

Chardon

East Cleveland

South Euclid

322

Cleveland

Cleveland Heights

Mayfield Heights

SEE "CUYAHOGA VALLEY NATIONAL PARK REGION" MAP

Mosquito Creek State Wildlife Area

Garfield Heights

Shaker Heights

Grand River State Wildlife Area

Parma

Maple Heights

Solon

Bainbridge

LaDue Reservoir

LaDue State Wildlife Area

Mosquito Creek Lake

Bedford Reservation

North Royalton

Twinsburg

422

Brecksville Reservation

271

Aurora

CUYAHOGA VALLEY NATIONAL PARK

NATIONAL PACKARD MUSEUM

YOUNGSTOWN-WARREN REGIONAL AIRPORT

Warren

Cuyahoga Valley National Park

Hudson

Streetsboro

80

EASTWOOD FIELD

VERNON'S CAFE

71

77

Stow

Kent

Ravenna

Niles

Girard

80

Cuyahoga Falls

Michael J Kirwan Reservoir

SEE "YOUNGSTOWN" MAP

Youngstown

STAN HYWET HALL AND GARDENS

Tallmadge

76

Austintown

BUTLER INSTITUTE OF AMERICAN ART

Akron

SEE "AKRON" MAP

224

Mill Creek Park

Struthers

Boardman

76

Wadsworth

Barberton

Berlin Lake

PIER 619

New Franklin

Green

AKRON-CANTON AIRPORT

Alliance

SEBRING MANSION AND SPA

Salem

Canal Fulton

North Canton

62

Orrville

MCKINLEY NATIONAL MEMORIAL AND PRESIDENTIAL LIBRARY AND MUSEUM

PRO FOOTBALL HALL OF FAME

Beech Creek Botanical Garden & Nature Preserve

30

Massillon

Canton

SEE "CANTON" MAP

J M SMUCKER CO STORE & CAFE

Perry Heights

154

250

Navarre

77

0   10 mi

0   10 km

© MOON.COM

the Detroit of the rubber industry for decades, with the four largest companies all headquartered in the city. The co-founder of Goodyear Tire and Rubber Company, F. A. Seiberling, built the Stan Hywet Hall and Gardens, today one of the largest houses in the United States open to the public. A meeting in a sweltering car showroom in Canton led to the birth of the National Football League, today one of the most lucrative sports leagues on the planet. President William McKinley was born in Niles near Youngstown and lived in Canton; McKinley's assassination paved the way to his vice president Theodore Roosevelt's presidency. Though it's tempting to label this region "basically Cleveland," the people of Northeast Ohio have carved their own niche in the state's, and the country's, history.

PLANNING YOUR TIME

Akron, Canton, and Youngstown are all good for a day or two each—Stan Hywet, the Pro Football Hall of Fame, and the Butler Institute of Art are the only attractions that demand more than an hour or two of your time. Akron is best situated for a longer stay, with Cuyahoga Valley National Park to the north and Canton to the south for excursions. The national park doesn't take more than a weekend to see, and even a day trip might suffice for those uninterested in long hikes.

Geneva-on-the-Lake and the surrounding wine country are best suited for leisurely meanderings. Three or four days would allow time for ample relaxation and some winery-hopping or covered bridge exploration. Bear in mind that this part of Ohio is part of the snow belt; due to its position east of Lake Erie, it gets much more snow than the rest of the state.

A popular resort, Geneva-on-the-Lake fills up fast in summer; book months in advance and prepare for higher rates Memorial Day-Labor Day. Otherwise, you shouldn't have much trouble booking hotels in this region except during large events such as Canton's Pro Football Hall of Fame Enshrinement Festival in August.

Cuyahoga Valley National Park Region

It may seem odd to find a national park in the middle of a metropolitan area. In the 1960s, with the polluted Cuyahoga River on fire upstream and urban sprawl encroaching on the land between Cleveland and Akron, locals sought to preserve the rural valley and the history within—most notably the remnants of the Ohio & Erie Canal. In 1974, President Gerald Ford signed into existence the Cuyahoga Valley National Recreation Area, which was upgraded to a national park in 2000.

What you get, then, is a markedly different experience than at most national parks. Cuyahoga Valley National Park intermingles with small towns and farms, even a major outdoor music venue. There are also miniature gorges, leafy woodland trails, waterfalls, and rock features, all within an easy drive from Cleveland, Akron, and Canton. The combination is an altogether pleasing mix of wilderness, history, and culture. It's really a recreational paradise, with ample options to hike, bike, and paddle. The park's wilderness is supplemented by contiguous metro parks, offering more opportunities to enjoy the outdoors. The centrally located town of **Peninsula** is a hub for visitors, with food, rentals, and a visitors center.

Previous: Stan Hywet Hall and Gardens in Akron; Ledges loop trail in Cuyahoga Valley National Park; Mechanicsville Covered Bridge in Ashtabula County.

Cuyahoga Valley National Park Region

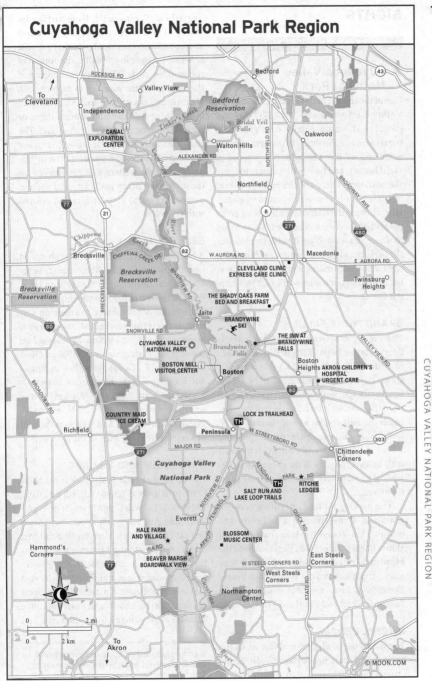

SIGHTS

★ Cuyahoga Valley National Park

One of the smaller national parks, **Cuyahoga Valley National Park** (330/657-2752, nps. gov/cuva, dawn-dusk daily, free) protects a rural corner of Northeast Ohio teeming with woodland wildlife and songbirds, steeped in canal history, and flush with excuses to enjoy the outdoors. There are 125 miles (201 km) of hiking trails that lead visitors to waterfalls, cliffs, and wetlands. With several entry points and a network of roads, it's easy to get to where you want to go. It's also free to enter the park. Bear in mind the area's rolling hills, tall trees, and winding roads if you're driving in low light or winter—this isn't pancake-flat Ohio.

BRANDYWINE FALLS

The most picturesque spot in the park is **Brandywine Falls** (8176 Brandywine Rd., Northfield). This 60-foot (18.3-m) waterfall is Ohio's tallest and is easily accessed by a short boardwalk (partially wheelchair-accessible) from the parking lot. The angled rock underneath the falls creates a lovely bridal veil effect, making this a popular photo spot. The 1.5-mile (2.4-km) **Brandywine Gorge loop trail** follows the edge of the gorge before descending to the creek, a moderate, hilly effort for hikers.

The parking lot tends to fill up between 10am and 4pm—consider a moderate 3.8-mile (6.1-km) round-trip hike from Stanford House (6093 Stanford Rd., Peninsula) via the **Stanford Trail** or a moderate 5-mile (8-km) round-trip hike from the Boston Mill Visitor Center (6947 Riverview Rd., Peninsula) via the **Towpath Trail** and **Stanford Trail.**

RITCHIE LEDGES

The most spectacular natural feature in the park other than Brandywine Falls is the crumbling cliffs of the **Ritchie Ledges** (405 Truxell Rd., Peninsula). A large parking lot and open field (perfect for a game of frisbee) sit atop a plateau encircled by the easy 1.8-mile (2.9-km) **Ledges loop trail** at the bottom of the wooded cliffs. The northeast corner of the loop trail is the most fun to explore, with gigantic chunks of bare rock that tumbled off the ledge (you can hike around them, or scramble among them at your own risk). The cliffs are a little more put together, but no less impressive, as the trail wanders directly underneath on the western side. An overlook on the southwest corner, easily accessed without descending to the loop trail, is best enjoyed with fall colors.

BEAVER MARSH

A brief, easy walk, the **Beaver Marsh** sits on land that was once an auto mechanic's shop. The site was cleaned up in the 1980s and beavers did the rest of the heavy lifting, building dams that restored the land to a teeming wetland. Today it's a diverse marsh, with beavers, otters, muskrats, and waterfowl observed on the regular. Park at the Ira Trailhead (3801 Riverview Rd., Cuyahoga Falls) and head north on the crushed limestone **Towpath Trail** for about 0.25 mile (0.4 km) to the wheelchair-accessible **wetland boardwalk.** Watch out for joggers and bikers on the trail by keeping far to the right of the path.

HALE FARM AND VILLAGE

On the southern end of the park is the **Hale Farm and Village** (2686 Oak Hill Rd., Bath, 330/666-3711, wrhs.org, 10am-5pm Wed.-Sun. June-Aug., 10am-5pm Sat.-Sun. Sept.-Oct., $12 adults, $6 children, free for children 2 and under), a living history museum featuring an 1825 homestead, working farm, and re-created village comprised of relocated historic buildings. Costumed interpreters demonstrate chores and craftwork, live animals lend authenticity to the farm, and

---

1: Ledges loop trail in Cuyahoga Valley National Park **2:** Worden's Ledges in Hinckley Reservation **3:** Brandywine Falls in Cuyahoga Valley National Park

events throughout the year add more activity to the historic site. Café 1810 serves light lunch options as well as beer and wine. The Marketplace sells handcrafted items such as pottery, apparel, and home decor from over 40 Ohio artists.

Cuyahoga Valley Scenic Railroad

An alternative way to experience the national park is via the **Cuyahoga Valley Scenic Railroad** (330/439-5708, cvsr.org, $15-60 pp). Scenic tours, murder mystery dinners, beer tastings, and other themed tours on historic railcars leave from three different stations between Independence and Akron, journeying down the spine of the national park. Five additional stops along the route allow cyclists to board by waving both their arms in the air. A Bike Aboard fee ($5 one-way) allows you to stow your bike on the train, and the Coach All-Day Pass ($20 adults, $15 children) allows on- and off-boarding privileges. Round-trip rides are 2.5-3.5 hours, depending on the season. Though the railroad connects the visitor centers and towns of the national park, most of the popular hiking trails are not along the route.

ENTERTAINMENT AND EVENTS
The Arts

At the south end of the national park, **Blossom Music Center** (1145 W. Steels Corners Rd., Cuyahoga Falls, 330/920-8040, clevelandamphiteater.com) is Northeast Ohio's marquee outdoor music venue. The pavilion seats 5,700, with space for an additional 13,000 fans on the lawn behind. On top of big-name musical guests, the center is the summer home of the Cleveland Orchestra.

RECREATION
Hiking

Cuyahoga Valley National Park offers 125 miles (201 km) of hiking trails. In addition to the trails at popular sights Brandywine Falls, the Ritchie Ledges, and the Beaver Marsh,

suggested trails include the combined **Salt Run and Lake Loop Trails** at the Kendall Lake Shelter (1000 Truxell Rd., Peninsula), a good workout at just over 4 miles (6.4 km) total, consisting of 1 easy mile (1.6 km) with lake views and 3 miles (4.8 km) of significant up-and-down terrain through woods, and **Blue Hen Falls,** a moderate, 4-mile (6.4-km) round-trip from the Boston Mill Visitor Center (6947 Riverview Rd., Peninsula) through the woods to one of the more tranquil corners of the park, with a steep hill down to a 15-foot (4.6-m) waterfall at the end.

Several metro parks and reservations abut the national park, making it tricky to discern when you're in land operated by the National Park Service and when you're not. Along the northern borders of the national park, the steep-walled Tinkers Creek Gorge in **Bedford Reservation** (18753 Egbert Rd., Bedford, 216/635-3200, clevelandmetroparks.com) prevented loggers from cutting down the trees, leaving a more mature forest than most in Ohio. The hike to lovely **Bridal Veil Falls** is a fairly easy out-and-back, 0.4 mile (0.6 km) one-way, with some wooden stairs. The trailhead is on the opposite side of Gorge Parkway from the parking lot.

Farther afield, due west of the national park but worth a side trip, is **Hinckley Reservation** (432 Bellus Rd., Hinckley, 330/278-2160, clevelandmetroparks.com). The 1-mile (1.6-km) **Whipp's Ledges loop trail** is similar to Cuyahoga Valley's Ledges trail, with bluffs and rock formations to explore. The moderately difficult trail can be reached via either the Whipp's Ledges or Top O'Ledges picnic areas. Another interesting feature is the 0.7-mile (1.1-km) **Worden's Ledges loop trail.** Local bricklayer Noble Stuart carved folk art into the cliff faces on this trail in the 1940s. There is some mild downhill hiking from the trailhead off Ledge Road, which is located on the southern border of the park.

Cycling

Century Cycles (1621 Main St., Peninsula, 330/657-2209, centurycycles.com) offers bike

Ohio & Erie Canal Towpath Trail

From 1827 to 1913, mules tugged canal boats along the Ohio & Erie Canal via a towpath parallel to the canal. Today, the recreational **Ohio & Erie Canal Towpath Trail** (ohioanderiecanalway.com) follows most of the original path, starting in Cleveland, running through the length of Cuyahoga Valley National Park, continuing on through Akron and Stark County, and concluding at the Tuscarawas County border. Made of crushed limestone, asphalt, or other paved materials depending on the location, the flat, 87-mile (140-km) multiuse trail can be accessed via 50 trailheads. Connections to other bike trails, part of the larger Ohio & Erie Canalway National Heritage Area system, link to Downtown Cleveland to the north and New Philadelphia to the south. Portions of the Towpath Trail are used as a bridle trail, but the path is primarily frequented by cyclists, joggers, and hikers. It passes by quaint towns, breweries, parks, and idyllic scenery.

Ohio & Erie Canal Towpath Trail

- The house used in the film *A Christmas Story* (3159 W. 11th St., Cleveland) is one block off the trail and is now a museum.

- The town of **Peninsula** is one of the best places in Cuyahoga Valley National Park to rent a bike, grab a bite to eat, or hop on the Cuyahoga Valley Scenic Railroad.

- The **Beaver Marsh** in Cuyahoga Valley National Park is right on the path, with a boardwalk running through the middle of a pristine wetland.

- The **Lock 15 Brewing Company** (21 W. North St., Akron) brewpub is right across the North Street bridge from the towpath.

- **Lock 3 Park** (200 S. Main St., Akron) in downtown Akron is the site of frequent live concerts and festivals.

- The Canton suburb of **Canal Fulton** is a preserved canal town with shops, restaurants, and the *St. Helena III* canal boat ride.

- The trail skirts downtown Massillon, with the **Massillon Museum** (121 Lincoln Way, Massillon) four blocks away from the trail.

rentals. It's located near the Lock 29 Trailhead of the Ohio & Erie Canal Towpath Trail and right off the Peninsula Depot train stop.

Kayaking, Canoeing, and Paddleboarding

The Cuyahoga River flows through the national park. It is not open to commercial use, but you can bring your own equipment and paddle at your own risk. There are five access points within the park, including the Lock 29 Trailhead (1648 Mill St. W., Peninsula) and

next to the Boston Mill Visitor Center (6947 Riverview Rd., Peninsula).

Skiing

A five-minute drive separates **Boston Mills** and **Brandywine ski resorts** (bmbw.com), sister resorts within the national park. Boston Mills (7100 Riverview Rd., Peninsula, 800/875-4241) is the more advanced of the two, with the steepest slopes in Ohio. Brandywine (1146 W. Highland Rd, Northfield) caters to a younger crowd, with snowboarding and tubing. Between the two resorts, there are 18 ski trails. Lift tickets and passes are valid at both resorts and start at $49.

FOOD

The little town of Peninsula is centrally located within the park and has a couple of places where you can grab a bite to eat. Bustling **Fisher's Café and Pub** (1607 Main St., Peninsula, 330/657-2651, fisherscafe. com, 11am-10pm Mon.-Thurs., 11am-11pm Fri., 8am-11pm Sat., 8am-10pm Sun., $9-16) has a homey interior, a large patio, and an American menu.

Across the street from Fisher's is a larger patio belonging to **Winking Lizard Tavern** (1615 Main St., Peninsula, 330/467-1002, winkinglizard.com, 11am-11pm Sun.-Thurs., 11am-midnight Fri.-Sat., $6-14). This Northeast Ohio chain has standard pub food—wings, burgers, wraps—as well as 26 beers on tap and dozens more available by the bottle.

Just west of Peninsula and the park borders, **Country Maid Ice Cream** (3252 Streetsboro Rd., Richfield, 330/659-6830, countrymaidicecream.com) has been making small-batch ice cream on-site since 1948. The ingredients are local, the ice cream is fresh, and the atmosphere is down-to-earth.

The national park is surrounded on most sides by suburbia; if you're game to drive outside the park for a meal, there are a variety of options in Cuyahoga Falls, Hudson, and Brecksville.

ACCOMMODATIONS

The suburb of Northfield, northeast of the park, features a handful of bed-and-breakfast options.

The Inn at Brandywine Falls (8230 Brandywine Rd., Northfield, 330/467-1812, innatbrandywinefalls.com, $175-300) is a historic, well-appointed bed-and-breakfast steps away from Brandywine Falls. The farmhouse in which it resides dates back to 1848.

The Shady Oaks Farm Bed and Breakfast (241 W. Highland Rd., Northfield, 330/468-2909, shadyoaksfarmbnb.com,

$154-189) is a colonial-style mansion with four suites appointed with antiques and period re-creations. The grounds are separated from neighbors by horse pastures and woods.

INFORMATION AND SERVICES

There are two primary visitors centers, the largest and most centrally located being the **Boston Mill Visitor Center** (6947 Riverview Rd., Peninsula, 440/717-3890, 10am-4pm daily). The second, the **Canal Exploration Center** (7104 Canal Rd., Valley View, 10am-4pm daily Memorial Day-Labor Day, 10am-4pm Sat.-Sun. early May-Memorial Day and Labor Day-Nov.), operates north of the park. The Cuyahoga Valley Scenic Railroad operates the **Peninsula Depot** (1630 Mill St., Peninsula, 330/439-5708, 9am-4pm daily) in the middle of the park and is another good spot to get information.

There are several urgent care facilities around the park, including a **Cleveland Clinic Express Care** (8210 Macedonia Commons Blvd., Ste. 40, Macedonia, 330/468-0190, 8am-8pm Mon.-Fri., 8am-4pm Sat.-Sun.) and an **Akron Children's Hospital Urgent Care** (328 E. Hines Hill Rd., Hudson, 2pm-9:30pm Mon.-Fri., 10am-5:30pm Sat.-Sun.). The nearest full-service hospital is **Western Reserve Hospital** (1900 23rd St., Cuyahoga Falls, 330/971-7000).

TRANSPORTATION

Because of the park's size, distances and time are relative. From Columbus, centrally located Peninsula is a nearly two-hour drive (128 mi/206 km) northeast up I-71 and I-271. From Downtown Cleveland, it's a 30-minute drive (23 mi/37 km) south down I-77. From Akron, it's a 25-minute drive (16 mi/26 km) north up SR 8 to SR 303, or through the park on Riverview Road. From Canton, it's a 45-minute drive (37 mi/60 km) north on I-77 to SR 8 to SR 303.

The best way to get around within the park is by car, bike, or the Cuyahoga Valley Scenic Railroad (cvsr.org).

Akron and Vicinity

"The Rubber Capital of the World" was the fastest-growing city in the United States in the early 20th century, powered by 25 rubber companies producing untold amounts of rubber for tires, flooring, airplane parts, and more. The city was also the site of the 1851 Women's Convention, during which Sojourner Truth gave her now famous "Ain't I a Woman?" speech (a historical marker at the United Way of Summit County's entrance at 37 N. High Street identifies the spot). Unexpectedly hilly, Ohio's fifth-largest city is still home to the Goodyear Tire and Rubber Company and surprises with an urbane downtown district and the stunning Stan Hywet estate.

With Cuyahoga Valley National Park just north of town (you can take a train there from downtown, in fact) and Canton 30 minutes south, Akron is an ideal place from which to explore this corner of Northeast Ohio.

SIGHTS

★ Stan Hywet Hall and Gardens

To get an idea of the money flowing through Akron during its time as the Rubber Capital of the World, spend time at the astounding 70-acre **Stan Hywet Hall and Gardens** (714 N. Portage Path, 330/836-5533, stanhywet.org, 10am-6pm Tues.-Sun. Apr.-Nov., limited hours Dec., self-guided tour $15 adults, $6 children 6-17). This immaculate Tudor Revival mansion and estate was constructed between 1912 and 1915 and belonged to F. A. Seiberling, cofounder of the Goodyear Tire and Rubber Company, and his wife, Gertrude. At its peak, Stan Hywet (named after the Old English term for "stone quarry" and pronounced HEE-wit) employed 20 domestic and 12 estate employees and was at the forefront of modern home conveniences. Today, it remains one of the largest houses in the United States and is the sixth largest of those open to the public.

A standard self-guided tour grants you access to the house as well as the grounds, which include expansive gardens, lagoons, a conservatory, and the Gate Lodge, inside which F. A. and Gertrude's daughter-in-law conducted the earliest incarnations of Alcoholics Anonymous. Interpretive placards are found inside the mansion, and friendly and informative volunteers are on standby to answer your questions about the 65-room building, which includes 18 luxurious bedrooms, 23 fireplaces, 23 bathrooms, and an opulent 2,700-square-foot (251-sq-m) music room; 98 percent of the furnishings and items on display in the house are authentic to the Seiberling family. Plan to spend half a day wandering the grounds. Fans of the hit show *Downton Abbey* may want to budget more time to soak in the U.S. equivalent of a similar lifestyle.

In-depth guided tours (prices vary) are available for interested parties, and there's a busy calendar of special events and holiday activities. All tours start at the carriage house, which now operates as the admissions and visitors center. Molly's Shop and Café serves light sandwiches, coffee, and snacks, with patio and picnic tables outside in view of the house.

Akron Zoo

In a state with several world-class zoos, little **Akron Zoo** (500 Edgewood Ave., 330/375-2550, akronzoo.org, 10am-5pm daily Apr.-Oct., 11am-4pm daily Nov.-Mar., $13 adults, $11 seniors, $10 children) struggles to stand out. That's not to say this hillside zoo is without its charms. The exhibits are quite good, in fact, just smaller-scaled. There's a bit of everything, with a particularly strong collection of North American animals including injured bald eagles that will perch inches away from the exhibit's glass. Visitors can slip down a see-through slide in the middle of the river otter exhibit, allowing them to briefly pass through a watery, otter-y world without

Akron

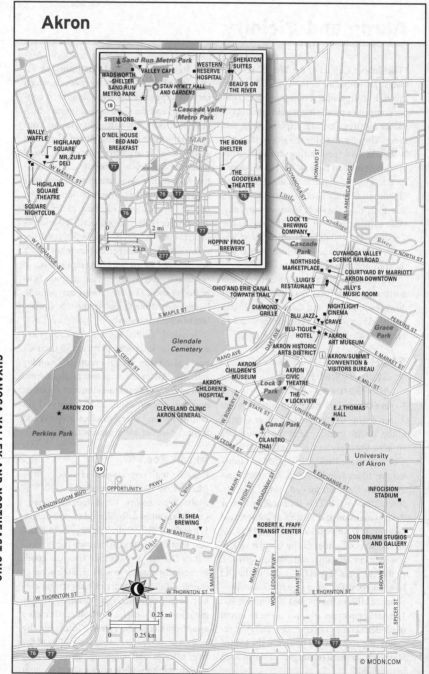

Sand Run Metro Park

SHERATON SUITES

WESTERN RESERVE HOSPITAL

VALLEY CAFÉ

WADSWORTH SHELTER SAND RUN METRO PARK

BEAU'S ON THE RIVER

STAN HYWET HALL AND GARDENS

18

SWENSONS

Cascade Valley Metro Park

O'NEIL HOUSE BED AND BREAKFAST

WALLY WAFFLE

HIGHLAND SQUARE

MR. ZUB'S DELI

MAP AREA

THE BOMB SHELTER

77

W MARKET ST

HIGHLAND SQUARE THEATRE

76

77

THE GOODYEAR THEATER

SQUARE NIGHTCLUB

76

77

0   2 mi

0   2 km

277

HOPPIN' FROG BREWERY

W EXCHANGE ST

HOWARD ST

CUYAHOGA ST

ALL-AMERICA BRIDGE

Little

Cuyahoga

River   E NORTH ST

LOCK 15 BREWING COMPANY

Cascade Park

CUYAHOGA VALLEY SCENIC RAILROAD

NORTHSIDE MARKETPLACE

COURTYARD BY MARRIOTT AKRON DOWNTOWN

LUIGI'S RESTAURANT

JILLY'S MUSIC ROOM

OHIO AND ERIE CANAL TOWPATH TRAIL

S MAPLE ST

PERKINS ST

DIAMOND GRILLE

NIGHTLIGHT CINEMA

BLU JAZZ+

CRAVE

BLU-TIQUE HOTEL

AKRON ART MUSEUM

Grace Park

Glendale Cemetery

DART AVE

RAND AVE

AKRON HISTORIC ARTS DISTRICT

E MARKET ST

AKRON/SUMMIT CONVENTION & VISITORS BUREAU

W CEDAR ST

AKRON CHILDREN'S MUSEUM

Lock 3 Park

AKRON CIVIC THEATRE

E MILL ST

AKRON ZOO

AKRON CHILDREN'S HOSPITAL

CLEVELAND CLINIC AKRON GENERAL

W BOWERY ST

W STATE ST

THE LOCKVIEW

E.J. THOMAS HALL

UNIVERSITY AVE

Perkins Park

Canal Park

W CEDAR ST

CILANTRO THAI

University of Akron

E EXCHANGE ST

59

OPPORTUNITY PKWY

S MAIN ST

S HIGH ST

S BROADWAY ST

INFOCISION STADIUM

VERNON ODOM BLVD

Ohio and Erie Canal

R. SHEA BREWING

ROBERT K. PFAFF TRANSIT CENTER

DON DRUMM STUDIOS AND GALLERY

W BARTGES ST

MIAMI ST

WOLF LEDGES PKWY

GRANT ST

BROWN ST

SPICER ST

W THORNTON ST

W THORNTON ST

S MAIN ST

E THORNTON ST

0   0.25 mi

0   0.25 km

76

77

76   77

© MOON.COM

getting wet. In 2021, Wild Asia opened, with Sumatran tigers, red pandas, and gibbons. Be prepared to walk uphill for half of your time at the zoo, then downhill the rest. Parking is $3.

Akron Art Museum

Specializing in contemporary and modern art, the **Akron Art Museum** (1 S. High St., 330/376-9185, akronartmuseum.org, 11am-5pm Tues.-Wed. and Fri.-Sun., 11am-9pm Thurs., $12 adults, $10 seniors, $8 students, free for children 17 and under) is divided into two buildings: The small, 1899 Italian Renaissance Revival building holds the modern collection, including examples of American impressionism, and the postmodern John S. and James L. Knight Building, which tripled the size of the museum, holds large gallery spaces for the contemporary collection. There's a small gift shop and a café with light lunch options, beer, and wine. Admission on Thursdays is free, in conjunction with the museum's Downtown@Dusk summer concert series, which is also free.

Akron Children's Museum

In the middle of a rejuvenated corner of downtown is the **Akron Children's Museum** (216 S. Main St., 330/396-6103, akronkids.org, 10am-4pm Tues.-Fri., 10am-5pm Sat.-Sun., $5 adults and children, free for infants under 12 months). Catering to small children, this little museum might be better thought of as an inexpensive, interactive assortment of play stations, with plenty of hands-on activities and opportunities for creativity. Park in the State Street parking lot (51 W. State St.) and bring your ticket to get validated.

Kent State University

In the suburb of Kent, 14 miles (22.5 km) northeast of the city, is the university notoriously associated with the May 4 massacre in 1970, when the Ohio National Guard opened fire on students protesting the escalating Vietnam War, killing four. A memorial plaza and garden is on the campus's main quad, commemorating the tragic moment in U.S. history. Steps away is the **May 4 Visitors Center** (300 Midway Dr., Kent, 330/672-4660, kent.edu/may4visitorscenter, 9am-5pm Mon.-Fri., noon-5pm Sat., free), which you can visit when the school is open. Its small exhibit reverentially interprets what happened that day, with photographs, contextual artifacts, and information depicting the events surrounding the shooting. There are designated visitors center parking spots in the Taylor-Prentice Hall lot.

In a completely different realm is the **Kent State University Museum** (515 Hilltop Dr., Kent, 330/672-3450, kent.edu/museum, 11am-5pm Tues.-Sat., noon-4pm Sun., $6 adults, $5 seniors, $4 ages 5-18), which holds a respected collection of decorative arts, fashion, and period clothing dating back to the 18th century.

ENTERTAINMENT AND EVENTS

The Arts

Lock 3 Park (200 S. Main St., 330/375-2877, lock3live.com) utilizes its canal-side greenery as an outdoor amphitheater. Next door, the unusually medieval **Akron Civic Theatre** (182 S. Main St., 330/253-2488, akroncivic.com) is a former movie palace that hosts touring shows and concerts. The **Akron Symphony Orchestra** (akronsymphony.org) performs at the University of Akron's **E. J. Thomas Hall** (198 Hill St., 330/972-7570, uakron.edu/ej). The **Goodyear Theater** (1201 E. Market St., 330/690-2307, goodyeartheater.com) occupies a formerly private theater space used by Goodyear employees at the company's headquarters and hosts traveling rock acts.

The **Nightlight Cinema** (30 N. High St., 330/252-5782, nightlightcinema.com) is a small, non-profit cinema near the art museum that shows independent, foreign, and cult films and organizes discussions and film festival screenings. It has a small but well-stocked bar. The **Highland Square Theatre** (826 W. Market St., 330/253-0100, highlandsquaretheatre.com) opened in 1938 and shows more conventional fare. Tickets are $5 and the

concessions stand serves the usual fare, plus beer and wine.

Festivals and Events

Rib, White and Blue (downtownakron.com) attracts barbecue competitors and consumers over the Independence Day weekend and includes a fireworks display. The **All-American Soapbox Derby** (soapboxderby.org) holds its week-long world championships in mid-July.

RECREATION
Cycling

The **Ohio & Erie Canal Towpath Trail** (ohioanderiecanalway.com) runs straight through the center of town, connecting Akron to the national park and Cleveland to the north and Canton to the south. Bike rental shops in town are few and far between; best to bring your own.

Kayaking, Canoeing, and Paddleboarding

Pier 619 (399 Stutz Ave., 330/644-9704, pier619.com) and **Dusty's Landing** (401 W. Turkeyfoot Lake Rd., 330/644-3220, dustyslanding.com) offer pontoon, kayak, and paddleboard rentals for the small Portage Lakes region south of the city.

Hiking

Besides nearby Cuyahoga Valley National Park, there are some decent metro parks closer to town. **Cascade Valley Metro Park** (837 Cuyahoga St., 330/867-5511, summitmetroparks.org/cascade-valley-metro-park) hugs the Cuyahoga River north of town with attractive overlooks and hiking trails. The ravines and wetlands of nearby **Sand Run Metro Park** (330/867-5511, summitmetroparks.org/sand-run-metro-park) harbor rare plant and amphibian species. There are several trailheads to the hilly trails; one is at the centrally located Wadsworth shelter (1440 Sand Run Pkwy.).

1: Akron Art Museum **2:** Stan Hywet Hall and Gardens

Spectator Sports

The **Akron RubberDucks** (milb.com/akron) are the AA-affiliate of the Cleveland Guardians and play baseball at the downtown **Canal Park** (300 S. Main St., 330/253-5153). The **University of Akron Zips** (gozips.com) compete in the Division I Mid-Atlantic Conference. The university supports a number of men's and women's sports programs, the largest being the football Zips who play at **InfoCision Stadium** (375 Exchange St.).

SHOPPING

The **Northside Marketplace** (21 Furnace St., 234/542-6627, northsidemarketplace.com) is an urban incubator of dozens of local shops and brands. Put your Akron pride on at **Rubber City Clothing** (330/434-4722, noon-6pm Tues.-Sat.), which carries unique Akron-related apparel and accessories. You'll also find quirky designs that capture the latest cultural or political zeitgeist. Or check out the latest in streetwear at **7th Floor Clothing** (234/542-6627, 11:30am-6:30pm Tues.-Sat.), whose first big fan was none other than the hometown King himself: LeBron James. The clothing line has been featured in national publications such as *Inc. Magazine* and the *New York Times*.

Not your average antique store, **The Bomb Shelter** (923 Bank St., 330/258-0088, 11am-5pm Mon.-Sat.) specializes in mid-century modern furniture, home accessories, vintage clothing, and other relics of the past.

Don Drumm Studios and Gallery (437 Crouse St., 330/253-6268, 10am-6pm Mon.-Fri., 10am-5pm Sat.) offers an impressive array of handcrafted metalworks, ceramics, glass, and other artwork and home decor pieces by Drumm as well as a curated list of artists.

FOOD
Central Akron

Everyone raves about the Arts District's ★ **Crave** (57 E. Market St., 330/253-1234, eatdrinkcrave.com, 11am-10pm Mon.-Thurs., 11am-11pm Fri., 5pm-11pm Sat., $11-30), a trendy American restaurant with a classy vibe, well-stocked bar, and diverse menu lineup. The kitchen is especially well-known for its gouda mac and cheese.

Cilantro Thai (326 S. Main St., 330/434-2876, cilantrothai.com, 11am-2:30pm and 5pm-9:30pm Mon.-Thurs., 11am-2:30pm and 5pm-10pm Fri., 4:30pm-10pm Sat., $10-23) is equal parts upscale Thai and Japanese cuisine, with noodles, fried rice, ramen, and an extensive sushi menu. This bright, contemporary spot is next door to the baseball stadium.

The Lockview (207 S. Main St., 330/252-5128, thelockview.com, 11am-midnight Mon.-Wed., 11am-1am Thurs.-Fri., noon-2am Sat., 4pm-2am Sun., $7-11) specializes in gourmet grilled cheese sandwiches. There's an eclectic craft beer draft list and a rooftop patio, though there's not much to see.

Diamond Grille (77 W. Market St., 330/253-0041, diamondgrille.com, 11am-10pm Mon.-Thurs., 11am-11pm Fri., 5pm-11pm Sat., $28-47) has been one of Akron's go-to white-tablecloth establishments since the Roosevelt administration. The unassuming exterior and vibe is a bit understated given the prices on the steak and seafood menu.

Luigi's Restaurant (105 N. Main St., 330/253-2999, luigisrestaurant.com, 11am-midnight Mon.-Thurs., 11am-2am Fri., 3pm-2am Sat., 3pm-midnight Sun., $6-12), near the Arts District, has been an Akron favorite since 1949, serving Italian American dishes in a lively, down-to-earth atmosphere. The main draws are the pizza and spaghetti; subs, pasta dishes, and salads round out the menu. Prices on the lunch menu are hard to beat. The place is cash only, but there's an ATM inside.

Famous for a signature Galley Boy burger that features special barbecue and mayo-based sauces, local drive-in chain **Swenson's** (40 S. Hawkins Ave., 330/864-8416, swensonsdriveins.com, 11am-1am Sun.-Thurs., 11am-1:30am Fri.-Sat., $6-10) began life in 1934 at this Hawkins Avenue location and has since expanded into the Cleveland, Canton, and Columbus markets.

Find a parking spot, turn on your headlights to grab a car hop's attention, and wait for your order in your car.

Belgian waffles and waffle sandwiches are the highlights at Highland Square's **Wally Waffle** (845 W. Market St., 330/374-4915, wallywaffle.com, 7am-3pm Mon.-Fri., 7am-4pm Sat.-Sun., $6-11), a contemporary space full of happy people enjoying breakfast, even if when it's not morning. There are three locations throughout Akron's northern environs, but this one is closest to the center of town.

Need some late-night grub? Highland Square's **Mr. Zub's Deli** (795 W. Market St., 330/252-0272, mrzubs.com, 11am-3am Mon.-Sat., 11am-2am Sun., $6-12) has a lengthy list of sandwich options in addition to pizza and wings. They don't skimp on the portions, and there are 20 beers on tap.

Around Akron

Brightly colored **Valley Café** (1212 Weathervane Ln., 330/865-0101, valley-cafe.com, 8am-2pm Tues.-Fri., 8am-3pm Sat.-Sun., $6-12) prides itself on its family ownership and friendly atmosphere, serving up dishes described as "diner food with a gourmet twist and a hint of southern roots." Breakfast and lunch are served during all hours.

The northern suburb of Cuyahoga Falls has a number of noteworthy restaurants, with a central business district hugging the edge of the Cuyahoga River. **Beau's on the River** (1989 Front St., Cuyahoga Falls, 330/920-7530, beausontheriver.com, 4pm-11pm Tues.-Fri., 8am-11am and 4pm-11pm Sat., 8am-1pm Sun., $12-39) has floor-to-ceiling windows and overlooks a cascading stretch of the river (ask for a view when making reservations). The American menu includes steaks, seafood, and a handful of sandwiches that offer a more affordable option. The restaurant is inside a Sheraton Suites hotel and puts on a mean Sunday brunch (11am-1pm).

If you find yourself out in Kent, northeast of the city, check out **Mike's Place** (1700 S.

Water St., Kent, 330/673-6501, mikesplaceres-taurant.com, 7am-9pm daily, $7-19). A Star Wars X-wing replica beckons visitors from the parking lot into this quirky restaurant that also features a castle, a painted bus, and memorabilia-packed walls. The menu, with about every imaginable American staple, is as resistant to a theme as the restaurant.

BARS AND NIGHTLIFE

The taproom at Canal Place's **R. Shea Brewing** (540 S. Main St., 234/571-5036, rsheabrewing.com, 11am-9pm Tues.-Thurs., 11am-11pm Fri.-Sat., 11am-8pm Sun.) over-looks the production facility, allowing you to sip as you watch the brewers hard at work. The food menu focuses on burgers and pizza.

Just off the Ohio & Erie Towpath Trail is **Lock 15 Brewing Company** (21 W. North St., 234/900-8277, lock15brewing.com, 11am-10pm Tues.-Thurs., 11am-11pm Fri.-Sat., 11am-9pm Sun.). This family-friendly brew-ery keeps a good variety of beer on tap year-round and offers a food menu that straddles the line between the usual grill options and a more upscale surf-and-turf selection.

It's a bit of an outlier distance-wise, but **Hoppin' Frog Brewery** (1680 E. Waterloo Rd., 330/352-4578, hoppinfrog.com, 5pm-10pm Mon., 11am-10pm Tues.-Wed., 11am-11pm Thurs.-Sat.) southeast of town receives some of the best beer ratings in the area. This popular brewery is especially known for its stouts and beer shakes, and the small food menu ditches the typical brewpub fare for vegetarian-friendly shareables and a small helping of salads and sandwiches.

Jilly's Music Room (111 N. Main St., 330/576-3757, jillysmusicroom.com, 5pm-close Wed.-Thurs., 5pm-1am Fri., 11am-1am Sat., 11am-3pm Sun.), just north of the Arts District, is an intimate live music and perfor-mance space showcasing a wide variety of acts. It has a full-service bar stocked with over 100 beers and a tapas and brunch menu. There's no cover charge unless otherwise noted.

Pull up a seat at the retro **BLU Jazz+** (47 E. Market St., 330/252-1190, blujazzakron.com, 6:30pm-1am Tues.-Sat.) in the Arts District for a low-key evening of jazz. It has a full bar, somewhat industrial ambience, and a small bistro menu.

Square Nightclub (820 W. Market St., 330/374-9661, squarenight.club, 5pm-2:30am daily) in Highland Square is the region's pre-miere LGBTQ club. This contemporary dance club also receives high marks for its karaoke.

ACCOMMODATIONS

There are chain motels scattered through-out the region, primarily in the suburbs. The largest cluster is along the Medina Road exit off of I-77, fairly far west of the center of ac-tion. Stow, due north of town, has an addi-tional cluster off of SR 8 and puts you closer to Cuyahoga Valley National Park.

Located in the Akron Historic Arts District, the **BLU-Tique Hotel** (1 S. Main St., 330/983-4905, blu-tique.com, $169-219) has a mid-century modern vibe and piano bar to complement its sister venue, BLU Jazz+, across the street. Overnight parking is $7.

At the other end of the Arts District, next to the Northside Marketplace, is the **Courtyard by Marriott Akron Downtown** (41 Furnace St., 330/252-9228, marriott.com, $139-159), a contemporary three-star hotel with spacious rooms suited to both business and relaxation.

If you wish to supplement a visit to the grand Stan Hywet estate with a night at a 1920s-era Tudor-style mansion, look for the **O'Neil House Bed and Breakfast** (1290 W. Exchange St., 330/867-2650, oneilhouse.com, $75-200); this house also once belonged to a rubber magnate. It features four guest rooms with period-appropriate furnishings.

The **Sheraton Suites Akron Cuyahoga Falls** (1989 Front St., Cuyahoga Falls, 330/929-3000, marriott.com, $169-249) is perched next to a scenic, rushing portion of the Cuyahoga River in downtown Cuyahoga Falls. There are even better waterfront views from the hotel's restaurant, Beau's on the River. You'll also find an indoor pool with floor-to-ceiling windows. The 212 modern suites are spacious, with separated living rooms and bedrooms.

INFORMATION AND SERVICES

The **Akron/Summit Convention and Visitors Bureau** (77 E. Mill St., 330/374-7560, visitakron.summit.org) is located in the John S. Knight Center.

Cleveland Clinic Akron General (1 Akron General Ave., 330/344-6000) is centrally located, as is **Akron Children's Hospital** (214 W. Bowery St., 330/543-1000). Nearby Tallmadge has two urgent care centers: **UH Akron** (145 West Ave., Tallmadge, 330/633-7090, 9am-8pm Mon.-Fri., 9am-5pm Sat.-Sun.) and **Cleveland Clinic Express Care** (33 North Ave., #104, Tallmadge, 330/344-3990, 8am-8pm Mon.-Fri., 8am-4pm Sat.-Sun.).

TRANSPORTATION
Getting There

Akron is in the middle of a tangle of major highways, accessible via **I-77** from Cleveland, which is 50 minutes (39 mi/63 km) north of Akron, and Canton, 30 minutes (24 mi/39 km) south of Akron. **I-76** crosses the city horizontally, connecting to I-71 to the west for access to Columbus, which is two hours away (125 mi/201 km), and heading east toward Youngstown, 50 minutes away (50 mi/81 km).

Akron-Canton Airport (CAK, 5400 Lauby Rd., North Canton, 888/434-2359, akroncantonairport.com), a reliever airport for Northeast Ohio, is 20 minutes (15 mi/24 km) south of downtown. American Eagle, Delta, Spirit, and United mainly connect to hubs along the eastern United States. Several car rental companies have set up shop in the airport. Additionally, you can grab a rideshare, taxi, or the 110 Akron Metro bus (though stops are infrequent).

Greyhound (greyhound.com), **Barons Bus** (baronsbus.com) and **GoBus** (ridegobus.com) stop at the **Robert K. Pfaff Transit Center** (631 S. Broadway St.) downtown. Tickets are available for purchase on-site.

Getting Around

The **Akron Metro** (akronmetro.org) bus system connects Akron with surrounding suburbs and offers express service to Downtown Cleveland. Fares are $1.25 per ride, or a day pass is $2.50. You can pay on the bus or purchase ahead of time on the EZfare mobile app or at the Robert K. Pfaff Transit Center (631 S. Broadway St.). The **DASH** is the city's free weekday shuttle service that loops around downtown and the University of Akron. The bus stops every 10 minutes 7am-7pm and every 15 minutes 7pm-11pm. Uber also operates in Akron.

The **Cuyahoga Valley Scenic Railroad** (cvsr.org) stops at the **Akron Northside Station** (27 Ridge St.) for journeys into Cuyahoga Valley National Park.

Canton and Vicinity

Though often lumped in with Akron as a region (they even share an airport named Akron-Canton), Canton is technically the center of its own metropolitan area. This former industrial city, like so many in Northeast Ohio, has had to reshape its economy to fit a 21st-century economic landscape. These days, you'll find trendy restaurants alongside old stalwarts in the rebounding downtown area. You'll also find some unique historic sites: the McKinley Presidential Library and Museum and the First Ladies National Historic Site. And of course, as the birthplace of the National Football League, you'll find the massive Pro Football Hall of Fame.

SIGHTS

★ Pro Football Hall of Fame

What better city to put the **Pro Football Hall of Fame** (2121 George Halas Dr. NW, 330/456-8207, profootballhof.com, 9am-8pm daily, $28 adults, $24 seniors, $21 children 6-12) than the birthplace of the National Football League? This expansive museum is both a tribute to the league's greatest players and coaches and a museum covering the game's history, greatest hits, and changing play style, as well as the league's development. Football fans will revel in the memorabilia, including countless jerseys and cleats belonging to big names, footballs from timeless games, and more. Interactive stations allow visitors to learn more about particular moments in NFL history. The Hall of Fame itself is reverential, a large room holding the busts of the inductees over the years. Special exhibits such as the *Game for Life* show—starring a Joe Namath hologram giving a star-studded halftime pep talk in a simulated locker room—are nearly Disney-esque in production quality. Non-fans may find it all overwrought, but there's no denying the seriousness the museum takes in honoring the history of an important element of the nation's culture. A massive gift shop at the end of the tour sells apparel representing all 32 NFL franchises.

The adjacent Johnson Controls Hall of Fame Village is under construction in phases and, when completed, will be a 200-acre sports and entertainment complex with retail, a hotel, and a football-themed waterpark. The completed Tom Benson Hall of Fame Stadium, looming over the museum, is an early phase of the project.

★ McKinley National Memorial and Presidential Library and Museum

Side by side are the **McKinley National Memorial** and the **McKinley Presidential Library and Museum** (800 McKinley Monument Dr., 330/445-7043, mckinleymuseum.org, 9am-4pm Mon.-Sat., noon-4pm Sun., $10 adults, $9 seniors, $8 children). Serving as president from 1897 until his 1901 assassination (which led to vice president Theodore Roosevelt ascending to the nation's highest office), William McKinley helped the United States enter the 20th century as a rising power on the world stage. McKinley made Canton his home, where he built his career in law and politics, and it also serves as his final resting place.

The monument will catch your eye first, an impressive domed mausoleum of granite and marble holding the remains of President McKinley, his wife, Ida, and their daughters. Inside, in the center of the dome, is a 12-foot (3.6-m) red, white, and blue skylight with 45 stars—one for each of the states at the time of McKinley's passing—with the sarcophagi for the president and his wife directly underneath. Free of charge, the monument sits atop a hill; the 108 steps to the top are a popular exercise spot for locals. Sneak your car past the museum to the left to go around the hill to a small parking lot just behind the monument. You can view the outside of the monument

Canton

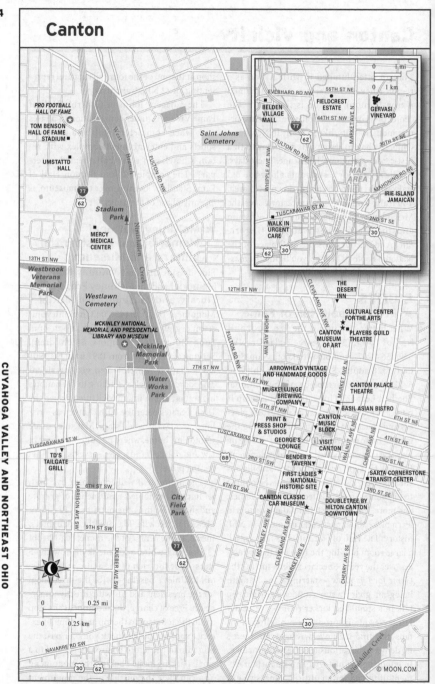

PRO FOOTBALL HALL OF FAME

TOM BENSON HALL OF FAME STADIUM

UMSTATTD HALL

Saint Johns Cemetery

EVERHARD RD NW
55TH ST NE
BELDEN VILLAGE MALL
FIELDCREST ESTATE
GERVASI VINEYARD
44TH ST NW
MARKET AVE N
FULTON RD NW
30TH ST NE
WHIPPLE AVE NW
MAP AREA
MAHONING RD NE
IRIE ISLAND JAMAICAN
TUSCARAWAS ST W
2ND ST SE
WALK IN URGENT CARE

West Branch

FULTON RD NW

Stadium Park

MERCY MEDICAL CENTER

13TH ST NW

Westbrook Veterans Memorial Park

Westlawn Cemetery

Nimishillen Creek

MCKINLEY NATIONAL MEMORIAL AND PRESIDENTIAL LIBRARY AND MUSEUM

Mckinley Memorial Park

12TH ST NW
THE DESERT INN
CLEVELAND AVE NW
CULTURAL CENTER FOR THE ARTS

SHORE AVE NW

FULTON RD NW

CANTON MUSEUM OF ART
PLAYERS GUILD THEATRE

7TH ST NW

Water Works Park

6TH ST NW

ARROWHEAD VINTAGE AND HANDMADE GOODS

MARKET AVE N

CANTON PALACE THEATRE

MUSKELLUNGE BREWING COMPANY

4TH ST NW

BASIL ASIAN BISTRO

6TH ST NE

PRINT & PRESS SHOP & STUDIOS

CANTON MUSIC BLOCK

TUSCARAWAS ST W

GEORGE'S LOUNGE

VISIT CANTON

WALNUT AVE NE

CHERRY AVE NE

4TH ST NE

TUSCARAWAS ST W
88
3RD ST SW

BENDER'S TAVERN

2ND ST NE

TD'S TAILGATE GRILL

FIRST LADIES NATIONAL HISTORIC SITE

SARTA CORNERSTONE TRANSIT CENTER

HARRISON AVE SW

6TH ST SW

City Field Park

CANTON CLASSIC CAR MUSEUM

DOUBLETREE BY HILTON CANTON DOWNTOWN

3RD ST SE

9TH ST SW

McKINLEY AVE SW

CLEVELAND AVE SW

MARKET AVE S

DUEBER AVE SW

77
62

CHERRY AVE SE

0   0.25 mi
0   0.25 km

NAVARRE RD SW

30
62

Nimishillen Creek

© MOON.COM

The Birth of the National Football League

In the early part of the 20th century, professional football was a Wild West of endless bidding wars for players and franchises bleeding cash. Many of the teams were located in small- to mid-size industrial cities in the Midwest, and the college game was more popular than the professional one. Eager to establish a central league to govern the mechanics of the game and the managerial aspects behind the scenes, representatives from area teams came to Canton at the invitation of Ralph Hay, owner of the Canton Bulldogs. The 14 men met at Hay's Hupmobile auto dealership and hammered out the basic outlines for a league, which they called the American Professional Football Association. On September 17, 1920, the deal was made with 32-year-old star Jim Thorpe of the Canton Bulldogs named the league's first president. The first game under league play took place a week later.

The league, and the game, was still quite different from what we know today. Athletes played both offense and defense. The forward pass was a rarity. Teams created their own schedules (and sometimes played college teams). In 1922, the league changed its name to the National Football League, and the professional game gained popularity as the years went on and the gameplay changed. Today, the National Football League is the most watched professional sports league in North America.

any time; the inside is open during museum hours April-November.

The library and museum is a combination McKinley museum, science center, and local history museum. The small Discover World science portion is skippable unless you have children in need of hands-on time, though there is an impressive mastodon skeleton. Elsewhere in the museum, the McKinley Gallery re-creates William and Ida's parlor, with their furniture and personal effects as well as an animatronic Mr. and Mrs. McKinley to welcome you. The highlight is the Street of Shops, a life-size replica of a 19th-century town. Unlike many similar exhibits in other museums, visitors can walk through the shops and really step into the past.

First Ladies National Historic Site

Ohio lays claim to more presidents than almost any other state. It stands to reason, then, that Ohio had a lot of first ladies. The First Ladies National Historic Site (205 Market Ave., 330/452-0876, nps.gov/fila, 9am-4pm Tues.-Sat., free) operates a small education center highlighting the accomplishments of first ladies over the years and displaying a small collection of their personal effects.

The highlight is a tour of the restored Saxton McKinley House, the Victorian family home of first lady Ida Saxton McKinley and also where she and eventual president William McKinley both lived from 1878 to 1891. Tours ($7 adults, $6 seniors, $5 children 17 and under) leave from the education center a short block away from the house and last approximately 45 minutes.

Canton Classic Car Museum

The Canton Classic Car Museum (123 6th St. SW, 330/455-3603, cantonclassiccar.org, 10am-5pm daily, $7.50 adults, $6 seniors, $5 children, $3 children 4 and under) is as much a nostalgia museum as it is a car museum. Over 45 vintage cars are on display, with corresponding ads, posters, antique toys, and other odds and ends from Canton's yesteryear. A gift shop sells model cars and other items in the spirit of the museum.

Canton Museum of Art

The Canton Museum of Art (1001 Market Ave., 330/453-7666, cantonart.org, 10am-8pm Tues.-Thurs., 10am-5pm Fri.-Sat., 1pm-5pm Sun., $8 adults, $6 seniors, free for children 12 and under) focuses on American art from the 19th century to the present, as well as

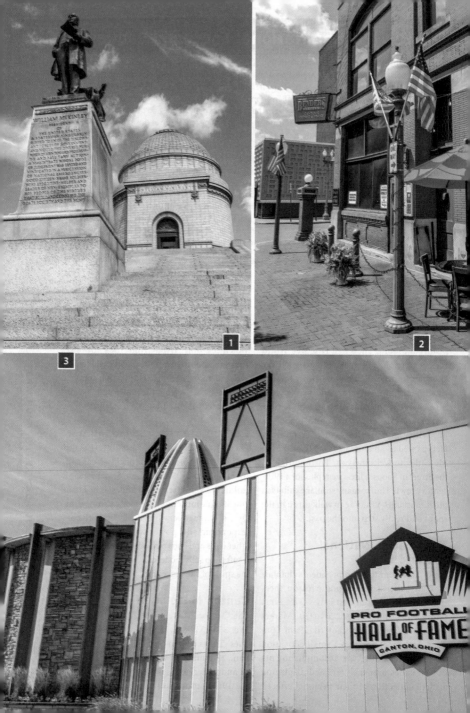

contemporary ceramics. The museum is known for its watercolor collection, including works by Hopper, Homer, and Sargent. The Artisan Boutique gift shop sells a curated assortment of locally made crafts, stationery, and apparel. Admission is free every Thursday and the first Friday of every month.

Canal Fulton

Nearby **Canal Fulton** is a preserved canal town 15 miles (24 km) northwest of Canton. The small, strollable town is a stop on the Ohio & Erie Canal Towpath Trail and features ice cream shops, boutiques, and restaurants in historic 19th-century and early-20th-century buildings. The *St. Helena III* canal boat (125 Tuscarawas St. NW, Canal Fulton, 330/854-6835, cityofcanalfulton-oh.gov/canal-boat-operations, 10am-4pm daily May-Sept., 10am-4pm Sat.-Sun. Oct., $9 adults, $8 seniors, $5 children ages 6-17) runs hour-long tours along the canal, with the boat pulled by two horses.

Massillon Museum

Canton's nearest neighbor to the west (and main high school football rival), Massillon, is home to the **Massillon Museum** (121 Lincoln Way, Massillon, massillonmuseum. org, 9:30am-5pm Tues.-Sat., 2pm-5pm Sun., free). The local art and history museum is mostly noteworthy for its permanent exhibit on famous football coach Paul Brown, who grew up and coached in Massillon before moving on to collegiate and professional football heights.

ENTERTAINMENT AND EVENTS

The Arts

The **Canton Symphony Orchestra** (cantonsymphony.org) performs at William McKinley High School's **Umstattd Hall** (2323 17th St. NW). The historic **Canton Palace Theatre** (605 Market Ave. N.,

330/454-8172, cantonpalacetheatre.org) hosts concerts, movie screenings, and touring shows in its 1,500-seat auditorium. **The Players Guild Theatre** (playersguildtheatre. com) is one of the oldest continually operating theater companies in the country and performs musicals and dramas at the **Cultural Center for the Arts** (1001 Market Ave.), the same venue that houses the Canton Museum of Art.

Festivals and Events

Early August's **Pro Football Hall of Fame Enshrinement Festival** (profootballhof-festival.com) is a week-long celebration of the latest inductees to the Hall of Fame. Over 700,000 people enjoy the annual festivities, which include a parade, a 5K run/walk, photo ops, autograph sessions, and the Hall of Fame game.

Canton First Fridays of the month are a monthly themed evening of live music, art, and extended hours for the downtown Canton Arts District's galleries and restaurants. The action is mostly concentrated along 6th Street and Cleveland Avenue from 6pm to 10pm, though the bars and live music go into the night.

RECREATION

Parks

A string of parks follows Nimishillen Creek near I-77, starting near the Pro Football Hall of Fame at **Stadium Park** (1200-2500 Stadium Park Dr. NW) and heading south to the McKinley National Memorial. Walking trails, playgrounds, and a garden center pull people to the outdoors for a leisurely walk or bike ride.

Cycling

The **Ohio & Erie Canal Towpath Trail** (ohioandereicanalway.com) skirts the west side of Stark County, heading through Canal Fulton and Massillon. You'll find a handful of bike rental shops along the trail in both towns.

1: McKinley National Memorial **2:** Bender's Tavern **3:** Pro Football Hall of Fame

Kayaking, Canoeing, and Paddleboarding

The **Canal Fulton Canoe Livery and Campground** (219 Cherry St. W., Canal Fulton, 330/854-4008, cfcanoe.com) offers canoe and kayak rentals as well as shuttle services for self-guided trips ranging 3-11 miles (4.8-17.7 km) on the Tuscarawas River. The livery also offers affordable bike rentals. **Sippo Lake Park** (5300 Tyner St., 330/479-2358) has a kayak/canoe launch area.

Spectator Sports

Canton has seen a number of sports teams come and go over the decades, but the high school football rivalry between the **Canton McKinley Bulldogs** (cantonmckinley.com) and **Massillon Washington High School Tigers** (massillontigers.com) has outlasted them all and is regarded as one of the most competitive—and most fervently supported—high school rivalries in the country. Both schools carry on the mascots of their respective towns' long-gone professional teams. Both schools have enormous stadiums, with the Bulldogs playing at the 23,000-seat **Tom Benson Hall of Fame Stadium** (1835 Harrison Ave. NW) and the Tigers playing at **Paul Brown Tiger Stadium** (1 Paul E. Brown SE, Massillon).

SHOPPING

Print & Press Shop and Studios (429 4th St. NW, 330/451-6574, noon-5pm Thurs.-Fri., 11am-3pm Sat.) is a good place to find Canton- and Ohio-related apparel or handcrafted souvenirs, quirky stationery, and gifts from makers both local and national.

Irreverent **Arrowhead Vintage and Handmade Goods** (534 Cleveland Ave. NW, 330/817-6723, 10am-5pm Tues.-Fri., 10am-4pm Sat.) stocks apparel, accessories, magnets, and more, steeped in snark. The shop also specializes in altered art imbued with incongruous pop culture references.

Between Wooster and Massillon off US-30 is the town of Orrville, home to **The J. M.** **Smucker Company Store and Café** (333 Wadsworth Rd., Orrville, 330/684-1500, jmsmucker.com/smucker-cafe-store, 9am-5:30pm Mon.-Sat.), which sells all manner of jams, jellies, and other delicious products from the Smucker empire. Sample limited or unusual flavors while you're here.

FOOD

Canton's food scene boasts a good variety of old staples, family-owned international eateries, and trendy newcomers.

Though the National Football League's birth occurred in an auto showroom, the gentlemen in attendance reportedly carried the meetings over to ★ **Bender's Tavern** (137 Court Ave. NW, 330/453-8424, benderscanton.com, 11am-9pm Mon.-Thurs., 11am-10pm Fri., 5pm-10pm Sat., $20-47). This classy fine-dining steak and seafood restaurant is Canton's oldest, operating since 1902. Lunch is much more affordable than dinner, with salads and sandwiches.

It's hard to know where to start with the 55-acre, Tuscany-inspired ★ **Gervasi Vineyard** (1700 55th St., 330/497-1000, gervasivineyard.com), north of town. The vineyard offers tours and has three elegant restaurants and multiple accommodations. Located in a historic barn, **The Bistro** (5pm-8pm Tues.-Thurs., 4pm-9pm Fri.-Sat., noon-8pm Sun., $12-38) is an upscale Italian eatery with steak, pasta, and pizza. **The Crush House** (11:30am-8:30pm Mon.-Thurs., 11:30am-9:30pm Fri.-Sat., $12-24) serves a focused menu of Italian entrées at a cheaper price point in a more industrial setting. **The Still House** (7am-5pm Mon.-Tues., 7am-10pm Wed.-Thurs. and Sun., 7am-midnight Fri.-Sat.) starts the day as a café, with coffee and pastries, and ends as a cocktail lounge.

Keep the sports vibe going after your visit to the Pro Football Hall of Fame at **TD's Tailgate Grill** (2234 Tuscarawas St. W., 330/451-2140, tdstailgategrill.com, 11am-10pm Mon.-Thurs., 11am-11pm Fri.-Sat., 11am-9pm Sun., $9-16). Self-labeled a "sports bistro," it takes its menu a little more seriously than most sports bars but still comes with all the TVs, beer, and patio seating you're after. There's a second location on the north side of town.

The relaxed **Basil Asian Bistro** (585 Market Ave. N., 330/452-3888, basilasianrestaurant.com, 11am-8pm Tues.-Fri., noon-8pm Sat., $9-19) has assembled a terrific menu of upscale, pan-Asian entrées representing Chinese, Japanese, and Southeast Asian cuisines. Coconut spaghetti is a house specialty. The bar serves a good mix of beer, wine, and cocktails.

Off the beaten path is **Irie Island Jamaican** (3407 Mahoning Rd. NE, 234/360-8964, noon-8pm Tues.-Sat., noon-6pm Sun., $7-12). Choose from one of four dinners (curry, chicken, beef, or fish) in three entrée sizes at this unassuming restaurant. Portion sizes are a bargain for the prices.

The Desert Inn (204 12th St. NW, 330/456-1766, desertinncanton.com, 2pm-9pm Tues.-Sat., noon-7pm Sun., $14-31) is a festive Mediterranean restaurant that serves its entrées, most notably shish kebabs, family-style. The Arabic-inspired dining room has been a family-owned and operated establishment since 1970.

BARS AND NIGHTLIFE

The **Canton Music Block,** along Cleveland Avenue between 2nd and 4th Streets, features several venues that, collectively, put on 15-20 live performances on weekends. For more information, visit cantonmusicblock.com.

The laid-back **George's Lounge** (229 Cleveland Ave. NW, 330/452-0029, georgescanton.com, 4pm-2am Tues.-Thurs., 11am-2am Fri.-Sat.) has been a Canton staple for live music and late-night bites since 1959, with grass-fed burgers, hand-cut fries, and craft brews.

Muskellunge Brewing Company (425 5th St. NW, 513/802-3417, muskellungebrewingcompany.com, 5pm-11pm Thurs.-Fri., noon-11pm Sat., noon-6pm Sun. during

football season) is a freshwater fish-inspired nanobrewery in downtown Canton with a small but bright taproom.

ACCOMMODATIONS

The biggest group of motels is north of town near the Belden Village Mall off I-77.

Downtown's only significant accommodation is the former McKinley Grand Hotel, renovated and rebranded as the **Doubletree by Hilton Canton Downtown** (320 Market Ave. S., 330/471-8000, hilton.com, $103-163), with sleek, modern rooms and an indoor pool.

North of town, **Gervasi Vineyard** (1700 55th St., 330/497-1000, gervasivineyard.com, $199-389) has a variety of accommodation options, including The Villas and The Casa, a 24-suite boutique hotel. Both are luxuriously rustic and come with fireplaces, heated tile floors, and complimentary breakfasts. The Villas are reservable as either individual suites or entire units.

INFORMATION AND SERVICES

Visit Canton (227 2nd St. NW, 330/454-1439, visitcanton.com, 9am-4pm Mon.-Fri.) operates a visitors center in downtown Canton.

Mercy Medical Center (1320 Mercy Dr. NW, 330/489-1000) is a large, multidisciplinary hospital right off I-77 near the Pro Football Hall of Fame. **Walk In Urgent Care** (4135 Tuscarawas St. W., 330/546-0913, 9am-9pm Mon.-Fri., 10am-6pm Sat.-Sun.) is west of downtown Canton.

TRANSPORTATION
Getting There

Canton is 30 minutes south of Akron (24 mi/39 km) and one hour south of Cleveland (60 mi/97 km) via I-77. From Columbus, take I-71 north to US-30 east; the trip takes roughly two hours (130 mi/209 km).

Akron-Canton Airport (CAK, 5400 Lauby Rd., North Canton, 888/434-2359, akroncantonairport.com) is a reliever airport for northeast Ohio. American Eagle, Delta, Spirit, and United mainly connect to hubs along the eastern United States. Several car rental companies have set up shop in the airport. Additionally, you can grab a rideshare, taxi, or the 81 SARTA bus to downtown Canton's Cornerstone Transit Center. The airport is 15 minutes (10 mi/16.1 km) north of downtown.

Greyhound (greyhound.com), Barons Bus (baronsbus.com), and GoBus (ridego-bus.com) stop at the Cornerstone Transit Center (112 Cherry Ave. SE, 330/477-2792) in downtown Canton. There are no ticket sales on-site.

Getting Around

The Stark Area Regional Transit Authority (SARTA) (sartaonline.com) connects Canton with surrounding Stark County communities. Regular routes are $1.50, with an unlimited day pass setting you back $3. Tickets can be paid with exact cash on board, or you can purchase a ticket or pass online or at any transit station. United Taxi Services (330/915-9338) operates throughout Stark County. Uber also operates in Canton.

Youngstown and Vicinity

"We make steel and we talk steel."

So says the narrator in the 1944 documentary *Steel Town* about Youngstown's then-burgeoning steel industry. There's no getting around the fact that because of the U.S. steel industry's decline, today's Youngstown doesn't look like 1944's Youngstown. The city has lost more than half its population (though the surrounding Mahoning Valley metropolitan area hasn't fared as badly) and steel is no longer the myopic focus of the region's economy.

But Youngstown is a city with good bones, with restaurants that have been around for generations, beautiful parks, and an art museum that punches way above its weight. Given the large waves of Italian immigrants who came in the early part of the 20th century, Youngstown may be the best place in Ohio to enjoy Italian American food. Both unpretentious and cultured, Youngstown represents the gems and the challenges of Rust Belt America.

SIGHTS

Youngstown Historical Center of Industry and Labor

A good place to get your bearings in terms of what Youngstown used to be is the Youngstown Historical Center of Industry and Labor (151 W. Wood Ave., 330/941-1314, youngstownohiosteelmuseum. org, 10am-4pm Wed.-Fri., noon-4pm Sat., $7 adults, $6 seniors, $3 students). Walk counterclockwise through this small museum's exhibits to chronologically learn about how the area's natural resources led to Youngstown's steel prominence, what life was like for steel workers and their families, and how steel is made. Images and artifacts fill the space and the imagination, transporting visitors to a city built on one industry and populated by waves of immigration.

★ Butler Institute of American Art

While everyone else was collecting European art, industrialist Joseph G. Butler, Jr. was collecting what his fellow Americans were creating. Founded in 1919 next to Youngstown State University's campus, the Butler Institute of American Art (524 Wick Ave., 330/743-1107, butlerart.com, 11am-4pm Tues.-Sat., noon-4pm Sun., free) was the first museum dedicated solely to American art and is the best excuse to venture out to Youngstown. The building itself is impressive, constructed of fireproof marble to protect Butler's priceless collection. The galleries are arranged chronologically, starting with Hudson River

Youngstown

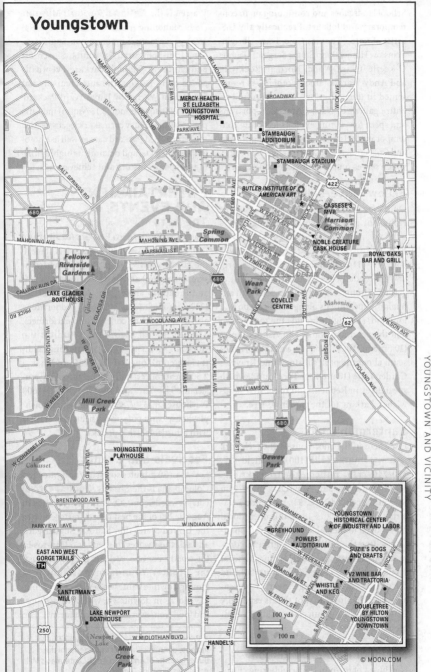

© MOON.COM

School landscapes and continuing on to contemporary and folk art. Practically any U.S. artist of note—Thomas Cole, Ivan Albright, Winslow Homer, John Singer Sargent, Georgia O'Keeffe, Grant Wood, Norman Rockwell, and Andy Warhol, among others—is represented in the collection. You'll also find an entire gallery of Native American portraits and space for visiting exhibits featuring contemporary artists. There is a small gift shop and Collections Café (7:30am-2pm Mon.-Fri.), which serves soups, sandwiches, and coffee.

Fellows Riverside Gardens

On the northern end of Mill Creek Park—a ribbon of green space and Youngstown's primary park—is the gorgeous **Fellows Riverside Gardens** (123 McKinley Ave., 330/740-7116, millcreekmetroparks.org, dawn-dusk daily, free). This 12-acre botanical garden is immaculately landscaped, with annuals and perennials alongside a gazebo and fountain. Highlights include the rose garden and the perennial walk. The visitors center (10am-5pm Tues.-Sun.) has a gift shop, a museum about the park's history, and Kravitz's Garden Café (10am-4pm Tues.-Sun.), which specializes in Reubens and other deli sandwiches. Parking for the gardens is free.

Lanterman's Mill

Elsewhere in the enormous Mill Creek Park is **Lanterman's Mill** (1001 Canfield Rd., 330/740-7115, millcreekmetroparks.org, 10am-5pm Tues.-Sun. May-Oct., noon-4pm Sat.-Sun. Apr. and Nov., $2), set beside a waterfall. Dating back to 1845, this operational mill is open to the public, with a gift shop inside selling the mill's freshly ground cornmeal, buckwheat, and flour, along with local crafts and wares. The mill, the waterfall, and the nearby covered bridge together present a historic, photogenic spot that is especially striking against autumn colors. Call to schedule a tour.

National Packard Museum

Northwest of town in the neighboring city of Warren is the **National Packard Museum** (1899 Mahoning Ave. NW, Warren, 330/394-1899, packardmuseum.org, noon-5pm Tues.-Sat., 1pm-5pm Sun., $8 adults, $5 seniors and children). Though Packard eventually ended up in Detroit, the auto company was founded in Warren by James Ward Packard. The 23,000-square-foot (2,137-sq-m) museum preserves the luxury carmaker's legacy, featuring refurbished Packard cars as well as photographs, artifacts, and documents highlighting the company's history and achievements.

ENTERTAINMENT AND EVENTS
The Arts

The impressive art deco **Powers Auditorium** (260 W. Federal Ave., 330/744-0264) is home to the **Youngstown Symphony** (youngstownsymphony.com) and hosts touring musicians and Broadway shows. The **Covelli Centre** (229 E. Front St., 330/746-5600) indoor arena also hosts traveling concerts and performers. The neoclassical **Stambaugh Auditorium** (1000 5th Ave., 330/747-5175, stambaughauditorium.com) opened in 1926 and has a 2,500-seat concert hall that hosts touring musicians. **The Youngstown Playhouse** (600 Playhouse Ln., 330/788-8739, theyoungstownplayhouse.com) puts on musicals and dramas with affordable ticket prices.

Festivals and Events

Less than 30 minutes south of Youngstown in Columbiana is the **Shaker Woods Festival** (shakerwoods.com). Over three weekends in August, 200 of the best juried craftspeople in the United States don historic Shaker garb and sell their wares in sheds and lean-tos in the woods. For one weekend in early August, the **Greater Youngstown Italian Fest** (youngstownitalianfest.org) takes over four city blocks in downtown, with music, shops, and food from over 40 Italian restaurants. The

---

1: Winslow Homer's *Snap the Whip* in the Butler Institute of American Art **2:** the exterior of the Butler Institute of American Art **3:** Lanterman's Mill **4:** Fellows Riverside Gardens

Canfield Fair (canfieldfair.com) has been running strong since 1846 and is the largest county fair in Ohio, drawing 350,000 people and big-name entertainment for Labor Day weekend.

RECREATION

Parks

Mill Creek Park (330/702-3000, millcreek-metroparks.org) is over 2800 acres of urban oasis, cutting through the western edge of Youngstown all the way to Boardman, 5 miles (8.1 km) south, with scenic drives, hiking trails, three lakes, and a golf course. Glenwood Avenue runs somewhat parallel east of the park.

Cycling

The MetroParks Bikeway (millcreekme-troparks.org) is an 11-mile (17.7-km) paved trail skirting the rural western edge of the Youngstown metropolitan area. Passing through farms, fields, and woodlands, the bikeway has three trailheads, including at Trailside Bicycle Rental (6685 Kirk Rd., Canfield, 330/503-4690) and at the intersection of Mahoning Avenue and Harold Street, nearer the center of Canfield southwest of Youngstown.

Hiking

Mill Creek Park's moderately difficult East and West Gorge Trails snake along either side of Mill Creek Gorge. Together they form a 1.7-mile (2.7-km) loop, with the trail passing sandstone cliffs and a historic suspension bridge in the middle. The trail can be accessed from Lanterman's Mill (1001 Canfield Rd.). The park has 10 miles (16.1 km) of hiking trails in total. Learn more at millcreekme-troparks.org/visit/hiking.

Kayaking, Canoeing, and Paddleboarding

Mill Creek Park's Lake Glacier Boathouse (330/740-7114 ext. 289) and Lake Newport Boathouse (330/740-7114 ext. 290) offer access areas for privately owned kayaks and canoes. You can also rent by the hour.

Spectator Sports

The Covelli Centre (229 E. Front St., 330/746-5600) is home to junior league hockey team the Youngstown Phantoms (youngstownphantoms.com). Minor league baseball team Mahoning Valley Scrappers (milb.com/mahoning-valley) are affiliated with the Cleveland Guardians and play at Eastwood Field (111 Eastwood Mall Blvd., Niles, 330/505-0000), north of Youngstown.

Youngstown State University's Penguins (ysusports.com) compete in NCAA Division I men's and women's sports, notably the men's football team, which plays at Stambaugh Stadium (577 5th Ave., 330/941-1978).

SHOPPING

The Amish Market (6121 South Ave., Boardman, 330/248-9933, theamishmarket. net, 9am-6pm Thurs.-Fri., 8am-4pm Sat.) brings Amish delights such as home furnishings, baked goods, produce, and deli meats and cheeses together under one roof. The limited hours give the vendors days to prepare the best-quality goods. The Market Restaurant serves Amish food for breakfast, lunch, and perhaps an early dinner.

FOOD

Take your pick of established neighborhood Italian eateries.

Cassese's MVR (410 N. Walnut St., 330/746-7067, youngstownmvr.com, 11am-11pm Mon.-Sat., $8-15) traces its history back to 1927 and features a large menu of Italian favorites and sandwiches, patio seating, and four bocce courts. The bocce season starts in April and goes to August. No experience is necessary to play!

The more upscale Vernon's Café (720 Youngstown Warren Rd., Niles, 330/652-1381, vernonscafe.com, 11am-10pm Mon.-Thurs., 11am-11pm Fri., 4pm-11pm Sat., $12-31) has a few more traditional Italian trattoria dishes and a full bar, if you can manage to get past the enormous wine list.

Good luck making a choice at **Jimmy's Italian Specialties** (3230 Belmont Ave., 330/759-2904, jimmysitalianspecialties.com, 10am-6pm Mon.-Fri., 10am-5pm Sat., $5-10). This market of imported Italian goods is encircled by a deli, bakery, and counters serving pizza, salad, soup, and build-your-own pasta. There's a small dining area and a Tuscan-inspired patio to enjoy your selections.

If you're not in the mood for Italian, there's **Suzie's Dogs and Drafts** (34 N. Phelps St., 234/228-9158, 11am-midnight Mon.-Wed., 11am-2:30am Thurs., 11am-4am Fri.-Sat.). Choose from one of the specialty dogs or build your own from 60 topping options. The spacious restaurant's bar has a good craft beer selection to boot. A second location is in nearby Boardman.

Long-time haunt **Rip's Café** (614 Youngstown Poland Rd., Struthers, 330/755-0057, ripscafestruthers.com, 11am-midnight daily, $5-12), southeast of town, and has been open since 1933. Rip's menu mixes Polish dishes in with its dirt-cheap hamburgers and sandwiches. Equal parts bar and restaurant, this neighborhood hole-in-the-wall has a beer list that mixes no-nonsense essentials with a handful of Ohio craft beers.

Local ice cream chain **Handel's** got its start in 1945 and has since proliferated to 50 locations in 10 states. The likes of *USA Today*, *National Geographic*, and others have labeled Handel's as some of the best ice cream in the United States. The ice cream was originally sold in a gas station, but the first shop—a walk-up ice cream stand—still sits on the south side of town (3931 Handel's Ct., 330/788-0356, handelsicecream.com, 11am-10pm daily). There are five other locations in the Youngstown area.

BARS AND NIGHTLIFE

V2 Wine Bar and Trattoria (100 W. Federal St., 330/742-5595, v2byvernon.com, 11am-9pm Mon.-Wed., 11am-2:30am Thurs.-Fri., noon-2:30am Sat., noon-8pm Sun.) is brought to you by the folks at Vernon's Café. Along with some of that restaurant's staples and some pizza, you'll find a long wine list, martinis, 21 craft beers, and a friendly, casual atmosphere.

The "don't judge a book" adage applies to **Royal Oaks Bar and Grill** (924 Oak St., 330/744-5501, 11am-2am Mon.-Fri., noon-2am Sat.). Dive-y looking on the outside and only slightly less dive-y looking inside, this bar serves some of the best barbecue and wings in the city.

Pour your own beer at **Whistle and Keg** (101 W. Federal St., 330/747-3661, whistlekeg.com, 4pm-11pm Tues.-Thurs., 1pm-11pm Fri.-Sat.), which charges by the ounce. Exchange your credit card and ID for a wristband that activates any of the bar's 44 taps and try as much or as little as you'd like. The modern, casual bar curates a list of national and regional beers as well as some of its own creations. There are additional locations in Cleveland and Columbus.

Noble Creature Cask House (126 E. Rayen Ave., 234/719-1827, noblecreaturebeer.com, 4pm-10pm Wed.-Thurs., noon-11pm Fri.-Sat., noon-6pm Sun.) serves 12 of its own brews and a menu of sandwiches and snacks from the cozy brick sanctuary of the former Butler Memorial Presbyterian Church.

ACCOMMODATIONS

The lone option in the center of Youngstown is **DoubleTree by Hilton Youngstown Downtown** (44 E. Federal St., 330/333-8284, hilton.com, $132-179), which resides in the neoclassical Stambaugh Building built in 1907. Hilton revamped the interior in 2012 to provide 125 contemporary guest rooms.

Julia's Bed and Breakfast (6219 W. Liberty St., Hubbard, 330/534-1342, juliasbb.com, $110-278) is on the grounds of the Pine Lakes Golf Club northeast of Youngstown. Six rooms and suites come with in-room Jacuzzis and a modern country sensibility.

Otherwise, the biggest groups of motels are along Boardman Poland Road off I-680 south of town and N. Canfield Niles Road, off I-80 near Austintown west of the city.

INFORMATION AND SERVICES

There is no visitors center in Youngstown, but for tourist information or to have tour guides mailed to you visit the **Mahoning County Convention and Visitors Bureau's website** at youngstownlive.com.

Mercy Health–St. Elizabeth Youngstown Hospital (1044 Belmont Ave., 330/746-7211) is located near downtown. If you're just looking for an urgent care clinic, the closest to downtown is **QUICKMed Urgent Care** (3499 Belmont Ave., 330/476-2260, 8am-8pm Mon.-Fri., 9am-6pm Sat.-Sun.).

TRANSPORTATION
Getting There

Youngstown is a bit of an outlier in terms of Ohio's major cities, managing to separate itself from the densely populated Northeast Ohio region. It's a straight shot from Akron to Youngstown, which is a 50-minute drive (51 mi/82 km) east on I-76. From Cleveland, take I-77 south to I-480 south to the I-80 turnpike east; the total trip is about 1.25 hours (74 mi/119 km). SR 11 is a divided highway that shoots straight down from Ashtabula on Lake Erie to Youngstown an hour south (57 mi/92 km).

The **Youngstown-Warren Regional Airport** (YNG, 1453 Youngstown Kingsville Rd., Vienna, 330/856-1537, yngairport.com) is north of the city; as of this writing, it does not have any commercial flights going through the terminal. In the past, low-cost airlines such as Allegiant have flown through, so it's worth checking the website to see if anything has changed. For now, the next closest airport is actually **Pittsburgh International Airport** (PIT, 1000 Airport Blvd, Pittsburgh, PA, 412/472-3525, flyp-ittsburgh.com), just under an hour southeast. The **Akron-Canton Airport** (CAK, 5400 Lauby Rd., North Canton, 888/434-2359, akroncantonairport.com) is nearly the same distance, to the west, but sees far fewer flights.

Greyhound (greyhound.com) and **Barons Bus** (baronsbus.com) stop at the **Youngstown Mercer Bus Stop** (340 W. Federal St.) in downtown Youngstown.

Getting Around

The Western Reserve Transit Authority (WRTA) (wrtaonline.com) serves Youngstown, Warren, and nearby suburbs. Regular fares are $1.25. You can purchase tickets or day passes online, at the main terminal (340 W. Federal St.), or using the EZfare smartphone app. Most routes run 6am-7pm during the week and 7am-6pm on Saturday. **Independent Radio Taxi** (330/746-8844) serves the Youngstown area.

Alliance

Industrial town Alliance has a few oddities in its pocket if you're in transit between Youngstown and Canton. The struggling downtown is seeing renewal in the form of quirky, one-of-a-kind museums.

SIGHTS
Troll Hole Museum

The Guinness record for world's largest collection of trolls belongs to Sherry Groom and her **Troll Hole Museum** (228 E. Main St., 330/596-1157, thetrollhole.com, 10am-4pm Tues.-Sun., $10 adults, $8 seniors, $6 children ages 2-12). Whether acquired by Sherry or donated by troll lovers, the museum holds over 25,000 troll dolls and memorabilia arranged in playful rooms, with displays covering the mythological origins of trolls. A large gift shop sells vintage troll dolls and other accessories, and there's a café in the back. Sherry also runs a cat café and an escape room on the block, all of which she uses to support Arts for Alzheimer's.

Feline Historical Museum

The **Feline Historical Museum** (260 E. Main St., 330/680-4444, felinehistoricalfoundation.org, 11am-3pm Tues.-Fri., free) sits in a stately former bank building and is best described as an inventory of cat-related art, knick-knacks, and books. The displays feature hundreds of ceramic, glass, and otherwise breakable felines that young children probably ought to stay clear from. Put together, they present a history of man's infatuation with cats. The museum's library is stocked with over 8,500 feline-related books and magazines, a veritable resource for cat lovers.

Glamorgan Castle

The oldest oddity in Alliance is the **Glamorgan Castle** (200 Glamorgan St., 330/238-8787, glamorgancastle.com), an incongruous chateau in the middle of town. Built in 1904 as a private residence, the mansion is currently used by Alliance City Schools. It's not typically open to the public,

but there are guided tours on Fridays at 1pm and 2pm for $10 per person.

Beech Creek Botanical Garden and Nature Preserve

Kids will enjoy the natural playgrounds and butterfly house at the **Beech Creek Botanical Garden and Nature Preserve** (11929 Beech St. NE, 330/829-7050, beechcreekgardens.org, 10am-4pm Mon.-Sat., noon-5pm Sun. May-mid-Sept., $9, limited hours and reduced prices mid-Sept.-Apr.). This botanical garden combines nature, play, and art, with a caterpillar nursery, short hiking trails, and oversized Lincoln logs. Keep an eye on the event calendar for weekly or special events including Critter Features, a close encounter with local or exotic wildlife under the care of an area rehabilitation center or sanctuary.

FOOD

Most of Alliance's best restaurants can be found on the southwest end of town, along US-62/W. State Street between the University of Mount Union and where US-62 turns into a divided highway headed toward Canton.

The College Inn (935 W. State St., 330/823-3332, collegeinnalliance.com,

Glamorgan Castle

11am-8pm Mon.-Sat., 11am-7pm Sun., $6-12) is a small, simple diner within walking distance of the university. The straightforward menu includes burgers, sandwiches, and hot meals.

In business since 1940, **Heggy's Confectionery** (1306 W. State St., 330/821-2051, heggysalliance.com, 7am-8pm Mon.-Sat., 9am-2pm Sun., $5-10) is both a soda fountain-style diner and a candy store, with over 40 varieties of Heggy's chocolates and roasted nuts. Breakfast is served until 11am and nothing on the menu is going to break the bank.

Papa Gyros (320 W. State St., 330/823-7773, papagyros.com, 11am-9pm daily, $10-17) serves authentic Greek entrées alongside gyros, with salads, souvlaki, and seafood filling out a well-rounded menu. And, of course, there's baklava (and baklava cheesecake). There are four other locations in the Akron/Canton area.

ACCOMMODATIONS

East of Alliance, the exquisite **Sebring Mansion and Spa** (385 W. Ohio Ave., Sebring, 330/938-0423, sebringmansion.com, $225-400) belonged to businessman Frank Sebring; he enjoyed Italy so much he had his new house, constructed in 1900, built entirely of Italian materials by imported Italian craftsmen. Choose from nine immaculate suites with Jacuzzi tubs and the most high-end of furnishings.

There are a handful of chain motels off US-62/W. State Road on the west side of town for something more down to earth.

TRANSPORTATION

Alliance is a 30-minute drive (21 mi/34 km) northeast of Canton via US-62. It's 45 minutes (37 mi/60 km) southwest of Youngstown, though the route isn't very straightforward: Take I-80 west to I-76 west to the SR 225 exit. Head south and turn right at the roundabout in Deerfield to stay on SR 225 and then keep an eye out for the left turn to remain on the route 2.5 miles (4 km) down the road. SR 225 will bring you to Alliance.

The **Stark Area Regional Transit Authority (SARTA)** (sartaonline.com) connects Alliance with Canton and the rest of Stark County. Regular routes are $1.50, or an unlimited day pass costs $3. Tickets can be paid with exact cash on board, or you can purchase a ticket or pass online or at the **Phyllis Beyers Alliance Transit Center** (10 Prospect St.).

There is no long-distance intercity bus to Alliance, but **Amtrak** (Amtrak.com) stops at the **Alliance Station** (820 E. Main St.) platform in the middle of the night.

Ashtabula County

As far northeast as you can go in Ohio, Ashtabula County distinguishes itself from most of the state with its lake-effect snow, wineries, and numerous covered bridges. The latter two pull in visitors yearning for a relaxing, rural respite. Add the Lake Erie shoreline and its beaches, and a handful of colorful towns, and Ashtabula County might be the most unique corner of the state.

★ GENEVA-ON-THE-LAKE

Established in 1869, Geneva-on-the-Lake was Ohio's first summer resort, complete with dance halls and amusement parks. Changing preferences wiped out similar resort towns along the coast, but Geneva-on-the-Lake remains, albeit in a mellower incarnation than its early-20th-century heyday. Wander down to "The Strip" portion of Lake Road for

Ashtabula County and Wine Country

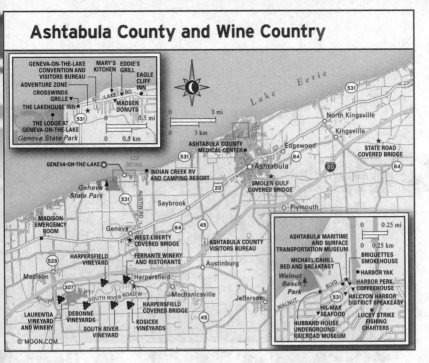

arcades, fried food vendors, tacky gift shops, and libations. Bring the family to Geneva State Park Lodge with its pools and walking paths along the Lake Erie shore. Or book a vacation home and spend the weekend reading in the lake breeze. The simple pleasures and basic motels that dominate the town make this a down-to-earth spot for a family vacation among Ohio's Lake Erie destinations; it's not as raucous as Put-in-Bay with its nightlife, not as thrilling as Sandusky with its water parks and roller coasters. This is a place to relax, to do as much or as little as you'd like, next to a big, beautiful lake.

Erosion in recent years due to warm temperatures and high-water levels have eaten away at the entire Lake Erie shoreline, but Geneva-on-the-Lake seems to have been especially affected. Plans are underway to fight erosion and restore the private beaches in town, so long as the money shows up. As of this writing, the sole beach in town—public or private—is in Geneva State Park.

Keep in mind that the town is pretty seasonal and that many businesses are closed or have reduced hours outside May-September.

Sights
ADVENTURE ZONE
Reminiscent of 80s- and 90s-style arcades, old-school entertainment center **Adventure Zone** (5600 Lake Rd., 440/466-3555, adventurezonefun.com, hours vary by season, prices vary by activity) offers a fun assortment of indoor and outdoor activities for the family. The arcade, indoor playground, miniature golf, go-karts, merry-go-round, batting cages, a zipline, and more are available à la carte or as part of combo packages. Concessions include snacks, sodas, pizzas, and pretzels. The place also does bicycle, golf cart, and surrey rentals to further explore the town's main strip.

Recreation

GENEVA STATE PARK

The center of recreation and main attraction in town is **Geneva State Park** (4499 Padanarum Rd., 440/466-8400, ohiodnr.gov, dawn-dusk daily, free) on the shore of Lake Erie. The park's 700 acres include just about anything you'd think to do next to a giant, scenic lake—and some things you wouldn't.

The 300-foot (91-m) natural **beach,** the only one left in Geneva-on-the-Lake, is a draw, as is the 2-mile (3.2-km), mostly flat **Orange Trail,** a multiuse trail that skirts along the shoreline between the beach and the park lodge. There are over 7 miles (11.3 km) of trails in total, some open for snowmobiling in the winter.

The **Geneva Marina** (genevamarina.com) holds 370 docking spaces and offers fishing charters and Jet Ski rentals. The **North Coast Outpost** (thenorthcoastoutpost.com) offers kayak and paddleboard rentals on the lake. **Lake Erie Canopy Tours** (lakeeriecanopy-tours.com) offers a zipline over a creek and a ropes course.

Accommodations range from camping and cabins right on the shore to the Lodge at Geneva-on-the-Lake and its cottages.

Food

Open since 1950, **Eddie's Grill** (5377 Lake Rd. E., 440/466-8720, eddiesgrill.com, 11am-10:30pm daily May-Sept., $4-10) is a staple for the families who have been coming to Geneva-on-the-Lake for decades. Three generations of the Sezon family work the open-air counter, including Eddie himself. The hot dog and hamburger menu is simple, the prices are cheap, and the place doesn't look like it's changed since it opened. The eatery takes cash only.

Unassuming **Mary's Kitchen** (5023 New St., 440/466-8606, maryskitchengotl.com, 7am-8pm daily summer, $7-17) has been around since 1946, quietly serving quality

meals from a small, old house removed from the hubbub of The Strip. The restaurant features a three-season porch and a diner-type menu including breakfast favorites and a popular and hefty perch sandwich.

Besides Mary's Kitchen, another popular breakfast spot is **Madsen Donuts** (5426 Lake Rd. E., 440/466-5884, madsendonuts. com, 8am-3pm Mon.-Thurs., 8am-6pm Fri. and Sun., 8am-10pm Sat., $2-4), a presence on The Strip since 1938. It serves donuts and coffee from a simple counter.

Probably the most upscale place in town is the Lakehouse Inn's **Crosswinds Grille** (5653 Lake Rd. E., 440/466-8668, thelakehouseinn.com/crosswinds-grille, 5pm-8pm Sun.-Thurs., 5pm-9pm Fri.-Sat., $14-34), with a gorgeous lakeside patio and a menu of pizzas, burgers, and steaks. Reservations are recommended.

Accommodations

The vast majority of accommodations in Geneva-on-the-Lake are basic 1950s-era motels (some in better shape than others), rental homes and cottages, and campgrounds. However, there are some attractive, alternative outliers. Prices skyrocket during summer weekends so book months in advance.

The ★ **Lodge at Geneva-on-the-Lake** (4888 N. Broadway, 866/806-8066, thelodgeatgeneva.com, $199-399) is Ohio's newest state park lodge, opened in 2004. Situated right on the shore of Lake Erie in Geneva State Park, this comfortable four-season resort includes an indoor and outdoor pool, firepits, wine country shuttles, bike rentals, and restaurants. The grounds are well-maintained, with relaxing walking paths along the lake. Come winter, snowshoes, skis, and snow bikes are available free of charge for overnight guests. There are also 25 two-bedroom lakeside cottages.

The landscaped back patio at **The Lakehouse Inn** (5653 Lake Rd. E., 440/466-8668, thelakehouseinn.com, $199-279) may be the best place in town to enjoy views of

---

1: Geneva State Park beach **2:** perch sandwich at Mary's Kitchen in Geneva-on-the-Lake

☆ Ohio Wine Country

The rich soil and Lake Erie breeze of extreme Northeast Ohio lend themselves to a microclimate suited to growing grapes. Thus, a small Ohio wine country emerged around Ashtabula and Lake Counties. The wineries range from quiet tasting rooms to expansive patios and dining rooms. Among the dozens of picturesque vineyards you'll find quaint towns, historic bed-and-breakfasts, and scenic covered bridges.

Most of the wineries are concentrated around the Grand River, with many in and around Geneva and Madison, both south of Geneva-on-the-Lake. Recommended wineries include, from east to west:

- **Kosicek Vineyards** (636 SR 534, Geneva, 440/361-4573, kosicekvineyards.com) is a long-established vineyard, with grapes growing since 1929 and a tasting room with a small menu of shareables and treats. The estate cabernet sauvignon and merlot are favorites. One-ounce tasting samples are $1 each.

- **Ferrante Winery and Ristorante** (5585 SR 307, Geneva, 440/466-8466, ferrantewinery. com) is one of the more established wineries in the area. A lodge-like dining room and large patio overlook the vineyards and serve an upscale Italian menu. The ice wine is popular, as is the award-winning vidal blanc. Sweet and dry tasting trays are available for $10 and come with six varieties.

- **South River Vineyard** (6062 S. River Rd. W., Geneva, 440/466-6676, southrivervineyard. com) features a tasting room inside an old 1892 church and a large, temple-like covered patio with expansive views of the vineyards and woods. The same family runs a distillery on the other side of the vineyard . . . you can walk there with your wine, including the only estate malbec in Ohio. There are three wine-tasting flights available (each $7 and including four selections): dry white, dry red, and sweet.

- **Harpersfield Vineyard** (6387 SR 307, Geneva, 440/466-4739, harpersfield.com) serves its estate-grown wine and small plates from a cozy tasting room, or take your picks out on the patio. Guest musicians play in the evenings and Sunday afternoons.

- **Debonné Vineyards** (7840 Doty Rd., Madison, 440/466-3485, debonne.com) is one of the bigger operations and offers over 50 wines, including an award-winning chardonnay and ice

the lake. Choose from eight modernized B&B rooms, three two-bedroom cottages, or a private beach house. There's a spa on-site, as well as the upscale Crosswinds Grille restaurant, which takes full advantage of the lake view.

Another bed-and-breakfast option on the opposite side of The Strip is **Eagle Cliff Inn** (5254 Lake Rd., 440/466-1110, eaglecliffinn. com, $139-189), with six rooms (some quite small) and three cottages, all with rustic but modern charms. The three suites are more contemporary. A highlight is the wrap-around porch.

CAMPING

Geneva State Park (4499 Padanarum Rd., 440/466-8400, ohiodnr.gov, from $27) maintains a campground with 93 electric sites, including 19 full hookup sites. A ring of 12 cabins sits next to the shore.

Indian Creek RV and Camping Resort (4710 Lake Road E., 888/726-7802, sunrvresorts.com/resorts, from $82) is a 110-acre, well-maintained resort near the lake with full RV hookup sites and cottage rentals. Amenities include miniature golf, a bar and grill, small fishing lakes, and a swimming pool.

South River Vineyard

wine. The winery offers seven different tasting flights ($10 each) that come with 6-8 varieties. There's frequent live entertainment and an expansive patio extends out into the lawn. The food is more "bar and grill" than "ristorante" and there is a craft brewery on-site as well.

- **Laurentia Vineyard and Winery** (4599 S. Madison Rd., Madison, 440/296-9175, laurentiawinery.com) features a log cabin-inspired tasting room and sunny patio to enjoy your small plates and wine, including the award-winning cabernet sauvignon and dry riesling.

Information and Services

The **Geneva-on-the-Lake Convention and Visitors Bureau** (5540 Lake Rd. E., 440/466-8600, visitgenevaonthelake.com) operates a small visitors center on the western edge of The Strip.

The **Madison Emergency Room** (6270 North Ridge Rd., Madison, 440/428-0280, 24 hours daily) is about a 20-minute drive west of Geneva-on-the-Lake on US-20.

Transportation

Geneva-on-the-Lake is about an hour's drive (53 mi/85 km) from Cleveland taking I-90 east and then heading north on SR 534. Taking SR 2 and US-20 east is about the same distance and time. The town is an hour and 20 minutes (75 mi/121 km) from Akron via I-77 north, I-271 north, and I-90 east to the SR 534 exit, from which you'll head north. From Youngstown, take SR 11 north to I-90 west to the SR 534 exit and head north for a total ride of just over an hour (70 mi/113 km). There is no bus service to the city.

Sunset Taxi and Transportation (440/855-5314) operates in the Geneva area and also can arrange larger group transportation for wine tours or parties. **Premier**

☆ Ashtabula County's Covered Bridges

Harpersfield Covered Bridge

What is a covered bridge and why is it covered?

Though there have been covered bridges for centuries, the economical truss design became popular in the United States in the 19th century, especially between 1825 and 1875. The timber used for the bridges was susceptible to the elements, so a covered roof was integrated for structural integrity. These covered bridges have a lifespan of about 100 years and are appreciated for their unique appearance and the aesthetic choices made by architects later in the game who added flourishes to the basic design.

Ashtabula County's 19 covered bridges are the most you'll find in any Ohio county and include the country's longest and shortest covered bridges, as well as nine that predate 1900. Adjacent parks, cafés, and restaurants allow you to make a road trip out of the experience, and the bridges have become popular destinations in their own right. The town of Jefferson hosts the **Ashtabula Covered Bridge Festival** (coveredbridgefestival.org) every October, with crafts, a parade, and food, along with self-driving tours of the bridges (17 of the 19 bridges are still operational and open to car traffic).

Here are some of the more noteworthy bridges:

- The **Smolen Gulf Covered Bridge** (7001 State Rd., Ashtabula) is the longest in the United States at 613 feet (187 m). Built in 2008, the bridge is 93 feet (28.3 m) above the Ashtabula River and has a parking lot.

- Clocking in at a whopping 18 feet (5.5 m) is the **West Liberty Covered Bridge** (92 W. Liberty St., Geneva), a replacement for a cement bridge and the country's shortest covered bridge.

- The **Harpersfield Covered Bridge** (1122 Harpersfield Rd., Geneva) dates back to 1868 and has a steel supplement on one end, added after a flood washed away the shoreline. A park and café are on the north side of the river.

- The **State Road Covered Bridge** (5899 State Rd., Conneaut), east of Ashtabula, has a classic covered bridge look. There's no parking lot, so you'll have to pull over to the side of the road.

Visit visitashtabulacounty.com/things-to-do/covered-bridges for more information on the bridges and their locations.

Transportation Service (440/466-1515) does the same.

ASHTABULA

Ashtabula, meaning "river of many fish" in Iroquois and Algonquin, is on the rebound. This rough-and-tumble Great Lakes port has seen successful reinvestment both in its 19th-century **Ashtabula Harbor Historic District** and the **Ashtabula River**, which was horribly polluted coming into the 21st century. Over 70,000 cubic yards (53,519 cubic m) of contaminated sediment were dredged, opening the Ashtabula River again to commercial and recreational traffic as well as returning fish and wildlife. You can watch said traffic travel under the **Ashtabula Lift Bridge,** which operates every 30 minutes. Pull in for a bite, take a fishing charter, watch the lift bridge, and appreciate the lifestyle of an unpretentious port town, a stark contrast to most Ohio communities.

Sights
ASHTABULA MARITIME AND SURFACE TRANSPORTATION MUSEUM
Situated inside the original 1871 lightkeeper's house, the **Ashtabula Maritime and Surface Transportation Museum** (1071 Walnut Blvd., 440/964-6847, ashtabulamaritime.org, noon-4pm Fri.-Mon., $9 adults, $8 seniors, $3 children) holds 25,000 artifacts detailing the area's maritime and railroad shipping and industry. Odds and ends of ships, including anchors and hulls, sit outside the museum, which has a commanding view of the Ashtabula River and the lift bridge.

HUBBARD HOUSE UNDERGROUND RAILROAD MUSEUM
Ashtabula played a pivotal role in the Underground Railroad, helping enslaved people escape to Canada. The small **Hubbard House Underground Railroad Museum** (1603 Walnut Blvd., 440/964-8268, hubbardhouseugrmuseum.org, 1pm-5pm Fri.-Sun.

Memorial Day-Labor Day, $5 adults, $4 seniors, $3 children) interprets this history with exhibits on local abolitionists and the Underground Railroad system itself. Volunteer-led tours help visitors appreciate the local history museum's artifacts and stories.

Entertainment and Events
FESTIVALS AND EVENTS
Neighbor to the east and fellow Lake Erie town Conneaut puts together **D-Day Conneaut** (ddayohio.us), an impressive reconstruction and reenactment of the 1944 D-Day invasion of Normandy, complete with hundreds of volunteer reenactors, transports, and WWII airplanes. Since its inception in 1999, it's grown to become the world's largest living history event, held over two days in mid-August.

Recreation
Being a Lake Erie port, there are plenty of opportunities to get yourself out on the water.

Walnut Beach Park (Lake Ave. and Walnut Blvd., 440/993-7036, ohiodnr.gov) is one of the nicer, sandier beaches on Lake Erie. There's a concession stand, large picnic shelters, a playground, and the Ashtabula Harbor Lighthouse visible in the distance.

Lucky Strike Fishing Charters (Marina Dr., 440/997-7010, lake-erie-walleye-fishing-charters.com) is one of several charters available downstream on the Ashtabula River for a venture out to Lake Erie, which is dubbed "the walleye capital of the world." Novice and experienced anglers alike are welcome.

Harbor Yak (1 Ferry Dr., 440/990-0161, harboryak.com) offers guided tours and rentals of kayaks, canoes, hydro-bikes, and paddleboards for exploring the harbor.

Food
Right off the harbor is **Harbor Perk Coffeehouse** (1003 Bridge St., 440/964-9277, harborperk.com, 7am-7pm daily), a handsome space with high ceilings, brick walls, and large

tables ready for good conversation. A small selection of bagels and pastries are available.

Briquettes Smokehouse (405 Morton Dr., 440/964-2273, briquettessmokehouse. com, 11am-10pm Tues.-Thurs., 11am-11pm Fri.-Sat., noon-8pm Sun., $9-26) has the best view of the harbor in town, with a large patio facing the river. A strong craft brew game includes beers from Ohio brewers and beyond.

Hil-Mak Seafood (449 Lake Ave., 440/964-3222, hilmakseafoods.com, 4pm-9pm Tues.-Sat., $10-33) does fresh seafood plus ribs and hamburgers in a friendly, vaguely seafaring-themed dining room. There's also a fish market behind the restaurant on 5th Street, with an exclusively seafood menu of sandwiches, dinners, and seafood by the pound. There's no seating in the market.

Halcyon Harbor District Speakeasy (1119 Bridge St., 440/536-4291, harborhalcyon.com, 11:30am-9:30pm Mon.-Wed., 11:30am-11pm Thurs., 11:30am-1:30am Fri.-Sat., noon-8pm Sun., $9-25) is an upscale American restaurant specializing in pasta and burgers with an alleyway patio and live music.

Accommodations

Just uphill from the historical district is **Michael Cahill Bed and Breakfast** (1106 Walnut Blvd., 440/813-0572, cahillbb.com, $130-140), which has four antique-filled rooms with private baths, plus a certified chef on hand for breakfast.

Information and Services

The **Ashtabula County Visitor Bureau** (440/275-3202, visitashtabulacounty.com) operates a visitors center (1850 Austinburg Rd.) off the SR 45 exit from I-90. **Ashtabula County Medical Center** (2420 Lake Ave., 440/997-2262) is Ashtabula's primary hospital.

Transportation

Ashtabula is an hour's drive (58 mi/93 km) east of Cleveland via I-90 and SR 11. From Youngstown, Ashtabula is a straight shot north on SR 11, again about an hour's drive (56 mi/90 km). From Geneva-on-the-Lake, it's about a 20-minute drive (10 mi/16.1 km) east on SR 531. There is no scheduled bus service to Ashtabula.

City Taxicab (440/992-2156) serves the Ashtabula County area.

1: The Lakehouse Inn in Geneva-on-the-Lake **2:** Ashtabula Harbor Historic District **3:** Ashtabula Lift Bridge

Lake Erie and Northwest Ohio

Northwest Ohio is perhaps the state's most in-congruous region. On one hand, you have a four-county area on the shores of Lake Erie known as "Vacationland," a popular summer destination with a vast supply of rental homes, cottages, campgrounds, and bed-and-breakfasts eager to host folks looking for a simple break from the city. The lake is the shallowest, warmest, and most productive of the Great Lakes, supporting the greatest numbers of fish and therefore ample angling opportunities for perch and walleye. The Marblehead Peninsula is steeped in maritime culture, with the fishing towns of Port Clinton and Marblehead and historic lighthouses dotting the shore. There's the archipelago of tiny islands in Lake Erie led by Put-in-Bay, known for its boisterous party atmosphere, and the quieter

Highlights

Look for ★ to find recommended sights, activities, dining, and lodging.

© MOON.COM

★ Join the fun at **South Bass Island and Put-in-Bay,** which sport a rollicking party scene (page 213).

★ Ride the record-breaking roller coasters at **Cedar Point,** known as "America's Roller Coast" (page 222).

★ Bird-watch at **Ottawa National Wildlife Refuge,** a major stopover for migrating species and one of the top birding sites in the nation (page 229).

★ View over 700 animal species and brave a ropes course over an African-style savanna at the **Toledo Zoo and Aquarium** (page 230).

★ See works from old masters and contemporary glass art at the **Toledo Museum of Art,** one of the best art museums in Ohio (page 231).

★ Explore **Fort Meigs Historic Site,** the largest wooden fort in North America and one of the country's few War of 1812 sites (page 233).

★ Learn about the 19th U.S. president at the **Rutherford B. Hayes Presidential Library and Museums** and see a replica of the Oval Office's Resolute desk (page 242).

★ Trace the journey of astronaut Neil Armstrong from Wapakoneta to the moon at the **Armstrong Air and Space Museum,** chronicled with artifacts and spacecraft (page 245).

Lake Erie and Northwest Ohio

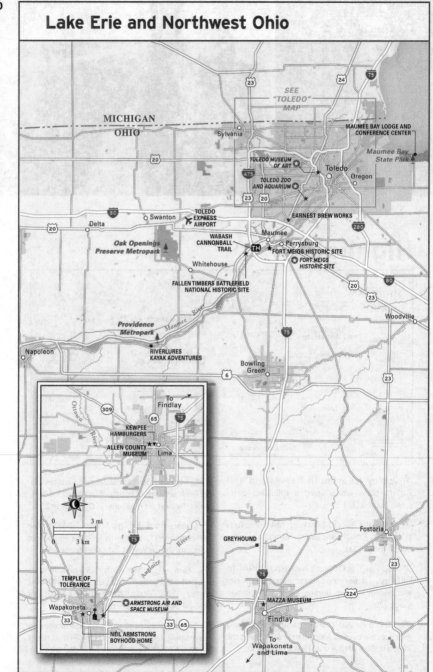

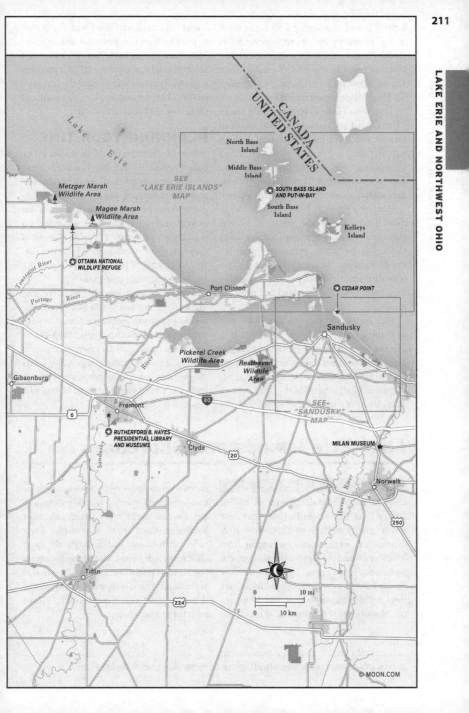

© MOON.COM

Kelleys Island. Anchoring it all is the small city of Sandusky and its amusement park, Cedar Point, arguably Ohio's greatest attraction and home to more roller coasters than almost anywhere on earth (only California's Six Flags Magic Mountain has more).

Then there's Toledo. West of Vacationland, "The Glass City" is only an hour south of Detroit and every bit as industrial, though a more diversified economy has kept things better afloat here. Such industry has afforded the city a wealth of quality attractions unique for a metropolitan area of only half a million.

Once you get away from the lake, things quiet down considerably. Small, industrial cities line I-75 from Toledo all the way down to Dayton. None are particularly noteworthy destinations on their own, but they do offer distractions to pull you off the highway for a break from flat farmland and two-lane monotony.

This region also played a significant role in shaping the United States as we know it. The late 18th century saw continued struggles between American Indian nations and encroaching white settlers. Northwest Ohio became the frontline of the War of 1812, when a confederacy of nations led by famed Shawnee leader Tecumseh partnered with the British to push back on U.S. positions. Toledo's Fort Meigs and Put-in-Bay's Perry's Victory and International Peace Memorial interpret how a mostly forgotten war enabled the country's westward expansion, and how this corner of Ohio bore the brunt of that war.

PLANNING YOUR TIME

Toledo can be experienced in 2-3 days. The Lake Erie islands and shoreline are best enjoyed in summer, when all the attractions and restaurants are open and maintain their longest operating hours. You could spend a day or long weekend in Sandusky, depending on your budget and interest in rides. The rest of the region is an as-much-or-as-little-time-as-you'd-like kind of place, with few sights but ample recreational opportunities.

Because of the seasonality of attractions like Cedar Point and Put-in-Bay, many venues close or greatly reduce their hours by winter. Spring and fall can be a mixed bag—some businesses open April-October, weather permitting. It's worth confirming specific hours of operation before you go anywhere in this region if you're visiting outside Memorial Day-Labor Day.

Lake Erie Islands and Shoreline

TOP EXPERIENCE

Dubbed Vacationland, the western half of Ohio's Lake Erie shore features maritime towns, plenty of fresh perch, marina after marina, and accommodations ranging from RV campgrounds to mega-waterpark resorts. **Sandusky** is the primary gateway, with the **Cedar Point** amusement park pulling in over three million visitors per season. Heading into the **Marblehead Peninsula,** things quiet down with campgrounds, motels, and bed-and-breakfasts offering lakeside views and quick access to the area's attractions, most notable of which are the tiny islands a few miles off the coast. **Put-in-Bay** is the party choice, though there's something for everyone. **Kelleys Island** has a deserved reputation as the family friendly choice. All told, most of this area qualifies as a quiet, coastal escape from the workaday life.

Previous: Cedar Point beach; Marblehead Lighthouse; the Hippoquarium at the Toledo Zoo.

Which Island?

There are four primary inhabited islands in Lake Erie that belong to Ohio. Which you choose to visit depends on your preferences in terms of atmosphere, numbers of people, and activities. None of the islands are particularly heavy on "sights"; these are small islands which most seek out to get away from the crowds, or to revel in them in one island's case. So, which to visit?

- **South Bass Island:** A summertime party scene in Put-in-Bay pulls droves to the town's bars and small resorts. There are quiet corners, with bed-and-breakfasts, wineries, and the commanding presence of Perry's Victory and International Peace Memorial lending some respectability to the island's proceedings.

- **Kelleys Island:** The quieter version of South Bass Island, Kelleys Island is best known for its glacial grooves and numerous bed-and-breakfasts. A handful of restaurants and wineries are on hand.

- **Middle Bass Island:** Farmland and vineyards dominate this island, which offers little in the way of attractions but much in bird-watching and quiet.

- **Isle St. George:** Undeveloped and sparsely populated, this tiny island offers birds, lake views, and solitude.

★ SOUTH BASS ISLAND AND PUT-IN-BAY

Hardly anybody calls South Bass Island by its name, with most simply calling it Put-in-Bay, which is the name of the lively town on the island's north side. Something between Mackinac Island and Key West in both geography and attitude, Put-in-Bay attracts a party crowd both young and old who come for the island's playful bars, the novelty of driving rental golf carts (the primary way to get around the island), and to enjoy themselves on a Midwest island. There are some quieter spots—Perry's Victory and International Peace Memorial stands somewhat contradictorily near party central. There are bed-and-breakfasts away from the hubbub, as well as the campsites of South Bass Island State Park. All told, almost anything you can do in Put-in-Bay you can do on the mainland, but it's always more fun on an island. Keep in mind that the island pretty much shuts down to visitors in the winter (though not entirely) and hours are seasonal, with the typical tourist season stretching April-October and peak season running June-August.

Sights
PERRY'S VICTORY AND INTERNATIONAL PEACE MEMORIAL

The waters of Lake Erie saw intense naval fighting during the War of 1812. Buoyed by the motto "don't give up the ship," Commodore Oliver Hazard Perry and his U.S. navy turned what looked set to be a stumbling defeat into a victory during the Battle of Lake Erie, which took place only miles from the shores of Put-in-Bay. The victory turned the tide against the British, who had embarrassed U.S. forces in the Great Lakes region up to that point. Visible from miles in any direction and finished in 1915, **Perry's Victory and International Peace Memorial** (93 Delaware Ave., 419/285-2184, nps.gov/pevi, grounds 24 hours daily, visitors center 10am-6pm daily May-early Sept., free) is, at 352 feet (107 m) tall, the largest Doric column in the world. A small visitors center includes a brief Battle of Lake Erie video and some interpretive exhibits on the battle and the construction of the granite memorial. At the base inside the column are the remains of six officers—three British and three

Lake Erie Islands

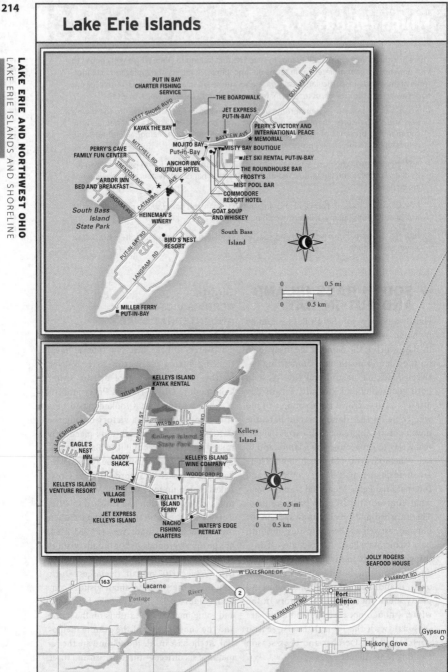

South Bass Island map:

PUT IN BAY CHARTER FISHING SERVICE

THE BOARDWALK

JET EXPRESS PUT-IN-BAY

KAYAK THE BAY

PERRY'S VICTORY AND INTERNATIONAL PEACE MEMORIAL

MOJITO BAY Put-in-Bay

MISTY BAY BOUTIQUE

PERRY'S CAVE FAMILY FUN CENTER

JET SKI RENTAL PUT-IN-BAY

ANCHOR INN BOUTIQUE HOTEL

THE ROUNDHOUSE BAR

FROSTY'S

ARBOR INN BED AND BREAKFAST

MIST POOL BAR

COMMODORE RESORT HOTEL

HEINEMAN'S WINERY

GOAT SOUP AND WHISKEY

South Bass Island State Park

South Bass Island

BIRD'S NEST RESORT

WEST SHORE BLVD

MITCHELL RD

TRENTON AVE

NIAGARA AVE

CATAWBA AVE

PUT-IN-BAY RD

LANGRAM RD

BAYVIEW AVE

COLUMBUS AVE

MILLER FERRY PUT-IN-BAY

0   0.5 mi
0   0.5 km

Kelleys Island map:

KELLEYS ISLAND KAYAK RENTAL

TITUS RD

WARD RD

DIVISION ST

MONAGAN RD

Kelleys Island State Park

Kelleys Island

W LAKESHORE DR

EAGLE'S NEST INN

CADDY SHACK

KELLEYS ISLAND WINE COMPANY

WOODFORD RD

KELLEYS ISLAND VENTURE RESORT

THE VILLAGE PUMP

KELLEYS ISLAND FERRY

JET EXPRESS KELLEYS ISLAND

NACHO FISHING CHARTERS

WATER'S EDGE RETREAT

0   0.5 mi
0   0.5 km

JOLLY ROGERS SEAFOOD HOUSE

W LAKESHORE DR

E HARBOR RD

163

Lacarne

Portage   River

2

Port Clinton

W FREMONT RD

Gypsum

Hickory Grove

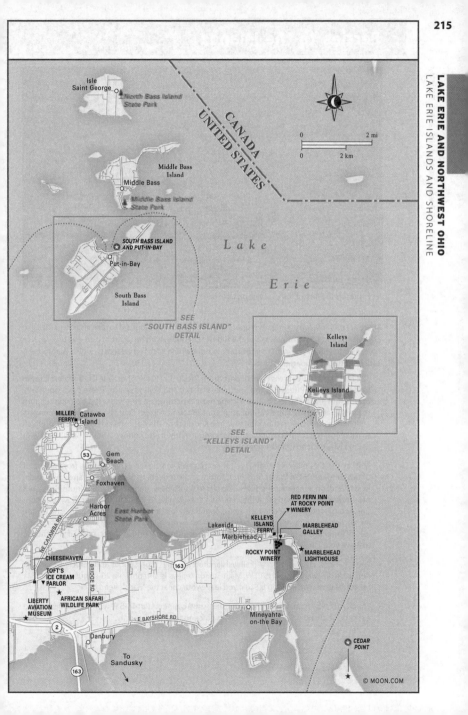

Isle
Saint George

*North Bass Island
State Park*

CANADA
UNITED STATES

0   2 mi
0   2 km

Middle Bass
Island

Middle Bass

*Middle Bass Island
State Park*

**SOUTH BASS ISLAND
AND PUT-IN-BAY**

Put-in-Bay

South Bass
Island

L a k e

E r i e

*SEE
"SOUTH BASS ISLAND"
DETAIL*

Kelleys
Island

Kelleys Island

*SEE
"KELLEYS ISLAND"
DETAIL*

MILLER
FERRY Catawba
Island

53

Gem
Beach

Foxhaven

Harbor
Acres

*East Harbor
State Park*

RED FERN INN
AT ROCKY POINT
▼WINERY

Lakeside

KELLEYS
ISLAND
FERRY

Marblehead

MARBLEHEAD
GALLEY

ROCKY POINT
WINERY

★ MARBLEHEAD
LIGHTHOUSE

CHEESEHAVEN

TOFT'S
ICE CREAM
▼PARLOR

163

LIBERTY
AVIATION
MUSEUM

★ AFRICAN SAFARI
WILDLIFE PARK

E BAYSHORE RD

Mineyahta-
on-the-Bay

2

Danbury

CEDAR
POINT

163

To
Sandusky

© MOON.COM

Ferries to the Islands

Jet Express is the fastest ferry service on Lake Erie.

There are multiple ferry companies operating throughout Vacationland to take visitors to the Lake Erie islands and back. Summers see the fullest schedules, with reduced or non-existent service the closer to winter you get. It's important to note where each ferry departs, which islands each serves, and the comparative costs.

- **Jet Express** (jet-express.com) departs from Sandusky (101 W. Shoreline Dr.) and Port Clinton (3 Monroe St.) to Put-in-Bay (on South Bass Island) and Kelleys Island. These passenger-only catamarans are the fastest option and the most expensive—a 30-minute trip from Port Clinton to Put-in-Bay runs $20 one-way for adults or $33 round-trip. Jet Express also drops passengers off in Put-in-Bay itself, rather than the Lime Kiln dock on the opposite side of the island, which saves time if the town is your destination. Importantly, it also connects South Bass Island with Kelleys Island for an island-hopping day.

- **Miller Ferry** (millerferry.com) is a passenger and vehicle ferry that departs from the tip of Catawba Island (5174 Water St., Port Clinton) and connects to South Bass Island and Middle Bass Island, on separate schedules. The trip to South Bass Island is only 18 minutes long, but passengers are dropped off at the Lime Kiln dock 2 miles (3.2 km) from Put-in-Bay, so to continue on passengers need to rent a bike or golf cart, call a taxi, take a bus, or walk. The upside is that tickets are significantly cheaper than Jet Express at $8 one-way to South Bass Island ($10.50 one-way to Middle Bass Island), and there's free parking at the terminal if you choose to leave your car.

- The **Kelleys Island Ferry** (kelleysislandferry.com) is a passenger and vehicle vessel and departs from Marblehead (510 W. Main St.) for Kelleys Island only—a 20-minute ride and $11 for adults one-way. Parking is $10 if you leave your car at the Marblehead dock.

- The **Sonny-S Boat Line** (middlebassferry.net) connects Put-in-Bay with Middle Bass Island a short ride away, at $7 one-way. It ferries passengers and bikes only.

U.S.—and stairs to an open-air deck ($10 admission) that has a view of the islands and mainland coast. An elevator also makes the journey to the top. Check the calendar for special events, including the annual Historic Weekend in mid-September that commemorates the conflict and the peace the U.S.-Canada border has seen since.

PERRY'S CAVE FAMILY FUN CENTER
For families visiting the island, **Perry's Cave Family Fun Center** (979 Catawba Ave., 419/285-2283, perryscave.com, 10am-5pm Mon.-Thurs., 10am-6pm Fri.-Sun. May-Sept., $5-10 per attraction) has quite the assortment of activities on offer: miniature golf, a butterfly house, gemstone mining, and a maze, among others. Everything sits above the eponymous limestone cave, which is on the small side; tours are about 20 minutes long. There are combo tickets for three attractions ($21 adults, $13 children) or all attractions ($28 adults, $20 children), including the cave tour.

HEINEMAN'S WINERY
The oldest operating winery in Ohio is family-owned **Heineman's Winery** (978 Catawba Ave., 419/285-2811, heinemanswinery.com, 11am-7pm Mon.-Sat., noon-7pm Sun. mid-Apr.-late Oct., tours 11am-5pm daily May-Sept.). Established by German immigrant Gustav Heineman in 1888, the winery features a suitably old-world tasting room and is best known for its pink catawba. Underneath the building is the unusual **Crystal Cave,** which is not a cave at all but the world's largest geode. Tours ($7 adults, $3.50 children) last 10 minutes and run irregularly throughout the day and include a glass of wine. A separate tour of the wine cellar can be combined with the cave tour. There are no official tastings, so sample the wine at the bar, which offers five-ounce tasting glasses for $2.75.

Recreation
Put-in-Bay Watercraft Rentals (419/285-2628, pibjetski.com) operates from South Bass

Island State Park's dock and provides Jet Ski, stand-up paddleboard, and kayak rentals.

On the town side of the island are **Jet Ski Rental Put-in-Bay** (14 Bath St., 419/285-7547, putinbayjetski.com); **Kayak the Bay** (760 Bayview Ave., 419/967-0796, kayak-thebay.net), which offers kayak rentals and guided tours; and **Put-in-Bay Charter Fishing Service** (609 Bayview Ave., 419/341-2805, putinbayfishingcharterservice.com), which takes groups up to six out on the lake to catch walleye, bass, and perch.

Shopping
Souvenir stores along harbor-facing Delaware Avenue sell Put-in-Bay memorabilia and apparel. **Misty Bay Boutique** (246 Delaware Ave., 419/285-7925, lovinputinbay.com, 9am-9pm daily May-Sept., limited hours daily Apr. and Oct.) is one of the more established, with women's apparel and nautical gifts and decor.

Food
They say "fine dining meets flip flops" at ★ **Goat Soup and Whiskey** (820 Catawba Ave., 419/285-4628, soupandwhiskey.com, 11:30am-9pm Sun.-Thurs., 11:30am-10pm Fri.-Sat. May-Sept., $13-41), which features an eclectic menu of seafood, sandwiches, and hearty entrées. Portions are well worth the price (the perch tacos and Reuben balls are local favorites), and there's plenty of seating between the covered patio and the hunting lodge-like dining room. Downstairs is an additional biergarten.

The best place in Put-in-Bay to eat out on the water is **The Boardwalk** (341 Bayview Ave., 419/285-3695, the-boardwalk.com, 11am-9pm Sun.-Thurs., 11am-10pm Fri.-Sat. Memorial Day-late Sept., reduced weekend-only hours early May and Oct.-Nov. weather permitting, prices vary by location). A conglomeration of five bars and restaurants at different price points, this collection of sociable eateries sits on a pier and offers everything from easy bowls of lobster bisque (a popular choice) to fine-dining surf-and-turf options.

A bit more everyperson is **Frosty's** (252 Delaware Ave., 419/285-3278, frostys.com, 8am-10pm Mon.-Fri., 7am-10pm Sat.-Sun. Apr.-Oct., $5-15), which does lunch and dinner sandwiches, burgers, and specialty pizzas, as well as breakfast for half the week. Around since 1949, this bar and grill is known for its drinks served in frosty mugs. Look for live music in "The Backyard."

Bars and Nightlife

Befitting the party scene, there is absolutely no shortage of drinking holes on the island.

Located at the Commodore Resort, **MIST Pool Bar** (272 Delaware Ave., 419/285-3101, commodoreresort.com) is one of the liveliest party spots in town and open to 21-and-over resort guests as well as non-guests. The Caribbean vibe and swim-up bar transport partiers away from Ohio. DJs play mixes 9pm-2am Thursday-Sunday.

Another "tropical" spot is **Mojito Bay** (389 Catawba Ave., 419/285-5282, mojitobaypib.com), a tiki bar with a floor of sand and swings instead of bar stools. The bar features live music at night.

The Roundhouse Bar (228 Delaware Ave., 419/285-2323, theroundhousebar.com) is a distinctive red, round tavern and has been a presence on the island since 1873. The Americana interior features live entertainment and an older clientele than, say, the pool bar.

Accommodations

Party resorts, bed-and-breakfasts, rental condos—there's quite the variety for such a small island. Prices are their highest on summer weekends. The farther you go from town, the quieter your stay is likely to be.

If you're here to party, then it's the **Commodore Resort Hotel** (272 Delaware Ave., 419/285-3101, commodoreresort.com, $229-425) for you, with two popular bars and rooms and suites of various sizes to accommodate groups. Rooms are basic but clean.

For those who want to leave the party at the party and return to a quiet bed, there's the couples' hotel, **Anchor Inn Boutique Hotel** (500 Catawba Ave., 419/285-5055, anchorinnpib.com, $219-271), with nine spacious, comfortable rooms and a hot breakfast included.

A much more sedate option in the middle of the island is **Arbor Inn Bed and Breakfast** (511 Trenton Ave., 419/285-2306, arborinnpib.com, $165-215), a modern bed-and-breakfast with four rooms, each with a king bed and private bathroom.

Birds Nest Resort (1371 Langram Rd., 419/285-6119, birdsnestresort.com, $145-185) offers simple cottages that sleep 2-8 people. A pool is on the property, which sits in the middle of the island near the small airport.

CAMPING

The main feature of **South Bass Island State Park** (1523 Catawba Ave., 419/285-2112, ohiodnr.gov, May-mid-Oct.) is the seasonal campground. It has 125 non-electric sites, 10 full-hookup sites, and four "cabents" with sturdy cabin-like walls and a canvas roof. Rates start at $29, and some sites are perched right along the low cliffside, with stellar views of the mainland.

Transportation

The only way to get to Put-in-Bay is by ferry service or charter plane. There are two ferry docks: the downtown Put-in-Bay marina and the Lime Kiln dock on the opposite end of the island, 2 miles (3.2 km) from town. **Jet Express** (jet-express.com) drops you off downtown and connects with Port Clinton, Kelleys Island, and Sandusky, but is a passenger-only service and the priciest option; the 30-minute ride from Port Clinton to Put-in-Bay costs $20 one-way. The cheaper option that also ferries vehicles—though having a car on the island is much more of a hindrance than a help—is **Miller Ferry** (millerferry.com); the trip from Catawba to South Bass Island costs $8 one-way. Miller Ferry drops you off at the Lime Kiln dock on the opposite side of the island from town, so you must rent a bike or golf cart, catch a taxi, take a bus, or walk to Put-in-Bay. A handful of taxi services operate passenger vans on the island, including Island Club Taxi (419/285-5466).

The main way to get around the island is by golf cart; rental rates run about $12 per hour or $60 per day for a four-person cart. You can find several rental agencies next to either of the island's ferry docks or on Delaware Avenue in town. You will also find bike rentals in these spots. Island Transportation (putinbaytrans.com) runs a tour trolley ($12) as well as a bus ($3) that connects the Lime Kiln ferry dock with downtown.

KELLEYS ISLAND

A quieter alternative to Put-in-Bay, Kelleys Island is best known for the unusual glacial grooves of Kelleys Island State Park. It's also the largest of the Lake Erie islands, with thick forests, historic wineries, and disused quarries (the island was once one of the world's largest exporters of limestone). While you'll still find some bars and nightlife, it's easy to avoid the noise.

Sights and Recreation

Kelleys Island State Park (920 Division St., 419/746-2546, ohiodnr.gov, dawn-dusk daily, free) is best known for the world's largest glacial grooves—35 feet (10.7 m) wide and 400 feet (122 m) long—carved by retreating glaciers during the last ice age. The otherworldly limestone bedrock can be viewed via a footbridge and stairs. Otherwise, the park offers a lakeside campground and 8 miles (12.9 km) of hiking trails through forest, wetlands, and old quarries. The **North Pond trail,** an easy 1-mile (1.6-km) loop hike, is the best for bird-watching; keep an eye out for bald eagles and migrating waterfowl. A small 100-foot (30-m) public swimming beach is available.

Kelleys Island Kayak Rental (920 Division St., 419/285-7433, kelleysislandkayakrental.com) operates out of the state park and rents kayaks and stand-up paddleboards.

Nacho Fishing Charters (733 W. Lakeshore Dr., 419/656-4951, nachofish.com) offers walleye and perch fishing trips and also arranges sightseeing boat trips, water taxis to anywhere nearby (including Canada), and accommodations on the island.

Food

Local stalwart **The Village Pump** (103 W. Lakeshore Dr., 419/746-2281, villagepumpkioh.com, 11am-2:30am daily, $9-20) stays open most of the year and serves an inexpensive menu of sandwiches and seafood, as well as some large surf-and-turf dinners for an island splurge.

Outdoor bar **Caddy Shack** (115 Division St., 419/746-2518, 11am-2am daily Memorial Day-Labor Day, limited hours daily Labor Day-Nov. and Apr.-Memorial Day, $9-16) is best known for pizzas and its weekday special of grilled wings. There are 30 beers on tap and, in theme with the name, miniature golf. Daily hours may fluctuate depending on how busy they are, so call ahead.

Kelleys Island Wine Company (418 Woodford Rd., 419/746-2678, kelleysislandwineco.com, 11am-10pm Mon.-Sat., 11am-8pm Sun., $8-16) is a full-service winery with two restaurants on the premises—one specializing in pizza and the other in tacos—and frequent live music. All the wines are produced on-site by the Zettler family.

Accommodations

Kelleys Island Venture Resort (441 W. Lakeshore Dr., 419/746-2900, kiventureresort.com, $275-460) is the only true hotel on the island, with 31 modern, comfortable suites of various sizes, lake-facing porches, and a pool. Prices decrease considerably outside summer weekends.

Water's Edge Retreat (827 E. Lakeshore Dr., 419/746-2333, watersedgeretreat.com, $199-289) is a brightly colored Queen Anne house right on the shore with excellent views of the lake. This bed-and-breakfast features seven antique-appointed guest rooms.

Alternatively, the **Eagles Nest Inn** (216 Cameron Rd., 419/746-2708, theeaglesnestinn.com, $140-170) is situated in the quiet woods away from the lake. There are three guest rooms here, all appointed with country decor, and an above-ground pool.

CAMPING

Kelleys Island State Park (920 Division St., 419/746-2546, ohiodnr.gov) has a lakeside campground with 126 sites, including 35 with a full hookup, along with four cabins and two yurts. Rates start at $27 a night.

Transportation

The only way to get to the island is by ferry. The **Kelleys Island Ferry** (kelleysislandferry. com) connects the island with Marblehead on the mainland and accommodates vehicles; the 20-minute ride costs $11 one-way. **Jet Express** (jet-express.com) makes a stop in-between Sandusky and Put-in-Bay but does not ferry vehicles; one-way tickets start at $15.

Once on the island, many rent bikes or golf carts at any of the several services within steps of the ferry dock. There is also the **Jolly Trolley** (419/746-2377), which can take up to 14 people; reservations are required. The trolley also does an island loop on weekends; fares are $5 and don't require a reservation.

MIDDLE BASS ISLAND

Middle Bass Island is closer in sensibility to Kelleys Island than South Bass Island but with much less to do. Dominated by private farms and vineyards, the island offers a handful of accommodations and **Middle Bass Island State Park** (1719 Fox Rd., 419/285-0311, ohiodnr.gov), which features a 184-slip marina, a primitive campground with sites reservable free of charge, and the shell of the historic Lonz Winery, clearly visible from Put-in-Bay. The winery, once a popular party spot, fell into disrepair after a terrace accident closed the facility. Today, visitors can find museum-like displays of old wine-making equipment in the cellars. Bikes, paddleboards, and kayaks are available to rent at the Harbormaster building. The serene island is a quiet choice for birders.

Transportation

Miller Ferry (millerferry.com) takes passengers and vehicles to Middle Bass from Catawba on the mainland, a 40-minute trip ($10.50 one-way). From Put-in-Bay, take the **Sonny-S Boat Line** (middlebassferry.net) for the short ride ($7 one-way); only passengers and bikes are allowed.

ISLE ST. GEORGE

Isle St. George, or North Bass Island, is the least accessible and therefore least visited of the inhabited Lake Erie islands. Only 2 miles (3.2 km) from the border with Canada, the island is only accessible by private boat or airplane and has not been commercially developed. Roughly two dozen people live here year-round to farm and look after the vineyards. **North Bass Island State Park** (Isle St. George, 419/734-4424, ohiodnr.gov) has primitive camping sites, which require a permit, and the four-bedroom Lake House for rent. Fishing and birding are the activities of choice, as is looking for local reptiles such as the Lake Erie water snake in Fox's Pond.

SANDUSKY

Charles Dickens famously visited Sandusky in 1842 on his tour through Ohio, saying the town was "sluggish and uninteresting enough . . . like the back of an English watering-place out of the season." The city has grown sprightlier since, with the arrival of Cedar Point in 1870 and its development into "The Roller Coaster Capital of the World" cementing Sandusky as the gateway to Ohio's Vacationland. There are ferries to Lake Erie's islands and marinas from which to set off on a lake adventure—but there's also plenty to keep you in town. The presence of the nation's most popular seasonal amusement park has attracted far

1: Perry's Victory and International Peace Memorial on South Bass Island 2: the indoor waterpark at Kalahari Resorts Sandusky 3: Put-in-Bay on South Bass Island

Sandusky

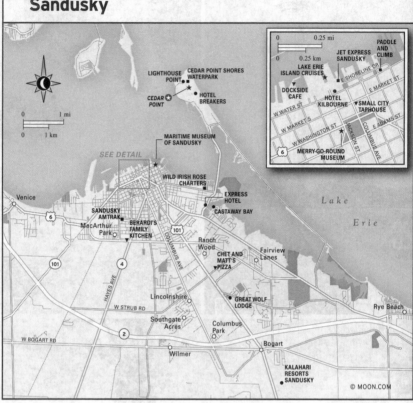

more waterpark resorts, restaurants, museums, and retail shops than a city of 25,000 normally claims. Downtown overlooks Sandusky Bay and has seen reinvestment throughout the 21st century, with restaurants and craft breweries reclaiming 19th-century storefronts.

Cedar Point's seasonality affects the entire city. If you're visiting anytime other than summer, it's worth double-checking hours of operation for attractions and restaurants.

Sights and Recreation

While Cedar Point is by far the largest draw to the area, it's worth noting that the arrival of indoor waterpark resorts has transformed Sandusky into a year-round destination.

TOP EXPERIENCE

★ CEDAR POINT

You don't win *Amusement Today*'s Golden Ticket Award for "Best Amusement Park in the World" 16 years consecutively for nothing. A glistening metropolis of roller coaster hills along the Lake Erie waterfront, **Cedar Point** (1 Cedar Point Dr., 419/627-2350, cedarpoint.com, May-Oct., check website for seasonal hours calendar, $72 general admission) is the country's most visited seasonal amusement park and its second oldest in operation, having opened as a lakeside resort in 1870. This massive 364-acre park sitting on a peninsula off Lake Erie is home to 17 roller coasters, the second most of any park

Cedar Point: "America's Roller Coast"

You'll be hard pressed to find anywhere in the world with as many quality roller coasters as Cedar Point. The park's 17 roller coasters—ranging from classic wooden coasters to state-of-the-art record-breakers—have inspired Cedar Point to bill itself as "America's Roller Coast." Six of them are over 200 feet (61 m) tall, more than any other park in the world. How do you prioritize which to ride?

riding on Millennium Force

- When **Millennium Force** opened in 2000, it was the world's first "giga" coaster—topping 300 feet (91 m)—as well as the tallest and fastest. The hill and drop are directly adjacent to the lake, and it is one of the longest roller coasters in the country. This behemoth has been ranked the first- or second-best steel roller coaster in the world every year of its existence.

- **Maverick** is unusual for its 95-degree drop. The quick twists and flips recall a ride on an obstinate stallion.

- Opened in 2018, **Steel Vengeance** was billed as the world's first "hybridcoaster" as the park took the bones of popular wooden coaster Mean Streak and infused a new steel track with other adjustments.

- Another record-breaker when it opened in 2003, **Top Thrill Dragster** launches riders to 120mph (193 km/h) in less than four seconds and shoots up 400 feet (122 m) in the air only to come down again for a 30-second trip. The tallest and fastest roller coaster in the world when it opened, it still remains in the top three for both.

- One of the more unique coasters in the park is **Valravn.** The train stops at the edge of the drop for a few hair-raising seconds before diving at a 90-degree angle.

in the world, and each new addition seems to break a new record for height, twists, and screams. There are over 70 rides total, with thrills for little ones as well, including the Planet Snoopy children's area. There are also live shows and a nightly laser show. Included in admission are the 18 water attractions at **Cedar Point Shores Waterpark,** including various enclosed and open-air slides and a 500,000-gallon wave pool.

If you can pull yourself away from the rides, there's a mile-long (1.6-km) sand **beach** on the eastern edge of the peninsula open to ticketholders and guests of any of Cedar Point's accommodations. **North Coast Parasail and Watersports** (440/315-3479, northcoastparasail.com) offers parasailing and watercraft rentals on the lake.

There's enough to do on the peninsula for an entire vacation. To that end, Cedar Point operates its own lodgings: Adjacent to the park at the same address (1 Cedar Point Dr.) are **Hotel Breakers,** with over 600 guest rooms, and **Lighthouse Point,** which offers a campground and lakeside cottages. A short drive away is the park's **Express Hotel** (1201 Cedar Point Dr.) and indoor waterpark resort **Castaway Bay** (2001 Cleveland Rd. W.), a destination of its own. All can be reached at 419/627-2106.

Tickets are significantly cheaper if purchased on the website, where you can also purchase Fast Lane wristbands, meal plans, and other add-ons. Refreshment options in the park are plentiful and pricey. There is a large picnic shelter outside the front entrance for those who packed lunches (get your hand stamped to get back into the park). Parking is $20.

WATERPARK RESORTS

The resorts' nightly rates include passes to their respective waterparks. The resorts also offer waterpark day passes for non-guests, though the price can fluctuate depending on the season.

Kalahari Resorts Sandusky (7000 Kalahari Dr., 877/525-2427, kalahariresorts.com, $200 and up/night) is the second largest indoor waterpark in the United States, occupying an enormous campus on the southern edge of town. On top of a 174,000-square-foot (16,165-sq-m) safari-themed indoor waterpark included with nightly rates, the complex includes an escape room, a spa, an outdoor waterpark, miniature golf, and a small zoo, some of which come with an extra admission cost. Accommodation options range from typical guest rooms to five-bedroom suites. Day passes are $75 and up for adults.

Sandusky is home to the second-oldest **Great Wolf Lodge** (4600 Milan Rd., 800/641-9653, greatwolf.com, $169-429/night), complete with a frontier-themed 30,000-square-foot (2,787-sq-m) indoor waterpark with slides, pools, and a lazy river. There are five restaurants on-site (with a dining plan available) and an outdoor pool open during summer months. Some suites have a sleeping area with a log cabin or "wolf den" theme and feature bunk beds. Day passes are $50 for adults.

Cedar Point got into the indoor waterpark game in 2004 when it opened **Castaway Bay** (2001 Cleveland Rd. W., 419/627-2106, castawaybay.com, $149-379/night). The 38,000-square-foot (3,530-sq-m) waterpark includes a lazy river, a wave pool, kids' splash areas, and a handful of slides. Visitors will also find a large arcade, restaurants, and a fitness center. The rooms are basic, with a slight tropical tinge to match the waterpark. Day passes are available for $29 for adults.

MERRY-GO-ROUND MUSEUM

The **Merry-Go-Round Museum** (301 Jackson St., 419/626-6111, merrygoroundmuseum.org, 10am-4pm Mon.-Sat., noon-4pm Sun. Memorial Day-Labor Day, $6 adults, $5 seniors, $4 children) is dedicated to collecting and refurbishing the festive animals of antiquated carousels. Housed in Sandusky's old post office, the museum holds over 70 original carousel animals—all from the golden age of merry-go-rounds between 1880 and 1930—lovingly restored by the museum's volunteers in a shop visible on the main floor. Admission includes a ride on a restored 1939 Allan Herschell Company carousel.

MARITIME MUSEUM OF SANDUSKY

It hasn't always been about resorts and roller coasters in Sandusky. The small **Maritime Museum of Sandusky** (125 Meigs St., 419/624-0274, sanduskymaritime.org, 10am-4pm Tues.-Sat., noon-4pm Sun. June-Aug., $7 adults, $6 seniors and children) covers the city's commercial fishing, ice harvesting, shipwreck, shipbuilding, and Underground Railroad history with interactive displays and artifacts including antique Lyman boats—locally made sport boats that influenced the industry early. A sailboat station allows kids to build their own model to take home. Parking is free and there's a nice nautically themed gift shop.

LAKE ERIE ISLAND CRUISES

Hop aboard the *Goodtime I* with **Lake Erie Island Cruises** (109 W. Shoreline Dr., 419/625-9692, goodtimeboat.com, May-Oct., $10-28 pp). This family-owned company offers a variety of tours out into Lake Erie, including sunset, island-hopping, party, and themed dinner cruises.

OTHER RECREATION

Several fishing charters depart from Sandusky's docks. **Wild Irish Rose Charters** (613 Bimini Dr., 419/357-4625, wildirishrosecharters.com) arranges walleye and perch fishing charters or private cruises to the islands.

Outdoor gear store **Paddle and Climb** (305 E. Water St., 419/502-1044, paddleandclimb.com) offers kayak and stand-up paddleboard rentals as well as a 32-foot (9.8-m) rock climbing wall, in addition to selling outdoor adventure apparel, accessories, and equipment suitable for life on the trail or the water.

Food

The popular **Small City Taphouse** (202 Columbus Ave., 419/502-0099, smallcitytaphouse.com, 3pm-10pm Mon.-Thurs., noon-11pm Fri.-Sat., $10-17) marries a pan-Asian menu of sushi, pho, fried rice, and more with 80 taps of local, national, and international craft beer. The large, bright dining room and extensive bar make for a festive gathering spot.

Seasonal walk-up counter **Dockside Café** (611 W. Shoreline Dr., 419/503-2296, 11am-9pm daily Memorial Day-Labor Day, $9-15) occupies a sunny spot on the end of a marina. The simple menu covers burgers, tacos (notably walleye tacos), salads, and quesadillas. There's outdoor seating only, and the view covers the entire bay, with Cedar Point in the distance.

It all started in 1942 with a hand-cut French fry stand in Cedar Point. **Berardi's Family Kitchen** (1019 W. Perkins Ave., 419/626-4592, sanduskyberardis.com, 6am-8pm Mon.-Sat., 7:30am-1:30pm Sun., $9-14) has since relocated and expanded to a full-service restaurant but remains a local favorite. Despite the Italian last name, the restaurant's menu mainly focuses on burgers, sandwiches, and salads with a small Italian menu tossed in. The hand-cut fries are still there.

Easy-going **Chet and Matt's Pizza** (1013 E. Strub Rd., 419/626-6000, chetmattspizza.com, 11am-10pm Mon.-Thurs., 11am-11pm Fri.-Sat., 10am-10pm Sun., $5-12) pairs well with a family day of fun. Choose from one of the unusual pizza pies to share, build your own individual pizzas, or go for the lunch or dinner buffet. Wings and burgers round out the inexpensive menu.

Accommodations

It's not typically cheap to stay in Sandusky—even quite ordinary motels can fetch a pretty penny for their proximity to Cedar Point. There's quite a range of options, from dumpy two-star motels to historic downtown boutique hotels to waterpark resorts. Most of the many chain motel options are found along Milan Road southeast of town near SR 2 or close to Cedar Point. It's best to reserve early or visit during a weekday for more options and cheaper rates.

CEDAR POINT HOTELS

Guests at any of Cedar Point's accommodations enjoy early entry to the park and access to discount ticket packages or room/ticket combination rates.

Wedged between the park and the beach, the historic **Hotel Breakers** (1 Cedar Point Dr., 419/627-2106, cedarpoint.com, $324-403) features over 600 rooms and suites—fairly basic but spacious. The complex includes two outdoor pools, an indoor pool, hot tubs, and several bars and restaurants, including a hibachi grill.

Five minutes south of the park is the **Express Hotel** (1201 Cedar Point Dr., 419/627-2106, cedarpoint.com, $129-219), with simple but updated two-bed guest rooms. Outside is a pool and splash pad.

DOWNTOWN HOTELS

Hotel Kilbourne (223 W. Water St., 844/373-2223, hotelkilbourne.com, $275-375) is right on the waterfront in downtown Sandusky. Five luxurious suites are outfitted with king beds and walk-in showers. Prices decrease considerably on weeknights. A rooftop bar is on the premises.

CAMPING

On the far end of the peninsula behind Cedar Point is **Lighthouse Point** (1 Cedar Point

Thomas Edison's Birthplace

Thomas A. Edison Birthplace Museum

Famous inventor Thomas Alva Edison—responsible for game-changing devices such as the lightbulb and motion picture camera—was born in tiny Milan on February 11, 1847. He only spent the first seven years of his life here before his family moved to Port Huron, Michigan, where Edison grew up. Milan operates the Thomas A. Edison Birthplace Museum (9 N. Edison Dr., 419/499-2135, tomedison.org, 10am-5pm Tues.-Sat., 1pm-5pm Sun., $15 adults, $10 seniors and children) in the modest brick house of the Edison family, who donated era-appropriate furnishings; the house looks much as it would have while Edison lived there. You'll also find early versions of many of Edison's inventions.

You can make an afternoon out of Milan, about 25 minutes (13 mi/20.9 km) southeast of downtown Sandusky. Steps away from the Edison birthplace is the Milan Museum (10 N. Edison Dr., 419/499-2968, milanhistory.org, 10am-5pm Tues.-Sat., 1pm-5pm Sun. June-Aug., 1pm-5pm Fri.-Sun. Sept.-Dec. and Feb.-May, $9 adults, $8 seniors, $5 children), a collection of historic buildings that feature exhibits on the town's former inland port days and more about Edison. The small central square of the Milan Historic District is surrounded by 19th-century buildings with antique stores, boutiques, and inviting restaurants such as the suitably themed Invention Restaurant (15 N. Main St., 419/499-0478, 6am-2pm Mon., 6am-8pm Tues.-Sat., 7am-2pm Sun., $5-12), which serves diner-like breakfasts, lunches, and dinners in a family-friendly setting decorated with pictures of Edison. You can even stay the night at Angel Welcome Bed and Breakfast (2 E. Front St., 419/499-0094, angelwelcome.com, $140), nicely situated in a Federal 1828 home between Edison's birthplace and the historic district. Three suites find an effective balance between history and comfort.

Dr., 419/627-2106, cedarpoint.com, $121-359), with 156 cottages and cabins as well as 145 attractive RV campsites with full hookups. Tent camping is not permitted. There's a shower/restroom facility and an outdoor pool available May-Labor Day.

Transportation

Sandusky is a little over an hour's drive west from Cleveland (62 mi/100 km) via I-90 and SR 2. The trip east from Toledo is also just over an hour (54 mi/87 km) via SR 579 and SR 2. It's a little less straightforward from

Columbus, with multiple routes possible. The most straightforward is heading north on US-23 and then exiting past Marion to head north on SR 4, which bumps right into Sandusky. All told the journey is an easy 2.25- to 2.5-hour drive (111 mi/179 km), a workable day trip from Central Ohio.

The **Amtrak Station** (1200 N. Depot St., amtrak.com) sees a few stops, primarily in the middle of the night. **Greyhound** (greyhound.com) also stops at the station.

The **Jet Express** (jet-express.com) leaves from 101 W. Shoreline Drive for Put-in-Bay and Kelleys Island.

The **Sandusky Transit System** (sandusky.oh.us) is primarily suited for residents but does have some fixed routes of interest to visitors. Fare is $1.50 and can be paid with exact change or the EZfare app. None of the lines go directly to Cedar Point but they can take you downtown or to the Milan Road strip of resorts, hotels, and shops. **A Sandusky Taxi** (419/366-7918) operates throughout the city.

MARBLEHEAD

Tiny Marblehead is most notable for its iconic Marblehead Lighthouse, from which there are excellent views of the Lake Erie islands and shoreline: Put-in-Bay to the west, Kelleys Island to the north, and Cedar Point to the south.

Sights
MARBLEHEAD LIGHTHOUSE
Lake Erie smashes into the rocky shore next to **Marblehead Lighthouse** (110 Lighthouse Dr., 419/798-2094, marbleheadlighthouseohio.org, free), the oldest U.S. lighthouse in the Great Lakes and reportedly the most photographed site in Ohio. Built in 1821, the red and white lighthouse is open for tours ($3 pp) that allow visitors to ascend the 77 steps up to the top for panoramic views of the islands and shoreline. The original keeper's house next door is home to a small museum and gift shop. Within the park is also the Lifesaving Station Museum, educating visitors on the town's role as a Coast Guard station. The lighthouse, keeper's house, and museum are open noon-4pm daily Memorial Day-Labor Day, and the grounds are open dawn-dusk daily year-round.

Recreation
East Harbor State Park (1169 N. Buck Rd., 419/734-4424, ohiodnr.gov, dawn-dusk daily, free) features coastal hiking trails, wetlands, a disc golf course, and a sandy swimming beach. It also has one of the largest campgrounds in Ohio. The marina offers charters for a day on the lake.

Food and Accommodations
Set in an 1893 limestone building, **Rocky Point Winery** (111 W. Main St., 419/967-5344, rockypointwinery.com, 10am-8pm Mon.-Sat.) offers small plates along with a dozen or so local wines and live music. The same family runs the **Red Fern Inn at Rocky Point Winery** (419/515-1494, redferninn.com, $189-299) within the building. There are four guest suites, each with one or two bedrooms and a full kitchen. Rates include complimentary bicycle rentals and a bottle of wine.

Next door is **Marblehead Galley** (113 W. Main St., 419/798-5356, marbleheadgalley.com, 7am-9pm Sun.-Thurs., 7am-10pm Fri.-Sat., $6-16), setting the table for breakfast, lunch, and dinner with diner classics as well as seafood, including local perch and walleye. There's indoor and outdoor seating at this nautically themed bar and grill.

CAMPING
The campground at **East Harbor State Park** (1169 N. Buck Rd., 419/734-4424, ohiodnr.gov) offers over 500 electric and non-electric sites (including 23 full-hookup sites suitable for RVs), flush toilets, and hot showers, though privacy between the sites is practically nonexistent. Try to reserve a spot on the edge if possible. Rates start at $27.

Transportation
From Toledo, Marblehead is just over an hour's drive (52 mi/84 km) east. Take SR 579

Birding in Northwest Ohio

The southern coast of Lake Erie is a natural stopping point for migratory birds exhausted from their long journey north during springtime. Birds are apt to rest in the shore's wetlands before venturing across the lake. During spring, Ohio's trees are still bare, which makes spotting as many as 280 species of waterfowl, songbirds, shorebirds, and raptors relatively easy. As such, Northwest Ohio has established a reputation as a birding hotspot.

Mid-April through May is peak season, when the most birds are making their way through the area. It's also when the region hosts **The Biggest Week in American Birding** (biggestweekinamericanbirding.com), a nine-day festival in early May celebrating the hundreds of thousands of winged visitors that descend upon Northwest Ohio. Particularly popular are the more than 40 species of colorful, fluffy warblers that arrive in such numbers at times that they may come within feet of patient visitors, an experience that has earned the region the moniker "Warbler Capital of the World" in birding circles. Registration is required for the festival's events, but many are free. It's quite the to-do for nature lovers; in addition to visiting the parks, thousands attend field trips, guided walks, lectures, and other events during the festival.

Where are the best places in Northwest Ohio to do some birding?

- **Magee Marsh Wildlife Area** (13551 SR 2, Oak Harbor, 419/898-0960, ohiodnr.gov) features a long boardwalk that passes through the marsh and forested beach.

- **Ottawa National Wildlife Refuge** (14000 SR 2, Oak Harbor, 419/898-0014, fws.gov) has a large visitors center and the safari-like Wildlife Drive, which is open on scheduled days throughout the year.

- **Metzger Marsh Wildlife Area** (Bono Rd. off SR 2, Curtice, 419/424-5000) is adjacent to the Ottawa National Wildlife Refuge and is a continuation of the marshy wilderness, albeit with few amenities or facilities.

- **Maumee Bay State Park** (1400 State Park Rd., Oregon, 419/836-7758, ohiodnr.gov) features an extensive boardwalk through lakeside marsh and woods.

- **Oak Openings Preserve Metropark** (4139 Girdham Rd., Swanton, 419/360-9179, metroparkstoledo.com) preserves a unique Northwest Ohio ecosystem of oak savanna and vegetated dunes that is a popular stop for migrating songbirds.

to SR 2 to the SR 269 exit. Turn right at SR 163 and the town is at the end of the peninsula. It's a simpler drive from Cleveland, roughly 1.25 hours away (78 mi/126 km) west on I-90 and SR 2 until the SR 269 exit.

The **Kelleys Island Ferry** (kelleysislandferry.com) departs from Marblehead for Kelleys Island at 510 W. Main Street.

Black Taxi (419/707-3718) operates throughout the Marblehead Peninsula.

PORT CLINTON

The "Walleye Capital of the World," Port Clinton boasts a small but historic downtown, a Jet Express ferry dock, and plenty of opportunities to get in on the fishing action. A

secondary gateway to the area after Sandusky, it's a solid choice as a base to enjoy the area's recreation and sights, with several restaurant and accommodation options.

Sights
AFRICAN SAFARI WILDLIFE PARK
The **African Safari Wildlife Park** (267 S. Lightner Rd., 419/732-3606, africansafariwildlifepark.com, 9am-7pm daily Memorial Day-Labor Day, 10am-5pm daily late Feb.-Memorial Day and Labor Day-early Dec., $29.95 adults, $20.95 children) provides two zoo experiences. The drive-through safari takes you through enclosures teeming with animals such as giraffes, zebras, antelope,

and llamas, which you can feed (one cup of food per car is provided with admission). The walk-through safari more closely resembles a typical zoo-going experience, with small animals displayed in small habitats. You're free to enjoy both as many times as you like, and there are side experiences such as an aviary and educational programs as well. A gift shop and café are on-site. Parking is free. Admission prices are lower on weekdays and in the off-season.

LIBERTY AVIATION MUSEUM

The **Liberty Aviation Museum** (3515 E. State Rd., 419/732-0234, libertyaviationmuseum.org, 10am-4pm Mon.-Fri., 10am-5pm Sat.-Sun., $10 adults, $8 seniors and children) features two hangars and multiple galleries of functional WWII aircraft, vehicles, and artifacts. Highlights include a B-25 bomber and a Ford Tri-Motor. In front of the museum is the vintage **Tin Goose Diner** (419/732-0236, tingoosediner.com, 7am-7pm daily, $7-11), built in the 1950s by the Jerry O'Mahony Diner Company and still featuring old-school bar stools and booths and a fitting diner menu.

★ OTTAWA NATIONAL WILDLIFE REFUGE

A veritable safari for bird lovers, **Ottawa National Wildlife Refuge** (14000 SR 2, Oak Harbor, 419/898-0014, fws.gov/refuge/ottawa, dawn-dusk daily, free) harbors 6,500 acres of wetlands, coastal grasslands, and woods frequented by flocks of migrating waterfowl, colorful songbirds, and several nesting pairs of bald eagles. Both the American Bird Conservancy and Audubon Ohio have designated the refuge an Important Bird Area for its location on migratory routes. Start at the large visitors center (9am-4pm daily), where helpful rangers can tell you what to see and where to find them, then head out to hike atop the 10 miles (16.1 km) of dikes that help control the water levels. Bring binoculars to survey the unobstructed views, as well as sunscreen; you're pretty exposed in the sun and Lake Erie breeze. Like an actual safari,

you can take your car through the one-way Wildlife Drive (check the schedule for open days) to spot trumpeter swans, eagles, sandhill cranes, wading birds, and other critters in the open wilderness. Deer, foxes, mink, turtles, and water snakes also call the refuge home. While there's something to see in any season, spring is the busiest time of year as migratory birds stop on the lakeshore for a rest before soldiering on. The visitors center and nearby trail are handicap accessible.

Recreation

There are many fishing charters available in Port Clinton. Try **Sassy Sal Charters** (40 Jefferson St., 419/732-7755, sassysalcharters.com) or **Shore Nuf Charters** (247 W. Lakeshore Dr., 419/734-9999, shore-nuf.com).

Food

A quick walk from the Jet Express ferry dock, the turquoise house of **Coffee Express** (128 W. 2nd St., 419/734-2089, 6am-3pm Mon. and Sat., 6am-5:30pm Tues.-Fri., 7am-3pm Sun., $4-8) offers pastries, quiches, and cookies baked in-house as well as a light lunch menu. There's outdoor seating on either side of the building.

Unfussy **Jolly Rogers Seafood House** (1737 E. Perry St., 419/732-3382, 11am-8pm daily, $9-15) does counter-service fried fish platters, with fresh walleye and perch battered before your eyes while you're in line to order your food. There's indoor and outdoor seating in this low-key joint.

In the Knoll Crest Shopping Center is the peninsula's location of local institution **Toft's Ice Cream Parlor** (4016 E. Harbor Rd., 419/732-8857, toftdairy.com, 11am-9pm Sun.-Thurs., 11am-10pm Fri.-Sat.). Originating in Sandusky in 1900, the parlors feature 52 varieties of ice cream and scoop out large portions. There is a limited amount of seating inside.

To the east of town is **Cheesehaven** (2920 E. Harbor Rd., 419/734-2611, cheesehaven. com, 10am-7pm daily). Open since 1949, this roadside market sells over 100 varieties of domestic and imported cheeses and spreads, as well as classic and unusual candies, taffy, homemade fudge, and other snacks. This is a must if you're putting together a picnic.

Accommodations

Right in the center of town since 1886 is the **Island House Hotel** (102 N. Madison St., 419/734-0100, port-clinton-ohio-hotel.com, $99-199). There are 10 different configurations of modernized guest rooms which have seen the likes of sitting presidents, sports stars, and other celebrities who have stopped through town.

OurGuest Inn and Suites (220 E. Perry St., 419/734-7111, ourguestinnandsuites.com, $79-159) offers basic, inexpensive rooms near

downtown. The grounds include a heated pool and a firepit.

There are a handful of chain motels a couple minutes east of the center of town along the water.

Transportation

Port Clinton is a little under an hour's drive (38 mi/61 km) east from Toledo via SR 579 and SR 2. From Cleveland, take I-90 to SR 2, a little over an hour's drive (77 mi/124 km) west.

The **Jet Express** (jet-express.com) leaves from 3 Monroe Street for Put-in-Bay and then on to Kelleys Island and Sandusky.

After Hours Taxi (419/732-6151) operates throughout Port Clinton and the Marblehead Peninsula.

Toledo and Vicinity

Every industrial city in Ohio seems to have its "thing," and Toledo's is glass. Already a major Great Lakes port, sitting on Lake Erie at the mouth of the Maumee River, Toledo benefitted from the arrival of glassmaking companies in the 1880s (led in size and stature by the Libbey Glass Company), all of which manufactured glass products of various sizes and shapes: dishware, windshields, and lightbulbs among them. Such was the volume and quality of production that the city earned the nickname "The Glass City," which it still goes by today. Automobile manufacturing arrived too, with Toledo well-positioned only an hour south of Detroit and on the railroad between New York and Chicago. The money made from these industries went into beautiful parks, a large and free art museum, and other cultural amenities that few cities of its size enjoy. Today, Ohio's fourth largest city after the Three C's has faced the decline of population and industry so prevalent in Rust Belt America. Yet, the city's attractions linger and prosper as beloved entities that, sadly, don't always receive much attention outside of the metropolitan area. Visitors will also find two

unique museums: the National Museum of the Great Lakes and Fort Meigs, a rare War of 1812 historic site and the largest wooden fort in North America. Put together, Toledo offers a uniquely Ohioan perspective on the Great Lakes region and an attractive, alternative base from which to explore the Lake Erie area away from the high prices of Vacationland.

SIGHTS

★ Toledo Zoo and Aquarium

A much larger and more complete zoo than a city the size of Toledo has any right to, the **Toledo Zoo and Aquarium** (2 Hippo Way, 419/385-5721, toledozoo.org, 10am-6pm daily with last admission at 5pm Memorial Day-Labor Day, reduced hours Labor Day-Memorial Day, $22 adults, $19 seniors and children) is well-loved by locals, highly regarded by the zoo world, and home to 10,000 animals of over 700 species. Historic, Spanish-inspired architecture dots the park, including an outdoor auditorium and the aquarium. The zoo was more or less put on the map in the 1980s when it opened a then-innovative "Hippoquarium," which let visitors view the aquatic pachyderms from underwater. The exhibit is part of the **Tembo Trail,** which also features African elephants, yaks, grizzly bears, and other critters from across the globe (there's not a real theme to the exhibit). The five-acre open savanna of **Africa!** is home to favorites such as giraffes, zebras, wildebeest, and several species of antelope. Uniquely, visitors have the opportunity to view the exhibit from a bird's-eye perspective via the **Aerial Adventure Course,** a three-story-tall high ropes course and zip line that stands behind the enclosures. Other highlights include **Arctic Encounter,** with polar bears, seals, and grey wolves, and **Kingdom of the Apes,** which has orangutans and gorillas.

The zoo is split in half by the Anthony Wayne Trail highway, with a handicap-accessible pedestrian bridge straddling it. There are plenty of food options, including the Carnivore Café, which serves typical grill fare as well as some Mexican options. Parking is $8.

Toledo Botanical Garden

A free asset to the community, the **Toledo Botanical Garden** (5403 Elmer Dr., 419/270-7500, metroparkstoledo.com, dawn-dusk daily, free) is a 60-acre "museum for plants." Less intensively landscaped than many other botanical gardens, these gardens feel more pastoral than manicured, such as in the Woodland Garden, with rhododendrons, hostas, and native wildflowers. There is also a perennial garden, rose garden, and elegant sculptures dotted throughout. The Doneghy Inclusive Garden was designed with accessibility in mind, including sensory components and wheelchair-accessible flower beds. Picnic tables and restrooms can be found at the main Elmer Drive entrance.

★ Toledo Museum of Art

Like the zoo, you might arrive at the **Toledo Museum of Art** (2445 Monroe St., 419/255-8000, toledomuseum.org, 10am-4pm Tues.-Sun., free) scratching your head: *this* is in Toledo? It's free, to boot. The museum's Greek Revival building, opened in 1912, houses more than 30,000 pieces of art in its collection, though only a small percentage is on display at any given time. The 45 galleries cover a lot of ground, from an antiquities room designed to appear like a Roman atrium to spartan rooms holding postmodern sculptures. Within the collection are pieces from masters such as Rembrandt, Renoir, Van Gogh, and Monet. A truly one-of-a-kind room holds a recreated medieval cloister reconstructed from the arcades of three monasteries. The Museum Café (11am-4pm Wed., Thurs., and Sun., 11am-7pm Fri.-Sat.) serves gnocchi, sandwiches, and a half-pound burger of the week. In accordance with the city's glass reputation, the Museum Store sells a large selection of glassworks.

Across Monroe Street from the main building is the **Glass Pavilion** (2444 Monroe St.), an annex opened in 2006. The galleries here display the museum's glass collection, including a Dale Chihuly piece and a chronological exhibit of glass art through the millennia. The coffee bar (noon-3:30pm Tues.-Wed., noon-8:30pm Thurs.-Fri., noon-4:30pm Sat.-Sun.) fronts the street.

Parking for the museum campus is $8. There are several parking lots. The closest to a front door of the main museum is Lot 1, which hides behind the museum on Art Museum Drive and is accessible from Monroe Street via Glenwood Avenue or Oakwood Avenue.

Imagination Station

Science museum **Imagination Station** (1 Discovery Way, 419/244-2674, imaginationstationtoledo.org, 10am-5pm Tues.-Sat., noon-5pm Sun., $13 adults, $12 seniors, $11 children) sits right on the riverfront in downtown Toledo. The museum's mission is to provide interactive STEM learning experiences for children (note that adults are listed as "big kids" on the website). Many exhibits are hands-on, such as the Idea Lab, where visitors can design, create, and tinker with various projects involving animated cartoons, air-powered cars, and marble tracks. Extreme Science Theater hosts shows throughout the

Toledo

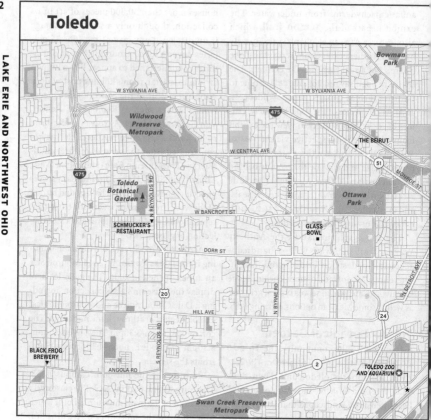

day demonstrating key scientific principles. Experience some serious weather and try to control water in the Water Works exhibit.

The museum features a gift shop and the Atomic Café, selling sandwiches and pizza. The Vistula Parking Garage (at Summit St. and Cherry St.) and Superior Street Garage (between Madison Ave. and Adams St.) are the closest parking options, unless you're lucky enough to find metered street parking closer. On the third Thursday of the month, the museum stays open until 8pm, with $5 admission after 5pm.

National Museum of the Great Lakes

Perhaps the most unique museum in Toledo, the **National Museum of the Great Lakes**

(1701 Front St., 419/214-5000, nmgl.org, 10am-5pm Mon.-Sat., noon-5pm Sun. May-Oct., reduced hours and ships closed Nov.-Apr., $10 adults, $8 children, additional $6 ship admission fee) chronicles the natural, cultural, and economic history of the Great Lakes region. The relatively small museum is stocked with quality interactive exhibits, interesting pieces of ships and artifacts, and fascinating information about the world's largest freshwater resource, which has seen its fair share of battles, shipwrecks, and commerce. Profiles of the lakes highlight each body of water's unique characteristics and how the country's "Third Coast" has shaped the progress of the United States. Those who remember the sinking of the *Edmund Fitzgerald* in 1975 (or Gordon Lightfoot's lengthy ballad)

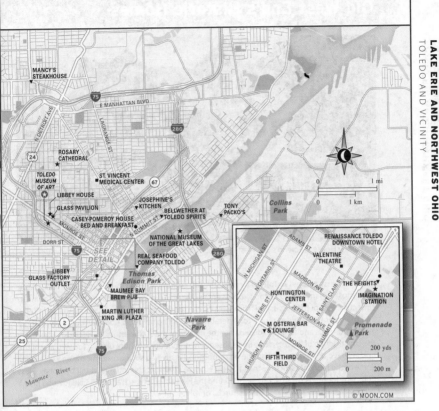

can check out artifacts from the ship as well as a submarine simulation exploring the wreckage. The highlight of the museum is exploring inside the two ships docked in the Maumee River next to the building: the tugboat *Ohio*, built in 1903, and the 617-foot (188-m) freighter *Col. James M. Schoonmaker,* with its cozy guest suites and massive cargo holds dating back to 1911.

A small gift shop sells books, nautically themed art, and souvenirs. Parking is plentiful and free.

★ Fort Meigs Historic Site

Southwest of town, the **Fort Meigs Historic Site** (29100 W. River Rd., Perrysburg, 419/874-4121, fortmeigs.org, fort 9:30am-5pm Wed.-Sat., noon-5pm Sun. Apr.-Oct., museum 9:30am-5pm Wed.-Sat., noon-5pm Sun. year-round, $10 adults, $8 seniors, $5 children) was reconstructed over the earthworks of the original fort, which was built in 1813 as Ohio's primary defense along the Maumee River. This historic site preserves 65 acres encompassing the fort and surrounding grounds where U.S. troops repelled two sieges from combined British and American Indian forces during the War of 1812. The fortification—the largest wooden fort in North America—features seven spartan blockhouses, including four that are open to the public and host to exhibits interpreting life inside the fort. A small but interesting museum outside the fort details the establishment of Ohio, conflicts with American Indians, and the war, with artifacts excavated from the site such as

Old West End's Historic Homes

the Libbey House in Toledo's Old West End neighborhood

The swankiest address in Toledo by the late 19th century, the Old West End holds many of the city's most expansive and historic houses and is one of the largest collections of late Victorian architecture east of the Mississippi. The styles range from Victorian to Edwardian to Arts and Crafts, and the size of the houses range considerably as well. The neighborhood fell out of favor in the 1920s and 1930s and sank into disrepair in the middle of the 20th century, its decline hastened by the construction of the interstate and subsequent demolition of entire blocks. Today, many of the houses have been restored and the neighborhood is diverse socioeconomically and culturally. Some of the highlights include the **Libbey House** (2008 Scottwood Ave.), built by Libbey Glass Company founder Edward Libbey in 1895, and the **Rosary Cathedral** (2535 Collingwood Blvd.), a unique Spanish Plateresque-style church completed in 1931.

weapons, cannonballs, and tools. Find a costumed interpreter, or Manager of Historic Programs John Thompson in his office in the middle of the fort, to add further dimension to this hallowed ground—one that advocates for peace rather than celebrating war as it stewards a painful piece of U.S. history. The gift shop is well-stocked with history books on the American Revolution, American Indian people native to Ohio, and the War of 1812. Check the website to see the busy calendar of engaging historical, holiday, and evening events.

Fallen Timbers Battlefield National Historic Site

There's not a lot to see in the present day at **Fallen Timbers Battlefield National**

Historic Site (5601 Anthony Wayne Trail, Maumee, 419/407-9700, dawn-dusk daily, free), which was established by a partnership between the National Park Service, Toledo Metroparks, and Ohio History Connection, but this ground witnessed a fateful moment in U.S. history that enabled westward expansion and removal of American Indians. Southwest of the city, the precise location of the 1794 battle was only correctly identified by archaeologists in 1995. The spot previously thought to be the battleground is home to the Fallen Timbers State Memorial, a handsome monument commemorating

1: Fort Meigs Historic Site 2: Toledo Museum of Art
3: Arctic Encounter at the Toledo Zoo

Battle for the Northwest Territory

Established in 1787 by Congress, the Northwest Territory was the first territorial expansion of the new United States of America and incorporated much of present-day Ohio, Michigan, Indiana, Illinois, and Wisconsin. As the closest part of the Northwest Territory to the original 13 colonies, Ohio saw many of the formative struggles between American Indians, who by this point saw the value of banding together to fight for their homes, and settlers traveling to this coveted territory to build a new life.

Tensions grew as settlers flocked to what would become Ohio. American Indians who had largely remained either peaceful or passive grew more hostile, with settlers retaliating in kind. In 1791, 1,000 U.S. militia members and regulars marched north from Cincinnati to establish forts and quell an American Indian confederacy that had violently and successfully opposed raids into their territory. The force was led by Northwest Territory governor General Arthur St. Clair, whose military record was marked by controversy and whose fitness for battle was questionable. Led by Miami chief Little Turtle and Shawnee chief Blue Jacket, a confederacy force of 2,000 Indigenous warriors ambushed and decimated the poorly trained U.S. force in western Ohio near the headwaters of the Wabash River. With nearly the entire army killed or wounded, the Battle of the Wabash, or **St. Clair's Defeat** as it came to be called, is still considered one of the greatest disasters in U.S. military history.

The war continued to go badly for the United States as allied American Indians attacked forts and disrupted supply lines. While peace negotiations ensued, President George Washington ordered General "Mad" Anthony Wayne to train and lead the new Legion of the United States, a forerunner of the U.S. Army. The force left Cincinnati a much larger and better-trained unit than St. Clair's force and met the confederacy at a site where hundreds of trees were felled by a recent tornado near the Maumee River, just south of present-day Toledo. On August 20, 1794, about 3,000 men under Wayne met Blue Jacket's force of 1,300, and the **Battle of Fallen Timbers** ended with a U.S. victory, a temporary disintegration of the Indigenous confederacy, and the signing of the Treaty of Greenville, which forced the American Indians to cede southern and eastern Ohio to the United States. The Shawnee retreated north or resettled in Missouri. Though American Indians would again band together under the leadership of Shawnee chief Tecumseh over a decade later, the defeat and treaty marked the beginning of their removal from the Northwest Territory.

the soldiers, American Indians, and settlers who sacrificed their lives on these sacred grounds. North of this location, a 1.5-mile (2.4-km) loop with interpretive signs meanders through the woods of the battle's correct site, which sits on the other side of the Anthony Wayne Trail highway from the memorial and next to, somewhat discouragingly, a shopping mall. To go straight to the battlefield and path, go to the parking lot at 4949 Jerome Road, where there is a small visitors center. A 0.5-mile (0.8-km) pedestrian and bike trail connects the two spots with a bridge over Anthony Wayne Trail.

Sauder Village

In the vicinity of Toledo, **Sauder Village** (22611 SR 2, Archbold, 419/446-2541, saudervillage.org, 10am-5pm Wed.-Sun., $20 adults, $18 seniors, $14 children) is something of a history theme park, with a historic village of relocated buildings and reconstructions covering Ohio history from 1803 to 1928, working craftspeople, a farm, and costumed guides to educate visitors. There's plenty of country-style shopping and eating to do while you're here (note some of the shops and restaurants keep their own hours). There is also a campground and hotel in the complex, which is west of town.

ENTERTAINMENT AND EVENTS

The Arts

The **Toledo Symphony Orchestra** (toledo-symphony.com) performs at the **Peristyle** concert hall in the Toledo Museum of Art (2445 Monroe St., 419/246-8000).

The Toledo Cultural Arts Center manages the 900-seat **Valentine Theatre** (410 Adams St., 419/242-2787, valentinetheatre. com), which was built in 1895 and today hosts local theater and musical acts, including the **Toledo Jazz Orchestra** (toledojazz.org).

The **Huntington Center** (500 Jefferson Ave., huntingtoncentertoledo.com) is an 8,000-seat multipurpose arena that hosts touring musicians and other acts.

Festivals and Events

The greater Northwest Ohio area is the center of the birding world during the **Biggest Week in American Birding** (biggestweek-inamericanbirding.com), which takes place over 10 days in early May.

The **Toledo Jeep Festival** (toledojeep-fest.com) attracts over 70,000 people over one weekend in early August with off-road courses, food trucks, and live music.

The area's oldest and largest ethnic festival, the **German American Festival** (gafsociety. org) features authentic German food and beer as well as festive competitions for a weekend in late August.

RECREATION
Parks

Promenade Park (400 Water St., 419/245-3357, toledo.oh.gov) is a stretch of green space wedged between downtown Toledo and the Maumee River with walking paths, public art installations, and a calendar of live music and festivals throughout the year.

Providence Metropark (13827 S. River Rd., 419/360-9187, metroparkstoledo.com) features over a mile (1.6 km) of the original 19th-century Miami and Erie Canal and its only remaining working lock. Costumed interpreters staff the **Canal Experience,** which allows visitors to ride aboard a mule-drawn canal boat ($7) through the lock May-October. Boat rides last approximately one hour.

Maumee Bay State Park (1400 State Park Rd., Oregon, 419/836-7758, ohiodnr. gov, dawn-dusk daily, free), 20 minutes east of Toledo, has two swimming beaches, boardwalks over coastal wetlands, a golf course, and a nature center. A variety of accommodations include a campground, cabins, and a large lodge.

Cycling

The **Wabash Cannonball Trail** (metropark-stoledo.com) offers 64 miles (103 km) of mostly paved multiuse paths connecting several of the metro area's southwestern parks, including Fallen Timbers and Oak Openings. Note bike rentals in the area are few and far between.

Kayaking, Canoeing, and Paddleboarding

Riverlures Kayak Adventure (24287 Front St., Grand Rapids, 419/832-0989, riverlures-kayaking.com) offers kayak rentals on the Maumee River southwest of Toledo. The **Maumee River Water Trail** (metropark-stoledo.com) has 39 access points starting from Maumee Bay State Park and continuing to Riverside Park in Antwerp, a total of 107 miles (172 km).

Hiking

Oak Openings Preserve Metropark (4139 Girdham Rd., Swanton, 419/360-9179, metroparkstoledo.com) is the largest remaining tract in Ohio of the rare oak savanna ecosystem, with sandy forest and vegetated dunes. There are over 50 miles (81 km) of trails within the 5,000-acre park, southwest of the city.

Spectator Sports

The **Toledo Mud Hens** (milb.com/toledo) are one of the oldest minor league baseball teams in the country, with a history going back to 1896. They play at downtown's **Fifth Third Field** (406 Washington St., 419/725-4367), which is surrounded by a number of lively bars and restaurants. The **Toledo Walleye** (toledowalleye.com) play minor league hockey at **Huntington Center** (500 Jefferson Ave., huntingtoncentertoledo.com).

The **University of Toledo Rockets** (utrockets.com) compete in the Mid-American Conference and support men's and women's teams, including the men's football team that plays at the **Glass Bowl** (1745 Stadium Dr., 419/530-3790).

SHOPPING

Shop for glass in the "Glass City" at the **Libbey Glass Factory Outlet** (205 S. Erie St., 419/254-5000, libbey.com/outlet, 9:30am-5:30pm Mon.-Fri., 8am-5pm Sat., 10am-5pm Sun.) near downtown. It has an ample selection of tableware, serving dishes, and decorations.

The **Town Center at Levis Commons** (3201 Levis Commons Blvd., 419/931-8888, shopleviscommons.com) is an upscale, outdoor shopping mall.

FOOD
Central Toledo

*M*A*S*H* fans will recall that Klinger has a thing for ★ **Tony Packo's** (1902 Front St., 419/691-6054, tonypacko.com, 10:30am-10pm Mon.-Thurs., 10:30am-11pm Fri.-Sat., 11:30am-9pm Sun., $10-14), a Hungarian hot dog restaurant that's been open since 1932. The joint retains a classic atmosphere with old bar chandeliers and checkerboard tablecloths. Glass cases throughout the restaurant display hot dog buns signed by celebrities (everyone from Larry King to Margaret Thatcher). A decent beer selection complements the simple menu of hot dogs, chili, and stuffed cabbage. There are five other locations throughout town, but this is the original.

Experimental without being pretentious, **M'Osteria** (611 Monroe St., 419/214-4222, mosteriatoledo.com, 11:30am-11pm Mon.-Thurs., 11:30am-2am Fri., 5pm-2am Sat., $10-26) balances an innovative Italian menu with an Ohio farm-to-table sensibility. Ingredients are locally sourced, the atmosphere is sociable, and the drink menu includes 8-10 drafts and a sizeable selection of wine.

The **Maumee Bay Brew Pub** (27 Broadway St., 419/243-1302, mbaybrew.com/brew-pub, 11am-10pm Mon.-Thurs., 11am-midnight Fri.-Sat., 11am-9pm Sun., $9-17) of the Maumee Bay Brewing Company serves burgers, pizzas, salads, and beer-infused soups in a historic brick building, formerly a hotel.

Overlooking downtown Toledo on the Maumee River is **Real Seafood Company**

The Toledo Mud Hens play at Fifth Third Field.

(22 Main St., 419/697-5427, realseafoodcorestaurant.com, 4pm-9pm Mon.-Thurs., 11:30am-10pm Fri.-Sat., noon-9pm Sun., $23-45), a high-end establishment with a surf-and-turf menu, raw bar, and patio with the river and city in full view.

Another great view of the city is from indoor/outdoor rooftop restaurant and lounge **The Heights** (444 N. Summit St., 419/243-7565, theheightstoledo.com, noon-9pm Mon.-Thurs., noon-10pm Fri., 10am-10pm Sat., 10am-2pm Sun., $11-17), with 360-degree views of downtown Toledo from the 12th floor of the Renaissance Hotel. The menu features upscale pizzas, sandwiches, and a small list of entrées, while the lineup for weekend brunch (10am-2pm Sat.-Sun.) includes exciting twists on chicken and waffles and eggs Benedict.

Just east of downtown is **Josephine's Kitchen** (902 Lagrange St., 419/242-6666, 12:30pm-9pm Thurs.-Sun., $11-15), a tiny, down-to-earth neighborhood outfit with a soul food menu.

Around Toledo

The Beirut (4082 Monroe St., 419/473-0885, beirutrestaurant.com, 11:30am-9pm Mon.-Thurs., 11:30am-10pm Fri.-Sat., $11-26) is a long-established, festive choice for Middle Eastern and Italian favorites, with sumptuous decor and a vibrant atmosphere.

A Toledo destination since 1921, **Mancy's Steakhouse** (953 Phillips Ave., 419/476-4154, mancys.com/steakhouse, 11am-2pm and 4:30pm-9pm Mon.-Thurs., 11am-2pm and 4:30pm-9:30pm Fri., 4pm-9:30pm Sat., $25-65) serves a focused menu of steak and seafood in an almost whimsically old-fashioned dining room with stained glass, brick walls, and dark wood features.

The menu is bigger than the restaurant at authentic diner **Schmucker's Restaurant** (2013 N. Reynolds Rd., 419/535-9116, schmuckersrestaurant.com, 8am-9pm Mon.-Wed., 8am-10pm Thurs. and Sat., 7am-10pm Fri., $5-15). Chugging along since 1948, the joint is known for its homemade pies—

choose the "full course" option to add pie to your entrée.

The "Kevin Bacon" is the best-selling pizza at **Basil Pizza and Wine Bar** (3145 Hollister Ln., Perrysburg, 419/873-6218, basilpizzaandwinebar.com, 11am-10pm daily, $10-24), southwest of Toledo. The 13-inch thin-crust Neapolitan-style pies are easily splitable between two, especially paired with one of the intriguing small plates such as street corn toast. The wine list is enormous.

BARS AND NIGHTLIFE

The craft brewery **Earnest Brew Works** (4342 S. Detroit Ave., 419/340-2589, earnestbrewworks.com, 4pm-9pm Mon.-Thurs., 2pm-10pm Fri., noon-10pm Sat., 1pm-7pm Sun.) is a regional favorite, with relaxed digs and 18 taps carrying a nice variety of home brews. A rotation of food trucks brings the chow.

The microbrewery **Black Frog Brewery** (831 S. McCord Rd., 567/318-4672, blackfrogbrewery.com, 4:30pm-10pm Wed.-Fri., 3pm-10pm Sat.) is also highly regarded, with a small, unpretentious taproom and an easy-going vibe.

Bellwether at Toledo Spirits (1301 N. Summit St., 419/662-9521, toledospirits.com, 4pm-10pm Tues.-Thurs. and Sun., 4pm-1am Fri.-Sat.) builds inventive drinks with homespun batches of vodka, gin, and more. There's a hip, fun-spirited dining room and a relaxed patio of picnic tables.

ACCOMMODATIONS

There's one hotel downtown: the **Renaissance Toledo Downtown Hotel** (444 N. Summit St., 419/244-2444, marriott.com, $143-188), with a sleek lobby, comfortable rooms sporting big-screen TVs, and two restaurants, including The Heights indoor/outdoor rooftop lounge.

The **Casey-Pomeroy House Bed and Breakfast** (802 N. Huron St., 419/243-1440, casey-pomeroyhouse.com, $125-185) and its six guest rooms live in a restored 1873 house.

The restoration is ongoing in this charming Victorian home.

Set in Maumee Bay State Park 20 minutes east of downtown, the **Maumee Bay Lodge and Conference Center** (1750 State Park Rd., Oregon, 419/836-1466, maumeebaylodge. com, $169-289) allows you to enjoy the state park as well as the lodge's pools, racquetball courts, two restaurants, and other amenities. The guest rooms are modern and comfortable, with some patios facing Lake Erie.

A few of Toledo's attractions are located on the south side of town, so it makes sense to stay in the cluster of chain motels in the Maumee and Perrysburg area.

CAMPING

Maumee Bay State Park (1400 State Park Rd., 419/836-7758, ohiodnr.gov) offers a campground with 29 full-hookup sites and over 200 electric sites, as well as cabins near the waterfront. Rates start at $29.

INFORMATION AND SERVICES

Destination Toledo (visittoledo.org) is the best resource for things to do and see in Toledo.

St. Vincent Medical Center (2213 Cherry St., 419/251-3232) is the closest general hospital to the center of town. The same network runs a **walk-in primary care** location (2238 Jefferson Ave., 419/251-4696, 8am-8pm Mon.-Fri., 10am-4pm Sat.-Sun.).

TRANSPORTATION
Getting There

Toledo is well-connected by highway. Via I-75, Toledo is a little over 2 hours north (149 mi/240 km) from Dayton and nearly 3 hours north (202 mi/320 km) of Cincinnati. From Cleveland, take I-90 west to I-75 north

for about a 1.75-hour (114 mi/184 km) trip. From Columbus, take US-23 north (which turns into SR 15 by Carey) to I-75 north. The total trip is just over 2.25 hours (142 mi/ 229 km).

Allegiant Air and American Airlines operate a handful of routes out of **Toledo Express Airport** (TOL, 11013 Airport Hwy., 419/865-2351, toledoexpress.com), 25 minutes west of downtown Toledo. Six car rental companies operate counters at the airport. Check with the airport website for hours. Most people coming in and out of Toledo utilize the **Detroit Metropolitan Wayne County Airport** (DTW, 11050 Rogell Dr., Detroit, MI, 734/247-7678, metroairport.com), 40 minutes to the north of Toledo via I-75 and I-275. The large airport sees a number of international flights and is a hub for Delta Airlines and Spirit Airlines. To get from the airport to Toledo, grab a rental car from one of the many available agencies. A taxi will run you at least $150.

Greyhound (greyhound.com) and **Barons Bus** (baronsbus.com) stop at the **Martin Luther King Jr. Plaza** (415 Emerald Ave.), which also sees three **Amtrak** (amtrak. com) trains come through during the night.

Getting Around

The **Toledo Area Regional Transit Authority (TARTA)** (tarta.com) operates a bus system connecting the city with area suburbs. Fares are $1.50, or passes can be purchased via the EZfare app. Though the system is helpful for getting around central Toledo, you'd best be served by a private vehicle to access the outlying attractions.

Black and Yellow Taxi Cab (419/699-4545) serves the region. **Uber** (uber.com) and **Lyft** (lyft.com) also operate in the metro area south to Bowling Green.

1: brunch at The Heights **2:** downtown Toledo from The Heights rooftop patio **3:** Hungarian hot dogs at Tony Packo's **4:** a boardwalk through coastal wetlands at Maumee Bay State Park

Fremont

With a population of about 16,000 and a major Heinz plant, Fremont bustles along reasonably well. The Wyandot village of Junquindundeh sat on the site of the modern city, as did Fort Stephenson, built during the War of 1812. The fort repelled a siege by a much larger combined force of British and American Indians during the war. The Wyandot people lingered as white settlers built a town around the fort; they were the last American Indian nation to leave Ohio, in 1843. Historical markers and a monument outside the Birchard Public Library on Croghan Street note the former site of the fort.

Today, the town is most known as the home of President Rutherford B. Hayes, whose legacy is on full display at the Rutherford B. Hayes Presidential Library and Museums. The historic downtown boasts 19th-century buildings, boutiques, and a handful of restaurants to pull you away from the chains that line the roads coming into town.

SIGHTS
★ Rutherford B. Hayes Presidential Library and Museums

The **Rutherford B. Hayes Presidential Library and Museums** (Spiegel Grove, 419/332-2081, rbhayes.org, 9am-5pm Mon.-Sat., noon-5pm Sun., museum and mansion $20 adults, $18 seniors, $10 teens, $5 children, free admission to library and grounds), on the southwest end of town off Buckland Avenue, chronicles the life and accomplishments of the 19th U.S. president, who spent his formative, career-building years in Fremont. Hayes' children deeded their father's estate, Spiegel Grove, to the state of Ohio to construct what became the country's first presidential library upon its opening in 1916. Within the two-story museum and research center, renovated in 2016, are 19,000 artifacts related to Hayes' life, family, and military and political career. Highlights include a presidential carriage, original White House china, and a photograph-friendly replica of the Resolute desk—the original was given to President

The Spiegel Grove estate is part of the Rutherford B. Hayes Presidential Library and Museums.

Hayes by Queen Victoria in 1880 and has been used by almost every president in the Oval Office since.

Behind the museum is the Spiegel Grove mansion on 25 acres of what remains of the estate. The 31-room Victorian mansion was constructed during the Civil War, with additions made later as Hayes returned to Fremont after his stints as governor of Ohio and president of the United States. The house is open for tours and reflects how it would have appeared and been furnished with the Hayeses at home. The surrounding estate grounds are lovely, with large, stately trees and a path leading to a granite tomb in which the former president and Mrs. Hayes are interred.

You can purchase a cheaper ticket to the museum if you're uninterested in going inside the house.

FOOD AND ACCOMMODATIONS

The Garrison (209 Garrison St., 419/333-8260, the-garrison.net, 11am-9pm Mon.-Thurs., 11am-10pm Fri.-Sat., $11-24) offers a fine menu of upscale tavern staples and European meals along with 20 taps filled with local craft beer in a historic 19th-century storefront.

A more inexpensive choice a few buildings down is **Down Thyme Café** (115 S. Front St., 419/332-4334, 6:30am-5pm Mon.-Fri.,

7am-3pm Sat., $4-7), a spacious coffee shop that also does breakfast sandwiches, wraps, and quinoa bowls. Grab some Toft's Ice Cream, a specialty out of Sandusky, while you're at it.

Your best bet for a place to sleep is one of the handful of chain motels you pass on your way into town on SR 53 coming in from the turnpike.

INFORMATION AND SERVICES

The **Sandusky County Convention and Visitors Bureau** (sanduskycounty.org) is a good resource on area attractions.

ProMedica Memorial Hospital (715 S. Taft Ave., 419/332-7321) is the area's general hospital. There is also a **Walk In Urgent Care** (2180 Sean St., Ste. 6B, 419/355-8343, 8am-8pm Mon.-Fri., 10am-6pm Sat.-Sun.) on the north side of town off SR 53 near Walmart.

TRANSPORTATION

Fremont is an easy 45-minute drive (35 mi/56 km) east of Toledo via the I-90 turnpike, or US-20 which does not have tolls. From Cleveland, I-90 is your best bet, a roughly 1.5-hour drive west (85 mi/137 km) to the SR 53 exit. There is no bus service to Fremont.

Since you require a car to reach Fremont, a car is also your best bet in getting around this small city.

Along I-75

Western Ohio's flat farmland is likely the image of Ohio you conjure in your mind if you've never visited. Indeed, much of the terrain in this part of the state—the eastern edge of the corn belt that stretches all the way to Nebraska—matches that image. The towns and cities along this corridor of I-75 between Toledo and Dayton, fine places as they are to live and do business, are not typically seen as destinations, with perhaps the exception of

Neil Armstrong's Wapakoneta. But hop off the highway to stretch your legs and grab a bite to eat at a local favorite.

FINDLAY

Findlay has slowly and quietly grown into a prosperous city of over 40,000 people, buoyed by the presence of bigwigs such as Whirlpool, Marathon Oil, and Cooper Tire and Rubber. For travelers, it doesn't offer much more than an excuse to jump off the highway for a bite to eat and, for art appreciators, a museum of children's book art.

Sights
MAZZA MUSEUM
Fans of the whimsical artwork of children's picture books will want to stop by the University of Findlay's **Mazza Museum** (201 College St., 419/434-4560, mazzamuseum. org, noon-5pm Wed.-Fri., 1pm-4pm Sun., free) which holds the world's largest collection of original children's book illustrations. Even if you don't know your Maurice Sendak from your Marc Brown, the walls of colorful illustrations are a delightful respite from the steering wheel. As hours are somewhat sporadic, it's best to call to arrange an appointment, just in case.

Food and Accommodations
Dietsch Brothers (400 W. Main Cross St., 419/422-4474, dietschs.com, 9am-9pm Tues.-Fri., 10am-9pm Sat., noon-5pm Sun.) has been a Findlay institution since 1937, selling fine candies and ice cream from two locations in town (this location is the older of the two, though not the original). Take your selections to the seating area or buy a box for later.

Findlay's central business district has quite a few restaurants, though none cover as much culinary geography as **Circle of Friends** (125 W. Sandusky St., 567/294-4274, circleoffriendsfindlay.com, 11am-9pm Mon.-Sat., $9-16), whose menu includes Greek, Middle Eastern, Indian, and Southeast Asian choices. Special "around the world" plates sample the various regions in this laid-back, multicultural spot.

The US-224/Trenton Avenue exit off I-75 has quite a few chain hotels. Otherwise, there are two solid alternatives in downtown Findlay if you're tired of run-of-the-mill freeway hotels.

Findlay Inn and Conference Center (200 E. Main Cross St., 419/408-5343, findlayinn.com, $112-127) features fairly basic but comfortable rooms. There's a full-service bar and restaurant on-site, and a continental breakfast is included with the rate.

The **Hancock Hotel** (621 S. Main St., 419/423-0631, hancockhotel.com, $119-139) has contemporary guest rooms and walk-in glass showers. For an upcharge, breakfast at classic Mancy's on-site is included.

Information and Services
The **Hancock County Convention and Visitors Bureau** (visitfindlay.com) is the best resource for the Findlay area.

Blanchard Valley Hospital (1900 S. Main St., 419/423-4500) is the city's general hospital. There's also helpfully the **Physicians Plus Urgent Care** (3949 N. Main St., 419/423-3888, 8am-8pm Mon.-Fri., 9am-5pm Sat.-Sun.) very near I-75 north of town.

Transportation
Findlay is a 50-minute drive (46 mi/74 km) south of Toledo on I-75 and just under 1.75 hours (107 mi/172 km) north of Dayton via the same road. **Greyhound** (greyhound.com) and **Barons Bus** (baronsbus.com) stop at a **Pilot Travel Center** (11471 SR 613) north of the city.

USA Cab (419/788-6206) serves the Findlay area. There's no bus system in the city.

LIMA
A city of 36,000, Lima (pronounced "lie-ma," unlike the Peruvian city) is where many in this corner of Ohio go for shopping and services. The city was a major railroad center in the 19th century thanks to the Lima Locomotive Works, whose steam engines were shipped across the world. As the halfway point between Dayton and Toledo it's a natural stop for gas and food beyond the typical golden arches landscape—and Kewpee Hamburgers, a relic from the early 20th century, is worth stopping for.

Sights

ALLEN COUNTY MUSEUM

The **Allen County Museum** (620 W. Market St., 419/222-9426, allencountymuseum.org, 1pm-5pm Tues.-Fri., 1pm-4pm Sat.-Sun., $5 suggested donation) is one of the nicer local history museums in Ohio. There are the usual exhibits that depict the area in decades past, the industries that put Lima on the map, and local geology, but also unexpected highlights such as John Dillinger's jail cell (the gangster did time in the Allen County Prison), a replica of Noah's Ark, and a collection of taxidermied albino animals. A massive No. 10 Shay locomotive engine celebrates Lima's history as a railroad and locomotive manufacturing center.

Food and Accommodations

At its zenith before WWII, there were more than 400 locations of ★ **Kewpee Hamburgers** (111 N. Elizabeth St., 419/228-1778, kewpeehamburgers.com, 5:30am-10pm Mon.-Thurs., 5:30am-11pm Fri.-Sat., 3pm-10pm Sun., $4-7), the second-oldest hamburger chain in the United States after White Castle. An early pioneer of the drive-through, there are only five Kewpee Hamburgers left today, and three of them are in Lima. While there is a location right off I-75 on Bellefontaine Avenue, it's worth it to visit the iconic 1939 diner downtown. Prices are dirt cheap, and the refreshingly simple menu features hamburgers, fries, and malts, plus 10 varieties of freshly baked pie.

A good casual dining option is **Hunan Gardens** (723 Saratoga Ave., 419/228-1995, 11am-10pm Mon.-Thurs., 11am-10:30pm Fri.-Sat., 11am-9:30pm Sun., $8-14), a Chinese American family eatery that hits the sweet spot on portion size, quality, and price point.

The best cluster of chain motels is off the SR 309 exit from I-75.

Information and Services

Visit Greater Lima (144 S. Main St., 419/222-6075, visitgreaterlima.com, 8am-5pm Mon.-Fri.) operates a visitors center near the center of town.

Lima Memorial Hospital (1001 Bellefontaine Ave., 419/228-3335) is only a couple minutes' drive from I-75 and has an emergency room.

Transportation

Lima is the halfway point between Dayton and Toledo, a little over an hour's drive north on I-75 from Dayton (74 mi/119 km) and the same heading south from Toledo (77 mi/124 km). **Greyhound** (greyhound.com) and **Barons Bus** (baronsbus.com) stop at a station (218 E. High St.) near downtown.

The **Allen County Regional Transit Authority (ACRTA)** (acrta.com) serves the area with eight fixed bus routes. Fares are $1, payable in exact change on the bus.

WAPAKONETA

Small-town Wapakoneta is most notable for its famous native son: first man on the moon Neil Armstrong. His sites, as well as the peculiar Temple of Tolerance, make Wapakoneta the most interesting excuse to pull off I-75 to stretch the legs. The historic downtown has a solid number of restaurants, antique shops, and boutiques.

Sights

★ ARMSTRONG AIR AND SPACE MUSEUM

The smallish **Armstrong Air and Space Museum** (500 Apollo Dr., 419/738-8811, armstrongmuseum.org, 9:30am-5pm Mon.-Sat., 11am-5pm Sun. Apr.-Sept., hours vary Oct.-Mar., $10 adults, $9 seniors, $4 children) is located right off I-75 and pays homage to the humble beginnings and career of Neil Armstrong. The exhibits portray NASA's struggle to catch up with the Soviet Union's space program leading up to 1969's Apollo 11 mission as well as the significance of Armstrong's contributions. The building's center dome houses the Astro Theater, which plays a 25-minute video about the Apollo 11 lunar landing. Highlights of the museum's collection include a moon rock, Armstrong's space suits, and the Gemini VIII spacecraft that Armstrong piloted prior to his landmark mission to the moon. The museum's small gift shop is stocked with spacecraft models, astronaut ice cream, and other suitably themed souvenirs.

To commemorate the Apollo 11 moon landing, the museum hosts the annual **Summer Moon Festival** (summermoonfestival.com) for a weekend in mid-July, which brings a long list of programs, food trucks, and vendors to the museum grounds as well as four blocks of Wapakoneta's historic town center.

NEIL ARMSTRONG'S BOYHOOD HOME

Neil Armstrong's boyhood home (601 W. Benton St.) is a private residence and does not allow tours, but you can still appreciate from the sidewalk the modest, small-town beginnings of a man who set a new course for human exploration.

TEMPLE OF TOLERANCE

Philosopher and artist Jim Bowsher's house, with ivy and rusty knick-knacks, might look like the kind of house you walk past a little faster, but you'd be missing the hidden gem that sits behind it. Bowsher has spent the last few decades building a free-spirited secret garden in his backyard, which he calls the **Temple of Tolerance** (203 S. Wood St., 24 hours daily, free). Curious memorabilia, random statues, and shady trees lead to an open area with the temple structure itself, constructed from mounds of rocks and building debris, evoking jungle ruins. It offers a tranquil, offbeat retreat from the real world. Walk up the driveway and enter through the gate at your leisure. You're not obligated to pay anything to wander around, but there is a donation box in the front porch

of the house if you feel moved to contribute something.

Food and Accommodations

For super-cheap eats and some local ice cream, there's **Max's Dairy** (901 Bellefontaine St., 419/738-7712, 11am-9pm Mon.-Sat., 3pm-9pm Sun., $2-5), a walk-up counter offering soft serve and hard dip ice cream, cookie dough by the cup, and a small food menu that includes hamburgers, hot dogs, and walking tacos (taco ingredients in a chip bag). There's a small sitting area outside.

Another cheap option is **The Alpha Café** (7 E. Auglaize St., 419/738-2013, alpha-cafe.biz, 8am-1am Mon.-Thurs., 8am-2:30am Fri., 11am-2:30am Sat., $4-10). This local haunt features a simple breakfast menu, à la carte burgers, sandwiches, and sides, and an unbeatable daily lunch special rotation. The main attraction aside from the prices in this otherwise no-frills establishment is the 1893 hand-carved oak bar. The café takes cash only.

There are a handful of chain motels off the SR 501 exit from I-75.

Information and Services

Visit the **Wapakoneta Chamber of Commerce website** (wapakoneta.com) for more information on the area.

There is a **Walk In Urgent Care** (1321 Bellefontaine St., 567/356-4054, 8am-8pm Mon.-Fri., 10am-6pm Sat.-Sun.) near the Armstrong Air and Space Museum.

Transportation

Wapakoneta is a straight shot north of Dayton on I-75, about an hour's drive (59 mi/95 km). From Toledo, I-75 curves somewhat to the southwest until you arrive at Wapakoneta 1.5 hours later (91 mi/147 km). From Columbus, take US-33 northwest for about a 1.5-hour drive (89 mi/143 km).

There are no public transportation options in Wapakoneta.

Cincinnati and Vicinity

Sitting on the banks of the Ohio River within walking distance of the American South, Cincinnati balances regional identities, at times clearly Midwestern and others more Southern or even Appalachian. There's also a faint aura of the Old World, a glimmer of a European river town due to heavy German immigration in the 19th century. With colorful Victorian architecture, craft beer at every corner, and a peculiar but tasty definition of "chili," Cincinnati is a true American original.

If the story of Ohio is the sequel to the American Revolution, Cincinnati is chapter one. The first major American city founded after the Revolutionary War in 1788, Cincinnati was also the first true American boomtown, nicknamed the Queen City (or the Queen

Highlights

Look for ★ to find recommended sights, activities, dining, and lodging.

★ Learn about the history of slavery in the Americas and the heroic Underground Railroad, laid bare on the banks of the Ohio River in the **National Underground Railroad Freedom Center** (page 251).

★ Explore Victorian **Over-the-Rhine,** the largest historic district in the United States and the city's premier neighborhood for dining, drinking, and shopping (page 255).

★ Experience three museums for one price at the **Cincinnati Museum Center at Union Terminal,** set in a stunning art deco train station (page 257).

★ View art spanning thousands of years at the free **Cincinnati Art Museum,** known especially for its collection of American art (page 259).

★ Observe rare manatees, bonobos, and the world's most famous hippo, Fiona, at the **Cincinnati Zoo and Botanical Garden,** frequently listed among the best zoos in the country (page 260).

★ Get a goetta sandwich at **Findlay Market,** Ohio's oldest continuously running local market (page 273).

★ Toast the bounty of **craft breweries**— Cincinnati, one of the top beer cities in the nation, has more than 50 (page 277).

★ Have a close encounter of the watery

kind at the intimate **Newport Aquarium** (page 287).

★ Seek thrills at **Kings Island,** which offers 14 roller coasters. The world's longest wooden roller coaster, The Beast, tears through a dense forest (page 289).

of the West). Steamboats chugged along the Ohio River, bringing settlers from the original 13 colonies at first and then large numbers of German and Irish immigrants. The population doubled every decade of the early 19th century until it was the sixth-largest city in the United States. Had Chicago not come around and taken over the meatpacking industry, Cincinnati might look a little more like the Windy City in terms of size and stature. The arrival of trains, too, would take some wind out of the city's sails as transportation no longer relied on the highway of the Ohio River. Still, "The Paris of America" would remain in the top 10 cities by population up until the turn of the 20th century, shaped by monied families such as the Procters, Gambles, Krogers, and most of all the Tafts . . . chief among them our 27th president, William Howard Taft.

The city's population peaked in the 1950s, after which the story is the same as for so many urban areas. White flight, suburban sprawl, and rising crime led to a sharp decrease in population, but urban renewal projects and a commitment to development in the center of the city have turned things around dramatically. Starting in the 2010s, Cincinnati has been increasing in population once again. With the return of citizens (and money) came a horde of innovative restaurants, craft breweries, and boutique shops to accompany the cultural institutions that have outlasted the city's downturn—establishments like the Cincinnati Zoo and Botanical Garden, Cincinnati Art Museum, and Findlay Market, which are among the oldest and most respected of their kind in the country. The city's architectural heritage goes largely overlooked but holds some spectacular gems such as the art deco Carew Tower, the Brooklyn Bridge-in-miniature Roebling Suspension Bridge, and the gothic Cincinnati Music Hall, which stands in bustling Over-the-Rhine, one of the country's premier historic neighborhoods and featuring one of the largest collections of original Italianate architecture in the world.

Today, Cincinnati has developed a culture of its own. It is unique among the large Ohio cities, with its devotion to Cincinnati-style chili, fervent sports fandoms (especially for baseball), and long, storied history with beer. Other than a few far-flung must-dos, most of Cincinnati's best attractions, restaurants, and shopping can be found close to the city center, making this a good walking town. Let your curiosity get the best of you and explore one of the Midwest's most interesting cities.

PLANNING YOUR TIME

Three days is enough time to see the best of the city. Four or five days gives you more time to explore and the ability to spend a day at Kings Island. It's also easy to combine sightseeing in Cincinnati with a day trip to Dayton, or vice versa, depending on your priorities. A good number of restaurants and attractions are closed on Mondays. Just enough are closed or have reduced hours on Sundays to make you wish you'd come on Saturday.

As with all of Ohio, the best times to visit Cincinnati are in the in-between months of May-June and September-October. Winters here are Ohio's mildest but can still bring chilly temperatures and snow. Summers will certainly bring the heat and humidity, though the festival season is in full swing. Keep an eye out on the calendar for Opening Day (March/April), Taste of Cincinnati (May), the Flying Pig Marathon (May), Bunbury Music Festival (June), and the Cincinnati Music Festival (July); prices for accommodations can jump quite high during these events.

ORIENTATION

While the metropolitan area is sprawling, Cincinnati proper is manageable and most of the main attractions lie in the center of town. Downtown and the adjacent Over-the-Rhine,

---

Previous: Black Brigade Monument in Smale Riverfront Park; Cincinnati Music Hall; Camp Washington Chili.

Cincinnati

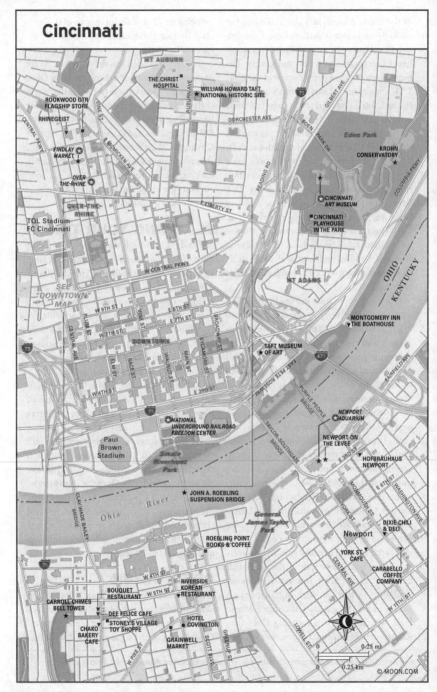

© MOON.COM

just to the north, lie in a river valley on a walkable grid network. The grid continues somewhat in the surrounding neighborhoods, though note their names—Mount Adams, Walnut Hills, and so forth—mark the sort of elevation change that pedestrians may find obstructive. Roads on a map, though relatively straight, may head uphill, so a quick hop on public transportation or a rideshare may be in order. The University of Cincinnati is relatively close to the center of gravity as well, but trips to the outlying Northside, Hyde Park, or Oakley neighborhoods are best made by car. Two interstates, I-71 and I-75, helpfully converge downtown and head north toward these neighborhoods; I-71 runs northeast to Hyde Park and Oakley, while I-75 runs north to Northside.

Sights

DOWNTOWN

Cincinnati's downtown is attractive and compact, a walkable central business district of corporate headquarters, swanky hotels, fine dining, and historic structures complemented by The Banks mixed-use development to the south, complete with major league stadiums, an assortment of attractive restaurants, and the National Underground Railroad Freedom Center.

★ National Underground Railroad Freedom Center

Wedged between the southern slave states and the promise of safety in Canada, Cincinnati, and Ohio in general, played a significant role in the famed Underground Railroad during the years of slavery, with active abolitionists and several routes crossing through the state. Equal parts horrific and inspiring, the National Underground Railroad Freedom Center (50 E. Freedom Way, 513/333-7739, freedomcenter.org, 10am-5pm Tues.-Sat., noon-5pm Sun.-Mon., $15 adults, $13 seniors 60+, $10.50 children ages 3-12, free for children under 3) sits in the center of The Banks development and is a museum of conscience and reconciliation, detailing the evil of slavery in the Americas, the Underground Railroad that rose to challenge the system, and the current state of slavery in the world. The museum's exhibits share the stories of freedom seekers, abolitionists, people of power who sought the end of slavery, and those that fought to keep it. Powerful accounts of brave resistance, both past and present, highlight the "freedom" aspect of the museum's name. There are relatively few artifacts on display; the largest by far is an early 1800s slave pen from Kentucky, haunting to walk through. The museum features a few multimedia attractions, including *Brothers of the Borderland*, a 25-minute film about abolitionists in Ripley, Ohio, narrated by Oprah Winfrey, and the brief *Suite for Freedom*, an animated introduction to the museum. The text-heavy exhibits and somber subject matter make this a challenging museum for little ones, but children of elementary school age and above will discover an eye-opening window into the country's complicated past.

Smale Riverfront Park

A series of terraces descends from The Banks down to Smale Riverfront Park (166 W. Mehring Way, 513/352-6180, cincinnatiparks.com/smale-riverfront-park, 6am-11pm daily, free), completed in 2015 to reconnect the industrial city with its riverfront. The park features a playful collection of water features and splash pads, climbable sculptures, and educational pieces all next to a splendid view of the Ohio River. Highlights include a foot piano, flying pig sculpture, and swinging chairs underneath a shady pergola. A particularly moving display is the Black Brigade Monument, with sculptures and relief panels chronicling the part

Downtown Cincinnati

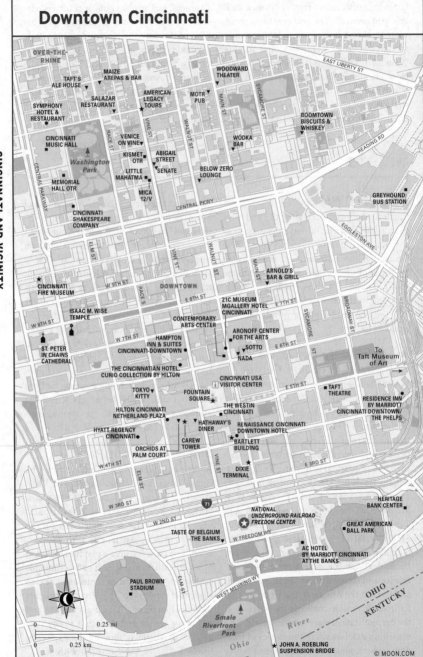

OVER-THE-RHINE

TAFT'S ALE HOUSE
MAIZE AREPAS & BAR
WOODWARD THEATER
EAST LIBERTY ST

SYMPHONY HOTEL & RESTAURANT
SALAZAR RESTAURANT
AMERICAN LEGACY TOURS
MOTR PUB
MAIN ST
SYCAMORE ST
BOOMTOWN BISCUITS & WHISKEY
READING RD

CINCINNATI MUSIC HALL
VENICE ON VINE
VINE ST
WALNUT ST
WODKA BAR

Washington Park
RACE ST
KISMET OTR
ABIGAIL STREET
SENATE
BELOW ZERO LOUNGE

MEMORIAL HALL OTR
LITTLE MAHATMA

MICA 12/V

CINCINNATI SHAKESPEARE COMPANY
CENTRAL PARKWAY
CENTRAL PKWY

GREYHOUND BUS STATION

ELM ST
EGGLESTON AVE

CINCINNATI FIRE MUSEUM
W 9TH ST
DOWNTOWN
ARNOLD'S BAR & GRILL

ISAAC M. WISE TEMPLE
RACE ST
E 8TH ST
MAIN ST
E 7TH ST
21C MUSEUM MGALLERY HOTEL CINCINNATI
BROADWAY ST

W 8TH ST
W 7TH ST
CONTEMPORARY ARTS CENTER
ARONOFF CENTER FOR THE ARTS
SYCAMORE ST

ST. PETER IN CHAINS CATHEDRAL
HAMPTON INN & SUITES CINCINNATI-DOWNTOWN
E 6TH ST
SOTTO
NADA

THE CINCINNATIAN HOTEL, CURIO COLLECTION BY HILTON
CINCINNATI USA VISITOR CENTER
To Taft Museum of Art

TOKYO KITTY
FOUNTAIN SQUARE
E 5TH ST
TAFT THEATRE

HILTON CINCINNATI NETHERLAND PLAZA
THE WESTIN CINCINNATI
RESIDENCE INN BY MARRIOTT CINCINNATI DOWNTOWN/ THE PHELPS

HYATT REGENCY CINCINNATI
HATHAWAY'S DINER
RENAISSANCE CINCINNATI DOWNTOWN HOTEL

ORCHIDS AT PALM COURT
CAREW TOWER
BARTLETT BUILDING
VINE ST
E 3RD ST

W 4TH ST
ELM ST
DIXIE TERMINAL

W 3RD ST

71
HERITAGE BANK CENTER

W 2ND ST
NATIONAL UNDERGROUND RAILROAD FREEDOM CENTER
GREAT AMERICAN BALL PARK

TASTE OF BELGIUM THE BANKS
W FREEDOM WY
AC HOTEL BY MARRIOTT CINCINNATI AT THE BANKS

PAUL BROWN STADIUM
ELM ST
WEST MEHRING WY
OHIO
KENTUCKY

Smale Riverfront Park
River

0   0.25 mi
0   0.25 km
Ohio
JOHN A. ROEBLING SUSPENSION BRIDGE
© MOON.COM

this volunteer unit of Black soldiers played in the city's defense during the Civil War. Carol Ann's Carousel overlooks the park from the top of the bank, next to the entrance to the Roebling Suspension Bridge.

Carew Tower

As splendid a French art deco skyscraper as you're likely to find anywhere, the **Carew Tower** (41 W. 5th St., 513/579-9735, cincinnatiusa.com, 9am-5:30pm Mon.-Thurs., 9am-6pm Fri., 10am-7pm Sat.-Sun., $6 ages 12 and up, $3 ages 6-11, free for children 5 and under, cash only) was completed in 1930 and only lost its status as the city's tallest skyscraper in 2010 when the Great American Tower went up a few blocks away. Though primarily an office building, visitors can shop or dine in the arcade, stay at the elegant **Hilton Cincinnati Netherland Plaza,** or go up to the outdoor **observation deck** at the very top of the building. To get to the deck, take the elevator from the arcade up to the 45th floor. From there, you can take the stairs or a small, somewhat rickety elevator up to the 48th floor, and then walk the final flight of stairs to the 49th. Take note before you go up: admission is cash only. The view is lovely, with Kentucky, the Ohio River valley, and much of the city in plain view. Those scared of heights may not appreciate the unobstructed view and the look down.

Fountain Square

Fountain Square (520 Vine St., 513/621-4400, myfountainsquare.com) has been the center of gravity in downtown Cincinnati since 1871. Though it has moved and gone through renovations over the years, the space has continued its role as a central gathering space. In the middle sits the bronze and granite Tyler Davidson Fountain, with the central figure, known as the Genius of Water, showering water from her outstretched arms down to the pool below. In the warmer months, the square maintains a busy schedule of farmers markets, free live music, and exercise activities. Look for weekly events like Salsa on the Square on Thursday evenings from May to September, World Fare lunches with ethnic food trucks on hand, and the Fifth & Vine Live music series. Several restaurants operate along the square's perimeter year-round, with plenty of outdoor seating.

Cincinnati Fire Museum

Cincinnati touts itself as the birthplace of professional firefighting, and the **Cincinnati Fire Museum** (315 E. Court St., 513/621-5553, cincyfiremuseum.com, 10am-4pm Tues.-Sat., $8 adults, $7 seniors, $6 ages 7-17, free for children 6 and under) is there to prove it. Housed in the former Engine Company No. 45 Fire House built in 1904, the museum chronicles the history of firefighting in the United States from the mid-19th century to the present. Kids can slide down a fire pole, observe old firefighting equipment, and see the full protective gear of modern firefighters. Fire safety education is another crucial part of the museum's mission. The Safe House exhibit allows visitors to experience a house fire and provides education on best safety practices.

Taft Museum of Art

A stately 1820 Federal-style mansion adjoining grassy Lytle Park and its statue of a young, clean-shaven Abraham Lincoln, the **Taft Museum of Art** (316 Pike St., 513/241-0343, taftmuseum.org, 11am-4pm Wed.-Fri., 11am-5pm Sat.-Sun., $12 adults, $10 seniors, free for children 18 and under) houses the private collection of Anna and Charles Phelps Taft, half-brother of President William Howard Taft, who accepted his party's nomination on the house's front steps in 1908. The small but impressive collection includes Chinese porcelains and works from Rembrandt, Gainsborough, and Sargent. Space in the modern annex allows the museum to host special exhibitions. Also on offer is the Lindner Family Café, open during museum hours, whose menu changes monthly and includes sandwiches, salads, and a weekend brunch. Parking is free with admission, and admission

1

2

3

NATIONAL UNDERGROUND RAILROAD FREEDOM CENTER

Roebling Suspension Bridge

Visitors passing by the riverfront may view the old bridge crossing the Ohio River with suspicion: "Where have I seen that before?" It's no mistake that the **John A. Roebling Suspension Bridge,** renamed in 1983 for its designer, bears a remarkable resemblance to New York City's Brooklyn Bridge. Roebling designed Cincinnati's bridge first, opening as the Cincinnati-Covington Bridge in 1866. Citizens were ecstatic about the architectural feat; in the first three days after its opening, over 120,000 pedestrians walked across the bridge. It was the first bridge to cross the Ohio River and at the time was the longest suspension bridge in the world at 1,057 feet (322 m), only to be outdone by Roebling's own Brooklyn Bridge in 1883, which came in at a then unprecedented 1,595 feet (486 m).

Alas, Cincinnati cannot quite claim the bridge as its own, as much of the Ohio River is owned by the Commonwealth of Kentucky. However, University of Cincinnati graduate and Cincinnati native Joseph Strauss grew up inspired by the bridge. Years later, he would serve as the chief engineer of the Golden Gate Bridge in San Francisco.

John A. Roebling Suspension Bridge

on Sundays is free. Advance admission is a reduced price.

TOP EXPERIENCE

★ OVER-THE-RHINE

At 362 acres, Over-the-Rhine claims to be the largest historic district in the United States, a claim contested only by Savannah, Georgia. The neighborhood gets its name from its early German inhabitants, who likened crossing the canal separating the neighborhood from downtown to going "over the Rhine." The canal is gone, paved over to become Central Parkway, but the effect is the same: high-rises give way to a dense grid of colorful Victorian storefronts and houses ranging from Italianate to Queen Anne to Greek Revival.

The victim of early-20th-century German xenophobia, Prohibition (when the economy relied on breweries), white flight, racist public

1: Carew Tower 2: Fountain Square 3: National Underground Railroad Freedom Center

housing policies, and ill-planned attempts to reverse course, the neighborhood entered the new millennium synonymous with drugs, crime, and indifferent landlords. Things radically turned a corner with the help of corporate funding, and Over-the-Rhine has returned to its status as a center of culture, cuisine, and lots and lots of beer drinking. The transformation has been stunning. In 2009, the neighborhood was named the most dangerous in the country. Just a single decade later, Over-the-Rhine had become the city's greatest asset. It's where Cincinnatians take out-of-towners and is named in the same breath as Greenwich Village, the French Quarter, and Charleston, South Carolina, in travel articles regarding preserved architectural heritage. Boutiques, coffee shops, and a wide variety of upscale restaurants all beckon the pedestrian, who will find no shortage of options. Two long-standing institutions—bustling Findlay Market and the gothic Cincinnati Music Hall—anchor the area and have drawn locals and tourists for over

Downtown's Historical Architecture

Cincinnati's prominence was greatest toward the end of the 19th century and into the early 20th century. As such, many of the city's greatest architectural treasures come from this era. Downtown boasts the greatest concentration of these gems.

- **The Bartlett Building** (24-42 E. 4th St.) is one of four buildings in Cincinnati designed by notable Chicago architect Daniel Burnham, who is famous for New York's Flatiron Building, Washington D.C.'s Union Station, and Chicago's 1893 Columbian Exposition. Built in 1901, it was the city's first skyscraper and once housed the Union Savings Bank. Today, visitors can appreciate the neoclassical building with a stay at the **Renaissance Cincinnati Downtown Hotel,** which, though modernized, maintains some of the bank's original features.

- Across the street from the Bartlett Building is the 1921 **Dixie Terminal** arcade (49 E. 4th St.). Once a station for streetcars and then buses, the building, designed by Cincinnati firm Garber and Woodward, is now an office building. The intricate art deco atrium is open to the public during business hours.

- The corner of 8th and Plum is home to two impressive places of worship. Dedicated in 1845, **St. Peter in Chains Cathedral** (325 8th St.) is the city's second oldest church after St. Mary's in Over-the-Rhine, which dates from 1841. Built in the Greek Revival style, unusual for a Catholic church, the cathedral was designed by architect Henry Walter, who was also a designer for the Ohio Statehouse. Look for a Venetian glass mosaic built by German craftsmen on the apse wall. Not to be outdone, the **Isaac M. Wise Temple** (720 Plum St.), a synagogue built in 1866, sports a Moorish facade with squared roofs and rose windows and is a National Historic Landmark.

- On 9th Street between Plum and Vine Streets is the **Ninth Street Historic District,** with over 40 buildings dating from the late 19th and early 20th centuries along the streetscape representing Italianate, Greek Revival, and Queen Anne architecture.

a hundred years. Gentrification, for better or worse, continues to transform the neighborhood, which will be one to watch on the national radar in the coming years.

Common sense about walking in inner-city neighborhoods applies here. The area around Liberty Street in particular still has some work ahead of it, which it means there are fewer people around.

★ Cincinnati Museum Center at Union Terminal

West of Over-the-Rhine in the West End is Cincinnati's Union Terminal, an impressive 1933 art deco train station that inspired the design for DC Comics' Hall of Justice and now holds the **Cincinnati Museum Center** (1301 Western Ave., 513/287-7000, cincymuseum.

org, 10am-5pm daily, $14.50 ages 13-59, $13.50 age 60+, $10.50 ages 3-12, $5.50 ages 1-2, free for children under 1). The station's abundant space holds the Museum of Natural History, the Cincinnati History Museum, and the Duke Energy Children's Museum, all offered under one admission ticket. None of the museums are particularly large or comprehensive, which is part of the allure; there's no need to stick to one museum for long.

At the **Museum of Natural History**, the Neil Armstrong Space Exploration Gallery features, among other artifacts celebrating the 50th anniversary of the Apollo 11 moon landing, one of the moon rocks collected at Tranquility Base. The museum also includes an ancient Egyptian mummified child with a sarcophagus; a dinosaur hall; and an elaborate re-creation of a cave system complete with water features, fake stalactites, and displays on geology and cave critters. Done

1: colorful storefronts in Over-the-Rhine
2: Cincinnati Museum Center at Union Terminal
3: Cincinnati Art Museum 4: Taft Museum of Art

with natural history? Cross to the other side of the building to the **Cincinnati History Museum,** where you can walk through Cincinnati in Motion, an enormous miniature streetcar display depicting Cincinnati of the 1940s. In the lower level is Public Landing, where you can walk through the Cincinnati riverfront as it looked in the mid-1800s and board a steamboat. If you have kids in tow, take them to the **Duke Energy Children's Museum** to burn some energy climbing in The Woods, a forest-themed playground. Also in residence in the building for an additional cost is the Robert D. Lindner Family Omnimax Theater, Nancy & David Wolf Holocaust and Humanity Center, and the Cincinnati History Library and Archives. Various combo tickets allow you to package these experiences into one price.

Because the museum was originally designed as a train station and not a museum, the labyrinthine layout can get confusing. Helpful staff are eager to point you in the right direction. Also, escalators and elevators make exploring the multiple levels less daunting.

There are several food options on-site. Off the main lobby is the Rookwood Ice Cream Parlor, covered in locally produced Rookwood Pottery's pastel subway tiles and serving

Graeter's Ice Cream, also locally made. Cup & Pint serves pizza, coffee, and beer in the lobby as well. In the lower level outside the main entrance to the Children's Museum is Bean Sprouts, serving health-conscious sandwiches.

Parking in the museum center's parking lot is $6.

Washington Park

Backed by the impressive Cincinnati Music Hall across the street, **Washington Park** (1230 Elm St., 513/621-4400, washington-park.org, 6am-11pm daily, free) is the neighborhood's front lawn. The park hosts over 500 events throughout the year including concerts, markets, fitness classes, and more. The playground is helpfully fenced in and the interactive water fountain attracts scores of local kids in the warmer months.

The Porch is an outdoor bar that offers favorites from Rhinegeist, Taft's Ale House, and other local breweries. Check the park's website for hours—the bar is closed during the winter but may open for unseasonably warm temperatures.

Underneath the park is a 450-space parking garage with affordable rates, though special event pricing can bump the rates to $15.

Washington Park, backed by Cincinnati Music Hall

American Legacy Tours

Interested in digging a little deeper into Cincinnati's history? Join **American Legacy Tours** (1332 Vine St., 859/951-8560, americanlegacytours.com, check website for tour times, $29 and up) on a guided walking tour. The company offers 17 different itineraries that cover the area's beer, baseball, and gangster history. Haunted tours take a look at the spooky side of town, and a wine and dessert tour makes the hard choices for you in the area's finest dining destinations. The Queen City Underground Tour takes a look at Over-the-Rhine's brewing history and includes a stop in a rediscovered brewing tunnel 30 feet (9.1 m) below ground. Tours last 90 minutes to two hours depending on the tour.

WALNUT HILLS

Northeast of downtown, Walnut Hills is a diverse, mixed-income neighborhood that is beginning to see some of the changes Over-the-Rhine experienced in the 2010s. Long-time residents and newcomers alike tread carefully to ensure the neighborhood's cultural and historic heritage are not lost in the process. The neighborhood abuts Eden Park, a favorite among locals.

Eden Park

One of the most popular parks in Cincinnati, **Eden Park** (950 Eden Park Dr., 513/352-4080, cincinnatiparks.com, 6am-10pm daily, free) is an excellent choice for an amble outside between museums. Mirror Lake and the Bettman Fountain, installed in 2001, stand where a vast reservoir once stood. The 1894 Eden Park Stand Pipe, sitting on top of a hill and visible from much of the central part of the city, once stored water for the Walnut Hills community but has been obsolete for more than a hundred years. Near the stand pipe is the Presidential Grove. What began as a commemorative grove of trees has evolved into one of active participation by living presidents who are at their leisure to choose a tree to represent them. Thus, you have President Bill Clinton's swamp white oak sandwiched by magnolias, the tree of choice for both Bushes. Next to the Twin Lakes and their overlook of the Ohio River is a Capitoline She-wolf statue. The statue was a gift to the city from Benito Mussolini; in 1932, to commemorate the 10th year of his fascist regime, he sent such statues to American cities with Roman names. Mussolini supposed that Cincinnati was named after the Roman statesman Cincinnatus, which is not quite right—the city is actually named after the Society of the Cincinnati, a club of Revolutionary War veterans (which in turn took its name from Cincinnatus).

★ CINCINNATI ART MUSEUM

Overlooking downtown Cincinnati on a hill from within Eden Park, the **Cincinnati Art Museum** (953 Eden Park Dr., 513/721-2787, cincinnatiartmuseum.org, 11am-5pm Tues.-Wed. and Fri.-Sun., 11am-8pm Thurs., free) is one of the oldest art museums in the country and the oldest west of the Allegheny Mountains. The collection spans 6,000 years of artistic endeavor and includes works from Asia, Africa, Europe, and the Americas. Highlights include Titian's portrait *King Philip II of Spain,* Rubens' *Samson and Delilah,* and Van Gogh's *Undergrowth with Two Figures.* Paintings from Matisse, Picasso, and Miró round out a fine modern art display. The museum is especially known for American art, including an impressive collection of portrait miniatures and a large collection from portraitist and Cincinnati native Frank Duveneck.

There's not much food within walking distance of the museum, but the Terrace Café (11am-3pm Tues.-Wed. and Fri.-Sun., 11am-7:30pm Thurs.) is at your service, with a full menu of soups, salads, and sandwiches and seating in the warmer months on—you guessed it—a terrace. CAM Coffee Bar (open during regular museum hours) is in the front lobby.

Outside the building, be sure to save a few minutes to walk down the driveway for a great view of downtown. Additionally, Art Climb is a series of stairs that connect the museum to the bottom of the hill at Gilbert Avenue, through which pedestrians can enjoy gardens and outdoor art.

KROHN CONSERVATORY

A welcome splash of tropical color in the dreary Ohio winter, the **Krohn Conservatory** (1501 Eden Park Dr., 513/421-5707, cincinnatiparks.com, 10am-5pm Tues.-Sun., $7 adults, $5 ages 5-17, free for children 4 and under) has been an educational asset for the city since its inception in 1933. Housed in art deco digs in Eden Park, the conservatory puts on seasonal shows including a summer butterfly garden and a fine holiday railroad display utilizing botanical architecture. Permanent displays feature palms, desert plants, bonsai, and plants that produce food. There's no café on site, but there is a small gift shop. Check the website for an event calendar.

Harriet Beecher Stowe House

Author Harriet Beecher Stowe spent 18 formative years in Cincinnati, from 1832 to 1850. The stories she collected from former slaves during this time inspired her most famous work, *Uncle Tom's Cabin,* published in 1852. The displays in the **Harriet Beecher Stowe House** (2950 Gilbert Ave., 513/751-0651, stowehousecincy.org, 10am-4pm Thurs.-Sat., noon-4pm Sun., $6 adults, $5 seniors/students, $3 ages 6-17, free for children 5 and under), where she lived with her father and other Beecher family members before her marriage to professor Calvin Stowe, focus on her life as an author and abolitionist. The Hattie and Eliza Stowe Educational Center, named for her two oldest children, allows young kids to play with era-appropriate toys, write with simulated quill and ink, and experience other elements of 19th-century life.

Ohio's Lucky Cat Museum

You've seen the porcelain maneki-neko cat. It sits up and waves its paw, beckoning you inside what is probably a Chinese or Japanese restaurant. Well, if you want to see a whole lot of them, the **Lucky Cat Museum** (2511 Essex Pl. #150, 513/633-3923, luckycatmewseum.com, 3pm-6pm Tues.-Sat., free) holds over 2,000 variations, curated by artist Micha Robertson in her space at Essex Studios, an artist co-op. Wall hangings, wearables, books, teapots, original pieces from Japanese artists, and more are on display, all playfully spinning off the design that dates back to Japan's late Edo period. You don't need long to peruse the collection, and admission is free, but donations are always accepted.

UNIVERSITY OF CINCINNATI

Named one of the country's most beautiful campuses for its modern architecture, the University of Cincinnati north of downtown offers a good walk for those in a collegiate mood. The school's buildings reflect the university's reputation as a center of design. Indeed, the College of Design, Architecture, Art, and Planning is considered among the world's best. Buildings from contemporary architects such as Frank Gehry and Peter Eisenmann are the result of a master plan dating back to the 1990s.

The area surrounding campus features a couple of noteworthy attractions not affiliated with the university: the city's highly regarded zoo and William Howard Taft's birthplace and boyhood home.

TOP EXPERIENCE

★ Cincinnati Zoo and Botanical Garden

In 2019, a reader's choice competition in *USA Today* ranked the **Cincinnati Zoo and Botanical Garden** (3400 Vine Rd., 513/281-4700, cincinnatizoo.org, 10am-5pm daily Sept.-May, 10am-6pm daily Memorial Day-Labor Day, $19-27 adults, $15-21 children and seniors, children under 2 free) as the best zoo in the United States. Opened in 1875 and one of the oldest zoos in the country, this compact park packs a lot into its 75 acres, with over 500 animal species represented within its

University of Cincinnati

EAST
WALNUT
HILLS

THE VIDEO
ARCHIVE

JUST QIN
BARBECUE
RESTAURANT

HARRIET
BEECHER STOWE
HOUSE ★

LINCOLN AVENUE

GILBERT AVE

GOMEZ SALSA
WALNUT HILLS ▼

E MCMILLAN ST

READING ROAD

WASHINGTON AVE

Fleischmann
Gardens

CINCINNATI
CHILDREN'S HOSPITAL
MEDICAL CENTER

UNIVERSITY OF CINCINNATI
MEDICAL CENTER:
■ EMERGENCY ROOM

FOREST AVE

BURNET AVE

READING RD

OHIO'S
LUCKY CAT
MUSEUM ★

Hauck
Botanic
Gardens

BURNET AVE

CINCINNATI ZOO &
BOTANICAL GARDEN ✿

ERKENBRECHER AVE

MARTIN LUTHER KING DRIVE

CORRYVILLE

WILLIAM HOWARD TAFT RD

E MCMILLAN ST

To
Downtown
Cincinnati

VINE ST

E UNIVERSITY AVE

■ ISLAND
FRYDAYS ▼

BOGART'S ▼

W CORRY ST

Inwood
Park

VINE STREET

WOOLPER AVE

LUDLOW AVE

JEFFERSON AVE

Burnet
Woods

UNIVERSITY OF
CINCINNATI

■ FIFTH
THIRD
ARENA

NIPPERT
STADIUM ■

CALHOUN ST

CLIFTON AVE

CLIFTON AVE

GASLIGHT BED
& BREAKFAST

MCALPIN AVE

MIDDLETON AVE

LUDLOW AVE

TERRACE AVE

WHITFIELD AVE

CLIFTON
HOUSE

PROBASCO ST

CLIFTON AVE

W MCMILLAN AVE

CUF

WARNER STREET

Edgewood Grove
Park

MARTIN LUTHER KING DR W

Coy
Park

STRAIGHT ST

Fairview
Park

0.25 mi

0.25 km

0

0

CENTRAL PKWY

75

AMERICAN
SIGN MUSEUM ★

CAMP
WASHINGTON
CHILI ▼

CAMP
WASHINGTON

SPRING GROVE AVE

© MOON.COM

exhibits. Species such as manatees, bonobos, and Komodo dragons are found in few other zoos in the country. Though the zoo's exhibits have been modernized, historic buildings such as the 1906 Taj Mahal-like Elephant House and the original 1875 Reptile House are impressive relics from the zoo of yesteryear. There are 3,000 species of plants on the zoo grounds, dispersed throughout exhibits and small horticultural displays, providing a lush backdrop in the warmer months.

In 2017, the zoo found itself the subject of national attention when baby hippo Fiona was born prematurely. Hand-raised by her keepers, Fiona grew tremendously and is still a popular figure with her own book and Wikipedia page. You can find Fiona happily floating in her enclosure in Hippo Cove. Other popular attractions include Gorilla World, with a simulated jungle habitat, and the Africa section, whose Cheetah Encounter allows guests to view cheetahs running at top speed.

Approaching its 150th birthday in 2025, the zoo has tremendous expansion plans that include more space for its elephants, polar bears, and Australian critters. The zoo is a good choice any time of year (especially since admission can be as much as half off during the winter). Tickets vary based on day of the week and projected attendance and weather. Purchase discounted tickets online. Parking is $10.

William Howard Taft National Historic Site

The 27th president of the United States and 10th chief justice of the Supreme Court, William Howard Taft is an illustrious native son of Cincinnati. The **William Howard Taft National Historic Site** (2038 Auburn Ave., 513/684-3262, nps.gov/wiho, 8:30am-4:45pm daily, free) preserves the hilltop Greek Revival house where Taft was born and spent his childhood. Taft's life and his family's political dynasty reflect a period of transition for the United States as it became a world power. Start your visit at the Taft Education Center, with interpretive exhibits, a gift shop, and a 15-minute film about Taft's legacy. The house itself has been restored to resemble its appearance around 1857-1877, during Taft's adolescence. The portraits, among other items, belonged to the Tafts, but many of the furnishings are there only as era-appropriate additions. Guided tours run every 30 minutes until 4pm. Parking on-site is free.

Fiona the Hippo at the Cincinnati Zoo and Botanical Garden

NORTHSIDE

Racially and socioeconomically diverse, Northside has gained a reputation as both a dining destination and an LGBTQ-friendly community. Visitors will find an eclectic assortment of ethnic restaurants, quirky shops, and some of the city's coolest drinking establishments in this neighborhood north of downtown and the University of Cincinnati. Second Saturdays—the second Saturday of every month—are the best time to come, when shops and restaurants offer extended hours in conjunction with art gallery openings.

Spring Grove Cemetery and Arboretum

One of only five cemeteries in the country designated a National Historic Landmark, **Spring Grove Cemetery and Arboretum** (4521 Spring Grove Ave., 513/681-7526, www.springgrove.org, 8am-6pm daily, free) is the resting place of Civil War generals, statesmen, and the families that built Cincinnati. Stunning mausoleums, obelisks, and headstones dot the picturesque woods, rolling hills, and ponds. Of particular note is the private mausoleum and chapel of the Dexter family, who prospered in the liquor business. Built in 1869, this Gothic Revival structure features flying buttresses, a rarity as far as family resting places go. Historic figures interred in the cemetery include Civil War officer and poet William H. Lytle and Salmon P. Chase, who was Lincoln's treasury secretary among his many political accomplishments. Restrooms and maps for a self-guided walking tour can be found in the visitors center at the entrance. If you take a car through the cemetery, park to the right of the pavement and not on the grass.

American Sign Museum

Hidden in an industrial corner of town between Northside and the Camp Washington neighborhood to the south, the **American Sign Museum** (1330 Monmouth Ave., 513/541-6366, americansignmuseum.org, 10am-4pm Wed.-Sat., noon-4pm Sun., $15 adults, $10 seniors, students, active military, free for children 12 and under) chronicles America's history through flashy signage. The collection spans eras of signs including painted, lightbulb, neon, and porcelain and is split about 50/50 between donated and purchased signs dating from the early 20th century to the present. A neon-filled Main Street room is the highlight, with giant signs from the likes of McDonald's and Howard Johnson's. The free guided tours are quite detailed and are at 11am and 2pm Wednesday through Saturday and 2pm on Sunday. While at the museum, visitors can also peek into a neon sign workshop and sign restoration shop, with some signs available for purchase. A small gift shop up front sells vintage-style signs and old-fashioned candy. Parking onsite is free.

HYDE PARK

Northeast of downtown and one of Cincinnati's most desirable neighborhoods, Hyde Park's streets boast a fine display of stately houses and upscale retail. In the center of these streets is historic Hyde Park Square with its collection of boutique apparel shops, art galleries, cafes, and restaurants that match the area's wealthy clientele.

Cincinnati Observatory

Atop the Mount Lookout neighborhood adjacent to Hyde Park is the "Birthplace of American Astronomy," the **Cincinnati Observatory** (3489 Observatory Pl., 513/321-5186, cincinnatiobservatory.org, noon-4pm Mon.-Fri., check the website for additional programs and prices). Previously located on Mount Adams—named after President John Quincy Adams, who laid the cornerstone at the original building's dedication in 1843—the Cincinnati Observatory is a fully functional 19th-century observatory and the country's oldest open to the public. There are two buildings here, built in 1873 and 1904, each with a telescope. The newer and smaller of the two, the Mitchel Building, holds the original 1845 Merz

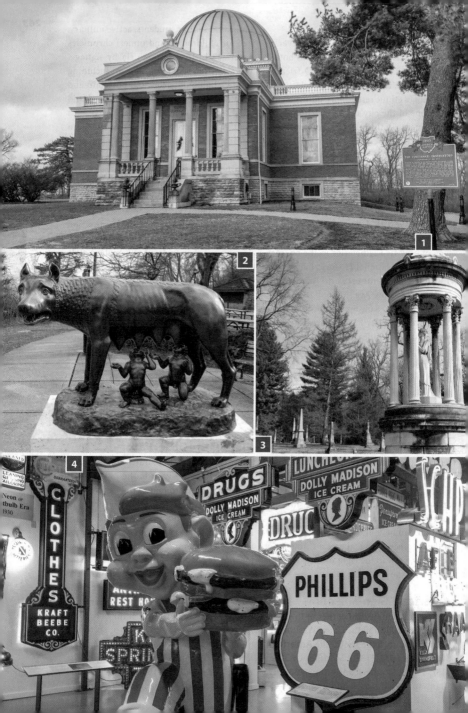

Coney Island Amusement Park

Though Kings Island dominates the amusement park scene in Southwest Ohio these days, the big name used to be **Coney Island Amusement Park** (6201 Kellogg Ave., 513/232-8230, coneyislandpark.com, check seasonal hours on the website, $17.95 adults, $13.95 seniors, $9.95 children). This spot southeast of town has been an amusement center of one kind or another since 1870 and has rotated through names: Parker's Grove, Ohio Grove, The Coney Island of the West, and now simply Coney Island. Its location right off the Ohio River has left it prone to flooding. Taft Broadcasting, which bought the park in 1969, intended to move the park to a larger space away from flooding. That park opened in 1972 as Kings Island. As you can see, Coney Island is still here. Over time, however, the park has decided to remove its amusement park rides and focus on its strengths as a waterpark.

The highlight of the park is, as it has been since 1925, the two-acre, three million-gallon Sunlite Pool. This massive, shallow water playground inspires play with in-pool slides, inflatables, and obstacle courses. Also on hand in the park are waterslides, a diving pool, and Typhoon Tower, an interactive water playground that is frequently inundated with 1,300 gallons of water from 33 feet (10 m) above.

und Mahler telescope, one of the oldest in operation in the world. Daytime tours of the buildings and their telescopes are on Tuesday, Thursday, and Saturday at noon, 1pm, and 2pm. Tickets are $5 per person and, at the time of writing, required advance reservations.

The dedicated staff maintain a multitude of weekly events year-round, including stargazing nights most Thursdays and Fridays and historical tours on the second and fourth Sundays of the month. Keep an eye out for astronomy courses, date nights, and other special events on the schedule.

Entertainment and Events

THE ARTS

Cincinnati enjoys an active arts scene with several highly regarded performing groups, some of which rank among the oldest of their kind in the United States.

Over-the-Rhine is host to several prominent performing arts centers, but foremost in town is **Cincinnati Music Hall** (1241 Elm St., 513/621-2787, cincinnatiarts.org/musichall), a stunning Gothic Revival behemoth and an icon of the city. A National Historic Landmark, the center was constructed in 1878 and is the home base of some of the oldest musical organizations in the country including the **Cincinnati Symphony Orchestra** (cincinnatisymphony.org), **Cincinnati Opera** (cincinnatiopera.org), **Cincinnati Ballet** (cballet.org), and the annual choral **May Festival** (mayfestival.com). The Friends of Music Hall operate 60-minute walking tours ($15), bringing visitors through public and private spaces within the building, which also has the reputation of being notoriously haunted. Tours are added every month, so check the website for tour dates and times.

The adjacent **Memorial Hall** (1225 Elm St., 513/977-8838, memorialhallotr.com), a beaux arts venue built in 1908 and itself no aesthetic slouch, hosts **Chamber Music Cincinnati** (cincychamber.org) and visiting acts. A block south of Memorial Hall is **Cincinnati Shakespeare Company** (1195

1: Cincinnati Observatory **2:** Eden Park **3:** Spring Grove Cemetery **4:** American Sign Museum

Elm St., 513/381-2273, cincyshakes.com), whose repertoire extends beyond the Bard.

Away from Over-the-Rhine in downtown, the more modern **Aronoff Center for the Arts** (650 Walnut St., 513/621-2787, cincinnati-arts.org/aronoff-center) or simply the Aronoff, does the rest of the heavy lifting when it comes to performance venues. Designed by famed architect Cesar Pelli and opened in 1995, the Aronoff has three auditoriums and is home to a number of smaller professional theater and dance companies. The center is best known, though, as the place to find traveling acts such as touring Broadways shows.

Across the street from the Aronoff is the **Contemporary Arts Center** (44 E. 6th St., 513/345-8400, contemporaryartscenter.org), a sleek, modern counterpart to the area's turn-of-the-20th-century architecture. This non-collecting art museum rotates visiting exhibitions and artists-in-residence.

Not to be overlooked is the 1928 **Taft Theatre** (317 E. 5th St., 513/232-6220, taft-theatre.org) and its resident performance company, **The Children's Theatre of Cincinnati** (thechildrenstheatre.com). An important distinction: this well-established group performs exquisite shows exclusively *for* children, but not *by* children. Founded in 1919, it's the oldest children's theater in the country.

One of the first regional theaters in the country, Eden Park's **Cincinnati Playhouse in the Park** (962 Mt. Adams Cir., 513/421-3888, cincyplay.com) is well regarded in the theater community and is known for bringing new plays to Cincinnati.

FESTIVALS AND EVENTS

It seems there's always something going on in town. In the summer months in particular, every weekend is booked with major music festivals, cultural celebrations, and plain excuses to get outside while the weather's fine.

Early March's funky **Bockfest** (bockfest. com) celebrates the arrival of spring and the city's beer-brewing heritage with a parade, 5K, the crowning of the Beard Baron and Sausage Queen, and bock beer from local breweries over the course of a weekend.

Cincinnati's long history with baseball culminates on **Opening Day** (cincinnati-usa.com), marking the start of the Cincinnati Reds' season in late March/early April. It's been an unofficial city holiday since the 1880s, with people skipping work and school to watch the parade make its way from Findlay Market to downtown. Parks, shops, and restaurants add their own celebrations in the mix to make this a citywide party.

Celebrating the city's 19th-century affiliation with pork is the **Flying Pig Marathon** (flyingpigmarathon.com) that attracts over 40,000 runners and 150,000 spectators in early May, making this the largest sporting event in the city. The race continually ranks among the best in the country.

If you'd rather come to eat than run, late May's **Taste of Cincinnati** (tasteofcincinnati. com) is the longest-running culinary event in the United States and features more than 250 dishes to try over one weekend.

Signaling the end of summer is the **Riverfest** (cincinnatiusa.com), a massive Labor Day party ending with a 30-minute fireworks display on the riverfront.

German food aficionados can't miss **Oktoberfest Zincinnati** (oktoberfestzincin-nati.com), America's largest Oktoberfest, featuring wiener dog races, the World's Largest Chicken Dance, plenty of oompah music, and of course beer over one mid-September weekend.

Music gurus put two Cincinnati events on their calendars. In early June, **Bunbury Music Festival** (bunburyfestival.com) is a three-day music extravaganza on the riverfront that features over 100 acts and four stages. Headliners in the past have included Snoop Dogg, Muse, Post Malone, Florence and the Machine, and Twenty One Pilots. Likewise, late July's long-running **Cincinnati Music Festival** (cincymusicfestival.com) brings the best in R&B, soul, jazz and hip-hop. Past performers in this two-day event include Aretha Franklin, Miles Davis, Whitney Houston, Luther Vandross, and Janet Jackson.

Recreation

PARKS

Most of Cincinnati's best parks for hiking are along the I-275 outerbelt.

Northwest of downtown, **Mt. Airy Forest** (5083 Colerain Ave., cincinnatiparks.com), an early urban reforestation project, features an 18-hole disc golf course, hiking, mountain biking paths, bridle paths, and a handicap-accessible tree house among 1,500 acres of woods, wetlands, and prairies.

Farther north, the popular **Glenwood Gardens** (10397 Springfield Pike, 513/771-8733, greatparks.org) is 335 acres of woods, wetlands, and formal gardens including a moderate 1.6-mile (2.6-km) **Wetland Loop** nature trail. The whimsical **Highfield Discovery Garden** ($5.25 per person, under 2 free) features themed storybook gardens and a 25-foot (7.6-m) play tree. You can purchase tickets or pick up a map at the English-inspired Cotswold Visitor Center.

Northeast of the city, one of the most comprehensive parks in the area is **Sharon Woods** (11450 Lebanon Rd., Sharonville, 513/521-7275, greatparks.com). Trails include an easy 2.6-mile (4.2-km) paved **multiuse trail** along the lake and the moderate **Gorge Trail** (0.7 mi/1.1 km one-way) into 100-foot-tall (30-m) Sharon Gorge, where 450-million-year-old trilobite fossils have been found. At the **Sharon Centre** are live animals, nature displays, and the two-story **Adventure Station indoor playground** ($4.75 per child ages 2-12, under 2 free), which incorporates natural themes and an 1800s town into the design. Kids 2-5 will especially enjoy the large ball pit.

Also northeast of the city, **Summit Park** (4335 Glendale Milford Rd., Blue Ash, 513/745-8443, summitparkblueash.com) is an innovative community gathering space with a sprawling, creatively designed playground, 150-foot (46-m) observation deck, and four local restaurants on-site. A giant lawn is perfect for throwing a Frisbee or catching one of the many events the park hosts throughout the year.

Closer to the center of town is historic **Ault Park** (5090 Observatory Ave., 513/357-2604, cincinnatiparks.com), with trails, flower gardens, an impressive 1930 Italian Renaissance-style pavilion, and panoramic views of the Little Miami River valley. The park is 8 miles (12.9 km) east of downtown.

CYCLING

Northwest of the city and close to Indiana, **Mitchell Memorial Forest** (5401 Zion Rd. Cleves, 513/521-7275, greatparks.org) offers 8 miles (12.9 km) of mountain biking paths designed per International Mountain Biking Association standards. The two paths—one intermediate and the other advanced—wind through steep terrain and technical features.

The **Little Miami Scenic Trail** ends (or begins, depending on your perspective) at Beechmont Avenue in Anderson Township east of town. This paved trail weaves through Southwest Ohio's villages, state parks, and rural farmland. Work is being done to connect this trail with the **Ohio River Trail,** also paved, which is currently limited to the downtown riverfront.

KAYAKING, CANOEING, AND PADDLEBOARDING

Fifty West Canoe & Kayak (7605 Wooster Pike, 513/479-0337, fiftywestcanoe.com), across the street from the well-regarded brewpub of the same name, operates on the Little Miami River east of the city. The Facebook page maintains up-to-date information on conditions and hours depending on the season. **Green Acres Canoe and Kayak** (10465 Suspension Bridge Rd., Harrison, 513/353-4770, greenacrescanoe.com) to the northwest offers canoes, kayaks, tubes, and rafts for 3-mile (4.8-km) and 8-mile (12.9-km) self-guided paddling excursions down the melodramatically named Whitewater River. Passenger buses run frequently to return travelers to the livery, which can get busy on weekends and holidays.

ROCK CLIMBING

Indoor rock climbing gym **Climb Time** operates two locations: the original in suburban Blue Ash and the newer one in the Oakley neighborhood (4460 Orkney Ave., 513/818-8017, ctoba.com), opened in 2019. The 45-foot-tall (13.7-m) facility offers equipment rental and $17 day passes. Additionally, there's **RockQuest** (3475 E. Kemper Rd., 513/733-0123, rockquest.com), with $15 day passes and lessons available for kids and adults.

SPECTATOR SPORTS

There's no shortage of sports in Cincinnati, with professional and collegiate sporting events occurring year-round. Even better, three of the main venues are lined up in a row in The Banks district between downtown and the riverfront, so adding a game to your itinerary is a breeze.

Major League Baseball's Opening Day is a city holiday around here, with parade and all. The city traces its history to the first professional baseball team in the country, the Cincinnati Red Stockings. The **Cincinnati Reds** (mlb.com/reds) play their home games at **Great American Ball Park** (100 Joe Nuxhall Way, 513/765-7400). Numerous features adorn this stadium, a must for baseball history fans. Two smokestacks, evoking the steamboats that pulled into the city for over a century, stand behind the outfield and emit

fireworks and other displays when the home team is doing well. Other highlights include mosaics near Crosley Terrace that depict the original 1869 Cincinnati Red Stockings and the Big Red Machine teams that dominated the 1970s, as well as the Rose Garden symbolizing Pete Rose's record-breaking hit, a single against the San Diego Padres. The garden is located approximately where the famous ball landed in what was then the left-center field of Riverfront Stadium.

The National Football League's **Cincinnati Bengals** (bengals.com) play on the other side of The Banks in the sleek **Paul Brown Stadium** (1 Paul Brown Stadium, 513/621-8383). **FC Cincinnati** (fccincinnati.com), which leveled up from the United Soccer League to Major League Soccer in 2019, plays in **TQL Stadium** (1501 Central Pkwy., 513/977-5435) just west of Over-the-Rhine.

The **University of Cincinnati Bearcats** (gobearcats.com) compete in the NCAA American Athletic Conference. The school's basketball team plays at **Fifth Third Arena** (2700 Bearcat Way, 513/556-2287) and is one of the most competitive programs in the country, as is the team's crosstown rival **Xavier University Musketeers** (goxavier.com) who play at the **Cintas Center** (1624 Herald Ave., 513/745-3900). Both basketball teams have seen many successful seasons and deep runs into the NCAA Basketball Tournament, Xavier in particular of late.

Minor league hockey team the **Cincinnati Cyclones** (cycloneshockey.com) are affiliated with the Buffalo Sabres and play at **Heritage Bank Center** (100 Broadway St., 513/421-4111) along the riverfront.

1: Great American Ball Park **2:** brunch burger at Taste of Belgium

Shopping

OVER-THE-RHINE

Many long-standing local shops operate satellite locations in OTR, including women's boutique **Kismet** (1233 Vine St., 513/906-7796, 11am-7pm Mon.-Thurs., 11am-8pm Fri.-Sat., noon-5pm Sun.). The store's selection of eclectic yet affordable clothing and accessories is geared for the "past Forever 21, but not yet Ann Taylor" crowd, as the knowledgeable employee behind the counter put it.

A favorite souvenir shop is **MiCA 12/v** (1201 Vine St., 513/533-1974, www.shop-mica.com, 10am-8pm Mon.-Sat., 10am-5pm Sun.), stocked with stationery, accessories, and other take-homeables made by local artists, as well as locally themed T-shirts.

If you're looking for something truly original, then **The Little Mahatma** (1205 Vine St., 513/723-1287, 11am-8pm Mon.-Thurs., 11am-9pm Fri.-Sat., 11am-5pm Sun.) is your place. Originally located in the Carew Tower, the aromatic little shop now takes up residence in OTR and pulls in jewelry, artifacts, and other handmade one-of-a-kind pieces from 30 countries. The shop works with fair-trade companies to acquire their wares.

Based in Cincinnati, the ceramics company **Rookwood Pottery** (1920 Race St., 513/381-2510, 10am-4pm Mon.-Sat., 11am-4pm Sun.) has been synonymous with elegance and quality since its establishment in 1880. Many prominent buildings and homes in the area (and elsewhere, including NYC's Grand Central Station) sport tiles or pottery from the company, which folded in 1967 but was revived in 2004. There are outposts in Kenwood Towne Centre and Liberty Center, but the flagship location is here in Over-the-Rhine, with a spacious showroom. Prices for the tableware and decor aren't cheap, but you're buying the best in the business.

OAKLEY

If you're in the area for MadTree Brewing, itself a family-friendly destination for most hours of the day, there are a couple of quality kid-oriented stores worth a look in the Oakley neighborhood.

The Blue Manatee Literacy Project, which runs children's bookstore **Blue Manatee Bookstore** (3094 Madison Rd., 513/257-0774, 9am-5pm Tues.-Thurs., 9am-6pm Fri.-Sat., 10am-3pm Sun.) has been a mainstay in supporting child literacy for decades, through various iterations. For every book purchased, one is donated to a disadvantaged young reader in the Cincinnati region. The shop's cozy digs host a busy schedule of story times and high-profile author visits.

If you're passing through for books, you might as well browse some toys too. **King Arthur's Court** (3040 Madison Rd., 513/531-4600, 10am-7pm Mon.-Sat., 11am-6pm Sun.) has been selling a curated assortment of toys for 40 years, including a robust selection of LEGO sets that cover Harry Potter, architecture, and more. There's a play area for young kids.

HYDE PARK

In the center of these streets of fine, old houses is historic Hyde Park Square, with its collection of boutique apparel shops, galleries, cafés, and restaurants that cater to the area's wealthy clientele.

Fans of unique stationery and decor ought to head to **Poeme** (3446 Michigan Ave., 513/321-4999, 10am-6pm Mon.-Fri., 10am-5pm Sat.), which specializes in custom stationery and design services. The shop offers an eclectic collection of greeting cards, notebooks, and the cutest assortment of clocks in Ohio.

Delamere & Hopkins (2708 Erie Ave., 513/871-3474, 10am-8pm Mon.-Thurs., 10am-6pm Fri.-Sat., 11am-5pm Sun.) is a long-running outfitter and outdoor clothing store operating in a historic space that once housed a grocery. The store specializes in fly-fishing and upland hunting gear and sports the largest selection of quality Barbour apparel outside of Barbour retail stores.

Food

Eating in Cincinnati is a treat. You have established fine-dining options, trendy newcomers pushing the envelope, and neighborhood haunts that have changed little in decades. The international food scene comes with its own standouts too, and you're never far from a chili parlor. Prices run the gamut from pocket change to very expensive.

DOWNTOWN
Bar and Grill
Arnold's Bar and Grill (210 E. 8th St., 513/421-6234, arnoldsbarandgrill.com, 11am-1am Tues.-Wed., 11am-2:30am Thurs.-Sat., $12-24) traces its history to 1861 when Simon Arnold opened a tavern in this building that dates back to the 1830s. As such, it's the city's oldest bar and something of a timepiece in Cincinnati history. Inside is Arnold's old bathtub, once used for gin. The menu is best known for its signature Greek spaghetti but covers the salads, burgers, and meaty entrées you expect to see at a bar, albeit at an elevated level and with outliers like Moroccan cauliflower steak. Vegan and gluten-free options are available too. The place maintains a busy schedule of live music that includes country, bluegrass, jazz, and Americana.

Barbecue
The famous barbecue ribs at the **Montgomery Inn Boathouse** (925 Riverside Dr., 513/721-7427, montgomery-inn.com, 11am-9:30pm Mon.-Thurs., 11am-10:30pm Fri.-Sat., 3pm-9pm Sun., $12-33) have attracted politicians, athletes, and entertainers over the decades. Though the original is in the suburb of Montgomery, the Boathouse location has a view right on the Ohio River. It also has a solid drink menu with local craft beer.

French
The epitome of fine dining in Cincinnati, **Orchids at Palm Court** (35 W. 5th St., 513/564-6465, orchidsatpalmcourt.com, 5:30pm-9pm Sun.-Thurs., 5:30pm-10pm Fri.-Sat., $42-94) is in the exquisite French art deco lobby of the Hilton Cincinnati Netherland Plaza in the Carew Tower. The restaurant is the only AAA Five-Diamond-rated establishment in Ohio, and the menu is suitably upper-crust. For a slightly more affordable option, the restaurant offers the three-course Taste of Orchids special from Sunday through Thursday for $45. Valet parking is available on the Race Street side of the hotel and is complimentary with dinner for up to 12 hours. Business attire is suggested. Next to Orchids, The Bar at Palm Court reflects the same culinary experience and is stocked with an extensive wine list, selection of bourbon, and craft beer.

Mexican
The corner of Walnut and 6th Streets is probably the glitziest in Cincinnati, what with the Aronoff Center for the Arts, 21cMuseum Hotel, and Contemporary Arts Center drawing people looking for high-end entertainment. Smack-dab in the middle of the action is **Nada** (600 Walnut St., 513/721-6232, eatdrinknada.com, 11am-10pm Mon.-Thurs., 11am-midnight Fri., 10:30am-11pm Sat., 10:30am-10pm Sun., $10-21), a trendy Mexican restaurant and bar known for its margaritas. Everything's delectable, but the quesadillas come crusted shut with tastefully burnt cheese. Portions are on the small side.

Goetta and Cincinnati Chili

a four-way chili at Camp Washington Chili, a mainstay in the Cincinnati chili world

Cincinnati features not one, but two regional specialties that are worth a try.

When Cincinnati's 19th-century German immigrants needed a way to stretch their meat supply for the week, they added oats and onions to their pork, seasoned it with rosemary, thyme, or whatever else they had in their cupboard, and came up with **goetta** (pronounced "get-uh"). Typically served for breakfast, goetta may also be found on sandwiches or as a topping on pizza. Many diners in the Cincinnati area offer goetta as a breakfast meat. Some places serve their goetta crunchier than others, some maintaining the sausage-ness more than others. Either way, it's available in most places that serve breakfast.

Perhaps more widely known is **Cincinnati chili**, which, according to most definitions, is not chili at all but rather more like a meat sauce. Cincinnati chili parlors are the great equalizer—in each you'll find old, young, rich, poor, families, friends, couples, and individuals enjoying this unique dish. The chili was developed by Greek immigrants in the 1920s looking to expand their restaurant menus with something less obviously ethnic. While local chains Skyline Chili and Gold Star Chili are as common as Starbucks here, there are dozens of independent parlors, each guarding their secret recipes, that draw their own devoted fans. The chili includes an unusual array of spices, including cinnamon and even chocolate, and is primarily eaten on spaghetti. Be ready to make a few choices when ordering, denoted by what "way" you want it:

- **Two-Way:** Spaghetti and chili

- **Three-Way:** Spaghetti, chili, and a heap of shredded cheese

- **Four-Way:** Spaghetti, chili, shredded cheese, and either diced onions or kidney beans

- **Five-Way:** Spaghetti, chili, shredded cheese, diced onions, and kidney beans

Another popular way to eat Cincinnati chili is on Coney dogs, again with shredded cheese piled on top. Oftentimes, people order both.

Italian

Rustic is the first word that comes to mind at **Sotto** (118 E. 6th St., 513/977-6886, sottocincinnati.com, 5pm-10pm Mon.-Thurs., 5pm-11pm Fri.-Sat., 4pm-9pm Sun., 11am-2pm Mon.-Fri., $18-36), where the wood and brick decor, lit softly by candlelight and elegant fixtures, sets the mood for intimate dining. Similar to its basement dwellings, Sotto's menu is down-to-earth. This is one of the most popular spots in town and just steps away from the Aronoff Center for the Arts, so reservations are a good idea. Sotto is underneath sister Italian restaurant **Boca** (513/542-2022, bocacincinnati.com, 5pm-10pm Tues.-Sat., $25-45), where the modern elegance comes at a price.

Brunch

There are multiple locations around town, but the downtown outpost of ★ **Taste of Belgium** (16 W. Freedom Way, 513/396-5800, authenticwaffle.com, 7am-3pm Mon., 7am-10pm Tues.-Thurs., 7am-11pm Fri., 8am-11pm Sat., 8am-8pm Sun., $11-24) offers a great view of the Ohio River and Roebling Suspension Bridge. The restaurant's rustic-chic digs are a friendly space to enjoy some of the finest brunch the city offers, including their signature waffles. The firm, disc-sized waffles come in many variations, including a brunch burger with hamburger, bacon, egg, Havarti, and syrup. A couple of menu items feature Cincinnati's signature goetta meat, including goetta hash. Not in the mood for brunch? The menu also includes salads, sandwiches, and Belgian appetizers. The restaurant features a bar with an extensive draft list as well as a take-out espresso bar with waffles by the bag.

Restaurants in downtown Cincinnati tend to skew upscale or fast food. For something in the middle, check out **Hathaway's Diner** (441 Vine St., 513/621-1332, 8am-2pm Sun.-Thurs., 7:30am-4pm Fri.-Sat., $7-14), a place that frequently shows up on lists of best diners in the country. Inside the Carew Tower arcade, the diner is an authentic greasy spoon with checkerboard floors and Formica tables like they had when the diner opened in 1956. It's a seat-yourself kind of joint, with daily specials, including free pie with an entrée purchase on Tuesdays. Breakfast is served during all business hours.

OVER-THE-RHINE
★ Findlay Market

Named by *Newsweek* in 2019 as one of the "10 Best Food Markets in the World" (and

Findlay Market

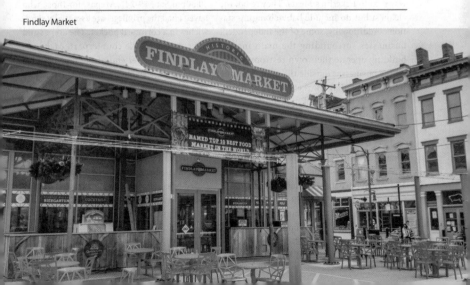

the only one representing the United States), **Findlay Market** (1801 Race St., 513/665-4839, findlaymarket.org, 9am-6pm Tues.-Fri., 8am-6pm Sat., 10am-4pm Sun.) is a city treasure. Over a million people come to the market annually, from all socioeconomic and cultural walks of life. Open since 1855 and the oldest continuously running public market in Ohio, Findlay Market draws crowds for its produce vendors and food stalls and is the best place in town to find cheap eats. The market not only occupies the central market building but the surrounding colorful storefronts as well. Start at butcher **Eckerlin's Meats** (eckerlinmeats.com) for a $4 goetta sandwich, available all day, every day. Only have time for a quick coffee and pastry? There are several good options. **Deeper Roots Coffee** (deeperrootscoffee.com) is intentional about the relationships they form with coffee farmers. There's also a strong international food scene at the market. **Pho Lang Thang** (pholangthang.com) serves up an extensive menu of piping-hot pho and crunchy banh mi sandwiches. Additionally, **Saigon Market** (findlaymarket.org) fills the Asian grocery niche, providing necessities from Vietnam, China, Thailand, and beyond.

Public restrooms are available down a hallway next to Eckerlin's Meats. They're not the cleanest but do include baby changing stations. Additionally, some of the independent businesses surrounding the main market building operate their own restrooms. Not all the businesses outside the main building follow the Findlay Market operating hours, so it's worth taking a look at their websites for more information.

Gastropub

Trendy **Senate** (1212 Vine St., 513/421-2020, senatepub.com, 4:30pm-10:30pm Wed.-Fri., 11:30am-10pm Sat., 11:30am-9pm Sun., check for longer summer hours, $9-16) specializes in gourmet hot dogs. Being in Over-the-Rhine, the beer selection is on point and pulls from within the city, state, and elsewhere. A second location is in the suburb of Blue Ash.

Comfort Food

It's right there in the name at **Boomtown Biscuits and Whiskey** (1201 Broadway, 513/381-2666, boomtownbiscuitsandwhiskey. com, 9am-9pm Tues.-Thurs., 9am-10pm Fri.-Sat., 9am-3pm Sun., $9-13), a contemporary take on frontier food. Barn doors, old saws, and other trappings of frontier life are juxtaposed with modern lighting and furnishings. The menu relies on biscuits, with the option of a biscuit sandwich or ordering various jams, gravies, and other goodies to pair with the bread.

New American

Upscale **Salazar** (1401 Republic St., 513/621-7000, salazarcincinnati.com, 5pm-10pm Mon.-Thurs., 5pm-11pm Fri.-Sat., brunch 10:30am-2pm Sat.-Sun., $18-37) sports an exciting New American menu and drink list, perfect for a romantic dinner before a show at nearby Cincinnati Music Hall. A popular brunch keeps the place busy on the weekends.

Venezuelan

An international standout in Over-the-Rhine is Venezuelan **Maize Arepas and Bar** (1438 Race St., 513/381-1608, maizeotr.com, 5pm-10pm Tues.-Thurs., 5pm-10:30pm Fri., 4pm-10:30pm Sat., $9-24). Arepas, for those who haven't had the privilege, are essentially sandwiches in a cornmeal pocket. The arepas and their corn pancake counterpart, *cachapas,* are on the cheaper end of the menu, which includes more elaborate dinner entrées. Pull up a stool and try this South American staple.

Mediterranean

Abigail Street (1214 Vine St., 513/421-4040, abigailstreet.com, 5pm-10pm Tues.-Thurs., 5pm-11pm Fri.-Sat., $12-17) serves multicolored tapas dishes in a stylish interior of exposed brick, hanging lightbulbs, and subway tile. Turkish coffee and Moroccan mint tea are on hand to sip with your nosh.

Italian

Sadly, the recent success of the neighborhood

has not been shared by everyone and there is still a high level of poverty in the community. Enter **Venice on Vine** (1301 Vine St., 513/221-7020, veniceonvine.com, 11am-3pm Mon.-Thurs., 11am-3pm and 5pm-9pm Fri., 11am-9pm Sat., $8-11), which provides training and jobs for those facing barriers to employment such as homelessness and criminal records. Pizza comes in 9-inch or 16-inch sizes alongside a handful of salad and sandwich options.

WALNUT HILLS
Barbecue
Would you like a side of social justice with your dinner? **Just Q'in** (975 E. McMillan St., 513/452-MEAT, justqin.com, 11am-8pm Mon.-Sat., $8-16) hires folks with barriers to employment to smoke its meat in-house with cherry and sugar maple wood, make its sides (which are all vegetarian and mostly gluten-free) from scratch, and staff the restaurant. You can also check the restaurant's social media for the whereabouts of its food truck.

Mexican
A must-try is a "turtle" at **Gomez Salsa** (2437 Gilbert Rd., 513/954-8541, gomezsalsa.com, 11am-10pm Tues.-Sat., $9), essentially a burrito with the added blessing of being sealed shut by toasty cheese. The typical selection of tacos, burritos, and burrito bowls are available as well, both at this location and at their pop-up window in Over-the-Rhine.

UNIVERSITY OF CINCINNATI
Jamaican
Featured on Food Network's *Diners, Drive-Ins and Dives*, **Island Frydays** (2826 Vine St., 513/498-0680, islandfrydays.com, 11am-7pm Mon.-Wed., 11am-8pm Thur.-Sat., $9-16) is a labor of love for native Jamaican and former Cincinnati Bearcat Leo Morgan. The decor delightfully matches the palette of the Jamaican flag and complements the authentic jerk chicken and fish dinners.

NORTHSIDE
Chili
Technically in the Camp Washington neighborhood to the south, ★ **Camp Washington Chili** (3005 Colerain Ave., 513/541-0061, campwashingtonchili.com, 24 hours Mon.-Sat., $5-10) is a mainstay in the Cincinnati chili world. It's occupied the corner of Colerain and Hopple since 1940, though the original parlor was demolished in 2000. Newspaper and magazine clippings on the walls will tell you just how much press the place has received for its chili, which is helpfully offered in several sizes in case you'd like to sample other menu items. Breakfast is served all day on Saturdays, and there is a satisfying menu of burgers and other sandwiches for those uninterested in chili.

Senegalese
Not much to look at from the outside, **Darou Salam** (4163 Hamilton Ave., 513/681-3663, 10am-9pm Mon.-Sat., 11am-8pm Sun., $8-12) is a spartan hole-in-the-wall serving up some of the best West African food in the city, if not the state. The entrées, including popular jollof rice and chicken dishes, are hearty and portions are well-sized.

Nepali
Bridges Nepali Cuisine (4165 Hamilton Ave., 513/374-9354, bridgesnepalicuisine.com, 11am-9pm Mon.-Thurs., 11am-10pm Fri.-Sat., 11am-8pm Sun., $8-14) is celebrated as one of the best international restaurants in town. The colorful menu of *momo* dumplings, samosas, and rice bowls complement the warm atmosphere and are accessible dishes for those familiar with Indian food.

HYDE PARK
Burgers
Neighborhood standby **Arthur's Cafe** (3516 Edwards Rd., 513/871-5543, arthurscincinnati.com, 11am-midnight daily, $9-14) is best known for its burgers, long considered some of the city's best. The restaurant maintains a Burger Madness special on Sundays,

Mondays, and Tuesdays that allows visitors to add most toppings free of charge. The crispy fish-and-chips is also well regarded. The diner's well-worn furnishings and old-school ambience mark the sort of local joint that relies on good food and the devotion of regulars. In fact, a mural of some long-time regulars adorns an entire wall next to the bar.

Deli

Open since 1938, **Carl's Deli** (2836 Observatory Ave. A, 513/871-2275, carlsdeli. com, 8am-10pm Mon.-Sat., 11am-9pm Sun., $7-10) is a couple of blocks removed from Hyde Park Square and offers over 30 sandwiches, though you can also design your own. The neighborhood spot has been named a "Best of the City" by *Cincinnati Magazine*.

Ice Cream

Cincinnati ice cream chain ★ **Graeter's Ice Cream** (2704 Erie Ave., 513/321-6221, graeters.com, 9am-10:30pm Sun.-Thurs., 9am-11pm Fri.-Sat.) has been going strong since 1870 and is ubiquitous throughout southwestern and central Ohio, with locations stretching to Chicago. The original parlor no longer exists, but Hyde Park Square's is the oldest still in operation and maintains a classic feel with tiled floors and small tables. The company uses a French-pot process to produce a dense ice cream. Black Raspberry Chocolate Chip is the perennial favorite, accounting for 20 percent of the company's sales alone.

OAKLEY
Cafés

There are other locations in Blue Ash and downtown, but Oakley's ★ **Sleepy Bee Cafe** (3098 Madison Rd., 513/533-2339, sleepybeecafe.com, 7am-2:30pm Mon.-Fri., 8am-3pm Sat.-Sun., $9-12) was the first, and it has been selling health-conscious meals with local ingredients since 2013. The pancakes are fluffy and rich, hot tea is sold by the pot, and the crowd-pleasing Avi Omelet comes stuffed with fresh vegetables. The decor

leans delightfully into the bee theme, including a wall of bee-inspired artwork by the restaurant's littlest patrons.

Though the coffee at Sleepy Bee Café will do you just fine, it's worth stopping in **Redtree Art Gallery and Coffee Shop** (3210 Madison Rd., 513/321-8733, redtreegallery.net, 7am-6pm Mon.-Fri., 8am-6pm Sat., 9am-3pm Sun.) for a wider selection and a glance at the local artwork, which makes an enticing souvenir. Famed Cincinnati hippo Fiona is the subject of many pieces. T-shirts are also available. The menu includes bagels, quiches, and burritos from local vendors.

PRICE HILL

It's not that far off the beaten path, but there isn't much that will pull you to the Price Hill neighborhood west of downtown other than dining destinations that are both affordable and open on Sundays and Mondays, something of a rarity outside of fast food around here.

Chili

Topping many "best chili" lists alongside Camp Washington Chili is **Price Hill Chili** (4920 Glenway Ave., 513/471-9507, pricehillchili.com, 6am-11pm Mon.-Thurs., 6am-1am Fri.-Sat., 7am-3pm Sun., $7-17). The extensive breakfast, lunch, and dinner menus make this one of the few places in town you can enjoy both of Cincinnati's specialties: goetta and chili. This casual joint, popular with comfort food fans of all types, has been family owned and operated since 1962.

Gastropub

For casual dinner and a view, consider **Incline Public House** (2601 W. 8th St., 513/251-3000, inclinepublichouse.com, 11am-midnight Mon.-Sat., 10am-11pm Sun., $10-18), situated on the edge of a hill, with a panorama of downtown Cincinnati. Pizza, burgers, and sandwiches dominate the straightforward menu. The draft beer list focuses on local Ohio brews.

Bars and Nightlife

Cincinnati boasts the kind of beer scene befitting a town with 200 years of German immigrant influence, with over 60 craft breweries in the region. Beer has played an integral role in the city's economy, nightlife, and culture for nearly the entirety of its history. Besides beer, you'll find innovative clubs, hopping independent music venues, and glamorous cocktail bars.

★ CRAFT BREWERIES

The big name in Cincinnati craft breweries right now is ★ **Rhinegeist** (1910 Elm St., 513/381-1397, rhinegeist.com, 3pm-midnight Mon.-Thurs., 3pm-2am Fri., noon-2am Sat., noon-9pm Sun.), whose quality beers can be found throughout Ohio. Housed in the former bottling facility for Christian Moerlein Brewing Co. (another prominent Cincinnati beer), Rhinegeist offers a family-friendly taproom (before 8pm) and convivial rooftop mingling space (weather dependent). No food is served, but outside food is encouraged, especially with Findlay Market just steps away. The brewery pumps out quite the variety of quality brews, but their fruit beers such as Bubbles and Slangria are particularly a strong suit.

Speaking of Christian Moerlein Brewing Co., their **Moerlein Lager House** (115 Joe Nuxhall Way, 513/421-2337, moerleinlager-house.com, 11am-10pm Mon.-Thurs., 11am-11pm Fri.-Sat., 11am-10pm Sun.) keeps this historic brand alive. The company started life in 1853 and was one of the largest breweries by volume in the United States, exporting to Europe and South America. Prohibition ended all of that in 1919. The company was revived in the 1980s and operated a historic brewery and taproom in Over-the-Rhine until 2020. Today, this brewpub serves an assortment of meaty entrées, burgers, and a small selection of German dishes next to their over 80 brews on hand. Big windows and outdoor seating provide open views of the baseball stadium and riverfront.

A worthwhile brewpub is ★ **Taft's Ale House** (1429 Race St., 513/334-1393, taftsbeer.com, 11:30am-10pm Mon.-Wed., 11:30am-11pm Thurs., 11:30am-midnight Fri.-Sat., 11:30am-9pm Sun.). Since 2015, Taft's has occupied a rehabbed 1850 church. The atmosphere is relaxed and casual, with ample seating on the main floor as well as the balcony, where a second bar keeps things running smoothly. The Gavel Banger IPA has won awards in the beer world and was named "Cincinnati's Favorite Beer of 2019" by the *Cincinnati Enquirer*. Taft's has expanded with two **Taft's Brewpourium** locations—one in Northside and one in Columbus—that add pizza to the mix.

Urban Artifact (1660 Blue Rock St., 513/542-4222, artifactbeer.com, 4pm-10pm Mon., 4pm-midnight Tues.-Thurs., 11am-1:30am Fri.-Sat., 11am-10pm Sun.) is another brewery in a former church building, utilizing the church's former gymnasium as the brewery and courtyard as the biergarten. The beer list skews toward sours and fruity beers, though guest beers from other breweries are quite diverse. The brewery is also a live music venue and maintains a busy and diverse schedule. Check the Facebook page for upcoming shows. Food is not served on-site.

Perhaps the main draw to the Oakley area is popular **MadTree Brewing** (3301 Madison Rd., 513/836-8733, madtreebrewing.com, 11am-11pm Mon.-Thurs., 11am-1am Fri., 10am-1am Sat., 10am-11pm Sun.), a massive brewery, taproom, and biergarten complex just north of the main Oakley Square area. A hangar encloses the brewery, adjacent to the airy taproom and the sprawling, dog-friendly biergarten, which is tented and heated in the cold winter months. Over 30 of MadTree's beers are on tap. Chef-owned **Catch-A-Fire Café** (513/441-8565, catchafirepizza.com, 11am-10pm Mon.-Thurs., 11am-midnight Fri., 10am-midnight Sat., 10am-10pm Sun., $8-25) takes up residence inside and serves pizza and brunch with locally sourced ingredients.

Outdoorsy types will like **Fifty West Brewing** (7668 Wooster Pike, 513/834-8789, fiftywestbrew.com, 11am-9pm Mon., 11am-10pm Tues.-Thurs., 11am-11pm Fri.-Sat., 10am-9pm Sun.), one of the more prominent craft breweries in the Cincinnati area. Aside from the quality beers and the burger bar menu, the brewery promotes an active lifestyle with volleyball and pickleball leagues, kayak rentals, and, being located off the Little Miami Scenic Trail, bicycle rentals.

BARS AND CLUBS

If you can't decide which brewery to visit, you can take your pick of over 500 craft beers and 100 wine varieties at Northside's **Higher Gravity** (4106 Hamilton Ave., 513/813-3523, highergravitycrafthaus.com, 4pm-11pm Mon., 2pm-11pm Tues.-Wed., 2pm-midnight Thurs., 2pm-1am Fri., noon-1am Sat., 1:30pm-11pm Sun.). This relaxed beer store and bar makes a point to create a casual, kid-friendly atmosphere in which people can take their time to explore the wide selection. They rotate local, state, and national beers from 14 taps.

A tiki-themed speakeasy, you say? The front for Walnut Hills' **Tiki Tiki Bang Bang** (965 E. McMillan St., 513/559-9500, gorillacinemapresents.com, 5pm-midnight Tues.-Thurs., 5pm-2am Fri.-Sat.) is a movie rental business, but beyond the doors is a tropical cocktail bar catering to cinephiles with their Friday night Disney karaoke and Saturday sundown patio movies. Rum is the liquor of choice here.

In the middle of downtown, Japanese-style karaoke concept **Tokyo Kitty** (575 Race St., 513/744-0909, thattokyobar.com, 5pm-2am Mon.-Fri., 1pm-2am Sat., 5pm-midnight Sun.) is a 21-and-over neon-infused club that combines karaoke, cocktails, and dancing. The public front room is boisterous, though private karaoke rooms can be reserved by the hour for groups of up to 18. It's owned by the same folks that run Tiki Tiki Bang Bang.

Below Zero Lounge (1120 Walnut St., 513/421-9376, 4pm-2am Thurs.-Sat., open Sun. for Bengals games, check the events schedule for Mon.-Wed. openings) is a proud martini bar in the middle of beer-focused Over-the-Rhine with over 100 vodkas, all served at 6°F (-14.4°C). Dressing smartly is encouraged. Check the website's schedule for an ongoing rotation of live DJs, karaoke, and more.

Another member of the Over-the-Rhine vodka club is **Wodka Bar** (1200 Main St., 513/381-3739, wodkabarotr.com, 4pm-midnight Tues.-Thurs., 4pm-2:30am Fri., 2pm-2:30am Sat., noon-10pm Sun.), though this time with a strictly Eastern European slant. The bar's interior maintains an old-world charm to match the drinks on offer. Also on hand to accompany your vodka is a full menu of pierogi, cabbage rolls, and other delights from the motherland.

LIVE MUSIC

MOTR Pub (1345 Main St., 513/381-6687, motrpub.com) is an intimate 150-person concert venue in the heart of Over-the-Rhine that catches up-and-coming indie rock bands as they come through the area. Best of all, there's no cover charge. Ever. The happy hour from 4pm to 7pm offers half-off beers. Across the street and operated by the same owners is the **Woodward Theater** (1404 Main St., 513/345-7986, woodward-theater.com). Originally a movie theater dating to the early 1900s, the Woodward reopened as a music venue in 2014 when the acts booked at the MOTR Pub were getting a little too popular. Even though this 600-person auditorium holds a larger audience than MOTR, it still maintains an intimate feeling.

Bogart's (2621 Vine St., 513/872-8801, bogarts.com), next to the University of

Cincinnati campus, pulls in regional and national acts in a 1,500-seat former vaudeville theater.

Looking for a little more grit? Head to Northside for a show at **The Comet** (4579 Hamilton Ave., 513/541-8900, cometbar. com). As eclectic as they come, The Comet has an all-vinyl reggae dance party the second Friday of the month, biker nights on Tuesdays, and two sets from The Comet Bluegrass All-Stars every Sunday night. The dive bar is also known for its burritos. Check the website's calendar for recurring and visiting acts.

The big outdoor concert venue in town is the **Riverbend Music Center** (6295 Kellogg Ave., 513/232-6220, riverbend.org), which attracts everything from A-list tours to heavy metal festivals to orchestral concerts.

Accommodations

Most of Cincinnati's best and most convenient accommodations are downtown or across the river on the Kentucky riverfront. These are also by far the area's priciest options. For more budget-minded travelers, a handful of guesthouses and bed-and-breakfasts are in the thick of the city's most interesting neighborhoods. Additionally, a cluster of chain hotels is available in the Sharonville/Blue Ash area near the outerbelt that puts you nicely between Kings Island and the city, making an easy base for area travels. Rates across the city drop significantly in the winter.

DOWNTOWN
$150-200

In the former 1920s *Cincinnati Enquirer* building is the **Hampton Inn & Suites Cincinnati-Downtown** (617 Vine St., 513/354-2430, hilton.com, $161-219), though the interior has been thoroughly modernized. Rates include a free hot breakfast.

The **Hyatt Regency Cincinnati** (151 W. 5th St., 513/579-1234, hyatt.com, $152-252) is a practical, relatively affordable downtown hotel in a modern high-rise across the street from Duke Energy Convention Center. Rooms are neutral, clean, and come with good views of downtown. On the 5th floor is an enclosed saltwater pool with an outdoor sundeck.

Over $200

The boutique ★ **21c Museum Hotel Cincinnati** (609 Walnut St., 513/578-6600, 21cmuseumhotels.com/Cincinnati, $269-449) is an ultramodern restoration of the historic Metropole hotel. As part of the 21c Museum Hotel brand, the building features a contemporary art gallery with rotating exhibits on the first two floors (free and open to the public) and artwork from a private collection in each of the otherwise minimalistic 156 rooms. The Spa at 21C offers an extensive menu of relaxing services, and there are two fashionable dining and drinking options in the building: the first floor's **Metropole** (513/578-6660, metropoleonwalnut.com, 7am-10pm Mon.-Thurs., 7am-11pm Fri.-Sat., 7am-9:30pm Sun.) and the rooftop **Cocktail Terrace** (open at 5pm). The hotel is within steps of the Aronoff Center and Contemporary Arts Center.

Inside the art deco Carew Tower is the AAA Four-Diamond ★ **Hilton Cincinnati Netherland Plaza** (35 W. 5th St., 513/421-9100, hilton.com, $210-339). The lobby's dark wood walls and marble staircases transport visitors to a bygone era of elegance. The modern rooms come with excellent views of downtown, Fountain Square, and the riverfront. Fine dining is just an elevator ride away at the **Orchids at Palm Court** (513/564-6465, orchidsatpalmcourt.com, 5:30pm-9pm Sun.-Thurs., 5:30pm-10pm Fri.-Sat., $42-94), located just off the lobby.

The chic **Renaissance Cincinnati Downtown Hotel** (36 E. 4th St., 513/333-0000, renaissance-hotels.marriott.com, $246-259) has the distinctive honor of occupying a building designed by turn-of-the-20th-century Chicago architect Daniel Burnham. The guest rooms are sleek and contemporary but the lobby and other shared spaces maintain many of the original features of the bank that originally occupied this space, including the walnut front doors.

Another historic option is the **Cincinnatian Hotel** (601 Vine St., 513/381-3000, hilton.com, $234-284), a Curio Collection by Hilton property containing 146 contemporary suites. The French Second Empire-style building dates to 1882, when it was the premier hotel in the city.

The lone hotel option in The Banks development on the riverfront is, fortunately, a good one and the best option for visitors attending a Reds or Bengals game. The contemporary **AC Hotel by Marriott Cincinnati at the Banks** (135 Joe Nuxhall Way, 513/744-9900, marriott.com, $227-439) offers rooms with balconies to catch the great view of downtown, the baseball stadium, and the Ohio River.

Centrally located right off Fountain Square is **The Westin Cincinnati** (21 E. 5th St, 513/621-7700, marriott.com, $204-249), with 456 rooms remodeled in 2015. A pool and workout room are on the 17th floor.

Grab-and-go cafeteria **Ingredients** offers convenient breakfast and lunch options.

The Residence Inn by Marriott Cincinnati Downtown/The Phelps (506 E. 4th St., 513/651-1234, marriott.com, $246-399) is in a quieter corner of downtown, a block away from the Taft Museum of Art. This historic building, known as The Phelps, was an upscale apartment building that counted former president William Howard Taft's aunt, whom he would frequently visit, as one of its former tenants. Today, the suites come with kitchenettes and are suited for extended stays. A porch overlooks Lytle Park. The hotel offers a complimentary breakfast buffet and a rooftop restaurant with excellent views.

OVER-THE-RHINE
$150-200

Across 14th Street from Cincinnati Music Hall is **Symphony Hotel** (201 W 14th St., 513/721-3353, symphonyhotel.com, $159-229). This bed-and-breakfast in an 1871 townhome has nine rooms, each themed and appointed according to a different classical composer. Each room also comes with a flat-screen TV with complimentary streaming services. There's live jazz in the bar every Thursday, Friday,

view from the top of the Carew Tower, which houses the Hilton Cincinnati Netherland Plaza

and Saturday night and breakfast—continental during the week and gourmet during the weekend—is included in the rate. Parking is free and a restaurant is on-site.

UNIVERSITY OF CINCINNATI

If you're in town primarily for a function on campus, there are chain hotels next to the university, or you can stay in a historic bed-and-breakfast.

$150-200

The Clifton House (500 Terrace Ave., 513/221-7600, thecliftonhouse.com, $155-235) sits in the Gaslight District, a neighborhood of historic homes and gaslit lamps, and is within spitting distance of campus. There are six rooms available, all furnished in accordance with the B&B's 1900 build date. The Midwest Culinary Institute provides the gourmet breakfast and baked goods are always available in the pantry.

Also within the Gaslight District is Gaslight Bed & Breakfast (3652 Middleton Ave., 513/861-5222, gaslightbb.com, $150-170) with four antiques-filled rooms, a sauna and weight room, and a gigantic willow tree to greet you. The two cheaper rooms have shared bathroom facilities. The large deck is a relaxing place to sit with friends.

NORTHSIDE
$100-150

Six Acres B&B (5350 Hamilton Ave., 513/541-0873, sixacresbb.com, $139-169) sits in a secluded 1850 house that belonged to abolitionist Zebulon Strong, who used the property as a stop on the Underground Railroad. Today, the bed-and-breakfast maintains five rooms and ample common space with era-appropriate furnishings and decor. A bit removed from the bustle of town, Six Acres is only a few minutes' drive from the nightlife and restaurants of the Northside neighborhood.

Information and Services

TOURIST INFORMATION

The Cincinnati USA Visitor Center (511 Walnut St., 513/534-5877, cincinnatiusa.com, 11am-5pm daily) provides information on events, dining options, and other current tips that might come in handy during a visit. The office is right on Fountain Square next to Chipotle.

HEALTH AND EMERGENCY SERVICES

The emergency services nearest the center of town are located at The Christ Hospital (2139 Auburn Ave., 513/585-2000, thechristhospital.com) and the University of Cincinnati Medical Center (234 Goodman St., 513/584-1000, uchealth.com). For those with kiddos that need specialized help, nearby is the Cincinnati Children's Hospital Medical Center (3333 Burnet Ave., 800/344-2462, cincinnatichildrens.org), one of the best of its kind.

Transportation

GETTING THERE

Cincinnati is well connected to the rest of country via road and air. Though direct flights exist from Toronto and Paris, most international travelers will likely connect via a major hub such as Chicago or Atlanta.

Air

The **Cincinnati/Northern Kentucky International Airport** (CVG, 3087 Terminal Dr., Hebron, KY, 859/767-3151, cvgairport. com) offers direct flights to most major American airports and six destinations in Canada, Europe, and Central America. A 20-minute drive southwest of the city along I-275, the airport is served by 10 airlines, including mainstays like Delta and United along with increasing service from ultra-low-budget airlines Allegiant and Frontier.

Train

Cincinnati is served by one Amtrak line, the *Cardinal* (amtrak.com/cardinal-train), which stops at **Union Terminal** (1301 Western Ave., 513/287-7000) three times a week. Check the Amtrak website for a timetable.

Long-Distance Bus

Megabus (us.megabus.com) connects Cincinnati with Indianapolis and Chicago, with somewhat removed stops at the parking lot of 691 Gest Street and the University of Cincinnati outside French Hall. Otherwise, **Greyhound** (greyhound.com), **Barons Bus** (baronsbus.com), and **GoBus** (ridegobus. com) stop at both the University of Cincinnati and the bus station at 1005 Gilbert Avenue, the latter offering on-site ticket sales.

Car

Cincinnati is well connected to the region by interstate highways. **I-71** and **I-75** converge south of the city in Kentucky and separate again in downtown. Outerbelt **I-275** makes an enormous loop around the area, venturing into northern Kentucky and taking a sniff of Indiana before returning to Ohio, though for most visitors this road will likely be useless unless coming from the airport.

Columbus and Indianapolis are equidistant from Cincinnati, both just under two hours' drive (107 mi/172 km northeast, 112 mi/180 km northwest, respectively). Dayton is about an hour (54 mi/87 km) north on I-75.

Lexington is 1.5 hours (82 mi/132 km) south on I-75. Louisville, southwest on I-71, is just over 1.5 hours (100 mi/161 km). Driving into town on I-71/I-75 north from Kentucky is by far the most dramatic entrance into the city as the highway heads down a hill overlooking the river valley.

GETTING AROUND

To and from the Airport

Executive Transportation (800/990-8841, executivetransportation.org) provides service to hotels, sights, and other stops throughout the metro area. A $26 fare gets you to downtown Cincinnati or Covington, Kentucky. Round-trip is $40.

A taxi to or from the airport to downtown is $34. Lyft and Uber are also authorized to operate at the airport. The ride is about 30 minutes.

The **Transit Authority of Northern Kentucky (TANK)** (859/331-8265, tankbus. org) runs an express route, the 2x Airporter, connecting the east end of baggage claim to Covington (20 minutes) and downtown Cincinnati (30 minutes) 5am-midnight daily. One-way fares for TANK's express routes are $2. Visit the website for a timetable and options to purchase tickets. You can also pay with cash on the bus, though no change is given.

Car

In general, driving in Cincinnati is not difficult outside of downtown and

Over-the-Rhine. Downtown, though a grid, can be aggravating because of one-way streets and difficult-to-read road signs. If you're planning on spending the majority of your time in the center of the city exploring downtown, the surrounding neighborhoods, and across the river to Covington or Newport, then a car may not be necessary. Public transportation and rideshare companies like Uber and Lyft will serve you well. However, if you have plans to venture further, say to Kings Island, a car is your best bet, though there are less-than-ideal public transportation options available.

Parking is generally not difficult nor expensive in Cincinnati, compared to larger cities. Downtown is the most expensive place to keep your car. Be wary of event pricing in riverfront parking garages—prices can spike to $20 for the day. Parking overnight can cost over $20 and more than $30 if doing valet.

All the major car rental companies operate in the Cincinnati area. It's generally more expensive, though more convenient, to rent straight from the airport. Hertz, Budget, and Avis maintain downtown locations. Enterprise appears to have more locations in the region than others.

Streetcar

The **Cincinnati Bell Connector** (cincinnati-oh.gov/streetcar, 6:30am-midnight Mon.-Thurs., 6:30am-1am Fri., 8am-1am Sat., 9am-11pm Sun. and holidays) is a 3.6-mile (5.8-km) loop that connects the riverfront, downtown, and Over-the-Rhine with 18 stops and service every 12-15 minutes. A ticket vending machine is available at each stop for you to purchase and validate your ticket. Only prepurchased tickets need to be validated; tickets purchased at the machine are automatically validated. Fares are $1 for a two-hour pass or $2 for a day pass.

Local Bus

The **Southwest Ohio Regional Transit Authority (SORTA)** (go-metro.com) operates a complex network of bus routes connecting downtown Cincinnati with surrounding neighborhoods and communities along the outerbelt. Fares are determined by what zone you are in and what zone your destination is in. All of the City of Cincinnati is in one zone and fare is $1.75. Fares go up to $4.25. Transfers are $0.50 and valid for two hours. Exact change is required for fare boxes. Thirty-day passes or Stored Value Cards can be

Cincinnati Bell Connector

purchased at ticket vending machines at any of the Cincinnati Bell stops as well as at Government Square (5th St. and Walnut St.), Clifton Heights (Calhoun St. and Clifton Ave.), Med Center (Burnet Ave. and Goodman St.), and Oakley Transit Center (corner of Isben and Marburg).

Taxi

There aren't a ton of taxis patrolling the streets as they do in much larger cities, so if you are relying on taxi service it's best to call one. **Towne Taxi** (513/761-7700, townetaxi-inc.com) and **Riverfront Taxi** (513/886-0256, riverfronttaxicincinnati.com) are two companies that operate 24/7.

Bike

Cincinnati Red Bike (cincyredbike.org) is a bike-share system with 59 stations and over 500 bikes between the Kentucky riverfront and Northside. Single-ride ($3) and day passes ($10) can be purchased online or at the kiosk at any station.

Across the Ohio River

Cincinnati is only a river away from the state of Kentucky and the northern border of what has traditionally been considered the South. The communities across the river—chief among them Covington and Newport—have significant histories of their own and practically operate as busy neighborhoods of Cincinnati with proximity to downtown.

COVINGTON, KENTUCKY

Covington possesses an impressive stock of 19th-century homes and commercial buildings along two primary corridors: downtown Covington in and around Madison Avenue, and mixed-use MainStrasse Village primarily along Main Street. Along both you'll find boutique shops, bars, and restaurants to rival what's across the river in Cincinnati. MainStrasse Village's story is in some ways a precursor to Over-the-Rhine's. It too was a largely German neighborhood that was all but neglected by the middle of the 20th century. Inspired by the successful resurrection of German Village in Columbus, the community reshaped the area as a German storybook-inspired neighborhood spearheaded by the construction of the Carroll Chimes Bell Tower in 1979. Today, it's a pleasant area with upscale restaurants, bars, and gift shops.

Covington is connected to downtown Cincinnati by the John A. Roebling Suspension Bridge, opened in 1866 and a precursor to the Brooklyn Bridge, which shares Roebling as the chief architect. Travelers can drive, bike, or walk across the historic bridge, though most of Covington's main attractions and restaurants are several blocks from the bridge.

Sights and Recreation

DEVOU PARK

Devou Park (1201 Park Dr., 859/292-2160, exploredevoupark.org) is a massive hilltop park near the Ohio River. Its 8 miles (12.9 km) of paved or backcountry trails provide scenic opportunities to stroll, hike, jog, or mountain bike through forested hills. In the middle of the park is an 18-hole golf course. Bike rentals are available at the welcome center 8am-9pm. Drive to the Memorial Overlook next to Drees Pavilion for an outstanding panoramic view of downtown Cincinnati, the Ohio River, and Covington.

BEHRINGER-CRAWFORD MUSEUM

Within Devou Park is the **Behringer-Crawford Museum** (1600 Montague Rd., 859/491-4003, bcmuseum.org, 10am-5pm Tues.-Sat., 1pm-5pm Sun., $9 adults, $8 seniors, $5 ages 3-17), a natural and local history museum that opened in 1950 and is based on the private, eccentric collection of William

Behringer, an avid traveler. Through his assortment of fossils, animal specimens, Native American artifacts, and subsequent additions, the museum chronicles the history of northern Kentucky from prehistoric times to the present day. Highlights include a miniature railroad display, a stuffed two-headed calf, and a replica of the Roebling Bridge across the Ohio River.

Outside the museum is the free NaturePlay@BCM playground, complete with tot-sized replicas of log cabins and flatboats as well as typical playground equipment with natural elements incorporated.

CARROLL CHIMES BELL TOWER

The highlight of Goebel Park, at the edge of MainStrasse Village, is the **Carroll Chimes Bell Tower** (605 Philadelphia St.), a faux German Gothic clock tower. The Pied Piper glockenspiel runs from April through November at times posted next to the tower but is roughly every two hours from the late morning into the evening.

Shopping

Near the Roebling Bridge, **Roebling Point Books & Coffee** (306 Greenup St., 859/815-7204, roeblingpointbooksandcoffee.com, 7am-6pm Mon.-Fri., 8am-6pm Sat.-Sun.) is a cozy place to browse the new arrivals and pick up a cup of fair-trade coffee. Inviting sofas and chairs are on hand to test-drive both. The store's location close to the bridge makes this an enticing excuse to make the walk from The Banks.

There's woodworking and then there's *woodworking*. **Grainwell Market** (33 W. Pike St., 859/261-6600, grainwell.com, 11am-6pm Tues.-Fri., 10am-4pm Sat.) in downtown Covington is the latter. Three sisters run a workshop down the street and produce striking décor that you didn't know you needed until you saw it. Wonderful craftsmanship goes into items like city names in graceful script, city skylines, cute quotes, and coasters.

MainStrasse Village's **Stoney's Village Toy Shoppe** (323 W. 6th St., 859/655-9571, noon-5pm Thurs.-Fri., noon-4pm Sat.-Sun.) wins the award for the building with the best color (kind of a seafoam green with a purple porch). The old house is stocked with ukuleles, games, and creativity-inspiring toys.

Food

A standout in MainStrasse Village is Japanese ★ **Chako Bakery Café** (611 Main St., 859/609-0166, chakobakerycafe.com, 11am-5pm Tues.-Sun.). Order one of its sweet or savory pastries at the counter or enjoy some onigiri from the small lunch menu. The most popular lunch item is the first-come, first-served Katsu-Sando fried pork sandwich, limited to 20 per day. There is a small, calm dining room in the back to enjoy your selections.

Also in MainStrasse Village, **Bouquet** (519 Main St., 859/491-7777, bouquetrestaurant.com, 4:30pm-10pm Mon.-Sat., $19-32) was one of the area's early adopters of farm-to-table thinking. This upscale American bistro changes its menu frequently but features appetizers, small plates, entrees, and dessert all crafted from products from over 50 farmers. The drink menu is extensive, especially the bourbon and wine.

For a slice of New Orleans food and jazz, step into **Dee Felice Café** (529 Main St., 859/261-2365, deefelicecafe.com, 5pm-10pm Mon.-Thurs., 5pm-midnight Fri.-Sat., $15-38), also located in MainStrasse Village. The menu covers a lot of ground from relatively inexpensive sandwiches to Cajun classics and steak plates. Jazz is on Wednesday and Thursday nights. Dress is casual, though reservations are recommended. The bar portion opens at 4pm.

Voted the best Korean food in the Cincinnati area four years in a row is **Riverside Korean** (512 Madison Ave., 859/291-1484, riversidekoreanrestaurant.com, 11:30am-2pm and 5pm-9pm Mon.-Thurs., 11:30am-2pm and 5pm-10pm Fri., 5pm-10pm Sat., 5pm-9pm Sun., $15-25) in downtown Covington. The restaurant has a full menu of authentic Korean dishes, including some hot pot dinners for two. All dinners come with

the expected banchan side dishes. The lunch menu is cheaper.

Accommodations

A smattering of chain hotels can be found along the riverfront. Though none are particularly special, they're cheaper options than what's on offer in downtown Cincinnati and a quick ride, perhaps even a walk, away from most downtown destinations. For something more distinctive, try the 114-room **Hotel Covington** (638 Madison Ave., 859/905-6000, hotelcovington.com, $219-332). Housed in Kentucky's first skyscraper, which was home to Coppin's Department Store for 70 years, Hotel Covington is a contemporary twist on boutique style. Ownership has gone to great lengths to keep things as local as possible: coffee at its **Artisan Coffee Bar** (6:30am-10pm Sun.-Thurs., 6:30am-11pm Fri.-Sat.) comes from Newport's Carabello Coffee. An impressive woodworking piece shaped like the United States in New American **Coppin's Restaurant** (breakfast and brunch Sat.-Sun., lunch Mon.-Fri., dinner daily) comes from the masters at nearby Grainwell.

Transportation
GETTING THERE

Covington is connected to downtown Cincinnati via the John A. Roebling Suspension Bridge and, to the west, I-71/I-75 just south of where the two highways split.

GETTING AROUND

The **Transit Authority of Northern Kentucky (TANK)** (859/331-8265, tank-bus.org) connects the suburbs of northern Kentucky with each other, downtown Cincinnati, and the Cincinnati/Northern Kentucky International Airport. Day passes are $3.50. Otherwise, local fare is $1.50 and express routes are $2. The 2x Airporter express route connects the airport with Covington

(20 minutes). You can pay with exact change on the bus, or purchase ahead of time at locations listed on the website. The Southbank Shuttle, also operated by TANK, keeps things simple by sticking to the riverfront area near hotels and frequented attractions and crossing the river to downtown Cincinnati; fares are $1.

Executive Transportation (800/990-8841, executivetransportation.org) provides service from the airport to Covington for $26 ($40 round-trip). Other airport transportation options include taxis as well as Lyft and Uber.

NEWPORT, KENTUCKY

Newport is smaller than Covington. Once you leave the riverfront, it feels a bit more working class, a touch more Southern, than its larger neighbor to the west. Most visitors come to Newport for the Newport-on-the-Levee riverfront entertainment complex—connected to downtown Cincinnati by the pedestrian-only Purple People Bridge—but there's more restaurants and shops to explore inland along Monmouth Street and the East Row Historic District's elegant Victorian homes on the east side of town.

Sights
★ NEWPORT AQUARIUM

The smallish **Newport Aquarium** (1 Levee Way, 800/406-3474, newportaquarium.com, 10am-6pm daily, $25.99 adults, $17.99 ages 2-12) combines creative exhibit design with close animal encounters, making this one of the more intimate aquarium experiences you're likely to have. Several of the exhibits incorporate tunnels into the design to allow for immersive views into aquatic habitats, where colorful fish, friendly sea turtles, and other creatures lurk. At Stingray Hideaway, kids can touch two species of rays in a 17,000-gallon pool. Gator Alley is home to two rare albino alligators, Snowball and Snowflake. The most impressive exhibit is Surrounded by Sharks, which offers two exciting ways to view these stunning creatures: through the tank in a long, acrylic tunnel or above the tank from a 75-foot (22.9-m) rope bridge. Also popular

---

1: Stoney's Village Toy Shoppe in Covington, Kentucky **2:** Grainwell Market in Covington, Kentucky **3:** Newport Aquarium in Newport, Kentucky

are the penguins, and the Newport Aquarium boasts one of the best collections in the country with six species showing off their style.

The aquarium uses a timed entry system to control the number of people in the aquarium, so purchasing tickets ahead of time is best (and you won't have to wait in line). There's one food option in the building, Sharky's Café, which serves the standard grilled food, wraps, snacks, and drinks that you find at animal parks.

The aquarium is an anchor of the **Newport-on-the-Levee** (newportonthe-levee.com) entertainment district, which includes a 20-screen AMC movie theater and several dining options. As such, the closest parking for the aquarium is in the 24/7 Newport-on-the-Levee parking garage, which is an affordable parking option in general but also a consideration if you're headed to a Reds game across the river and don't mind a bit of a walk.

Food

For a city that focuses so much on its German heritage, there are strangely few German restaurants in Cincinnati. Enter **Hofbräuhaus** (200 E. 3rd St., 859/491-7200, hofbrauhausnewport.com, 11am-11pm Sun.-Wed., 11am-1am Thurs.-Sat., $10-24). A convivial restaurant and brewery associated with the legendary biergarten in Munich, Hofbräuhaus features live German music and entertainment, a full menu of traditional dishes and Americanized sandwich and sausage plates, and beer by the liter (or half liter, if you're not that committed), all enjoyed from long, communal tables. There are also locations in Columbus and Cleveland, but this is the only one by a riverfront. Most hours are family friendly, though the good-natured fun gets louder as the night goes on.

One of the older and better-regarded chili parlors in the Cincinnati area is **Dixie Chili** (733 Monmouth St., 859/291-5337, dixie-chili.com, 9am-1am Mon.-Thurs., 8am-3am Fri.-Sat., 10am-1am Sun., $5-10). Tracing its history back to 1929, this place still feels like a no-frills family establishment. Patrons order at the counter, get in line past the register with trays, and wait as the dutiful employees fill them with their orders. The menu is more focused than other parlors—no breakfast or double-decker burgers here. There are sandwiches available, but chili is really the attraction.

Quirky **York St. Café** (738 York St., 859/261-9675, yorkstonline.com, 11am-10pm Tues.-Sat., $12-25) is in an 1880s Queen Anne building that was formerly a pharmacy. The menu is wide-ranging but leans American and Mediterranean. An interesting take on appetizers is the "conversation boards," shareable platters that encourage noshing with friends. There's a lounge on the 2nd floor, an art gallery on the 3rd floor, and a private art studio on the 4th, so the vibe is definitely eclectic.

Pull up a stool and drink coffee for a good cause. Easily spotted in a bright blue building, **Carabello Coffee** (107 E. 9th St., 859/415-1587, carabellocoffee.com, 7am-8pm Mon.-Fri., 8am-8pm Sat.) roasts fair-trade and farm-direct coffee and then supports children's programs in developing, coffee-producing countries with the profits. Check their website for a list of places that sell their coffee.

Transportation

GETTING THERE

Newport is directly across the Ohio River from downtown Cincinnati via the Taylor Southgate Bridge or the pedestrian-only Purple People Bridge. I-471 runs past Newport and connects the town with I-71 to the north and I-275 to the south.

GETTING AROUND

As with Covington, Newport is served by the **Transit Authority of Northern Kentucky (TANK)** (tankbus.org), with the Southbank Shuttle being especially useful for visitors staying along the riverfront or heading to a Reds game.

Vicinity of Cincinnati

Cincinnati's suburbs offer their own charms, including some enticing dining options of their own and satellite locations for some of Cincinnati's favorite haunts. The biggest attraction outside of city limits is Kings Island amusement park.

MASON

A sprawling suburb north of Cincinnati's outerbelt, Mason is on the map primarily for its proximity to major amusement park Kings Island and the accommodations and attractions that have opened surrounding it.

Sights and Recreation

TOP EXPERIENCE

★ KINGS ISLAND

Any attention Ohio receives for roller coasters is typically reserved for Cedar Point. While this may have been a fair judgment at the turn of the 21st century, Cedar Point's parent company, Cedar Fair, purchased this park in 2006 and has since devoted significant resources to help bridge the gap. Today, Kings Island (6300 Kings Island Dr., 513/754-5700, visitkingsisland.com, see the website for seasonal hours, $41.99 for adults and kids online, considerably more at gate) has 14 roller coasters and is the nation's second most attended seasonal amusement park behind Cedar Point.

The park, which sprawls across 364 acres, offers a good variety of rides and attractions for any age group. *Amusement Today* awarded the park "Best Kids Area" for 18 years straight beginning in 2001 for its area that is now called Planet Snoopy. Older visitors may fondly remember the wooden roller coaster The Racer from their childhood (or from the TV shows *The Partridge Family* and *The Brady Bunch,* which both filmed episodes here). Thrill riders should seek out roller coasters Orion, Mystic Timbers, Flight of Fear, and Diamondback. My money for best roller coaster experience of all time (eclipsing even Cedar Point's best coasters) is riding the park's forest-dwelling The Beast—the world's longest wooden roller coaster since its 1979 inception—at night.

Adjacent to the amusement park and included with admission is Soak City Water Park. Tropical Plunge is a seven-story tower with six waterslides to choose from. The thrill ride Rendezvous Run spins you around in the dark. Those with toddlers can stay removed from the screams and waves at Castaway Cove. In all, there are over 50 water attractions to keep everyone properly cooled down.

Food in both the amusement and waterpark does not come cheaply—expect typical theme park prices. Parking is also pricey at $17 a car. Keep an eye on the website for bundles that include parking and food. One theme park not enough? There is a two-park ticket that grants you admission to both Kings Island and Cedar Point at a heavily reduced rate.

Shopping

Liberty Center (7100 Foundry Row, Liberty Twp., 513/644-0900, liberty-center.com) is a mixed-use shopping center with upscale dining options, a comedy club, and a movie theater. It's outside the outerbelt in the Kings Island vicinity.

Food

Critics seem to agree that one of the region's best Mediterranean restaurants is Phoenician Taverna (7944 Mason Montgomery Rd., 513/770-0027, phoenicianterverna.com, 11am-2pm and 5pm-9pm Tues.-Thurs., 11am-2pm and 5pm-10pm Fri., 5pm-10pm Sat., 5pm-9pm Sun., $9-21). The authentic Lebanese menu and modern decor make this a sought-after destination tucked amid a strip mall.

Vicinity of Cincinnati

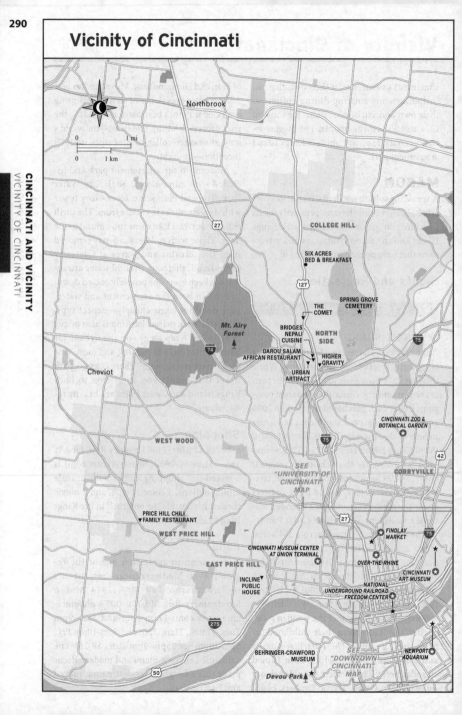

Northbrook

0   1 mi
0   1 km

COLLEGE HILL

SIX ACRES
BED & BREAKFAST

SPRING GROVE
CEMETERY ★

THE
COMET

BRIDGES
NEPALI
CUISINE

NORTH
SIDE

Mt. Airy
Forest

DAROU SALAM
AFRICAN RESTAURANT

HIGHER
GRAVITY

URBAN
ARTIFACT

Cheviot

CINCINNATI ZOO &
BOTANICAL GARDEN

WEST WOOD

SEE
"UNIVERSITY OF
CINCINNATI"
MAP

CORRYVILLE

PRICE HILL CHILI
FAMILY RESTAURANT

WEST PRICE HILL

FINDLAY
MARKET

CINCINNATI MUSEUM CENTER
AT UNION TERMINAL

OVER-THE-RHINE

EAST PRICE HILL

CINCINNATI
ART MUSEUM

INCLINE
PUBLIC
HOUSE

NATIONAL
UNDERGROUND RAILROAD
FREEDOM CENTER

SEE
"DOWNTOWN
CINCINNATI"
MAP

NEWPORT
AQUARIUM

BEHRINGER-CRAWFORD
MUSEUM

Devou Park

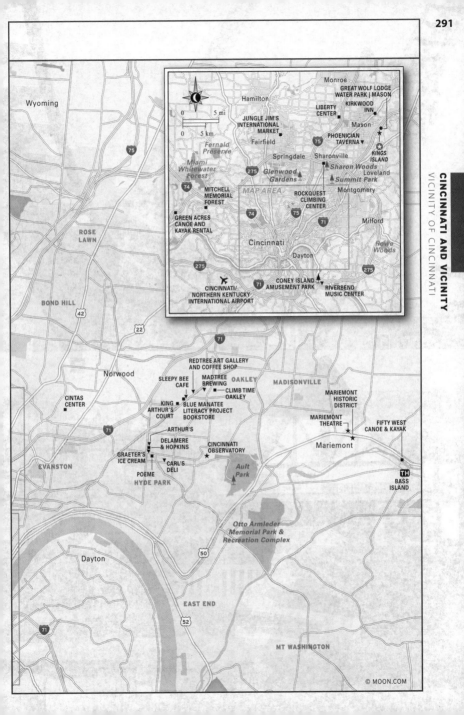

Wyoming

Monroe

Hamilton

GREAT WOLF LODGE
WATER PARK | MASON

LIBERTY
CENTER

KIRKWOOD
INN

JUNGLE JIM'S
INTERNATIONAL
MARKET

Mason

Fernald
Preserve

Fairfield

PHOENICIAN
TAVERNA

Miami
Whitewater
Forest

Springdale

Sharonville

KINGS
ISLAND

Glenwood
Gardens

Sharon Woods

MITCHELL
MEMORIAL
FOREST

MAP AREA

ROCKQUEST
CLIMBING
CENTER

Summit Park

Loveland

Montgomery

GREEN ACRES
CANOE AND
KAYAK RENTAL

ROSE
LAWN

Milford

Cincinnati

Howe
Woods

BOND HILL

Dayton

CINCINNATI/
NORTHERN KENTUCKY
INTERNATIONAL AIRPORT

CONEY ISLAND
AMUSEMENT PARK

RIVERBEND
MUSIC CENTER

REDTREE ART GALLERY
AND COFFEE SHOP

SLEEPY BEE
CAFE

MADTREE
BREWING

OAKLEY

MADISONVILLE

Norwood

CLIMB TIME
OAKLEY

MARIEMONT
HISTORIC
DISTRICT

CINTAS
CENTER

KING
ARTHUR'S
COURT

BLUE MANATEE
LITERACY PROJECT
BOOKSTORE

MARIEMONT
THEATRE

FIFTY WEST
CANOE & KAYAK

ARTHUR'S

Mariemont

DELAMERE
& HOPKINS

CINCINNATI
OBSERVATORY

GRAETER'S
ICE CREAM

CARL'S
DELI

EVANSTON

POEME

Ault
Park

TH

BASS
ISLAND

HYDE PARK

Otto Armleder
Memorial Park &
Recreation Complex

Dayton

EAST END

MT WASHINGTON

© MOON.COM

1

2

Jungle Jim's International Market

Ever visited a restaurant, a far-flung state, or even another country where you wished you'd bought that specialty sauce, that strange fruit, that mocha-flavored bubble gum? **Jungle Jim's International Market** probably has it. What began as a simple roadside produce stand has ballooned into an amusement park of a grocery experience. Jungle Jim's stocks hundreds of thousands of items from 70 different countries. The building is so humongous, they offer maps at the front door. There are even guided "safari" tours Monday-Friday. To put it plainly, this isn't the kind of store you run into for a carton of eggs. It's a bona fide foodie attraction.

There are two Jungle Jim's International Market locations, one close to **Kings Island** (5440 Dixie Hwy., Fairfield) and the other close to **Mariemont** (4450 Eastgate S. Dr., Cincinnati). You can find more information about both locations at junglejims.com or at 513/674-6000. Hours at both are 8am-10pm daily.

Accommodations

Hotels in Mason are of the inexpensive motel variety off the Kings Mills Road exit from I-71. One notable exception is the **Kirkwood Inn** (4027 S. US-42, 513/398-7277, kirkwood-inn.com, $109-259), a 1970s roadside motel turned country inn a couple of miles away from I-71 and Kings Island. The Jacuzzi suites are quite a bit pricier than the standard rooms, which compare favorably to other rooms in the region price wise. Plus, there's six acres to explore and a full hot breakfast at the historic Kirkwood House on-site.

For alternative accommodation (or a weatherproof amusement option in the winter months), there's **Great Wolf Lodge** (2501 Great Wolf Dr., 800/913-9653, great-wolf.com/mason, $229-475). Like the company's other locations, this resort combines an 84°F (29°C) indoor waterpark, cabin-in-the-woods themed suites, and dining and shopping options in a massive building. The waterpark manages to fit the caliber of slides and other water attractions from outdoor parks into a relatively small space. Admission to the waterpark is included in the nightly rate. There are non-water attractions available for an additional cost including a bowling alley, arcade, and miniature golf. Day passes are also available, though

prices are subject to availability and can surge quite high, so buying earlier is best.

Transportation

GETTING THERE

The best way to get to and around Mason is by car. The town is about 25 minutes (23 mi/37 km) northeast of downtown Cincinnati by car on I-71. A handful of Cincinnati's bus routes, operated by the **Southwest Ohio Regional Transit Authority (SORTA)** (go-metro.com), stretch their way to parts of Mason including the 71X Kings Island Express, but service is infrequent.

MARIEMONT

Anglophiles, take note. Just a 15-minute drive east on US-50 from downtown Cincinnati is the charming suburb of Mariemont (pronounced "Mary-mont"). Founded in the early 1920s by philanthropist Mary Emery, the town was designed to resemble an English garden town with Tudor Revival architecture and ample green space. Mariemont's quiet streets, stately homes, and relaxed pace are its main attractions. This place is for those whose idea of a night well-spent is a hearty dinner, a film at an independent theater, and a good book by the fireplace.

1: Diamondback roller coaster at Kings Island in Mason **2:** Mariemont Theatre in Mariemont

Sights

MARIEMONT HISTORIC DISTRICT

Much of the village lies within the Mariemont Historic District, designated a National Historic Landmark in 2007. The peaceful residential streets and small, stylized town center, most of which follows the original plan's English architecture, offer one of the area's most pleasant walking experiences. Dogwood Park, on the western edge of town, features the stone Emery Carillon, with performances at 4pm on Sundays.

MARIEMONT THEATRE

One of the few remaining independent cinemas in the Cincinnati area is the Mariemont Theatre (6906 Wooster Pike, 513/272-2002, mariemonttheatre.com, check online for showtimes, $7.75-10.25), a commanding presence on the village's main square. The theater's five screens are a good place to scope out the latest Oscar bait, foreign films, and independent cinema. Weekly specials include $5 tickets on Tuesdays and $6 tickets for those 60 and over on Boomer Mondays. Concessions are reasonably priced and the bar is stocked with local beer.

Shopping

A handful of shops and boutiques are situated in the town square, notably gift shop Pomegranate and Lime (6804 Wooster Pike, 513/271-1012, 11am-4pm Mon.-Sat.). The store carries fashionable lines of décor, accessories, jewelry, and other gifts.

Food and Accommodations

Perhaps the best excuse to visit Mariemont is to stay at the ★ Mariemont Inn (6880 Wooster Pike, 513/271-2100, mariemontinn. com, $189-254). In operation since 1926, the timber and brick inn is managed by the Best Western Premier brand and went through an extensive renovation in 2009. The cozy lobby transports guests to the kind of lodge you'd expect to see after a day's hike in the English moors, with mounted animals on the walls and reading nooks adorned with era-appropriate furniture. Rooms come with Tempur-Pedic beds, original artwork, and a fireplace. Intimate Southerby's Pub (4pm-close daily) opens to the lobby and is an inviting place for a pint when the weather is rough. Local favorite The National Exemplar (6880 Wooster Pike, 513/271-2103, nationalexemplar.com, 7am-2:30pm and 5pm-9:30pm Mon.-Thurs., 7am-2:30pm and 5pm-10pm Fri.-Sat., 7am-2:30pm and 5pm-9pm Sun., $16-42) is attached to the hotel and serves American cuisine for breakfast, lunch, and dinner. The dinner menu, which includes an extensive draft beer and wine list, offers salad, pasta, and an array of meaty entrées. The restaurant helpfully displays showtimes for the Mariemont Theatre, less than a block away, though the inn's comfy aesthetic and multiple drinking and dining options may tempt you not to leave.

Transportation

Car is the best way to get to and around Mariemont, which is 15 minutes (10 mi/16.1 km) east of downtown Cincinnati via US-50. The Southwest Ohio Regional Transit Authority (SORTA) (go-metro.com) has one route that passes through Mariemont, the 29X Milford Express, which stops in front of the Mariemont Inn.

Dayton and Southwest Ohio

History is part of the landscape in Southwest

Ohio, home to many of the state's oldest towns and some of its most impressive earthworks. The terrain switches between flat farmland and gently rolling hills and woods, with the region's far eastern side kissing the edge of rugged Appalachia. This same area is devoid of major cities and is one of the least accessible parts of Ohio. Indeed, unless you are coming from Cincinnati, getting to the southern edge of Ohio can be a chore. The reward, though, is the state's largest expanses of wilderness, most mysterious mounds, and some of its most historic places. The Serpent Mound in remote Peebles, to name the best example, is the

Highlights

Look for ★ to find recommended sights, activities, dining, and lodging.

★ Tour four enormous hangars commemorating military, space, and presidential aviation history at the **National Museum of the United States Air Force** (page 300).

★ Learn about the pioneering Wright brothers and their friend, poet Paul Laurence Dunbar, at the **Dayton Aviation Heritage National Historical Park** (page 300).

★ View an incredible assortment of vehicles, buildings, and manufactured goods that illustrate Dayton's history at **Carillon Historical Park**—the 1905 Wright Flyer III is a highlight (page 301).

★ Amble around **Yellow Springs,** a quirky little town with funky shops, free-spirited restaurants, and ample outdoor opportunities (page 317).

★ Experience some of the state's best **hiking** on Southwest Ohio's superb trails (page 322).

★ Traverse 300 acres of woods, hills, and unusual sculptures by foot or car at the **Pyramid Hill Sculpture Park and Museum** (page 327).

★ Ponder the mysterious origin of the undulating, 1,300-foot (396-m) effigy mound at the **Serpent Mound Historical Site** (page 332).

Map labels:
- Dayton Aviation Heritage National Historical Park
- National Museum of the United States Air Force
- Springfield
- Carillon Historical Park
- Yellow Springs
- Dayton
- Yellow Springs
- 70
- 75
- 71
- 22
- Middletown
- Hamilton
- Wilmington
- Fairfield
- Pyramid Hill Sculpture Park and Museum
- Montgomery
- OHIO
- Cincinnati
- 275
- Serpent Mound Historical Site
- Covington
- Ohio
- Hiking
- Peebles
- River
- 0   20 mi
- 0   20 km
- Augusta
- Ripley

Dayton and Southwest Ohio

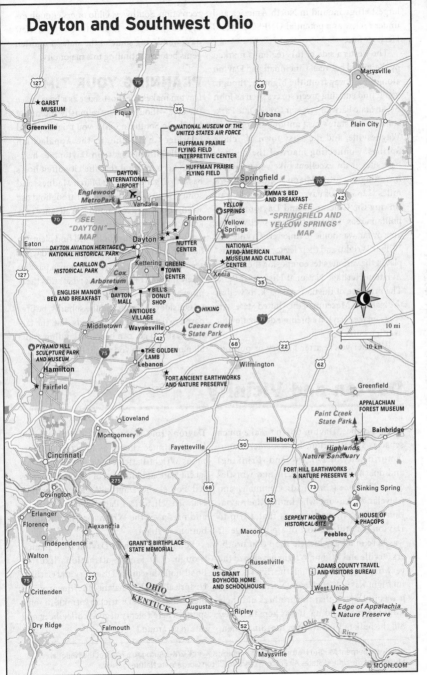

Marysville

127
Piqua
75
36
GARST MUSEUM
Greenville
68
Urbana
Plain City

NATIONAL MUSEUM OF THE UNITED STATES AIR FORCE
HUFFMAN PRAIRIE FLYING FIELD INTERPRETIVE CENTER
HUFFMAN PRAIRIE FLYING FIELD
DAYTON INTERNATIONAL AIRPORT
Springfield
70
42
EMMA'S BED AND BREAKFAST

Englewood MetroPark
Vandalia
YELLOW SPRINGS
Yellow Springs
SEE "SPRINGFIELD AND YELLOW SPRINGS" MAP

Eaton
70
SEE "DAYTON" MAP
Fairborn
Dayton
NUTTER CENTER

DAYTON AVIATION HERITAGE NATIONAL HISTORICAL PARK
NATIONAL AFRO-AMERICAN MUSEUM AND CULTURAL CENTER

CARILLON HISTORICAL PARK
Kettering
GREENE TOWN CENTER
Xenia
35

Cox Arboretum
ENGLISH MANOR BED AND BREAKFAST
DAYTON MALL
BILL'S DONUT SHOP
HIKING
71
10 mi
10 km

ANTIQUES VILLAGE
Middletown
Waynesville
Caesar Creek State Park

PYRAMID HILL SCULPTURE PARK AND MUSEUM
75
THE GOLDEN LAMB
Lebanon
68
22
Wilmington
62
Greenfield

Hamilton
Fairfield
42
FORT ANCIENT EARTHWORKS AND NATURE PRESERVE
Paint Creek State Park
APPALACHIAN FOREST MUSEUM
Bainbridge

Loveland
Montgomery
Fayetteville
50
Hillsboro
Highlands Nature Sanctuary
FORT HILL EARTHWORKS & NATURE PRESERVE

Cincinnati
275
62
73
Sinking Spring
41
HOUSE OF PHACOPS

Covington
68
SERPENT MOUND HISTORICAL SITE
Peebles

Erlanger
Florence
Alexandria
Macon
ADAMS COUNTY TRAVEL AND VISITORS BUREAU

Independence
GRANT'S BIRTHPLACE STATE MEMORIAL
Russellville
West Union

Walton
27
US GRANT BOYHOOD HOME AND SCHOOLHOUSE
Edge of Appalachia Nature Preserve

75
Crittenden
OHIO
KENTUCKY
Augusta
Ripley
52
Ohio River

Dry Ridge
Falmouth
Maysville

© MOON.COM

largest effigy mound in North America and under review as a potential UNESCO World Heritage Site.

The western side of this region is marked by the sprawl between Cincinnati and Dayton along I-75. Away from the highway, though, you'll find enticing green spaces such as John Bryan State Park and Caesar Creek State Park, some of the state's best antique shopping in Waynesville, and the artsy town of Yellow Springs. Connecting many of the region's best sites is an excellent bikeway network, including the Little Miami Scenic Trail—78 miles (126 km) of paved multipurpose trail linking the Cincinnati and Dayton metropolitan areas. Dayton, the largest city in the area by far, was home to tinkerers Orville and Wilbur Wright, and their legacy is on full display at the various sites composing the Dayton Aviation Heritage National Historical Park. The presence of the national park, as well as the National Museum of the United States Air Force, makes Dayton a premier destination for aviation buffs.

Whether you're after history or outdoor recreation, Southwest Ohio offers enough excuses to veer off the interstate and spend a few days wandering some of the state's forgotten gems before continuing to a major city.

PLANNING YOUR TIME

Dayton makes the most sense as a base to see the area—though if you're mostly intending to hike in Southern Ohio, you might instead consider Chillicothe (in the Appalachian foothills). If you do stay in Dayton, it's helpful to keep in mind that the city often hosts basketball games during March Madness and some large-scale youth events throughout the spring. Booking a few months in advance may keep costs down.

History and nature buffs will find plenty to do in this region; expect to spend 3-4 days to see the highlights. Those with only a passing interest would be fine to pick what suits them most and spend a weekend exploring.

Outside of Dayton and the suburbs, be prepared to drive on country roads that, the farther east you go, can become winding and a bit narrower than you might like.

Dayton and Vicinity

At first glance, Dayton doesn't make much sense as a destination. It's a former manufacturing city of 140,000 (and shrinking) and doesn't have all the bells and whistles of the Three C's (Cincinnati, Columbus, and Cleveland). Anyone who knows their aviation history, though, knows that a trip to Dayton is nothing short of a pilgrimage. It was here in a busy bicycle shop that brothers Orville and Wilbur Wright developed the very first airplane. Though the first successful flight was at Kitty Hawk, North Carolina, it was in Dayton that the brothers did their thinking and building. It was here that they did the bulk of their testing, too. Since then,

Dayton's role as a major center of aviation has continued, home as it is to the enormous Wright-Patterson Air Force Base, adjacent National Museum of the United States Air Force, and Dayton Aviation Heritage National Historical Park, which chronicles and preserves the Wright brothers' contributions to flight.

You'll find more in Dayton than planes, though. Fun family attractions like the Boonshoft Museum of Discovery and Carillon Historical Park help balance the itinerary, and there's the Oregon District to sprinkle in some spunk. There's plenty of good coffee, beer, and eats to go around, too.

Previous: Serpent Mound Historical Site in Peebles; Kellett K-2/K-3 Autogiro aircraft at the National Museum of the United States Air Force in Dayton; Clifton Gorge State Nature Preserve.

Dayton

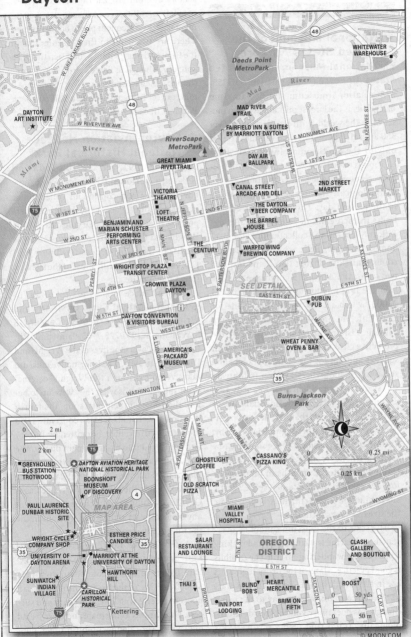

WHITEWATER WAREHOUSE

Deeds Point MetroPark

River

Mad River

DAYTON ART INSTITUTE

W RIVERVIEW AVE

MAD RIVER TRAIL

E MONUMENT AVE

N KEOWEE ST

WEBSTER ST

FAIRFIELD INN & SUITES BY MARRIOTT DAYTON

E 1ST ST

RiverScape MetroPark

DAY AIR BALLPARK

GREAT MIAMI RIVER TRAIL

W MONUMENT AVE

Miami River

CANAL STREET ARCADE AND DELI

2ND STREET MARKET

W 1ST ST

VICTORIA THEATRE

E 2ND ST

THE DAYTON BEER COMPANY

E 3RD ST

N JEFFERSON ST

LOFT THEATRE

THE BARREL HOUSE

W 2ND ST

BENJAMIN AND MARIAN SCHUSTER PERFORMING ARTS CENTER

N MAIN ST

THE CENTURY

WARPED WING BREWING COMPANY

W 3RD ST

S PATTERSON BLVD

S PERRY ST

WRIGHT STOP PLAZA TRANSIT CENTER

SEE DETAIL

E 5TH ST

CROWNE PLAZA DAYTON

W 4TH ST

EAST 5TH ST

DUBLIN PUB

WAYNE AVE

W 5TH ST

DAYTON CONVENTION & VISITORS BUREAU

WEST 6TH ST

S LUDLOW ST

WHEAT PENNY OVEN & BAR

AMERICA'S PACKARD MUSEUM

WASHINGTON ST

35

Burns-Jackson Park

0   0.25 mi

0   0.25 km

Inset (bottom left)

0   2 mi

0   2 km

75

GREYHOUND BUS STATION TROTWOOD

DAYTON AVIATION HERITAGE NATIONAL HISTORICAL PARK

BOONSHOFT MUSEUM OF DISCOVERY

4

PAUL LAURENCE DUNBAR HISTORIC SITE

MAP AREA

WRIGHT CYCLE COMPANY SHOP

ESTHER PRICE CANDIES

35

35

UNIVERSITY OF DAYTON ARENA

MARRIOTT AT THE UNIVERSITY OF DAYTON

SUNWATCH INDIAN VILLAGE

HAWTHORN HILL

CARILLON HISTORICAL PARK

75

Kettering

Inset (bottom center)

S PATTERSON BLVD

S MAIN ST

WARREN ST

GHOSTLIGHT COFFEE

CASSANO'S PIZZA KING

OLD SCRATCH PIZZA

WYOMING ST

MIAMI VALLEY HOSPITAL

Inset (bottom right — Oregon District)

SALAR RESTAURANT AND LOUNGE

PINE ST

OREGON DISTRICT

CLASH GALLERY AND BOUTIQUE

E 5TH ST

THAI 9

BROWN ST

BLIND BOB'S

HEART MERCANTILE

JACKSON ST

ROOST

CLAY ST

INN PORT LODGING

BRIM ON FIFTH

0   50 yds

0   50 m

© MOON.COM

★ National Museum of the United States Air Force

The **National Museum of the United States Air Force** (1100 Spatz Dr., 937/255-3286, nationalmuseum.af.mil, 9am-5pm daily, free) is the largest military aviation museum in the world, with a collection of over 360 aircraft, spacecraft, and missiles rivaled only by the Smithsonian Institution. Four enormous hangars show the evolution of military, reconnaissance, and exploratory craft, chronologically taking visitors from WWI to the present day. Though there are highlights in each exhibit, some especially significant items in the collection include B-17 bomber *Memphis Belle,* which completed 30 combat missions during WWII and inspired two films; the Apollo 15 command module from the 1971 mission to the moon; and SAM 26000, which served as Air Force One for eight different presidents, from Kennedy to Clinton. Visitors can walk inside (though the protective glass makes this experience a tight squeeze and not for the claustrophobic) and stand in the spot where Lyndon B. Johnson was sworn in as president after Kennedy's assassination. In fact, the Presidential Gallery features several craft that have ferried presidents, royalty, and other dignitaries. Nearby, visitors can view inside a space shuttle Crew Compartment Trainer, where astronauts trained for up to six months in preparation for the real deal. A replica of a space shuttle sits behind the compartment to approximate the size of a real shuttle.

The scale of the museum cannot be overstated, so wearing walking shoes and making a plan before wandering off into the exhibits is good practice. Many of the major highlights are in the fourth hangar, so you might start in the back and make your way to the front, though this does move you backwards chronologically. You'll find plenty of diversions along the way, including simulators ($8-16);

the Air Force Museum Theatre ($8 adults, $7 seniors, $6 children), with a rotating schedule of aviation, military, and space-related documentaries; and frequent photo opportunities. There are two cafés in the museum: one in the front and one, helpfully, between the third and fourth hangars. There's also a massive gift shop in which to find the perfect souvenir. All told, expect to spend at least a half day here. Parking, like admission, is free.

★ Dayton Aviation Heritage National Historical Park

Opened in 1992, the **Dayton Aviation Heritage National Historical Park** (nps.gov/daav) is a non-contiguous collection of important sites around the city that interpret the lives of brothers Orville and Wilbur Wright and their pursuit of flight, as well as the life of their friend, acclaimed poet Paul Laurence Dunbar. While most of the sites are free, some require a fee.

The best place to start is west of downtown at the **Wright Cycle Company** and **Wright-Dunbar Interpretive Center** (16 S. Williams St., 937/225-7705, 9am-5pm daily, free), which covers the lives of the Wrights and Dunbar up to 1903. The informative museum takes visitors through the Wrights' original print shop, which is what they were up to before they opened their bike shop, the fourth iteration of which sits across a courtyard from the interpretive center. Forgotten by history and converted into an apartment duplex, the building was slated for demolition until a historian rediscovered its significance. Brief tours of inside the bike shop, arranged as if Orville or Wilbur might come into work at any moment, start at the top of the hour inside the interpretive center.

A few blocks northwest is the **Paul Laurence Dunbar Historic Site** (219 N. Paul Laurence Dunbar St., 10am-4pm Fri.-Sun., free). One of the first African American poets to receive widespread acclaim and success, Dunbar was a classmate and close friend of Orville, who, along with his brother, published some of Dunbar's earliest writing from their print shop. The site is located in Dunbar's two-story brick house, which appears much as it did when he lived at this address, with many of his original furnishings and books. The last tour of the day starts at 3:30pm. A separate visitors center features additional displays on Dunbar's life, poetry, and association with the Wright brothers.

The **John W. Berry Sr. Wright Brothers National Museum** is located south of downtown inside the Carillon Historical Park, which requires admission to enter. Here you'll find the original 1905 Wright Flyer III housed inside a building of Orville's design.

Now that you have your bearings on the Wrights' accomplishments, head to the **Huffman Prairie Flying Field Interpretive Center** (2380 Memorial Rd., 937/425-0008, 9am-5pm daily, free) east of the city, which chronicles how Wilbur and Orville perfected their original Flyer to become the first practical airplane. Next to the building is the **Wright Brothers Memorial,** which overlooks the pasture, obscured by woods, where the Wrights flew their tests and where they truly learned how to fly. Or you can drive east from the interpretive center down to the **Huffman Prairie Flying Field** (Pylon Rd.; take Gate 16A off SR 444), where there's a replica hangar and launching catapult. A roughly 1-mile (1.6-km) nature trail loops through tallgrass prairie and wildflowers. Parking is on Marl Road, west of Symmes Road.

Completed in 1914, the Colonial Revival mansion **Hawthorn Hill** (901 Harman Ave., 937/293-2841, www.daytonhistory.org, tours 10am and 12:30pm Wed. and Sat., $14) is the house that Orville built after the success of the aviation business. Luminaries such as Charles Lindbergh and Henry Ford visited the Wrights at this address on the southern end of the city, which is the last place Orville lived. Tours, which last approximately 90 minutes and explore some of Orville's personal touches to the house, start from Carillon Historical Park via shuttle. Hawthorn Hill is part of the National Aviation Heritage Area (which also encompasses the national

historical park as well as Carillon Historical Park) and is managed by a partner of the National Park Service.

★ Carillon Historical Park

Not your average regional history museum, the multifaceted **Carillon Historical Park** (1000 Carillon Blvd., 937/293-2841, daytonhistory.org, 9:30am-5pm Mon.-Sat., noon-5pm Sun., $12 adults, $10 seniors, $8 ages 3-17) pulls together an incredible assortment of vehicles, buildings, and manufactured goods that illustrate Dayton's history, which in some cases is internationally relevant. The park is easy to spot thanks to the 151-foot (46-m) Deeds Carillon, built in 1942 and a symbol of the city.

Your visit begins in the **Heritage Center of Dayton Manufacturing and Entrepreneurship,** which covers Dayton's evolving manufacturing prowess with displays including dozens of fancy cash registers and a fully functioning carousel. Behind the building is a roomy park with historical buildings plucked from the area and moved here for safekeeping from the bulldozer. These include the **Newcom Tavern,** built in 1796 and Dayton's oldest existing building. In the **William Morris House,** you may find staff dressed in period clothing busy preparing food as settlers did 200 years ago (check the museum's calendar for special events). In the very back of the park is the **James F. Dicke Family Transportation Center,** an airy building with stagecoaches, steam engines, train cars, and buses from yesteryear.

The star of the show is the **John W. Berry Sr. Wright Brothers National Museum.** This museum within a museum is part of the Dayton Aviation Heritage National Historical Park and houses the original 1905 Wright Flyer III, the first of the Wright brothers' planes that they considered a practical airplane. Orville himself had a hand in designing the building that houses the plane, as well as the restoration of the plane itself. It was one of his last projects before he passed away in 1948. The museum also includes a replica of the Wrights' bike shop and artifacts pertaining to their businesses and airplanes.

The **Carillon Brewing Company** (937/910-0722, 11am-9pm Sun.-Thurs., 11am-10pm Fri.-Sat.) is located at the front of the complex and does not require park admission to enter. The employees, all in 1850s garb, brew their beers according to 19th-century methods and recipes. You're likely to find your beer a bit spicier than you're used to, with unusual hints of coriander and ginger, among other things. There's a full menu of German food as well.

Boonshoft Museum of Discovery

Part children's museum, part science museum, and part zoo, the **Boonshoft Museum of Discovery** (2600 Deweese Pkwy., 937/275-7431, boonshoftmuseum.org, 9am-5pm Mon.-Sat., noon-5pm Sun., $14.50 adults, $12.50 seniors, $11.50 ages 3-17) is an attractive option for regional families as well as visitors with young ones in need of a break from the area's aviation heritage. There are plenty of opportunities for muscle and motor skill development here, with a multistory climbing tower in Oscar Boonshoft Science Central and a long water table for toddlers in the Kids Place. Older kids will enjoy the ice age fossils in the main lobby and Science on a Sphere, a globe with a diameter of 6 feet (1.8 m) that displays worldwide data chosen from a kiosk—anything from alarming ice melt in the Arctic to Facebook friendships. The Discovery Zoo wing features over 100 small critters and insects, with accessible viewing for youngsters; residents include otters and meerkats. Tip: The museum is AZA-accredited, meaning you may qualify for a hefty discount if you are a member at a fellow accredited zoo; call ahead to confirm. Discoveries Gift Shop offers a robust selection of DIY science kits, plush dolls, and toys for your inner geek. There's no cafeteria in the museum, but there is a small selection of snacks in the gift shop.

Dayton Art Institute

A much better art museum than you'd expect from a city the size of Dayton, the **Dayton Art Institute** (456 Belmonte Park N., 937/223-4278, daytonartinstitute.org, 11am-5pm Wed. and Fri.-Sat., 11am-8pm Thurs., noon-5pm Sun., $15 adults, $10 seniors, $5 students and ages 7-17, free for children 6 and under) wields an impressive collection that includes works from Bierstadt, O'Keeffe, Rubens, Degas, and more. The museum traces its history back to 1919 but has been in its current home, an Italian Renaissance-style building overlooking downtown Dayton, since 1930. There are four primary wings dedicated to European, American, Asian, and visiting art. The Dayton Art Institute is also recognized as a great art museum for children, with programs for kids as young as two. The Museum Store lets you bring some art home with you, along with accessories, books, and jewelry.

America's Packard Museum

America's Packard Museum (420 S. Ludlow St., 937/226-1710, americaspackardmuseum.com, noon-5pm daily, $6 adults, $5 seniors, free for students) displays restored and running Packard cars in a former Packard dealership showroom and is the largest such collection in the world. The showroom maintains its early-20th-century charm, complete with checkered floors and original ceiling lights. Docents are on hand to provide tours, depending on your interest level. Some of the cars in the showroom belonged to the rich and famous, including Perry Como and Al Capone (reportedly, the last car he ever owned). There's free two-hour parking along Ludlow Street, a relatively quiet road for downtown.

Oregon District

A pocket of blue-collar hipsterdom just east of downtown, the quirky **Oregon District**

1: Wright-Dunbar Interpretive Center at the Dayton Aviation Heritage National Historical Park 2: Boonshoft Museum of Discovery 3: Vectren Dayton Air Show 4: cash registers at Carillon Historical Park

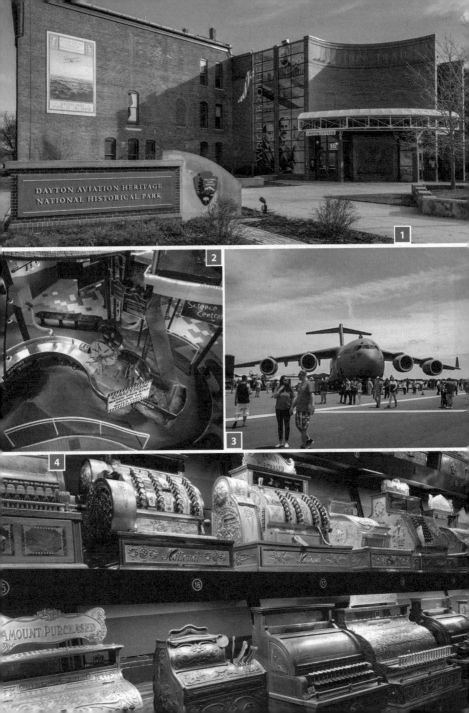

is home to a cluster of many of the city's best dining and drinking experiences. Brick roads denote when you've entered the quirk zone, which is replete with gritty bars, vintage shops, boutiques, and a diverse restaurant lineup. The housing stock south of 5th Street, the 'hood's main drag, is a mix of Victorian styles and is worth a stroll.

SunWatch Indian Village
SunWatch Indian Village (2301 W. River Rd., 937/268-8199, sunwatch.org, 9am-5pm Tues.-Sat., noon-5pm Sun. Apr.-Nov., $7 adults, $6 seniors and ages 6-17, free for children 5 and under) is a reconstructed Fort Ancient village on an archaeological site, just south of downtown. The last of the mound-building cultures in the Ohio Valley, the Fort Ancient people thrived from AD 1000 to AD 1650. They lived in small villages centered around plazas and relied on hunting and farming. Re-creations of the village's structures stand on the exact locations based on excavations. An interpretive center includes a theater with an introductory film, artifacts, and displays depicting life 800 years ago in the village. It also houses a gift shop. The Boonshoft Museum of Discovery holds additional artifacts interpreting the site.

ENTERTAINMENT AND EVENTS
The Arts
The modern **Benjamin and Marian Schuster Performing Arts Center** (1 W. 2nd St., 937/228-7591, daytonlive.org) is the largest performing arts center in town and is home to the **Dayton Philharmonic Orchestra** (daytonperformingarts.org/philharmonic), **Dayton Opera** (daytonperformingarts.org/opera), and **Dayton Ballet** (daytonperformingarts.org/ballet). The historic **Victoria Theatre** (138 N. Main St., 937/228-7591, victoriatheatre.com) is an impressive 1866 Italianate theater with 1,150-seats that hosts touring shows and concerts. The professional **Human Race Theatre Company** (937/461-3823, humanracetheatre.

org) performs at the intimate **Loft Theatre** (126 N. Main St., 937/228-7591).

Festivals and Events
A unique international festival held at the Dayton Convention Center (22 E. 5th St.) is **A World A'Fair** (aworldafair.org), which hosts over 35 non-profit organizations representing over 50 countries. Food, performances, and educational opportunities draw over 25,000 people to this three-day celebration in mid-May, making this the convention center's largest annual event.

The biggest show of the year is the **Vectren Dayton Air Show** (daytonairshow.com), celebrating the region's contributions to aviation and one of the most prestigious air shows in the country. The festival is held over a weekend in late June at the Dayton International Airport.

The **Dayton Celtic Festival** (daytoncelticfestival.com) is held at RiverScape MetroPark (237 E. Monument Ave.) and is a popular family outing to eat, drink, and listen to traditional music acts. Activities during this weekend-long celebration in late July include book readings, a Celtic breakfast, and Sunday mass in Gaelic and English.

The Dayton Art Institute (daytonartinstitute.org) hosts the area's largest **Oktoberfest**, held the fourth full weekend in September as a fundraiser for the museum. German food, music, and gifts are abundantly available, as is beer, with 40 selections on offer. There's also a "TV Cave" with big screens to watch the weekend's football.

RECREATION
Parks
Five Rivers MetroParks (937/275-7275, metroparks.org) operates 19 parks in the Dayton metropolitan area.

Peak activity at the downtown **RiverScape MetroPark** (237 E. Monument Ave., 937/274-0126, metroparks.org/riverscape, 24 hours daily) is during the warmer months when the interactive fountain is operating, concessions are open, and the pavilion hosts a summer concert series. Swinging chairs overlook the river. There's not a lot happening in the park during the colder months.

Cox Arboretum (6733 Springboro Pike, metroparks.org/cox-arboretum, 8am-8pm daily) features 2.5 miles (4 km) of hiking trails through meadows and woods, a butterfly house, and the Tree Tower, an observation tower that offers panoramic views of the park from 65 feet (19.8 m) above ground.

Cycling

Dayton seems to keep its distance from its rivers, understandably so after a devastating 1913 flood. Massive levees separate the downtown area from the Great Miami River. What this means for cyclists is space for a built-in network of parkland and paved trails through the center of town on the **Great Miami River Trail** and **Mad River Trail**. In fact, Dayton is extremely well-connected by bike trails in general, with over 300 paved miles (485 km) connecting Dayton to many of its MetroParks and onward to Springfield, Waynesville, and even Cincinnati via the **Little Miami Scenic Trail.** For more information on bike paths, visit miamivalleytrails.org. There are a handful of bike rental shops in the area, along with the **Link** (linkdayton.org) bike-sharing network in the central part of the city.

Kayaking, Canoeing, and Paddleboarding

Eight MetroParks offer kayaking, canoeing, or stand-up paddleboarding opportunities, most as entry points to the **Great Miami River Water Trail.** You will need to rent from another location, however, as most MetroParks do not offer liveries; the exception is **RiverScape MetroPark** (237 E. Monument Ave., 937/274-0126, metroparks. org/riverscape), which rents kayaks and paddleboards on the Great Miami River June through August. **Whitewater Warehouse** (104 Valley St., 937/222-7020, kayakdayton. com, 1pm-6pm Mon.-Fri., 11am-4pm Sat.) offers rentals along Mad River, not far from RiverScape. It provides stand-up paddleboard

rentals from Memorial Day to Labor Day and has offered kayak rentals in the past. Call to check what its rental offerings are for the summer season.

Hiking

Most of the MetroParks have hiking trails through woods, meadows, and wetlands. The largest of the parks is **Englewood MetroPark** (4361 National Rd., www.metroparks.org/englewood, 8am-8pm daily), north of the city, with over 1,900 acres accessible from four entry points: East Park (4361 W. National Rd., Vandalia), North Park (500 Old Springfield Rd., Vandalia), South Park (9331 Meeker Rd., Dayton), and West Park (100 E. National Rd., Englewood). The East Park entrance puts you closest to the most trailheads and activities. Within the park are three waterfalls and good birding opportunities.

Spectator Sports

Dayton does not have any top-tier professional sports, but there are some alternative options. The Cincinnati Reds affiliate **Dayton Dragons** baseball team (milb.com/ dayton) plays in **Day Air Ballpark** (220 N. Patterson Ave., 937/228-2287), formerly Fifth Third Field.

Additionally, two large universities support NCAA Division I teams. The **Wright State University Raiders** basketball team (wsuraiders.com) play at the **Nutter Center** (3640 Colonel Glenn Hwy., 937/775-3498). More notable is the **University of Dayton Flyers** basketball team (daytonflyers.com), who make some noise now and then during tournament season. The team plays at **University of Dayton Arena** (1801 Edwin C. Moses Blvd., 937/229-4433), which is often a host of NCAA Tournament games during March.

SHOPPING

There's plenty of shopping in the Dayton area. **Greene Town Center** (4452 Buckeye Ln., Beavercreek, 937/490-4990, thegreene.com) is a mixed-use upscale lifestyle center with three anchor stores, over a hundred shops, a movie theater, and several dining options.

Oregon District

Boutiques and vintage shops line 5th Street, the Oregon District's main drag. Some of the shops are less than kid-friendly, though most are perfectly fine.

In the middle of the Oregon District is **Heart Mercantile** (438 E. 5th St., 937/250-6020, heartmercantile.com, 11am-8pm daily), an irreverent gift shop that refuses to conform to social norms (read: swear words on stuff). You can find apparel, mugs, and other items with some sass inserted.

Nearby, **BRIM on fifth** (464 E. 5th St., 937/222-4287, brimonfifth.com, 11am-8pm Tues.-Sat., 11am-4pm Sun.) is painted bright yellow and hard to miss. Inside you'll find a dog-friendly hat and apparel shop, with a curated collection of headwear, bags, socks, and ties for men and women.

Clash Gallery and Boutique (521 E. 5th St., 937/259-8986, clashdayton.com, noon-6pm Tues.-Thurs., noon-8pm Fri.-Sat., noon-5pm Sun.) specializes in unique jewelry, art, and clothing made by local artists. It also carries vintage clothing and apparel lines carried by few if any stores in the Dayton area. There's something for men, women, and children here.

South of Downtown

Though you're likely to find some boxes in local gift shops and grocery stores, you ought to head to regional favorite **Esther Price Candies** (1709 Wayne Ave., 937/253-2121, estherprice.com, 8am-5:30pm Mon.-Fri., 9am-5pm Sat.) for a much wider assortment. Here, candies are available in boxes or in bulk. Don't miss the chocolate-covered potato chips. There are several locations in Southwest Ohio, but this one is the closest to central Dayton.

Antiques Village (651 Lyons Rd., 937/291-5060, antiquesvillage.net, 10am-8pm daily) is an enormous antique mall with over 350 shops including dedicated bookstore, candle, and

framed art areas. There's plenty of decor and furniture to boot.

FOOD

Downtown

A one-stop shop for groceries, locally made handiworks, and lunch is **2nd Street Market** (600 E. 2nd St., 937/228-2088, metroparks.org/2nd-street-market, 11am-3pm Thurs.-Fri. and Sun., 8am-3pm Sat.). Five Rivers MetroParks operates this indoor marketplace, open since 2001 in a former railroad freight depot. It hosts over 50 local vendors selling baked goods, produce, crafts, and prepared food options. Among them are some selections unique to Dayton and perhaps the entire state. **Cheeky Meat Pies** serves New Zealand-style meat pies. **Maria's Unique Foods** sells Amish and Mennonite-made products such as jams, pie fillings, and pickled foods. An outdoor **farmers market** (8am-3pm Sat. June-Oct.) is also held seasonally. Parking outside the long, skinny building is plentiful and free.

Canal Street Arcade and Deli (308 E. 1st St., 937/220-9333, canalstreetarcadeanddeli.weebly.com, 11am-1am Mon.-Thurs., 11am-1:30am Fri.-Sat., 11am-11pm Sun., $6-10) is a combination deli counter/dive bar/beer-and-wine carryout/arcade a couple of blocks from the river and baseball stadium. Sandwiches, salads, and naan pizzas dominate the menu. You can build your own breakfast or grilled cheese sandwich as well. Supervised children are permitted before 3pm, but the place is for the 21-and-over crowd after 5pm. Seating is limited.

Oregon District

Upscale Italian restaurant ★ **Roost** (524 E. 5th St., 937/222-3100, roostitalian.com, 5pm-10pm Tues.-Thurs., 5pm-11pm Fri.-Sat., 5pm-9pm Sun., $20-37) serves traditional dishes using modern recipes in an intimate setting.

1: Day Air Ballpark, home of the Dayton Dragons **2:** BRIM on fifth in the Oregon District **3:** Esther Price candies **4:** Heart Mercantile in the Oregon District

Rather than pasta, the menu focuses on well-prepared meats and seafood, with entrées such as a butter-poached filet mignon and mushroom-crusted scallops. Rolling garage doors open when the weather warrants.

Another Italian-ish option in the Oregon District is **Wheat Penny Oven & Bar** (515 Wayne St., 937/496-5268, wheatpennydayton. com, 11am-10pm Mon.-Fri., 10am-10pm Sat., 10am-3pm Sun., $13-34). The menu is stuffed with California-style pizzas, pastas, and sandwiches, all served in a large, relaxed dining room. A handful of "Family Pack" menu options are on hand, with portions large enough for four adults. You'll also find a robust menu of beer, wine, and cocktails.

A classy option for dinner is **Salar Restaurant and Lounge** (400 E. 5th St., 937/203-3999, salarrestaurant.com, 5pm-9pm Sun.-Thurs., 5pm-10pm Fri.-Sat., $21-39). This Peruvian fusion restaurant embraces the influence immigration has had on that country's food, with hints of southern European, West African, and Japanese flavors. Take your pick among the seating choices, which include two outdoor patios, two bars (open at 4pm daily), the main dining room, and a comfortable lounge. The menu is awash in gluten-free and vegetarian options.

For a rock-solid Irish pub experience, there is **Dublin Pub** (300 Wayne St., 937/224-7822, dubpub.com, 11am-midnight Mon.-Wed., 11am-1am Thurs., 11am-2am Fri.-Sat., 10am-11pm Sun., $8-20). A full menu of Irish favorites and pub-style sandwiches and burgers are on offer, as are thick-cut "pub fries," slathered in cheese, bacon, and a white wine reduction—they were voted some of the best fries in Ohio. Though there is a giant selection of Scotch and whiskey as well as beer, the pub reportedly imports the second most Guinness in Ohio. Live music frequents the front stage, and the somewhat tight seating makes this a warm, jovial establishment.

Thai 9 (11 Brown St., 937/222-3227, thai9restaurant.com, 11:30am-2:30pm and 5pm-9:30pm Mon.-Thurs., 11:30am-2:30pm and 5pm-10pm Fri., 5pm-10pm Sat., 5pm-9:30pm Sun., $13-25), as its name suggests, serves high-end versions of your favorite Thai dishes but devotes at least as much space on the menu to Japanese cuisine, with udon and an extensive sushi list. The lunch menu is substantially cheaper at this large, airy establishment that maintains a business casual dress code (jeans are fine, but check the website for more details).

South of Downtown

Cassano's Pizza King (430 Warren St., 888/294-5464, cassanos.com, 10:30am-11pm Mon.-Thurs., 10:30am-midnight Fri.-Sat., 11am-11pm Sun.), a local favorite, serves up square-cut, thin-crust pizza. It has over 30 locations around Dayton, Springfield, and other towns in the region, but this one is closest to central Dayton.

Cassano's doesn't completely own the pizza world around here. **Old Scratch Pizza** (812 S. Patterson Blvd., 937/331-5357, oldscratchpizza.com, 11am-10pm Tues.-Thurs., 11am-11pm Fri.-Sat., 11am-9pm Sun., $8-12) has its own devoted following. Personal Neapolitan-style pizzas are the specialty here, with menu offerings divided into "reds" and "whites." There are 20 beers on tap to pair with your choice, along with cocktails and wine sold by the half or full liter. There is a second location in Centerville.

There are plenty of local coffee houses to choose from in the central Dayton area. Try ★ **Ghostlight Coffee** (800 S. Patterson Ave., 937/985-2633, ghostlightcoffee.com, 6:30am-6:30pm Mon.-Fri., 8am-4pm Sat.-Sun.), which serves Cincinnati's Deeper Roots Coffee. There are two locations, in Midtown and South Park; the modern, industrial-looking Midtown location on Patterson Avenue has a larger food menu to accompany its coffee. The bagels are baked to perfection using beer from Fifth Street Brewpub. The salt-and-pepper one is especially divine. Other menu items include tartines, salads, and breakfast sandwiches.

information center in Yellow Springs, right off the Little Miami Scenic Trail

Meandering 78 miles (126 km) between Cincinnati suburb Newtown and Springfield, the **Little Miami Scenic Trail** (miamivalleytrails.org/trails) is the longest paved trail in the Miami Valley network and one of the longest such trails in the country. This multipurpose path connects many of the region's highlights and is popular with hikers and cyclists alike. The southern half hugs the Little Miami River through forests and hills while the northern half follows disused rail lines. Visitors along the trail will roll past charming towns, craft breweries, state parks, and ancient historical sites. Additional regional favorites such as Young's Jersey Dairy and Kings Island are within spitting distance as well.

Major stops along the trail, going north to south, include:

- Springfield's **Heritage Center** building (117 S. Fountain Ave., Springfield) is the northern terminus of the trail. A stately office building occupying an entire city block, the Heritage Center houses a museum, city archives, and a coffee shop.

- **Yellow Springs** is a funky town of boutiques, cafés, and historic bed-and-breakfasts, with excellent hiking opportunities at **Glen Helen Nature Preserve** (405 Corry St., Yellow Springs) and **John Bryan State Park** (3790 SR 370, Yellow Springs).

- **Waynesville**'s small main street is occupied by country restaurants and numerous antique shops.

- **Fort Ancient Earthworks and Nature Preserve** (6123 SR 350, Oregonia) is accessible from the trail via a steep hiking path, on top of which is an overlook and a 2,000-year-old Hopewell culture ceremonial enclosure.

- The trail cuts through the center of **Loveland,** which has an excellent selection of bars and restaurants steps off the trail.

- The **Bass Island Trailhead** across the street from Horizon Community Church (3950 Newtown Rd., Cincinnati) is the southernmost trailhead, though the path continues until it dead ends near Beechmont Avenue in Cincinnati. Another reason to make this place the end of the line is the Fifty West complex, which includes a canoe livery and **Fifty West Brewing** (7668 Wooster Pike, Cincinnati, 513/834-8789, fiftywestbrew.com, 11am-9pm Mon., 11am-10pm Tues.-Thurs., 11am-11pm Fri.-Sat., 10am-9pm Sun.), one of the more prominent craft breweries in the Cincinnati area.

Around Dayton

Not technically in Dayton but in southern suburb Centerville is ★ **Bill's Donut Shop** (268 Main St., Centerville, 937/433-0002, billsdonutshop.com, 24 hours daily). A Centerville tradition since the 1960s, this no-frills donut joint specializes in cake donuts, in particular its sour cream version, but has a wide assortment available at all hours. The donuts have appeared on "Best of" lists from *USA Today* and Business Insider. This particular location, the only one left, opened in 1979 and looks like it hasn't changed much, with wood-paneled walls and changeable-letter menus.

BARS AND NIGHTLIFE

There are a few notable craft breweries in and around downtown and the Oregon District. Relaxed **Warped Wing Brewing Company** (26 Wyandot St., 937/222-7003, warpedwing.com, 3pm-10pm Mon.-Thurs., 3pm-midnight Fri., noon-midnight Sat., noon-8pm Sun.) and its taproom are located in the industrial digs of the former Buckeye Brass & Iron Foundry. It offers a refreshingly diverse range of beers as well as its own root beer and ginger beer, plus a food menu that includes burgers, sliders, wings and tacos.

A block away from the baseball stadium is **The Dayton Beer Company** (41 Madison St., 937/228-2337, thedaytonbeerco.com, 4pm-10pm Tues.-Thurs., 4pm-midnight Fri., noon-midnight Sat., noon-6pm Sun.), which led the charge of new craft breweries in Dayton when, in 2010, it was the first brewery to open in 50 years. Its German-style biergarten, inside a former industrial site, has 36 taps serving its own brews alongside the best of Ohio.

Dayton's drinking scene isn't entirely new. Recognized as one of the country's best bourbon bars by *The Bourbon Review,* downtown's **The Century** (18 S. Jefferson St., 937/223-3382, centurybourbon.com, 3pm-2:30am Mon.-Fri., 3pm-2:30am Sat., 6pm-2:30am Sun.) has been serving bourbon and whiskey from behind its cherrywood and stained-glass bar since 1942 (the bar itself dates to 1862).

Decked out in dark wood and with some barrels used for tables, the bar maintains a decidedly old-school aesthetic.

Downtown's **The Barrel House** (417 E. 3rd St., 937/222-4795, barrelhousetap.com, 11am-midnight Tues.-Thurs. and Sun., 11am-1am Fri.-Sat.) earns high marks for its beer selection from around the country and its warm, comfortable digs, complete with couches. Operated by a husband-and-wife duo, the bar sells beer by the taster, draft, or growler. On Sundays, guests are encouraged to bring their favorite vinyl to play on the bar's music system.

Blind Bob's (430 E. 5th St., 937/938-6405, blindbobs.com, 11am-2:30am daily) in the Oregon District is a dingy-in-the-best-way dive with a full menu of wings and burgers. The most popular menu item is the creamy pickle soup—a highlight of the city, really. The beer list is long and there's live music on the weekends to match the eclectic clientele. The kitchen closes at 11pm.

ACCOMMODATIONS

Accommodations in Dayton are almost exclusively chain hotels, of which there are a couple of helpful clusters. A good number have staked out a spot near Wright-Patterson Air Force Base, which puts you nicely between Dayton's attractions and side excursions to Yellow Springs or Springfield. On the south side is another large cluster, near the Dayton Mall between Centerville and Miamisburg. Staying down here puts you closer to Cincinnati if you're headed in that direction.

$100-150

For something outside brand-name hotels, try **Inn Port Lodging** (22 Brown St., 937/224-7678, innport.com, $129-159) in the heart of the Oregon District. There are three guest rooms in this Victorian house, and some or all of them can be reserved at the same time to enjoy the house with a larger group at a discounted rate. All rooms have a private bathroom and two of the three have king-sized beds. A wine shop and bar are on-site.

For something a little different, and a little out of the way, try **English Manor Bed and Breakfast** (505 E. Linden Ave. Miamisburg, 937/866-2288, englishmanorohio.com, $126-139). In the quiet suburb of Miamisburg south of Dayton, this 1920s Tudor mansion has six rooms appointed with era-appropriate antiques. Breakfast is served 6am-10am and the owners will help you plan your stay.

$150-200

There are relatively few accommodation options in the center of town. **Crowne Plaza Dayton** (33 E. 5th St., 937/224-0800, ihg.com, $156-165) has a foot both in downtown and the Oregon District and is connected to the convention center. The hotel offers parking in an attached garage, a rooftop restaurant and lounge, and clean, though unremarkable, rooms. The slightly more upscale **Fairfield Inn & Suites by Marriott Dayton** (305 E. Monument Ave., 937/331-9330, marriott. com, $166-219) is steps away from the river, its parks, and the baseball stadium. A breakfast buffet is included in the rate.

The area near the University of Dayton south of downtown also supports a couple of brand-name hotels. **Marriott at the University of Dayton** (1414 S. Patterson Blvd., 937/223-1000, marriott.com, $180-219) offers comfortable, modern rooms in a location convenient to most of the city's attractions.

INFORMATION AND SERVICES

The **Dayton Convention and Visitors Bureau** (22 E. 5th St., 937/226-8211, dayton-cvb.com, 8am-5:30pm Mon.-Fri.) is located at the front of the Dayton Convention Center and can assist with itinerary planning.

Dayton is known for its quality healthcare, with two primary networks maintaining several hospitals throughout the region. **Miami Valley Hospital** (1 Wyoming St., 937/208-8000) has over 800 beds and is centrally located. **Soin Medical Center** (3535 Pentagon Blvd., 937/702-4000), part of the Kettering Health Network, is a full-service hospital on the east side of town near Wright State University.

TRANSPORTATION
Getting There

Dayton is 70 minutes (73 mi/118 km) west of Columbus on I-70 (and then SR 4 or I-75 to reach downtown). From Cincinnati, take I-75 north for just under an hour (54 mi/87 km). From Toledo, take I-75 south for 150 miles (242 km), which takes about 2.25 hours. US-35 is useful if you're coming from southern Ohio.

Dayton's **Greyhound bus terminal** (5136 Salem Ave., 937/837-6251) is on the northwest side of town.

Dayton International Airport (DAY, 3600 Terminal Dr., 937/454-8200, flydayton. com) serves about 2.5 million passengers a year and is the third largest airport in Ohio after Cleveland and Columbus. The airport is a 15-minute drive (13 mi/20.9 km) north of the city on the other side of I-70 and is served by Delta, American, United, and Allegiant airlines.

Charter Vans (937/898-4043, chartervans. com) and **Callahan's Premium Car Service** (937/789-3829, callahanspcs.com) offer private transportation between the airport and destinations within the region. Uber and Lyft are both licensed to operate within the airport. All the large car rental companies maintain offices near baggage claim. Taxis are also available 7am-midnight, or 30 minutes past the last flight, whichever is later. Otherwise, the RTA regional transit system operates bus route 43, which connects the airport with downtown Dayton.

Getting Around

It's easy to drive around Dayton, which is great because a car is by far the best method for sightseeing in the area. I-75 cuts a swath through the middle of the city going north-south. I-70 skirts the top edge of town. I-675 is a bypass on the east side, connecting the air force base with many of the area's wealthier suburbs. SR 4 is an under-used divided highway that also connects downtown Dayton with I-70, with the air force base and museum in the middle. US-35 cuts through town going east-west, connecting I-675 with downtown. Parking is inexpensive and abundant.

Uber and Lyft both operate in Dayton.

The **Greater Dayton Regional Transport Authority (RTA)** (i-riderta.org) serves the area with public bus routes, including some of the few remaining trolley bus routes in the country. Regular adult fare is $2 and can be paid on-board; exact fare is recommended, though change will be administered in the form of change cards redeemable for future use. Day passes are available for $4. Passes can be purchased at any of the authority's five transit centers, including downtown's **Wright Stop Plaza Transit Center** (4 S. Main St.).

Springfield

Springfield was the "City at the End of the Road" when the National Road (now US-40) temporarily stopped construction in 1839 in the middle of town, picking back up a decade later. The city prospered up through the first half of the 20th century, during which a number of impressive civic buildings and houses were constructed. Today, the substantial loss of jobs and population has taken its toll on the city. Some of those impressive buildings remain, some in better shape than others.

There's not a lot going on in musician John Legend's hometown, but if you're passing through on your way to Columbus or Dayton there are a couple diversions, depending on your interests, that could pull you off I-70. This blue-collar city of 60,000 is a major stop on the Little Miami Scenic Trail and is thus an excellent place to stock up on supplies, grab a beer or coffee, or treat yourself to a decent meal.

SIGHTS

Frank Lloyd Wright's Westcott House

Frank Lloyd Wright fans will certainly appreciate the **Westcott House** (85 S. Greenmount Ave., 937/327-9291, westcotthouse.org, 11am-5pm Tues.-Sat., 1pm-5pm Sun., $18 adults, $15 seniors and students). Built in 1908, the house had fallen into a state of disrepair and was threatened with demolition. In 2001, the Frank Lloyd Wright Building Conservancy and the Westcott House Foundation funded a massive restoration, and today the house is open for tours. This is the only Prairie-style house Wright built in Ohio and features a unique pergola feature rare in his designs. Tours lasting roughly 90 minutes start in the garage and leave every couple of hours, but check the website for seasonal schedules.

Hartman Rock Garden

In a quiet residential neighborhood on the south side of town is the quirky **Hartman Rock Garden** (1905 Russell Ave., no phone number, hartmanrocks.org, dawn-dusk daily, free). A testament to the doldrums of unemployment, the rock garden is the result of a Great Depression layoff. In 1932, unemployed factory worker Ben Hartman put his free time to use building a cement fishing pond in his backyard. He enjoyed the work and just kept going, constructing entire worlds out of rock, concrete, and metal. Miniature villages, structures with religious iconography, and a castle with a moat fill the yard, creating a funky roadside attraction for the neighborhood. Today, the volunteer group Friends of the Hartman Rock Garden own and maintain the space. The group offers 45-minute tours for $12, but you need to book in advance. Self-guided tours are free (donations encouraged).

Springfield Museum of Art

An affiliate of the Smithsonian, the small **Springfield Museum of Art** (107 Cliff Park

Springfield and Yellow Springs

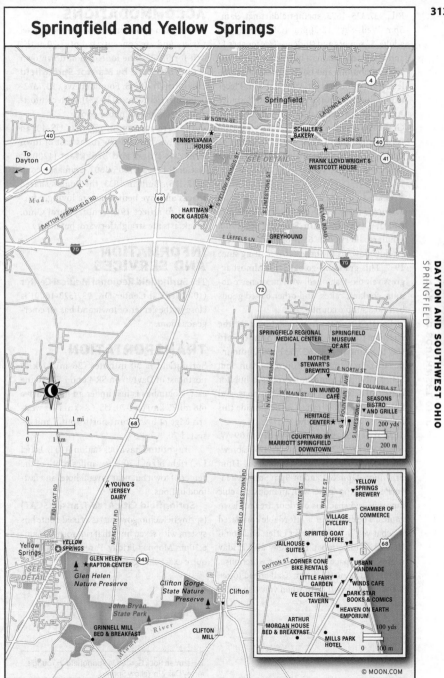

Springfield

To Dayton

Mad River

PENNSYLVANIA HOUSE

SCHULER'S BAKERY

FRANK LLOYD WRIGHT'S WESTCOTT HOUSE

HARTMAN ROCK GARDEN

E LEFFELS LN

GREYHOUND

SEE DETAIL

0   1 mi

0   1 km

YOUNG'S JERSEY DAIRY

POLECAT RD

MEREDITH RD

SPRINGFIELD JAMESTOWN RD

Yellow Springs

YELLOW SPRINGS

GLEN HELEN RAPTOR CENTER

Glen Helen Nature Preserve

John Bryan State Park

Clifton Gorge State Nature Preserve

Clifton

GRINNELL MILL BED & BREAKFAST

Little Miami River

CLIFTON MILL

Detail 1 (Springfield):

SPRINGFIELD REGIONAL MEDICAL CENTER

SPRINGFIELD MUSEUM OF ART

MOTHER STEWART'S BREWING

N YELLOW SPRINGS ST

E NORTH ST

E COLUMBIA ST

W MAIN ST

UN MUNDO CAFE

FOUNTAIN AVE

SEASONS BISTRO AND GRILLE

HERITAGE CENTER

S LIMESTONE ST

COURTYARD BY MARRIOTT SPRINGFIELD DOWNTOWN

0   200 yds

0   200 m

Detail 2 (Yellow Springs):

YELLOW SPRINGS BREWERY

N WINTER ST

WALNUT ST

CHAMBER OF COMMERCE

VILLAGE CYCLERY

SPIRITED GOAT COFFEE

JAILHOUSE SUITES

DAYTON ST

CORNER CONE BIKE RENTALS

URBAN HANDMADE

LITTLE FAIRY GARDEN

WINDS CAFE

DARK STAR BOOKS & COMICS

YE OLDE TRAIL TAVERN

HEAVEN ON EARTH EMPORIUM

ARTHUR MORGAN HOUSE BED & BREAKFAST

MILLS PARK HOTEL

0   100 yds

0   100 m

© MOON.COM

Rd., 937/325-4673, springfieldart.net, 9am-5pm Wed.-Sat., 12:30pm-4:30pm Sun., $5 adults, $3 seniors and students, free for ages 17 and under) maintains a busy schedule of visiting exhibitions and holds a permanent collection that focuses on American art. Pieces from Ohioans George Bellows and Berenice Abbott are present, as are highlights from Grant Wood and A. T. Bricher. The museum is in the middle of Veterans Park alongside Buck Creek, a pleasant setting that also makes for a good place to walk.

FOOD

There are three locations, but the **Schuler's Bakery** (457 E. Main St., 937/323-4900, schulersbakery.com, 6am-8pm daily) nearest downtown is the original, operating since 1937. This grab-and-go bakery is almost aggressively old-fashioned, with inexpensive donuts, cookies, cakes, and other baked goods behind a simple counter.

Located under the clock tower of the Heritage Center building, **Un Mundo Café** (117 S. Fountain Ave., 937/323-8355, unmundocafe.com, 7am-3pm Mon.-Fri., 8am-1pm Sat., $5-10) is a community-focused hub for coffee, beer, paninis, gourmet hot dogs, and local art. There is limited seating inside this breakfast-and-lunch joint.

Mother Stewart's Brewing (109 W. North St., 937/717-0618, motherstewartsbrewing.com, 3pm-10pm Tues.-Thurs., 3pm-11pm Fri., noon-11pm Sat., noon-9pm Sun.) is a favorite gathering space, with an industrial chic taproom and spacious outdoor area for lawn games. The craft beer is affordable compared to what you'll find in larger cities, and you'll find live music most Thursday and Friday nights. The space is in a former warehouse, adding to the rustic charm. Call ahead to see if a food truck will be in when you visit.

ACCOMMODATIONS

Most accommodations are of the chain hotel variety and are concentrated off I-70 at the exit for SR 72. The lone option downtown is the **Courtyard by Marriot Springfield Downtown** (100 S. Fountain Ave., 937/322-3600, marriott.com, $137-174), with comfortable rooms and an indoor pool.

If you're passing through via US-40, an alternative option a few miles east of town is **Emma's Bed and Breakfast** (4200 E. National Rd., 937/505-3602, emmasbb.com, $132-175). Built in 1833, the home's shared spaces and five bedrooms are lovingly furnished to reflect 19th-century rural Ohio. Breakfasts are straightforward, but hearty.

INFORMATION AND SERVICES

The **Springfield Regional Medical Center** (100 Medical Center Dr., 937/523-1000) is close to the center of town and has an emergency room.

TRANSPORTATION

Springfield is 30 minutes (26 mi/42 km) northeast of Dayton on SR 4 and I-70. To the east, Columbus is just under an hour's drive (48 mi/77 km) on I-70. US-68 skirts the western edge of town, runs north-south, and bisects I-70.

Greyhound has a bus station (110 E. Leffel Ln.) right off of I-70, a few miles south of the center of town but near several hotel and fast-food options.

Springfield City Area Transit (SCAT) (springfieldohio.gov/scat) is a fixed-route bus system with seven lines that run roughly 6am-6:30pm Monday-Friday. Fares are $1 and require exact change.

1: Hartman Rock Garden in Springfield 2: Young's Jersey Dairy in Yellow Springs

Yellow Springs

A hippie mountain town without a mountain, Yellow Springs sticks out in what is otherwise a solidly red part of the state. Comedian Dave Chappelle's hometown resembles the kind of quirky resort village you'd expect to find outside a national park, and it has been a left-leaning hotspot for over a century as home to a failed 19th-century utopian community and social justice-oriented Antioch College. Take a stroll down the town's main street, Xenia Avenue, and you'll find free-spirited cafés, bookstores, and shops. On weekends, vendors set up booths throughout town and sell organic and artisan this and that.

If you're looking for outdoor adventure, east of town is a contiguous area of woodsy wilderness comprised of Glen Helen Nature Preserve, John Bryan State Park, and Clifton Gorge State Nature Preserve. The Little Miami Scenic Trail runs through the town, making this a colorful stop on a long trip through rural Ohio.

With such a variety of activities in a relatively small region, Yellow Springs has become a popular day trip among Ohioans. Offering numerous bed-and-breakfasts and guesthouses, it's also an alternative place to stay if nowhere in Dayton is striking your fancy and you want to explore the region from a wider perspective.

SIGHTS

Young's Jersey Dairy

You thought you were just in it for the ice cream, but **Young's Jersey Dairy** (6880 Springfield-Xenia Rd., 937/325-0629, youngs-dairy.com, 11am-9pm daily) offers so much more. Working the dairy farm since 1869, the Young family began selling their produce directly to consumers in the 1950s from a modest 10-foot by 10-foot (3-m by 3-m) room. Today, that operation has exploded into a mini-amusement park, with two restaurants,

a petting zoo, miniature golf, batting cages, a driving range, and other family activities unaffiliated with cows. Special events add more to the mix throughout the year—especially autumn, with a corn maze, pumpkin patch, and haunted wagon rides. Of course, you can still go just for the ice cream, which is sold in the dairy mart alongside a small menu of burgers and sandwiches. If you're itching for some fun, purchase wristbands at either of the restaurants or the miniature golf station for three ($16.95) or five ($23.95) activities.

Glen Helen Raptor Center

The nonprofit Glen Helen Ecology Institute runs the **Glen Helen Raptor Center** (1075 SR 343, 937/767-7648, glenhelen.org/raptor-center, 9am-7pm daily summer, 9am-6pm daily spring and fall, 9am-5pm daily winter, free), a small rehabilitation facility that cares for over 200 injured birds a year, half of which end up back in the wild after their recovery. The center houses around 15-20 species at any given time within its rows of flight cages, including great horned owls, bald eagles, and red-tailed hawks. The facility appreciates donations; see the website for details.

National Afro-American Museum and Cultural Center

The tiny town of Wilberforce, 7 miles (11.3 km) south of Yellow Springs, is named after British statesman and abolitionist William Wilberforce and home to two historically Black universities: Wilberforce University and Central State University. On the campus of the latter is the **National Afro-American Museum and Cultural Center** (1350 Brush Row Rd., 937/376-4944, ohiohistory.org, 9am-4pm Wed.-Sat., $6 adults, $5 seniors, $3 children ages 6-17). The museum, operated by Ohio History Connection, rotates exhibits of photographs and artifacts that celebrate and acknowledge the historical, artistic, and cultural achievements of African Americans. Over 9,000 items spanning the 18th-21st centuries are in the permanent collection, including a Buffalo Soldier coat, an original manuscript of *Roots,* and Gregory Hines' tap shoes. Allow roughly one hour to soak in the exhibits of this small museum, which celebrated its 30th anniversary in 2018.

RECREATION
John Bryan State Park
The 752-acre **John Bryan State Park** (3790 SR 370, 937/767-1274, ohiodnr.gov, dawn-dusk daily, free), 2 miles (3.2 km) southeast of town, hugs the Little Miami River as it passes through limestone Clifton Gorge. Hiking trails take you along either the rim or the river, passing rock formations and spring wildflowers as the 130-foot-deep (40-m) gorge narrows to the east. The park features nearly 10 miles (16.1 km) of mountain bike trails, opportunities for rock climbing (call the park office to register for a site), and a campground.

Clifton Gorge State Nature Preserve
John Bryan State Park's rim and river trails continue east into **Clifton Gorge State Nature Preserve** (2381 SR 343, 614/265-6453, ohiodnr.gov, dawn-dusk daily, free), where the gorge becomes shallower and tighter until it reaches The Narrows, a tight squeeze of rapids (too narrow for rafting). The gorge trail passes cliffs, seasonal waterfalls, and wildflowers. There is a parking lot on SR 343 as well as another on Jackson Street in the town of Clifton, which puts you closer to The Narrows.

Glen Helen Nature Preserve
Charming **Glen Helen Nature Preserve** (405 Corry St., 937/769-1902, glenhelen.org, dawn-dusk daily, free) is immediately east of town and features over 20 miles (32 km) of hiking trails through new- and old-growth forest and ravines. The moderate **Inman Trail** (1.2-mi/1.9-km loop) passes many of the highlights, including the diminutive yellow springs for which the town is named (they're actually more orange-ish) and a Hopewell culture mound. The Inman Trailhead is located at the preserve's main entrance, near the **Trailside Museum** (9am-5pm Sat.-Sun.), which features hands-on displays, animal ambassadors, and a gift shop. The preserve's entrance is only a few blocks from the middle of Yellow Springs, making it possible to enjoy a stroll through town and a hike without jumping in the car. Parking is $5.

★ SHOPPING
Yellow Springs offers a colorful assortment of shops, mainly on Xenia Avenue.

Free-spirited **Heaven on Earth Emporium** (253 Xenia Ave., Unit C, 937/767-2000, noon-4pm Mon., 11am-4pm Tues.-Thurs. and Sun., 10am-6pm Fri., 11am-6pm Sat.) is a deceptively large boutique hiding at the end of an alley. The labyrinthine store offers apparel (primarily for women), jewelry, and other accessories celebrating an eclectic fashion sense and lifestyle.

Along with a wide selection of used books and a collection of comic books both common and rare, **Dark Star Books & Comics** (237 Xenia Ave., 937/767-9400, 11am-6pm daily) sells board games and pop culture accessories related to everything from Studio Ghibli to literature.

People who enjoy T-shirts with controversial statements ought to check out **Urban Handmade** (113 Corry St., 937/319-6049, 10:30am-5:30pm Wed.-Fri., 10:30am-6pm Sat., 11am-5pm Sun.), which specializes in irreverent and political shirts, along with local art.

The adorable **Little Fairy Garden** (224 Xenia Ave., 714/785-5876, noon-6pm daily) is tucked behind the main street near Ye Olde Trail Tavern. This garden decor specialty shop focuses on miniature houses and props for your garden beds. A magical forest space in the front hosts fairy garden workshops and parties.

FOOD

One of the nicer places for a bite in town is **Winds Café** (215 Xenia Ave., 937/767-1144, windscafe.com, 11:30am-2pm and 5pm-10pm Tues.-Sat., 10am-3pm Sun., $15-35), a European-inspired bistro with a seasonal menu that changes bimonthly to match the available local ingredients. The dining room is casual and the lunch menu significantly cheaper than the dinner menu.

Billed as "Ohio's Oldest Tavern," **Ye Olde Trail Tavern** (228 Xenia Ave., 937/767-7448, oldetrailtavern.com, 11am-10pm Sun.-Thurs., 11am-11pm Fri.-Sat. Easter-Halloween, 11am-9pm Sun.-Thurs., 11am-10pm Fri.-Sat. Halloween-Easter, $9-12) traces its history back to 1827 and feels like it inside, with its rustic antiques, exposed wood beams, and a fireplace. Outside, on an expansive patio that's good for people-watching on the main drag, the vibe is a bit more modern. The menu includes an extensive appetizer list, typical pub fare, some German staples, and pizza.

Right off the Little Miami Scenic Trail is the popular **Yellow Springs Brewery** (305 Walnut St., 937/767-0222, yellowspringsbrewery.com, 3pm-9pm Thurs.-Sun.). The taproom features over a dozen craft beers in a friendly, art-filled setting. A rotating list of food trucks provides the grub.

Any hippie town worth its mettle will have a handful of eclectic coffee shops to discuss takes on the latest political news, and Yellow Springs is no exception. **Spirited Goat Coffee House** (118 Dayton St., 937/767-1514, 7am-7pm Mon.-Wed., 7am-10pm Thurs.-Fri., 8am-10pm Sat., 8am-7pm Sun.) serves fresh-brewed coffee and tea in an open, comfortable sitting area with colorful walls. A stage in the back hosts live music and open mic nights.

Just east of Yellow Springs, Clifton's historic ★ **Clifton Mill** (75 Water St., Clifton, 937/767-5501, cliftonmill.com, 9am-4pm Mon.-Fri., 8am-5pm Sat.-Sun., $8-13) was established in 1802 and remains one of the largest water-powered grist mills in existence. The mill still grinds flour, but the main attraction is now the restaurant, in business since the 1980s, which serves up country-style breakfasts and lunches. Also on the grounds is a covered bridge and enough land to put up a spectacular Christmas display every holiday season. Near the trailhead for Clifton Gorge State Nature Preserve, the restaurant makes a good before- or after-hike meal. Tables fill up, so expect a wait during the lunch rush. The

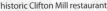

historic Clifton Mill restaurant

gift shop up front sells country decor, candy, and the restaurant's pancake mix.

ACCOMMODATIONS

Constructed in 2016 to resemble a 19th-century mansion, **Mills Park Hotel** (321 Xenia Ave., 937/319-0400, millsparkhotel. com, $165-315) is located right on the south end of the Xenia Avenue strip, with a spacious, shady porch and 28 well-appointed rooms reminiscent of an old inn. In each room and suite you'll find custom furniture and plush bedding. In the lobby, the Southern-themed **Ellie's Restaurant & Bakery** offers indoor and porch seating.

The **Arthur Morgan House Bed & Breakfast** (120 W. Limestone St., 937/767-1761, arthurmorganhouse.com, $145-180) is a cheaper option and also near the southern end of the main drag. The six modern rustic guest suites are bright and spacious, and each comes with a private bathroom. During summer, the breakfast gurus procure their ingredients from the Yellow Springs Farmers' Market. Reservations require a minimum two-night stay.

Built in 1878, **Jailhouse Suites** (111 N. Winter St., 937/319-1222, jailhousesuites. com, $110-125) is a collection of four suites housed in the town's old jailhouse, plus a cottage about 100 yards (91 m) away. In the property's quaint little garden, you can enjoy a seat and good view of the historic green jailhouse building (though little identifies the building as a prison).

The **Grinnell Mill Bed & Breakfast** (3536 Bryan Park Rd., 937/767-0131, grinnellmill-bandb.com, $115-125) is situated in a red 1811 grist mill near the entrance to John Bryan State Park and offers three guest rooms and a continental breakfast. The spacious central area includes a fireplace and quiet spaces to read or enjoy a boardgame.

CAMPING
John Bryan State Park (3790 SR 370, 937/767-1274) offers 17 electric campsites and 43 non-electric sites, accommodating both tents and RVs. Rates start at $21.

INFORMATION AND SERVICES

The **Chamber of Commerce** building (100 Dayton St., 937/767-7202, yellowspringsohio.org), right off the Little Miami Scenic Trail, has an information center and public restrooms in a replica of an 1880s railroad depot.

Your best bet for medical services is heading west to Dayton. The nearest urgent care center is **Doctors' Urgent Care** (2131 Gateway Dr., Fairborn, 937/873-9500, amca-reinb.com) near the intersection of I-675 and Dayton Yellow Springs Road. The nearest hospital is **Greene Memorial Hospital** (1141 N. Monroe Dr., Xenia, 937/352-2000), 8 miles (12.9 km) south of town off US-68.

TRANSPORTATION
Getting There
Yellow Springs is 10 minutes (7 mi/11.3 km) south of I-70 along US-68. The town is 25 minutes (20 mi/32 km) east of downtown Dayton via I-675 and Dayton Yellow Springs Road.

Greene CATS (937/708-8322, co.greene. oh.us/253/greene-cats-public-transit) is a Demand Responsive service connecting Yellow Springs with Beavercreek, Xenia, and Fairborn with flex routes and scheduled rides. Call at least two business days in advance to schedule your transportation.

Getting Around
There are no public transportation options exclusive to Yellow Springs. Cars are your best option, though you can get to most places on foot. Since Yellow Springs is a stop on the Little Miami Scenic Trail, bicycles are another good option. Bike rentals are available at **Corner Cone Bike Rentals** (101 S. Walnut St., 937/817-0724) and **Village Cyclery** (110 Dayton St., 937/767-9330, vcbikes.com) during the warmer months.

Who Was Annie Oakley?

Popularized for modern audiences by the Irving Berlin musical *Annie Get Your Gun*, 5-foot-tall (1.5-m) Annie Oakley (1860-1926) was born Phoebe Ann Mosey north of Greenville. She was possibly as young as 15 (accounts differ) when she entered the limelight for her unbelievable shooting skills. It was at the Baughman & Butler shooting act, traveling through Cincinnati, that Oakley answered hot shot Frank Butler's $100 bet that he could outshoot anybody who dared challenge him. Oakley outshot the guy, who over time became smitten with the young woman and eventually married her.

The two lived in Cincinnati at the beginning of their marriage, residing in the Oakley neighborhood. They performed in circus acts, including the Sells Brothers Circus out of Columbus, first with Butler as the headliner and eventually the other way around. In 1885, Butler and Oakley joined Buffalo Bill to perform in his elaborate Wild West show for 16 years. They performed for royals and dignitaries from around the world, with Oakley allegedly shooting the cigarette out of Kaiser Wilhelm II's mouth. She could shoot the thin side of a playing card from 30 paces. She became the star of the show, second only to Buffalo Bill himself. Throughout her life, Oakley supported the idea of women learning to use firearms as both a hobby and means of protection. She lobbied for the ability of women to join the military, even writing a letter to President William McKinley, offering a unit of 50 female sharpshooters who would provide their own ammunition and arms should the call come. The call never came.

Oakley continued to perform off and on as she aged. She passed away in Greenville at the age of 66. Her ashes are buried at Brock Cemetery, north of town near the village of Versailles. Butler, who died 18 days later, is buried next to her.

Greenville

Lost in a sea of cornfields, Greenville is on tourists' radar for two reasons: as the hometown of gunslinger Annie Oakley and as the location of the signing of the Treaty of Greenville in 1795, a fateful document that momentarily ended frontier hostilities and pushed Native Americans out of much of Ohio. The town also boasts a handsome 19th-century main street with a good number of interesting restaurants and shops.

SIGHTS

Garst Museum

A county history museum on steroids, the **Garst Museum** (205 N. Broadway St, 937/548-5250, garstmuseum.org, 10am-4pm Tues.-Sat., 1pm-4pm Sun. Feb.-Dec., $10 adults, $9 seniors, $7 ages 6-17, free for children 5 and under) is a 35,000-square-foot (3,252-sq-m) compendium of Darke County history, with special focus on the life of Annie Oakley and the circumstances surrounding the Treaty of Greenville, which opened much of Ohio to settlement and confined Indigenous tribes to the northwest corner. Miniatures and other displays depict the original Fort Greenville (built in 1793 and no longer standing) and the tense situation on what was then the western frontier of the United States. Throughout the large rooms of the museum are odds and ends depicting the history of the county, including old-timey bicycles, mastodon fossils, and American Indian spearheads dating back to 14,000 BC. Annie Oakley's guns are on display in an exhibit devoted exclusively to her. If you're keen to explore more sites related to Annie Oakley, the museum staff can provide maps to locations around town connected to her life.

FOOD

If you're still in an Annie Oakley mood after the Garst Museum, grab an Annie Oakley burger at **The Merchant House** (406 S. Broadway St., 937/459-4405, tmh-greenville.com, 11am-10pm Tues.-Thurs., 11am-11pm Fri.-Sat., $9-19). The restaurant occupies a high-ceilinged 1876 building that used to be a department store. The menu covers typical bar-and-grill territory, including flatbreads, sandwiches, salads, pizzas, and burgers, all with decent portions and affordable prices. The sizeable draft menu pulls from a variety of local and national breweries.

The first name in cheap eats in Greenville is **Maid-Rite Sandwich Shoppe** (125 N. Broadway St., 937/548-9340, maidrite-greenville.com, 10am-10pm Mon.-Thurs., 10am-11pm Fri.-Sat., 11am-10pm Sun., $5). Open since 1934, this diner serves a small menu of loose-meat sandwiches, shakes, and chips. Super cheap beer is available, as is a gum wall for you to either contribute to or gag at. Your choice.

A cool space for a cup of coffee is **The Coffee Pot** (537 S. Broadway St. #101, 937/459-5498, ourcoffeepot.com, 6:30am-8pm Mon.-Fri., 7:30am-4pm Sat., 10am-4pm Sun.). Like The Merchant House, it was formerly a department store, and the inviting building has lots of seating and a pulley-system operating the ceiling fan. Along with coffee, offerings include Ohio-made Velvet Ice Cream, baked goods, and a small lunch menu of soups and sandwiches.

ACCOMMODATIONS

There are a handful of chain motels on the outskirts of Greenville. A lone bed-and-breakfast, **Wayman's Corner B&B** (633 Central Ave., 937/316-6074, waymanscorner. com, $99-139), has four rooms with antique and lace decor, Serta mattresses, and private bathrooms. The Rooftop Retreat room adds a Jacuzzi to the mix.

INFORMATION AND SERVICES

The **Darke County Visitor's Bureau** (421 S. Broadway St., 937/548-5158, visitdarkecounty. org, 10am-5pm Mon.-Fri.) is available to point you in the right direction toward sights, food, and essentials.

Wayne HealthCare (835 Sweitzer St., 937/548-1141) is a general medical and surgical hospital on the south end of town.

TRANSPORTATION

Greenville is 50 minutes (41 mi/66 km) northwest of Dayton via I-75, I-70, and SR 49.

Though you're unlikely to need it if you made it to Greenville on your own, the **Greenville Transit System (GTS)** (937/547-1811, cityofgreenville.org) is a shared-ride public transportation system that services the town. Call to make transportation arrangements.

Waynesville

Founded in 1797, this tiny town is, as the "Antique Capital of the Midwest," one of the state's best antiquing spots. There are over 60 antique shops and boutiques in and around Main Street. In the fall, swordplay and Shakespeare (or something like it) abound at the annual Ohio Renaissance Festival, and sauerkraut is served by the ton at the Ohio Sauerkraut Festival.

ENTERTAINMENT AND EVENTS
Festivals and Events

Running on weekends September-October, the **Ohio Renaissance Festival** (renfestival.com) is one of the largest renaissance festivals in the country. The re-created 16th-century village—30 acres in size—is chock full of ye olde this and that, turkey drumsticks,

Though not as rugged as southeastern Ohio's unglaciated Appalachia, much of Southwest Ohio is comprised of rolling hills and deep ravines cutting through a patchwork of woods and fields. The terrain trends downward the closer you get to the Ohio River, which is the lowest elevation of the state. The best hikes are a bit spread out, so it may be helpful to choose one or two and make a plan based on your choice.

yellow springs at Glen Helen Nature Preserve

- **South Gorge Trail to Narrows Trail— John Bryan State Park/Clifton Gorge State Nature Preserve** (3790 SR 370, Yellow Springs/2381 SR 343, Yellow Springs): This 5.6-mile (6.2-km) out-and-back hike starting in John Bryan State Park and connecting to Clifton Gorge State Nature Preserve takes you through a weathered limestone gorge, past trickling waterfalls and rock formations, and to the top of the gorge when the Little Miami River becomes a little too big for its britches. The path is, for the most part, an easy one, minus the climb out of the gorge, which is moderately difficult. Plan your time accordingly so you can eat lunch at the historic **Clifton Mill** (75 Water St., Clifton, 937/767-5501, cliftonmill.com) before turning around and heading back the way you came. Plan for 3-4 hours, or longer if you grab lunch.

- **Inman Trail/Lower and Upper Birch Creek Trails/Talus Trail—Glen Helen Nature Preserve** (405 Corry St., Yellow Springs): This scenic preserve is only a couple of miles from John Bryan State Park. The trails here are pretty intertwined, and thus customizable. Starting at the Inman Trailhead and doing the **Inman Trail** loop (1.2-mi/1.9-km loop) takes

jousting tournaments, and irreverent shows. Era-appropriate costumes are encouraged, and plenty of apparel and gifts are for sale; prices are a bit steep.

Hundreds of thousands of people descend upon Waynesville in mid-October for the **Ohio Sauerkraut Festival** (sauerkrautfestival.waynesvilleohio.com), which takes over Main Street with over 450 craft booths and food vendors. Throughout the festival weekend, over seven tons of sauerkraut are served.

RECREATION
Caesar Creek State Park
One of the state's best state parks for aquatic adventures, **Caesar Creek State Park** (8570 SR 73, 513/897-3055, ohiodnr.gov, dawn-dusk daily, free) is a 3,741-acre natural playground surrounding Caesar Creek Lake, an artificial lake created in the 1970s. Five boat ramps and a marina are available around the lake, which does not have a restriction on horsepower. There are ample camping opportunities as well. A 1,300-foot (396-m) swimming beach sits on the north shore of the lake. Not interested in the water? There are 20 hiking, mountain biking, and bridle trails that circle the lake, ranging from moderate to difficult. The rock here is some of the oldest in the state, making the dry spillway for the dam a unique spot to search for fossils, which you can take home (pick up a free permit at the visitors center). Other attractions include a nature center and the Pioneer Village, a hodgepodge of 18th- and early-19th-century log cabins and other buildings that were relocated here for preservation.

you past the yellow springs (more orange-ish, really) for which the town is named, as well as a waterfall and Hopewell culture mound. Extend the loop by heading south on the Lower Birch Creek Trail (0.7 mi/1.1 km one-way) and then the Upper Birch Creek Trail (0.7 mi/1.1 km one-way), which takes you to a covered bridge down a short spur (0.2 mi/0.3 km one-way) across Grinnell Road. Head back north to where you started via the Talus Trail (1.4 mi/2.3 km one-way) past dolomite rock cliffs. The entire loop is a mostly flat and easy-to-moderate 4.4 miles (7.1 km), taking approximately 2 hours.

- Fort Trail to Gorge Trail Loop—Fort Hill Earthworks and Nature Preserve (13614 Fort Hill Rd., Hillsboro): This hilly, moderate-to-difficult trek follows a stone and earthen-walled Hopewell culture hilltop enclosure along the Fort Trail (2.2-mi/3.5-km loop). You'll loop back to the parking lot on the Fort Trail, or you can elect to extend the loop 1.4 miles (2.3 km) in via the Gorge Trail (3 mi/4.8 km one-way), which follows Baker Fork past rock formations and overhangs and passes right through an old log cabin. This larger loop is 4.4 miles (7.1 km). This is some of Ohio's most pristine forest, and there are plenty of spring wildflowers. Plan on about 2 hours.

- Buzzardroost Rock Trail—Edge of Appalachia Nature Preserve (4274 Waggoner Riffle Rd., West Union): The trailhead for the moderately difficult Buzzardroost Rock Trail is off SR 125. It's an out-and-back trail (4.4 mi/7.1 km round-trip), past cliffs, rock formations, and prairie. The trail ends at a steep overlook of the Ohio Brush Creek valley. There aren't too many overlooks in Ohio this high up, making this a prime spot for fall colors. Plan on 2-3 hours.

- Perimeter Trail—Caesar Creek State Park (8570 SR 73, Waynesville): There's a lot to the Perimeter Trail (5 mi/8.1 km round-trip), but for the best bits start at Flat Fork Picnic Area and head east away from the dam. Through the woods you'll find a waterfall, a swinging bridge, and the dry rock bed of a river spillway, where you may encounter fossils. Take the trail to the Pioneer Village, a collection of 200-year-old cabins plucked from the area for preservation, and turn back the way you came. Plan on 2-3 hours.

SHOPPING
Antique Shopping

Lilly's Corner Mall (105 S. Main St., 513/897-0388, lillys-corner-mall.business.site, 11:30am-5pm Tues.-Sat., noon-5pm Sun.) is one of the larger antique stops in town, with over 7,000 square feet (650 sq m) and 28 antique and vintage shops. Built in 1917, the building housed Waynesville's first auto dealership and movie theater.

If you're crafty, you'd better head to Village Salvage (85 S. Main St., 513/914-4177, villagesalvage.com, 11am-5pm Mon.-Sat., noon-5pm Sun.). Though this home improvement store specializes in lock repair for old houses, it also has quite the stock of vintage hardware, lighting, and stained glass salvaged from old homes and factories.

Upcycled and repurposed home decor and gifts are the specialty at American Pie (43. S. Main St., 513/897-7437, 11am-4pm Tues.-Fri., 10am-5pm Sat., noon-4pm Sun.). This family-owned shop is full of one-of-a-kind "rustic refined" pieces. It's also the flagship store for Jason Thomas Designs, a handcrafted furniture line.

FOOD

As its name suggests, Village Family Restaurant (144 S. Main St., 513/897-8835, villagefamilyrestaurant.com, 7am-9pm Mon.-Fri., 7:30am-9pm Sat., 8am-9pm Sun., $8-12) is an unfussy country diner offering an inexpensive selection of hot meals, sandwiches, salads, and pizza. Daily specials such as fried catfish and barbecued ribs spice things up. The restaurant is known for its peanut butter pie.

A touch more sophisticated is **Cobblestone Village Café and Interiors** (10 N. Main St., 513/897-0021, cobblestonevillageandcafe.com, 11am-3:30pm Tues.-Sun., $9-16), with a simple menu of French-inspired sandwiches, salads, and chef specialties you probably weren't expecting to find in Waynesville. The well-lit interior and wood cathedral ceilings are a comforting respite, whatever the weather. The extensive gift shop features mostly interior decor items that'll match the antiques you find in town.

ACCOMMODATIONS

There's not a lot going in Waynesville during the evening, which may be why there are few accommodations options. Waynesville is also conveniently located between Dayton, Cincinnati, and Columbus and only a few minutes from two interstate highways, making this an easy day trip for many.

No one would call the **Creekwood Motel** (401 S. Main St., 513/897-1000, creekwoodmotel.com, $70) fancy, but it's a basic and clean motel option close to the shops and restaurants. It's also a convenient stop for weary travelers on the Little Miami Scenic Trail. Note that check-in and check-out must

occur during office hours, which are roughly 7am-7:30pm.

CAMPING

Caesar Creek State Park (8570 SR 73, 513/897-3055, parks.ohiodnr.gov) offers 252 electric sites, 35 full-hookup sites, and six group camp sites together accommodating both tents and RVs. Rates start at $29.

INFORMATION AND SERVICES

Waynesville Urgent Care (4353 E. SR 73 #150, 513/855-4336, waynesvilleuc.com) is available for minor needs. Otherwise, the closest major hospitals to Waynesville are in Lebanon, Middletown, and Dayton. The closest are **Miami Valley Hospital South** (2400 Miami Valley Dr., Centerville, 937/438-2400) in a Dayton suburb to the north and Lebanon's **TriHealth Bethesda Arrow Springs** (100 Arrow Springs Blvd., Lebanon, 513/282-7000) to the southwest.

TRANSPORTATION

Waynesville is at the junction of US-42 and SR 73, 8.5 miles (13.7 km) west of I-71 and 11 miles (17.7 km) east of I-75. From Dayton, take US-35 east to US-42 south, for a drive of just over 30

Caesar Creek State Park

minutes total (28 mi/45 km). Waynesville is 45 minutes (40 mi/64 km) northeast of Cincinnati via I-71 north to SR 48 north to US-42 north. From Columbus, Waynesville is just over an hour's drive (71 mi/114 km) via I-71 south to SR 73 west. There are no public transportation options to the town.

Pretty much anything you want to see in Waynesville, other than Caesar Creek State Park, is along walkable Main Street. Otherwise, a car is your best bet. There is plenty of on-street parking in town.

Lebanon

Historic Lebanon, today a growing town of about 20,000, was a stagecoach and railroad stop for the likes of Mark Twain, Charles Dickens, and too many presidents to name, all coming to stay at the famous Golden Lamb, Ohio's oldest inn. Though the Golden Lamb is undoubtedly the star, visitors will find a quaint town center with antique and decor shops, bookstores, cafés, and more, in buildings pushing or over 200 years old. Ancient earthworks and plentiful recreation abound on the periphery, and the town is a stone's toss from Kings Island amusement park, just off I-71 in the Cincinnati suburbs. Lebanon is well-connected by major roads, making this an interesting alternative base for exploring the area.

SIGHTS AND RECREATION
Fort Ancient Earthworks and Nature Preserve

Heading along SR 350 past rural homesteads east of Lebanon, you may suddenly find yourself driving through what appears to be an earthen gate to some long-forgotten fortress. This is the entrance to **Fort Ancient Earthworks and Nature Preserve** (6123 SR 350, Oregonia, 800/286-8904, fortancient.org, 10am-5pm Wed.-Sat., noon-5pm Sun. Apr.-Nov., 10am-5pm Sat., noon-5pm Sun. Dec.-Mar., museum and park $7 adults, $6 seniors and youth, grounds only $8 per car), one of the most impressive earthworks in the state. Embankments extending 3.5 miles (5.6 km) are what remain of a massive 2,000-year-old Hopewell culture complex situated 235 feet (72 m) above the Little Miami River. Trees now grow atop the mounds, so this is one of the few Ohio sites that benefits from a winter viewing, when the leaves are less concealing. Gaps in the walls align with key lunar and solar events, which suggest that rather than a military fort, this enclosure was more ceremonial in nature and likely a regional destination for Native Americans across the eastern part of the continent. Smaller conical mounds and stone circles dot the interior, which can be driven through. Several hiking paths offer alternative vantages on the mounds, and a 0.1-mile (0.2-km) connector trail makes the steep descent to the Little Miami Scenic Trail. The museum out front chronologically lays out the history of Native Americans in Ohio, with informative displays of pottery, ornaments, tools, and weapons discovered in Ohio's archaeological sites. Shelters and tables scattered throughout the plateau encourage picnics amid the natural scenery.

Lebanon Mason Monroe Railroad

The historic **Lebanon Mason Monroe Railroad** (16 E. South St., 513/933-8022, lebanonrr.com, schedules and prices vary) offers themed train rides, primarily for children, complete with costumed characters and staff members. A few adult-themed itineraries exist as well, including a murder mystery and a pizza-and-beer trip. The Turtle Creek Valley Flyer is the basic non-themed tour, where the conductor provides historical context about the railroad. Most trips last 1.25 hours and take passengers through rural Warren County's woods, hills, and rivers. The train offers two car choices: the climate-controlled deluxe class with reclining seats or the heated but not air-conditioned Lackawanna coach class. Both allow access to the Queen City Tavern dining car, which includes concessions and gifts.

Glendower Historic Mansion

Atop a hill in a neighborhood of stately 19th- and early-20th-century homes is the older and statelier **Glendower Historic Mansion** (105 Cincinnati Ave., 513/932-1817, wchsmuseum. org/glendower, noon-4pm Fri.-Sun. June-Labor Day and Dec., $10 adults, $6 students). This 1836 Greek Revival home once belonged to a wealthy area merchant. Tour guides interpret the 14 elegant rooms and their furnishings. Though you can reach the mansion from Orchard Avenue via a private alley, the far better view coming in is from the main entrance off Cincinnati Avenue. Visitors in December can come see the house fully decked out for Christmas. Admission is cash only. The house is full of stairs, so this attraction is not wheelchair-accessible at present, though funds are being raised to improve accessibility.

FOOD

The **Black Horse Tavern** (27 S. Broad St., 513/932-5065, goldenlamb.com/dine, 11am-9pm Mon.-Sat., noon-8pm Sun., $14-38), on the ground floor of The Golden Lamb inn, serves the same menu as the hotel's private dining rooms and is the nicest place in town for dinner, offering sandwiches, salads, hamburgers, and entrées of the meat-and-potatoes variety with an upscale flourish in a historic setting.

The Village Parlor (22 S. Broadway St., 513/932-6918, villageparlor.com, 11am-8pm Sun.-Thurs., 11am-9pm Fri.-Sat., $5-12) is a classic, affordable lunch or dinner choice. Open since 1969, The Village Parlor preserves the town's soda fountain and ice cream parlor. Sandwiches dominate the menu—but leave

room for ice cream. The restaurant was used as a location shoot for the films *Harper Valley, PTA,* and *Milk Money.*

Lot No. 1 (9 E. Main St., 513/836-3103, 7:30am-6pm Mon.-Fri., 8am-6pm Sat., noon-6pm Sun.) is a terrific coffee shop inside the town's oldest building, built between 1807 and 1814. Order your coffee downstairs and perhaps peruse the sizeable gift shop, complete with specialty mugs, and then head upstairs to the cozy seating space featuring a fireplace. There's an outdoor patio in the back as well.

For Asian cuisine, check out **Roll On In** (44 E. Mulberry St., 513/228-0069, rollonin.com, 11am-9pm daily, $7-14) for hibachi bowls, sticky rice bowls, salads, and the specialty: sushi burritos. There are menu options, or you can build your own. A small selection of craft brews is available, as well as a large selection of side dishes.

ACCOMMODATIONS

There are no chain hotels in Lebanon, but a small list of interesting historic inns, bed-and-breakfasts, and independent motels.

Anchoring downtown with its Italianate facade and portico, ★ **The Golden Lamb** (27 S. Broad St., 513/932-5065, goldenlamb.com, $129-170) is the first word in accommodations in Lebanon. Open since 1803, the Golden Lamb is not only Ohio's oldest inn, it's the state's oldest continuously operating business. The owners added floors to the building as the inn's success grew, first as a stagecoach stop and then as a railroad inn. Charles Dickens stayed here in 1842, as did Mark Twain in 1856. Too many presidents and politicians to name have stayed the night throughout the decades. There are also frequent reports of paranormal activity from resident ghosts. The rooms, the lobby, and the popular Black Horse Tavern maintain a 19th-century ambience with period furniture and decor.

The Golden Lamb's not the only game in town. **Hardy's Bed and Breakfast Suites** (212 Wright Ave., 513/932-3266, hardysproperties.com, $112-140), in a pink Victorian house within walking distance of downtown

Lebanon, offers four suites. Extended-stay rates are available.

The best independent motel option is **Shaker Inn** (600 Cincinnati Ave., 513/932-7575, shakerinnmotel.com, $65-130), an affordable alternative to the more historic options in the middle of town. Rooms are basic and vary from single units to family suites. Complimentary juice, coffee, and pastries are available, as is a pool in the summer months.

INFORMATION AND SERVICES

CareFirst Urgent Care (1000 Columbus Ave., Ste. B, 513/934-7171) is the town's only urgent care facility. **Bethesda Medical Center** (100 Arrow Springs Blvd., 513/282-7000) is a full-service hospital with emergency care.

TRANSPORTATION

Lebanon is a 40-minute drive (35 mi/56 km) north from Cincinnati via either I-71 or I-75. Take I-71 north to SR 48 north, or I-75 north to SR 63 east. From Dayton, it's a similar 40-minute (27 mi/43 km) drive south via I-75 and SR 123. There's no bus service to Lebanon.

There are no public transportation options in Lebanon, so a car is your best bet.

Hamilton

Founded as a fort in 1791 (and named after then-Secretary of the Treasury Alexander Hamilton), Hamilton is a former industrial city that has managed to escape the heavy population loss of its peers. The city has invested heavily in the arts and in conserving its cultural heritage, with a number of well-preserved 19th-century homes and the unique Pyramid Hill Sculpture Park and Museum. A small but attractive downtown of 19th- and early-20th-century buildings is anchored by the 1889 Butler County Courthouse, which is on the National Register of Historic Places, and the impressive Butler County Soldiers Monument dedicated in 1906 to commemorate the Civil War.

SIGHTS
★ Pyramid Hill Sculpture Park and Museum

One of the most unique parks in Ohio is the **Pyramid Hill Sculpture Park and Museum** (1763 Hamilton Cleves Rd., 513/868-1234, pyramidhill.org, 8am-5pm daily, $8 adults, $3 children 6-12, free for children 5 and under). More than 300 acres, this scenic park with woods, hills, and over 80 contemporary outdoor sculptures by national artists is designed to be enjoyed either by car, foot, or rentable "ArtCart" golf carts. Paved roads, paved trails, and unpaved trails alike zigzag through the grounds. Most of the sculptures are visible from the Gallery Loop road. Some of the hills are quite steep so, unless you're game for a hike, a set of wheels is probably for the best. ArtCarts are available on a first-come, first-served basis and can be rented at the visitors center. Inside the park and included with admission is the **Ancient Sculpture Museum** (noon-5pm daily), an ancient Roman-styled building with some odds and ends of antiquity. Picnics with outside food are encouraged, though there are some snacks available in the gift shop at the visitors center.

FOOD

When it comes to food, Hamilton is a place of budget-friendly hometown favorites. Open since 1938, **Jolly's Drive-In** (210 N. Erie Blvd., 513/894-7541, 11am-9:30pm Sun.-Wed., 11am-10pm Thurs.-Sat., $5-10) is an old-school drive in with hamburgers, hot dogs, and root beer by the gallon. The prices are hard to beat. A second location is on the far northwestern side of town.

Nearly as old as Jolly's Drive-In is **Hyde's Restaurant** (130 S. Erie Blvd., 513/892-1287, hydespies.com, 6:30am-9pm Mon.-Sat., 7:30am-9pm Sun., $5-11), operating since 1946. You'll find all your favorite diner dishes and then some, but what keeps people coming back is the pie. Daily pie and dessert specials rotate throughout the week. The aesthetic is as unpretentious as the menu, with old benches and hanging lights.

Serving comfort food since 2014 is **High Street Café** (250 High St., 513/805-7428, highstcafe.com, 7am-2:30pm Sun.-Fri., $6-10). This easygoing restaurant in the heart of downtown serves a straightforward menu of breakfast staples, soups, salads, and sandwiches. The bakery churns out impossible-to-ignore cookies, cakes, and pies, and the whole place is decked out in fun decor and stuff to buy for your kitchen.

ACCOMMODATIONS

There are a handful of lodging options in Hamilton itself. Otherwise, your best bet is to stay closer to Dayton or the Cincinnati outerbelt. The lone chain hotel in town is **Courtyard by Marriott Hamilton** (1 Riverfront Plaza, 513/896-6200, marriott.com, $183-265), which sits conveniently on the riverfront in downtown Hamilton, steps away from restaurants. This contemporary hotel includes spacious rooms and an indoor pool.

For a more unique option, try the old-timey **Rossville Inn** (117 S. B St., 513/868-1984, rossvilleinn.com, $120-159), a pre-Civil War house turned bed-and-breakfast with five guest rooms, each with a private bathroom (and one with a Jacuzzi). The inn, with its twisty stairs, billiards parlor, and peaceful backyard, is one block away from the Main Street Bridge and downtown.

INFORMATION AND SERVICES

The **Hamilton Welcome Center** (1 High St. #2, 513/844-8080, visithamiltonohio.com, 10am-4pm Mon.-Fri.) offers area information.

Fort Hamilton Hospital (630 Eaton Ave., 513/867-2000) is part of the highly regarded Kettering network and is closest to the center of town. There is also **TriHealth Bethesda Butler Hospital** (3125 Hamilton Mason Rd., 513/894-8888) on the east side of the city.

TRANSPORTATION
Getting There

Hamilton is a little off the beaten path, interstate-wise. Luckily, 10 miles (16.1 km) of divided highway SR 129 cuts through suburban Cincinnati to connect the center of town to I-75; it's about a 40-minute drive (35 mi/56 km) from downtown Cincinnati to Hamilton.

The nearest **Greyhound** bus station is in Oxford, which is connected to Hamilton via the BCRTA regional bus system. Hamilton is about a 50-minute drive (52 mi/84 km) from **Dayton International Airport** (DAY, 3600 Terminal Dr., 937/454-8200, flydayton.com) and about a 45-minute drive (43 mi/69 km) from **Cincinnati/Northern Kentucky International Airport** (CVG, 3087 Terminal Dr., Hebron, KY, 859/767-3151, cvgairport. com).

Getting Around

The **Butler County Regional Transit Authority (BCRTA)** (butlercountyrta. com) exists mainly to connect the cities of Hamilton, Middletown, Oxford, and Cincinnati's northern suburbs west of I-75. Most routes are $2 and can be paid with exact change. Passes are available for purchase online, on the Transit App, or at the BCRTA Administrative Office (3045 Moser Ct., 10am-3pm Mon.-Fri.).

1: The Golden Lamb inn in Lebanon 2: stone circle at Fort Ancient Earthworks and Nature Preserve 3: Ohio River waterfront in Ripley 4: John Rankin House in Ripley

Ripley

Sleepy Ripley could be, pound for pound, the most historic town in Ohio—it was a major stop on the **Underground Railroad.** Due to its large number of abolitionists, the community was known by slave holders in Kentucky as the "Hell Hole of Abolitionism." Two historic sites here—the John Rankin House and the John Parker House—encapsulate this heritage, with tours and small museums. Sitting right along the Ohio River, Ripley offers a chance to stretch your legs on a drive down the Ohio River Scenic Byway (US-52 in these parts), with its Front Street wedged between stately houses and the river itself. River traffic and the surrounding hills make for a serene backdrop to contemplate what it took for enslaved people to cross the river over 150 years ago.

SIGHTS

John Rankin House

Overlooking a commanding view of Ripley and the Ohio River is the brick **John Rankin House** (6152 Rankin Hill Rd., 937/392-4044, ohiohistory.org, 10am-4pm Wed.-Sat., noon-4pm Sun. Apr.-Oct., $6 adults, $3 students and children). Reverend Rankin was an early abolitionist and used his farm and modest home as a station on the Underground Railroad. Over the course of 40 years, he and his family of 13 children managed to aid over 2,000 freedom seekers. Among those who sought shelter here was Eliza Harris, whose harrowing account of crossing the Ohio River from Kentucky was immortalized in Harriet Beecher Stowe's novel *Uncle Tom's Cabin*. Guided tours of the house, appointed with era-appropriate furniture, run every hour on the hour (the last leaves at 3pm) from the small visitors center, which houses a couple of displays about the family, as well as a gift shop. It costs nothing, however, to walk the grounds and take in the lovely vista.

John Parker House

The other major abolitionist in town was entrepreneur John Parker. The two-story **John Parker House** (300 N. Front St., 937/392-4188, johnparkerhouse.net, 10am-5pm Fri.-Sat., 1pm-5pm Sun. May-Oct. or by appt. year-round, $5 adults, $3 children) celebrates the contributions Parker, formerly enslaved himself, made to the Underground Railroad as a conductor, as well as to the local economy. With a $1,000 bounty on his head, he ventured into Kentucky numerous times to escort freedom seekers to Ripley. An avid inventor, Parker patented improvements to the tobacco press and soil pulverizer and ran a successful foundry. Artwork depicts his journey from an enslaved youth to a patent-holding businessman. Upstairs, informative displays cover more about his life's pursuits and the Underground Railroad. The house sits near the river and is a good starting point for a walk along the riverside park.

FOOD

Homey **Cohearts Riverhouse** (18 N. Front St., 937/392-4819, 11:30am-9pm Thurs.-Sat., 11:30am-7pm Sun., $5-15) serves an unfussy menu of sandwiches, soups, salads, and a handful of hot dishes. The restaurant is right on the river; to enjoy the scenery, sit on the porch rather than the dining room, or order takeout and grab a bench near the river.

INFORMATION AND SERVICES

The best place to get information about the area is the **John Rankin House visitors center** (6152 Rankin Hill Rd.).

The nearest major medical facilities are actually down the river in Maysville, Kentucky. The **Fast Pace Health Urgent Care Center** (420 Martin Luther King Hwy., Maysville, KY, 606/375-4817, 8am-8pm Mon.-Sat., 1pm-5pm

President Grant's Stomping Grounds

US Grant Boyhood Home

This area of Ohio lays claim to both the birthplace and childhood home of Ulysses S. Grant, 18th president of the United States. If you're passing through toward Ripley or headed east on SR 32 to cut across the southern part of the state, and you happen to appreciate history, these stops may be worth your time.

Grant's Birthplace State Memorial (1551 SR 232, Point Pleasant, 513/497-0492, ohiohistory.org, 10am-5pm Wed.-Sat., 1pm-5pm Sun. May-Sept., $3 adults, $2 seniors, $1.50 children 6-12) is the tiny Point Pleasant cottage that the Grant family lived in when little Hiram Ulysses was born in 1822 (he later changed his name while at West Point). There's no grand estate or lush gardens here, just evidence of the humble beginnings of a two-term president. Period furnishings depict the modest life of the family at the time. The Grant Birthplace is west of Ripley right off the Ohio River Scenic Byway, and it's an easy stop on the way to or from Ripley.

In Georgetown, 30 minutes (23 mi/37 km) east of Point Pleasant and 17 minutes (13 mi/20.9 km) north of Ripley, is the **US Grant Boyhood Home** (219 E. Grant Ave. #1311, Georgetown, 937/378-3087, usgrantboyhoodhome.org, noon-5pm Wed.-Sun. May-Oct., $5 adults, $3 children). This two-story brick house is quite an upgrade from the cottage by the river, but still reflective of the man's rural early life. The interior, which underwent a $1.4 million restoration in 2011, looks much as it did during Grant's early days and displays furnishings and other memorabilia belonging to the family, including binoculars Grant used as a Union general during the Civil War. An animatronic 15-year-old Grant is on hand to explain more about his life in the small town. The old **schoolhouse,** also simple, is six blocks away at 508 S. Water Street. Admission covers both the home and schoolhouse. Tours in both locations are run ad hoc as visitors arrive, led by dutiful staff members. The weekend-long **Grant Days** is an event held at the end of April throughout town and celebrates the life of Grant with lectures, historical displays, and military reenactments.

Sun.) and the **Meadowview Regional Hospital** (929 Medical Park Dr., Maysville, KY, 606/759-5311) are both about a 15- to 20-minute drive from town.

TRANSPORTATION

Ripley is an hour's drive (52 mi/84 km) east of Cincinnati via SR 52. There is no public transportation here, so a car is your best option.

Peebles

There are few compelling reasons to stick around tiny Peebles except to gas up and grab a bite to eat before continuing on empty country roads. So what brings people to the area? The largest effigy mound in North America.

SIGHTS

★ Serpent Mound Historical Site

Historians are unsure who built the 1,300-foot (396-m) **Serpent Mound** (3850 SR 73, 800/752-2757, ohiohistory.org, 10am-4pm daily, free entry, $8 parking fee), a National Historic Landmark north of Peebles. The original assumption was that the Adena culture built the effigy mound over 2,000 years ago, based on the presence of an Adena burial mound nearby. However, separate carbon-dating studies have yielded conflicting results, with some supporting the Adena theory and others suggesting the Serpent Mound was built more recently, roughly 900 years ago, by the Fort Ancient culture. Either way, the mound was likely built for ceremonial purposes and already a mystery to the Indigenous population when white settlers arrived in the area.

The mound's clear, undulating serpentine shape makes this the most unusual and interesting mound in Ohio, and perhaps the United States. A paved path orbits the grassy mound and an observation tower allows visitors to get a more comprehensive look, though for a full picture you'll need to find an aerial shot. A small, somewhat dated museum behind the gift shop depicts what life was like for the Adena people and the process of building a burial mound (three of which remain on the park grounds). Ample picnic tables are available for a sit and a meal among the ancient remnants of these fascinating cultures. Note that the park's roads can be impassable in snow and ice, though you're welcome to park by the gate and walk 0.4 mile (0.6 km) to the mound. The mound is up for consideration as a UNESCO World Heritage Site.

House of Phacops

Between Peebles and the Serpent Mound is the quirky **House of Phacops** (29894 SR 41, 937/205-3810, alternateuniverserockshop.com, call for hours). Proprietor Thomas Johnson runs this roadside rock-and-fossil shop, with a collection of trilobites (horseshoe crab-looking fossils) that is affiliated with the Smithsonian Institution and includes the largest-known specimen. The shop's minerals, carvings, and herbs celebrate the fact that it sits atop a deep fault line, which the shop proclaims emits a flow of positive energy.

FOOD

White Star Restaurant (38 N. Main St., 937/587-5750, 6am-7pm Mon.-Sat., 7am-3pm Sun., $6-14) offers simple meals in a simple setting. Rows of wooden tables flanked by booths on either side accommodate families and regulars eating country diner food at reasonable prices.

Small-batch coffee roaster **The Greene Beanery** (25675 SR 41, 937/798-4023, greenebeanery.com, 7am-5pm Mon.-Fri., 8am-2pm Sat.) catches you off guard as you enter town from the south side. This blue country house offers an enticing porch or a warm, hardwood interior to enjoy your java. The café also offers a small menu of sandwiches.

INFORMATION AND SERVICES

The **Adams County Travel and Visitors Bureau** (509 E. Main St., West Union, 937/544-5639, adamscountytravel.com, 9am-1pm Mon.-Fri.) is located in West Union, 20 minutes south of Peebles, and provides information about local attractions, activities, and restaurants. You'll also find the nearest urgent care in West Union, the **SOMC West Union Family Health Center** (90 CIC Blvd., West Union, 937/544-8989, somc.org, 8am-8pm daily). The nearest hospital is **Adams County Regional Medical Center** (230 Medical Center Dr., Seaman, 937/386-3400).

TRANSPORTATION

Peebles is just over an hour (69 mi/111 km) east of Cincinnati via SR 32. The town is served by a **Greyhound** (greyhound.com) bus stop right off SR 32 at 25191 SR 41, though you'll have to purchase your ticket online or elsewhere as there's no ticket service here. **Barons Bus** (baronsbus.com) and **GoBus** (ridegobus.com) also utilize the stop.

Long-distance Uber and Lyft are really the only options for getting around. You'd be better served by driving yourself.

Bainbridge

Teensy Bainbridge finds itself in the middle of a wealth of hiking and other recreational opportunities. There's not much to the town, but it's the best stop nearby to find food and supplies for whatever adventure you're headed for.

SIGHTS AND RECREATION

Paxton Theatre

Ohio's longest running country music show, the **Paint Valley Jamboree**, plays in historic **Paxton Theatre** (133 E. Main St., 740/634-3333), an intimate 347-seat opera house. The music show plays the second Saturday of every month and has attracted the likes of Waylon Jennings, Conway Twitty, Merle Haggard, and Loretta Lynn over the years. Other events at the theater include live gospel, bluegrass, and country performances.

Highlands Nature Sanctuary

West of town, there's plenty to see at **Highlands Nature Sanctuary** (7660 Cave Rd., 937/365-1935, arcofappalachia.org/highlands-nature-sanctuary, dawn-dusk daily, free), operated by Arc of Appalachia, a nonprofit that purchases and preserves forested land in Southern Ohio. With its bountiful wildflowers and hidden waterfalls, this is one of the best places to do springtime hiking in Ohio. The tiny **Appalachian Forest Museum** (9:30am-4:40pm daily Apr.-Oct.) serves as the primary visitors center and tells the story of deciduous forests through large oil murals. The sanctuary has 15 trails that snake out from nine trailheads into old-growth forests, unique rock formations, and the 100-foot (30-m) Rocky Fork Gorge. Some of the shortest yet most spectacular hikes leave from the museum trailhead (open during museum hours), including the 0.5-mile (0.8-km) one-way **Valley of the Ancients trail**, a moderately difficult path that passes limestone grottoes (bring a flashlight or cell phone to explore!) as you descend to the riverbed, surrounded by patches of trillium in early spring. Elsewhere, the 2-mile (3.2-km) **Kamelands Trail** is a loop that includes an optional spur that descends to the Rocky Fork Gorge floor. Trails are narrow, so wearing long pants is a good idea. The sanctuary also offers a handful of affordable lodging options, including cabins and unusual dome houses. Note that Cave Road, which connects many of the trailheads and lodges, is narrow and largely unpaved.

Fort Hill Earthworks and Nature Preserve

Southwest of town and also operated by Arc of Appalachia is the **Fort Hill Earthworks and Nature Preserve** (13614 Fort Hill Rd., Hillsboro, 800/283-8905, arcofappalachia.org/fort-hill, dawn-dusk daily, free), encompassing over 1,300 acres preserving mature forests and a 2,000-year-old earthen-walled fort atop a flat ridge. Constructed by the Hopewell culture and likely used for ceremonial or religious purposes rather than war, the fort is accessible by hiking the moderate 2.2-mile (3.5-km) **Fort Trail loop,** which connects to the park's other trails if you'd like to extend your hike through additional rock formations and forests. Along the trails, old-growth forests protect a number of wildflowers and fungi representing an unusually high amount of biodiversity for Ohio. A small education center provides interpretive exhibits on the area's geological and archaeological features.

Paint Creek State Park

5,600-acre **Paint Creek State Park** (280 Taylor Rd., 937/981-7061, ohiodnr.gov, dawn-dusk daily, free) west of Bainbridge straddles the transition between flat Ohio and hilly, unglaciated Ohio. The park surrounds a large reservoir and has a little bit of everything, including a campground, a marina, a sand beach, bridle trails, a disc golf course, and hiking trails. The area behind the Paint Creek dam is a popular fishing spot.

FOOD

The Paxton Restaurant (108 W. Main St., 740/634-2922, thepaxtonrestaurant.com, 6am-8pm Mon.-Sat., 7am-3pm Sun., $6-12) operates out of a Sunoco gas station, but is a clean, inexpensive place to enjoy country diner food after a weekend of roughing it in the woods. Dessert includes homemade pies and "Possibly the World's Greatest Cheesecake" from local Mystical Cheesecake.

The seafood meals come with hush puppies, a rarity this far north.

ACCOMMODATIONS AND CAMPING

There are no accommodations in town; most people are coming to these parts to camp. Highlands Nature Sanctuary and Paint Creek State Park offer camping grounds and/or cabins on grounds.

Highlands Nature Sanctuary (7660 Cave Rd., 937/365-1935, arcofappalachia.org/highlands-nature-sanctuary, $95-155) features a motley assortment of cabins, dome house cottages, and suites. A minimum two-night stay is required.

Paint Creek State Park (280 Taylor Rd., 937/981-7061, ohiodnr.gov) has nearly 200 campsites for tents and RVs, and a handful of cabins and full-hookup sites. Rates start at $28.

INFORMATION AND SERVICES

The **Visitors Bureau of Highland County** (130 S. High St., Hillsboro, 937/393-1111, visithighlandcounty.com) and the **Ross-Chillicothe Convention and Visitors Bureau** (230 N. Plaza Blvd., Chillicothe, 740/702-7677, visitchillicotheohio.com, 8:30am-5pm Mon.-Fri.) are on either side of Bainbridge near SR 50 and can provide visitor information on the wider region.

The closest medical facilities to Bainbridge are in Greenfield, 12 miles (19.3 km) north, at **Adena Greenfield Medical Center** (550 Mirabeau St., Greenfield, 937/981-9400).

TRANSPORTATION

Bainbridge is a 90-minute drive (76 mi/122 km) east of Cincinnati via SR 50 and 80 minutes (72 mi/116 km) southeast of Dayton via US-35 and SR 41. You will need a car to get to Bainbridge.

The nearest taxi companies are in Chillicothe, 23 miles (37 km) away, including **Chillicothe Cab** (740/775-7433).

1: Serpent Mound Historical Site in Peebles **2:** Paint Creek State Park

Appalachian Foothills

Welcome to Ohio's hinterland.

The unglaciated Appalachian plateau of southeast Ohio is by far the state's most rugged corner, with unending hills, winding roads, deep woods, and a lack of major cities (the largest in the area, college town Athens, clocks in at about 24,000 people). Like Cincinnati and Southwest Ohio, this region includes much of Ohio's earliest settled history. River town Marietta was the first American settlement in the Northwest Territory, established by Revolutionary War veterans in 1787. Likewise, Ohio University was the territory's first university, founded in 1803. Predating them are missionary villages in the New Philadelphia area—Schoenbrunn and Gnadenhutten—around during the Revolutionary War. Farther west is Chillicothe, the state's

Highlights

Look for ★ to find recommended sights, activities, dining, and lodging.

★ Hop in a safari-style truck at **The Wilds** conservation center and travel through open grasslands, where you'll spot giraffes, rhinos, bison, and more (page 348).

★ Do a little bit of everything at **Salt Fork State Park,** which comes with boating, hiking, golf, and a popular lodge (page 349).

★ Hike past recess caves, cliffs, and waterfalls at **Hocking Hills State Park** (page 352).

★ Sweat on hiking trails by day and hit brew-pubs by night in progressive **Athens,** home to the oldest university in Ohio (page 359).

★ Dive into history in **Marietta,** the Northwest Territory's first U.S. settlement, at the confluence of the Muskingum and Ohio Rivers (page 365).

★ Learn about Ohio's ancient mound builders at the **Hopewell Culture National Historical Park** (page 371).

★ Tour the **Adena Mansion and Gardens Historic Site,** which includes a grand 1807 house designed by the "father of American architecture" (page 372).

Appalachian Foothills

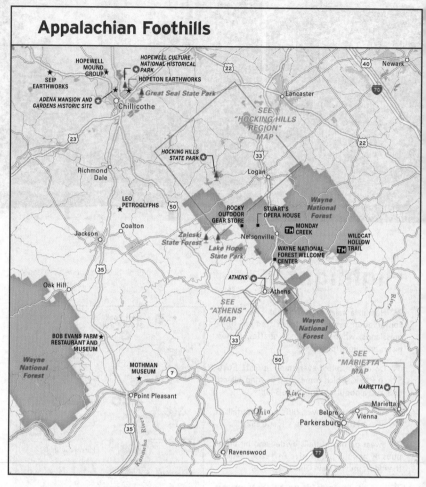

Newark

Hopewell Culture National Historical Park

Hopeton Earthworks

Hopewell Mound Group

★ Seip Earthworks

★ Adena Mansion and Gardens Historic Site

Great Seal State Park

Chillicothe

Lancaster

SEE "HOCKING HILLS REGION" MAP

Richmond Dale

Hocking Hills State Park

Logan

★ Leo Petroglyphs

Rocky Outdoor Gear Store

Stuart's Opera House

Wayne National Forest

Coalton

Jackson

Zaleski State Forest

Monday Creek

Nelsonville

Lake Hope State Park

Wildcat Hollow Trail

Wayne National Forest Welcome Center

Oak Hill

ATHENS

Athens

SEE "ATHENS" MAP

★ Bob Evans Farm Restaurant and Museum

Wayne National Forest

Wayne National Forest

★ Mothman Museum

SEE "MARIETTA" MAP

MARIETTA

Point Pleasant

Marietta

Belpre

Vienna

Parkersburg

Ohio River

Kanawha River

Ravenswood

first capital and home to Hopewell Culture National Historical Park and the Adena Mansion and Gardens, a seemingly misplaced East Coast Federal-style estate designed by one of the U.S. Capitol's architects.

History aside, Appalachian Ohio features arguably the state's greatest density of recreational fun: state parks, a national forest, and nature preserves offer hundreds of miles of hiking through gorges, cliffs, and forests.

There is an unlimited number of camping, cabin, and other accommodation options, and a growing number of adventure sport parks to supplement your hiking adrenaline boost. The area's rivers—the Ohio, Muskingum, and Hocking among them—present agreeable options for paddling tours via canoe, kayak, or raft.

In short, you've found Ohio's outdoor paradise.

Previous: Ash Cave in Hocking Hills State Park; Ernest Warther Museum and Gardens in Dover; Cutler Hall at Ohio University in Athens.

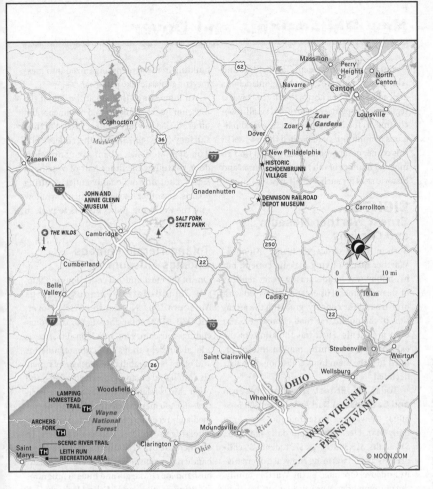

PLANNING YOUR TIME

There are unlimited recreational choices in this corner of Ohio. If your primary goal is to sample trails and maybe spend a day or two on a lake, decide which parks are most appealing and then choose a base from there. The Hocking Hills region and Athens are the most centrally located and nearest the most options in terms of Appalachian Ohio's attractions. Athens is particularly convenient, with abundant recreation options and easy connections to Marietta or Chillicothe. New Philadelphia, Cambridge, and Steubenville lie a bit farther from this cluster of state parks, national forestlands, and historical towns.

The Hocking Hills region is one of Ohio's most popular summer and fall destinations, so plan ahead. Making weekend reservations for accommodations and campgrounds months ahead of time is a good idea.

This part of Ohio is by far the hilliest, so make sure your car is prepared for constantly climbing up and down steep grades. While there's something to appreciate about this region in every season, keep ice in mind during the winter.

New Philadelphia and Dover

About halfway between Cambridge and Akron on I-77 are the city of New Philadelphia and, adjoined to the north, the city of Dover, a region rich in pioneer history and small-town charms. In the late 18th century, several religious communities established themselves in this corner of the woods. Today you'll find an unusual number of interesting museums and historic sites for such a small area.

SIGHTS
Ernest Warther Museum and Gardens

Born in 1885, woodcarver Ernest "Mooney" Warther made a living making cutlery, but his hobby was hand-carving exact replicas of steam engines. His creations traveled with him around the country, grabbing the attention of the public, railroad companies, and even presidents. Such was the allure of the carvings that the Smithsonian Institution offered to place them in its collection. Warther declined.

Today, the **Ernest Warther Museum and Gardens** (331 Karl Ave., Dover, 330/505-6003, thewarthermuseum.com, 9am-5pm daily Mar.-Dec., 10am-4pm daily Jan.-Feb., $15 adults, $13.50 seniors, $7 students, $5 children) is a heartwarming showcase of creativity and love. Operated by the Warther family, the museum houses nearly 80 years' worth of hand-carved steam engines and other creations. Follow along Warther's life chronologically from the start of his hobby to the passing of the torch to his children. Guided tours start at 10am, noon, and 2pm; self-guided tours are available all day.

The museum is on the grounds of the Warther family house, with a small, friendly garden evoking their Swiss heritage. Warther's wife, Frieda, had her own unusual hobby—collecting over 100,000 buttons. A small percentage of these are on display in a small

building in the gardens, organized into mesmerizing mosaic-like patterns.

An interesting gift shop at the end of the museum stocks family-carved ornaments and other small decor items. Otherwise, **Warther Cutlery** (330/343-7513, warthercutlery.com, 9am-5pm Mon.-Sat., 10am-4pm Sun.) next door continues the other half of Warther's legacy, churning out quality cutlery, cutting boards, and other kitchen utensils. A window into the workshop allows visitors to peek in while they shop.

Toland-Herzig Famous Endings Museum

One of the most unusual collections in Ohio, the **Toland-Herzig Famous Endings Museum** (803 N. Wooster Ave., Dover, 330/343-6132, tolandherzig.com/famous-endings-museum, 9am-5pm Mon.-Fri., free) is a local funeral parlor's collection of bulletins and other memorabilia from celebrity funerals. You'll find photos, gravesite markers, and other things related to the passing of celebrities—far too many to name but including immediately recognizable presidents, Hollywood elite, singers, athletes, and world leaders. In all, there are over 2,500 artifacts, including a handwritten note to Marilyn Monroe from ex-husband Joe DiMaggio and funeral programs for Princess Diana and Michael Jackson. Call ahead to arrange a tour.

Historic Schoenbrunn Village

In 1772, Moravian missionary David Zeisberger founded Schoenbrunn with a handful of white settlers and Christian converts of the Lenape tribe, as many as 400 at the village's peak. The settlers' neutrality came under pressure from the British and

---

1: Dennison Railroad Depot Museum near New Philadelphia **2:** Tuscora Park in New Philadelphia **3:** Sublime Smoke Fine BBQ in Bolivar **4:** Zoar Wetland Arboretum near Bolivar

their Indigenous allies as well as American authorities during the Revolutionary War, and in 1777 the inhabitants abandoned the settlement, which included many Ohio firsts such as the first schoolhouse and church. Today, **Schoenbrunn Village** (1984 E. High Ave., New Philadelphia, 740/922-6776, ohiohistory.org/schoenbrunn, 9:30am-5pm Tues.-Sat., noon-5pm Sun., $7 adults, $5 seniors, $4 children) has been re-created over the foundations of the original village. Seventeen structures, including the schoolhouse and church, interpret what life was like for this utopian society. Tours are typically self-guided, starting from the small and somewhat outdated visitors center and museum that briefly covers life for the settlers and Lenape villagers, but guided tours are available Wednesday and Saturday (10am-1pm). Costumed volunteers may be on hand to interpret the re-created buildings. Check the website for an events calendar, which includes a Legend of Sleepy Hollow drama and Colonial Trade Faire with over 150 reenactors, both in October.

Dennison Railroad Depot Museum

The **Dennison Railroad Depot Museum** (400 Center St., Dennison, 740/922-6776, dennisondepot.org, 10am-5pm Tues.-Fri., 11am-4pm Sat., 11am-3pm Sun., $8 adults, $6 seniors, $4 children ages 6-17) captures a moment in time: The depot served as a canteen for 1.3 million servicemembers on the way to the front during World War II. Located halfway between Columbus and Pittsburgh, Dennison was the third largest canteen stop in the country during the war. This museum, housed in the 1873 train station and a line of attached train cars, includes an interactive railroad car for kids to climb around and a WWII hospital car. A small theater plays a film about Dennison's days as a canteen, and a model train display depicts the town during WWII. The Over the Rail Diner inside the station serves some seriously inexpensive lunch and dinner plates.

Dennison is a 15-minute drive (11 mi/17.7 km) southeast of New Philadelphia via SR 250.

RECREATION

Old-fashioned **Tuscora Park** (161 Tuscora Ave., New Philadelphia, 330/343-4644, tuscorapark.com, 11:30am-7pm daily, free) is small-town fun at its most delightful. Three pools, terraced picnic areas, miniature golf, ample playground space (including a train-themed, handicapped-accessible playground), and seasonal amusement rides beckon families to spend summer nights outside. Ride tickets are $1 each or 10 tickets for $8. The rides, which include a carousel, small Ferris wheel, and a tiny roller coaster, are best suited for young children. Check the website for the various amusements' seasonal hours (most run Memorial Day to Labor Day, though the park is open year-round) and for an events calendar that includes live music in the bandstand.

The 20-mile (32-km) **Zoar Valley Trail** (tuscazoar.org/zoar-valley-trail), traversed both by hikers and bikers, skirts many of the area's attractions via a combination of roads, old canal towpaths, and abandoned railroad beds. Parking is at Schoenbrunn Village (1984 E. High Ave., New Philadelphia; closes at 5pm), Camp Tuscazoar (6066 Boy Scout Rd. NE, Dover), Canal Lands Park (8645 Dover Zoar Rd. NE, Dover) next to Zoar Village, and Fort Laurens (11067 Fort Laurens Rd. NW, Bolivar).

FOOD

Dough Co. Doughnuts and Coffee (801 Boulevard St., Ste. B, Dover, 6am-2pm daily) is in a nondescript redbrick building, but you won't want to pass up the delectable yeast and cake doughnuts inside, including "honeymooners" with jelly on top. There's coffee, of course, and a decent-sized seating area, but breakfast options outside the realm of fried dough are limited.

For a more robust breakfast menu, check out old-fashioned **Dee's Restaurant** (1109 C Bowers Ave., New Philadelphia, 330/364-9221,

6am-2pm Mon.-Sat., 8am-1pm Sun., $4-12). With vinyl booths and a small patio, this popular diner serves breakfast favorites as well as pork mush patties known as krepples, similar to Cincinnati's goetta. The restaurant also serves lunch with a menu that includes hot meals, sandwiches, and salads.

Just off I-77 is **El San Jose Mexican Restaurant** (1240 W. High Ave., New Philadelphia, 330/308-8928, 11am-10pm Mon.-Thurs., 11am-10:30pm Fri., 11:30am-10pm Sat., 11:30am-9pm Sun., $8-14), serving up reliable Tex-Mex favorites for affordable prices. The large dining room features wood tables and booths and festive wall decor.

Brickyard Dining Co. (140 Commercial Ave. SE, New Philadelphia, 234/801-4519, brickyardco.com, 11am-9pm Mon.-Thurs., 11am-10pm Fri.-Sat., $8-14) puts together an all-American lineup of individual wood-fired pizzas, burgers, sandwiches, and salads in a modern, high-ceilinged dining room. Housemade desserts, including a crushed Oreo ice cream sandwich, round out a large menu.

ACCOMMODATIONS

There are name-brand motels in both Dover and New Philadelphia off I-77. An outlier is **The Schoenbrunn Inn and Conference Center** (1186 W. High Ave., New Philadelphia, 330/339-4334, theschoenbrunninn.com, $104-159), with simple, Ikea-like guest rooms and an indoor pool. A hot breakfast is included in the rate.

Also consider staying in Amish Country, which is just on the other side of I-77 from this area.

INFORMATION AND SERVICES

The **Tuscarawas County Convention and Visitors Bureau** (124 E. High Ave., New Philadelphia, traveltusc.com, office 9am-5pm Mon.-Fri.) has a visitor kiosk open 6am-10pm daily.

The **Cleveland Clinic-Union Hospital** (659 Boulevard St., Dover, 330/343-3311) is the area's main hospital. It also runs an urgent care center (110 Dublin Dr., Dover, 330/343-0753).

TRANSPORTATION
Getting There

New Philadelphia and Dover are easily accessible via I-77. New Philadelphia is about a 30-minute drive (27 mi/43 km) south of Canton and 80 minutes south of Cleveland (86 mi/138 km).

Greyhound (greyhound.com), **Barons Bus** (baronsbus.com), and **GoBus** (ridegobus.com) stop at the Eagle Truck Stop (217 County Hwy. 21, New Philadelphia). The CVB lists the address at 217 16th St. SW, but either way you should end up at the truck stop just off I-77. It's best to purchase tickets online, though you can buy GoBus tickets at Joe's Shoe Repair (130 E. High Ave., New Philadelphia, 330/364-4131).

Getting Around

Performance Taxi (330/204-7393) is a 24/7 taxi service located in New Philadelphia serving the greater area.

BOLIVAR

This former canal town of scarcely 1,000 souls has a well-looked-after central area ("downtown" seems generous). If you're driving down I-77 and ready for a meal or an excuse to stretch your legs, Bolivar is prepared with some suggestions along Canal Street.

Sights
ZOAR VILLAGE

A six-minute (3 mi/4.8 km) drive southeast from Bolivar is the tiny former utopian settlement of **Zoar Village** (800/262-6195, historiczoarvillage.com). In 1817, German religious dissenters established a communal village that lasted for over 80 years. Today, the village is a lived-in community maintained by its residents and on display for people looking for a quiet stroll among log cabins, old brick homes, and restored 19th-century artisan shops.

While it's free to wander the town—including the central **Zoar Gardens**

The Gnadenhutten Massacre

Gnadenhutten Museum and Historical Park

"A stain on frontier character that the lapse of time cannot wash away." That was what Theodore Roosevelt called the Gnadenhutten atrocity, more than a century later.

The late 18th century saw a number of missionary settlements established in this part of Ohio, led primarily by the Moravians. Gnadenhutten was such a settlement, populated by members of the Lenape (also known as the Delaware people) who had converted to Christianity. During the Revolutionary War, this region of Ohio sat directly between the Americans' Fort Pitt (Pittsburgh) and the British Fort Detroit. Tensions were so high that villagers abandoned the nearby Moravian settlement of Schoenbrunn a mere five years after it was established. The inhabitants of Gnadenhutten stayed put.

In 1781, the Lenape villagers at Gnadenhutten were forcibly removed by the British and their Indian allies to the Upper Sandusky area under suspicion of being spies for the Americans. When food at the camp was low, around 100 of them were allowed to return to Gnadenhutten to harvest their crops and gather their stores. While there, a raiding party of Pennsylvania militia rounded up the townspeople, accusing them of aiding raids on white settlers in western Pennsylvania. The militia held a council and determined to massacre the Lenape they had rounded up, even though they belonged to the peaceful Moravian religion and were not involved with the raids. Informed of the decision, the Lenape spent the following night praying and singing hymns, awaiting their fate the next morning. On March 8, 1782, the militiamen separated the Lenape by men and women and scalped them. In total, 28 men, 29 women, and 39 children were killed. Two boys managed to escape and share the dreadful news with Moravian missionaries.

The massacre's brutality did not sit well with frontier settlers, or even some of the Pennsylvania militia who abandoned the unit before the massacre took place. The outrage was never put toward justice, however, and the militiamen who carried out the massacre were never tried for their crimes.

Today, the sleepy village of Gnadenhutten maintains the somber **Gnadenhutten Museum and Historical Park** (182 Cherry St., 740/254-4143, traveltusc.com/directory/listing/gnadenhutten-museum-historical-park, 1pm-5pm Tues.-Sun., 10am-5pm Sat., free), which preserves the burial site of the Lenape. A small interpretive museum, with artifacts related to Gnadenhutten, and a 35-foot (10.7-m) monument near the burial site commemorate a truly dark chapter of the American Revolution.

Gnadenhutten is a 20-minute drive (15 mi/24 km) south of New Philadelphia via SR 250 and US-36.

(198 E. 3rd St., Zoar), in bloom all summer—if you want to enter any of the historic buildings and watch costumed volunteers perform craft demonstrations, you'll need to sign up for a tour (10am-4pm Wed.-Sat., 11am-4pm Sun., $8 adults, $4 children). Tours leave from the **Zoar Store** (198 Main St., Zoar, 10am-5pm Wed.-Sat., noon-5pm Sun. Apr.-Dec., 10am-5pm Fri.-Sat., noon-5pm Sun. Mar., closed Jan.-Feb.), a sort of general store with souvenirs, books, pottery, and old-fashioned candy and toys.

A free option is the pleasant **Zoar Wetland Arboretum** (end of Lake Dr., zoarwetland.org, dawn-dusk daily). A shelter overlooks a gorgeous, shallow marsh full of lilies and wildlife. The park has 2 miles (3.2 km) of easy, shaded trails along the water.

There are a couple of food options while wandering the village including **Tin Shop Coffee House** (395 Main St., Zoar, 330/874-2793, tinshopcoffeehouse.com, 7am-6pm Mon.-Fri., 8am-6pm Sat., $5-9), which provides soups, salads, and made-from-scratch baked goods alongside its coffee. The front of the house faces the Zoar Gardens, but for an even more serene break, there's a back-porch seating area.

Food

Sublime Smoke Fine BBQ and Craft Brew (110 Water St. SE, 330/227-8118, sublimesmoke.com, 11am-9pm Tues.-Sat., $9-19) is the best option along Bolivar's Canal Street. This relaxed neighborhood establishment does excellent barbecue as well as pizza. Budget-minded or less-hungry folks, take note: there are two sandwich sizes here. The place has a Boylan soda fountain, a dozen beers on tap, and a covered patio.

On the east side of I-77 is **Lockport Brewery** (10748 Wilkshire Blvd. NE, 330/874-6037, 3pm-9pm Wed.-Thurs., noon-10pm Fri.-Sat., noon-9pm Sun., $11-18), a bright, modern brewpub started by a husband-and-wife duo. The brewery features award-winning beers and a simple, enticing menu of half-pound burgers, pizza, and street tacos. The small patio's wall is adorned with an Instagram-worthy mural celebrating Bolivar.

Transportation

Bolivar is just off I-77, about 15 minutes (15 mi/24 km) north of New Philadelphia and 15 minutes (12 mi/19.3 km) south of Canton. The closest long-distance bus options are in New Philadelphia.

Steubenville

Dean Martin's hometown is an industrial Ohio River city that attracted and retained Italian, German, and Polish immigrants and traditions, though it was first a pioneer outpost on the western edge of the United States. In 1786, American forces built Fort Steuben—named after the colorful Baron Friedrich Wilhelm von Steuben, a Prussian officer who assisted Washington in training the Continental Army—to protect land surveyors working in the area. Settlers built homes around the fort and the area came to be known as Steubenville. Today, you'll find a reconstructed fort and a curiosity known as Steubenville-style (or Ohio Valley-style) pizza.

SIGHTS
Fort Steuben

The "Gateway to the West" before St. Louis, reconstructed **Historic Fort Steuben** (120 S. 3rd St., 740/283-1787, oldfortsteuben.com, 10am-4pm Mon.-Sat., 11am-4pm Sun. May-Oct., $10 adults, $9 seniors, $7 children ages 6-12) sits along the Ohio River and interprets what life was like for settlers and surveyors during the late 18th century. The first federal land office west of the Alleghenies, built in 1801, also sits here and looks much as it would have inside when it was used. The visitors center hosts a small museum including artifacts excavated from the site and a gift shop selling pioneer-related souvenirs. Most just do a self-guided tour, but an interpreter can be scheduled upon request. A lineup of events keeps the fort busy, including early June's **Frontier Days,** which invites artisans and reenactors to bring the fort's history to life with demonstrations and performances.

ENTERTAINMENT AND EVENTS

Starting in 2015, the **Steubenville Nutcracker Village and Advent Market** (steubenvillenutcrackervillage.com) has pulled significant crowds to downtown Steubenville from late November to early January. Over 150 locally made, life-size nutcrackers—reportedly the world's largest collection—are placed throughout Fort Steuben Park and nearby blocks. The Advent Market includes festive music, visiting artisans, local food vendors, and general merrymaking during the holiday season.

FOOD

DiCarlo's Pizza (318 Adams St., 740/282-1081, dicarlospizza.com, 11am-9pm Mon.-Fri., 2pm-9pm Sat.-Sun., $4-10) is the granddaddy of Steubenville-style pizza. Order by the "cut" (how many 4-by-4-inch squares

you want). There's not a frill to be had in this take-out and delivery-only space, but you can take your pizza to Fort Steuben Park a block away and eat under the shadow of the impressive Jefferson County Courthouse. This place is cash only, but there's an ATM inside if you need it.

Open since 1927, old-school **Naples Spaghetti House** (329 North St., 740/283-3405, naplesspaghettihouse.com, 11am-7pm Mon.-Thurs., 11am-8pm Fri., noon-8pm Sat., noon-7pm Sun., $9-16) serves inexpensive Italian American favorites. Portions are good-sized and the no-nonsense wood-paneled dining room is decorated with paintings and photographs of Italy, Dean Martin, and Steubenville of yesteryear. The stuffed bread roll "heels" are a popular take-out choice with local teenagers, particularly the Poor Boy Heel which comes with meat sauce, provolone cheese, and a giant meatball.

A charming part of Steubenville's revitalization effort is the conversion of the aptly named Renaissance building into the duo **Steubenville Popcorn Company** (157 N. 4th St., 740/275-4714, steubenvillepopcorn.com, 9:30am-6pm Mon.-Sat.) and **Leonardo's Coffeehouse** (159 N. 4th St., 740/792-4426, leonardoscoffee.com,

Frontier Days at Fort Steuben

Steubenville-Style Pizza

squares of Steubenville-style pizza at DiCarlo's Pizza

Steubenville-style (or Ohio Valley-style) pizza is one of the more unusual iterations of the pie, appearing rudimentary, even unfinished.

During the early 20th century, the DiCarlo family ran an Italian grocery followed by a bakery in Steubenville. When the oldest son, Primo, returned after World War II, he brought back tales of a dish he'd eaten in Italy: crispy bread with tomato sauce and grated cheese on top. The family took their already popular bakery bread, crafted a pizza recipe, and opened the Original DiCarlo's Pizza in 1945. They opened a second store in Wheeling, West Virginia, in 1949, and the brand continued to expand.

What makes the pizza so unusual, other than the square shape and the delightful crisp to the thick crust, is the method in which it's made. The crust is cooked on a sheet pan with a layer of sauce, comes out after it rises for another layer of sauce, and doesn't receive the grated provolone cheese or toppings until the very end. The result is a sloppy, perfect mess that does its final "cooking" in the takeout box.

DiCarlo's Pizza has since expanded to several states, and other pizzerias have emulated the style, but it all started in Steubenville.

7am-10pm Mon.-Fri., 8am-10pm Sat.). The two operations share space and ownership in the cavernous commercial building that has housed more than 75 businesses over the years, most notably a ballroom and dance studio. That space—adorned with stained glass windows and chandeliers—now belongs to giggling friends, board games, and students dutifully studying. Gourmet popcorn, ice cream, coffee, and candy are on hand for a midday treat or evening snack.

ACCOMMODATIONS

Bayberry House Bed and Breakfast (741 N. 4th St., 740/632-2899, bayberryproperties. com, $109-189) occupies two fine Victorian homes on a historic residential street near the center of town. The eight rooms between the two houses each have private baths and are appointed with antiques.

A handful of chain motels sit near the Franciscan University of Steubenville on the north side of town, with convenient access to SR 7. Try the **Best Western Plus Franciscan Square Inn and Suites** (200 Franciscan Square, 740/792-8050, bestwestern.com, $110-140). It's a newer building with spacious rooms, an indoor pool, and a full breakfast.

INFORMATION AND SERVICES

The **visitors center** at Fort Steuben (120 S. 3rd St., 740/283-1787) includes information on the area as well as the Ohio River Scenic Byway, which continues as SR 7 and US-22 in these parts.

Trinity Health runs two hospitals in Steubenville, **Trinity East** (380 Summit Ave., 740/264-8000) and **Trinity West** (4000 Johnson Rd., 740/264-8000).

TRANSPORTATION
Getting There

Steubenville is 23 miles (37 km) north of I-70 via SR 7 right along the Ohio River and West Virginia border. The city is just over an hour (58 mi/93 km) east of New Philadelphia. There is no bus service to Steubenville.

The closest major airport to Steubenville is actually **Pittsburgh International Airport** (PIT, 1000 Airport Blvd., Pittsburgh, PA, 412/472-3525, flypittsburgh.com), which is 25 miles (40 km) to the east via US-22 and Pennsylvania SR 576.

Getting Around

Weir-Cove Taxi (304/748-1515) offers 24/7 service throughout the area and to Pittsburgh International Airport.

Cambridge

You're likely to pass through Cambridge if you're spending a significant amount of time in eastern Ohio—it sits at the junction of I-70 and I-77 and is the largest town for about 45 minutes in any direction. While the town itself doesn't boast many attractions, the surrounding area includes some true highlights of this region.

SIGHTS AND RECREATION
★ The Wilds

In 1984, a subsidiary of the American Electric Power Company handed over more than 9,000 acres of surface-mined land southwest of Cambridge to be restored and converted to a wildlife conservation center. Today, **The Wilds** (14000 International Dr., Cumberland, 740/638-5030, thewilds.columbuszoo.org, 10am-4pm daily May-Oct., 10am-4pm Sat.-Sun. early Nov., last tour leaves at 4pm, $30) is one of the largest conservation centers in North America, stewarding the care and recovery of over 500 animals representing 25

mostly endangered species, some of them critically so. This nonprofit open-air safari through vast enclosures has been affiliated with the Columbus Zoo and Aquarium since 2001.

There are several tours available but the most popular is the **Open-Air Safari,** a two-hour-plus journey in a large open-air vehicle through the expansive fields and pastures of the park. The guide will help you spot giraffes, rhinos, and large herds of bison, takin (a kind of goat-antelope), and exotic deer, though sometimes this is hardly difficult; the animals may come close to the vehicle on their own. The only traditionally zoo-like section is the Carnivore Center, for which visitors disembark from the vehicle to view cheetahs, African painted dogs, and dholes (Asiatic wild dogs) in large natural enclosures.

There are three snack/café options in the park, including the Terrace Grill at the Carnivore Center midway through the tour. There's also a gift shop at the park entrance.

A multitude of additional experiences

beyond the Open-Air Safari are available for those willing to spend some money, including behind-the-scenes tours, a zipline, and horseback tours. Want to wake up in the morning to the sight of exotic wildlife? There are cabins and luxury yurts on the premises for overnight stays.

★ Salt Fork State Park

Ohio's largest state park, **Salt Fork State Park** (14755 Cadiz Rd., Lore City, 740/432-1508, ohiodnr.gov, dawn-dusk daily, free) is northeast of Cambridge and holds over 20 miles (32 km) of hiking and bridle trails, a nature center, and an 18-hole golf course, all centered on Salt Fork Lake and surrounded by woods. Spanning 2,500 feet (762 m), one of the state's largest inland beaches curves around the lake with soft sand and is complete with changing rooms, outdoor showers, and a concession stand.

The hiking trails run on the short side. At only 0.5 mile (0.8 km) long one-way, the hike to **Hosak's Cave**—a recess cave similar to those found in Hocking Hills State Park—is an option for a short, fairly easy hike. A 50-foot (15.2-m) waterfall descends from the top seasonally. The 1.8-mile (2.9-km) **Stone House Loop Trail** features mature trees, abundant spring wildflowers, and the Kennedy Stone House at the end of a spur. Built in 1837, the stone house is open to visitors on weekends from May until October.

Sugartree Marina (740/439-4009) holds a new fleet of pontoons, jet boats, fishing boats, and kayaks to enjoy on the lake, which allows unlimited horsepower in certain parts of the water. There are 215 campsites, 54 cottages, and a lodge with indoor and outdoor pools, tennis, volleyball, and basketball courts, and a game room.

John and Annie Glenn Museum

The **John and Annie Glenn Museum** (72 W. Main St., New Concord, 740/826-0220, ohiohistory.org, 10am-4pm Wed.-Sat., 1pm-4pm Sun. May-Oct., $7 adults, $6 seniors, $3 children) sits 9 miles (14.5 km) west of town. This humble house, where astronaut John Glenn spent his childhood, holds exhibits telling the story of the lives of John and his wife, Annie. There's memorabilia of John's military and NASA career as well as personal effects from both. Some rooms are set up museum-style with displays while others recreate what the house would have looked like during John's childhood. Guided tours are one hour long and start with a video.

FOOD

With a history dating to 1931, family-operated **Theo's Restaurant** (632 Wheeling Ave., 740/432-3878, theosrestaurant.us, 10am-9pm Mon.-Sat., $5-11) has been a local favorite for a long time. Expect typical diner fare with the added bonus of Coney Island hot dogs (hot dogs with meat sauce), one of the restaurant's original draws.

The same family has ties to **The Forum** (2205 Southgate Pkwy., 740/439-2777, theforumrestaurant.com, 11am-9pm Tues.-Thurs. and Sun., 11am-10pm Fri.-Sat., $9-21), a Greek and Italian place closer to the town's main exit off I-70. The restaurant is a step up in terms of a formal sit-down restaurant experience, and in price, from their main street diner.

Behind the John and Annie Glenn Museum is quaint **Chapman's Coffee House** (68½ Main St., New Concord, 740/826-0299, chapmanscoffee.com, 7am-6pm Mon.-Fri., 8am-2pm Sat., $5-8). Aside from the expected coffee and tea selections, the coffeehouse does hot breakfast sandwiches, paninis, wraps, and salads. The house has plenty of good nooks and crannies to claim as your own, or there's a small, shady patio in front.

ACCOMMODATIONS

The secluded **Salt Fork Lodge and Conference Center** (14755 Cadiz Rd., Lore City, 740/439-2751, saltforkparklodge.com, $170-260) is within Salt Fork State Park and offers 148 guest rooms, all with balconies or patios facing either the outdoor pool or the woods and lake beyond. The rooms mix a rustic sensibility with modern convenience and comfort, and the lodge includes two pools, basketball and volleyball courts, and the Timbers restaurant and lounge with floor-to-ceiling windows. The lodge also maintains a good number of cabins, including some lakeside units.

The **Colonel Taylor Bed and Breakfast** (633 Upland Rd., 740/432-7802, coltaylorinnbb.com, $135-160) is an interesting Queen Anne-style house in residential Cambridge. Four historic rooms come with private baths and working gas fireplaces. On top of breakfast, there's the option to add a fine dinner to your experience.

There are quite a few name-brand motels off the Southgate Parkway exit on I-70, just west of the interchange with I-77.

CAMPING

The **Salt Fork State Park** campground (14755 Cadiz Rd., Lore City, 740/439-2751, ohiodnr.gov) features 215 campsites including full hookup, RV, and tent-only spots. Rates start at $29.

INFORMATION AND SERVICES

The **Cambridge/Guernsey County Visitors and Convention Bureau** (627 Wheeling Ave., 740/432-2022, visitguernsey-county.com, 8am-5pm Mon.-Fri., 9am-5pm Sat.) runs a tourist information center that has details on the area's attractions.

The **Southeastern Ohio Regional Medical Center** (1341 Clark St., 740/439-8000) is the area's primary hospital with an emergency room.

TRANSPORTATION
Getting There

Cambridge is directly east of Columbus on I-70, about an 80-minute drive (80 mi/129 km). The town is also due south of Cleveland, Akron, and Canton on I-77; it's a nearly two-hour drive from Cleveland (118 mi/190 km), 85 minutes (83 mi/134 km) from Akron, and an hour's drive from Canton (60 mi/97 km). Cambridge is a 50-minute (48 mi/77 km) drive north from Marietta on I-77.

Greyhound (greyhound.com), **Barons Bus** (baronsbus.com), and **GoBus** (ridego-bus.com) stop at the BP gas station at 2246 Southgate Parkway, near a number of retail and motel accommodations.

Getting Around

Noble Taxi Cabs (740/509-6089) services the Cambridge area. **South East Area Transit** (seatbus.org) runs a lap around town with buses stopping every hour. Fares are $1 and paid on the bus.

1: The Wilds near Cambridge **2:** Old Man's Cave in Hocking Hills State Park **3:** Salt Fork State Park near Cambridge

Hocking Hills Region

TOP EXPERIENCE

Arguably Ohio's favorite state park, Hocking Hills State Park preserves unusual rock formations, cliffs, caves, waterfalls, and thickly forested land that epitomizes the dense foothills of Appalachian Ohio. The dominant formation is the recess cave, a large cliff overhang that is hundreds of feet long.

Around the state park are an overwhelming number of rental cabins and accommodations, exciting outdoor adventure parks, and other excuses to enjoy the great outdoors in the hinterland. The nearby town of Logan is the best place to gas up, stock up on supplies, and grab a bite to eat before venturing into the hills.

SIGHTS AND HIKES

★ Hocking Hills State Park

Hocking Hills State Park (740/385-6842, ohiodnr.gov, dawn-dusk daily) draws millions of visitors every year to its miniature gorges, cliff faces, and waterfalls. The park is noncontiguous, broken into seven segments that are only sometimes connected by trails. All individual sites within Hocking Hills State Park are free of charge.

OLD MAN'S CAVE

The starting place for most people at Hocking Hills State Park is **Old Man's Cave** (19988 SR 664, Logan, 740/385-6842). Not a cave at all but a giant overhanging cliff, Old Man's Cave got its name from a hermit who lived in the rock shelter in the early 19th century.

Park in the Old Man's Cave parking lot (where there's a large visitors center) and start at the Upper Falls, from which the **Grandma Gatewood Trail** descends into the gorge and snakes past waterfalls, intriguing rock formations, and the "cave" itself. You can return to the parking lot for a loop (about 0.5 mi/0.8 km in total), but foot traffic drops

considerably after Old Man's Cave as you continue on the Grandma Gatewood Trail and head toward the Lower Falls. For an extended hike, the trail continues along the bottom of the gorge to the larger **Cedar Falls** roughly 2 miles (3.2 km) away, and **Ash Cave** another 2.5 miles (4 km) after that—moderate-to-difficult trails based on length rather than significant elevation gain. The easier **Gorge Rim Trail** (2.5 mi/4 km one-way) also connects the Old Man's Cave area with Cedar Falls; other than a peek at Rose Lake it mostly stays in the woods.

Old Man's Cave is by far the most popular stop in the state park, so it behooves travelers to arrive early, especially on weekends. While most trails are well marked and fairly wide, it's worth remembering these are cliffs and water we're dealing with: small children should be kept close at hand. Steps into the gorge can be on the steep side so while the trails are not long, they are moderate in difficulty based on the need to hike back out of the gorge. The large visitors center is the best place within the state park to use the restroom, grab a snack, and get information on the area's attractions and accommodations.

ASH CAVE

Old Man's Cave is better known, but **Ash Cave** (SR 56, Logan, 740/385-6841) to the south is more impressive. Some 700 feet (213 m) long and 100 feet (30.5 m) high, Ash Cave is the largest recess cave east of the Mississippi River. Two out-and-back trails lead to the cave from the parking lot through leafy forest. The 0.25-mile (0.4-km) wheelchair-accessible **Gorge Trail** leads to the bottom of the stunning site, which also features a trickling waterfall depending on recent rainfall. The 0.5-mile (0.8-km) **Rim Trail** gradually makes its way to the top of the cave, from which hikers can pick up the **Grandma Gatewood Trail** to

Hocking Hills Region

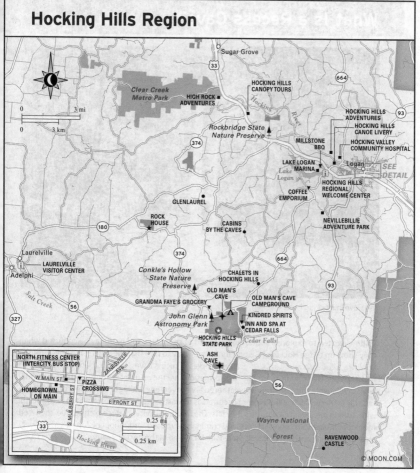

Cedar Falls 2.5 miles (4 km) away and on to Old Man's Cave, another 2 miles (3.2 km). Restrooms are available near the parking lot, which tends to fill up on weekends.

ROCK HOUSE

The only rock feature in Hocking Hills State Park that could possibly qualify as a cave is the Rock House (16350 SR 374, Laurelville, 740/385-6841), northwest of much of the rest of the park. Unlike the other recess caves of the park, the Rock House maintained some of its outer walls, creating a unique,

200-foot-long (61-m) corridor inside the cliff, with seven "windows" and 25-foot-high (7.6-m) ceilings. It looks the part of a secret base, which is how thieves, murderers, and other criminals used the cave in the past, creating the nickname Robbers Roost. The Rim Trail from the parking lot to the cave is downhill with a moderate number of stairs. Climbing back up to the parking lot from the Rock House, either back the way you came or up the Gorge Trail, is moderate to strenuous. All told, there's about 1 mile (1.6 km) of hiking round-trip.

What Is a Recess Cave?

Ash Cave in Hocking Hills State Park

Visitors excited to explore a subterranean world of stalactites and bats may be confused when they show up to see Hocking Hills and its "caves," only to find that the trails stay above ground. Old Man's Cave and Ash Cave are examples of recess caves, perhaps better thought of as rock shelters. These auditorium-like rock formations are the result of erosion; a cliffside's middle layer of relatively soft sandstone is weathered away over time while sturdier layers of rock at the top stay in place. Much of this erosion occurred as the last ice age's glaciers retreated to the north, with rushing meltwater carving into the cliffs. The resulting cavity creates a picturesque, sheltered room that Indigenous tribes, settlers, and criminals have used throughout history. It's a relatively rare rock feature, and Hocking Hills State Park has some of the best anywhere.

CONKLE'S HOLLOW STATE NATURE PRESERVE

There are two trails at **Conkle's Hollow State Nature Preserve** (24858 Big Pine Rd., Rockbridge, 740/385-6841), located between Old Man's Cave and Rock House. The easy out-and-back **Gorge Trail** (0.75 mi/1.2 km one-way) traverses a 200-foot (61-m) gorge—one of the deepest in Ohio—past rock formations and cliffs until you reach a *Fern Gully*-like hidden world with a waterfall. About half of this trail is wheelchair accessible. The strenuous 2.5-mile (4-km) **Rim Trail** loops around the gorge, providing wider views as it hugs the cliff's edge.

John Glenn Astronomy Park

Not part of the state park but just down the street from Old Man's Cave is the **John Glenn Astronomy Park** (20531 SR 664, Logan, 877/403-4477, jgap.info, 24 hours daily, free). A dedicated dark-sky park, this unique gem is operated by the nonprofit group Friends of the Hocking Hills State

Park. Weekly programs manned by volunteers offer presentations on the night sky in an 80-foot (24.4-m) solar plaza designed to highlight equinoxes and solstices. Enthusiasts, happy to share, bring their high-powered telescopes and point them toward planets in the sky. There's also a permanent 28-inch (71-cm) telescope under a foldaway observatory roof. Check the website for a program schedule. It's recommended to reserve a parking space on the website, and to bring your own chairs or blankets.

Rockbridge State Nature Preserve

A little removed from the state park's sites (but closer if you're coming from Columbus) is **Rockbridge State Nature Preserve** (11475 Dalton Rd., Rockbridge, no phone number, dawn-dusk daily, free). As the name suggests, this off-the-beaten-path park features a natural rock bridge over a ravine, this one being about 100 feet (30.5 m) long and 10-20 feet (3-6.1 m) wide. An attractive waterfall to the side of the bridge makes for quite the photo opportunity. The park itself is not large; walk from the parking lot trailhead through some fields and choose between two moderately difficult loop trails: the **Natural Bridge Trail** (1 mi/1.6 km), to find the eponymous rock formation, and the **Rock Shelter Trail** (0.75 mi/1.2 km), which winds through the woods to a small cliff overhang.

The address is a bit arbitrary—from US-33, travel north on Dalton Road until it comes to the At Boulder's Edge cabin retreat. There's a small parking lot on the left and a sign for the preserve.

OTHER RECREATION
Adventure Sports

Hocking Hills Canopy Tours (10714 Jackson St., Rockbridge, 740/385-9477, zipohio.com, 9am-6pm daily) offers several zip-lining experiences, including the "original tour" that takes guests over cliffs and the Hocking River. This adventure park also offers off-road Segway tours, tours of Rockbridge State Nature Preserve, and more. Check the website for which tours run through which months of the year (most run from spring to fall and even into December).

Hocking Hills Adventures (26633 Main St., Rockbridge, 740/385-4449, hockinghillscanoeing.com/funcenter) offers a go-kart track, as well as an 80s-style arcade and miniature golf. Not to be outdone, **NevilleBillie Adventure Park** (15155 Sauer Kraut Rd., Logan, 740/380-1775, nevillebillieadventurepark.com) provides 16 miles (26 km) of private off-road ATV trails. There's also a paintball area and a massive ropes course.

Kayaking, Canoeing, and Paddleboarding

Logan is home to two canoe liveries along the gentle Hocking River. **Hocking Hills Canoe Livery** (12789 SR 664, Logan, 740/385-0523, hockingriver.com) offers an unguided 5-mile (8-km) tour with canoes, kayaks, or rafts. A shuttle service drives you to the drop-off and you paddle your way back to the start—and your car. Look for nighttime tours that end with a bonfire and live music. Hourly rentals are also available. Unguided tours with **Hocking Hills Adventures Canoe Livery** (31251 Chieftain Dr., Logan, 740/385-8685, hockinghillscanoeing.com) range 5-7 miles (8-11.3 km) and can be taken with canoes, kayaks, tubes, or rafts. The longer tour gives you the chance to see the Rock Bridge a short hike from the water.

Lake Logan Marina (30443 Lake Logan Rd., Logan, 740/380-2956, lakeloganmarina.com) provides kayaks, paddleboards, paddleboats, and pontoons for rental by the hour on the eponymous Lake Logan.

Rock Climbing

High Rock Adventures (10108 Opossum Hollow Rd., Rockbridge, 740/385-9886, highrockadventures.com) provides climbing and rappelling fun on private land away from the hikers in the state park. Three experiences range from 35 feet (10.7 m) to 100 feet (30 m) high. Instruction and all equipment are included in the tours, which start at $50.

FOOD

An easy start to your day is found at **Millstone BBQ** (12790 Grey St., Logan, 740/385-5341, millstonebbq.com, 11am-9pm Mon.-Thurs., 11am-10:30pm Fri.-Sat., 10am-9pm Sun., $10-24). Right off US-33, this Southern-style restaurant smokes its meats on-site and features a large patio. The bar is stocked with craft beer and signature cocktails.

Roadside **Grandma Faye's Grocery** (20507 SR 664, Logan, 740/385-9466, no website, 8am-8pm Sun.-Thurs., 8am-10pm Fri.-Sat.) has a little bit of everything: thin-crust pizzas, simple subs, fudge, alcohol. You'll also find souvenirs and stuff you might want for your cabin or campsite. Nothing fancy here, but its location is convenient while driving between sites in the state park.

Logan's **Pizza Crossing** (58 N. Mulberry St., Logan, 740/385-8558, pizzacrossing.com, 11am-midnight Sun.-Thurs., 11am-1am Fri.-Sat., $7-10) is a popular spot. Besides square-cut pizza you'll find the usual pasta, salad, and sub options in this relaxed joint.

One of the more upscale places to eat in the area is the Inn and Spa at Cedar Falls' ★ **Kindred Spirits** (21190 SR 374, Logan, 740/385-7489, innatcedarfalls.com, breakfast 8am-10am daily, lunch [seasonal] 11am-2pm daily, dinner 5pm-7pm Sun.-Thurs., 5pm-8:30pm Fri.-Sat., $9-41), a fine-dining experience in an 1840s log cabin. The menu changes with the season, but the lunch menu (served late May-Oct.) is generally much more affordable than the high-end dinner menu.

The contemporary **Coffee Emporium** (13984 SR 664, Logan, 740/270-2697, hockinghillscoffeeemporium.com, 8am-4pm Sun.-Thurs., 8am-5pm Fri.-Sat., $4-8) features a small two-level patio and serves coffee from organic, fair-trade, and women-owned producers. Breakfast is served all day, though there is also a small lunch menu.

ACCOMMODATIONS

Cottages, cabins, and camping abound in and around Hocking Hills State Park. There are rental houses, treehouses, shipping-container Airbnb's, you name it. You can go as primitive or as luxurious as you'd like.

Possibly the most "treat yourself"-friendly accommodations in the Hocking Hills region is the ★ **Inn and Spa at Cedar Falls** (21190 SR 374, Logan, 740/385-7489, innatcedarfalls.com, $149-309). As the name suggests, this country-style bed-and-breakfast—comprising modern cabins, yurts, and lodges—is very near the Cedar Falls waterfall and the trails that lead to Old Man's Cave and Ash Cave. The spa itself is in an 1840s log cabin and offers a wide menu of services. Likewise, the restaurant on premises—Kindred Spirits—is also inside an 1840s log cabin and provides an exquisite dining experience. Reservations are recommended for all of the above well in advance.

One of the more unusual choices is **Ravenwood Castle** (65666 Bethel Rd., New Plymouth, 740/596-2606, ravenwoodcastle.com, $144-184), a faux-medieval castle southeast of the park with seven guest suites surrounded by cabins and medieval village-themed cottages. To match the festive atmosphere and continue the theme of unplugging while in the woods, there is an emphasis on gaming (of the role-playing and board game variety) within the castle's programming.

Glenlaurel (14940 Mt. Olive Rd., Rockbridge, 740/385-4070, glenlaurel.com, $249-399) is another themed accommodation, though admittedly more highbrowed. There are 21 luxurious Scottish-themed rooms, suites, crofts (small cabins), and cottages on the 140-acre estate, which includes a trail to a private gorge. Rooms and suites are located in the main Carriage House and Manor House buildings. Also on the grounds are a golf course, a spa, and a kitchen serving seven-course meals. A three-course breakfast is included with any reservation.

Not interested in themes? Family-owned **Chalets Hocking Hills** (18905 SR 664, Logan, 740/385-6517, chaletshh.com) rents more than 50 well-maintained cabins for groups sized 2-32. The cabins are divided across five locations throughout the region, the largest just down the road from Old Man's Cave. Rates start at around $140 a night, not including fees.

Cabins by the Caves (Logan, 614/322-2283, cabinsbythecaves.com) similarly features a mix of cabins and lodges, some of them equipped with hot tubs and game rooms. The company's properties are located throughout the region and start at around $189 per night; some are pet friendly.

CAMPING

There are hundreds of camping sites within the area. The most centrally located are within the state park's **Old Man's Cave Campground** (19852 SR 664, Logan, 740/385-6841, ohiodnr.gov). There are over 150 spots here, perhaps a little close together, ranging from primitive tent sites to full hookups with easy access to the trails. There are also 40 basic Sherman cabins. Rates start at $27.

INFORMATION AND SERVICES

There is an exhausting number of attractions, accommodations, and roadside adventures in the Hocking Hills region, so it's helpful to sort through them with a human being. The Hocking Hills Tourism Association operates three locations: the **Hocking Hills Regional Welcome Center** (13178 SR 664, Logan, 740/385-9706, explorehockinghills.

com, 9am-5pm Mon.-Sat., 11am-5pm Sun.) is helpfully located right off the US-33 exit to SR 664, more or less the entrance to the region. On top of helpful employees and tons of information, it includes the quirky and free **Paul A. Johnson Pencil Sharpener Museum** to spend a couple minutes in. The other two locations are **Homegrown on Main** (65 W. Main St., Logan, 740/216-4435, 10am-5pm Mon.-Sat.), a store in Logan that mixes information with local art, and the **Laurelville Visitor Center** (16197 Pike St., Laurelville, 740/385-9706, 10am-4pm Fri.-Sat., 11am-4pm Sun.), convenient if you're coming from the southwest. The **Old Man's Cave Visitor Center** (19988 SR 664, Logan, 740/385-6842, ohiodnr.gov, 9am-5pm daily) is also a useful place to find information.

Hocking Valley Community Hospital (601 SR 664 N., Logan, 740/380-8000) is the nearest hospital and emergency room to the park. There's an urgent care facility (10am-9pm daily) on the premises just inside the emergency entrance.

TRANSPORTATION
Getting There

US-33 is the main road traversing the Hocking Hills region, connecting the area with Columbus around 50 minutes (50 mi/81 km) to the northwest and Athens 30 minutes (25 mi/40 km) to the southeast.

There is a curbside bus stop in Logan outside North Fitness Center (4 E. Main St., Logan) that services **Greyhound** (greyhound.com) and **GoBus** (ridegobus.com).

Getting Around

The private **Hocking Hills Transportation Services** (740/274-2949) can provide transportation for groups up to 11. Reservations are recommended but not required.

Athens

Developed around Ohio University, established in 1804, Athens is part Appalachian cultural center, part notorious party college town, part progressive enclave. The town of 24,000 (not including the university's enrollment) caters to college students, locals interested in arts and culture, and those just looking for a good bite or drink. The hillside town is surrounded on all sides by recreational options—endless miles of hiking, reservoirs for swimming and boating, and camping in some of the state's remotest woods. Those wanting to sweat on the trails by day and enjoy a brewpub by night will find a good base in Athens.

SIGHTS
Ohio University

The first university in the Northwest Territory, the oldest in Ohio, and the eighth-oldest public university in the United States—a surprising list of superlatives for a university in the middle of the hills—**Ohio University** manages to retain some of the historic charm befitting its age. Though the school has expanded considerably into a modern university of 20,000 students (with an additional 15,000 at other branches), the College Green still reflects its early-19th-century beginnings, with Federal-style Cutler, McGuffey, and Wilson Halls all built between 1819 and 1839. Stately elm trees on the Green contribute to the picturesque collegiate environment. The best place to park on the campus is the **Baker University Center** (1 Park Pl.), from which you can grab a coffee, find a campus map, and wander wherever you desire.

While not quite as storied a tradition as the Ohio State Buckeyes, the **Ohio Bobcats** (ohiobobcats.com) put together competitive men's and women's teams in the Division I Mid-Atlantic Conference, especially men's basketball. Tickets for games are also considerably cheaper than Ohio State's. The **Marching 110** (marching110.com) is a looser, more uproarious counterpart to Ohio State's more buttoned-up marching band. Their iconic marching, cadences, and choreography have twice earned them spots in the Macy's Thanksgiving Day parade.

Kennedy Museum of Art

The **Kennedy Museum of Art** (100 Ridges Cir., 740/593-1304, ohio.edu/museum, 10am-5pm Mon.-Wed. and Fri., 10am-8pm Thurs., 1pm-5pm Sat.-Sun., free) resides in the impressive building known as the Ridges, previously the Athens Mental Hospital. The Victorian double-turreted entrance stands in the center of the complex, which also includes additional classrooms and administrative offices for the university. The museum itself is known for its collection of Southwest Native American art and ceramics as well as a strong collection of African art.

ENTERTAINMENT AND EVENTS
The Arts

The **Dairy Barn Arts Center** (8000 Dairy Ln., 740/592-4981, dairybarn.org, noon-5pm Tues.-Sat.), as its name suggests, is a 1914 dairy barn converted into a modern art gallery. This nonprofit attracts a rotating calendar of shows from local, regional, and visiting artists for little or no admission cost. The gallery shop stocks art from the artists themselves. The private **Ora Anderson hiking trail** (1 mi/1.6 km) leaves from the parking lot and loops through the woods for a mostly easy hike (a few steep sections might elevate this to moderate for some). A trailhead to the Ridges Trails is across the street up some steps.

Festivals and Events

The **Athens Halloween Block Party** (athenshalloween.com) is a raucous takeover of Court Street in downtown Athens by costumed students and visitors. DJs and bands

Athens

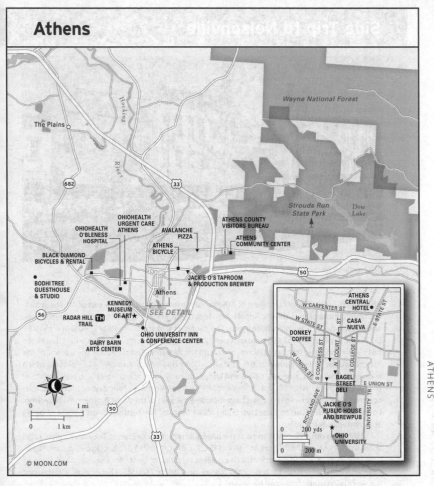

© MOON.COM

perform on stages throughout party central as the revelry has only increased since students first stormed Court Street to party in 1974. It's a party befitting a school with something of a party reputation.

★ RECREATION
Cycling

The **Hockhocking Adena Bikeway** (athensohio.com) follows the Hocking River and connects Athens with Nelsonville to the northwest—a total of 21 miles (34 km) of flat, paved bikeway. The trail begins at Athens Community Center (701 E. State St.), though

there is also parking at West State Street Park, where the street dead-ends after the Athens Public Transit building (397 W. State St.). A couple of bicycle shops rent bikes, including **Athens Bicycle** (4 W. Stimson Ave., 740/594-9944, athensbicycle.com) and **Black Diamond Bicycles and Rentals** (540 W. Union St., 740/249-4045), the latter located right off the trail.

Kayaking, Canoeing, and Paddleboarding

Strouds Run State Park has a boathouse (12927 Strouds Run Rd., 740/594-2628,

Side Trip to Nelsonville

Nelsonville's Historic Square Art District

About 14 miles (22.5 km) northwest of Athens is the town of Nelsonville, a sort of Athens in miniature with more of an authentic Appalachian feel, the tiny Hocking College, bed-and-breakfasts, and a respectable arts and culture scene. The center of said scene is **Stuart's Opera House** (52 Public Square, 740/753-1924, stuartsoperahouse.org), a 19th-century opera house that keeps busy with concerts, theater performances, and local events. The theater is the anchor of the historic public square known as the **Nelsonville Historic Square Art District**, which is rounded out with galleries, cafes, and shops. In early June, the theater also puts together the growing **Nelsonville Music Festival** (nelsonvillefest.org), four days of bluegrass, folk, country, soul, and other genres that have included the likes of the Avett Brothers, Willie Nelson, Loretta Lynn, The Head and the Heart, and Mavis Staples. The festival makes a point of being environmentally friendly.

Nelsonville's other claim to fame is as the headquarters of Rocky Brands. They have a giant retail shop, the **Rocky Outdoor Gear Store** (45 E. Canal St., 740/753-3130, rockyoutlet.com, 10am-7pm Mon.-Sat., 10am-6pm Sun.), with an excellent selection of boots, footwear, apparel, hunting gear, and other essentials for the rural, country, or outdoor lifestyle. There's even a restaurant inside, serving sandwiches and ice cream.

Depending on your interests—say, if you wanted a quieter weekend away from college students—you may choose to make your base Nelsonville rather than Athens, though there are far fewer accommodations and restaurants available.

ohiodnr.gov, dawn-dusk daily, free) that rents pontoons, canoes, kayaks, and pedal boats for affordable rates. It's recommended to make a reservation for the pontoons. The park also has hiking trails and a swimming beach along the Dow Lake reservoir, the centerpiece of the park.

Hiking

West of Athens are two parks providing ample hiking. **Zaleski State Forest** (29681 SR 278, Zaleski, 740/596-5781, ohiodnr.gov, dawn-dusk daily, free) features a 23-mile (37-km) backpacking trail through dense second-growth forest and hills. Surrounded by the state forest and with shorter hikes is **Lake Hope State Park** (27331 SR 278, McArthur, 740/596-4938, ohiodnr.gov, dawn-dusk daily, free), featuring a man-made lake popular with beavers, a dining lodge specializing in barbecue, and camping grounds.

Closer to town are the **Ridges Trails** (athensconservancy.org/aaorg/ou-theridges. html, dawn-dusk daily, free), which meander through 700 acres of woodlands and open hilltop fields that formerly belonged to the Athens Mental Hospital. There are four sometimes overlapping trails in all—the combined 2.9-mile (4.7-km) **Ridges Trail** and **River Valley Nature Trail** loop takes hikers to Radar Hill, the site of a former WWII radar station and the highest point in Athens for views of the town and surrounding hills. There are multiple trailheads, but the most useful is located on Dairy Lane west of the Dairy Barn Arts Center (8000 Dairy Ln.), from which you'll hike up old roads to the top of the hill. All hikes are moderate in difficulty; there is little shade in some parts, so sunscreen and a hat are a good idea. For a shorter hike, there's another trailhead for the Ridges Trail near the water tower on Water Tower Road near the Kennedy Museum of Art that is a shortcut to the River Valley Nature Trail. Additionally, the 1.3-mile (2.1-km) one-way **Ridges Cemetery Nature Walk** starts across the street from the Dairy Barn Arts Center.

FOOD

Casa Nueva (6 W. State St., 740/592-2016, casanueva.com, 8am-11pm Mon.-Tues., 8am-2am Wed.-Fri., 9am-2am Sat., 9am-11pm Sun., $8-15) is a worker-owned co-op that's been around since 1985. The Mexican-inspired menu includes a good number of vegetarian and vegan options, and the restaurant hosts live music and art shows.

You'll notice **Jackie O's** beer in many bars throughout the state of Ohio; the popular craft brewery is often ranked as one of the best in the state. The brand operates the **Public House and Brewpub** (22 W. Union St., 740/592-9686, jackieos.com, 11am-2am daily, $10-13), a full-service restaurant that uses ingredients largely sourced from area farms on its pizza and burgers; there is a full bar. The company also runs the **Taproom and Production Brewery** (25 Campbell St., 740/447-9063, jackieos.com, 2pm-9pm Mon.-Thurs., 11am-10pm Fri.-Sat., noon-7pm Sun.), which has a sunny patio and a small menu of snacks. The Public House and Brewpub are in the center of town while the taproom is located about 1 mile (1.6 km) northeast.

Bagel Street Deli (27 S. Court St., 740/593-3838, bagelstreetdeli.com, 7:30am-9pm Mon.-Fri., 9am-9pm Sat.-Sun., $4-8)

swimming beach at Strouds Run State Park

Hiking in Wayne National Forest

Wayne National Forest (fs.usda.gov/wayne) is Ohio's only national forest, protecting mostly reforested areas of southeast Ohio after settlers in the 19th century cleared most of Ohio's original tree coverage. Nearly a quarter of a million acres are divided between three sections: the Athens Unit, Marietta Unit, and Ironton Unit, with all offering a variety of recreational options in the way of backcountry trails, hiking, fishing, ATV trails, and more. In general, hikers should be prepared for less-frequented, less-maintained trails that require a little more effort to find your way through. The Wayne National Forest Welcome Center (13700 US-33, Nelsonville, 740/753-0101, 8am-4:30pm Mon.-Fri.) in the Athens Unit is located directly off US-33 within the park headquarters and is a good place to find information on what's available and acquire any necessary permits. Some highlights of the national forest:

ATHENS UNIT

- The Monday Creek trailhead (Cheeseman Rd., Nelsonville), 20 minutes (15 mi/24 km) northwest of Athens, is a popular starting point for over 75 miles (121 km) of moderate trails used by ATV riders, mountain bikers, and hikers.

- The moderate Wildcat Hollow Trail (County Rd. 58, Glouster), 40 minutes (23 mi/37 km) north of Athens, makes a figure eight, allowing hikers to choose between a 15-mile (24-km) loop or a 5-mile (8-km) loop through dense forests, ridgetops, and meadows.

MARIETTA UNIT

- The moderate-to-difficult Lamping Homestead Trail (36998 Clearfork Rd., Graysville) is among the most remote places in Ohio. This 3.5-mile (5.6-km) loop, 35 miles (56 km) northeast of Marietta, sees climbs of 300 feet (91 m) and more from creek to ridge and passes by the old Lamping family cemetery from the mid-19th century.

- Also very secluded is the Archers Fork Trail (T411 Rd., Matamoras), a 9.3-mile (14.9-km) loop passing the Irish Run natural bridge, rock formations, and recess caves. The moderate-to-difficult trail, 23 miles (37 km) east of Marietta, has seven climbs of at least 250 feet (76 m).

- The strenuous 11-mile (17.7-km) Scenic River Trail leaves from Leith Run Recreation Area (44400 SR 7, Matamoras), 22 miles (35 km) east of Marietta, and ascends the bluffs near the Ohio River to loop through thick forest (the river is best viewed outside summer) and rock formations. You can connect to other paths for a longer journey.

IRONTON UNIT

- Nine miles (14.5 km) north of the small Ohio River town of Ironton (and a full hour southwest of Gallipolis), the Lake Vesuvius Recreation Area (County Rd. 29, Pedro) features the 7.8-mile (12.5-km) Lakeshore Trail, a moderate loop that begins and ends at the ruins of an old iron furnace and clings between Lake Vesuvius and wooded, rocky outcroppings.

offers a wide variety of bagel sandwiches, with over 25 types of bagels to choose from. The brick walls in the thin squeeze of a dining room bear the names of visitors who have taken a piece of provided chalk to leave their mark. There's also a takeout window for on-the-go bites.

Donkey Coffee (17 W. Washington St., 740/594-7353, donkeycoffee.com, 7am-6pm Mon.-Fri., 8am-6pm Sat.-Sun.) serves "caffeine with a conscience" in its cozy two-floor café. Fair-trade coffee, house-baked goodies, and health-conscious snacks are on offer, proceeds from which support a long list of charitable organizations. Check the website for music, poetry, comedy, and other live performances.

Avalanche Pizza (329 E. State St., 740/594-4664, avalanchepizza.net, 10am-1am Sun.-Thurs., 10am-4am Fri.-Sat., $6-12) puts together NYC-style pizza pies with unusual topping combinations and a fluffy crust (still foldable, though). Also unusual is the affordability, with an awesome three-pizza special ($16.99-30.99 for three pizzas, depending on size and toppings). For delivery or pick-up only.

ACCOMMODATIONS

There are several motel chains in town, mostly on the east side along State Street.

The **Athens Central Hotel** (88 E. State St., 740/595-0500, athenscentralhotel.com, $134-236) is Athens' only boutique hotel and is located in the center of town. The 22 luxuriously minimalist rooms come with rainfall showers, big-screen TVs, free continental breakfast, and a fridge of complimentary drinks.

The **Ohio University Inn and Conference Center** (331 Richland Ave., 866/593-6661, ouinn.com, $109-159) is located on the south end of campus. This clean business hotel has an outdoor pool and an onsite restaurant. The Bed and Breakfast rate includes breakfast at the restaurant.

Unwind west of Athens at **Bodhi Tree Guesthouse and Studio** (8950 Lavelle Rd., 740/707-2050, bodhitreeguesthouse.com, $100-150), which offers four clean, modern rooms, wi-fi, and no TV. Instead you'll find serene views of the surrounding woods and hills, locally sourced breakfast, yoga classes, massages, and a sensory-deprivation float tank.

CAMPING

The campground at **Lake Hope State Park** (27331 SR 278, McArthur, 740/596-4938, ohiodnr.gov) features nearly 200 full-hookup, electric, and non-electric sites for tents and RVs, as well as a variety of cabin accommodations. Rates start at $27.

INFORMATION AND SERVICES

The **Athens County Visitors Bureau** (667 E. State St., 800/878-9767, athensohio.com, 9am-5pm Mon.-Fri.) is in a little white cabin in front of the community center.

The **OhioHealth O'Bleness Hospital** (55 Hospital Dr., 740/593-5551) is the area's main hospital and includes an emergency room. **OhioHealth Urgent Care Athens** (265 W. Union St., 740/594-2456, 9am-9pm Mon.-Thurs., 9am-6pm Fri.-Sun.) is nearby.

TRANSPORTATION
Getting There

Athens is a 1.25-hour (77 mi/124 km) drive southeast from Columbus via US-33. US-50 connects Athens with Marietta, 50 minutes (49 mi/79 km) to the east, and Chillicothe, 70 minutes (58 mi/93 km) to the west.

Greyhound (greyhound.com), **Barons Bus** (baronsbus.com), and **GoBus** (ride-gobus.com) stop at the Athens Community Center (701 E. State St.) and at the Baker University Center on campus. Tickets are sold on-site at the community center but not the campus stop.

Getting Around

Athens Transit (athenstransit.org) is a fixed-route bus system serving Athens. Fares are $1. Lyft also operates in Athens. There are several cab companies in town, including **Athens Airport Express** (740/590-4686) that goes to John Glenn Columbus International Airport.

Marietta

If Cincinnati is chapter one of the American Revolution's sequel, Marietta is the first paragraph. In 1788—a mere four years after the Revolutionary War's end—the Ohio Company of Associates settled Marietta as the first town under the legal protection of the United States government within the newly created Northwest Territory. Many Continental Army veterans and officers were among the settlers, who were led by Revolutionary War hero General Rufus Putnam. The newcomers experienced oscillating tension and peace with the nearby Lenape (Delaware) tribe, who felt an increased threat to their land as white settlement expanded. The settlers' legacy, in terms of structures, has largely been washed away by the Ohio River's floods, but their history is preserved through leafy parks, museums,

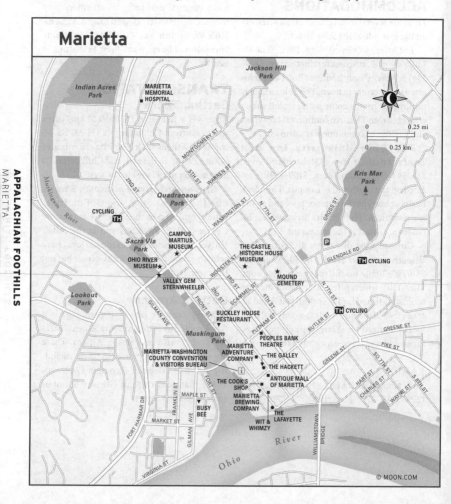

and a sense of place maintained by Marietta's dedicated inhabitants. The small city's historical allure is supplemented with endless recreational opportunities, a compact 19th-century downtown, and the pleasing Ohio River itself.

★ SIGHTS
Campus Martius Museum

The best place to get your bearings on the region's history is the **Campus Martius Museum** (601 2nd St., 740/373-3750, mariettamuseums.org, 9:30am-5pm Mon.-Sat., noon-5pm Sun., $7 adults, $4 students). Built over the site of Marietta's original Campus Martius civilian fortification constructed in 1788-1791, the museum chronicles the birth of the Northwest Territory, the establishment of Marietta, and the cultural history of Appalachia. Inside the well-organized building you'll find personal effects of some of the settlers; a copy of the Northwest Ordinance of 1787, the legislative act that opened the Northwest Territory to settlement; and displays interpreting the Indigenous cultures that lived here well before white settlement as well as life in early Marietta days. Three floors of exhibits pack in a lot of artifacts and relevant information in a relatively small space.

The last remaining part of the fortification—General Putnam's simple house—is on its original foundation, set up to appear as it did in the late 18th century, and enclosed within the museum. Tours of the house are at the top of the hour.

A small gift shop at the entrance is stocked with history books and some knickknacks. Parking at the rear of the building is free.

Ohio River Museum

While the Campus Martius museum covers a wide range of interests, the nearby **Ohio River Museum** (601 Front St., 740/373-3750, mariettamuseums.org, 9:30am-5pm Mon.-Sat., noon-5pm Sun., $7 adults, $4 children) is more single-minded, focusing on the Ohio River's importance in early American transportation. The museum, tellingly held aloft on concrete stilts for fear of flooding, holds dozens of scale replicas of the steamboats that traversed the Ohio River throughout the 19th century. The highlight of the museum is certainly the *WP Snyder Jr.,* the last steam-powered tugboat to work on the Ohio River and docked just outside the building on the Muskingum River. Tours of the boat are every hour starting at 10:30am, with the last tour at 3:30pm. Campus Martius and the Ohio River

the Valley Gem Sternwheeler on the Ohio River

Museum offer a combined ticket for $10 if you're interested in seeing both.

Mound Cemetery

When the Ohio Company settled Marietta, they found a large complex of ancient earthworks from what we now know as the Hopewell culture. In true pioneer spirit, much of it was leveled to make way for settlement, but early leaders did have enough forethought to save at least a few pieces of true American antiquity. They preserved a large conical burial mound, estimated to date from 100 BC to AD 500, in perpetuity by establishing the city's first cemetery around its base. Given that many of the original settlers were veterans of the American Revolution, there are more Revolutionary War officers buried in **Mound Cemetery** (514 Cutler St., no phone, 9am-5pm daily, free) than anywhere else in the United States. General Rufus Putnam is laid to rest in the back of the cemetery.

Additional mound remnants can be found in Quadranaou Park and Sacra Via Park less than 1 mile (1.6 km) northwest of the cemetery.

The Castle Historic House Museum

There are many lovely historic homes among Marietta's brick streets, but perhaps none as lovely as **The Castle Historic House Museum** (418 4th St., 740/373-4180, mariettacastle.org, 10am-4pm Mon.-Tues. and Thurs.-Sat., 1pm-4pm Sun., closed Jan.-Mar., check for fall and spring hours, $10 adults, $9.50 seniors, $7 children). This Gothic Revival home, constructed in 1856 by attorney and abolitionist Melvin C. Clarke, features an unusual octagonal turret and a garden of period-appropriate flowers and plants. Tours, lasting under an hour, begin in the carriage house and showcase the abundant red oak furniture, the lives of the various owners over the years, and the changes each made to the building.

Valley Gem Sternwheeler

Setting off from the Muskingum River next to the Ohio River Museum is the **Valley Gem Sternwheeler** (601 Front St., 740/373-7862, valleygemsternwheeler.com, check website for tour prices ranging $15-75). The company offers several boat tours down both the Muskingum and Ohio Rivers including historical sightseeing, dinner cruises, and murder mysteries. There's a bar on board (available only for Ohio River tours) and two levels—the lower, cafeteria-like dining level and an open second level for breezy views of the river and surroundings. If your tour doesn't include a lunch or dinner buffet, there's pizza and snacks for sale.

ENTERTAINMENT AND EVENTS
The Arts

Opened in 1919 and newly restored, the **Peoples Bank Theatre** (222 Putnam St., 740/371-5152, peoplesbanktheatre.com) is the area's primary destination for performing arts. This former vaudeville house has seen the likes of Frank Sinatra, Jimmy Stewart, and Judy Garland grace its stage. Today, the multiuse space is used for movie screenings, concerts, and theatrical performances.

Festivals and Events

The **Ohio River Sternwheel Festival** (ohioriversternwheelfestival.org) is the biggest event of the year. Over 100,000 people descend upon the city the weekend after Labor Day, with over 30 authentic sternwheel boats lining the riverbank on view as well as free entertainment and a major fireworks display. Outdoor enthusiasts will enjoy mid-August's **Rivers, Trails, and Ales Festival** (rtafest.com), which organizes group trips to the trails and rivers and invites regional craft breweries to set up shop in town.

1: The Castle Historic House Museum **2:** Mound Cemetery **3:** fireworks at the Ohio River Sternwheel Festival

RECREATION

Being located near woodsy hills and a major river has its advantages, and locals enjoy a long list of recreation opportunities. The big name in town for recreational supplies and rentals is **Marietta Adventure Company** (219 2nd St., 740/538-0801, mariettaadventurecompany.com, 10am-6pm Tues.-Sat.). The store, which occupies several floors of an old commercial building, includes a bike shop, kayak showroom, and accessories and apparel for getting your sweat on. The shop offers kayak, bike, and mountain bike rentals and shuttle service. It's also a good resource for area trails.

Cycling

There are over 30 miles (48 km) of **mountain biking trails** within Marietta city limits alone, including some very near downtown. There are about 3 miles (4.8 km) of mountain bike trails behind **Marietta Middle School** with a trailhead at the end of Butler Street near 7th Street. You can also park in the small gravel lot at Glendale Tennis Courts off Channel Lane. The trails in **Kris Mar Park** connect to a longer network. There's a trailhead with a small parking lot behind the Subway at 104 Gross Street.

The **Marietta River Trail** serenely follows along the Muskingum River and curves around downtown as it reaches the confluence with the Ohio River. Parking is at the northern trailhead in Indian Acres Park (Linwood Ave.), East Muskingum Park (310 Front St.), and Ohio Riverfront Park (off Ohio St.).

For more trails, visit mariettaadventurecompany.com/mountain-bike-rentals.

Kayaking, Canoeing, and Paddleboarding

With two rivers (Muskingum and Ohio) and a number of creeks in the area, there are several options for paddle itineraries on the water. **Marietta Adventure Company** (mariettaadventurecompany.com) sets up trips and shuttle services.

Hiking

The **Broughton Nature and Wildlife Education Area** (639 SR 821, 740/374-9396, thebroughtonfoundation.org, dawn-dusk daily, free) is just north of town and features several miles of trails through the wooded hills, including the difficult 2.7-mile (4.3-km) **Orange Loop** trail. Hikers share the path with mountain bikers.

The Marietta segment of **Wayne National Forest** (fs.usda.gov/wayne) manages and preserves some of the least developed land in Ohio and features some longer, more difficult trails for those interested in a daylong adventure or overnight backpacking excursion.

SHOPPING

The Cook's Shop (180 Front St., 740/538-6003, thecooksshop.com, 10am-5:30pm Mon.-Sat., noon-4pm Sun.) is set up something like a tool shop, only for the kitchen. You'll find a lot of American-made items, as well as cooking classes.

Nearby **Wit & Whimzy** (152 Front St., 740/371-5022, witnwhimzy.com, 11am-6pm Mon.-Fri., 10am-5pm Sat., noon-4pm Sun.) puts together a curated assortment of locally, regionally, and independently made gifts and apparel, much of it Marietta or Ohio themed.

The **Antique Mall of Marietta** (135 2nd St., 740/376-0038, 10am-6pm Mon.-Sat., 11am-5pm Sun.) has over 8,000 square feet (743 sq m) of space in a historic multistory building.

FOOD

Across the Muskingum River from downtown Marietta in the Harmar district is ★ **Busy Bee** (226 Gilman Ave., 740/373-3755, busybeerestaurant.com, 6:30am-2pm Mon.-Sat., 8am-2pm Sun., $6-12), a popular breakfast and lunch hole-in-the-wall with a patio overlooking some old train cars. This welcoming restaurant, open since 1944, prioritizes local ingredients; the wall tells you exactly where

---

1: mountain biking in Marietta **2:** The Cook's Shop **3:** The Lafayette hotel **4:** pancakes at Busy Bee in Marietta's Harmar district

they get what. The pancakes are large and the fresh-squeezed orange juice is a bargain.

On the ground floor of The Hackett boutique hotel is **The Galley** (203 2nd St., 740/374-8278, thegalleymarietta.com, 11am-10pm Mon.-Thurs., 11am-11pm Fri.-Sat., $11-34), a tavern-like American restaurant with a stately bar, stained glass, and a small covered patio. The menu covers a lot of ground including burgers, salads, pasta, and elevated surf n' turf entrees. The Alaskan halibut is especially popular. The craft beer selection is one of the most extensive around, including options from throughout Ohio.

Ask anyone in town for a dinner recommendation and they'll almost certainly mention **Marietta Brewing Company** (167 Front St., 740/373-2739, mbcpub.com, 11am-9pm Tues.-Thurs., 11am-10pm Fri.-Sat., $10-18). The family-friendly brewpub serves half-pound burgers, 10-inch personal pizzas, and other dishes to accompany craft beers made both here and elsewhere in Ohio.

The **Buckley House Restaurant** (332 Front St., 740/374-4400, bhrestaurant.com, lunch buffet 11am-2pm Mon.-Fri., dinner 5pm-9:30pm Mon.-Fri., 5pm-10pm Sat., $23-32) is the area's premier fine-dining spot. Located in a large 1879 house, the restaurant—led by master chef Emad Al-Masri—features a simple yet elegant Mediterranean menu and a classy Victorian setting.

ACCOMMODATIONS

Travel back in time to the steamboat era at **The Lafayette** (101 Front St., 740/373-5522, lafayettehotel.com, $75-170). The historic hotel dates back to 1892; its steamboat-themed lobby, blue awnings, and location near the confluence of the Muskingum and Ohio Rivers make this the most distinctive accommodation in the city. Rooms, some of them facing the water, come in all shapes and sizes and are not modernized (i.e., may possess both historical charm and quirks). There are two restaurants and a café serving Starbucks coffee within the building.

A more contemporary option is **The Hackett** (203 2nd St., 740/374-8278, the-hacketthotel.com, $129-169), a boutique hotel combining early-20th-century aesthetics and modern comforts. The five rooms come with high ceilings, exposed brick walls, and updated bathrooms.

In addition, there is a cluster of chain motels off the I-77 exit to SR 7.

INFORMATION AND SERVICES

The **Marietta-Washington County Convention and Visitors Bureau** (241 Front St., 740/373-5178, mariettaohio.org, 10am-5pm Mon.-Fri.) offers information and brochures about the area. There are also public restrooms in the building.

Marietta Memorial Hospital (401 Matthew St., 740/374-1400) is the closest hospital to Marietta's attractions. There's also an urgent care at **Quality Care Associates** (416 Front St., 740/236-4131, 8am-8pm Mon.-Sat.).

TRANSPORTATION
Getting There

Marietta is on the border with West Virginia right off I-77, about 50 minutes (48 mi/77 km) south of the junction with I-70 near Cambridge. It's 50 minutes (49 mi/79 km) east of Athens via US-50.

Greyhound (greyhound.com), **GoBus** (ridegobus.com), and **Barons Bus** (baronsbus.com) utilize a bus stop in front of the Armory building (241 Front St.) close to the action in the center of town.

Getting Around

Ohio Valley Cab (740/374-8294) serves the Marietta area with flat rates to surrounding major airports.

Marietta is compact, its roads are set on a grid, and most anything you want to do is within walking distance of downtown. Though parking is easy and cheap (or free), you could conceivably get around on foot or by bike.

Chillicothe

Ohio's first capital from 1803 to 1810 (and again from 1812 to 1816), Chillicothe boasts attractions that cover thousands of years of history, including the mounds of the Hopewell Culture National Historical Park and the stately Adena Mansion and Gardens Historic Site. You'll also find a handsome main street with interesting shops and enticing places to eat in this town of 21,000, located where the plains and the foothills meet.

SIGHTS
★ Hopewell Culture National Historical Park

One of the best places to learn about Ohio's mound builders is the **Hopewell Culture National Historical Park** (16062 SR 104, 740/774-1125, nps.gov/hocu, dawn-dusk daily, free). Built by the Hopewell culture sometime between AD 1 and AD 400, these ceremonial mound complexes intrigue with their peculiar geometry and are on a tentative list as a UNESCO World Heritage Site, and if accepted would by Ohio's first. Operated by the National Park Service, this park is actually four separate sites; start at the **Mound City Group Visitor Center** (16062 SR 104, 8:30am-5pm daily) north of town for a small museum with ceramics and other artifacts excavated from the park's grounds. The adjacent **Mound City** site itself is the most impressive, consisting of 22 mostly conical earthen mounds encircled by a low wall. Signs throughout help interpret the uses of the mounds, which included social, religious, and burial purposes. There is little shade while walking among the mounds, so come prepared with sunscreen or an umbrella during the hot summer months.

What remains at the **Hopeton Earthworks** (990 Hopetown Rd.) and **Hopewell Mound Group** (4721 Sulphur Lick Rd.), both within a 10-minute drive of Mound City, requires a bit more imagination because the mounds have been reduced to their foundations either from farming or erosion, but interpretive trails explain what archaeologists have discovered and what they believe the sites were used for. **Seip Earthworks** (7078 US-50, Bainbridge), 16

Mound City at Hopewell Culture National Historical Park

miles (26 km) southwest of the Mound City site, is one of the largest the Hopewell are known to have built, though the mound today is reconstructed.

★ Adena Mansion and Gardens Historic Site

On the northwest side of the city, the **Adena Mansion and Gardens Historic Site** (847 Adena Rd., 740/772-1500, adenamansion. com, 9am-5pm Wed.-Sat., noon-5pm Sun., $10 adults, $9 seniors, $5 children) preserves the 300 remaining acres of the once 2,000-acre estate of early Ohio politician Thomas Worthington. A senator and governor in the time of Jefferson's and Madison's presidencies, Worthington moved into the stone Federal-style house when it was constructed in 1807 and conducted his business from his estate, quite grand for a state then only four years old. The mansion was designed by Benjamin Henry Latrobe, one of the designers of the U.S. Capitol and whose work in Greek Revival architecture earned him the moniker "The Father of American Architecture." Today, the mansion has been restored to its 1807 appearance, complete with era-appropriate furnishings and original Worthington family belongings. One-hour tours of the mansion start in front of the house at the top of the hour.

In addition to the mansion are walkable floral and vegetable gardens, outer buildings such as a smokehouse and barn, and a modern visitors center and museum, which provides information on the Worthington family, the notable early-19th-century characters that visited the estate, and Ohio's road to statehood.

Leo Petroglyphs

Some 25 miles (40 km) southeast of Chillicothe are the mysterious **Leo Petroglyphs** (357 Township Hwy. 224, Ray, 800/600-0144, ohiohistory.org, dawn-dusk daily, free). It's not clear who carved the 40 or so figures into the sandstone boulder, though it's thought to be the work of the Fort Ancient people nearly 1,000 years ago. Covered from the elements

by a shelter, they can be hard to see, but the highlight is a figure with a human head, deer antlers, and bird feet. At any rate, the shelter and the trail behind to a small gorge could use some upgrading.

ENTERTAINMENT AND EVENTS
The Arts
TECUMSEH! OUTDOOR DRAMA

Since 1973, summer outdoor drama *Tecumseh!* (tecumsehdrama.com) has dazzled millions of viewers in the 1,600-seat Sugarloaf Mountain Amphitheatre (5968 Marietta Rd.), just north of Chillicothe, telling the story of Shawnee warrior and leader Tecumseh with pyrotechnics, battles, and horses in the giant outdoor stage. The story follows and sympathizes with the eponymous character as he builds a confederacy of Indigenous tribes to defend the Ohio country from encroaching settlement and broken promises. A few notches above your average outdoor drama, the show was penned by playwright and novelist Allan W. Eckert and features a score recorded by the London Symphony Orchestra and narration by actor Graham Greene of the Oneida Nation. Behind-the-scenes tours and a buffet, both available for additional charge, add to a memorable night.

RECREATION
Hiking

It's said that the image of wheat and low-lying mountains on Ohio's great seal was inspired by the view from Thomas Worthington's Adena estate looking toward Sugarloaf Mountain. You can hike the mountain and nearby ridges at **Great Seal State Park** (4908 Marietta Rd., 740/887-4818, ohiodnr. gov, dawn-dusk daily, free), with over 20 miles (32 km) of moderate-to-difficult trails. Print a map of the trails beforehand—it can be easy to get turned around.

1: downtown Chillicothe **2:** Ivy's Home and Garden **3:** Adena Mansion and Gardens Historic Site

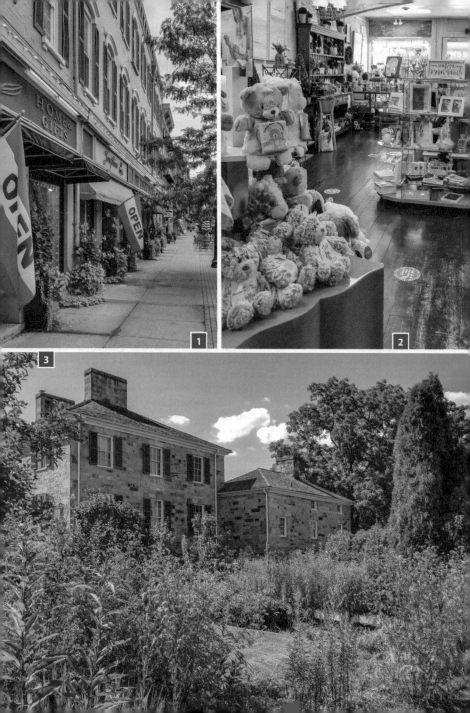

SHOPPING

Ivy's Home and Garden (105 N. Paint St., 740/779-9522, 10am-8pm Mon.-Sat., noon-5pm Sun.) boasts a beautiful brick-and-wood interior stocked with home accessories, fragrant soaps, and women's and children's clothing.

Next door is the unique **History Store** (101 N. Paint St., 740/775-7400, the-history-store.myshopify.com, 10am-8pm Mon.-Sat.), which specializes in military miniatures spanning centuries but also carries books and puzzles.

The Fort Collective (107 E. 2nd St.) has three clothing boutiques, including **Hometown Threads** (740/851-6103, thread-soh.com, 10am-7pm Mon.-Fri., 9am-7pm Sat.), which stocks Ohio- and Chillicothe-themed apparel.

FOOD

The **Old Canal Smoke House** (94 E. Water St., 740/779-3278, oldcanalsmokehouse. com, 11am-9pm Mon.-Thurs., 11am-10pm Fri.-Sat., 11am-8pm Sun., $9-24) is a casual, modern tavern in an 1850s forge with a long list of quality sides to choose from to go with your 'cue.

R Kitchen (66 N. Paint St., 740/775-4555, rkitchenonpaint.com, 11am-8pm Tues.-Thurs., 11am-9pm Fri.-Sat., $10-25) serves upscale comfort food in a historic space mixed with modern touches. Ingredients are locally sourced, as are the craft brews.

A couple of local celebrities—a best-selling author and a two-time Food Network champion—operate bakery **High Five Cakes** (81 N. Paint St., 740/775-2253, 10am-6pm Tues.-Thurs., 10am-7pm Fri.-Sat.). The crew specializes in cupcakes, but also serves cookies, brownies, and bubble tea. An adorable kids' nook will keep little ones occupied while you enjoy your selection.

Contemporary **Rost Coffee** (107 E. 2nd St., 740/779-3679, rostcoffee.com, 7am-7pm Mon.-Sat.) is part of the Fort Collective building, also home to three boutiques and coworking space. There's plenty of seating in this large space, which features pastries and specialty coffee drinks like the Brown Butter.

ACCOMMODATIONS

The biggest cluster of motels is off the Bridge Street/SR 159 exit from US-35.

The **Atwood House** (68 S. Paint St., 740/774-1606, atwoodhousebandb.com, $125-160) is an elegant 1843 Greek Revival home near downtown Chillicothe with four historic rooms. All come with private bathrooms except for the Hunt Room, whose bathroom is in the hallway.

INFORMATION AND SERVICES

The **Ross-Chillicothe Convention and Visitors Bureau** runs a tourist information center (230 N. Plaza Blvd., 740/702-7677, visitchillicotheohio.com, 8:30am-5pm Mon.-Fri.) on the north end of town.

The **Adena Regional Medical Center** (272 Hospital Rd., 740/779-7500) is the area's primary general hospital. The same system runs **Adena Urgent Care** (55 Centennial Blvd., 740/779-4000, 8am-9pm daily) on the west side of town. There's also **Family Urgent Care** (879 N. Bridge St., 740/772-5050, 9am-8pm Mon.-Fri., 9am-7pm Sat.-Sun.) a little closer to the center of town.

TRANSPORTATION
Getting There

Chillicothe is a straight shot south of Columbus on US-23, taking roughly an hour (47 mi/76 km) to drive. **Barons Bus** (baronsbus.com) stops at a BP gas station at 760 N. Bridge Street, helpfully near food and quality motel options.

Getting Around

The **Chillicothe Transit System** (chillicothe.com) runs infrequent routes through town and to nearby communities. Fares are generally $1, though it depends on your destination. Only the city routes run on Saturday, and there is no transit on Sunday. **Chillicothe Cab** (740/775-7433) operates in the area.

Who Was the "Mothman"?

"It was like a man with wings."

On November 12, 1966, gravediggers in Clendenin, West Virginia, witnessed a large flying creature swooping from tree to tree above them. Three days later, two couples in Point Pleasant, West Virginia, just across the Ohio River from Gallipolis, reported to the local newspaper that a grayish "man with wings" with a 10-foot wingspan and glowing red eyes chased them as they drove through the outskirts of town. "I'm a hard guy to scare," reported one of the men, "but last night I was for getting out of there."

More sightings around Point Pleasant popped up throughout the following year. People likened the eyes to bicycle reflectors when shining a light in the strange creature's eyes, if they managed to do so at all. The *Gettysburg Times* reported eight additional sightings, including two volunteer firemen who reported "a very large bird with red eyes." Perhaps the idea of this Mothman would have petered out if not for the tragedy that transpired on December 15, 1967, when the Silver Bridge connecting Point Pleasant and Gallipolis over the Ohio River collapsed during rush hour, killing 46. Paranoid locals wondered at the Mothman's appearance in conjunction with the tragedy: was the Mothman a harbinger of doom, or the creator of it?

While there could be simple explanations for these mysterious events (skeptics believe the Mothman was likely a sandhill crane, which can grow quite large, and the bridge was old and carrying a heavier load than it was designed for), the situation's spookiness hasn't left the imagination. In fact, it's celebrated. In Point Pleasant, the Mothman Museum (400 Main St., Point Pleasant, WV, 304/812-5211, mothmanmuseum.com, 10am-5pm Mon.-Thurs., 10am-6pm Fri.-Sat., noon-5pm Sun., $4.50 adults, $1.50 children) attracts the superstitious, the seekers of the paranormal, and those in search of quirky merchandise. In addition to exhibiting press clippings, eyewitness accounts, and other documents about the sightings and bridge collapse, the museum has a collection of props from the 2002 film centered on the legend, *The Mothman Prophecies*, starring Richard Gere. The third weekend of September, the town hosts the Mothman Festival (mothmanfestival.com) to celebrate all things Mothman. You'll also find a Mothman statue outside of the museum.

But will you find the Mothman?

Gallipolis

Gallipolis, or "City of Gauls," was established in 1790 by a group of French aristocrats fleeing their own Revolution. They'd been duped by a fraudulent land-development company into thinking they owned land in the Northwest Territory and made it all the way down to the Ohio River only to find out that they owned nothing. After some sorting out with the Washington administration and the Ohio Company in Marietta, the French immigrants were granted a plot of land further along the river. These city folks didn't come with the requisite skills necessary for pioneers, yet somehow they survived.

Today, Gallipolis is part of the Point Pleasant micropolitan area, which more recently is associated with the mysterious "Mothman" appearances in the 1960s. The town is also home of the original Bob Evans Farms, from which the Bob Evans restaurant chain developed.

SIGHTS
Bob Evans Farm, Restaurant, and Museum

Bob Evans, his wife, Jewell, and their six children lived on this 1,000-acre farm for 20 years, during which time they began a sausage-making business in 1948 that expanded to deliveries to 1,800 locations and

14 trucks. Today, Bob Evans restaurants are in 18 states and the **Bob Evans Farm, Restaurant, and Museum** (791 Farmview Rd., Bidwell, 740/245-5304, bobevans.com/about-us/the-farm, 10am-4pm daily, free), northwest of Gallipolis, celebrates the history of the family and the country restaurant chain they established. The land includes log cabins, mills, and a cemetery with Revolutionary War veterans. The homestead, originally a stagecoach inn and listed in the National Register of Historic Places, houses the museum, which chronicles the restaurant's history and shows old commercials that Bob and Jewell filmed in their kitchen. Of course, there is a Bob Evans restaurant on the premises.

Our House Tavern

In town is the restored **Our House Tavern** (432 First Ave., 800/752-2618, ohiohistory.org, 10am-4pm Wed.-Sat., 1pm-4pm Sun. Memorial Day-Labor Day, $4 adults, $3 seniors, $1 children). This Federal-style tavern and inn, built in 1819, hosted travelers and pioneers coming down the Ohio River, including French general and Revolutionary War hero Marquis de Lafayette, who visited in 1825 and left a jacket here that's now on display. View the dining room, taproom, and other facilities to get an idea of the many taverns that dotted the riverside in Ohio's early days. Call to arrange a tour.

FOOD

For a small town, Gallipolis has a solid variety of food options.

Tuscany Italian Restaurant (1308 Eastern Ave., 740/446-7800, tuscanygallipolis.com, 11am-9pm Sun.-Thurs., 11am-10pm Fri.-Sat., $10-20) covers a large range of pasta, meaty entrees, and seafood. The portions in this casual establishment are good sized, but save room for some of the chef's "secret recipe" carrot cake.

Family-run **Five Rivers Indian Cuisine** (234 3rd Ave., 740/441-5871, fiveriversoh.com, lunch 11am-2pm Wed.-Sat., dinner 5pm-9pm

Wed.-Sat., $9-15) prepares authentic Punjabi-Indian and Indo-Chinese dishes that you could easily spend twice as much money on in larger cities. There's a bar section with some popular Ohio craft beers and a back patio for additional seating.

ACCOMMODATIONS

There's a handful of motels, both chain and family-run, in Gallipolis. The nicest reviews go to **Hampton Inn Gallipolis** (444 Upper River Rd., 740/446-8000, hilton.com, $100-140), with a free hot breakfast, small indoor pool and hot tub, and basic but spacious rooms.

For a more distinctive experience across the river in Point Pleasant, West Virginia, there's the historic **Lowe Hotel** (401 Main St., Point Pleasant, WV, 304/675-2260, thelowehotel.com, $119-179). Continuously operating since 1901, this hotel offers a high-ceilinged lobby, family suites, a bar, an art gallery, libraries, and reading rooms. Located directly across the street from the Mothman Museum, the hotel sometimes attracts clientele looking for paranormal activity in the admittedly spooky building.

INFORMATION AND SERVICES

The **Gallia County Convention and Visitors Bureau** (441 2nd Ave., 740/446-6882, visitgallia.com, 8am-5pm Mon.-Fri.) provides information on the area.

Holzer Medical Center (100 Jackson Pike, 740/446-5201) has an emergency room. The center also runs an urgent care at **Fruth Pharmacy** (204 2nd Ave., 740/446-5110, 9am-7pm Mon.-Sat., noon-6pm Sun.).

TRANSPORTATION

Gallipolis is on the border with West Virginia at the intersection of SR 7 and US-35. It's about 50 minutes south of Athens (43 mi/69 km) using US-33 and SR 7 and an hour southeast of Chillicothe (60 mi/97 km) via US-35. There is no intercity bus service or nearby airport.

Background

The Landscape

GEOGRAPHY

Ohio is 220 miles (355 km) wide by 220 miles (355 km) long, making it the 34th-largest state in the United States at nearly 45,000 square miles (11,655 sq km). Its highest point is Campbell Hill near Bellefontaine at 1,549 feet (472 m) above sea level. Its lowest point is the Ohio River at 455 feet (139 m).

Over 14,000 years ago, Ohio's geography was marked by what was covered by glaciers and what was not. The unglaciated Appalachian plateau covering much of the south and east of the state consists of

rugged hills, though none are particularly high. The western half is known as the Till Plains, a mostly flat region that marks the beginning of the nation's corn belt, which stretches to Nebraska. The border around Lake Erie is part of the Great Lakes Plains, a fertile lowland that widens in the northwest into an area that was once known as the Great Black Swamp. This massive low-lying wetland was drained by settlers. Hugging the Ohio River in the state's southwest corner is the Bluegrass region, an area of rolling hills more commonly associated with Kentucky.

CLIMATE

Ohio's climate has traditionally been classified as humid continental, transitioning into humid subtropical the farther south you go. With ongoing climate change, much of the state can now be classified as the latter. Ohio is at the mercy of both cold, dry fronts from Canada and hot, moist fronts from the Gulf of Mexico, meaning potentially frigid and snowy winters and uncomfortably hot and humid summers. Generally, though, Ohio enjoys a temperate climate with four distinct seasons. Sunshine can be scarce in the winter months. In fact, Columbus, Cleveland, and Cincinnati are among the 10 cloudiest cities in the United States. Precipitation is fairly even year-round, averaging about 40 inches (102 cm) a year, including 28 inches (71 cm) of snow, though the north can get much more than this and the south can get much less. The snowbelt east of Cleveland averages as much as 100 inches (254 cm) of snow per year thanks to the lake effect. Though it is not located in "Tornado Alley," Ohio is victim to its fair share of tornados, some of them powerful and destructive. Flooding sometimes occurs, primarily in the Appalachian region's valleys and along the Ohio River.

ENVIRONMENTAL ISSUES

As a long-standing hotbed of agricultural and industrial activity, Ohio faces a number of environmental challenges, and has addressed some of them successfully. Ohio's waterways in particular have come a long way since Cleveland's Cuyahoga River caught fire in 1969. In 2019, the Ohio Environmental Protection Agency declared fish caught in the river safe enough to consume.

Of greatest concern is Lake Erie, the most diverse ecosystem of the Great Lakes and a source of drinking water for 11 million Americans and Canadians. Algae blooms caused by polluted runoff from large-scale farms and other industries decrease the quality and safety of the water, rendering beaches unsafe on occasion. When the algae dies off, the decomposition depletes oxygen and creates "dead zones" in the lake. Additionally, the lake is under threat from numerous invasive species that have either been introduced intentionally or that have hitched a ride along maritime ship traffic. An estimated 180 non-native species can be found in the lake including zebra mussels, goby, and even Pacific salmon. The most worrisome is the Asian grass carp, which threatens the entire Great Lakes ecosystem. Though breeding populations have not successfully invaded at this time, increased numbers could severely disrupt the existing food chain.

On land, Ohio has lost 90 percent of its original wetlands and much of its original forest cover. Historians estimate that the state was 95 percent covered by trees when pioneers arrived. By the early 20th century, that number was down to about 10 percent. The number has stabilized at around 30 percent in the 21st century.

Previous: Cleveland skyline on the Cuyahoga River.

Plants and Animals

TREES AND FLOWERS

About 100 species of trees can be found in Ohio's forests. Oak and hickory trees are the most common, with some maple, birch, sycamore, and pine as well. And of course there's also the buckeye, the state tree, which gives Ohioans their nickname (and the poisonous nuts to which The Ohio State University owes its mascot).

Wildflowers abound. Spring brings colorful blooms across the state, including bloodroot, trillium, and bluebells. Some 47 species of orchid can be found in the state's forests.

MAMMALS

When settlers first came to Ohio, the forests teemed with many of the continent's large mammals, including elk, cougars, wolves, and bears. Hunting and loss of habitat eradicated most of these populations early on. Today, Ohio is home to over 50 species of mammals, primarily rodents and small carnivores. Restored forest and the lack of major predators have caused white-tailed deer numbers to balloon to an estimated herd of at least 700,000. They are a dangerous presence on Ohio's roadways.

Black bears were among the extirpated species in the 19th century, but they're on the rebound. Around 50-100 individuals roam the eastern half of the state. Most sightings occur in the extreme northeastern counties. Likewise, after disappearing in the 19th century, bobcats have returned to their native land. While the cats remain elusive, sightings in the southeast forests have increased dramatically since the turn of the 21st century.

BIRDS

Over 400 species of birds have been reported in Ohio, though only about half breed in the state. Ohio's location on a major migratory route keeps the state on the birding world radar, with the northwest shore of Lake Erie in and around the Ottawa National Wildlife Refuge an area of particular focus. Birders "flock" to northwest Ohio, known as "The Warbler Capital of the World," to catch a peek of the colorful, diminutive songbirds.

In 1979, Ohio was home to as few as four breeding pairs of bald eagles, which came dangerously close to extinction in the state. Federal regulations and the banning of the chemical DDT helped eagle populations recover. By 2019, the estimated number of breeding pairs was up to 346. Eagles can now be spotted in nearly every county—a rewarding discovery in the state's parks and along its waterways.

REPTILES

Ohio is home to 47 species of snakes, turtles, and lizards. Three species of snakes—the northern copperhead, timber rattlesnake, and massasauga—are venomous. The northern copperhead and timber rattlesnake are primarily found in the southeastern portion of the state throughout the Appalachian foothills, while the massasauga is scattered in bogs and wetlands throughout the state. The copperhead is the most aggressive but typically delivers a nonlethal dose of venom. The timber rattlesnake is the largest and most dangerous, but is thankfully a shy fellow.

AMPHIBIANS

Nearly 40 species of amphibians, including 25 types of newts and salamanders, have been recorded in Ohio's wetlands and woods. Most notable is the largest species of salamander in North America, the eastern hellbender, also known as the "snot otter," which can grow to over 2 feet (0.6 m) in size (and is harmless, despite the scary-sounding name). It's one of five endangered amphibian species in the state, the others being the eastern spadefoot toad, green salamander, blue-spotted salamander, and the cave salamander. Most of Ohio's amphibian species are found in or near wetland habitats such as bogs and streams. In spring, newly filled vernal pools in the forests provide essential habitat for amphibians to lay their eggs away from the predators that reside in permanent bodies of water.

INSECTS AND ARACHNIDS

The usual cast of characters show up in the summer: bees, wasps, mosquitos, butterflies, moths, and various beetles. One in particular, the emerald ash borer, is an unwelcome invasive species wreaking havoc on Ohio's ash trees. Fireflies illuminate lawns and crop fields in early summer.

There aren't too many spiders in Ohio that pose a threat to humans, but the ones that do mostly fall under two categories: recluse and widow spiders. These are typically found in abandoned houses or small sheds in the southern half of the state, though confirmed sightings and/or bites come from all parts of Ohio. It doesn't hurt to check inside shoes and gloves that have been outside before inserting your appendages.

History

EARLY CIVILIZATION

Nomadic hunters arrived in the area now known as Ohio around 13,000 BC and maintained a hunter-gatherer lifestyle until around 800 BC, when the Adena people began to gather in small groups and cultivate crops such as squash and sunflowers. Pottery from this age suggests that the Adena stored food for long periods of time, offering further proof of permanent settlements. They were also mound builders, dotting central and southern Ohio with hundreds of conical burial mounds, some of which survive today. The Adena thrived until somewhere around AD 1200.

A second group, the Hopewell culture, lived alongside the Adena between 100 BC and AD 500. Like the Adena, the Hopewell built burial mounds but also constructed enormous, geometric earthworks for ceremonial and social purposes. The culture maintained a vast trade network, stretching from the Rocky Mountains to the Atlantic Ocean, utilizing the Ohio River and Great Lakes as transit routes. Their settlements were larger than those of the Adena and they cultivated additional crops such as corn.

Perhaps around AD 900, groups in Ohio including the Fort Ancient people, Whittlesey people, and Monongahela people began to build larger permanent villages, housing up to 200 people near prime corn-growing land. These groups remained in Ohio until the 17th century, when the Iroquois tribes of upland New York sought to expand their hunting grounds to accommodate their growing trade with Europeans. These Beaver Wars, as they came to be called, wiped out the existing cultures in Ohio as far as historians can tell. Remnants of these cultures likely evacuated the area as the Iroquois used the land to hunt pelts. It was around this time that French explorers first set foot in Ohio, finding a land largely devoid of people. The name "O-Y-O" (the Seneca term for the Ohio River, meaning "great river") stuck. As the Iroquois Confederacy waned, historical Ohio tribes such as the Shawnee, Wyandot, Delaware, and Miami moved back in from the east and south.

The French claimed the Ohio Country for themselves but weren't especially interested in setting up permanent populations, so they got along reasonably well with the local people. However, when the French lost the French and Indian War and signed the Treaty of Paris in 1763, they ceded all claims to the land to

Great Britain without consulting the tribes who lived there. Unlike the French, the British and their colonists viewed settlement in Ohio longingly. As settlers encroached, tensions flared and led to sporadic violence. Both sides committed horrific massacres, notably at the Moravian mission village of Gnadenhutten in 1782, where U.S. militiamen massacred 96 Christian Delaware people, justifying the violence as retaliation for raids in Pennsylvania. The evidence that the murdered people were guilty of the raids was scant enough that some of the militia refused to take part and the massacre was controversial even among frontiersmen.

NORTHWEST TERRITORY

Twenty years after the 1763 Treaty of Paris, American patriots John Jay and John Adams traveled to France to hash out the details to end the Revolutionary War between Great Britain and its American colonies. As part of the 1783 Treaty of Paris, the British wanted to keep their land northwest of the Ohio River, which they had won from the French. The Americans felt differently. "Rather than relinquish our claim to the western territory, I will go home and urge my countrymen to take up arms again and fight until they secure their rights, or shed the last drop of blood!" John Adams warned. The British yielded, and the territory became the property of the new United States of America.

Though the United States had earned its freedom through victory in war, the fledging country was financially strapped. The government's thin resources and near-worthless currency wrecked the economy and made it impossible to pay Revolutionary War veterans their due. Frustrated, indebted farmers in Massachusetts—veterans among them—stormed an armory during Shays' Rebellion, highlighting the tensions between the government and citizens. The government speculated that Ohio's land could be used as payment to veterans for their services.

Ohio was sitting there looking pretty. Thomas Jefferson himself called the Ohio River "the most beautiful river on earth," though he'd never seen it personally. Ohio had been romanticized by Europeans and colonists for more than a hundred years. Early French explorer St. John de Crevecoeur had described the land as "without doubt, the most fertile country, with the most varied soil, the best watered, and that which offers to agriculture and commerce, the most abundant and easy resources, of all those which the Europeans have ever discovered." On July 13, 1787, the Confederation Congress passed the Northwest Ordinance, opening the Northwest Territory as a legal place to settle. Many of the most ardent supporters of opening up the land to settlement were of New England Puritan stock. They successfully argued to make slavery illegal in the new territory.

Shortly after in 1788, the Ohio Company of Associates—comprised largely of former officers in the Continental Army and led by Revolutionary War hero Rufus Putnam—founded Marietta, the first settlement in the new Northwest Territory under the legal protection of the United States government. (Indigenous tribes, pre-existing French settlements, and squatters already occupied the area that is now Ohio, Indiana, Michigan, Illinois, and Wisconsin.) When Putnam and crew arrived at the mouth of the Muskingum River, they found a vast complex of mounds and earthworks near their intended settlement. When they asked the local tribes about the mounds, they more or less shrugged and said the land was like that when they found it.

"No colony in America was ever settled under such favorable auspices as that which has just commenced at Muskingum," George Washington said of Marietta, which became the capital of the Northwest Territory. Though Marietta faced early challenges and threats from nearby tribes, the settlement's success only fueled "Ohio Fever." Newcomers coming down the Ohio River stopped at the settlement on the way to settling additional towns. Downriver, Cincinnati in particular grew at an astounding rate, swiftly surpassing Marietta in size. A small group of French craftsmen and city folk, fleeing the French Revolution and duped by the so-called Scioto Company into believing they owned land in the territory, arrived and settled Gallipolis, or "City of Gauls" in 1790. Meanwhile, groups consisting primarily of New Englanders settled the northeast part of the state near what is today Cleveland.

Increasing numbers of settlers encroached on lands held by the Indigenous population, who began to withdraw from their pioneer neighbors. Tensions further north prompted President Washington to order Major General Arthur St. Clair, who was the governor of the Northwest Territory, to amass an army and march north from Fort Washington near Cincinnati to establish forts and force the Indigenous population to abide by existing treaties. St. Clair's force was composed primarily of inexperienced, undisciplined militia. Facing unusually harsh autumn weather and low food supplies, the force camped near the Wabash River. On November 4, 1791, a force of 1,000 men of the Western Confederacy of Native Americans led by Miami warrior Little Turtle surrounded the camp and exacted a heavy toll on the surprised American force, who fled all the way back to Fort Washington. Nearly all of St. Clair's army was killed, wounded, or captured in what was to become known as St. Clair's Defeat. The Western Confederacy suffered no more than 60 total casualties.

In 1792, Washington appointed General "Mad" Anthony Wayne to train a more suitable army to accomplish what St. Clair could not. Wayne built additional forts in the northwest part of Ohio, inciting unrest in the Indigenous population. Things came to a head in 1794 at the Battle of Fallen Timbers, where Wayne soundly defeated Shawnee leader Blue Jacket and his force. In 1795, the Treaty of Greenville opened all of eastern and southern Ohio to settlement, while confining Indigenous tribes to the northwest corner. Bloodshed would continue for decades, but the Treaty of Greenville was the beginning of the end of Indigenous occupancy of Ohio.

EARLY STATEHOOD

In 1803, President Thomas Jefferson endorsed the United States Congress' decision to make Ohio the nation's 17th state, with Chillicothe as the state capital. Within the first decade, the state's citizens found themselves uncomfortably close to battle, with the War of 1812 raging just to the north on Lake Erie and in Michigan. One of the young nation's greatest victories occurred off the shores of Put-in-Bay when 28-year-old Oliver Hazard Perry's fleet defeated the British navy on Lake Erie. "We have met the enemy and they are ours," Perry famously dispatched.

With the arrival of steamboat technology, Ohio's population continued to climb rapidly, from 45,000 in 1800 to 500,000 in 1815. Cincinnati in particular became the nation's first western boomtown. Industry proliferated in the city, known as "Porkopolis" for its meat-processing plants. Breweries kept busy both employing and serving the substantial German immigrant population. Elsewhere in the state, agriculture was the primary pursuit. Political infighting among Ohio's different towns led to the creation of a new capital city in the center of the state, Columbus, in 1812. The Ohio and Erie Canal, completed in 1832, connected the Ohio River with Cleveland and Lake Erie, further promoting development within the interior. Traffic on the Ohio River and the canal made it easier for Ohioans to sell their products across the eastern half of North America.

Meanwhile, Indigenous occupancy in Ohio was all but finished. The Removal Act, passed in 1830, relocated what remained of the Indigenous population to specific villages elsewhere. The Wyandot were the last to leave the state in 1842.

Columbus remained small until the National Road connected it with Baltimore in 1831, bringing in Irish and German immigrants. The development of railroads in the 1840s and 1850s would further encourage growth and trade for Columbus, Cleveland, Akron, and Springfield. Ultimately, railroads would divert traffic from Cincinnati, which relied more on the Ohio River for trade, though the city continued to grow in both size and prominence throughout the 19th century. The canals too would fall victim to the proliferation, speed, and ease of the railroads. But the railroads also contributed to the development of further industry in the state, with iron an important driver of the economy for much of the century.

By the time the Civil War began, Ohio was a highly populated, centrally located state in the Union, making it a crucial logistics hub. Most Ohioans supported the Union cause. Some, notably the Peace Democrats, opposed Lincoln's policies. Nevertheless, Ohio played an important role in the Underground Railroad. It supplied more troops to the Union per capita than any other state, as well as many of its notable generals, including William Tecumseh Sherman and Ulysses S. Grant, who would later become president. After Grant's presidency, six of the following eleven presidents of the United States were born in Ohio. The war, burgeoning railroad system, explosion of industry, and continued immigration only buoyed the state's political and economic power.

CONTEMPORARY TIMES

Ohio entered the 20th century at the height of its strength relative to the rest of the country, with political influence, industrial vigor, and two cities in the top 10 by population. Akron was the "Rubber Capital of the World" with the four major tire-producing companies headquartered in the city. Toledo was similarly known as "The Glass City" for its glass manufacturers. Cleveland's John D. Rockefeller ran the gigantic multinational corporation Standard Oil, the largest oil refiner in the world, until 1897, making him the richest man in the world. Dayton was put on the national map when two bicycle shop owners, Orville and Wilbur Wright, managed the first successful airplane flight in 1903.

The Wrights' invention would soon be put to use in combat when World War I broke out in 1914. Ohio's still large and influential German immigrant population was eyed with suspicion, and the state lost many of its German-language schools and newspapers. In reality, the German immigrants were no less devoted to the United States than their neighbors. German American Eddie Rickenbacker from Columbus was the top American fighter pilot during the war, with 26 airborne victories. Since the turn of the century, though, it wasn't primarily Germans coming to Ohio. Poles, Hungarians, and Czechs came in droves, especially to Cleveland. The Irish came too, as did African Americans moving from the South. These newcomers were quickly put to work. Many of the state's most impressive public works and buildings were constructed during the first few decades of the 20th century.

The Great Depression hit the entire country hard. Ohio was no exception, though industry once again boomed during World War II. Roughly 12 percent of the state's population served in the military during the war. Columbus-based research center Battelle participated in the Manhattan Project, and Ohioan pilot Paul Tibbets flew the *Enola Gay* over Hiroshima, Japan, on August 6, 1945, and dropped an atomic bomb over the city, effectively ending the war.

In the following decades, Ohioans made substantial contributions during the space race between the United States and the Soviet Union. Notable astronauts John Glenn, Neil Armstrong, and Jim Lovell all hail from the state. The NASA John H. Glenn Research Center at Lewis Field in Cleveland made irreplaceable contributions to space exploration, including the development of the liquid hydrogen rocket engine.

Many of Ohio's cities peaked in population around 1950. The construction of the interstate system, suburbanization, white flight, and a newfound nationwide attraction to cities in the Sun Belt began a long, steady decline in the population of most Ohio cities. Longstanding degradation of the environment began to exact its toll on the state. Cleveland's polluted Cuyahoga River made embarrassing headlines in 1969 when it caught fire. Strip mining rendered parts of the Appalachian plateau unrecognizable. Pollution from factories, coal mining, and other industry threatened to devastate what remained of Ohio's natural resources. The changing global landscape of manufacturing and energy in the 1970s further cemented the decline of most of Ohio's cities as the number of blue-collar jobs plummeted. Only Columbus emerged relatively unscathed because its economy was more reliant on government and education than manufacturing.

With the turn of the 21st century, Ohio was ready for revitalization. Citizens looked at their inner cities with new interest and began to invest in urban renewal projects and housing. Further investment in public art, performing arts centers, and sports venues once again attracted crowds to Ohio's downtowns. New regulations and conservation movements have also improved Ohio's environment, though challenges remain. The economy has pivoted to finance, insurance, healthcare, and retail, though manufacturing and agriculture are still mainstays. Today, Ohio enjoys some of the nation's finest public libraries, zoos, and amusement parks alongside the treasures left behind from over 13,000 years of history.

Government and Economy

GOVERNMENT

Ohio has played an important, even essential, role in American politics for nearly its entire statehood. Eight presidents either were born or spent substantial percentages of their political lives in Ohio, giving the state the nickname the "Mother of Presidents." Only Virginia boasts more.

As its citizens are reminded every election cycle, Ohio is very much a swing state. Democrats maintain a firm grip on major cities, the northeast, and suburbs with high education levels. Republican strongholds include rural areas and affluent exurban areas surrounding Columbus and Cincinnati. Presidential candidates funnel millions into campaigns in Ohio, all knowing that the state can lean either direction on any given year. So too does the political landscape change on the state level, with power ping-ponging between the major parties. As of 2020, power sits with the Republicans. Ohio is also known as a bellwether state, voting for the victors in all but two presidential elections since 1896 (Dewey in 1944 and Nixon in 1960). No Republican has ever been elected to the presidency without winning Ohio.

ECONOMY

Measuring by gross domestic product, Ohio's economy is the 7th-largest state economy in the country and would be the 21st-largest global economy, sitting behind Saudi Arabia. The two long-standing stalwarts of the economy have been agriculture and manufacturing. Agriculture, though still important, has declined in prominence over the last several decades. Soybeans, corn, and dairy account for much of the agricultural output. Manufacturing is currently tied with financial services as the largest segment of the state's gross domestic product. Ohio is second to Michigan in automotive manufacturing jobs and is a major producer of chemicals, fabricated metal parts, rubber, and electrical equipment. Transportation and logistics also play an important role, as the state is within a day's drive of half the nation's population and manufacturing output. Ohio's contemporary economy is buoyed by healthcare, insurance, and retail. It is home to 25 of the Fortune 500 companies, including Kroger, Procter & Gamble, Marathon Petroleum, Nationwide Insurance, Goodyear Tire and Rubber, Macy's, American Electric Power, L Brands, Progressive Insurance, and Wendy's.

People and Culture

DEMOGRAPHICS
Population
Ohio is the seventh most populated state in the United States, with around 11.8 million people in the 2020 census. Population growth is slow, only increasing 2.3 percent between 2010 and 2020, with most of that growth occurring in the Columbus and Cincinnati areas. Columbus leads the pace as one of only 14 cities in the nation to gain more than 100,000 people in the 2010s, its metro area accounting for 90 percent of the state's growth during that period. Cincinnati turned a corner after decades of losing population and grew 4.2 percent. However, two-thirds of the state's 88 counties lost population during the same period, and the state's other cities all continue to lose population, albeit at a slower rate than the late 20th century. With this sluggish population growth, Ohio lost a congressional seat after the 2020 census.

The same period saw nearby states Illinois and West Virginia lose population and other Great Lakes states see similarly small rates of population growth. In a sense, then, Ohio is holding its own in a region still transitioning out of a manufacturing-focused economy.

Ethnicity
Though Ohio's population is diversifying, it remains one of the least ethnically diverse states in the country. 78.4 percent of the state's inhabitants identify as non-Hispanic white, 13.1 percent as Black, 4.0 percent Hispanic, and 2.5 percent Asian. About 4.6 percent of the population is foreign born.

Almost all of Ohio's diversity resides within its large cities and their suburbs. Nearly half of Cleveland's population identifies as Black, and another 12 percent as Hispanic. In Cincinnati, 42 percent of the population is Black. In Columbus, 5.8 percent identifies as Asian (nearly 20 percent do so in suburb Dublin) and over 12 percent of the city is foreign born, a higher percentage than the state's other cities. Columbus is quickly diversifying; the number of Hispanic residents increased by 58 percent and the number of Asian residents by over 75 percent between 2010 and 2020. Cleveland and some of its suburbs saw similar increases of Hispanic and Asian residents.

THE AMISH AND MENNONITES
The most widely known subculture in Ohio is the Amish, an agrarian, traditional Christian sect of Anabaptists that adhere to a code of simple living and dress. There are over 70,000 Amish in Ohio, 40,000 of which reside in Holmes County, the largest concentration of Amish in the world. Most Amish fall under the New Order Amish and the Old World Amish, both of which include smaller subgroups. Both groups reject most forms of modern technology, dress plainly, travel by horse-and-buggy, speak the Pennsylvania Dutch language (actually an old dialect of German), and worship in the home. Differences between the two groups appear in theology minutiae, which technologies are allowed in the home, and other details like grooming habits. The Amish are noted for

their agricultural prowess and their quality craftwork. Amish-built furniture is sought after by many Ohio households. Amish communities are growing rapidly thanks to large families and a high retention rate within congregations.

Closely related to the Amish are Mennonites. The majority of Mennonites also reject different levels of modern technology, although generally Mennonites are much more moderate than the Amish. Most drive cars, for example. Mennonites are seen as more integrated into the larger world. Like their Amish relatives, Mennonites are Anabaptists and pacifists.

RELIGION

Approximately 70 percent of Ohioans identify as Christian, with large numbers of Catholics, Methodists, and Lutherans. About 1.3 percent of the population is Jewish. Smaller minorities of Muslims, Hindus, Buddhists, and Mormons exist. About 40 percent of the population considers themselves religious, a few points below the national average. About 22 percent of the population does not identify with a religion at all.

LANGUAGE

English is the first language for 93.3 percent of Ohioans. Another 2.2 percent speak Spanish as their first language. Many in the Amish community speak Pennsylvania Dutch (German) as their first language, though nearly all are bilingual. While there aren't many "Ohioisms" that are distinguishable from the rest of the country, there are a few to learn. Keep in mind that Ohio is "The Buckeye State" and as such its people refer to themselves as "Buckeyes." Most say "pop" rather than "soda." Rather than saying "Excuse me" in an awkward encounter, Ohioans are often fully guilty of saying "Ope." Linguistically, Ohio is something of a crossroads for those sensitive to small differences in accents and pronunciation. The spectrum runs from upper Midwestern in the north, to Midland in the center, with a touch of Southern Appalachian toward the south.

LITERATURE

Ohio-born authors have made important contributions to American literature for decades. Early African American poet Paul Laurence Dunbar hailed from Dayton. His house is part of the Dayton Aviation Heritage National Historical Park, owing to his close friendship with the Wright brothers. *The New Yorker* humorist and cartoonist James Thurber was born in Columbus, where some of his short stories take place and his house is also open to visitors. His short story *The Secret Life of Walter Mitty* has been adapted twice for film.

The big name in Ohio literature, though, is undoubtedly Nobel Prize-winning author Toni Morrison, who was born and raised in Lorain. Morrison, who passed away in 2019, is one of the country's greatest fiction authors. Her debut novel, *The Bluest Eye*, told the story of young Pecola growing up in Lorain and facing the realities of racism and sexual abuse. It was followed by great acclaim for works such as *Song of Solomon* and *Beloved,* which both achieved national attention for chronicling not just the Black experience but the American psyche.

Other contemporary Ohio authors that have achieved some level of acclaim or success include R. L. Stine, Wil Haygood, Anthony Doerr, and Celeste Ng. J. D. Vance's memoir *Hillbilly Elegy* follows the hardships of working-class families in Middletown. Science-fiction novel *Ready Player One*, written by Ashland-born Ernest Cline, largely takes place in Ohio and pictures Columbus as the dystopian future's technology hub.

VISUAL ARTS

Early-20th-century realist painter George Bellows was born and raised in Columbus. Fellow realist—and Bellows' teacher—Robert Henri hailed from Cincinnati. Multimedia artist Aminah Robinson lived and worked in Columbus. Pop artist Roy Lichtenstein attended and taught at The Ohio State University. Other artists of various mediums associated with Ohio include portrait painter Frank Duveneck, early animator Winsor McCay, Superman co-creators Joe Shuster and Jerry Siegel, and Bill Watterson of *Calvin and Hobbes* fame.

Filmmakers frequently bring productions to Ohio to take advantage of its varied geography and cityscapes, not to mention the cheaper production costs. Cleveland in particular is a helpful stand-in for cities such as New York City, Washington D.C., and even Stuttgart, Germany, for films in the Marvel Cinematic Universe. Cincinnati has been the set for films such as *Rain Man*, *Carol*, and *Traffic*. The former Ohio State Reformatory in Mansfield was the primary shooting location for *The Shawshank Redemption*.

Hollywood is overrun by Buckeyes, including Steven Spielberg, Paul Newman, Clark Gable, Roy Rogers, Woody Harrelson, Josh Radnor, Dave Chappelle, Allison Janney, Beverly D'Angelo, Arsenio Hall, J. K. Simmons, Terrence Howard, Rob Lowe, Martin Sheen, Jonathan Winters, Halle Berry, George Clooney, Sarah Jessica Parker, Ed O'Neill, and John Lithgow. Little Denison University in Granville counts Steve Carell and Jennifer Garner among its alumni.

MUSIC

Though Ohio does not lay claim to the birth of any musical genres, Cleveland claims that its local disc jockey Alan Freed coined the phrase "rock and roll" and heavily promoted it in the early 1950s; thus the Rock & Roll Hall of Fame is located in the city today. The state has contributed numerous performers to a wide variety of music worlds, including Dean Martin, Doris Day, the Isley Brothers, Bobby Womack, Dave Grohl, Tracy Chapman, Marilyn Manson, and John Legend. Music groups originating from Ohio include Wild Cherry, Devo, Nine Inch Nails, Walk the Moon, Rascal Flatts, O.A.R., Twenty One Pilots, The Black Keys, 98 Degrees, and The National.

Essentials

Transportation

GETTING THERE
Air

Cleveland Hopkins International Airport (CLE, 5300 Riverside Dr., 216/265-6000, clevelandairport.com) and **John Glenn Columbus International Airport** (CMH, 4600 International Gateway, 614/239-4000, flycolumbus.com) are the state's two busiest airports. Cincinnati is served by the **Cincinnati/Northern Kentucky International Airport** (CVG, 3087 Terminal Dr., Hebron, KY, 859/767-3151, cvgairport.com) in Kentucky. As none of these are major hubs, international

routes are spotty, but all three travel to a fair number of domestic destinations and are serviced by the big airlines and low-cost carriers.

Train

It's certainly possible, though unlikely, that you'll arrive by train to tour Ohio. The **Amtrak** (amtrak.com) *Capitol Limited* and *Lake Shore Limited* lines skirt across the north of the state servicing Cleveland, Toledo, Sandusky, and a handful of small cities. Meanwhile, the *Cardinal* line stops in Cincinnati. Nearly all of the state's Amtrak stops are once-a-day affairs in the middle of the night, and there is no train service connecting the Three C's: Cleveland, Columbus, and Cincinnati.

Bus

Greyhound (greyhound.com), **Megabus** (megabus.com), **Barons Bus** (baronsbus.com), and **Flixbus** (flixbus.com) cross state borders to destinations in Ohio, with Greyhound and Barons Bus the most widespread.

Car

Ohio is well served by high-quality interstates crisscrossing the state. Running north to south are **I-75** to the west, connecting Toledo, Dayton, and Cincinnati, and **I-77** to the east, connecting Cleveland, Akron, Canton, Cambridge, and Marietta. Running diagonally southwest to northeast is **I-71,** connecting the three largest cities in Ohio: Cincinnati, Columbus, and Cleveland. Traversing the state east to west is **I-70,** cutting the state in half and connecting Cambridge, Columbus, and Dayton. Up north, **I-90** clings near Lake Erie connecting Cleveland and Toledo. **I-76** connects Akron and Youngstown before briefly becoming the Ohio Turnpike and heading into Pennsylvania. **I-80** similarly cuts east to west, skimming across the northern

part of Youngstown before picking up the Ohio Turnpike mantle from I-76. It cuts across northern Ohio between Akron and Cleveland and then dead-ends into I-90, which continues the Ohio Turnpike to the west.

U.S. highways and state routes reach areas in between the interstates. **US-23** makes an incision north to south, going through Columbus. **US-33** cuts diagonally northwest to southeast, again running through Columbus before reaching the rugged Appalachian foothills. **US-35** does a similar, more southerly route connecting Dayton with the southeast. **US-30** and **SR 2** travel east to west as alternatives to the Ohio Turnpike.

Boat

If you're arriving by private boat from Canada, refer to the **Ohio Department of Natural Resources** (ohiodnr.gov) for the proper procedures and paperwork. The website is also a resource with maps of public access, water conditions on Lake Erie, and more information on Ohio's waterways.

While there are no direct ferries from mainland Canada, you can take the seasonal **Pelee Islander** (ontarioferries.com) from Leamington or Kingsville to Canada's Pelee Island—and from there take another ferry to Sandusky.

GETTING AROUND

Bus

Greyhound (greyhound.com), and **Barons Bus** (baronsbus.com) are both as good at getting you around Ohio as getting you into it. Additionally, **GoBus** (ridegobus.com) connects the Three C's with smaller communities in between with daily service.

Car

Generally speaking, road-tripping through Ohio is simple and safe. With ample divided highways and attractions widespread across

---

Previous: the Ohio River in Marietta.

Coronavirus and Ohio

At the time of writing in fall 2021, the coronavirus pandemic had significantly impacted the United States, including Ohio, and the situation was constantly changing. Be mindful of the evolving situation when planning your trip.

BEFORE YOU GO

- Check local websites (listed below) for updated **local restrictions** and the **overall health status** of destinations in this area.

- If you plan to fly, check with your airline as well as the **Centers for Disease Control and Prevention** (cdc.gov) for updated **recommendations** and **requirements.**

RESOURCES

- **State of Ohio:** Ohio Department of Health (odh.ohio.gov), Ohio Department of Natural Resources (ohiodnr.gov)

- **National Park Service:** Cuyahoga Valley National Park (nps.gov/cuva)

- **U.S. Forest Service:** Wayne National Forest (fs.usda.gov/wayne)

both urban and rural landscapes, it's also the preferred method of traveling: Ohio is the perfect size for day trips. Roads are in fine condition and nearly all that you're likely to travel on are paved (remote country roads off major state highways may turn to gravel).

As for getting around by car in the cities, you can go either way. Parking is convenient enough and, depending on where you're coming from, relatively affordable. None of Ohio's cities are terribly dense, so the rush hour can get busy with cars heading to/from the suburbs. Avoiding city highways during the hours 7am-9am and 4pm-6pm is a good idea, though traffic isn't on the same level as the large coastal cities. If you'd rather leave the car behind, Columbus, Cleveland, and Cincinnati all have efficient public transportation systems to get you to some of the major attractions in the central part of the city, but venturing farther may be a chore. Plan on supplementing public transportation with ride-shares or taxi rides, especially in Columbus and Cincinnati.

Those unfamiliar with winter driving may find themselves in an uncomfortable situation, particularly in the snowbelt in northeast Ohio. Though municipalities generally do a good job of dealing with snow using salt and plow trucks, it's very possible to find yourself driving through snow, or worse, ice. Drive slowly, put more distance than usual between you and the car in front of you, and gently tap the brakes instead of hitting them once. It's not a bad idea to put some extra weight in your trunk, pack a shovel, and bring some extra blankets. While no place in Ohio is extremely remote, help may still take a couple of hours to reach you if a snowstorm is causing widespread problems.

The biggest danger on Ohio's roads are deer. Keep a sharp eye as you drive at dawn or dusk.

RV

With ample campgrounds and outdoor adventures, traveling Ohio by RV can be a rewarding way to appreciate the state's natural attractions. You can rent an RV with **Cruise America** (cruiseamerica.com) if you don't own one. Visit **Ohio Campers** (ohiocampers. com) for resources on Ohio's campgrounds.

Bicycle

Almost anywhere you go, cars reign supreme in this automobile-manufacturing state. But between lengthy multipurpose trails and designated bike lanes in the major cities, it's possible to get around by bicycle, though perhaps not as your primary mode of transportation. You should be comfortable riding your bike on winding country roads and busy city streets—but even with its hundreds of miles of trails and designated lanes, Ohio could still use more. Cleveland, Columbus, and Cincinnati are best suited for getting around by bike. Consult **Ohio Bikeways** (ohiobikeways.net) for more information on Ohio's bike trails.

Boat

If you're visiting the summer resort islands that dot Lake Erie, you'll likely spend a little time on a ferry from Port Clinton or Sandusky to one of the islands. The passenger-only **Jet Express** (jet-express.com) is the fastest option, and it's the only one that connects South Bass Island with Kelleys Island. The **Miller Ferry** (millerferry.com) is a passenger and vehicle ferry to South Bass Island at a more affordable rate; however, it drops you off on the far end of the island from the village of Put-in-Bay, which is where the action is. **Kelleys Island Ferry** (kelleysislandferry.com) is a passenger and vehicle ferry to Kelleys Island.

Recreation

PARKS

Ohio is home to one national park—**Cuyahoga Valley National Park,** between Cleveland and Akron—and a handful of national historical parks. The **Dayton Aviation Heritage National Historical Park** is a collection of sights interpreting the birth of aviation through the perseverance of Orville and Wilbur Wright. Chillicothe's **Hopewell Culture National Historical Park** preserves mound complexes constructed by the ancient Hopewell people. Ohio's only national forest, **Wayne National Forest** manages large tracts of wilderness in the southeast quadrant of the state, split into three sections, and features backpacking trails, mountain biking, and ATV courses.

The state is blessed with plentiful state parks, none more popular than **Hocking Hills State Park** in the southeast. Between the 83 state parks, you'll find preserved or restored beaches, marshes, coastline, forests, rock formations, and caves. These parks generally include well-maintained campgrounds, trails, and facilities, though some of the more remote spots may have less-than-desirable restroom options. Some parks offer cabin accommodations, and eight feature lodge resorts. Unlike some other states, there is no fee to visit an Ohio state park. For more information on what you can find, visit parks.ohiodnr.gov.

HIKING

With rolling hills and rugged terrain dominating the state's southern and eastern quadrants, Ohio has plenty of options when it comes to hiking. For day trips, stick to **Cuyahoga Valley National Park** or any of the state parks. For backpacking trips, the southern, sparsely populated part of the state is your best option, in particular **Wayne National Forest.**

For a really extended hike, over 1,000 miles (1,610 km) of the **North Country National Scenic Trail** (northcountrytrail.org) traverse Ohio's landscape, entering from Michigan to the north and heading south all the way to Cincinnati before turning east and eventually back north through Appalachia's hills and valleys. Much of this route is shared with the **Buckeye Trail** (buckeyetrail.org), which makes a loop around the state connecting several state parks.

BIKING

Ohio is continuously adding to its multipurpose trail system, making the state an attractive biking destination. In the southwest, the **Little Miami Scenic Trail** (miamivalleytrails.org) is 78 miles (126 km) of paved trail connecting Cincinnati to the Dayton area. Up in the northeast, the 87-mile (140-km) **Ohio & Erie Canal Towpath Trail** (ohioanderiecanalway.com) runs from Cleveland down through Cuyahoga Valley National Park, Akron, and Stark County. Connecting it all is the **Ohio to Erie Trail** (ohiotoerietrail.org), which takes riders through a mix of designated bike trails, city streets, and country roads to travel from Cincinnati to Columbus to Cleveland.

CANOEING AND KAYAKING

Canoeing and kayaking liveries dot the state—you're never too far from an afternoon paddling down a river or along a lakeshore. The Mohican region, centered on Mohican State Park, is considered the kayaking and canoeing capital of Ohio, with several options in a relatively small area among shady streams. Most of Ohio's waterways are gentle affairs, easy enough locations to lazily cruise or explore at your leisure, with relatively shallow Lake Erie and its occasionally pounding waves being the exception.

BOATING AND FISHING

With Lake Erie, the Ohio River, and numerous creeks, lakes, and reservoirs in between, boating is a popular summer pastime in Ohio. There are dozens of marinas offering boat rentals, typically pontoons and water sport units. If you're bringing your own boat, **Marinas.com** (marinas.com) features a list of public docks. For offerings within the state park system, turn to the **Ohio Department of Natural Resources** (ohiodnr.gov). If you were born after January 1, 1982, and want to operate a boat with 10 HP or more, you must complete the **Boat Safety Course for an Ohio Boating License** (boat-ed.com/ohio).

Along with boating, there are plenty of fishing options, too, from walleye and perch fishing charters on Lake Erie to the quiet bends of the Ohio River. A fishing license is required for people 16 and older to fish in Ohio's public waters and must be in their possession when fishing. Rates differ between residents and nonresidents, and nonresidents will need a separate Lake Erie fishing license. Visit the **Ohio Department of Natural Resources** (ohiodnr.gov) to purchase a license, consult a map of vendors selling physical licenses, and review fishing regulations.

BIRD-WATCHING

Ohio's main opportunity for wildlife observation comes in the form of bird-watching, particularly in the spring and fall. Migrating birds tend to pause on Ohio's shores before or after tackling the formidable Lake Erie, making the lakeshore—in particular the northwest—one of the nation's best spots for bird-watching, celebrated every year with **The Biggest Week in American Birding** (biggestweekinamericanbirding.com) in May. As many as 280 species of songbirds, shorebirds, waterfowl, and raptors—including many of the state's bald eagles—congregate on the coastal wetlands in and around **Ottawa National Wildlife Refuge** (fws.gov/refuge/Ottawa). For more on Ohio's Important Bird Areas and sighted species, refer to the **National Audubon Society** (audubon.org).

Food and Accommodations

FOOD AND DRINK

Ohio's eclectic assortment of ethnic enclaves, recent transplants, and rural traditions results in an appetizing array of farm-to-table restaurants, international food, and innovative new dining concepts. Restauranteurs take advantage of the state's expansive and productive farmland to source high-quality ingredients. Cleveland, Columbus, Cincinnati, and Dayton all feature a superb local market as proof of this bounty, creativity, and diversity. No other food exhibits these qualities better than Ohio's **ice cream.** In particular, Columbus's Jeni's Splendid Ice Creams and Cincinnati's Graeter's Ice Cream showcase what a chef can do with the best ingredients and an open mind.

As the "Buckeye" state, bakers have concocted a popular peanut butter and chocolate confectionary that resembles a buckeye nut. The **buckeye** dessert is delectable. The buckeye nut is poisonous.

There are a handful of local specialties as well. Columbus lays claim to **Columbus-style pizza**—edge-to-edge toppings on a cracker-thin-crust pie cut into squares. Tiny Steubenville has its own **Steubenville-style pizza** (sometimes called Ohio Valley-style), with cheese added *after* the pie comes out of the oven and sold by the square.

Cleveland is one of the best places in the United States to find Central and Eastern European food, Polish in particular. This ethnic background birthed the **Polish Boy** sandwich, a Cleveland specialty that sets a kielbasa topped with fries, slaw, and barbecue or hot sauce on a bun. Polish Boys are typically found in neighborhood watering holes and barbecue joints.

Above all of these, Ohio's best-known regional food is probably **Cincinnati-style chili**—a fine ground beef sauce that is typically seasoned with cinnamon and perhaps

even chocolate. Weirded out yet? They put it on spaghetti with diced onions and a pile of shredded cheese measured in inches. Century-old neighborhood chili parlors compete with chains Skyline Chili and Gold Star Chili, which are ubiquitous in the southwest quadrant of the state. Also popular in Cincinnati is **goetta,** a patty of ground pork, onions, oats, and spices that originated as a way to stretch the week's meat. Typically found on breakfast plates or on sandwiches, goetta also appears as a pizza topping in Cincinnati-area parlors.

Ohio is gaining a reputation as a **beer destination** with nearly 300 craft breweries in the state. Cincinnati's Rhinegeist and Cleveland's Great Lakes Brewing Company dominate the scene and are easy to find in bars and grocery stores across the state, but there's a plethora of options in between. Canal Winchester, just outside of Columbus, is the American headquarters of Scottish brewer BrewDog and home to the company's craft beer hotel.

ACCOMMODATIONS

Given Ohio's varied rural and urban landscapes, the state's accommodations cover the entire spectrum from posh four-star hotels to no-frills campgrounds. It's best to book well ahead of time, especially for summer visits and special large-scale events. Campgrounds can especially fill up during these times. The rates given in this guide reflect typical double occupancy rates for weekends in the summer (high season). You should expect to find lower rates for weekdays or off-season visits. The guide focuses on independent hotels, motels, and bed-and-breakfasts as much as possible, with mention of particularly useful clusters of chain motels, should you prefer that option. If you have a favorite hotel chain, it's often best to book straight through them rather than a third-party website. Either way, take notice of any cancellation or change policies before making a reservation. **TourismOhio** (ohio. org) is a good compendium of the state's accommodation options, from mainstream hotels to unique getaways.

Motels and Hotels

It should come with no surprise that Ohio's many highways come with many, many chain hotels off busy (and not busy) exits. Nicer hotels congregate in central business districts, whereas you'll find basic, independent motels—some tidy and some not—in the rural areas. The Lake Erie shoreline has the largest concentration of these, some hardly changed (for good and possibly bad) since their construction in the 1940s to 1960s.

Bed-and-Breakfasts

Ohio is peppered with bed-and-breakfasts, from cozy neighborhood retreats in major cities to small-town or farm accommodations. Most towns with a population of, we'll say, at least 10,000 have a bed-and-breakfast or two, with some smaller towns boasting one as well. The areas nearest Lake Erie have the most, well suited for quiet weekends enjoying wineries, bird-watching, or sunsets along the water. Some require a minimum two-night stay during weekends or high season.

Resorts

Ohio's resorts primarily fall under two categories: **state park lodges** and **indoor waterparks.**

Several of Ohio's state parks have large, resort-like lodges that often feature swimming pools, basketball or racquetball courts, golf, dining, and other amenities in proximity to swimming beaches, hiking trails, and lakes. They include Maumee Bay in the northwest, Mohican in the central part of the state, and Salt Fork in the Appalachian foothills. For more information on the state park lodges, visit **Great Ohio Lodges** (greatohiolodges.com).

Ohio's indoor waterpark resorts, featuring on-site restaurants, gaming rooms, and other indoor activities, are mainly concentrated in the Sandusky area, though there are a handful elsewhere.

Camping and Cabins

With nearly 10,000 campsites within state park boundaries alone, Ohio is a welcoming destination for campers. The state parks' well-maintained campsites range $17-39 per night, can be booked six months ahead, and are (mostly) open year-round. Some state parks also come with cabins with varying degrees of modernity or rusticity. Browse the campgrounds and cabins on the **Ohio Department of Natural Resources** (ohiodnr.gov) website. Throughout Ohio, you'll also find plenty of private campgrounds: giant RV resorts, KOAs, and family-operated land.

Hundreds of rental cabins, particularly in the Hocking Hills and Mohican regions, are popular alternatives to camping in these recreational hot spots. As with hotel rooms and campgrounds, these book quickly for the summer months. The sooner you book, the less headache you'll have making a reservation.

Travel Tips

WHAT TO PACK

The contents of your suitcase highly depend on the season. If traveling during the winter, be sure to bring a heavy winter jacket, hat, gloves, and perhaps even snow boots if you're planning on hiking. Wearing layers is best practice. Bring a blanket to stow in your trunk in case of a breakdown, as well as ice scrapers for your car.

You will need none of this in the summer. Instead, pack sunscreen, insect repellent, and water bottles to combat the sticky summer swelter. If traveling between March and June or September and November, come prepared for anything! It's not unusual to prefer shorts and T-shirts in the afternoon and switch to jeans and a hoodie for the evening. An umbrella or light rain jacket is helpful. Nasty cold fronts in the spring or fall can bring a little bit of everything in a short span of time, so keep apprised of the forecast before traveling.

TOURIST INFORMATION

TourismOhio (ohio.org) is the statewide tourism agency that can give you a general idea of what there is to see. Additionally, there are convention and tourism bureaus for nearly every county and major city, offering itinerary assistance, maps, profiles on local attractions and restaurants, and coupons. Some especially useful ones for your Ohio trip: **Destination Cleveland** (thisiscleveland.com), **Experience Columbus** (experiencecolumbus.com), **Cincinnati USA** (cincinnatiusa.com), **Dayton Convention and Visitors Bureau** (daytoncvb.com), **Destination Toledo** (visittoledo.org), **Lake Erie Shores and Islands** (shoresandislands.com), **Akron Summit Convention and Visitors Bureau** (visitakron-summit.org), and **Hocking Hills Tourism Association** (explorehockinghills.com).

There are also some good local publications that will give you an idea of Ohio's current goings-on. Articles in *Ohio Magazine* (ohiomagazine.com) cover the big attractions as well as the hidden gems. *Columbus Underground* (columbusunderground.com) is a local publication covering news, events, and food in Ohio's capital city and a good resource on what's happening and what's hot. *Cincinnati Magazine* (cincinnatimagazine.com) does much the same for Cincinnati. *Cleveland Traveler* (clevelandtraveler.com) is a relatively new blog covering all corners of the Cleveland-area scene.

INTERNATIONAL TRAVELERS
Entering the United States

With limited international flights and the only international crossing a little-used ferry hop from Ontario's Pelee Island, it's unlikely you'll arrive directly to Ohio from another country. Like anywhere else in the United States, Ohio may require international arrivals to obtain a travel visa. The U.S. government's Visa Waiver Program allows citizens of many countries to visit the United States without a visa for up to 90 days. However, those citizens will need to apply within the Electronic System for Travel Authorization (ESTA), which comes with a $14 fee. Consult the **U.S. Department of State's Bureau of Consular Affairs** (travel.state.gov) for visa and other pertinent information for international travelers, and bring your passport regardless.

Customs

Upon entering the United States, international arrivals must declare any dollar amount over $10,000 as well as the value of any gifts you plan to leave in the country. For information on what Customs may confiscate, including illegal substances or agricultural products, consult the **U.S. Department of Homeland Security's U.S. Customs and Border Protection** (cbp.gov).

Money

Ohioans use the United States dollar as currency. You'll find currency exchanges in airport lobbies and banks, though you'll get the best exchange rate by using ATMs to draw cash from your account at home. Research foreign ATM fees with your bank ahead of time. Credit cards are used widely, though it may be useful to draw some cash for Amish Country.

The rule of thumb for tipping restaurant servers is, like the rest of the United States, 15-20 percent of the pretax bill. Bartenders should get $1 per beer and $2-3 per mixed drink. Tip taxi and shuttle drivers 15 percent of the fare, and a couple of bucks to valets and porters. Remember to tip tour guides as well, perhaps 10-15 percent of the cost of your tour, though there is no hard-and-fast rule.

Electricity

Electrical outlets operate on the North American standard 120 volts, 60 hertz, and are either two-pronged or three-pronged. International visitors ought to buy adapters before arriving or leaving the airport, though they are easily found in large stores such as Walmart and Meijer.

ACCESS FOR TRAVELERS WITH DISABILITIES

Ohio's aging population ensures a consistent supply of ADA-compliant attractions, restaurants, and hotels for travelers. Old storefronts are the least likely to be accessible. When in doubt, call your destination ahead of time to see what their setup is.

The National Park Service provides accessibility information for **Cuyahoga Valley National Park** (nps.gov/cuva); popular attractions that offer accessibility include Brandywine Falls, the Beaver Marsh, and the Ohio & Erie Canal Towpath Trail. Consult the **Ohio Department of Natural Resources**

(ohiodnr.gov) for information on accessible activities and facilities in state parks, wildlife areas, and other public areas.

TRAVELING WITH CHILDREN

With beaches, playful museums, and some of the best zoos and amusement parks in the country, Ohio is an easy, relatively affordable, and attractive family vacation destination—you'll have no trouble finding kid-friendly things to do. Most attractions offer discounted children's rates. Unless you stay in the central business districts of the major cities, hotel parking for your large family vehicle is free and plentiful.

WOMEN TRAVELING ALONE

Ohio's well-connectedness is both a blessing and a curse: its many highways serve both road-tripping travelers and human traffickers. This vulnerability makes Ohio one of the worst states in terms of human trafficking. While the chance you will be affected is low, it's best to be aware and take commonsense precautions. Don't accept drinks from strangers. If you feel someone is stalking you, don't hesitate to contact police.

Keep in mind that cell phone reception gets spotty in the remote, rugged hills of southern and southeast Ohio.

SENIOR TRAVELERS

With its mixture of major cultural amenities and pastoral countryside, Ohio is an excellent travel choice for senior citizens. Most attractions offer senior discounts.

LGBTQ TRAVELERS

In a place as diverse in geopolitical identity as Ohio (Is it the South? The Midwest? The North?), you're bound to find a mosaic of informed and uninformed opinions regarding LGBTQ rights, though gay marriage is perfectly legal here as it is in the rest of the United States. All the major cities sport gay-friendly nightlife scenes, with Columbus's

Short North neighborhood especially catering to the LGBTQ community. Liberal outposts Athens and Yellow Springs are also accepting communities. Attitudes remain conservative outside cities, though typically with a libertarian "to-each-their-own" indifference.

TRAVELERS OF COLOR

Travelers of color should have no problem enjoying themselves in Ohio, particularly in the cities. Consult **Soul of America** (soulofamerica.com) for relevant history, cultural sites, and a directory of Black-owned businesses. Most of the biggest cities have their own directories of Black-owned businesses as well. As of this writing, Soul of America does not cover Columbus, but a quick online search reveals several articles and directories.

Ohio's rural areas are not diverse places; travelers of color may find themselves the recipients of double takes and awkward glances, though you shouldn't expect anything less than friendliness. As with anyone, Ohioans typically respond to politeness with politeness.

HEALTH AND SAFETY
Crime

Like many urban areas in the United States, Ohio's cities include neighborhoods that struggle against underemployment, drug problems, and gun violence. Each city has its areas that are best avoided after dark. Having said that, these cities are no less safe than any other major metropolitan area in the country. Common sense is all the precaution you need for a safe and enjoyable trip. Even in rural areas and parking lots, lock your car and hide valuable items in the glove compartment or trunk.

Insects

Though not exactly Australia in terms of dangerous critters, Ohio's fauna does warrant a handful of precautions. Ticks are a major problem in Ohio's wooded areas. Often carrying icky diseases like Lyme disease, ticks wait patiently on blades of long grass until hitching a ride from an unwitting host to feed on blood. If you go out for a hike, especially in less-worn paths thick with underbrush, be sure to wear long pants and sleeves and make regular checks for ticks when you stop. If you do have a tick latched, take a pair of fine-tipped tweezers, squeeze the tick as close to your skin as possible, and pull upward with steady pressure until the tick detaches. Don't pull too dramatically or twist—this may cause the mouth to break off from the body and remain in your skin. Clean the spot on your skin with rubbing alcohol, or soap and water.

Additionally, there are two types of spiders—black widows and brown recluses—that are considered dangerous. They're not seen too often, but if you've been hanging around old barns or the woods and left a pair of shoes or gloves out, it might be an idea to give them a good shake just to be on the safe side.

Wild Animals

There are three species of venomous snake in Ohio: the northern copperhead, the eastern massasauga, and the timber rattlesnake. Between their mild-mannered shyness, preference for areas far from human activity, and general rarity, you're unlikely to encounter any on your trip to Ohio unless you're doing some serious backcountry hiking. If you do get bitten by a snake, call 911 and keep the bitten part of your body below the heart. Don't apply heat or ice or try to suck out the venom.

While rare, black bears are spotted in the state's eastern half, so take the necessary precautions if camping. Store food in airtight containers suspended between trees out of a bear's reach, or in your car. Never store food in your tent. If you encounter a bear while hiking, give it a wide berth, especially if there are cubs present. While bears are typically shy and nonaggressive, they may attack if they feel threatened. It's not agreed on how best to deter an attack, but the most common answer is to wave your arms and make a lot of noise to intimidate the bear.

By far the greatest danger that Ohio's fauna presents is wild-running deer sprinting across the road. Keep your eyes peeled on the side of the road, especially during dusk and dawn.

Extreme Temperatures

In terms of temperature, Ohio can and does experience extreme heat and cold from time to time. During the summer, protect yourself with sunscreen, applied liberally and often. Drink plenty of water and wear light-colored, loose-fitting clothing. Individuals who don't follow these steps on hot, sunny days set themselves up for dehydration, heat exhaustion, or worse, heat stroke. Alternatively, winter brings the possibility of hypothermia and frostbite. Dress in layers, including socks, and keep dry. On days of extreme cold, limit skin exposure as much as possible.

COMMUNICATIONS
Cell Phones

Being a relatively small and densely populated state, you shouldn't have much problem with cell phone reception in Ohio. One exception is southern and southeastern Ohio, where remote, wooded valleys in the Appalachian hills may prevent phones from maintaining a signal. Try to get to high ground to find service, or better yet, take screenshots of relevant maps or information before you head to the hinterland.

Media

Take your pick from any of Ohio's many media markets for newspapers and local news networks. Cleveland's *The Plain Dealer* (cleveland.com), the *Cincinnati Enquirer* (cincinnati.com), and the *Columbus Dispatch* (dispatch.com) are the three largest newspapers and will provide local channel listings.

TIME ZONE

All of Ohio sits near the western edge of the Eastern Time Zone, one hour ahead of the Central Time Zone and three hours ahead of the Pacific Time Zone.

Resources

Suggested Reading and Viewing

SUGGESTED READING
Fiction

Anderson, Sherwood. *Winesburg, OH*. Public domain: 1919. This classic collection of short stories is a portrait of the fictional town of Winesburg and its inhabitants and has emerged as one of the most respected pieces of American fiction from the 20th century.

Cline, Ernest. *Ready Player One*. New York: Broadway Paperbacks, 2011. Written by Ohio native Cline, this dystopian sci-fi novel, when not spending time in a virtual world, largely takes place in Columbus, envisioned as the tech capital of the world. Steven Spielberg directed the film adaptation, and Cline released a sequel in 2020.

Morrison, Toni. *Beloved*. New York: Vintage Books, 1987. Inspired by a true story of a slave who escaped to Ohio, Morrison's bitter story of a woman haunted by memories was adapted for film in 1997 starring Oprah Winfrey, though the book is better received.

Morrison, Toni. *The Bluest Eye*. New York: Vintage Books, 1970. The debut novel from Ohio's most famed author, *The Bluest Eye* is Morrison's semi-autobiographical coming-of-age tale about race and poverty in Lorain, a satellite of Cleveland.

Ng, Celeste. *Little Fires Everywhere*. New York: Penguin Press, 2017. Ng is one of the most high-profile of Ohio's contemporary authors. *Little Fires Everywhere* takes place in the Cleveland suburb of Shaker Heights and spawned a Hulu original series.

Stowe, Harriet Beecher. *Uncle Tom's Cabin*. Multiple publishers, 1852. Stowe wrote this controversial, historically significant piece of antislavery literature based on her interviews of former slaves while living in Cincinnati.

Nonfiction

Bauer, Jeni Britton. *Jeni's Splendid Ice Creams at Home*. New York: Artisan, 2011. Jeni of Columbus's Jeni's Splendid Ice Creams shares the recipes to some of her favorite scoop shop flavors, as well as some background information on the company, reflections on seasonal tastes, and her personal journey to ice cream.

Giffels, David. *Barnstorming Ohio: To Understand America*. New York: Hachette Books, 2020. Akron journalist Giffels, with Ohio's bellwether status in mind, travels the state talking to farmers, steelworkers, and others representing Ohio's many economic and cultural points of view to make sense of the 2016 election and make predictions for 2020's election.

Goldbach, Eliese Colette. *Rust: A Memoir of Steel and Grit*. New York: Flatiron Books, 2020. Goldbach's memoir is largely set around her time in the ArcelorMittal Steel mill, with her own economic and societal frustrations reflecting those often found in Rust Belt America.

Haygood, Wil. *Tigerland: 1968-1969: A City Divided, A Nation Torn Apart, and a Magical Season of Healing.* New York: Vintage Books, 2018. Journalist and author Haygood writes an account of segregated East High School in Columbus and its unprecedented basketball and baseball state championships in the same year.

McCullough, David. *The Pioneers: The Heroic Story of the Settlers Who Brought the American Ideal West.* New York: Simon & Schuster, 2019. McCullough chronicles the birth of Ohio's statehood largely from the point of view of Marietta's first settlers. Full of lively historical figures, and an excellent resource on early Ohio history in the southeast and Cincinnati.

McCullough, David. *The Wright Brothers.* New York: Simon & Schuster, 2015. McCullough follows the lives of Orville and Wilbur Wright, from their family beginnings to their success in creating the first airplane. Much of the book takes place in Dayton, where the Wright brothers lived and worked most of their lives.

Thurber, James. *My Life and Hard Times.* New York: Harper & Brothers, 1933. Famed humorist and *New Yorker* cartoonist James Thurber reflects on growing up in Columbus with short, amusing stories.

Vance, J. D. *Hillbilly Elegy: A Memoir of a Family and Culture in Crisis.* New York: HarperCollins, 2016. Vance's harrowing story of poverty, drug addiction, and unemployment puts a homegrown take on some of Middle America's struggles. Much of the book takes place in Middletown, between Cincinnati and Dayton.

Ohio Travel

Finch, Jackie Sheckler. *Ohio Off the Beaten Path.* Lanham, MD: Globe Pequot, 2019. This guidebook dreams up themed itineraries, sprinkling in some of the state's better-known attractions with hidden gems, restaurants, and accommodations.

Forster, Matt. *Backroads and Byways of Ohio: Drives, Day Trips, and Weekend Excursions.* New York: The Countryman Press, 2018. Another itinerary creator divided geographically, Forster's guide inspires exploration with concise historical and cultural background alongside area highlights.

Korman, Danny. *Walking Cincinnati.* Birmingham, AL: Wilderness Press, 2019. Korman's thorough exploration of the Queen City takes travelers on walking tours of the historic urban area, with recommendations on restaurants, shops, and attractions along the way.

Reed, Mary. *Hiking Ohio: A Guide to the State's Greatest Hikes.* Lanham, MD: Rowman & Littlefield, 2019. This excellent guide is a compendium of the state's best day hikes, with helpful, detailed descriptions of landmarks and trailheads, trail maps, and pertinent information on distance, difficulty, and water availability. A must if you plan on doing a lot of hiking.

SUGGESTED VIEWING

American Factory (2019). Directed by Steven Bognar and Julia Reichert. This Oscarwinning documentary depicts the opening of a Chinese Fuyao factory in a shuttered GM plant near Dayton, and the following cultural clashes between Chinese leadership and working-class Americans.

The Avengers (2012). Written by Joss Whedon and Zak Penn. Directed by Joss Whedon. Starring Robert Downey Jr., Chris Evans, Chris Hemsworth, Scarlett Johansson, Mark Ruffalo, Jeremy Renner, and Samuel L.

Jackson. The Marvel Cinematic Universe's first crossover film sees its heroes defend Earth from a planetary invasion. Shooting took place partly in Cleveland, with the most notable scene disguising Public Square as Stuttgart, Germany.

Captain America: The Winter Soldier (2012). Written by Christopher Markus and Stephen McFeely. Directed by Anthony and Joe Russo. Starring Chris Evans, Scarlett Johansson, Samuel L. Jackson, Robert Redford, and Anthony Mackie. Captain America exposes a plot within the S.H.I.E.L.D. agency from his former nemesis. Filming largely took place in Cleveland.

Carol (2015). Written by Phyllis Nagy. Directed by Todd Haynes. Starring Cate Blanchett, Rooney Mara, and Sarah Paulson. Based on the 1952 book *The Price of Salt* by Patricia Highsmith, aspiring photographer Therese Belivet begins a romantic relationship with older, glamorous Carol Aird. Filming took place throughout the Cincinnati area, taking advantage of the city's historic architecture. The film was on many Top 10 lists of 2015.

A Christmas Story (1983). Written by Jean Shepherd, Leigh Brown, and Bob Clark. Directed by Bob Clark. Starring Peter Billingsley, Melinda Dillon, and Darren McGavin. This holiday classic about a young boy who wants a Red Ryder BB gun for Christmas was largely filmed in the Cleveland area, with the iconic Parker family house now a museum.

Race (2016). Written by Joe Shrapnel and Anna Waterhouse. Directed by Stephen Hopkins. Starring Stephan James, Jason Sudeikis, Jeremy Irons, Carice Van Houten, and William Hurt. This biopic follows Jesse Owens and his journey from college sprinter at The Ohio State University to Olympic gold medal winner in the 1936 games in Nazi Germany.

The Shawshank Redemption (1994). Written by Stephen King and Frank Darabont. Directed by Frank Darabont. Starring Tim Robbins, Morgan Freeman, Bob Gunton, and Clancy Brown. Timid banker Andy Dufresne, convicted of murdering his wife, is sentenced to life and serves time in a corrupt prison. Though the film takes place in Maine, shooting took place almost entirely in the Mansfield area, with the former Ohio State Reformatory posing as Shawshank State Penitentiary.

Internet Resources

GENERAL INFORMATION

State of Ohio
ohio.gov
An overview of information on travel, arts and culture, and maps within a wider umbrella of information about jobs and services.

Ohio Department of Transportation (ODOT)
transportation.ohio.gov
ODOT's official website includes information on road conditions and closures as well as construction warnings.

CUISINE AND TRAVEL

Cincinnati Magazine
cincinnatimagazine.com
Publication focusing on Cincinnati's dining scene, cultural events, and local news. Compiles useful "Best Of" lists of area retail.

Cincinnati USA
cincinnatiusa.com

Cincinnati's tourism bureau features profiles on area attractions, nightlife, and accommodations.

The Cleveland Traveler
clevelandtraveler.com

A blog specializing in the Cleveland area, with posts on the top bars, restaurants, outdoor activities, and more in the Cleveland metropolitan area.

Columbus Underground
columbusunderground.com

Local independent journalism outlet keeping tabs on events, new bars and restaurants, and recent developments in the Columbus metro area.

Destination Cleveland
thisiscleveland.com

This website from Cleveland's tourism bureau compiles information on the region's sights, food, and adventures.

Experience Columbus
experiencecolumbus.com

This tourism bureau in Columbus directs people to the area's attractions, nightlife, and more for useful itinerary planning.

Ohio: Find it Here
ohio.org

Travel inspiration and profiles on things to see, do, eat, and experience throughout Ohio.

Ohio Magazine
ohiomagazine.com

A monthly publication with features on Ohio's attractions, history, and events, with emphasis on hidden gems as much as well-known entities.

Only In Your State
onlyinyourstate.com

A website specializing on unearthing hidden gems and out-of-the-way destinations undiscovered, perhaps, even by locals.

HISTORY AND CULTURE

Ohioana Library
ohioana.org

This library in Columbus specializes in literature written either about Ohio or by Ohioans. Peruse the website for recent award winners, a catalog of books reflecting Ohio's contributions to culture, and information on the Ohio Literary Trail.

Ohio History Connection
ohiohistory.org

Ohio's primary historical society maintains a website featuring profiles of its sites and ample information on a variety of Ohio history topics.

PARKS AND RECREATION

National Park Service
nps.gov

Learn about the sites in Ohio operated by the National Park Service, including up-to-date information on closures and construction.

Ohio Department of Natural Resources
ohiodnr.gov

Restructured in 2020, this website is the best resource on Ohio's state parks. Explore by activity, by camping options, or by specific park. You can also make camping reservations for state park campgrounds.

Ohio Ornithological Society
ohiobirds.org

This organization provides information on birding hot spots, recent sightings, and other helpful resources.

Index

List of Maps

Photo Credits

MAP SYMBOLS

═══	Expressway	○	City/Town	✈	Airport	⚲	Golf Course
───	Primary Road	◉	State Capital	✈	Airfield	℗	Parking Area
──	Secondary Road	✦	National Capital	▲	Mountain	▲	Archaeological Site
═══	Unpaved Road	✪	Highlight	✦	Unique Natural Feature	▲	Church
----	Trail	★	Point of Interest			▯	Gas Station
··········	Ferry	•	Accommodation	⌇	Waterfall	⬯	Glacier
═══	Railroad	▼	Restaurant/Bar	▲	Park	▨	Mangrove
═══	Pedestrian Walkway	▪	Other Location	⊞	Trailhead	⬯	Reef
▥▥▥	Stairs	∆	Campground	✗	Skiing Area	▭	Swamp

CONVERSION TABLES

°C = (°F - 32) / 1.8
°F = (°C x 1.8) + 32
1 inch = 2.54 centimeters (cm)
1 foot = 0.304 meters (m)
1 yard = 0.914 meters
1 mile = 1.6093 kilometers (km)
1 km = 0.6214 miles
1 fathom = 1.8288 m
1 chain = 20.1168 m
1 furlong = 201.168 m
1 acre = 0.4047 hectares
1 sq km = 100 hectares
1 sq mile = 2.59 square km
1 ounce = 28.35 grams
1 pound = 0.4536 kilograms
1 short ton = 0.90718 metric ton
1 short ton = 2,000 pounds
1 long ton = 1.016 metric tons
1 long ton = 2,240 pounds
1 metric ton = 1,000 kilograms
1 quart = 0.94635 liters
1 US gallon = 3.7854 liters
1 Imperial gallon = 4.5459 liters
1 nautical mile = 1.852 km

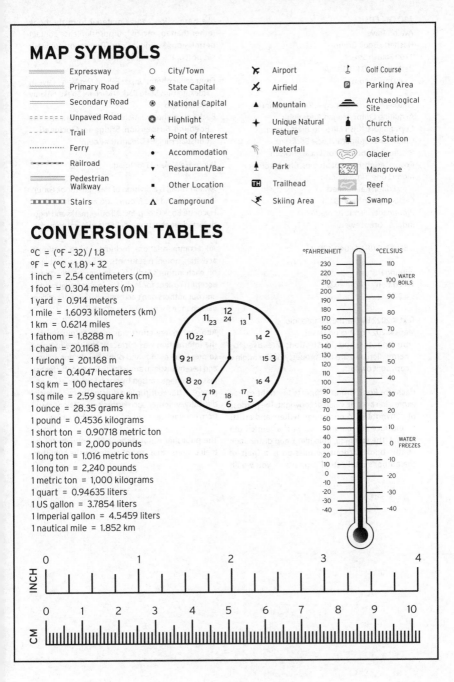

MOON OHIO

Avalon Travel
Hachette Book Group
1700 Fourth Street
Berkeley, CA 94710, USA
www.moon.com

Editor and Series Manager: Kathryn Ettinger
Acquiring Editor: Megan Anderluh
Copy Editors: Kristi Mitsuda, Brett Keener
Graphics Coordinator: Lucie Ericksen
Production Coordinator: Lucie Ericksen
Cover Design: Faceout Studios, Charles Brock
Moon Logo: Tim McGrath
Map Editor: Kat Bennett
Cartographer: Karin Dahl
Proofreader: Jamie Andrade
Indexer: Greg Jewett

ISBN-13: 978-1-64049-429-9

Printing History
1st Edition — April 2022
5 4 3 2 1

Front cover photo: Upper Falls at Old Man's Cave in Hocking Hills State Park © Michael Shake / Alamy Stock Photo
Back cover photo: Smale Riverfront Park and the Roebling Suspension Bridge in Cincinnati © Christian Hinkle | Dreamstime.com

Printed in Malaysia for Imago